THE MAN-LEOPARD MURDERS

THE MAN-LEOPARD MURDERS

HISTORY AND SOCIETY IN COLONIAL NIGERIA

DAVID PRATTEN

INDIANA UNIVERSITY PRESS
Bloomington and Indianapolis

For Emma, Hope and Grace

This book is a publication of

Indiana University Press
601 North Morton Street
Bloomington, Indiana 47404-3797 USA

http://iupress.indiana.edu

Telephone orders	800-842-6796
Fax orders	812-855-7931
Orders by e-mail	iuporder@indiana.edu

Originally published by Edinburgh University Press Ltd, 22 George Square,
Edinburgh

Manufactured in Great Britain

Cataloging information is available from the Library of Congress.

ISBN 978-0-253-34956-9 (cl.)

1 2 3 4 5 12 11 10 09 08 07

Cust/Add: 17028000/02	LSSC	SIERRA COLLEGE LIBRARY	
Cust PO No. 07-08		Cust Ord Date: 20-Dec-2007	
BBS Order No: C851020	Ln: 1 Del: 1	BBS Ord Date: 20-Dec-2007	
0253349567-33213665		Sales Qty: 1 #Vols: 001	
(9780253349569)			

The man-leopard murders

Subtitle: history and society in colonial Nigeria   Stmt of Resp: **David Pratten.**

HARDBACK   Pub Year: **2007**   Vol No.: _____   Edition:

Pratten, David.   Ser. Title:

Indiana University Press
                                        _____

Acc Mat:

Profiled	**PromptCat Barcode US**	**Mylar Dust Jacket (Clot**	
Tech	**Barcode Label Applicati**	**Spine Label Protector U**	
Services:	**Barcode Label Protector**	**Spine Label PromptCat**	
	Base Charge Processing		

Fund: **INTERDISC SOC ST**   Location:

Stock Category: Department:

Class #:   Cutter: Collection:

Order Line Notes:

Notes to Vendor:

Blackwell Book Services

CONTENTS

LIST OF FIGURES

ACKNOWLEDGEMENTS

Far too many people from the villages of Ikot Akpa Nkuk, Ikot Afanga and elsewhere in the southern Annang region have contributed to the making of this work to be mentioned here. I extend my sincere thanks to them for their patience and invaluable insights. I would, however, like to acknowledge my enormous debt to Obong Dr Frank A. Umoren, the Paramount Ruler of Southern Ukanafun, and his family for their generous hospitality during my fieldwork between 1996 and 1998 and again in 2001, 2002 and 2004. I also owe Imoh Frank Umoren my sincerest gratitude for his work with me during these years.

I would like to extend my thanks to those who assisted in my archival researches. By far the largest proportion of source material for this work was compiled from the Nigerian National Archives in Enugu. Mr U. O. A. Esse and his staff, including Comfort Umoh, Felicia Ibe and Isaac Iheakaram Amaechi, deserve special mention for their careful and patient assistance. Zofia Sulej and Mary-Ann Alho of the University of Witwatersrand were of enormous help in copying M. D. W. Jeffreys' papers, which are held in the library archives there. I must also mention the staff at Rhodes House Library, Oxford, at the Library of Congress, Washington D. C. and at the School of Oriental and African Studies, London, for their help. Thanks also to John Cardoo of the Qua Iboe Fellowship for facilitating my access to the Church's archives held at the Public Record Office in Belfast, and to Tim Hutchinson at the University of Saskatchewan Archive. I should also like to thank Ursula Jones for permission to consult Dr G. I. Jones' papers in Cambridge. Thanks also to John Messenger, Rosemary Harris, John McCall, Ken Barnes and John Manton for their observations and personal papers. For his friendship and his translation of the Spirit Movement papers I am especially grateful to Obong Walter Idem.

Along with colleagues at SOAS, Edinburgh, Sussex and Oxford, I am very grateful to Tom McCaskie, Richard Rathbone, Axel Harneit-Sievers, Charlie Gore, Ruth Ginio, Robin Horton, Kay Williamson, Turner and Miriam Isoun, Violetta Ekpo, Martin Lynn, Mike Rowlands, Peter Geschiere, Richard Fardon and Colin Murray for their help, insight and advice. During my fieldwork I enjoyed the hospitality of the Sociology Department at the University of Port Harcourt and the Faculty of Social

Sciences at the University of Uyo. I owe particular thanks to Steve Wordu for his amiable assistance during my first months in Port Harcourt. I am grateful to the Economic and Social Research Council for a studentship award which supported my initial research and to the British Academy for a postdoctoral research fellowship and fieldwork funding which saw the project through to this point.

For encouraging me many years ago to make the history I write 'my own', I should like to thank Cliff Davies. Since I had the good fortune of becoming John Peel's research student I have been inspired by his passion for a thoroughly historical ethnography, by his intimate knowledge of African societies and by the style and scholarship of his research. Most of all, though, I want to thank him for his belief in my work and for the persistence and generosity of his guidance over the many years of this project.

My research and writing would not have been possible without the support of my parents and family to whom I will always be grateful. My wife and daughters have borne the labours of authorship and the absences of an anthropologist with humour, grace and resolve and it is to them that I dedicate this book.

GLOSSARY

Where possible I have used Annang terms, and in this I have tried to maintain some consistency with Messenger's body of work on Annang studies. However, as there is no published Annang orthography or dictionary I have followed as far as possible the orthography used by Elaine Kaufman in her Ibibio Dictionary.

ŋ – ng
ɔ – or
tones – ` low, ´ high, ^ fall, ' lowered high
Ib. Ibibio
ábáŋ – pot
àbàsì – god
àbàsì ìkpá ísɔ̀ŋ – god of the soil
ábíà – specialist
àfáí – violence, brutality, wild
ákáì – forest
àkúkú (nkúkú pl.) – chief
álân áyôp – palm oil
áwíè òwò (ébíè òwò Ib.) – warrior society
àyèì – young shoot of a palm tree
áyéyìn – grandchild
áyôp – oil palm tree
èbé – husband, married
édíá – yam
èkóŋ – a men's society, a masquerade
ékóŋ – war, a society which celebrates war glories
ékpê – leopard
ékpê ówó – leopard man
ékpó – ancestral masquerade
ékpûk– lineage
ényɔ̀ŋ – sky
èsòp – court
èté – father

étî – good, beautiful
èwáŋá – final stage of marriage settlement
íbáàn – women
íbɔ́k – medicine; juju
ìbét – taboo
ídém – body
ídìɔŋ – diviner *(ábíà ídîɔŋ)*
ìdíók – malevolence, ugliness
ídúŋ – dwelling, village
ìfót – witch
íkɔ̀t – bush
ínòkòn – Igbo from Arochukwu
ísíp – palm kernel
ísɔ̀ŋ – soil
ísó ńdêm or *ísó íbɔ́k* – shrine
m̀bàkárà – ruler, European
m̀bét – laws
m̀bìàm – curse, oath
m̀bòbó (m̀bòpó Ib.*)* – fattening
m̀fòró – to change, to become
m̀kpàráwà – youth
m̀kpàtát – creeping plant *(Selaginella scandens)*
náám – to be influenced by
    ínáám – drunkenness
    ánáám – possession
ńdêm – spirit
ǹdɔ̀ – marriage
ǹdómó – testing
ǹdɔ̀k – end of year , harvest
ǹdúɔ̀hɔ̀ – a charm to delay or change expected actions
ǹkà – age group
óbɔŋ – *(ábɔ́ɔŋ* Ib.*)* – chief
óbíò – village
ódùdù – power
òkpɔ̀sɔ̀ŋ – powerful, strong
òkpòhò – manilla
òkpùngó – change
ówó – person
ùbén – witchcraft
údíá – food
údîm – group
úfɔk – house
úkáŋ – ordeal

ùkôt – in-laws
úkpɔ̂ŋ – soul
úkpèmé – protection
ùrùà – market
úsíó ǹdɔ̂ – divorce
úsûɔ – road
ùtíbè – contribution club

Market Days
édét ábô
ábô
ùrùàbôm
ófìɔŋ
édét
édítàhá
àtím
ékényɔ̀ŋ

1

INTRODUCTION:
THE MAN-LEOPARD MURDER
MYSTERIES

'MURDER AT IKOT OKORO – LEOPARD ALLEGED'
Leopards, or human leopards as some suspect, have been waging a
relentless war on the people of this division, particularly those living
in Ikot Okoro Area. Again and again the people have appealed to
Government for help. They have wailed for a long time, but no help
has been forthcoming. Day after day reports are made of loss of several
lives due to the ravages of these ferocious animals. Nobody knows
what Government thinks of this state of affairs. Recently the house
boy to Court Messenger Okon Bassey was attacked and killed while
on his way to tap palm wine near a riverside. The people are like sheep
without a shepherd.

Nigerian Eastern Mail, 10 March 1945

This newspaper article launched the official investigation into the 'man-
leopard' murders. From this moment, and for the next three years, the
Imperial gaze of police, press and politicians was focused on Calabar
Province in south-eastern Nigeria. At the time the police investigation was
reported as the 'biggest, strangest murder hunt in the world',[1] and it would
become the last major investigation in Africa into killings linked to a shape-
shifting cult. Three years later, when the police wound up their enquiries
in early 1948, they calculated that 196 men, women and children had
been victims of the man-leopard murders, though they also conceded that
there were almost certainly more murders that were never brought to light.
During this period ninety-six men were convicted of murder, seventy-seven
of whom were executed. Despite these facts, those closest to the investigation feared that the origin of the so-called 'man-leopard' murders would
probably never be discovered with any degree of certainty, and that the
events would remain shrouded in mystery.[2]

Every murder mystery starts with a body. Yet no one had reported the
suspicious circumstances surrounding the death of Dan Udoffia, Okon
Bassey's house-boy, until this article appeared in a weekly newspaper
published in Calabar, the provincial headquarters and coastal trading hub.
The first report of Udoffia's death was prompted by an anonymous tip-off
from two men, a court clerk and a school teacher, who were both stationed
in Ikot Okoro, the scene of Udoffia's death. They believed that he had been

murdered by 'human-leopards', and their intention was to alert the new Colonial Officer to their suspicions. The District Officer in question, Frederick Kay, had been posted to Abak that same month. His reputation as a stickler had preceded him. On reading the article in the *Nigerian Eastern Mail* Kay launched a preliminary enquiry. The victim's body was exhumed, and a post-mortem examination carried out in the nearby town of Ikot Ekpene revealed that Udoffia had died from shock and haemorrhage caused by two puncture wounds made by a sharp instrument. The doctor's autopsy report stated categorically that it was a man and not a leopard that had inflicted the wounds. With this evidence Kay began to believe that there was some substance to the suspicions voiced in the newspaper article and that, as he put it, murder was manifest.

Despite the medical evidence the initial investigation drew a blank. Kay spent fourteen hours taking twenty pages of statements from six witnesses, including an eye-witness to the fatal assault. In his statement Akpan Etuk Udo said that after tapping palm wine he had been walking home with Dan Udoffia on the evening of 22 February when he heard the sound of a commotion behind him. As he swung round he saw, just seven paces away, a leopard pinning Udoffia to the ground. He shouted and ran at the leopard, which disappeared into the bush. Though Udoffia was wounded he got to his feet and the two men ran home to the court compound in Ikot Okoro. The next day Udoffia's master and neighbour, Okon Bassey, took charge of the patient and moved him to his own house. Along with Akpan Etuk Udo and Frank Umoren, the court clerk, Okon Bassey marched several miles to fetch Nchericho, a 'native doctor', to attend to him, but before dawn on the following morning, 24 February, Dan Udoffia succumbed to his injuries.

So far so innocent, Kay reported. But the finger of suspicion had begun to point to the very person who had apparently tried to save the dying man, Okon Bassey. He was a head court messenger with seventeen years' service and had been at home on leave in Ikot Okoro at the end of February 1945. There was no direct evidence implicating Okon Bassey, but suspicion fell on him because of his role in a bizarre series of events on 23 February. When Udoffia was moved to Bassey's house that day several people were known to have visited the victim, including the local headmaster, other schoolteachers and the court clerk. Yet Bassey had refused to allow the local dispenser, James Ekpat Ekpo, who was the closest thing to a medical doctor in the vicinity and who lived just opposite, to see or treat the dying man. Then, when he died, Bassey buried Udoffia's body himself without making any report to the authorities. Perhaps, the District Officer reflected, the dispenser's intervention might have saved Udoffia's life; perhaps Okon Bassey had something to hide.

After ten days' investigation the police at Abak arrested Okon Bassey for manslaughter as he was not accused of physically taking part in the attack.

Local rumour had it, however, that he was in league with accomplices, two fellow members of a secret man-leopard society. 'It was commonly canvassed,' wrote the District Officer, 'that the man had met his death at the hands of the leopard society'. At the time Kay himself was no more convinced of this idea of a secret society having been employed to kill Dan Udoffia than he was of Akpan Etuk Udo's eye-witness evidence that he had seen a leopard at the scene of the attack:

> It may be that Akpan Etuk Udo's story is a tissue of lies – that there was not the semblance of a leopard or of a member of the leopard society, and that he and his associates destroyed deceased.[3]

A week later, however, the police investigation revealed a motive for the murder. Returning to his station in southern Ukanafun, Bassey was not only accompanied by his second of five wives, Maggie, but also by Dan Udoffia's widow, Unwa Obot. Plain-clothes police established that noisy quarrels were heard between the two women and Okon Bassey because he insisted on having sex with Udoffia's widow. Returning to his house in Ikot Okoro, the police took statements from Bassey's other wives, which would prove crucial to the prosecution's case against him. The police investigation was completed in July 1945 and although Kay remained sceptical about the leopard society theory and whether Bassey had himself ever been among its members, he was convinced that Okon Bassey had killed Dan Udoffia in order to carry on an affair with his wife.

Okon Bassey was subsequently charged with murder and the case was heard before a packed Supreme Court, with Mr Justice Manson presiding, on 27 November 1945. Prosecuting for the Crown, Barrister L. N. Mbanefo stated that Bassey had ambushed Udoffia on account of past disputes between them, and disguising himself as a man-leopard seriously wounded his neighbour with a sharp instrument and left him for dead. After the attack Bassey was further accused of refusing Udoffia medical treatment, of concealing him in his house, and of secretly and indecently burying him.[4] Bassey's defence counsel, Barrister J. M. Coco-Bassey, offered little to refute the charge. His case hinged on calling Bassey's wives as witnesses to establish his alibi, but their evidence on oath was dismissed under cross-examination as it was contradicted by statements the police had taken from them previously in Ikot Okoro. These statements claimed that Bassey had not been in the compound with his wives at the time of the attack as he had claimed. Bassey's senior wife, Edima, had stated that Bassey had threatened to kill Udoffia just hours before the murder and that he had taken her to Udoffia's grave the day after he was buried where he showed her faked leopard pad marks and where he had said that 'a leopard always dances on the grave of its victim'.[5] With his alibi broken the defence case collapsed and Okon Bassey was convicted on the evidence of his own wives. On 29 November 1945 he was sentenced to death by hanging.

In January 1946 the Resident of Calabar Province informed the regional Government of the unanimous desire among local councils and the District Officers for Okon Bassey, now a 'famous figure', to be hanged in public. Though he recognised that public executions had been abolished in 1943, the Resident endorsed this request in order to correct a widespread rumour that condemned murderers were not in fact hanged but taken to work as slaves in distant parts of the country or else exiled abroad.[6] At 9 o'clock on the morning of Saturday, 30 March 1946, just over a year after Dan Udoffia died, Okon Bassey was hanged in the yard of Abak prison. Thousands of people gathered outside and three chiefs were allowed to witness the execution along with a handful of officials, including Kay, who had requested to be there for 'political reasons'.

Apart from being the first man-leopard enquiry, the Udoffia case has a particular significance for the writing of this book. Fifty years after the man-leopard murders, by coincidence, the court clerk from Ikot Okoro who had anonymously written to the *Nigerian Eastern Mail* calling for the Government to act in the war against the human-leopards, Frank Akpan Umoren, became my guide to Annang history, and my friend. Umoren was the court clerk who, as a result of wartime under-staffing in 1945, covered both Ikot Okoro and Mbiakot Native Courts. DO Kay mentions that one 'Frank' along with Okon Bassey met Dan Udoffia and Akpan Etuk Udo returning from the attack, and that Frank trekked some distance to bring a 'native doctor' to treat Udoffia the day before he died. Umoren's own recollections of the Udoffia case are revealing. Though his junior within the Ikot Okoro court compound, Bassey had once threatened Umoren that he would soon be killed by a leopard believed to stalk the area. This was no mere insubordination, however, as to forecast death in this way was tantamount to a declaration of his own criminal intentions. Umoren had also heard Bassey threaten Udoffia that he would not live to marry a new wife. Umoren's account of the motive in the Udoffia case differs from that presented in court. He claimed that the dispute between Bassey and Udoffia was about wives as DO Kay had thought, but was not as straightforward. Udoffia owned land which he had rented on a pledge agreement to one of Bassey's wives. But Udoffia himself wished to marry again and needed money to complete his brideprice. He therefore redeemed his plot from Bassey's wife and re-pledged it to a man from Ikot Okoro called Abraham, at a higher rate. The reason for the master's ominous threat to his servant was this personal snub, and that he had been denied access to farmland at a time when food prices were especially high for poorly paid court auxiliaries.

Frank Umoren left the colonial service soon after the war to take up a more lucrative trade in piassava, palm oil and kernels. Fifty years on Obong (Dr) Frank Umoren is the paramount ruler, an officially recognised chief,

Figure 1.1 Obong (Dr) F. A. Umoren (© David Pratten)

of the southern Ukanafun clan in what is now Akwa Ibom State. On 29 December 2000, in a ceremony marked by the dispensation of honours upon his family and supporters, he celebrated his centenary. His recollections of the last century encompass histories of clan migration and knowledge of Annang social order prior to the violence of colonial arrival, along with a personal story of education, conversion, colonial service, and the rise and fall of political fortunes. All of these aspects would intrigue a curious new arrival to Chief Umoren's village of Ikot Akpa Nkuk, but none so much as the intimacies and accusations he revealed surrounding the man-leopard murder mysteries. It was this personal connection to the murders that led me to re-examine the published record, to try to exhume the colonial archive in Nigeria, Britain and America, and it was this introduction which suggested the possibility of unmasking further details of the murders from men and women of the villages in and around what was once known as the 'leopard area'.

★　★　★

The mysteries surrounding the man-leopard murders are of two distinct but related kinds: the immediate and the historical. The immediate problems of the criminal investigations are those related to the evidence available in particular cases: the means and the motive of each killing. The broader historical questions concern why these deaths happened when and where they did. Dan Udoffia's murder, though it was probably not the first man-leopard murder in Calabar Province during the 1940s, is nevertheless the natural beginning to this book. It was the first investigation to be launched, aspects of the case would shape subsequent inquiries, and as such it introduced many of the forensic puzzles of the man-leopard mysteries. The Udoffia case was indicative of a set of forensic questions concerning who or what was responsible for the deaths, questions that were complicated by problematic physical evidence and by contradictory witness statements.

How the killings might be seen as being of their time is the longer narrative of this work, but they were unquestionably of their place. The 'man-leopard' murders were committed in a landscape of flat, dense oil palm on the west bank of the Qua Iboe river. The physical landscape of this southern Annang territory was natural leopard habitat and the killers used this to their advantage. The location and timing of the attack on Udoffia and subsequent victims mimicked that of a leopard. Most of the murders happened on an isolated and deserted bush path. It was the sort of path villagers were known to pass regularly in the course of harvesting forest products, especially palm wine (as Udoffia had been) or *áfân* leaves used in preparing soup. The killers also attacked at dusk as leopards are known to do and as they had in the Udoffia case. Even if the victim's body was discovered quickly, the rapidly setting sun would soon discourage anyone sending for the police and would delay any search for clues or suspects until the following morning. It was not unusual, in fact, for crime scenes to be disturbed, sometimes with the addition of elaborate details to throw the police off track, between their discovery and any investigation.

In this habitat it was hard to distinguish between real leopard attacks and those which simulated them. The victims appeared to have been killed in the same way a wild leopard attacks its prey, from behind and biting at the neck and throat. Hence, the evidence of who or what was responsible for the attacks, leopard or man-leopard, is an enduring puzzle of the murders. The answer depended on the forensic medical evidence. The effectiveness of the techniques and tests of the 1940s, at least those available to doctors in Ikot Ekpene and Port Harcourt where most of the post-mortem examinations were carried out, was limited, especially when they were confronted with the severity of mutilation and decomposition which was typical of the victims' remains. It was not uncommon for victims to have been buried, as in the Udoffia case, and sometimes for years, before the police became aware of the suspicious circumstances surrounding the death. Udoffia's case, in which his wounds were consistent with stabs from a sharp pointed object, possibly a readily available farming tool like a yam spike or a file, was also similar to most of the subsequent deaths. The line in distinguishing between murder and mauling, between yam spike and leopard claw, was a fine one and required precision in its detection. The forensic evidence would swing overwhelmingly in favour of human agency, but the doctors had apparently been duped for several years prior to Kay's investigation into the Udoffia case and there remained sufficient room for further suspicions to emerge.

Nagging doubts regarding the physical evidence were compounded by inconsistencies in witness statements. The details of the eye-witness testimony in the Udoffia case, in which Akpan Etuk Udo claimed to have seen a leopard from the bush attack Udoffia, would be repeated with remarkable frequency throughout the investigations. For whatever reason, because they were telling the truth and this was how it appeared to them, or because they were concealing the identity of the killer, a high proportion of eye-witnesses testified to the police in their initial statement that they had seen a wild leopard attack the victim. In many instances, however, the eye-witnesses subsequently changed their stories. Again, whether they did so because the police allayed their fears or they spoke under duress would become a moot point, but these eye-witnesses invariably recollected, sometimes weeks later, that it was a man, sometimes two and usually someone they could name, whom they had seen stalking and assaulting the victim. In this context where witness evidence was inconsistent and unreliable, the main problem that arose was that of distinguishing between credible information and malicious accusation. Personal animosities, threats, grudges and resulting accusations, all of which emerged during the Udoffia case, would characterise almost every subsequent killing.

In two crucial respects Dan Udoffia's death differed from other man-leopard murders, and these features were probably why the case was the first to be exposed. Udoffia was not killed in the initial assault. His body was therefore not subject to the elaborate mutilations which served to disguise his wounds and simulate a leopard attack. As a result it was easier to establish pathologically the cause of his death. Yet these circumstances also expose a glaring evidential inconsistency. Since Dan Udoffia was well enough to walk home, why is there no mention of him definitely identifying who or what attacked him? Of course, this may well have been why Okon Bassey shielded his ward from outsiders; Bassey and others may well have conspired together; and the fear of being identified by this group may well be why the schoolteacher and the court clerk (who both saw Udoffia) alerted the authorities anonymously and rather circuitously.

If the means of murder in the Udoffia case were problematic, the question of motive was equally complex and bound up in a number of assumptions and suspicions. Local rumours fuelled colonial concerns that the strange deaths in western Calabar Province were the work of a secret leopard society. Experience of secret society 'revivals' across the Province and knowledge of Annang shape-shifting beliefs, coupled with the apparent conspiracy in the Udoffia case, suggested the operation of a covert network. Whether the murders were conducted by a secret society or a gang of hired assassins would became one of the most significant questions of the entire investigation. The reticence of local chiefs in providing information in the Udoffia case and those that followed further suggested that this was a subversive movement led by arch-conservatives within the village hierarchy.

Question marks over the precise organisation of the group conducting the killings were linked to the question of their intentions. Were the killers' motives ritual or revenge? The Udoffia case revealed marriage, brideprice, land tenure, debt and money to be central issues of dispute between the victim and the convicted. The puzzle, however, was this: could such apparently mundane motives, disputes which filled the court record books before, during and after the murders, account for all the killings? These commonplace disagreements might be expected to spill over into violence in only a handful of extreme and isolated instances, so was it feasible that they could explain almost 200 deaths in such a short space of time? There did not appear to be any ritual component to the Udoffia case, but the connection with secret societies meant the question was raised from the outset, as was the possibility that the killings were linked to performances at secret village shrines.

As more and more victims were discovered the question resurfaced. Was it possible that the wounds on the victims' bodies disguised more than the human hands that had inflicted them? Did the serial nature of the killings and the consistently precise pattern of mutilation not only conceal but reveal a ritual motive, the removal of human flesh and body parts for use in the performance of ceremonies to confer wealth or power on the killers and their confessors? This would become the most significant puzzle of the entire investigation, and for its three years' duration the debate over motives, whether ritual or revenge, would pass backwards and forwards from police posts to the provincial residency, and from Lagos to London.

These forensic puzzles, the identity of the killers and their means and motives, have provoked heated and long-running debates in which lives and careers have been lost. Yet this was not the first time such questions had arisen on the continent. To these puzzles from Calabar Province we may add a comparative context and an array of murder mysteries posed by 'human-leopards' and their crimes, actual or imagined, from elsewhere in Africa.

LEOPARD MEN IN FACT AND FICTION

From isolated anecdotes to widespread 'outbreaks', reports of the 'leopard' killing subterfuge have displayed a wide regional distribution and variation across the African continent over the past two centuries.[7] The cases from Sierra Leone at the end of the nineteenth century, from the Congo in the

1920s and from Tanganyika in the 1940s, however, are among the most well-known and reviewed cases. The sensational nature and high profile of these incidents and the way in which they seemed to confirm the most sinister of European colonial fantasies about Africa meant that the figure of the 'leopard man' featured prominently in fictional depictions of the continent in novels and films from the turn of the twentieth century onwards. Africa represented a blank space in Europe's collective imagination and could therefore be populated by all manner of invented creatures, sometimes noble, sometimes monstrous, that were the visual and visceral products of European fears and desires.[8]

Both the context of comparative 'big-cat' killings elsewhere in Africa and their fictional portrayal shaped the setting of the man-leopard killings in Nigeria and the range of ideas colonial investigators applied to them. From the mid-nineteenth century onwards reports of deaths disguised by the simulation of injuries inflicted by wild animals on their prey emerged from Sierra Leone to become the most notorious theriomorphic murders in West Africa. These deaths were linked to societies of human-leopards, human-alligators and human-baboons. Reports emerged from the Sherbro chiefdoms in the Sierra Leone hinterland in 1882 that 'the witches that transformed themselves into leopards, [had] destroyed and eaten over 40 persons'.[9] From the evidence presented in subsequent trials and investigations a common *modus operandi* emerged. The 'leopards' went out at night as a group and killings were conducted by one or two disguised with leopard skins over their heads and armed with five blades set as a claw-like instrument. After the killing, human flesh was cooked and consumed, it was alleged, and human fat was rubbed on a 'medicine' known as *bofima*.

The Sierra Leone 'human-leopards' posed a set of puzzles that would re-surface decades later along the coast in Nigeria. These included questions about what people meant when they referred to a 'leopard', what they meant when they claimed the killers 'ate' their victims, the origin and organisation of the human-leopard society, why those accused were often linked to chieftaincy politics, and how the colonial authorities would manage their response. The most significant feature of this episode, however, was the problematic ritual meanings that were attributed to the murders.

The underlying puzzle was the ontological status of the killers. In the Upper Guinea forest the generic Mende term referring to murders of this indeterminate type is *boni hinda* ('leopard business').[10] For some the victims were killed at night by witches with supernatural, theriomorphic powers, while others believed that the 'human-leopards' were men and women who disguised their crimes by simulating a wild leopard attack. The disparities between Mende and European modes of perception and understanding underpinned these contradictions. While European thought considers shape-shifting an interior process of altered consciousness, the peoples of the Guinea Coast perceive it as a change in objective reality and hence describe it as an exterior event.[11] European perceptions dismissed Mende accounts of supernatural causes in favour of finding a human culprit. In the murky space in between these views opportunities arose for political plotting, private intrigue and for lodging cynically motivated accusations. Indeed, for many, the crucial aspect of the investigation was not in understanding the murder motives so much as the motivations behind these accusations.

The accusations of *boni hinda* coincided with a particular historical moment of political crisis and social tension within rural Mende society. An underlying historical transformation was the shift in the centre of economic power during the late nineteenth century from the slave-trading coast to the palm oil-producing hinterland.[12] The subsequent colonial takeover of the Sierra Leone hinterland in 1886 was associated with an intersection of commercial rivalries, trade disputes, government backing for a new class of chiefs and the associated collapse of confidence in indigenous political structures. In the new colonial constitution chiefs were better able to exploit new opportunities to exact exorbitant levies and fines from their subjects. It was these exploited dependants who were willing witnesses in the colonial courts against their powerful patrons and other groups such as clerks, traders and missionaries who were accumulating wealth under the Protectorate. Accusations of leopardism against chiefs and headmen resonated with local conceptions of chieftaincy and its animal symbolism. Chiefs, like their counterparts elsewhere, were already 'human-leopards' of a sort since hunters were obliged to give them the skin, teeth and claws of a leopard they killed. The human-leopard murders may consequently be seen as resulting from the collapse of a system of egalitarian norms, from rampant political individualism of newly emergent classes, and from popular perceptions that the seizing of power involved the magical consumption of the vital organs of the most vulnerable in society.[13]

In contrast, some suggest that the human-leopard societies in Sierra Leone were a form of insurgency and rebellion in the face of the colonial encounter both in its political context and in terms of personal and psychological meanings. It has been argued that the magical manipulation of consciousness involved in shape-shifting embraced the ideals of personhood, of generosity and magnanimity represented by totemic animals such as the leopard. The different modalities of shape-shifting on the Guinea Coast revealed a personal agenda and a search for individual autonomy, meaning and control in a world that appeared unpredictable and ungraspable. Motivated by a 'concatenation' of personal grievances, political resentments and economic frustrations perhaps the leopard-men sought power and control over their own situation by realising 'the wildest imaginings and worst prejudices of their oppressors'.[14]

One of the key features of reports about human-leopards in Sierra Leone was their association with accusations of ritual cannibalism and the use of human body parts in the manufacture of charms. In order to make the *bofima* medicine's owner rich and powerful, it was thought to need to be anointed with human fat and smeared with human blood.[15] The link between the murders and the medicine led the investigation directly to the activities of the wealthy and powerful in Guinea Coast society. *Bofima* might be held collectively or it might be the personal charm of individuals aspiring to enhance their charisma, wealth and status. The human-leopards were therefore thought to be the cohorts of political aspirants, especially chiefs, and it was thought that the killing cycle reproduced itself. Each person who received power from the revitalised *bofima* incurred a 'flesh debt' which could be satisfied only with the death of a person whom they 'owned', like a slave, a ward or a consanguineous descendant; 'one eats what one is attached to', and this was usually a low-status adolescent.[16]

The cannibal might be perceived as an anti-colonialist, anti-modernist sign, as with other 'traditional' forms and poetics of violence.[17] The degree to which the extensive reports of human-leopard attacks on the Atlantic coast represented specific and real accounts of actual cannibalistic rites, however, is a key puzzle.[18] Eating and consuming are polysemic terms of the utmost ambiguity. Cannibalism can be taken as a metaphorical mode of explaining death, and as a politically motivated representation. Indeed, later enquiries with descendants of those from this region related how their ancestors had reported cannibalism cases to the District Commissioners in order to undermine the claims of their political rivals. Although contemporary informants may have their own reasons for not wanting to implicate their ancestors in 'leopard business', those who might take the archival records of these accusations at face value are therefore warned to exercise circumspection.[19]

The organisation and origin of the human-leopard society in Sierra Leone raised further problems. The human-leopard society was organised like the various sodalities of Mende, Temne and Sherbro society, including Poro, Sande and Thoma, and involved initiation, the use of 'medicine' and oaths of secrecy. In contrast to these groups, however, which stood for the social reproduction of the community in preparing children for adulthood, upholding the moral and physical order, and acting as the counterbalance to chieftaincy, the human-leopards were anti-social and stood for the accumulation of selfish, individual power.[20] The cases in Sierra Leone raised the question of whether the human-leopard society had formed a part of the social fabric in perpetuity, or whether reports of their crimes not only coincided with but were caused by colonial arrivals. The possibility of links between the 'leopard murders' and the Atlantic slave trade were never far from the surface. The *bofima* medicine was assumed always to have been the essential source of political power on the Sierra Leone coast and in the hinterland. Before the establishment of the Colony, when slaves and captives from internecine wars were more readily available, it was thought that there had been no need for the subterfuge of the leopard-style killing in securing victims for the *bofima* rites. Hence it was argued that the human-leopard society was of relatively recent origin, the early nineteenth century perhaps, and that its formation was linked not with the slave trade *per se* but with its abolition and the extension of colonial rule from Colony to Protectorate.[21] There was therefore a functional and literal colonial supposition that the human-leopard subterfuge was invented to conceal abduction and murder from watchful European eyes.[22]

More recent analyses of the murders in Sierra Leone also link the human-leopards to stories from the Atlantic slave trade era.[23] Memories of cannibalism linked to the Atlantic trade formed a lens, it has been suggested, through which the predatory and extractive relationships of the legitimate trade era could be evaluated.[24] The argument is that the 'leopard scare' in Sierra Leone at the end of the nineteenth century reworked the memories of earlier rumours of eating the vanquished in warfare and of European cannibals carrying away slaves to be consumed. This problematic re-historicising therefore tends to rework the very same narratives and fantasies that it is trying to contextualise. The danger indeed is that the reconstruction of a nineteenth-century political imagination begins to look suspiciously like the recirculation of a familiar narrative adopted by colonial commentators. In his 1915 account, for instance, one of the judges in Sierra Leone, K. J. Beatty, related historical precedents for stories of cannibalism from the 1600s onwards in order to signal a narrative of backwardness and barbarism.

The official response to reports of these murders in Sierra Leone was not against the leopard men specifically, but rather against those who accused and denounced them. The Tongo players' dance and performance was officially proscribed in 1892 because of the suspicion that it ordered punishments, including public burnings, of those accused of employing the leopard killing ruse for the purpose of cannibalism. Subsequent 'leopard-style' murders led to the introduction of extraordinary legislation in 1895, the year before Protectorate status was extended to the Sierra Leone hinterland. Between 1903 and 1912, seventeen cases were heard by a circuit court in which 186 people were charged with murder under the Human Leopard Society Ordinance. The scope of leopard society activities appeared to escalate in July 1912 when a murder was foiled in Imperri and one of the assailants turned King's evidence. The information he gave on a further thirty murders led to the arrest of almost 400 people, of whom 108, including several paramount chiefs (*mahawa*), were committed for trial before a Special Commission Court.

The ambiguities and uncertainties surrounding the events in Sierra Leone at the turn of the century compounded the difficulty of investigating accusations of covert assassination. The colonial investigations on the Guinea Coast therefore reveal a number of points which are of comparative insight. Despite the severe provisions of the legislation in place and the status of the judges shipped to the colony, the effectiveness of the colonial enquiry was undermined by the problematic nature of the evidence. Several cases, for instance, hinged on trying to identify human-leopards from supposed initiation marks on their buttocks.[25] In many ways the lack of corroborative evidence to support the accusations served precisely to confirm colonial fears about the covert nature of the human-leopards and the overwhelming and terrorising influence they had upon local people:

> In cases of this sort where the principal men are bound together by the bonds of guilt as well as of secrecy, where the victim is provided by the head of the family, who, instead of ferreting out the crime, uses all his influence to have the matter hushed up, and where the whole people cower down in dread of the terrible vengeance threatened by the awe-inspiring Borfima, it is not to be wondered at that it is exceptional to be able to procure independent evidence.[26]

Rather than investigate the motives behind the accusations, in fact, efforts were made to enquire into the reticence of informants and witnesses. A District Commissioner's Enquiry of 1913 believed that when government officers were making enquiries, an attempt was made 'to swear' the whole country and to put the entire population under an oath of secrecy.[27]

These difficulties were compounded by the presence of arch-sceptics who were unwilling to entertain the notion of human-leopards and who dabbled in the zoological sciences to prove their point. 'Leopard' murder inquiries were launched only when the authorities gave credence to the accusations, and when particular Colonial Officers refused to entertain the possibility of human-leopards the official murder rate declined. From 1912 to 1939 only three of the animal-related murders were reported in Sierra Leone. This period coincided with the tenure as Provincial Commissioner of Captain W. B. Stanley (based in Pujehun, Northern Sherbro) who was convinced that the cases of 'fetish murder' were in fact genuine cases of killing by wild animals – leopards, alligators and chimpanzees.[28] Stanley believed that his colonial predecessors had misjudged the situation because they refused to accept that Sierra Leone's wildlife was killing human beings and he sought to prove that chimpanzees were carnivorous. Stanley's intervention marks a striking parallel between events in Sierra Leone and those that would unfold in Nigeria.

Reports of the 'human-leopards' in Sierra Leone had a formative impact on conceptions of covert killings throughout the British colonies. The relationship between the knowledge of secret societies and human sacrifice along the West African Coast in the late nineteenth century became a regular topic of talks at Royal Anthropological Society meetings in London.[29] The human-leopards and lions in the eastern Congo which were involved in several 'outbreaks' had a similar effect on the francophone world. Belgian museum collections of human-leopard paraphernalia, including spotted 'leopard' costumes and knife-holding gloves, which came from the investigations in the eastern Congo, are responsible for much of the visual imagery of the big-cat killings.[30] There are two specific issues raised by accounts of human-leopards and lions from the Congo which have a bearing on subsequent events in Nigeria. The first is how they have been interpreted as the 'social heroes' of political resistance movements; the second is the way in which they have been seen as specialist assassins hired to intimidate rivals in local conflicts.

A series of outbreaks of human-lion killings in the Tabwa region of Congo near Baudonville (Moba) ran episodically from 1886 to 1942. The earliest coincided with European arrivals: those at the turn of the century took place against the background of the imposition of taxation, those in the inter-war period were set against famines, the influenza pandemic and the effects of the depression, and the last reported cases were associated with newly implemented British-style indirect rule, exacerbated by mobilisation efforts during the Second World War. Of these outbreaks, the murders during the 1890s have been interpreted within the broader historical process of colonial encounter and have been subject to claims that these lion-men attacks were 'a political strategy of terrorism'.[31] Tabwa lion-men (*visanguka*) had the power to make themselves invisible. They killed using iron claws while disguising themselves with animal skins and their crime scenes with carved pad prints.[32] During 1894 ten victims were killed near the White Fathers' mission station at Baudonville. Though other motives figured in these cases, including debt and adultery, it was the victims' connection to the missionaries that was perceived to be the critical feature. From April 1895 to March 1896 there was evidence of a concerted attack on mission followers, and the missionaries obtained permission from the Congo Free State forcibly to prevent converts from deserting their stations. This has led to the suggestion that the man-lion killers were 'social bandits' or 'heroic criminals' leading a liberation movement against colonialism and mission Christianity.[33] 'The whole movement', it was claimed, 'was a conservative reaction against ... collaborators with the colonisers'.[34] A common theme in the historiography and ethnography of human-leopards, indeed, is to link them with resistance to alien or indigenous elites. This leads us to consider the possibility that the leopard men were African social bandits or anti-heroes and to the question of whether they expressed pre-political sentiments and a desire for a just world.[35]

Two decades later, from 1919 to the mid-1930s, leopard-related killings emerged in the Bali region of Congo's Stanleyville District. Here, the leopard men were known as *anioto* (from the Bafwasea verb *nioto*, to scratch). The *anioto* functioned both as a weapon of war between rival chieftaincies, and as a means to right the wrongs of local justice, especially over brideprice cases.[36] Against a backdrop of administrative reforms in which the Belgian authorities sought to introduce British-style 'indirect rule' and in which customary law was afforded greater legitimacy, the *anioto* killings were seen as a political device by which rivals could undermine a chief's capacity to maintain law and order. As elsewhere, the leopard men were thought to be organised as a secret society, in this case as the exclusive upper-echelon of the *mambela* society. Initiation was said to involve practising the leopard method for the first attack, which was always to be on a relative in order to prove fealty to the association. The colonial response was to regulate secret societies, including the registration of members, and in 1936 the District Commissioner of Stanleyville insisted that women and children should see and therefore undermine the power of the otherwise secret regalia and practices of the *mambela*.

Congolese leopard men also became intimately linked with acts of political assassination. In 1933 and 1934 the Belgian authorities waged an extensive campaign against 'human-leopards' in north-eastern Congo. The 'aniotique campaign' began in 1933 with a mysterious death in Beni (Eastern Province) when a victim's left arm had been severed and a subsequent thirty-eight cases were investigated. A public prosecutor held an enquiry in January 1934 and a man known as Luluma was arrested. He denied having committed the murders but admitted to being a member of a sect, the human-leopards known as *wahokohoko*. A second magistrate's enquiry was launched in May 1934 (assisted by Joset, whose account is our main source). From the enquiries and the trials the killings appeared to be linked to inter-clan conflicts provoked by tensions over the payment of taxes and tribute, the installation of chiefs and disputes over land. The *wahokohoko*, then, were specialist assassins hired by prominent chiefs to further their ambitions, exact revenge, extract tribute or exert coercion during these inter-clan conflicts.[37]

Stories of the human-leopards in Sierra Leone encouraged the Nigerian investigators to look for ritual motives, while evidence from Congo pointed to assassination and resistance. Contrasting evidence of human-lion killings in Tanganyika, however, suggested two further issues that would dominate the investigations in south-eastern Nigeria: everyday motives for assassination and a connection between the killings and tensions within the household. The Usure area of central Tanganyika had apparently been visited by 'lion-men' in the 1920s, though investigations into over 200 deaths at the time were inconclusive. The suspicion was, however, that witch-doctors could control or turn themselves into wild lions (*mbojo* in Turu; *antu nsimba* in Swahili).[38] Evidence from deaths attributed to the *mbojo* which began to appear in the neighbouring Eastern Singida Province in 1946 was more revealing, and by July 1947 103 cases had been reported.[39]

The ambiguous identity of the killers was, as elsewhere, a key question. While the killers could have been men dressed in animal skins using iron claws, or men who had transformed themselves into a lion, the overriding explanation was that they were real lions controlled by a witch. These witches were usually women, since all women in Turu society were believed to possess latent witchcraft (*aroghi*) powers. Abnormal deaths, especially the *mbojo*-related deaths, were therefore attributed by men to women who had hated the victim and had commissioned the murder. Further evidence from later investigations revealed that the mode of the human-lion killings was peculiar. *Mbojo* assassins were named in the trials but never apprehended. They were people, many of them children, who had disappeared several years previously and who, it was claimed, had been abducted and trained to kill as a lion. These human-lions were hired for between 15 and 30 shillings and were assisted by the conspirators in mutilating the bodies of their victims to resemble a lion mauling. One man, for instance, claimed he had 'changed' a girl into the shape and habits of a lion by repeated doses of drugs (hashish the police thought) then hired her out to kill for 30 shillings.[40]

The Tanganyika cases were also explicitly linked to the shifting features of the colonial political landscape. First, the 1940s 'outbreak' followed a series of reforms which sought to empower decentralised traditional political structures. A government anthropologist, Hans Cory, who was brought in to investigate the murders, linked the deaths to local failings of indirect rule and argued that opposition to the human-lion practice was hampered by the recognition accorded village headmen by the German and then the British governments, which undermined the authority of more influential clan and sub-clan elders. Second, the deaths were linked to the impact and innovations of the colonial judicial systems.[41] Since witchcraft accusations could not be presented in these new courts it was suggested that perhaps local people substituted them with an embodied equivalent, a human-lion, whose identity could be revealed and who might be brought to trial not for nocturnal flights of imagination, but for plain murder.

Compared to the cases in Sierra Leone and Congo, the motives in the Tanganyika murders demonstrated marked differences. Fifteen of those who hired the *mbojo* were brought to court. The conclusion drawn from the evidence in these cases, which led to six executions, was that 'no mystical significance is attached to the despatch of the victims but this is done for the basest motives'.[42] In each of the cases in which convictions were upheld the apparent murder motives were petty and mundane, and included a woman's refusal to sell beer, a quarrel between relatives over a small debt and a wife's complaint that her husband was not supporting her. These motives, combined with accounts of how the lion-men were controlled by female witches,[43] have led to the conclusion that the human-lion killings in Tanganyika were the result of a collapse in gender relations and 'a coalescing of men against women'.[44]

All of the mysteries confronted in the big-cat killings elsewhere on the continent would figure in the man-leopard murders in Nigeria. The extent to which the investigators there were aware of the events in Sierra Leone, Congo and Tanganyika, however, is unclear. It seems unlikely that there was any formal liaison between the British colonial services. The Nigerian police files contained short press clippings and a copy of a report concerning the Singida lion-men. Senior officers in the Nigerian investigation tried in vain to consult accounts of events from Sierra Leone: one police officer on leave in London was frustrated in his efforts when he found that an account of the trials in Sierra Leone was out of print at Foyles bookshop.

★ ★ ★

While their knowledge of the details of these cases was limited, it is clear that the officers investigating the man-leopard cases in Nigeria nevertheless approached the murders armed with the vivid imagery of African leopard and lion-men. One of the magistrates sent to Opobo to hear the 'leopard murder' cases recalled having read an illustrated boys' magazine featuring the leopard men of Sierra Leone which 'depicted a group of hideous-looking monsters with cloaks and masks made of leopard-skin savaging their victims with specially fashioned steel claws'.[45] Fascination with African were-beasts and human-leopards was very much in vogue during the first half of the twentieth century. The leopard men began to appear in literature, comics and films from the 1900s onwards.[46] They became regular protagonists in dramatic tales set in the African colonies which played on the image of savage murder and barbaric rites, and served to embed popular perceptions of Africa among a European readership.

The leopard and lion men stories were popular allegories for both European encounters with the African continent, and of African encounters with Europe. They invariably portrayed characters who straddled these boundaries – Europeans in Africa and Africans who had been educated in Europe. The human-leopards of Sierra Leone became a stock in trade of colonial fiction. A 1900 novel by John Cameron Grant, *The Ethiopian*, claimed to be based on events of 1876 in Sierra Leone and tells the story of a chief's son, Jowé, who seeks to uncover the secrets of his culture deprived him by his missionary education in London but who, in the course of exploring his past, forms the Human Leopard Society of Westeria.[47] In Mary Gaunt's *The Arms of the Leopard*, an educated African, James Craven

MD, is engaged to an English woman. She falls for a political officer on the boat to West Africa and out of jealousy Craven enlists the Leopard Society to kill his rival.[48]

During the depression era the economic importance of the African colonies greatly increased, and authors and filmmakers in the 1930s were reinforcing and legitimising colonial political practices. For East Africa, lion-men societies figured as a feature of the safari genre, especially in novels relating the exploits of lone female explorers. John Crosbie's 1938 novel *The Lion Men*, for instance, is a Kenyan tale of game-hunters, colonial officers and a Russian countess and their encounter with the lion-men of Wa-Ndoro. With the initiation rites of aspiring warriors, which required the killing of a lion or a man, criminalised by the colonial government, the lion-men's underground society was overpowered by a punitive expedition, the burning of idols and the swearing of oaths of allegiance by the local chief.[49]

Two of the most popular figures of European boyhood fiction in the 1930s, Tintin and Tarzan, also encountered the leopard men in the pages of comics and pulp fiction of the period. In Hergé's 1931 comic, *Les aventures de Tintin: Reporter du Petit 'Vingtième' au Congo*, the eponymous hero's attempts to fend off diamond-smuggling gangsters led him to encounter the Anioto, a secret society of human-leopards organised, he is told, to halt the advance of the white men.[50] Rice Burroughs' *Tarzan and the Leopard Men* was serialised in the *Blue Book* magazine during 1932. The secret cult of the steel-clawed leopard men terrorised villages in the hunt for victims for their 'savage rites'. Only Tarzan could save Kali Bwana, the white woman held captive in the village of the Leopard Men. The book, first published in 1935, was made into a film by Kurt Neumann and released in 1946 as *Tarzan and the Leopard Woman*, in which trader caravans were ambushed by an 'evil leopard cult' led by the beautiful but deadly Priestess Lea.

Like the werewolf genre, leopard men as a literary subject became something of a standard for the horror adventure. Radio listeners in the United States heard Sherlock Holmes investigating the case of the 'African Leopard Man' in August 1944. In addition to the colonial narrative set in Africa, however, the detective dimension of the human-leopards, the unmasking of a cunning and lethal subterfuge, became a favourite for crime writers and movie-makers. The 1943 RKO movie *The Leopard Man*, directed by Jacques Tourneur, is a thriller set in New Mexico. A leopard (a panther in fact) belonging to a circus act is accidentally freed during a nightclub performance. A series of murders of young women killed at dusk is attributed to the prowling beast. It is the story of death foretold through prognostication and of outsiders confronting their colonial legacy. It is not a shape-shifting mystery, however, as the killer's ruse of murder in the style of a leopard is the key dramatic device. The real killer is not the leopard, the circus act or the glamorous nightclub performers. It is an expert in history and culture seconded to the investigation – the washed-up university lecturer!

By the 1950s human-leopard stories continued to figure prominently in both English and French fiction, especially in boys' stories and comics, in which young white men encountered the human-leopards in Africa and Europe. Many, including René Guillot's adventure set in a game reserve, involved the 'educated African' figure.[51] Through the 1950s and 1960s the leopard men continued to feature in European adventure comics, and as adversaries in the stories of Henri Vernes' Bob Morane and Victor Hubinon's Tiger Joe. The human-leopards of pulp fiction and 'B-movies' entered the television age in the late 1950s, featuring in an episode of *Sheena: Queen of the Jungle* in December 1956 when the heroine discovered uranium miners had been attacked not by leopards but by the 'dreaded and despised' 'Leopard Man'. As with novels set in Sierra Leone and East Africa, the leopard murders of Nigeria also became the subject of fiction. James Shaw's 1953 novel *The Leopard Men* was evidently influenced by the events described here and is an account of confrontations with human-leopards set on the English south coast and on the Cross River in south-eastern Nigeria.[52]

Just how significant these factual and fictional accounts were to the human-leopards or their pursuers in Calabar Province of Nigeria between 1945 and 1947 is difficult to say. Questions were asked at the time as to whether the various 'outbreaks' were linked by the secret knowledge and transmission of a pan-African leopard murder organisation. The trail on this line of enquiry in Nigeria went cold and the idea was dismissed. It is difficult to deny, however, that factual and fictional accounts contributed to a range of assumptions that came to the fore during the murder investigations. Ideas about the very possibility of shape-shifting 'leopard men', that the Annang leopard men used costumes and claws, and that there was a formula for the rites they performed at the murder scenes were assumptions derived from this body of evidence.

Despite the differences between the African 'big-cat killing' outbreaks in time, place, aesthetics and meanings, the comparative insights from colonial archives and fiction, set across the continent from the mid-nineteenth to mid-twentieth centuries, point to a broad set of 'man-leopard mysteries'. These range from understanding the meaning and motives of the leopard subterfuge to the organisational possibilities revealed in initiation and shadowy secret society-type organisations. The central themes of ritual and resistance and of the social cleavages of gender and generation are also shared by fictional and academic interpretations alike. The puzzles that surround the human leopards encompass the difficulties of establishing forensic proofs and are further underpinned by questions about the cultural construction of truth, perception and explanation. And common to all the human leopard accounts are apparently indeterminate links between murders and historical moments of social tension.

A SOCIAL HISTORY OF MURDER

The purpose of my account is not only to revisit the criminal and forensic dimensions of the murder enquiries suggested by events in Calabar Province and elsewhere across the continent, but also to place the murders in their historical context. My aim is to ask how life in colonial Nigeria, in its cultural, social, political and economic aspects, contributed to the murders, and in turn what the murders and their investigations say about life in colonial Nigeria:

> [This] ... does not imply that historians, disguised as judges, should try to re-enact the trials of the past ... The specific aim of this kind of historical research should be the reconstruction of the *relationship* between individual lives and the contexts in which they unfold.[53]

To hope that a synthesis of actors and their motives would expose the 'real', as yet uncovered, reason for the man-leopard murders would be to claim access to insights and information that are now buried secrets, and to fall into precisely the trap of expecting an overarching explanatory theory that beset the police at the time. Rather, faced with the complex and contradictory evidence, we have to countenance complex and contradictory analysis. The lure of the sensational murder in Africa as elsewhere, therefore, is to interrogate the broader social concerns revealed by the investigation of the crimes.[54] My account is informed throughout by this perspective and by the understanding that the murders reflected the historical trends of which they were a product. This lends itself to a way of writing which employs detailed investigation of individuals and their cultural worlds and of relating these to wider comparative and historical narratives.

The importance of narrative in this context, and more broadly for the writing of historical anthropology, cannot be underestimated:

> It is a critical instrument of human agency, for it is the principal means by which agents integrate the temporal flow of their activities. Putting it another way, human beings produce sociocultural forms through an arch of memories, actions and intentions. Narrative is the way in which that arch may be expressed, rehearsed, shared and commu-nicated. It is this which gives human action its inherent historicity or lived-in-timeness and which requires an anthropology that, to be adequate to its subject matter, should be essentially historical.[55]

Narrative, of course, offers the space for contradiction as well as tempo-ralisation.[56] Within such narrative discourse events serve as frames. Taking the murders as a single event, albeit an extended and complex one, is not a form of explanation in itself but 'permits an intelligibility' by framing and delimiting a cluster of historical analyses.[57] The event in this context serves less as a catalyst of change than to stage 'the mingling of the prescribed and the contingent'.[58]

What I also hope to show is that narrative and structure, contingency and culture, history and anthropology, are not discrete methodological options; narrative bends to structure and structure shapes narrative. The structuring here is not exclusively Annang, Christian or colonial in origin, but is rather a structuring of the encounter between them and concerns the 'existence and interaction between the cultural order as constituted in the society and as lived by the people: structure in convention and in action, as virtual and as actual'.[59] These encounters produced persistent, contradictory and often unresolved effects.

Recognising that history is re-authored, reinscribed and reconfigured, the emphasis on narratives and temporality in this account is an important check on a mode of historical anthropology that suggests resonances between past and present, but which elides an intervening period, and which avoids the forensic archive work necessary in accounting for historicity. This emphasis on historicity is especially important when we are reminded that colonialism was neither monolithic nor unchanging through history. As a result:

> We are confronted with the obvious fact that every document in a colonial archive – no matter how ignorant its author was of indigenous society or how unimportant his ideas were to future policy – is layered with the received account of earlier events and the cultural semantics of a political moment.[60]

Colonial conquest concerned both the territory of the 'oil rivers' hinterland, and the epistemological space associated with it. The exercise of power and the accumulation of knowledge were part of the same system. This project of documentation was both a product of the state bureaucracy and a set of technologies that bolstered state governance. It is in the colonial archives, the 'cross-sections of contested knowledge', therefore, that this study, in part, is based. The task here is twofold: to read between the lines and against its totalising classifications, but also to assess its rubrics of organisation and the continuities of its conventions:

> If a notion of colonial ethnography starts from the premise that archival production is both a process and a powerful technology of rule, then we need not only brush against the archives' received categories. We need to read for its regularities, for its logic of recall, for its densities and distributions, for its consistencies of misinformation, omission, and mistake *along* the archival grain.[61]

One reason why the leopard murders lend themselves to this mode of analysis and cast such particular light on Annang society was because the police had very little idea of why the murders were happening. They were so perplexed as to how the killings originated and how they could continue in the face of unprecedented surveillance that their search was extended over an ever-wider sociological and historical terrain. As reports of suspicious leopard-related deaths continued through 1946 and 1947 it became clear that the murders were linked not only to the ruses and rituals of the killers, but also to the broad impact of commercial, Christian and colonial relations on Annang society.

These stories begin with the global political economy of the nineteenth century whose shifting contours were reflected in the Annang political and symbolic landscape. Annang livelihoods had been intimately connected to the Atlantic slave trade and from the mid-nineteenth century onwards were dependent on palm oil exports. Annang concepts of personhood and agency, along with the cultural significance of animals, beliefs in shape-shifting and Annang ways of perceiving and explaining, became the subject of speculation and investigation during the murder enquiries, and were shaped in part by these economic trajectories. Leopards, palm fruit and oil became powerful signifiers of gendered contests within household agri-cultural production and of the transformations wrought by new sources of wealth. The relationships between human society and nature, between men and women, and between young and old are thus central to grasping the meaning of the murders as a whole.

Despite the economic significance of the palm oil-producing hinterland the villages in which the murders occurred constituted a remote adminis-trative backwater far from the political and commercial centre of Calabar. The effects of the fluctuations of the global palm oil market, however, were intensified in this region because of a peculiar economic feature: a dual currency of shilling and manilla. In 1948 the manilla was redeemed and demonetised at a rate of 1 per 3d, precisely the rate of exchange almost a century earlier in 1856. While this might suggest that the manilla had been an especially stable currency, it would overlook a volatile history of exchange rate fluctuations that would create clear winners and losers in the Annang economy and corresponding patterns of protest and violence.[62]

The complex nature of power and authority in the Annang past became crucial to questions about relationships and rights in the colonial present of the 1940s. Annang is a lineage-based society, and the narrative here traces the 'awkward fit' of lineage incorporation into the colonial state apparatus.[63] The rights in people and property, especially the rights of judicial sanction, which were contested by an Annang chieftaincy hierarchy would also prove central to an understanding of the murders. A feature common to 'outbreaks' of human leopard murders was that they appeared to coincide with historical moments of profound political disjunction in these 'lineage trajectories'. Specifically, they were associated with shifts in the constitution of British-style modes of indirect rule in which the identity and authority of chiefs in relatively decentralised societies was reconfigured. Indeed, two of the leopard murder 'outbreaks' were connected by the administrative legacy of one man. As Governor of Tanganyika and then Nigeria, Sir Donald Cameron had introduced to both countries during the 1920s and 1930s a blueprint of procedures to accommodate 'decentralised' societies within the scheme of indirect rule.[64]

The powers of leaders from lineages, villages and clans, however, were counterbalanced by those of secret societies, especially the leopard society (*ékpê*), the ancestral masquerade (*ékpó*) and the warrior cult (*áwiè òwò* or *ékóŋ*). The shady origin and organisation of the 'man-leopard society' linked the murders to another trajectory, that of the history of Annang secret societies. After initial ambivalence, secret societies were the subject of subsequent criminalisation and across Nigeria 'an organization that started off as the defender of traditional values ended up as a thorough-going criminal enterprise'.[65] Yet, throughout the period the secret society provided a powerful and persistent idiom to characterise the organisation behind nefarious acts, including rioting, prostitution, kidnapping, night guards and robbery gangs.

The murders were also set against a shifting religious landscape. Narratives of Annang religious encounters highlight the imperatives of conversion in the early years of the Qua Iboe Mission and stress the cultural continuity and localised meanings of religious change. The analysis of pathways to conversion in this context points to the critical role of brokers of religious power and knowledge, along with the dispossessed, the old and the young who first entered the enquirers' classes.[66] Despite the Qua Iboe Mission's predominance in this region, the murders took place amid an apparent crisis with the growth of prophetic Christian congregations which capitalised on the Mission's formalism and the syncretic charismatic impulse of the 'Spirit Movement' which had swept across the Province in 1927 and annually throughout the 1930s. Those most threatened by this development were the Annang diviners (*idíòŋ*) and their monopoly on healing and prognostication.

The colonial history of the Annang villages affected by the murders, like south-eastern Nigeria as a whole, was punctuated by three pivotal events: the Aro Expedition in 1901, the Women's War in 1929 and the Second World War of 1939–45. The legacy of each event would contribute directly to the way in which the murders were perceived. The British subjugation of the Aro's shrine at Arochukwu in 1901 had a direct impact on Annang populations by bringing Abak on the western bank of the Qua Iboe river within colonial circuits, and on the way in which Annang social organisation and religious practice were framed within long-running suspicions of slavery. The fallout of the Women's War would have profound implications for the governance of south-eastern Nigeria as reforms to the local courts and councils in its aftermath, which were designed to resolve an emerging intergenerational rift, instead turned them into spheres of intense political contest. The immediate backdrop to the murders was the fallout from the Second World War and an economic landscape of commodity shortages, cutbacks in administrative personnel and demobilisation. It was also a moment at which the antagonism of seniority which dominated political life throughout the colonial period appeared to shift decisively in favour of the educated nationalists at the chiefs' expense.[67]

As a political structure and a condition of being, the colonial state was riven by contradictions located between the imperatives of mission and mercantilism, and between stasis and reform.[68] As a cultural project of control colonialism transformed domination into a variety of effects that masked both conquest and rule.[69] As an ethnography of empire, my account is an attempt to focus on the contingencies of colonial rule, to understand how it altered the form and terrain of conflict and introduced 'new political languages, new powers, new social groups, new desires and fears, new subjectivities'.[70] Analysis of the tensions of empire is often limited by the failure to study critically indirect rule's discourse of representation and indigenous resistance and accommodation to it.[71] This study, therefore, looks beyond the grand oppositions and seeks to explore 'in the interstices of power structures, in the intersection of particular agendas, in the political spaces opened by new and renewed discourses and by subtle shifts in ideological ground'.[72] These included tension in relations between colonial rulers and their subjects, between norms of reciprocity and capitalist exchange, between young and old, and between men and women.

The underlying theme of this narrative is of tensions along the lines of gender and generation, though we are well reminded that:

> There is nothing surprising in the fact that 'women' and 'minors' should have turned the colonial change of scale to their advantage in order to further their ancestral struggle against social elders. We should beware of any teleological or populist *faux pas*.'[73]

Relations between the sexes are often the first aspects of social life to be affected by historical change.[74] Today it is widely held that, 'You cannot talk of the leopard men without talking of women'. This statement speaks to the uncertainties within the household that were current at the time of the murders. More generally, it relates to the need to analyse a series of contested discourses in which men sought to control or oppress women on the one hand, while women effectively challenged social and cultural restraints on the other.[75] Throughout the period covered in this account, marriage, divorce, adultery and prostitution were 'telling witnesses of the factors of power, ideology and differentiation'.[76]

The narrative of generation traces the shifting engagement of progressives and nationalists as critics of their fathers and their chiefs, and as the self-appointed intermediaries between society and the colonial state. Within this social history of Nigerian nationalism the role of the Ibibio Union's development during the 1930s was pivotal and should be seen in relation to a competitive imperative 'to fill the vacuum of leadership created by the conservatism and ineffectiveness of the colonial administration, and the poverty of missionary enterprise'.[77] The dichotomy of citizens and subjects – citizens in the racially segregated urban world of colonial civil society, and subjects in the 'decentralised despotism' of traditional rulers – is an overplayed distinction since these orbits were as interwoven then as they are today.[78] This analytic should not be confused with the emergence of a colonial public sphere, especially during the Second World War, which was constructed on the reification of these categories. This was a sphere of discourses and claims to the rights of citizenship during this period that was led by the 'been-tos', the 'Uncle Toms', the self-proclaimed 'reading public' and the 'improvement unions', which had long represented an attempt to attain some form of 'accommodation with modernity'.[79]

The significance of the man-leopard murders and the investigations into them is that they revealed the fault-lines that these encounters produced. To use a theatrical metaphor, the whole cast were present on stage simultaneously. It was an ensemble of husbands and wives, chiefs and elites, churchgoers and cult members, judges and litigants, nationalists and conservatives, criminals and policemen. And their script, though extraordinary, was also familiar. These characters' stories spoke most clearly of the ways in which social and political cleavages – gender, generation, religion, justice and relationships between society and state – were worked out in Annang society. A paradox of the murders, therefore, is the way in which some of the most mysterious and secretive events in colonial Nigerian history reveals rarely glimpsed intimacies of everyday life.

OF LEOPARDS AND LEADERS:
ANNANG SOCIETY TO 1909

This chapter concerns the constitution of Annang society and the intersections of corporate and individual modes of identification. It outlines
the key elements of Annang personhood in relation to lineage, initiation
and conceptions of the soul. It links the genealogy of shape-shifting beliefs
and a shifting symbolic landscape to gendered and generational tensions
wrought by a succession of changes from yams to slaves, and from slaves
to palm oil, in local modes of production during the eighteenth and nineteenth centuries. Finally, the chapter examines the relationship between
Christianity and colonialism in patterns of conquest and conversion within
Annang society at the turn of the twentieth century.

POWER AND PERSONHOOD

Identities in Annang society are conceived in intimate and intersecting
relationships between people, place and the past. Personhood concerns
ancestral relationships within the lineage, relationships with cohorts
through initiation, and relationships with the natural world through animal
affinities. Annang selfhood is therefore internally constituted of various
external elements.[1] These three main components, which are changing and
contingent, configure social and political identities, shape conceptions of
agency and explanation and, crucially in Annang beliefs, they configure a
further aspect of the self, power.

Ancestral links to the lineage (*ékpûk*) are established at birth when burial
of the umbilical cord connects the newborn to the village soil on which their
ancestors lived and in which they are buried.[2] Concepts of belonging in
Annang society are primarily conceived in terms of such associations with
the earth and of being a 'child of the soil' (*áyín ìsɔ̀ŋ*). The close proximity
between young children, earth and ancestors is captured in the saying '*ŋ́tɔ̀
áyín èdè ékpó*' ('children are the spirits of our ancestors').[3] Each person is a
reincarnation of the spirit of one such ancestor returning from a previous
life in the village of the ghosts (*óbìò ékpó*). This re-identification is acknowledged soon after birth because of a physical resemblance or familiar trait,
and is confirmed when the child assumes the ancestor's name (a relationship
known as *àkpɔ̀ŋ*).[4] An individual's sense of selfhood is therefore conceived in
relation to knowledge of the family's past, and to patterns of settlement that

constituted patrilineal identities. As individuals traced themselves through fathers and grandfathers in their personal names, so places were resonant of the past as farms, compounds and villages recalled the names of their founders. This 'landscape of names' was and remains a changing model of segmentary society, at once both topography and history.[5]

The lineage founders to whom these relationships are traced were the frontiersmen of southern Annang society, though they were often marginal characters. The first settlers were outcasts and refugees, along with hunters and hungry farmers. The founders of Annang villages were fleeing from inter-village skirmishing and chieftaincy disputes, and settled permanently in the lodges they had built for hunting trips and expanding yam farms. Though epic journeys involving heroic river-crossings form part of the narrative tradition, individually these settlers had not travelled far. Local accounts suggest that the primary centre of Annang distribution was the nucleus of villages around Abak from where the bulk of the population was derived.[6] Contemporary village and lineage charters suggest that expansion commenced at least twenty generations ago and ended fifteen generations later, when all the land to the west of Abak was occupied.[7] Abak represented the key axis of migration for both the Ibibio and Annang and was struc-turally divided into two parts which faced respectively east and west; the eastern became the Ibibio, the western the Annang.

In its simplest form the pattern of settlement and expansion consisted of a line of settlements reaching away from the parent village to occupy a strip of territory which widened only when it extended beyond the commu-nities on either side of it.[8] Unlike the Ibibio, however, who expanded along contiguous trajectories to form largely integral groups, the Annang expe-rience was more complex and resulted in a mosaic of villages and affilia-tions. Conflicts and inequalities in land supply led lineage segments with sufficient labour to sustain rotational slash-and-burn cultivation to break away and request land from the families of original settlers elsewhere.[9] The process by which settled lineages became divided between 'land-owners' (àmànà ísòŋ, first settlers) and 'latecomers' (àdídúŋ, strangers) then involved the exchange of a genealogical for a territorial definition of group identity. Consequently, this 'disjunctive' pattern of lineage expansion meant that equivalence and opposition between segments (in a pure segmentary system) was replaced by the principle of non-equivalence and complemen-tarity.[10]

A husband and his wife with their children formed an *idip*, literally the 'belly', and as this unit extended with the addition of wives and generations it formed a household (*úfɔk*). These family compounds combined as exog-amous patrilineages (*ékpúk*) in which the head of the most senior family was recognised as lineage head (*èté* or *óbɔŋ ékpûk*). They presided over a lineage meeting (*àfé úkɔt*), named after the day on which palm wine was presented

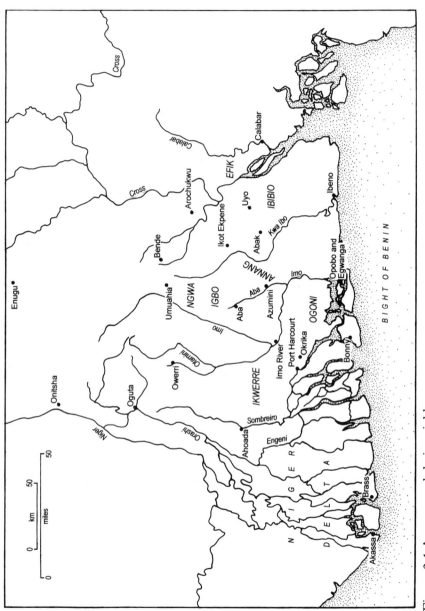

Figure 2.1 Annang and their neighbours

to them, and which distributed land and adjudicated in minor disputes between lineage members. As new lineages formed, either through fission or new arrivals, the *ékpûk* heads formed the core of a village council (*èsòp*) and the senior man of the founding lineage was recognised as the village head (*óbóŋ ísòŋ*).[11]

As this process reproduced itself, so new villages (*óbìò* or *ídúŋ*) were formed and allegiance to the parent village, the home of the original settlers, was expressed in common observance of a communal deity (*ńdêm*), food prohibitions (*ìbét*) and recognition of the *àkúkú* (pl. *ŋkúkú*), a descendant of the original settlers and the group's ritual and political head. The sphere of an *àkúkú*'s influence was mapped onto the landscape by an annual rite of 'first fruits' (*ndòŋò*).[12] Allegiance to the *àkúkú* was distinguished by attendance at his court (*èsòp ìkpá ísòŋ*), the fees and fines from which constituted the major part of his economic base. Intermediaries from each village (*áyáráfɔt* – literally, the 'man in-between') provided the physical and political link between parent and satellite villages which together formed a village group or clan (*ìkpá ísòŋ*).[13] *Àkúkú* chieftaincy, however, was subject to competing claims of genealogy (between factions within the parent village), of geography (as distances increased between parent and satellite villages) and of ritual performance (in which failure to redistribute incurred sanction and the loss of followers).[14]

As elsewhere along the West African coast the relationship between the symbols and vocabularies of animals and chiefs were intimately woven; animals were the 'ideal incarnations … that conjured forth intense onto-logical speculation'.[15] Allegiance to the *àkúkú* was also recognised in tribute in the form of hunted leopards. The right to receive a leopard and to carry out the appropriate purification and sharing rituals concerning it marked, as in Banyang society, the independent and superior status of the leader of one order of residential grouping above less significant groups.[16] Leopards were therefore a means of acknowledging a chief's authority, although the animal associations of Annang chieftaincy were not exclusively linked to the leopard in the same way as Banyang leaders where the leopard (*nkwo*) was associated so closely with leadership and political authority. Other animals – elephants and vultures – were also of symbolic importance to the Annang hierarchy. As messengers of the highest deity (*àbàssì ényòŋ*) vultures were necessary witnesses at the installation of a chief, and the elephant's tusk (*ńnûk énùìn*) was a key element of the chieftaincy regalia. Its physical possession staked a claim to the office, and it summoned the village to war and to peace. Nevertheless, by redistributing leopard meat on the basis of seniority between fellow village or lineage heads, chiefs could in turn mark out allegiances and obligations. This tribute also acknowledged the chief's position as the paramount public peacekeeper. In such a dynamic and fluid political context, the popular recognition accorded to those who settled cases, mediated in conflicts and supervised the disposal of poisons was a key index of power. Only a chief could remove those parts from a leopard which might be used in the preparation of poisons – its bile sack (èdídôt) and whiskers (ŋ́kám).[17] The leopard's whiskers are not in themselves poisonous. When ground up in a mortar and mixed into soup or stew, however, the chitinous powder becomes an undetectable and lethal cocktail since the shards can scarify the gut when consumed. Like all medicine (íbɔ́k) leopard's whiskers had to be rendered impotent by burning or by throwing them into a pit latrine. The python's (àsáwɔ̂) similarly potent properties also had to be disposed of publicly by the chief.

As the makers of this history of settlement, and the basis of individual and collective identity, ancestors and ancestral worship formed a key aspect of Annang religious life. From lineage and village founders onwards, generations of ancestors are recalled and invoked at household shrines (ísó ékpó – the face of spirits) in which they are represented by short wooden stakes (àkúà – from the ékɔ́m tree, Coula edulis). Successive male heads of household maintain such a shrine to the patrilineal ancestors by adding a new àkúà at the death of their father.[18] The transition of the disembodied spirit to ancestorhood was perilous. Extensive performances of separation and purification were linked with death,[19] including the construction of a highly decorated memorial structure (ŋ́wómó – see Figure 2.2),[20] and a ceremonial burial (íkpó) which was held between three and seven years later as an induction of the spirit into the village of the ancestors (óbìò ékpó). Without these obsequies the spirits became poor and emaciated, and would wander about causing harm, and they were necessary, therefore, to safeguard the status of lineage ancestors, the nature of their power, and the effect they have upon the living.

The distinction in the character of ancestors in Annang society was drawn between good spirits, those that were successful, and bad ones, those that were unsuccessful or notoriously malicious.[21] These categories were linked to both the status of the living person and the manner of their death; a natural death (mkpá) was contrasted with a sudden or violent one (àfái).[22] The ancestors were most commonly propitiated in libations. Drink was poured with the right hand to ancestors who had successfully entered óbìò ékpó to ensure safety, prosperity and fertility. Libations poured with the left hand sought to dispel vagabond spirits, a category of malevolent, restless and roaming ghosts (àfái ékpó) who had not made the transition.[23] This opposition expresses a common contrast in Annang belief between the right hand, associated with respect, authority, truth and good character, and the left, linked to disrespect, wrong-doing and malevolence. These practices also capture the inherent ambiguity of power and of powerful people in Annang society. The deliberate inversion of this right hand/left hand code, for instance, was a means by which malicious forces were imprecated into

Figure 2.2 *Ḿwómó* (Reproduced with kind permission of Kegan Paul)[24]

the self to do harm to another. Corpses and graves, especially those of a powerful person (a diviner, medicine-specialist or a chief), or of those who had been killed violently (those who were murdered, executed, killed in battle or who had died from the effects of false oath-swearing), were imbued with this order of power. These forces could be conjured to kill in graveside libations or in preparation of a charm, often a ring, which was left on the grave for seven days, after which its force was inflicted by touching the ring (*átúák túák ibɔk*) on the victim.[25]

The right/left, good/bad opposition corresponds to the aesthetic expression of concepts of beauty (*étî*) and ugliness (*idíók*). These terms are ways of relating character (*étî íĺo*, good person; *idíók íló*, bad person) and behaviour (*étî úsúŋ*, good way; *idíók úsúŋ*, bad way). The aesthetic representations of personhood are captured at their most figurative in the ancestral masquerade (*ékpó*) and in its use of beautiful and ugly masks.[26] At harvest time each year the ancestors return to their lineages in the form of the *ékpó* masquerade. *Ékpó* is indigenous to the Ibibio-speaking language cluster, and, in its simulation of ancestral presence, represents Annang cosmology writ large. Members of the society wear carved wooden masks, which impersonate and become possessed by the spirits of the ancestors. Beautiful masks are worn on the opening and closing performances of the masquerade in the market, and are painted white or yellow to represent good spirits (*mfɔ́n ékpó*). Beautiful masks portray the face in a human form and stress fertility, often with a series of smaller children's faces carved on the forehead. Ugly masks, in contrast, are painted in dark colours with exaggerated and distorted features representing malevolent wandering spirits (*idiók ékpó*). They are usually smaller, with non-human features such as jagged teeth and sometimes represent disfigurement and diseases such as gangosa.[27]

The fear of malevolent ancestral spirits, those invoked by enemies or provoked by disregard, featured prominently in the daily, and especially nocturnal, imagination. These spirits, like the masked players who represent them, are potent, dangerous and unpredictable. During the *ékpó* performance there is, consequently, a strong emphasis on the control of the fiercest spirits represented by the masks. These include categories of 'nonsense' spirits (*ńtímé ńtímé ékpó*) such as the deaf spirit (*inán ékpó*) who cannot hear the drum's directions or onlookers' pleas for mercy, and who delights in destroying farm crops.[28] The most awesome and dangerous of the masks, however, is that of the spirit of the ghosts (*ékpó ńdêm*). Wearing this mask is a form of ordeal and only a descendant of the society's founder can don it without suffering misfortune. Its highly ambiguous source of power contributes to *ékpó ńdêm*'s status. The initiate who wears the *ékpó ńdêm* mask sleeps in the forest (*ákái*) for seven nights where he must not eat food cooked by a woman. He will pour libations on the graves of seven 'wicked' people (*idiók iló* – ugly character), and will consume roots known as *ádûŋ àbàsì* (root of god) which make him feel as if he is flying.[29] His seclusion, invocations and consumptions each contribute to a state of possession once masked as *ékpó ńdêm* that exceeds the usual sense of possession (*náám* – 'not knowing oneself' and having a 'hot head') expressed and represented by other *ékpó* players. The malignancy of the possessed state of *ékpó ńdêm* is demonstrated in various symbolic forms, including the way the masked performer is tied at the waist with palm-tapper rope to prevent him from attacking onlookers, and the way he circulates round the market clockwise, by the left-hand side, thereby demonstrating his malicious intent.[30] Symbolic elements of the *ékpó* masquerade therefore illustrate not only how ancestors shaped individual identities, but also how the past possessed a potent influence over the lives of the living.

The ancestral masquerade (*ékpó*) marks the conjunction of modes of Annang identity and selfhood: descent and initiation, lineage and secret society. The second principal factor in the construction of Annang identities was membership, through initiation, of masquerades, secret societies and titles. By definition the mask and the masquerade concern the disguising of identities, but initiation into and membership of secret societies also marked social and physical transformations and created new boundaries of belonging and hierarchy. These identities also represent a differentiated expression of the articulation of power, and distinguished more sharply between identities and hierarchies constituted on the basis of access to knowledge.[31]

Initiation in Annang society comprised several of the classic elements of rites of passage. They were based on separation in the form of seclusion, they involved physical transformations through fattening, tests of character in public ordeals, the acquisition of new social roles sometimes expressed in liminal moments of rebirth, and processes of re-aggregation in performances at markets.[32] Both male and female identities were determined by a series of initiations. These included 'healing' initiations in which an affliction was cured by entering a secret society; 'protective' initiations which were common for children to ensure physical safety and to reduce later 'full' initiation costs;[33] 'coming of age' initiations of socialisation, 'joining a society' initiations to promote one's rank, and 'establishing a lodge' initiations to launch a new branch and by which societies were distributed and decentralised throughout the coastal hinterland.

Initiations often overlapped with transitions in a person's life-cycle, but they did not all define such moments. Without a recognised age-grade system, there was a nominal sequence to membership of the secret societies in an Annang man's life, of warriorhood (áwiè òwò) in the teen years, the ancestor society (ékpó) in adult years, and the leopard society (ékpê) subsequently.[34] In certain respects this cycle corresponded to the broad Annang generational categories of childhood (ǹtɔ áyín), youth (m̀kpàráwà), and elderhood (èté). Crucially, however, while this hierarchy captured levels of seniority and authority, it was based on the cost of initiation and in this way the societies offered an opportunity structure that cut across strict generational lines.

Initiation for young men into the warrior society (áwiè òwò – to cut head, known in Ibibio as ékóŋ – war) was a condition of male citizenship and a precondition of entry to other societies.[35] The smoothness of the carving and painting of áwiè òwò/ékóŋ masks denoted the youthfulness of its members. Unless a man was initiated he was nothing in the Annang village, and at death it was only members of áwiè òwò who were accorded full burial rites.[36] As the society's name suggests, entry into warriorhood was linked to the status accorded to those who took an enemy's head in combat.[37] Oral and written accounts of áwiè òwò initiation relate the use of a skull carried by a senior áwiè òwò member into the forest. He was chased by the novice

Figure 2.3 *Èkpó* (© David Pratten)[38]

who, upon finding him, acted out the process of beheading an enemy.[39] Following this performance initiates entered a period of seclusion for up to three months, during which they were fattened and taught the martial arts of combat.[40] Performances before conflict and during the new yam festival, which involved jumping over a fence of pots and palm leaves, provided a public test of the authenticity of a warrior's initiation.[41]

For most men who had reached social maturity, initiation into the ancestor society (*èkpó*) involved a simple presentation of food and money. Jeffreys provides a detailed account of early twentieth-century *èkpó* initiation costs. The first stage was to join the drum-beaters (*ádúk ìbît èkpó*). After that he provided the society with food (*étìmmé údíá èkpó* – pound yam for *èkpó*) in which the initiate prepared 100–150 balls of fufu yams (*ùsùŋ*), and spent 600 manillas to buy palm wine and 800 manillas to buy fish. He might wait two or three years before calling the *èkpó* members again to present them with between 100 and 150 manillas. Having paid each member, he became a full *èkpó* member.[42] In northern Annang villages *èkpó* was organised by the lineage and it was the lineage head who presided over the initiation.[43] In southern Annang there was more flexibility to this process and the *èkpó* society was based on a decentralised system of lodges (*àfé èkpó*) producing networks and alliances which cut across village lines and which bound lineages through the distribution of ritual offices. There was a premium on establishing a new *ékpó* lodge within a village, as this description illustrates:

> Before Ekpo starts in a town a man will buy a cow and give a feast to other intending members of the Society. He also will give to the chiefs of the town a big sum, about 2000 manillas. They in turn distribute this among the Ekpuks. The chiefs put round this man's neck ndan (raffia) [*ńdáám*]. This is the sign of his position. He gives the orders to other members of Ékpo to shoot non-members etc. When in his town many men have joined Ekpo and consequently much money has been paid to him he again gives a feast and his Ekpo men dance around the market. People of other towns then know who is the Ōbōŋ Ekpo.[44]

Several lodges from inside and outside the village formed a cluster around a prominent market where opening and closing performances were held. The annual performances of these lodges inscribed a set of village and inter-village allegiances onto the Annang political landscape. During the *ékpó* season masked players marched and sang songs along the boundary paths that defined an *ékpó* cluster, thereby mapping out the political landscape of the *ékpó* leaders and the relationships between them.

Violence too formed a central part of *ékpó* initiation. Before each *ékpó* performed in the market the *ékpó* leader (*èté ékpó*) blew a mouthful of 'hot' drink onto the performer's outstretched right hand, the hand with which they struck non-initiates (*àkpô ékpó*). The wounds they inflicted, with knives, swords or arrows, were injuries sent from the village of the dead (*óbìò ékpó*) and, however superficial, were treated most seriously. To heal the wounds non-initiates were forced to pay the initiation fees and join the society. There was, therefore, an incentive for *ékpó* to assault non-initiates in this manner during the dancing and parading since all the members shared the initiation fees, and the *èté ékpó* distributed eagle feathers and the rights to carve new masks to players who had inflicted such wounds. The physical intimidation of those who were prohibited from witnessing the performance, including non-initiates, women and strangers, reinforced the boundaries of belonging that secret societies like *ékpó* established, a central theme which is captured in *ékpó* songs:

> *àkpô ékpó kùnsé bàk ùdûdát ùnàn*
> non-initiate of *ékpó*, don't look at us unless you want a wound.[45]

The leopard society (*ékpê*) was more expensive to join.[46] Male children of *ékpê* members might be pre-initiated by their fathers in order to reduce later initiation costs and to protect their sons from harassment. As with *ékpó*, non-members of *ékpê* might be press-ganged into joining, especially if they were careless enough to witness the society's performance. These junior members were not privy to the inner secrets of the society. This knowledge

concerned the secret imitation of a leopard's roar.[47] The distinction between
those who had acquired this knowledge, who 'sat on the seat of the founder'
(ètìè ífùm ékpê), and those who did not, further reinforced the creation of
social hierarchies. Like other societies, ékpê membership was an investment
from which members could expect a return in the form of shared initiation fees and fines as well as prestige and political capital. As will be seen
below, ékpê ranked highly within the economic and political structure of the
Annang village and the region as a whole.

While initiation into the secret societies configured aspects of male status
and shaped a landscape of political identities, so other forms of initiation
framed moments of transition within the life-cycle, especially the preparation for ancestorhood (ínám) and the passage to womanhood (m̀bòbó).
Both forms of initiation were based on seclusion and fattening. Seclusion
(ákpé) marked a rejection of the mundane and a means of protecting the
self from the effects of one's enemies. Fattening typified the association in
Annang culture between bodily size, beauty, health, fertility and wealth.
The ínám (or ókù ínám) was a title taken by the most elderly members of a
community who were inducted when they became grandparents. Initiation
for both men and women involved a series of purifying rites in preparation
for the afterlife which marked their transition to near-ancestral status. The
ínám title could be re-entered to gain even greater status every seven years
in line with the bush-clearing and land-fallowing cycle. The centrepiece
of the initiation was an ordeal to prove innocence and good character by
which the initiate used a blunt matchet to decapitate a cow with a single
stroke (bìò) – one of the highest order of ordeals in Annang society.[48] The
initiate then entered a period of seclusion, and choosing just one person
to minister to them, usually a favourite wife or child, lived on the outskirts
of the village near the forest. Their public outing ceremony, a month later,
would coincide with the new yam festival and with the performance of the
women's initiation ceremony, m̀bòbó.

Mbòbó was the most important initiation in a woman's life.[49] This period
of seclusion and fattening occurred at the transition from adolescence to
womanhood prior to marriage and childbirth, though it also constituted a
means by which infertility, headaches and weight loss might be healed. By
entering the fattening room the initiate was displaying publicly not only
that she was a virgin but that she was also of good character (étî ílô). After
settling the final counting of the brideprice, a woman's prospective husband
commissioned a specialist in cicatrisation (ŋ̀kɔ́) and handed his bride over to
her mother to supervise the seclusion. Fattening was a form of conspicuous
consumption and a family's status might be reckoned by the girls' corpu-
lence at the 'coming out' display. Since the costs of food and the loss of
labour were high, fathers and husbands-to-be might share the expense.
While in seclusion the m̀bòbí was prepared for her new responsibilities to

the lineage and village and was instructed in the roles of wife, mother and daughter-in-law. After three months *ṁbòbó* ended with circumcision (for which the husband presented a gift of money known as *èwàná*), a cleansing rite (*ùdàrá ídém*) and an 'outing' performance (*ùrùà ṁbòbó* – market of *ṁbòbó*) in which all the village's initiates wore heavy brass rings (*àwɔ̀k*) on their legs and were paraded by the men's warrior society to their husband's compound.[50]

As soon as they left the fattening room most women were initiated into the senior women's association within the village. Holding authority over unmarried women and the rites of the fattening house, this secret society was named after the water yam (*èbrè*), a crop associated with women's cultivation.[51] Leadership positions within the society constituted a pathway to status and influence, and as with all secret societies *èbrè* founders were accorded a high status that could extend far beyond the village.[52] *Èbrè* played an important role in the public attribution of character within the village by parading and singing shaming songs (*ìkúɔ́ ówó* – to sing person). These songs were directed against thieves (*ìnɔ̀*), prostitutes (*àkpàrà*), murderers (*àwòt ówó*) and witches and poisoners (*ìfót*). The main *èbrè* performance on *ófìɔŋ* market day involved dancing round a yam basket (*àkpân èbrè*). The dancers rotated by the right-hand side to demonstrate that they were women of straight and true character (*ǹnèn ǹnèn ówó áŋwáàn*). This performance was an ordeal for the audience and various deviant categories, including thieves,

Figure 2.4 *Èbrè* society, Ikot Edem Ewa (© David Pratten)

men who had not joined *èkpó* and women who had had an abortion who were apprehended, paraded and shamed if caught watching.

Entry into the order of diviners (*idìɔŋ*) comprised many of the elements, including seclusion, ordeal and performance, that were common to these Annang initiation practices. Each was also concerned with access to knowledge, in the form of everyday skills (*úsɔ*) or knowledge of esoteric secrets (*ńdíp*). Becoming a diviner, however, concerned becoming a specialist in knowledge itself (*àbíà idìɔŋ* from *àbíà*, specialist, *dìɔŋɔ́*, to know). The onset of severe, recurring headaches was a sign that a person was being pursued by the *idìɔŋ* spirit for which the remedy was initiation. An elder *idìɔŋ* led them to the forest to 'open the eye of *idìɔŋ*' (*ńsàk ányên idìɔŋ*).[53] There the novice underwent a symbolic death and rebirth, dying in the forest before being carried to the *àfé idìɔŋ* where they were placed in a marked-out grave and covered with a burial cloth. When the elder *idìɔŋ* struck the ground with a plantain stem seven times the initiate returned to life.[54] The *idìɔŋ* was then paraded around seven markets before undertaking a period of seclusion. For some *idìɔŋ* the consumption of seven alligator peppers (*Afromomum melegueta*) during the initiation enabled and embodied their future prognosticative powers. The peppers are thought to remain within the upper body and in divinatory spirit possession move to cause a shaking sensation (*ńtúúk*). Such a shock at the back of the body predicts death, to the front, life, to the right, good fortune, and to the left, ill luck. This type

Figure 2.5 Ekpo Ubok Udom of Ikot Edem Ewa (© David Pratten) and Chief Inaw of Ikotobo (reproduced with kind permission of Kegan Paul)[55]

of consumed and embodied medicinal power is associated with the highest forms of sanction and is especially fraught with danger. Any lapse in the codes of behaviour and routine of worshipping the *idìɔŋ* spirit could kill the initiate. Indeed, it was common to substitute the human consumption of alligator peppers by placing them within a human skull. The skull itself, placed in a bag or a box, could speak with the 'small voice of *idìɔŋ*' (*ńyín ntie idìɔŋ*) and be interpreted by the initiate.[56]

Idìɔŋ divination was intimately tied to the routine of the market week and to the competitive stakes of the divination market. An *idìɔŋ* specialist might be initiated into the secrets of intercession, possession and prognostication of a number of further spirits in addition to *idìɔŋ*. Spirits of water, of ancestors and of medicine circulated around the coast and hinterland of the eastern Delta. Most southern Annang diviners saw clients according to a cycle of market days. On *ábô* market day, for instance, *idìɔŋ* would see those seeking the mediation of the spirit for medicinal cures (*ibɔk*). Those who sought prosperity and fertility (*ifá* or *mfá*)[57] would be seen on *ékényɔŋ* day. *Idìɔŋ* were consulted by those seeking wealth (*ékpó òmòmòm*) on *édét ábô* market day, and those seeking cures for madness (*ńdêm mɔ́ɔŋɔ́*) were treated on *édét* day. The various spirits with whom the *idìɔŋ* engaged did not represent different orders or grades as delineated in later colonial discourse, but the cost of initiation and sacrifices to maintain additional spirits, which were enough to cause men to sell wives and children, led to distinctions between them.[58] Such differentiation was crucial to *idìɔŋ*. They were primary mediators with the spirits of prosperity and fertility and key brokers in the knowledge of power. In a highly competitive market their livelihoods depended on innovation and on accessing esoteric, especially external, sources for healing and prognostication. As with diviners elsewhere an *idìɔŋ* initiate possessing such forces held a highly ambivalent position.[59]

The social transformations achieved through initiation therefore created and legitimated differences in status, power and authority. The nature of these ritual separators is central to understanding both the composition of Annang personhood, and the political constitution of Annang society at large. The orthodox analysis of stateless communities like Annang comprises a number of features. One is to stress the role of horizontal, cross-cutting associations, including secret societies, as unifying forces between otherwise fissiparous lineages. Another is to point to the way in which the regulation of particular fields of cultural and political life fall within the exclusive purview of specific societies.[60] Overall, however, these views of stateless societies are predicated upon a distinction, sometimes characterised as a constitutional balance, between an open sector over which lineage elders and village chiefs presided, and a closed sector which was the domain of secret societies[61] A further aspect, more recently argued, is that the control of access to the secret knowledge of the societies was a bulwark against the economic and political power of the elders.[62] Indeed, the evidence suggests that rather than political cohesion, the paramount feature of initiation-based secret societies was to create social differentiation.

While the Annang model of lineage-based chieftaincy was dynamic and shifting, its overriding feature was the absence of independent or autocratic authority. The diffuse distribution of power among various corporate entities can be seen as a strategy to resist the consolidation of power by individuals. Annang chieftaincy was highly contested and contingent, a principle captured in the phrase 'the chief does not rule by himself alone' (*'óbóŋ isibónó ikpɔŋ'*). The power of the secret societies was located outside the chieftaincy; chiefs were not above the laws of the societies,[63] and the spiritual beings to which the societies were dedicated provided independent legitimation for their activities. Hence, while elders led the societies, they shared power with those of independent wealth and status. The secret societies brought together constituencies of younger generations released from chieftaincy supervision who initiated and executed judgments as the 'impersonal manifestations of the collective will' since their anonymity was preserved by masks.[64] As an index of an individual's wealth, membership of the various secret societies consolidated independent status and prestige, and there was a strong impetus to join as many associations as possible.[65] The principles of secret society membership therefore contained a dynamic dialectic based on contesting issues of age and office, status and wealth, and the individual and the community:

> The purchase of the graded titles in the association provided advancement in status and power to the wealthy and ambitious, yet subjected them to the discipline of the association's rules, which reflected the norms of society at large.[66]

The social logics of lineage and secret society intersected as individuals invested exclusively in neither one mode nor the other, but in both simultaneously. Individual power holders could account for their position according to a matrix of social investment strategies. Seen as 'co-ordinates operating in the same system', the apparent ambiguities and oppositions between lineage and secret society dissolve.[67] On the one hand, this totalising analysis accounts for lineages 'owning' particular secret societies, lineage representation in the offices of secret societies, and for chiefs holding high office in the societies (not simply because they were chiefs but because they had wealth). On the other, the intersecting of principles explains the way in which lineage juniors could rise to seniority through the personal accumulation of secret society rank. In short, the complex of initiation outlined here represents a set of pathways to power for both men and women. These horizontal associations, incorporating secret societies and title groups, represented an important arena for the elaboration of displays of prestige and wealth which could be linked to political influence or used to channel wealth and ambition. Recent perspectives on the emergence of complex society suggest not only that African societies unsettle embedded evolutionary notions of political complexity, but emphasise horizontal complexity and internal segmentation as a counterpoint to conceptions of power which locate authority centrally in individuals.[68] Beyond the perspectives of descent, class or seniority, it is evident therefore that the outstanding intricacies and dynamics of status in Annang society are firmly linked to the economic structuring powers of the competitive ranking of persons.[69]

In addition to identities formed through lineage affiliation and through initiation, the third principal component of Annang personhood is the soul (*úkpɔ̀ŋ*), which is the vital breath or life-force. It has two parts: the bodily soul (*úkpɔ̀ŋ idém*) inhabits the individual, while the bush soul (*úkpɔ̀ŋ íkɔ́t*) occupies an object, usually a living form from the bush (a snake, a tree or a leopard). The term *úkpɔ̀ŋ*, however, defies a ready translation and its meaning has been entangled with a range of questions about identity in Annang society. The animal affinities to which the bush soul relates, for instance, have been linked with food prohibitions (the so-called 'clan totems' of later colonial discourse) which are common to the Ibibio-speaking communities. Information sent to Sir James Frazier claimed that marriages could be sanctioned only if the husband and wife shared the same bush-soul animal, and that entire families therefore shared an affinity with a particular animal.[70] The fact that *úkpɔ̀ŋ* could simultaneously refer to a shadow (from the sun), a person's 'vital spark' and an animal affinity led diffusionists to attribute the soul complex to the acquisition of these cultural features from 'children of the sun'.[71] The term has also invited comparison and contradiction with the idea of the ancestral spirit and the nature of the after-life.[72] The terms for the soul and the spirit of the dead, *úkpɔ̀ŋ* and *ékpó*, have been used interchangeably when in fact they capture the way in which Annang distinguish between the living and the dead. The spirit (*ékpó*) is of the dead while the soul (*úkpɔ̀ŋ*) concerns the living. The former may reincarnate; the latter's transient existence is bound to the living individual.

One of the oldest recorded definitions of the *úkpɔ̀ŋ*, from the mid-nineteenth century remains the clearest and closest match to everyday Annang usage:

1. The shadow of a person or thing which moves; not being stationary as *mfut*, the shadow of a tree.

2. The soul of a man. It is supposed that the soul may come out of the body and visit different places, and that it does so frequently in dreams: that an individual may be deprived of his soul, [and] a man's shadow may be caught, in which case he soon dies; and the soul of a healthy man may be transferred into the body of a sick man, the latter

recovering and the former dying.

3. An animal, with the existence of which the life of the individual is bound up. It may be a leopard, a fish, a crocodile, any animal whatever … If the *ukpön* gets sick or dies, so does the individual whose *ukpön* it is, and the *ukpön* is correspondingly affected by the individual. Many individuals, it is believed, have the power of metamorphosing themselves into their *ukpön*. *Ukpön anam enye uröñö*, His *ukpön* makes him sick. Said when an individual is seized with a temporary mania, and fancies himself his *ukpön*.[73]

It is within this concept of the soul therefore that people are most directly associated with the natural world. Within the Annang social and spiritual landscape, the forest (*ákáî*) was held in great fear. The boundaries between settlement and forest were defined in proscriptions, for instance, against sex in the forest, in seclusions during initiations and in the location of burial sites. Good ancestral spirits (*mfɔ́n ékpó*) were buried within the compound, while bad spirits (*idiók ékpó*) were disposed of in the forest.[74] The forest was a place braved only by hunters, but while it was associated primarily with secrecy and malevolence, it was also the site of considerable power and a font of creativity. Animal affinities tapped into this ambivalent source of power. Based on the principle of parallel injury the duality of the soul provided a powerful way of explaining human fate and fortune. Apart from the body, yet essential to its well-being, the bush soul is vulnerable, particularly to hunters and especially when the animal is drinking, since this is often when hunters will shoot.[75] Sores on the body (*idâŋ úkpɔ́ŋ* – arrow of soul), for instance, are attributed to wounds inflicted by a hunter on the animal that bears that person's soul. The *úkpɔ́ŋ*'s protection is therefore catered for within the space and routine of the household. To the rear of the household a large water pot (*ábáŋ úkpɔ́ŋ* – pot of soul) must remain filled so that *úkpɔ́ŋ* animals may drink in safety, and at the beginning of the dry season children of the compound must drink from it to revitalise their association (*úsɔ́rɔ́ ísó úkpɔ́ŋ*).[76] Despite the fact that the fates of person and animal are intertwined, such soul associations are usually unknown during a person's life. The identity of the creature may be revealed only through healing, divination or at death, when personal features, courage or cunning, strength or wisdom, will be deduced as deriving from this association. Strong men, including chiefs, for instance, may be found to have had the bush soul of a leopard (*áfák úkpɔ́ŋ ké èkpê* – 'his soul is in a leopard'). The leopard-soul reflected upon the person not only the powerful predations of the animal, but also its wily, trickster-like qualities. As a means of understanding human agency, the animal soul affinity, especially that of the leopard, was not only ambiguous in its identity, but ambivalent in its power.

The ambivalence in Annang conceptions of animal souls is reflected in the way that, as in the Banyang case, they are linked to notions of witchcraft.

The soul is transitory, and at night may leave the body while the breath itself (*úkpɔ́ŋ ibifík*) sustains the sleeping form. The detached soul was vulnerable to attack from an enemy, and victims were those whose souls were seized or 'trapped'. The aggressors, in contrast, were those who could wilfully project their bush soul to transform and manifest their animal affinities. This could take various guises and included assuming a were-form and conjuring an ostensibly real animal from leaves, woods and medicines.[77]

In Annang, *idíɔŋ* could conjure the leopard bush soul with an invocation at the household soul pot (*ábáŋ úkpɔ́ŋ*). Stories from the early twentieth century, for instance, recorded the belief that certain people could enter or project their bush soul (*úkpɔ́ŋ ikɔ́t*). After a concoction of leaves, eggs and water was prepared, the soul could depart from the body during sleep and take the form of a bird. The knowledge of preparing the medicine was said to be a secret of initiation, revealed only to chiefs' sons or the head of the secret societies, and that 'the power of metamorphosis [was] sometimes inherited, sometimes bought ... Since many believe that it is only used for evil purposes, the faculty is not often boasted of or admitted by its possessor.'[78] As this observation suggests, Annang beliefs conceived of those who could project their were-form as anti-social forces. Like the Banyang were-person (*mu debu*) they were represented within a witchcraft idiom as a 'person of the night'.[79] Beliefs in were-animals and witchcraft run into one another, but not universally. While everybody has a soul association, not all are malevolent witches and, as in the Banyang case from the Cross River, witchcraft can be performed with were-animals 'but not all were-animals are witchcraft'.[80]

Many accounts concerning malicious attacks on a person's soul involved a process of soul 'trapping'. By the early twentieth century it was reported that 'All Ibibio know charms such as this [to trap souls], but the Anang people are specially famous for their knowledge of these things ...'[81] Such accounts included ways in which diviners and specialists in the preparation of medicines (*ábíà ibɔ́k*) could 'trap' a bush soul by attracting it with familiar food, catching it in a wooden dish (*ùsàn úkpɔ́ŋ*), and then spearing it in order to kill the soul's human form.[82] Variations of this process relate ways in which a person's soul is drawn out and imprisoned within a pot, which is then hung over a slow fire so that the body of the victim withered.[83] These attacks on the bush soul therefore offered a range of explanatory possibilities of sickness and death since Annang concepts of good health are associated with the corpulent body (*ákpɔ́ŋ idém*) in contrast to the thin, dry body (*ńsíp idém*) of the sick person. Attacks on the soul also represented notions of seizure and capture. Jeffreys' account of such a witchcraft attack is remarkably detailed:

A man wishing to destroy another will pay an Abia Ibok to send the small bat called 'ékpêmion' by night into his enemy's house to seize his

Ukpon and fly off with it. … The bat is considered to have taken that person's Ukpon, who there and then sickens. The sick man consults an Abia Idiong who tells him what has happened and will make arrangements upon payment to have the Ukpon restored.[84]

The soul is not restored, in fact, but substituted. One of the most potent forms of healing in Annang society, a process shared by initiation practices, is soul-changing (*òkpùngó úkpɔ̀ŋ*). It is an important rite in the Annang healing repertoire and is performed when a person has fallen ill and when investigations reveal that the sickness is attributable to a witchcraft attack on the person's soul. The performance itself is identical to that of *idìɔ̀ŋ* initiation, and represents a ritual death and rebirth. This soul-changing rite further emphasises the possibilities of ritual substitution, and stresses the interchangeability of identity and forms in Annang culture.

★ ★ ★

The various elements of Annang personhood – lineage, initiation and animal affinities – shaped the construction of both identity and power. In Annang society, power (*ódùdù*) is transmitted from an omnipotent god (*àbàsì ényɔ̀ŋ*) who is remote and hidden deep in the sky. *Àbàsì ényɔ̀ŋ* is served in the worldly arena by numerous spirits (*ńdêm*). *Ńdêm* protect people and make women and crops fertile. They have fixed habitats in natural objects like springs, pools, rocks and inside great trees and are given physical representation in the form of clay or wooden statues and earthenware pots. Each spirit, especially important ones such as the village spirit (*ńdêm ídúŋ*) and market spirit (*ńdêm ùrùà*), has its own priest (*òkù*). The most significant *ńdêm* is the god of the soil (*àbàsì ikpá ísɔ̀ŋ*).

The duality of *àbàsì ényɔ̀ŋ* (god of the sky) and *àbàsì ikpá ísɔ̀ŋ* (god of the soil) is represented in numerous contexts in up-to-down, high-to-low movements (pointing, throwing, stepping and jumping), which are central elements of the Annang ritual repertoire. In libations, trials, secret society performances and marriage ceremonies, these gestures and motions constitute both ordeals of the self and invocations of the deities' moral sanction.[85] The most direct example of this earth–sky connection, which also contains a left–right opposition, is demonstrated in burial rites. When the deceased is entombed in the earth their right hand is tied to the roof beams of their house thereby raising the hand to point to the sky.[86] Deliberate infractions of this up-to-down motion constitute attempts to disrupt the natural order and transform the self. Falling down, for instance, is associated with spirit possession, while throwing items to land on a roof rather than the ground is linked to metamorphosis. In part, the failure to resolve the high–low opposition is also an invocation of the powers of the 'middle sky' (*ódùdù áfùm ényɔ̀ŋ*) the space inhabited by malevolent spirits (*àfái ékpó*).

The power of distant deities and their more proximate and more numerous intermediaries is not conceived in abstract or impersonal terms.[87] Rather, it is the transmission of power to human, personal and embodied forms that is significant in Annang thought as force, power and influence are conceived within personal relationships. Everyday strategies for success draw upon multiple sites of power. As we have seen, these sites include the forces of ancestral spirits, the influence derived from initiation into secret societies, along with the powers of the bush soul. Personhood and power are also conceived as being innate or invoked; power is either inherited (*màná ódùdù*), or manufactured and medicinally derived (*ódùdù íbɔ́k*). The origin of such power is a crucial question in a society where disruptions to personal and collective progress are perceived to be caused by individual competitors, rivals and enemies. Using power in this way is conceived as putting 'pressure' (*úfìk*) on another and of having 'influence' (*ábàyá* – to intimidate and frighten). Unless it is revealed in the specialist investigations of a diviner (*ídìɔŋ*), however, the source of a person's power remains secret. The recognition of power is therefore based on the public achievements of a person, a feature captured in the saying 'performance makes a person strong' ('*édínám ówó ánám ówó édí òkpɔ̀sɔ̀ŋ*'). Status and wealth must have been achieved as a result of overcoming the tests, trials and threats of a neighbour or a kinsman. Those who have suppressed a rival's power constitute a category of the strong and powerful (*òkpɔ̀sɔ̀ŋ ówó* – powerful person). Their status and identity were based on the accumulation of wealth, the moral calculus of which shifted dramatically from the sixteenth to the twentieth centuries.

TRADE AND TRANSFORMATION

The symbols of prestige and wealth within pre-colonial Annang society were multiple. They included wives, children, money, yams, livestock, buildings, palm trees, membership of secret societies, titles, skills, political positions and the ownership of slaves. The most significant path to accumulation within Annang society up to the mid-nineteenth century, however, is recalled in the following popular refrain:

> Yam is the greatness of a man,
> His child is his wealth.[88]

Trade, skills and titles aside, for Annang men yams and dependants were central to sustenance and status. This was the case throughout the region as a whole, which was split between southern riverside fishermen and northern upland farmers. The southern Annang region straddled the border between these two zones, but yam cultivation was the paramount crop.

The yam was central to the Annang economic and cultural world. The word for yam, *údìá*, is taken from the word to eat, *dìá*. The yam season once defined the Annang annual calendar. The first season of work (ìnì útóm) involved allotting, marking out and clearing plots of land which were farmed, in rotation, every seven years.[89] The heavy work of bush clearing for yam cultivation was carried out by lineage-based male work-groups (údìm).[90] After firing the cut and dried bush, seed yams were planted with the first rains, after which soil was heaped up around the yam roots and their vines were tied up. Women weeded during the 'time of hope' (ìnì m̀bék). Following the main rains restrictions against eating the new yams were lifted only after a round of feasts centred on the new yam festival (ìnì ǹsúúk údíá), after which yam barns were repaired and stacked before the harmattan season of ìnì ǹdɔk (time of closing) and the end of year itself (ìnì ùkàbà ísúâ).[91]

Yam cultivation gendered the relations of production. Several varieties were grown. Those harvested by men included àkpànà, ètém and m̀kpúk. Other varieties were associated with women's cultivation and included the sweet yam (ánêm), the water yam (èbrè) and the coco-yam (ikpɔ́ŋ), which was introduced in the nineteenth century. The marketing of yams was controlled by men.[92] The significance of yams was expressed in collective seasonal rites during the annual new yam festival (úsɔ́rɔ́ údíá), and in individual title-taking. Once harvested, yams were stacked in a barn (ísê) in which each vertical rack of yams (bàká) contained about forty yams.[93] When a man had accumulated twenty bars of yams he was eligible to invite senior title-holders to recognise his prowess in yam cultivation and take the title of údíá.[94] The theft of seed yams was considered a grievous offence, and the person who used a seed yam (m̀fít yam – reborn yam) for food was regarded as wicked and would not be welcomed in a house or offered hospitality.[95]

Time and its passing were marked and remembered by the yam season in both the shifts between farming activities and, in years, by the clearing of particular plots through the rotation cycle. In all matters concerning land, palm trees and farming, the óbɔ́ŋ ísɔ̀ŋ (senior lineage elder) was the immediate authority though the Annang political landscape was also differentiated by season and these responsibilities overlapped with those of the men's secret societies, áwìè òwò (ékóŋ), èkpê and èkpó. Áwìè òwò controlled the use of forest resources and firewood during the driest months after the harvest. During the planting season èkpê caught domestic animals straying onto farmland. The laws (m̀bét) of the ancestral society (èkpó) came into force after the rainy season, and it was èkpó that opened its performance immediately after the new yam festival and closed four weeks later when the ancestors were bid farewell at the year's end (ǹdɔk).

If yam cultivation was an index of a man's stature, then, as the song says, his dependants – wives, children and slaves – marked his wealth. Here the yam season also mapped out the reproductive cycle. The period of a prospective bride's seclusion, fattening and circumcision (m̀bòbó) began during the planting season and culminated, three months later, to coincide with the new yam festivities. The men's warrior society (áwìè òwò) marked each ṁbòbí with white chalk to signal her health and beauty before they were paraded in the village square and carried to their husband's compound. Marriages secured the most significant rights in people and labour in Annang society. The first marriage a man entered was arranged by his parents, who agreed an amount of brideprice (òkpòhò ńdɔ́) which was rendered in money, gifts of cloth and labour. The arrangement often occurred when the prospective spouses were only children and was settled with a series of instalments. The deferred reciprocity of these marriage contracts were guaranteed by the swearing of an oath (ákàn èbé – lit. to know husband) between parties arranging a marriage. Marriage links also established a set of alliances between exogamous lineages. Two forms were of particular importance, one based on symmetrical reciprocity (ùkôt – in-laws), and the other a system of complementary filiation through ties to the mother's kin (áyéyìn – lit. child's child) in which a status of social immunity was afforded to children within their mother's natal village.[96]

The lineage maintained its rights in women married into it with a range of devices. Adultery constituted a grave offence against the patrilineage because of the potential introduction of 'outside blood'. Women's sexual behaviour was regulated through the surveillance of an ancestral spirit invoked to ensure fidelity by both the wife's father and husband's lineage head at marriage. Sickness in the household, especially illness during pregnancy and stillbirth, would lead to the suspicion that a wife had committed adultery. The spirit was ékpó ńkà ówó (the spirit who goes to men) and its testing properties were invoked by suspicious husbands publicly on the weekly palm wine day, the annual day of labour service for a lineage head, or by passing wives food secretly sacrificed to ékpó ńkà ówó. With these grave consequences the public invocation of ékpó ńkà ówó provided an opportunity for confession and reconciliation. Ékpó ńkà ówó also regulated the sexual activities of widows, preventing them from having sex during the mourning seclusion.[97]

With extensive labour demands and ordeals to prove her character, a woman's rights and position within the lineage were far from secure. While they were retained by the lineage in the event of divorce, children secured a wife's albeit contingent position within the family. When children failed to materialise several strategies could be employed before 'barrenness' became grounds for the husband to seek divorce. Entering ṁbòbó seclusion and initiation into the èbrè society were both common steps by which a childless married woman might enhance her fertility. A further investment, usually made by women who had generated capital from trading, was to 'marry' a wife to her husband and pay brideprice on her husband's behalf. By 'marrying' a woman to their husband to compensate for their own infertility, wives were further ensuring their position within the household by having surrogate children who were dependent upon her (and not on their natural mother). Such children could therefore cultivate and secure a woman's claim to *ùdɔ̀ŋò* land gifted to her and her children by her husband, and thereby ensure that she had dependants to secure her ancestral status by performing burial rites.[98]

The accumulation of wealth in people also involved slaves (*áfûn*), though they were not held as commonly as other kinds of property in Annang society. Only the very prosperous possessed them, a person of wealth seldom owning more than twenty.[99] Unlike other systems of slavery in the region, Annang slaves were absorbed into the lineage within two generations; male slaves would be given their own plot to cultivate, while female slaves traded for their owners and eventually married within the lineage.[100] The general absence of economic slavery in this zone has been widely noted and is attributed to the low demand for external labour given the already high density of population.[101] In fact, the burden of labour fell on women and junior men within the lineage. In contrast, the coastal trading states of Old Calabar, Bonny and Opobo featured two forms of slavery: 'plantation' slaves to supply the ports and ships with foodstuffs; and trading slaves required to paddle the canoes of European goods to the inland markets. Plantation slaves were subject to a harsher regime than trading slaves for whom there were opportunities for individual promotion and assimilation within the 'houses' of the seaboard trading states.

The region as a whole, the Bight of Biafra, was the source of an increasingly high proportion of slaves for the Atlantic passage. The Portuguese were the first coastal traders along the Guinea Coast, exchanging cloth, spirits, gunpowder, guns, matchets, brass-rods, salt and old clothes for ivory and peppers. British commerce with the coast began in 1553 and was carried on in 'legitimate' goods until the slave trade expanded from 1590 onwards. From the 1740s, around 3,000 slaves annually were shipped from the coastal ports of Calabar, Opobo and Bonny. By 1750 the region had become the most important source of slaves from West Africa, and some 20 per cent of the trade, an estimated 175,400 slaves, left the Bight of Biafra between 1781 and 1790.[102]

The slave trade's impact on the hinterland was therefore crucially significant to the genealogy of Annang identity, economy and violence. The key debate concerning slavery in the Ibibio-speaking hinterland is the extent to which the numbers of slaves exported from Calabar and Bonny can be accounted for by slave-raiding. The established 'predatory state' theory of West African slavery, which argues that the major source of slaves came from the transfer of populations from 'weak' decentralised to predatory centralised states, has been questioned as a result of several regional examples, especially that of south-eastern Nigeria.[103] From Portuguese arrivals in the fifteenth century and the expansion of the outlets for slave-trading which they and their successors provided, there were three distinct phases in the development of the trade among decentralised societies. The first was a response to the violence of slave-raiding with the construction of physical defences or resettlement to higher ground. This was accompanied by an increased trade in arms. The second phase saw a decline in slave-raiding, an increase in kidnapping and a process by which communities began to sell their own. Judicial penalties such as beatings, execution, compensation and exile were converted to enslavement. The third phase saw the expansion of the internal market for slaves in which decentralised peoples not only sold but absorbed slaves and in which commercial transactions were increasingly based on the pawning or sale of dependants.[104]

Exceptionally among West African slaving systems, there was no initial phase of self-defence in which Igbo and Ibibio communities protected themselves by the construction of ditches and walls, or by resettlement. This suggests that the external threats of raiders in south-eastern Nigeria were negligible and that other mechanisms accounted for the bulk of the supply of slaves. It also illustrates that state formation was not as irresistible as the logic of the market.[105] The region's slave trade was also unusual in that the trading network that opened the hinterland was indigenous. Igbo-speaking Aro middlemen dominated the trade across the hinterland, including the western Ibibio markets where they were known as the 'children of the whitemen' (ǹtɔ̀ àfái ówó) because of their close association with the Portuguese. Significantly, however, though the Aro had access to the military might that they could muster from their trade in firearms and their capacity to hire Abam mercenaries, they were not slave-raiders.

One of the key factors contributing to the Aro's dominance was the flexible structure of the Aro commercial organisation. The Aro established overland trade routes, first with temporary shelters, then through arrangements made with Annang villages which became more permanent through marriage and kinship ties.[106] The Aro did not constitute a centralised state; rather Aro commercial success was based on a network of settlements in the western Ibibio-speaking region, of which Ndi Okoro was the largest, and which mirrored the village and lineage patterns of Arochukwu itself.[107] The Aro traders who specialised in the small-scale trade in goods and slaves in the western Ibibio region were known as ìnòkòn and came from the Aro community of Obinkita. Of the five Obinkita lineages, Ndi Akweke operated among the northern Annang and Ndi Chioka among the southern communities.

The Obinkita maintained commercial control through satellite settlements, the 'colonies' once described as 'divinely ordained trade centres'.[108] These settlements were established through agreements of mutual benefit and it is evident that the survival of the Aro trading network rested upon 'cordial relations with powerful non-Aro'.[109] This point is highlighted in the inability of Roger Casement's Aro guides from Ndi Okoro to secure passage through Annang territory in 1894. That a series of separate permissions was required to secure Casement's safety indicates the fractured structure to the Aro network which corresponded to the separate operations of the Obinkita lineages. During Casement's attempt to reach Esene and Opobo by land, in fact, he recorded that even Aro trade could be blockaded by the Annang: 'The Inokun come down trading to Esene, but often have trouble in passing the Anang towns.'[110]

Annang villages were attracted by the access the Aro presence offered to exotic trade goods, 'medicines' and, of course, the powers of the Aro oracle at Arochukwu. There has been considerable speculation that the Aro oracle, known variously as *ibini ukpabi* in Igbo, *ibritam* in Annang and later as the Long Juju of Arochukwu to the British, was originally an Ibibio shrine.[111] The oracle itself, as a judicial ordeal, was a significant channel for the disposal of criminals. It was also the premier regional fertility spirit, an important and neglected function given the increasing demand for labour as the yam and palm oil trades expanded. Inokun Uyo Ubong of the southern Annang village of Ikot Udo Obobo visited the oracle in the late nineteenth century:

> I went to Ibritam for though I had wives I had no sons, only daughters. I came back and had a son born to me a month later as predicted. So I have called one son Inokun and another Ibritam. I have now about forty sons. The Aros guided me. I was told at Ibritam to make a certain sacrifice in my town and sons would come. … I was taken to a place where there was a big rock and trees and water. I stood up to my knees in the water and Ibritam spoke to me.[112]

The Aro dealt with both the coastal middlemen, the Efik, Kalabari and Ubani, and with the Annang and Ibibio village hierarchy in overt and covert ways. Skirmishing and inter-village conflicts linked to succession disputes figure in local historical narratives in which rivals were seized and sold to the Aro. Yet, as this account illustrates, the supply of slaves was not their principal object:

> Disputes between villages and tribal sub-divisions, usually concerning boundaries and fishing rights, are frequent and persistent. The natives have little idea of open war but watch for an opportunity of catching and killing a solitary member of a hostile village, which, in its turn, will retaliate, perhaps several years later.[113]

Beyond this isolated skirmishing, there were a number of 'indirect' mechanisms by which the Aro supplied the coastal market with captives. In both Igbo and Ibibio communities the principal victims were those who had broken laws, those who were abducted and sold by individuals to enhance their own wealth or rid themselves of a rival, those who were considered deviant, and those sold or seized in settlement of debts. The proportion of children sold as slaves increased dramatically between the late eighteenth century when children accounted for 15 per cent of the trade, and the 1820s when their proportion had risen to 39 per cent. Most probably this was the result of kidnapping or of being sold by their families. Four out of six of Koelle's informants reported kidnapping.[114] Oral accounts recall that covert arrangements were made with the Aro to kidnap rivals. When the victim walked to the stream to fetch water or when a 'stubborn' child was sent on an errand, they would be abducted. The victim's family would carry on without knowing that people had 'collected money for his head'.[115] The Annang conception of the head-hunter is a vivid one. The killer remained hidden in the bush, painted his face with charcoal and carried a crook, a bag and a matchet with which he conducted his abductions.

Various categories of criminals and deviants were sold into slavery. The mid-nineteenth-century story of Udo Akpabio from Ikot Ekpene illustrates how debts, crimes and acts of deviance might each lead to seizure, ransoming and sale to the slave-traders.[116] Udo Akpabio had to mortgage land to cover the costs of the burial feasts for his father, a clan head (àkúkù). His mother remarried and gave birth to twins; as a result she was banished to the village of twin mothers (ìkɔ̀t ìbáàn ékpó) before being sold to Aro traders.[117] Left landless and alone, Udo Akpabio became a cloth trader, though travelling even ten miles during this period was difficult and required weapons and trusted contacts. He committed adultery and was fined 1,500 manillas: 'I had to hide myself and send some people to beg the offended husband to allow me to pay a fine as a ransom for my life.'[118]

A range of debt-servicing mechanisms also contributed to the supply of slaves. 'Pawns' (ùbíɔ́ŋ) were given as surety for payment in many transactions and when the debt defaulted they were sold into slavery.[119] Again, Udo Akpabio's comments on marriage and divorce in pre-colonial Annang society are of particular note. Fathers selected husbands for their daughters, who were severely dealt with or sold if they refused his choice:

> The repayment of the purchase money nearly always resulted in a sort of war between the villages. If a woman ran away the husband would catch any person from the village to which she had run and would sell them as a slave. If the wife died and money had been fully repaid another wife had to be given. This might be continued so long as the man desired to claim this privilege.[120]

In this context of the slave trade, therefore, clear pre-colonial trajectories of feuding, abduction and violence had emerged concerning the transfer and return of brideprice.

The demand for slaves led to the creation of institutions that provided for the elimination of unwanted persons.[121] The leopard society (*ékpê*) was one such institution which also helped to centralise trade and political power within those settlements in which it was formed. Its members included wealthy traders, heads of communities and even European traders. The Ekoi claim to have introduced the leopard society (*ngbe*) from the Cameroon bank of the Cross River estuary where it was adopted by the Ejagham (*mgbe*), the Efik (*egbo*), the Banyang (*ngbe*), Yakurr (*nkpe*), the Ibibio and Annang (*ékpê*) and the Ngwa (*okonko*).[122] This expansion should be understood in the context of trade links which penetrated the hinterland from the early eighteenth century onwards.[123] Dating the arrival of *ékpê* in Annang is problematic. As the *ékpê* society expanded northwards up the Cross River its westward diffusion was not direct but took place via the Aro traders. It has been suggested that the *ékpê* society's penetration of Ibibio and Annang communities was slowed by the presence of the *ékpó* masquerade and that *ékpê* arrived in the *ékpó* areas only at the end of the nineteenth century.[124] Not only do the histories of various local *àfé ékpês* trace their foundation to an earlier period, however, but it seems more probable that the violent sanctions and protection offered by *ékpê* membership were directly and intimately associated with the slave trade of an earlier period.[125]

The leopard society had the power to impose summary justice (to 'blow *ékpê*') and a set of sanctions, which included execution or seizure. The society was especially involved in recovering debts, in condemning debtors to enslavement and in policing other aspects of the slave trade such as settling and collecting 'comey' duties.[126] The commercial sanctions it imposed, plus the creditworthiness and freedom of travel it afforded members, contributed to the *ékpê* society's expansion into the hinterland. In the Abak area *ékpê* was the executive arm of village government and implemented judicial decisions in tandem with lineage heads and village chiefs. Any thief who was caught would be paraded through the market, beaten and either sold or killed at the execution grove (*úkâŋ ìnɔ̀* – place, thief). The fate of those executed was relayed to their relatives by the phrase the leopard had 'eaten' them (*ékpê òmùm enye átá* – 'leopard caught person chew'). Combined with their rights to catch and kill stray livestock on cultivated land, the lucrative privileges of status that membership of the leopard society conferred led to the saying that 'the leopard is food' (*ékpê édi údiá*).

The benefits of leopard society membership were seized upon by European traders who supported the society at Calabar because it was instrumental in the smooth running of commercial transactions. The sanctions of the *egbo* society were employed to reinforce the 'trust' system, particularly in the recovery of debts.[127] The following extract illustrates that *egbo* was used on behalf of the British to ensure that local traders would supply the supercargoes within five months of receiving their advance goods:

I, Duke Ephraim of Duke Town, River of Old Calabar, do hereby promise that in future, from and after this date, that [sic] a supercargo making a requisition to me to blow 'Egbo' on any native who may own a vesel [sic] that I will immediately blow such 'Egbo' on any such native, and enforce the payment of such debt in the course of five months from this date.[128]

James Holman, who was at Old Calabar in 1828, reported that masters of British ships were being admitted to *ékpê* in the 1820s. Between 1874 and 1880, when European traders were prevented from seizing property or persons to recover debts, several traders, including J. H. White, Harry Hartje, George Watts and Alex Henderson, joined *egbo* to secure their commercial position.[129] In 1877 James Walker calculated that the cost for a European joining all nine grades of *egbo* was between £1,000 and £1,300, for which they gained the following rights:

The only advantage to a European trader purchasing Egbo privileges, if it can be called an advantage, is thus: The individual so purchasing them can give out goods on credit to the native traders, and if any one who takes the goods fails in making payment of produce as stipulated, he can summon Egbo to take possession of his house property and slaves, and dispose of them to realise the amount of debt due.[130]

While southern Annang communities lay on the main arteries of the pre-colonial slave trade routes, they were so completely isolated by the monopoly of the middlemen that European accounts shed little light on the identity or internal dynamics of the hinterland groups. Monopolies of trade and power at the coast had served to organise space itself thereby creating inequality and hierarchy.[131] It is probable that the Annang were identified as early as the seventeenth century from reports written by missionaries working with African slaves in Latin America and the West Indies. These reports refer to a group known as the 'Moco' or 'Moko'.[132] Such evidence first appeared in 1627 when Alsonso de Sandoval referred to the 'Moco' as a group of 'Calabarians', thus linking the Moko to the port of Old Calabar.[133] The most significant eighteenth-century account of the hinterland is that of C. G. A. Oldendorp, a missionary who worked with slaves in the West Indies. In 1774 he placed the 'Mokko' near the Ijaw of New Calabar and produced a vocabulary of their language which bears a very close resemblance to modern Ibibio.[134]

The name Moko may have been lost when the slave trade moved from Obolo (Andoni) to Bonny, where the Ubani used the term Kwa to refer to the Ibibio. Koelle's 1854 study of the languages of liberated slaves in Sierra Leone does not use the term Moko or Kwa to refer to the Ibibio speakers of the Qua Iboe river but rather is the first to use the term 'Anan', which he listed as a separate language alternatively known by Europeans as

'Kalaba'.[135] Koelle found around 200 'Kalaba' people living in Sierra Leone originating from the districts of 'Anan, Bie or Bibie, Nkuo, Okua, Ekoe and Efik'.[136] In addition to the readily identifiable groups of Annang, Ibibio (Bibie) and Efik, the other groups in Koelle's records correspond to Ibibio villages located close to Arochukwu (Nkwot, Ukwa and Ekoi), from where large numbers of slaves originated.[137]

The expansion of the slave trade on the coast further articulated the calculus of accumulation in yams and people. A new imperative to yam production emerged with the provisioning of European slave-trading vessels which was to stimulate the internal agricultural market.[138] In Pereira's 1508 description of the estuary of the New Calabar and Bonny Rivers (the Rio Real), he mentions that hinterland inhabitants 'come from a hundred leagues or more up this river bringing yams in large quantities, which, in this district, are very good and nourishing; they also bring many slaves, cows, goats and sheep ... They sell all this to the natives of the village for salt, and our ships buy these things for copper bracelets, which are here greatly prized ...'[139] As the slave trade expanded, so these supply routes extended deeper into the Ibibio-speaking hinterland. In 1698, for example, Ibibio chiefs had become directly engaged in provisioning slave vessels. During *The Dragon*'s visit to Old Calabar, Barbot recorded that William and Robin, both kings of Agbisheria (Ibibio), were paid for the provision of plantain and game.[140]

It is unlikely that at first the uncertain and infrequent demands made by visiting overseas traders made a great difference to the hinterland economy.[141] By the late seventeenth century, however, the seasonal provisioning of ships with foodstuffs became very important, and slaving vessels timed their visits to the coast to coincide with the yam harvest. Supplemented with salted meat, European horse beans, and with maize and cassava meal from Sao Tomé and Principe, yams were the principal food consumed by slaves from the Bight of Biafra during the Atlantic crossing.[142] John Barbot recorded precise figures for the number of yams required to sustain a slave vessel leaving Bonny (Bandy-Point) for the Middle Passage at the turn of the eighteenth century, and he noted that the 'fittest time' to purchase slaves was determined by the supply of yams; delays during August and September had eased after the harvest by January and February:

> A ship that takes in 500 slaves, must provide above a 100,000 yams; which is very difficult, because it is hard to stow them, by reason they take up so much room; and yet no less ought to be provided, the slaves there being of such constitution, that no other food will keep them; Indian corn, beans and Mandioca disagreeing with their stomach; so that they sicken and die apace, as it happened aboard the Albion Frigat, as soon as their yams were spent, which was just when it anchor'd at St. Tome, after a fortnight's passage from Bandy-Point at Calabar.[143]

As the slave trade expanded, the demand for food – yams, maize and palm oil especially – increased to feed slaves and crew during the transatlantic voyage and during the long periods when ships remained in port. The expanding population of the coastal ports and the switch from agriculture and fishing to trade also placed greater demand on yam production in the hinterland. These yams were grown in the forest country bordering the Imo River, that is Annang, Ogoni and Ngwa territories, where they were available in July and August. Superior yams from the marginal savannah of the northern Niger riverain area were not ripe until late December to February.

The precise scale of this trade is difficult to gauge. Across the Bight of Biafra the annual shipment amounted to between 10,000 and 14,000 slaves between 1750 and 1810 and rose between 1820 and 1840.[144] During the mid-1820s sources indicate an average annual export of slaves from the Bight of Biafra of 20,000.[145] The large number of slaves shipped from the Bight of Biafra would therefore imply the export of a large tonnage of yams supplied from the lower Imo river and the Anambra and Lower Niger riverain to supply the ships anchored at Calabar, Opobo and Bonny. Based on Barbot's figures for the yam supply per vessel, conservative estimates would suggest that the demand for yams ran in excess of one million a year by the end of the eighteenth century.[146] At its peak in the mid-1820s, however, the annual demand for yams across the Bight of Biafra may have doubled.

The impact of this agricultural demand on Annang society can only be surmised. From the sixteenth century onwards the hinterland of the Bight of Biafra experienced a process of cumulative commercialisation in which the increase in trade at the coast stimulated trade within the hinterland. During this period there had been a marked continuity in the items traded, with food crops (especially yams) and livestock being as essential by the mid-nineteenth century as they had been when Periera made his observations at the beginning of the sixteenth.[147] Within the Lower Imo region the network of markets, the size of canoes, the introduction of higher units of currency, and investment patterns in livestock, farmland and tree crops would suggest that yam production was not for subsistence alone.[148] Since the annual cultivation of 800 yams (twenty racks) by an individual Annang farmer was considered exceptional enough to warrant an honorific title, the production of an agricultural surplus for export on such a large scale must have demanded a considerable number of producers. This has led to the suggestion that the demands of the overseas slave trade could have stimulated the initial southwards expansion of the southern Ngwa and Annang to their current settlements and the subsequent high population densities of this area.[149]

With the expansion of overseas trade and the shift from slaves and yams to palm oil during the nineteenth century, south-eastern Nigeria experienced arguably the most profound economic growth in all of West Africa.[150] The development of the palm oil trade was not a result of the abolition of slave-trading by the British in 1807 – an orthodox view of export substitution – but had also begun to develop earlier as a result of ship provisioning.[151] The first British fleet to enforce the ban on the slave trade arrived on the Cross River in 1821, and later, in 1827, sought to suppress the practice from its base on Fernando Po. The slave trade ceased to be vital to Calabar's economy from around 1830, and by 1841 Old Calabar signed a treaty ending the trade. By 1840, as the slave trade collapsed along the coast, the trade in palm oil continued to expand. In 1800, 223 tons of palm oil had been exported from the Niger Delta to Liverpool. By 1850 this had expanded to 21,723 tons.[152] When palm oil prices slumped in the 1860s and 1870s, the slack was partly taken up by a new trade in palm kernels.

This was a period of significant social transformation as Annang society witnessed a radical shift in the mode of production from the cultivation of yams to the production of palm oil. With the rise of the palm oil trade the Annang, along with their Ngwa neighbours, supplied the main local terminus of Ohambele on the Imo river until Azumini developed as an oil market in the 1860s. Annang and Ibibio households were more specialised in palm oil production. The higher population density of Ibibio and Annang communities, as compared to their Ngwa neighbours for instance, contributed to this economic specialisation along with the ready availability of water supplies that enabled processing techniques of fermentation which produced higher quality oil. As oil and kernel exports increased, so hinterland communities became ever more dependent upon both the overseas trade and internal trade in foodstuffs to compensate for the changes in production.

Palm oil did not replace yam cultivation but operated within the inter-stices of the existing agricultural year, with the main harvesting period being between January and May after the yam harvest in September to January. Nevertheless, labour burdens became more onerous and the adaptation of Annang society to oil palm production increased regional specialisation. North–south trade in particular became more pronounced as yams from the northern reaches of the Cross River in Ogoja, Abakaliki and Obubra were exchanged for palm oil, fish and salt from the coastal hinterland. Annang fortunes came to rest on the terms of trade in these two axes where exchange rates would prove critical. Food shortages in fact were reported from the late 1820s onwards. In 1828 the country around the Cross River was said to be 'barely able to supply itself with yams, plantains, etc.',[153] and by mid-century a missionary resident at Old Calabar reported that yam prices among the Ibibio west of the Cross River had jumped from five yams for a copper wire to five wires each and that 'prophets were warning of dire consequences if there was not a return to traditional prices'.[154]

The transformation from yam cultivation to palm oil production brought subtle but significant changes to the underlying sexual division of labour in which women had a central place in the subsistence and commercial economy, while men sought authority through ritual specialisation and ritual control.[155] The means of production remained broadly the same, with yams and palms both dependent on access to land and labour, but the nature of access to the crops themselves began to shift. Land was generally available for yam cultivation, either through physical expansion or fission, but access to it was controlled by elders and by one's place within the lineage. Palm oil trees, on the other hand, were subject to usufructuary rights which meant that it was not necessary to own the land in order to harvest the palm fruits. All palm trees were owned and cultivated by men, including the coconut palm (*isíp áyôp*), the palm oil tree (*áyôp*) and the palm wine tree (*úkɔ̀t áyôp*). Nevertheless, palm pledging systems introduced a flexibility which did not involve alienating the land and provided scope for greater inter-lineage and inter-village transactions.

The principles of access to labour were broadly similar for the successful production of the new cash crop, and access to labour, in the form of wives and children, remained critical. Where the yam was conceived as a 'male' crop, albeit with varieties delineated on a male and female basis and involving female labour in weeding, palm oil production served to inject a new commercial tension to male–female interdependence. Palm processing, the most labour-intensive aspect of palm oil production, was conducted by women and before heavier machinery was introduced it took place on a compound basis. While men owned the palm trees and were responsible for harvesting, control of the processing, marketing and profits of the palm oil crop rested with women.

The identity of those who benefited most from the new opportunities of the palm oil trade remained largely unchanged. Those who could assert rights in land by extending agricultural capacity (by renting land or palm trees) and by expanding their labour capacity (by marrying additional wives) were the senior office-holders of Annang society. Nevertheless, there was a fluidity to the palm oil export business and, by the turn of the century, this had translated into greater social and economic mobility for two dependent 'classes'. Young men exploited opportunities afforded by safer transportation to enter the preserve of the Aro middlemen and became palm oil traders. The Aro's regional trade monopoly was eroded during the late nineteenth century because of their failure to shift from overland trade routes to water transport to export the heavy oil puncheons. There are accounts, also, of direct trading pacts between Annang traders and coastal middlemen. Women also profited from the expansion of the oil trade as local marketing for domestic consumption was linked to the export market. Indeed, as women's autonomy derived from palm oil trading increased, so the gender relations of production shifted during the nineteenth century in ways that suggested the possibilities for a slackening of male control over the means of production. From this point on, access to and scarcity of female labour was a major factor in determining economic expansion.[156]A set of possibilities had emerged, therefore, which would expose tensions within the household, tensions that remained largely hidden while trade expanded steadily, while the exchange rate remained stable and trading routes and partners remained constant.

Before 1850, continuity rather than change was the chief characteristic of gender roles within the trade.[157] The rapid increase in the palm oil export market during the nineteenth century, however, was accompanied by an assertion of male rights to women's labour and the resulting proceeds. Laws of access to palm trees, especially those on communal land, may have been introduced during this period, along with restrictions on women climbing palm trees. Men also became involved in oil production, in pounding the palm fruit for instance, to relieve production bottlenecks and to exert their rights over the product. While men accrued profits from the palm oil that women processed and marketed, women themselves retained the kernels. Women used palm kernels as a 'bank', storing them for up to a year and selling small quantities to raise cash as required.[158] With the rise in demand for kernels for soap and margarine manufacture in the 1880s, both the expansion of the kernel trade and the increase in palm oil processing gave rise to commercial opportunities for women. Much depended, as has been argued elsewhere, on the degree to which individual women traded on their own account and retained exclusive rights over the profits of the kernel trade, but the rise in kernel output offset the impact on women of the fall in oil prices in the late nineteenth century which was felt most acutely by men.[159] This move away from a commodity that was primarily controlled by men to one that was controlled by women meant that kernels and the kernel trade became an important avenue for women to acquire wealth.[160] As a result the historical shift from palm oil to palm kernels marked a shift in gender relations.

As the mode of production shifted and pressure on the sexual division of labour intensified, so the symbolic repertoire of Annang society changed. The yam's symbolic associations, including the observance of yam-related festivals, the significance of yam titles, work groups and the recognition of yam production as an index of wealth and status, all declined.[161] In their place symbols of the oil palm (*Elais guineensis*) came to dominate domestic and political life. As palm fruit became the principal source and symbol of wealth and power during the nineteenth century, so palm symbols came to figure prominently in the Annang semantic field.

Palm symbols were especially linked to Annang chieftaincy. *Àyèì*, the new shoots of palm fronds that grow light green at the highest point of the tree, became a significant tool in the set of political instruments at the disposal of Annang chiefs. Plaited *àyèi* formed a garland (*ùnák*) which was a symbol of authority reserved for the highest order of Annang chieftaincy, *àkúkú ìkpá ísɔ̀ŋ*. *Àyèi* was sent by the various levels of chieftaincy and placed as an injunction to prevent trespass on disputed land, to broker peace during conflict, and to signify innocence in a tribunal or an ordeal.[162] Within the Ibesit and Ukanafun clans, chieftaincy rites included the annual preparation and burial of a pot of palm oil (*àlân óbɔ́ŋ*). This ritual combined the elements of earth, ancestors, palm and production. Each stage of its production was conducted by a different person, whose identity remained concealed, and culminated in a 'feeding' of the ancestors prior to the main palm oil harvest. Inokon Uyo Ubong's position at Ikot Udo Obobo, for instance, was confirmed annually by the sharing of oil produced from a special palm tree which was buried in an earthenware pot beneath the shrine house (*ńdêm*) in Ikot Akwa:

> This palm bore fruit but once a year and not like the other palms several times ... there was not another palm that had this peculiarity and from the ripening of its fruit were timed the seasons of the year. When the fruit was ripe a message was sent to two other towns [of Ukanafun] who sent back representatives. The fruit of the palm was then cut, palm oil prepared from it and buried in a pot in the ground of the Ndem's house, while the previous year's oil was dug up and a part sent to the Okukus of the other two towns to eat.[163]

The strong association between the products of the palm oil tree and political hierarchy also translated as an association between palm oil and the representation of power. Palm products were integral to preparations that were of direct malevolent intent at the same time as being central to the manufacture of healing and protective medicines. Basic 'recipes' for the preparation of medicines (*tèm ibɔ́k* – to cook medicine) and the ingredients they used varied from specialist to specialist and were subject to constant innovation. Nevertheless, there is a consistent pattern in which palm products, particularly those parts directly associated with the manufacture of palm oil such as the fruits, husks and kernels, were key components. The seed of a germinated palm fruit (*ńtípé ísíp*), for instance, is used to prepare 'good luck' or protective medicines (*úkpèmê*). In contrast, seven seedless kernel shells (*ùfógó ísíp*), which are hard to find, are used to produce the medicine of misfortune or bad luck (*ùjét úbɔ́k* – lit. wash hand, i.e. the passing of wealth through one's fingers). A variety of oil palm which produces a bright red fruit (*ìfíákù – Elaeis guineensis var. idolatrica or communis*) was especially potent and its oil was used in charms to protect against witchcraft.

Palm oil's impact on the distribution of wealth and political influence, and the new tensions it wrought within the household, were captured in this shifting symbolic landscape. As palm products were the medium of economic and political change, so they were also the medium of ritual performances representing physical transformations and shape-shifting which expressed tensions within the household. The kernel and the palm fruit were both signifiers of transformation – of raw into cooked and of nature into culture. For both men and women palm oil was symbolically associated with an aesthetic of health and beauty, but significantly the embodiment of oil's symbolic values was associated with key moments of transforming the self. Hence palm oil was a vital ingredient in the represen-tation of ancestral spirits as *ékpó* masquerade dancers smeared a mixture of palm oil and charcoal over their bodies to make them shiny and black. Women being initiated into womanhood during *m̀bòbó* fattening were also rubbed with oil and camwood every day.

The association between palm products and transformation, however, extended beyond initiation and masquerade performance, and expressed political conflict and mediation in further specific forms. The most potent medicines prepared from palm ingredients were for two modes of shape-shifting, *ùbén* and *ékpê m̀fòró*. *Ùbén* is a shape-shifter who drains the power of its victim through sexual intercourse. It articulates concepts of masculine power and of tensions between the sexes. A palm kernel is thrown onto the roof of a house which sends its occupant into a deep sleep. Metamor-phosing into an animal, a cat or lizard, the *ùbén* enters the room. When the victim wakes they recognise the form of the attack by scratches left on their body. These wounds are sometimes described as resembling a hawk's claw mark, and are often treated with cooked kernel oil (*álân ísíp*) as an antidote.[164] Should they disturb the intruder, the victim sees only a palm kernel spinning on the floor. Hence, the use of the palm kernel symbol in *ùbén* witchcraft mediates a transformation back from culture to nature, from human to animal, from the complementarity of production to indi-viduality, and from peace to violence within the household.

Early twentieth-century accounts of *ùbén* include a case in which a man was accused of witchcraft for entering his wife's locked room in the form of a rat through a hole in the roof:

> When he entered my room the first time in this secret manner, I was dreaming that I had gone up to Abassi's house, where Abassi himself dwelt among his chiefs. When I woke, I found the signs of what had happened, and on looking up, saw my husband scrambling along the roof like a big rat.[165]

Represented by transformations of the woman's palm product, the kernel, *ùbén* shape-shifting articulated male anxieties about power.[166] Since most accusations of this form of witchcraft were actually against women, *ùbén* represented the physical and spiritual weakening of male power through repeated acts of sexual intercourse, and of male fears of the heightened libido of women.[167] The belief that sex drained male power and potency permeated other male spheres. Warriors and night guards, for instance, would not have sex the day before conflict and contact with post-menopausal women would also serve as an antidote to male power.

Annang beliefs in shape-shifters conjured from the raw materials of the palm oil trade not only captured the tensions over power between men and women, they also suggested that considerable importance was attached to the spiritual apparatus with which to discipline the labour force. The empty bunch of palm fruit, the fibrous stems left behind once the fruit had been removed, was used by women as firewood. But it was also employed in preparations against women to render them infertile, to stop a woman menstruating and to make her look ugly like a man. The empty palm fruit bunch was also used to conjure up a leopard (*ékpê m̀fòró* – lit. change to leopard) which, among other applications, was used as an instrument of domestic sanction. Invoked by a household head to discipline children and wives, particularly if a wife was suspected of adultery, *ékpê m̀fòró* was summed up by striking the palm bunch with the blunt knife of Annang rituals (*ikúâ ibôm*) and by pouring a libation. The apparently real leopard that was conjured up was sent to bush paths on which wives suspected of adultery were passing on the way to their lovers, where it would scratch and startle but not savage them.[168] A variation of this practice was to use the empty bunch of the bright red *ifiákù* variety of palm. This had protective properties and could deter a bush leopard, 'cool down' a leopard or python soul affinity (*úkp̀ŋ ikɔ̀t*), and was thought to have protected *ékpê* society members as they travelled. *Ékpê m̀fòró* was thought originally to have been a war medicine and that it was subsequently adopted by thieves to make them disappear by becoming a tree or an anthill, by guards to make them immune from bullets, and in later years by tax evaders, traders of contraband and armed robbers.

★ ★ ★

The commercial opportunities of the palm oil trade, despite the domestic tensions they evoked, were jealously protected. The high costs of palm oil transportation made it essential for European middlemen to get as near as possible to the producing areas. 'Tapping', by which steamers intercepted produce directly, became a feature of Niger Delta trade by the 1870s, and 'factories' (trading posts) were established at Aboh, Onitsha and Lokoja (situated at the confluence of the Niger and Benue). The Efik at Calabar, however, employed a variety of tactics to restrict European contact inland to the Cross River trading axis with its markets at Itu, Ikot Offiong and Ikpa. These ranged from the provision of annual tribute (*utumo Ef.*) to confirm exclusive trading partnerships, the invocation of *egbo* (*ékpê*) society laws, as in 1862 to prevent young men from trading palm oil, and by the swearing of oaths, as Goldie reported in 1872, when an oath was sworn by traders from Duke Town and Creek Town to maintain the palm oil prices and measures.[169] In 1859, the United Free Church of Scotland mission was also prevented from working further upstream than the Efik trading post of Ikot Offiong under an agreement which stipulated that the missionaries would not engage in trade.[170]

At this crucial moment in the expansion of the palm oil business, as declining prices and demand in the 1870s forced traders to cut costs, those markets selling high-quality 'soft' palm oil, including the Annang and Ndokki (Ngwa Igbo) waterside markets on the Imo and Qua Iboe rivers, were subject to the most dramatic act of protectionism staged by the coastal middlemen: King Jaja's blockade from 1873 to 1887. In 1859 the Bonny houses of Annie Pepple and Manilla Pepple engaged in a civil war over the right to set trade 'comey'. Jaja, head of the Annie Pepple house, was driven out of Bonny by Oku Jumbo and withdrew first to Obolo (Andoni), and was later given territory which he called Opobo. In response, Jaja sought to usurp Bonny's position with the European traders. Through treaties and punitive actions against the Ibenos on the Qua Iboe river mouth, he monopolised access to the palm oil and kernel trade of the hinterland. In 1872 Consul Livingstone reported that Jaja controlled all the Igbo and 'Qua' markets, and that while the English firms in Opobo were flourishing, those in Bonny had been ruined.[171] By the treaty of 1873, in which the British recognised Jaja as King of Opobo, a ban was placed on European traders taking their ships up the Imo River beyond the port. Aware that recently introduced shallow draft steam vessels could enter the inland tributaries, Jaja had effectively annexed the Qua Iboe river-mouth territory by 1881.[172]

Jaja's blockade was secured both at the coast and through hinterland pacts. The biography of Uyo Ubong Udo Obobo and his family in the southern Annang village of Ikot Udo Obobo is significant in tracing these intersections of power between Jaja at the coast and wealthy Annang in the interior. Uyo Ubong was the son of the village's founder (Udo Obobo) and was reputed to have kept a stockade in which 'stubborn' people were held before being sold to the coast. Uyo Ubong traded slaves and oil with Jaja of Opobo at Akpa Alak ('come early') waterside market, one of a host of trading ports on the creeks and tributaries of the Qua Iboe and Imo rivers which traversed the Annang landscape frequented by Andoni, Opobo, Ibani, Ogoni and Ikwerre traders.[173] Jaja, known locally as Jojo, was reported once to have visited Ikot Udo Obobo in the company of an Ndokki trader from Akwete. Stories related today suggest that Jaja invested Uyo Ubong with powers to govern the interior region and secure his supply routes. Uyo Ubong was an old man by the 1870s, and his son, Inokun Uyo Ubong maintained the trading partnership with Jaja.[174]

Jaja's resistance to hinterland penetration continued as pressure on his trading monopoly grew in the 1880s with the arrival of European traders at the Qua Iboe estuary. Stores and factories set up by Watts, Holt and Harford (who started Sunday scripture-reading meetings) were ransacked and the villages they traded with were raided in 1880–81. In April 1881 Jaja petitioned Consul Granville for George Watts' removal from the river.[175] These events coincided with a shift in British policy towards the Delta rulers. From the 1840s the commercial relationship between the British merchants and local traders had been progressively defined by treaty, notably those negotiated by the British Consul John Beecroft after 1849. As part of this process Courts of Equity were established along the coast which regulated 'comeys', pilotage fees, the collection of debts and the settlement of commercial disputes. This commercial relationship shifted in the 1880s, however, as Britain's trade interests came under pressure from German territorial ambitions along the coast, and from 1884 Consul Hewett proceeded to conclude treaties of protection with African states in the Bights of Benin and Biafra. In June 1885 the British Government declared protectorate status over the 'Niger Districts' situated on the Old Calabar, Bonny, Cameroons, New Calabar, Brass and Opobo rivers. No attempts were made to establish local administration until 1891, however, when Calabar became the capital of the Oil Rivers Protectorate. A Commissioner and Consul General were appointed at Calabar, and Deputy Commissioners and Vice Consuls were posted to the main trading rivers.[176]

The blockade which had isolated the hinterland groups during the 1870s and 1880s was steadily dismantled after Protectorate status was proclaimed. Jaja, however, refused to sign the key treaty articles containing provisions for the opening up of the palm produce markets until 1887 when he was abducted and forced to send a chief with Consul Johnston to those markets he controlled and 'break the "ju-ju" which prevents the people of the interior from trading with the whitemen'.[177] The process of opening up the inland markets to trade, however, was resisted as subsequent British efforts to travel up the Qua Iboe river were thwarted by communities who denied access to creeks and landing points. In 1889, for instance, Opobo traders placed a boom across the Azumini creek at Mgbon Kwo. It was not until 1894 that, as a member of the Niger Coast Protectorate's survey department, the first explorer, Roger Casement, encountered Annang territory during his aborted exploration of the hinterland when, led by Aro guides, he was prevented from reaching Opobo by 'the king of the Anang'.[178] The identity of this 'king', of course, is elusive, though most likely he was a powerful chief or trader from near Abak, someone like Inokun Uyo Ubong, who was bound by pacts with the coastal middlemen and was wary of upsetting the delicate balance of the region's trading partnerships.[179]

CONVERSION AND CONQUEST

European missionary activity on the Qua Iboe river and its hinterland developed in the immediate aftermath of Jaja's reign at Opobo. It is necessary here, however, to examine the internal imperatives as well as the external dynamics of religious change on the Qua Iboe river. The links between missions and colonial orders, indeed, require a situational analysis since 'the mission situation is shaped by those whom a mission seeks to convert as well as by the power behind the mission'.[180] Harford's scripture meetings and the Ibeno traders' experience of the Scottish missions along the coast in Calabar led Ibeno chiefs to request a missionary of their own. The message was passed via merchants and the United Presbyterian Church of Scotland Mission in Calabar to several British training colleges. Set on a missionary path after the Sankey revival in his native Belfast several years previously, Samuel Bill, then studying at the Harley Missionary College in London, responded to the request. Bill arrived at the mouth of the Qua Iboe river in 1887 and established a non-denominational evangelical Protestant mission in those areas recently released from Jaja's blockade with the intention of expanding northwards up the river. Bill preached through a translator because he had learned Efik from his Scottish colleagues in Calabar which, although understood by younger converts, was not comprehended by the elders, who spoke the Ibeno dialect. A former Sierra Leonian trader, Williams, helped Bill with translation, while Elder Dempster, the steamer company, provided a free service to the fledgling mission outpost.

A year passed before there were any converts. The first was a young man called Min Ekong who was from one of the leading fishing families in Ibeno. His father had died when he was twelve. His grandfather was a shrine priest and Min would have succeeded to minister to several of the principal Ibeno spirits. From his own accounts, Min Ekong's initiation into the *nyena* shrine priesthood was well advanced; he had conducted full sacrifices at the shrine on his own, had mastered the means of producing the 'voice of the spirit' and was observing various food prohibitions. His grandfather warned him that divulging the shrine's secrets would incur a fine or worse from a certain Igbo village, which suggests that the shrine was part of a regional complex.[181] Soon after his initiation into the warrior society (*ékóŋ*), however, Min became the house-boy of the newly arrived Samuel Bill and assumed the Christian name of David. In 1891 he accompanied Bill on furlough to Belfast and on his return he became the mission's first preacher.

The chiefs, Egbo Egbo and Ukot Ibuno, who had initially requested the European missionary at Ibeno, proved reluctant converts. Both were traders whose livelihoods depended on the gin trade. After two years Egbo Egbo began to take instruction and was ministered to daily. Once he had renounced the gin trade and pensioned off eleven of his twelve wives he was baptised.[182] His power in village politics and in the 'palaver-house' fell considerably, but Egbo Egbo became one of the first church elders appointed to oversee the expanding congregation in Ibeno. Ukot Ibuno recanted while suffering from rheumatic fever.[183] He had been a renowned 'witch killer' and in this he was not alone among the Qua Iboe Mission's first converts. Asukpa Ikaeto, another renowned 'killer of wizards', had been accused of wizardry himself and had fled in fear that his life was to be taken on account of it.[184] He was an Ibibio sold to one of the Ibeno chiefs as a child, and had become a diviner and executioner. The palm grove to which he escaped was known as Mimbo Town near Eket and became a haven for former slaves and those fleeing accusations of wrong-doing. Influenced by Christian traders from Ibeno who rested at this spot, Asukpa built a small hut of bamboo and mats for evening services and had prepared a band of six enquirers for baptism. In 1899 he invited David Ekong to establish a mission station at Mimbo Town.[185]

Mission accounts exalted the moral and ethical characteristics of these early converts' prior 'heathen' lives. That Ukot Ibuno was a fair trader, well loved by his customers and who always returned money paid to him during his middleman dealings, indicated his basic decency. The wise counsel of David Ekong's grandfather – that he should have nothing to do with *egbo* men who dealt unjustly with a poor man, and that he should refrain from using charms to make himself brave, win a girl's love or make himself rich – were all presented as appropriate standards of conduct in preparation for his life as the church's most important messenger.[186] These accounts must be seen, however, as one among many devices by which the mission constituted their congregations as moral communities. Indeed, rather than illustrating prior moral proclivities towards Christianity, the conversion of Min Ekong, Ukot Ibuno and Asukpa Ikaeto suggests that those who were initially drawn to the mission were very powerful individuals who had a prior history of 'religious quest'.[187]

In the cases of Ukot Ibuno and Asukpa Ikaeto, illness and persecution were contributory factors, but it is intriguing, nevertheless, that 'witch killers' should be among the pioneer flock. What the missionaries meant when they referred to Ukot Ibuno as the 'elected leader in killing witches' or to Asukpa Ikaeto as the 'public executioner' is not clear. Most commonly it was the diviner (*idìɔŋ*) who detected witches, but another highly secret category of witch seer was known as *ukpòtia* or *ùkpòtiô*.[188] Goldie translates this word as headstrong and reckless. This definition is accurate in the sense that an *ùkpòtiô*'s fearlessness meant they considered themselves immune and all-powerful, but in general use it refers to a person of unassailable spiritual power. An *ùkpòtiô*'s power extended beyond the ordinary Annang and Ibibio sense of power as someone who has been tested (*òkpɔsɔ̀ŋ*), and beyond the prognosticative and spirit-invoking capacities of a diviner (*idìɔŋ*). Rather, an *ùkpòtiô* person was endowed with powers of a highly ambiguous nature and with very 'witch-like' capacities, including the ability to meet fellow *ùkpòtiô* in distant places, usually at night and often at the top of tall trees.[189] This points to the way in which brokers in knowledge and power, *ùkpòtiô* and *idìɔŋ*, who in indigenous terms were among the most power-fully protected, were also among the first to embrace Christianity.[190] They did not fear these new forces, but rather were interested in assimilating this new, exotic and foreign source of power.

Among the Qua Iboe converts there were those for whom the adage 'the nearer the Kirk the further from God' applied, yet in the main the reverse was true. Samuel Bill, Archie Bailie, John Kirk and later recruits to the mission focused on conversion at close quarters, especially in situa-tions where the mission profited from both the salvation of souls and from their labour. Qua Iboe evangelism was most effective among house staff of the mission quarters, and then among apprentices at the saw mill in Ibeno and the coffee plantation opened in Okat station.[191] Other indirect avenues, such as the government smallpox vaccination campaign, which Bill assisted in 1902, were also seen as a means of consolidating the mission, in this case to Eket. In other circumstances the demonstration of these powers of 'healing' might have expanded the congregation, but the vaccinations were mired in controversy. Men and women were injected at the same time in the same room, despite the fact that the exposure of women's buttocks to men was a potentially lethal act of spiritual sanction. Nevertheless, the provision of basic medical services and staffing the dispensaries that were established at the mission stations, were perceived, along with proficiency in Efik, as key requirements in the recruitment of European missionaries. Bill insisted that his missionaries 'work at the medicine' when they returned to Britain on furlough.

Figure 2.6 The Qua Iboe Mission 'pioneers'. Samuel Bill (*left*), John Kirk, Archie Bailie, Samuel Bill, Mrs Bailie, Mrs Bill and Miss Gordon (*centre*), David Ekong (*right*)[192]

The circle of converts at Ibeno was a tight one, and was extended in part by marriage among them. In 1895 the mission celebrated its first marriage when David Ekong married one of Chief Egbo Egbo's daughters, Mary, on whom he renounced his claim to brideprice. John Ewainan, appointed as a teacher at Impanek, was married to David Ekong's sister, Eka Ito. His cousin, Robert Anderson, also became a mission teacher. One of the eleven wives that Egbo Egbo 'put away' upon his conversion, Adiaha, who had been banished from Eket after giving birth to twins and had been enslaved before marrying Egbo Egbo, also went on to marry one of the Qua Iboe Mission's first preachers, Ibok. Marriages such as these consolidated the small congregation. It was this set of core families at Ibeno who trained and fostered the mission's recruits, and these marriages anticipated later initiatives with the founding of the Girls Institute in 1908, which sought to become a 'means of rescuing many from a life of heathenism', and of preparing them as the wives of mission teachers.[193]

The cultural continuity that underlay the process of Christian conversion saw Christianity's conceptions of God and Devil, Heaven and Hell, intersect with a complex duality of powers in Annang cosmology. In translations of the Bible and in everyday speech the remote, all-controlling, beneficial sky god, àbàsì ényòŋ, became Abasi, and was translated as God. The ancestral spirits, ékpó, as represented in masquerade performances, became the Devil.[194] This duality resonates with a structural distinction in Ibibio belief between the powers of up and down, earth and sky. Where the sky deity is linked to antidotes and protection, the earth's powers are associated with malevolence. Narratives of early converts illustrate something of their motivations for joining the Qua Iboe Mission fellowship, although very few dwell on non-instrumental factors.

The dominant orientation of Annang towards all religions was the search for individual and collective power, for personal protection, healing, fertility, and practical guidance through life's uncertainties.[195] Conversion was a choice, and the costs and benefits, which differed according to age and gender, were weighed up carefully.[196] The social advantages of belonging to the Christian community were especially relevant for those who had little to lose. The poor and marginalised included former slaves, strangers, and categories of social outcast in which mothers of twins predominated. Many had physically lived outside the Annang or Ibibio village in ad hoc settlements established by slaves, or in spaces such as the 'twin mothers' village' which were isolated by ritual embargoes. Conversion offered these groups haven and reintegration. At Ibeno and beyond, therefore, conversion appealed to the disempowered and those, like young men and women, who were least integrated into the social and religious networks of Ibibio life.

The majority of the small pioneer flock were a motley crew of social misfits. One of the terms under which Samuel Bill accepted land from the Ibeno chiefs was that any person accused of witchcraft, or who was being unlawfully sold as a slave, could take permanent and unmolested refuge on mission ground. Asukpa's community in Mimbo Town, and those who sought refuge at Ibeno, suggest that a significant proportion of the first converts were former slaves. Small parties of escaped slaves regularly swelled the 'refugee' population of the mission station. In March 1899 the missionaries received the largest group of these 'refugees', some 130, who were mainly women. Little was known of their origin – somewhere in the Niger Territories (300 miles to the north). Sold to 'Arab' slavers, they had been made to march from one town to another until they found themselves north of Old Calabar on the Cross River from where they made their escape in their owners' canoes. The mission housed them for six weeks, during which they were put to work by Bill, and cut firewood and processed oil in order to purchase food. Through the mission they were able to contact a British expeditionary force which sent two large canoes to carry them on the initial stage of a long journey back to the homes they had left months previously.[197]

By 1892, five years after Bill's arrival, there were thirty-five church members at Ibeno, and six inquirers living on mission ground.[198] Among them was the church's second convert, Etia, the first woman to enter the Qua Iboe Mission. The widow of a chief in the village of Impanek at the mouth of the Qua Iboe River, she fled to Duke Town, Calabar, where she saw the Scottish missionaries but was afraid of entering the church for fear of being bewitched. On her return she married again, but was accused of causing the death of a child in her new husband's family and of being a witch. Facing summary execution or the *esere* bean ordeal, Etia ate the poisonous bean and survived its effects. She was banished from Impanek, however, and settled near the Qua Iboe mission station. When her second husband died, she refused an offer of protection from the village chief, and requested land in the mission compound from Samuel Bill. Etia burned the wooden effigies representing her ancestors and the plate in which, at noon each day, she poured water for her bush soul to drink. Skilful in the use of herbs, Etia became famous as a children's healer, and when twin infanticide was prohibited in 1899 she nursed twin children until their mothers could accept them.[199]

The Christian congregation was especially appealing to older women like Etia, particularly those without children and with no one to support or bury them.[200] Fellowship within the Christian congregation became an important form of social insurance. A woman from Ibeno said, 'I seem to gain [a] great deal by being a Christian, friends give me presents every now and again to keep me from want.' Without a son or daughter of her own, becoming a Christian meant she had gained many friends who would bury her when she died.[201] Hearing that in heaven everything a person possesses will remain with them forever, an old woman who had entered the inquirer's class in Eket stated that:

> I have been a mother of many children fully trusting they will support me when I grow old [and] unable to work, but instead they all died and leave me without any child to care for me ... I will become a Christian that I may go to where there is no parting from friends and property.[202]

For senior men the costs of conversion involved social dislocation and sanctions. At the Okat station that Archie Bailie opened in 1895, a man who had been attending services for over a year, and seemed earnest in his conviction, suddenly stopped coming. When Bailie went to ask the reason for his absence, he said that his fellow *ékpó* members had threatened that if he returned to either church or class they would put him out of the society, prevent him cutting his palm fruit and deprive him of all the other privileges of that organisation, 'which to an Ibibio means so much'.[203] These were very real sanctions and could be invoked against the most well integrated within society, as the following story indicates. It is not clear precisely how, but Ekpo Uro Usoro had 'displeased a chief and incurred the wrath' of the *ékpó* society in Ikot Akpata. He fled to a Christian friend in Okat, where he received the news that his wife had been sold, his children appropriated, his farm plundered and his compound razed. Bailie's subsequent negotiation with the chiefs of Ikot Akpata to return the man's family and property proved futile. His suggestion that Ekpo Uro Usoro would be reconciled with the village if he was allowed to visit Okat Mission, not to work on Sundays, take no part in public sacrifices and not be forced to contribute to any 'heathen play' was met by a yell of derision. Ekpo did not go back to Ikot Akpata but built a house near the mission ground in Okat where he lived 'in peace and security'.[204]

This case points to the worldly costs incurred by the conversion of senior men whose investment in spiritual protection was also at risk. Protection through initiation and charms was especially significant in this context where conceptions of fortune were attributed to the covert actions of opponents. The risk faced by elders who considered conversion, therefore, would be to 'empty their body' of power and protection. In contrast to their seniors, young men who had yet to enter *ékpó* felt they had little to lose at the time of their conversion.[205] The high proportion of young men among the converts led deputations of chiefs to visit the mission stations and ask whether the church gospel compelled the young to be Christian. The young men saw being a Christian as their exclusive preserve, a sphere of religious and political opportunity not meant for the chiefs and elders. The widespread demand for schools was a reflection of young men's desire to improve themselves, and did not mean, as the mission recognised, that they were thirsting for the Gospel.

Nevertheless, these young men were influential in the spread of the church. One Sunday in Etinan in the early 1900s there were 1,268 members of the congregation of whom at least 800 were young men and boys, with the remainder all young women.[206] While there was clearly widespread appeal among young men in general, the role of influential individuals and of the ties binding groups of young men in bands of fellowship cannot be overestimated. At Ikot Akpan, the mission depended on a single young man who ran the school and who had attracted twenty others into the new church. Such positions were pathways to power and promotion, and in this case the young man's ambitions over-reached. He began to sell European gin, and wishing to raise himself up among the chiefs, he married additional wives. When he was removed from the church, only two of the twenty he brought with him remained.[207]

At Etinan, Kirk's account of the conversion of Akpan Udo Ema, who was one of the first young men to be baptised there, indicates that the 'bands of young' men came in various guises:

> Before we came he was one of the worst men in this town or for that matter in any of the towns in this neighbourhood, and he had a following of young men like himself for he was the son of a powerful chief and had therefore considerable standing in the place. Some of his past life could not be mentioned – 'let darkness cover it' … Shortly after we came here, he and his young men went to a town ten miles away and seized a lot of cattle and goats and as many yams as they were able to carry. These were all brought to his house where a division was made of the captured spoil. But in the mercy of God all this was soon to be changed. He and his companions settled down to learn to read in our little school, and he also came to the inquirers' class when there were only five names on the roll.[208]

Once Akpan Udo Ema had converted he made restitution for his robberies, and with eight of his gang learned to read the New Testament in seven months. His wife was baptised a few months later. On the morning of her baptism she became the first woman in the district to wear a dress, and for this reason the heads of the secret societies were said to have made an order that Akpan and his wife were to be killed.

It seems that there was a great deal of interest in the mission from young women too, but they were less able to follow up on this curiosity. The social pressures upon young girls to enter the pre-marital fattening society (ṁbòbó) were great, and the 'patriarchal panic' at the conversion of those responsible for the reproduction of the lineage was violent.[209] Reports that women were flogged by their husbands for going to church or attending inquirers' classes were widespread, and there were many accounts of more serious assaults. When in 1904 a man in Etinan heard that one of his wives had gone to church for the first time he cut her throat with a matchet.[210] Another Etinan man called his household together to make a feast and sacrifice, but one of his wives refused to take part and said she had heard in church that a man cannot serve two masters. Having decided 'to serve the true god, rather than the devil', her husband 'went to Ju-ju and told the God to kill her'. Three days later the woman died. He said 'ju-ju' killed her, but John Kirk, who had opened the Etinan station in 1898, claimed that the husband had poisoned her.[211]

Poisoning, in fact, became a common topic of discourse at the turn of the century. Kirk claimed that he knew of several people who had been poisoned at Etinan after his arrival, including the man who gave the ground on which the mission house itself was built. He also claimed that it was common knowledge that people poisoned for money. The man responsible for a series of poisonings in Etinan disclosed his complicity before a large crowd of people in the mission yard. He even named those who had paid him for his work, and said that the price he generally received was 1,100 manillas, or about £5. This discourse on poisoning was part of a significant innovation in the occult imagination of Ibibio and Annang society at the turn of the century.

The physical and social mobility of the period was associated not only with Christian conversion, but also with religious change more broadly as the western Ibibio-speaking areas witnessed the introduction of a new mode of witchcraft, ifót.[212] In everyday discourse ifót is a witch who kills by poisoning. This belief was linked to rumours that people in Calabar, its supposed source, did not live to an old age as they were consumed by a cycle of witchcraft flesh-debts. It has been argued that witchcraft accusations in Calabar during this period were the result of social and political tensions arising from the conflict between traditional status systems and the new status of wealth based on overseas trade.[213] In Calabar, those accused of ifót were subjected to a poison ordeal called esere made up of Calabar beans (Physostigma venenosum). The bean was considered ibét (ritually forbidden) to ifót in the same way as food prohibitions are ibét to Annang and Ibibio clans.[214] Hence stories of witchcraft familiar in Ikom folk tales as recorded by a District Commissioner, Dayrell, began to circulate in Ibibio and Annang. They related tales of 'bewitched' foods, of nocturnal transformations into a witch-bird (the owl), of chiefs and head men predominating among the witches, of witches' feasts and of the consumption of human flesh.[215]

As Christianity followed commerce north along the river, so the second Qua Iboe Mission station was opened on the site of a shop Harford had run at Okat in 1895.[216] This was the year that the Protectorate, which had been extended over the hinterland in 1893, was renamed the 'Oil Rivers and Niger Coast Protectorate'. Consuls and vice-consuls visited the Qua Iboe river for several years prior to the turn of the century, though their

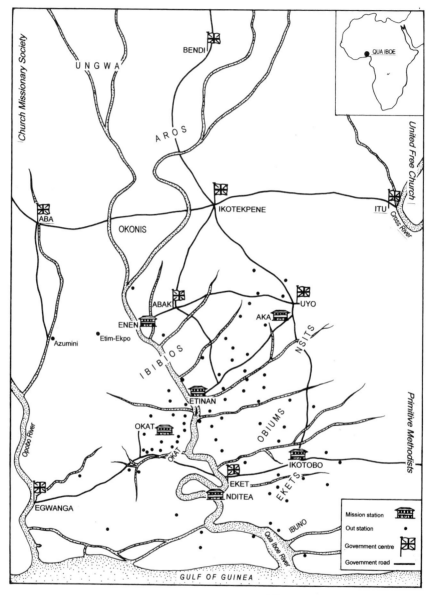

Figure 2.7 Qua Iboe Mission stations, c. 1912[217]

attempts to open interior roads and suppress 'obnoxious practices' had
little impact. It is important therefore to stress the historical contingency
with which Christianity and colonialism penetrated the palm oil-producing
hinterland. Nevertheless, sometimes in tandem, sometimes in spite of each

other, though often because of common fears, the forces of conquest and Christianity began to move inland. Two related anxieties developed in the years between Samuel Bill's arrival at Ibeno in 1887 and the opening of the colonial district office in the southern Annang town of Abak in 1909 – the British concern over the Aro traders determined the violent pattern of colonial conquest across the hinterland, and the missionaries' fear of the secret societies developed as a discourse on inter-generational conflict and judicial practice.

Samuel Bill did not have a close relationship with the British consuls on the coast. In 1898 Etinan chiefs implored him not to interfere with their customs of *idiɔŋ*, polygamy and twin infanticide. Bill replied that he was not disposed to constant appeals to the British Consul, but if reports of such practices came to his knowledge he would 'attempt to use or call in any force to aid us'.[218] On the subject of punitive expeditions staged by the British Government against hinterland communities he was equivocal. Bill allowed the mission's launch to be used to tow government troops between the coastal towns but refused to transport them if they were preparing an expedition. On one issue, however, Bill's antipathy for the *ékpê* ('egbo') society, he freely invoked the threat of the consul. Indeed, Bill had recommended the establishment of a Native Court at Ibeno for many years precisely because he saw it as the most effective way of breaking up 'Egbo law' in which, as he put it, 'the plaintiff is really also the judge and the executioner and the defendant has no chance'.[219]

The mission's perception of the secret societies was formative. To missionary minds, the secret societies, and the decentralised structure of Annang and Ibibio society more generally, were the residue of the ravages of the slave trade on a once unified people. The precise imagining of the secret societies, in fact, drew on contemporary stories from along the coast in Sierra Leone. Writing with a Belfast audience in mind, Archie Bailie, based at the Okat station, introduced the notion of human-leopard societies to the criminal landscape of the Qua Iboe hinterland. In October 1897 he wrote:

> The secret society of 'Human Tigers', which is prevalent in so many tribes on the West Coast has come into existence among the Ibibios again, to the dismay of all the inhabitants. These ferocious men prowl about on very dark nights looking for prey, which means any one they can get hold of. They also enter compounds and carry off the goats and yams, and so frightened are the people that they wouldn't, for all they possess, leave their houses to protect their property. These 'Human Tigers' are to be found in all the towns, and they roam about within call of each other; their cry, which is truly weird and frightful, sends terror to the native heart. Several young men here already have been seized by them, but they made their escape with only a few cuts.[220]

Although writing at exactly the same time as the human-leopard trials in Sierra Leone, Bailie was evidently referring here to the *ékpê* (leopard) society rather than to a 'human-leopard' cult, though these two groups would be consistently elided in such narratives. Indigenous words for leopards (*ékpê* in Annang, *ękun* in Yoruba) are commonly translated in Nigerian English as 'tiger', even though tigers are not found on the African continent.[221] These 'leopards' had caught thieves who had escaped from prison. *Ékpê* could collect goats with impunity, assault young non-initiates, seize goods in repayment of debts and, its most distinctive feature, which Bailie alludes to, was the secret manufacture of the leopard call. A few years later, in 1902, Samuel Bill described two murders whose details bore more in common with the later 'human-leopard' killings. He attributed to the secret society *ékpê* the murder of two young girls aged fifteen and sixteen who were killed and mutilated in broad daylight on the way to their farm.[222] 'It is dreadful that this society cannot be got at', Bill wrote in his daily journal.

For over a decade the secret societies would figure as the most serious obstacle to the spread of the Gospel, and as Bailie's 1906 reflections indicate, the spectre of the human leopard society had become a persistent feature:

> … the secret organisations are avowedly hostile and openly opposed to all Christian work. They are numerous and practically rule the country. Everyone lives in terror of them, and all their laws are readily obeyed. Their power is unlimited, they rob and oppress, they sell men and women into slavery and offer human sacrifices. I could tell of many dark crimes committed by them near my own station, but at present shall just say that from the Porrah, or Human Leopard Society of Sierra Leone, who tear and eat human victims, or the Silent Ones of the Lower Niger whose aim is to rid Africa of all white influence, down to the immoral Ekoŋ men, of our own tribe, they have all declared against the Gospel and use their great influence in retarding its progress.[223]

The most significant conjunction of colonial and Christian interests surrounded an event in the year following the opening of the Mission's third station at Etinan by John Kirk in 1898. The first incursion of Protectorate forces inland to the western Ibibio-speaking territory was triggered by the mission's direct opposition to Ibibio burial practices. The terms of the various treaties signed in the mid-1850s designed to prevent slavery on the coast had included provisions to stop certain social practices – the killing of twins, the *esere* bean ordeal and the sacrifice of human beings at burials. In March 1899, following the efforts of John Kirk to prevent the sacrifice of a young man as part of burial rites in the village of Mkpok in which Kirk and the District Commissioner Horace Bedwell were injured, a raid was approved.[224]

While the village of Mkpok was quickly overrun following these reports, the expedition force of seven officers, 180 troops and over 200 carriers led by Major Leonard met with surprising resistance. Leonard thought that with such a display of power, fighting would be unnecessary, but he was mistaken as the sortie to Eket which had been intended to last two or three days became protracted in a conflict with the neighbouring Afaha section of Ubium and lasted as many weeks.[225] Leonard's expedition penetrated a distance of 60 miles up the banks of the river, and claimed to have razed fourteen towns with 150 others who surrendered signing treaties by which they agreed to open and maintain roads, refrain from seizing people in 'palavers' and from all practices that would lessen the value of human life (including practices repeatedly referred to by the missionaries such as human sacrifices, twin murders, burial of widows alive and killing of supposed witches).[226] It quickly became apparent, however, that despite the advertised destruction of the 'Fetish Quae' (Eket), the area remained distinctly hostile and the Ekets regularly attacked soldiers and road-making parties, and rescued prisoners.[227]

Sir Ralph Moor, the Consul-General of the Niger Coast Protectorate, thought that a major force must have supported and stiffened the resistance displayed by the Ibibio villages during the expedition of 1899. It became the fashion from this point onwards to trace every local manifestation of opposition to British rule to Aro influence and gradually Aro enmity was built into an obsession.[228] In this conception the Aro's regional force was exaggerated as satellite trading settlements were mistaken for military garrisons. Moor became increasingly convinced that Ibibio leaders were compromised by their complicity in Aro slave-dealing atrocities, that the Aro had infiltrated their ranks, and that in order to bring the Ibibio under British rule the Aro should be subjugated. Colonial conceptions of Aro influence were spurred on by the Qua Iboe Mission's commentators and the link they drew between the Aro, the slave trade and the secret societies:

> Order has been restored and good government introduced so that the whole country is opened up, and now awaits the herald of the Cross to take possession in one King's name. About fifty miles farther up there is one of the most powerful tribes in Africa, called the Aroes ... They are the soldiers of the country, to whom the surrounding tribes pay tribute that they may fight for them ... They keep the trade of the interior from coming down to the coast, and have effectually [sic] resisted every overture of the Government for years, so that theirs is really the closed land of the West Coast. The Aroes are also the great slave traders of the coast, so that slavery cannot be abolished until they are dealt with. They are also the originators of the great secret societies of the country connected with witchcraft ... For several years

the Government have contemplated sending an expedition against them ... At the present time they are preparing for the long-looked-for advance ... It will be the largest thing of the kind that has ever been organised on the West Coast.[229]

The Aro Expedition was 'the severest single blow' that the British dealt to the Aro oligarchy, though its impact was considerably less decisive than the British had hoped for.[230] The punitive Aro expedition of 1901 was justified on the grounds of stopping slave-raiding, abolishing the 'fetish hierarchy' and stimulating legitimate trade. Initially, the British claimed to have freed the Protectorate forever from the evils of slave-dealing since they assumed, mistakenly, that slaves were procured by raids and that once law and order had been imposed, slave-dealing would cease. After the raid on the oracle, however, the Aro persisted in various subtle and illicit attempts to retain their trading oligarchy, including the trade in slaves. The British failed to understand the intricacies of the Aro trading system, and reports of revivals of the Long Juju and of ongoing slave deals and markets quickly suggested that their triumphalism was premature.

Distinguishing African resistance from colonial anxiety in this context is problematic. Yet, in this instance it is apparent that the British disquiet with the Aro was grounded in more than ignorance and suspicion. In concentrating their attacks on Ikot Ekpene, Aba, Owerri and Bende, the Aro Field Force had not attacked the Aro's north-western trading sphere around the market of Uzuakoli. It was from here that Aro slave-dealers were able to revive their business of moving slaves either through Enna, Edda, Biakpan and the Cross River to Calabar, or though Ibeku, Okokoro and Ikwerre to New Calabar (Degema) where, in spite of the government's anti-slavery policy, there was still some demand for slaves, especially children. It was probably because these areas fell under increased military scrutiny in 1905 and 1906 which served to curtail open slave-dealing that *ibini ukpabi*, the Long Juju, was revived at Aro by Chief Kanu Okoro in 1906. Taking advantage of the fact that Aro themselves were guides to the British and could forewarn kinsmen, that their import trade enabled them to disguise illicit transactions, and that slave-trade tracks bypassed new roads, the Aro system survived. The oracle was re-established in Okigwi Division at Isiagu in 1913 and returned to Arochukwu in 1915.[231]

The Aro Expedition had profound consequences for the region as a whole. After raiding Arochukwu, the four columns of the force led by Lt.-Col. Montanaro swept through Ikot Ekpene. Contemporary Annang reaction to the Expedition was one of surprise and resolve, 'Everyone of us said what a disgraceful thing it is for another people to come and fight us on our own land. We have no palaver with them. Let us find out where they are and fight with them.'[232] As a result, the Ikot Ekpene patrols were confined to the town's immediate surroundings as the Ukana clan was joined by

Adiasim in resisting the British forces. The subsequent battle at Anwa Oko near Ikot Ntuen, however, demonstrated the superiority of the maxim gun in British hands. The patrols themselves divided the region into divisions with Native Courts and Councils established at strategic locations. Political officers urged these Councils to undermine Aro standing further by passing bye-laws that would impress upon the Aro that their rights to trade and settle were conditional upon permission from local rulers.[233]

The relationship between the Qua Iboe mission and the institutions of colonialism became more explicit with the creation of these new courts. When it opened in December 1899, Bill became the clerk of the monthly Ibeno Native Court.[234] He also recommended fourteen chiefs from various towns to sit as assessors on the Court, of whom seven were Christians. They included Egbo Egbo, whose status was restored by his appointment as the Court's first president. The physical conjunction of church and court worked to the Mission's benefit in other ways too. At Etinan the church was located near the new Native Court and litigants would arrive from neighbouring communities on the Sunday to be ready for the opening of the court session on Monday morning. In this way the imposing external improvements of the church compound and congregation were widely advertised and those lodging for the night with converts would accompany their hosts to church.

Many proposed mission stations were abandoned because of local hostility. Nevertheless, by the end of 1899, as a result of the government expeditions, the towns and villages around Eket which had been closed to the Qua Iboe Mission began to invite the church in. Despite its misgivings about the punitive raids, there was considerable excitement within the mission in 1901 at the news that large tracts of densely populated country at the head of the Qua Iboe River (the Obium and Aro country) were being opened up 'to the entrance of the trader and the missionary' by the British military expeditions.[235] It was not only the expeditionary forces, however, that the Belfast missionaries followed up the river. Indeed, they were not the first Christians to penetrate the creeks and tributaries of the Qua Iboe. Many of the Opobo and Ibani trading settlements dotted along the creeks and tributaries that criss-crossed the southern Ibibio and Annang region had become small Christian communities of up to forty converts attending their own mud chapels built on the beaches. The churches of the coastal middlemen followed a familiar path of religious innovation within these host societies. Many protective cults, including *ànim èkìm*, had been introduced by middlemen from the coast who settled more or less permanently at Annang waterside trading posts. The Ibeno also traded deep up the Qua Iboe river and converts to the new mission church held meetings among the scattered Christians. In their northwards expansion these outposts, which were never visited by a preacher but which held prayers among themselves on Sundays, were a haven for the mission and a beacon of hope in its stuttering northern expansion.

Despite the fact that waterside markets were already home to Christian communities, and that the northern reaches had been 'pacified' by the expeditions, the mission's expansion was piecemeal and faltering. Crucially, the church did not have the resources to expand rapidly. It lacked significant finances from its home base, it could not raise funds from trade because of an existing trading monopoly agreed by the Ibenos, and it therefore lacked trained ministers and teachers for many years. Up to 1908 the mission was financed by both the local church and home funds.[236] Afterwards the church adopted a principle of self-sufficiency which severely handicapped its capacity since the majority of converts were young people, which as the European missionaries knew very well, was 'another way of saying that they are poor'.[237] What the young people demanded was schools, and the Qua Iboe Mission was therefore compelled to open numerous schools around each of the six central stations in response to the companies of young men 'whose anxiety for teachers is almost painful'.[238] These little schools lacked equipment and in the absence of a certified instructor many of the teachers were 'ignorant of any method of teaching'.[239]

Weekly cash offerings were supplemented by the sales of palm oil, which made the mission dependent on the fortunes of the export market. With the permission of the chiefs, young converts harvested palm oil plots, processed the oil and donated the proceeds of the sale to the church. Many chiefs, however, refused to grant access to communal palm to schoolboys, who were forced to resort to other means in order to raise funds for mission buildings or teachers' wages. Some learned carpentry from the mission and hired themselves out, giving a third, a half or even the whole of the money received to the church as an offering. At Ibeno, Bill raised funds by selling cut timber from his steam saw mill. Other donations were received from Qua Iboe graduates who had moved on to the government school in Bonny. The students there received a cup of rice and a ship's biscuit for their daily food ration. The biscuits could be sold at five a penny and twenty-four Eket boys studying at the school raised £1 2s 8d to be spent on a new church in their village of Atabong by saving and selling part of their daily allowance.[240] By these various means the church's annual donations from local Christians in Qua Iboe had risen slowly from less than £100 per year to £300 in 1908, £550 in 1909, and £1,000 in 1910.[241]

In addition to the lack of funds, rumours about the power of the mission, especially linked to explanations of illness and death, proved a powerful brake on mission expansion. News of illnesses related to conversion had a profound effect in keeping people away from the Mission house. In Okat during 1900, several relatives of converts had become ill and *idiɔŋ* attributed the cause to the mission. 'In fact', Bailie noted, 'every little trouble, and all sickness and deaths are blamed on this mission and on those who have burned their ju-jus'.[242] The examples of men such as Robert Eshett of Nung Oko and Bob Udo of Ikot Obong also demonstrate how illness and conversion coincided within local ontologies. After Robert Eshett renounced his *idìɔŋ* his two sons both died. His former *idìɔŋ* peers declared that the deaths were a visitation from his fathers' spirits and that they would slay him and his whole family if he did not sacrifice. After his baptism, Bob Udo was struck down by a disease that his village attributed to 'the Ju-ju's displeasure'. He was the first convert in Ikot Obong and the mission later surmised that the disease was brought on by a dose of poison slipped into his drink 'by the order of Idiong'.[243] For the expansion of the church, the illness of a prominent convert or supporter was disastrous: 'In Ikot sickness visited the house of the chief who was interested in opening an out-station. The Idiong men and all the man's relatives declare that this visitation is a direct punishment on him for wishing to build a schoolhouse and bring a teacher to the town.'[244]

While the attraction of Qua Iboe Christianity for young men was widespread, its path was far from smooth, and during this period young men's allegiances to the Qua Iboe Mission appeared to be highly provisional.[245] Two issues concerned young men most. One was gin-trading, the profits from which were quicker than on any other commodity. The other issue that was being 'seriously discussed among a lot of young men' was 'wife palaver'. It was not polygamy that the young converts wanted so much as flexibility regarding labour and divorce: 'The young men declare they don't want a number of wives, just one at a time. They wish an arrangement made by which when a wife displeases her husband, or turns out badly, or troubles him with too many palavers, he may dismiss her, and put another into her place.'[246] Since these were essentially economic grievances, the two issues, gin and marriage, would flare up as the principal cause of 'backsliding' whenever economic fortunes declined.

Conversion interrupted the initiatory cycle by which men's societies reproduced themselves. By the early 1900s those who converted to Christianity and resisted initiation into *ékpó* were therefore also the subject of concerted and violent coercion: 'The heathen people made palaver, because Christian young men were growing up without joining Egbo, or rather without paying fees to be made members of that powerful society.'[247] In 1905 *ékpó* 'made a strong stand for the old customs, and have practically blotted out the work at two of the out-stations, where they killed several enquirers'.[248] By 1906 the Christian converts 'grew cold', and there was a clamour for polygamy and liberty to trade in gin.[249] During the season of *ékpó* performances in 1907, the mission reported that young Christians had 'lately shown a disposition to return to playing'.[250] The following year the secret societies had 'resorted to their old trick of putting ju-ju signs in front of the Christians' houses with the idea of bringing some calamity on the home'.[251]

Despite these various constraints on the mission's progress, the balance began to shift in its favour, especially as a result of its strategic use of judicial and diplomatic devices. The right to settle cases was a key index of power in Annang society and the fact that the mission house became a place for the settlement of disputes for Christians and non-Christians alike meant that justice and arbitration became an important arena in which European missionaries consolidated their position. Settling cases at the mission house also offered converts opportunities to retaliate and to exploit their rivals by fabricating claims against their persecutors. Bailie reported how he had discovered that a deputation who claimed the chief of a neighbouring village intended to kill churchgoers, school children and women who wore dresses was in fact an attempt to discredit the chief.[252] This incident also captures something of the mission's ambivalent attitude towards Ibibio chiefs. Missionaries were quick to make the chiefs responsible for whatever dispute or breakdown had happened, and so a confrontation between *ékpó* and converts over women wearing 'decent' clothes, would be put at the chiefs' door. Yet the mission was also dependent upon and courted the favour of chiefs, who were especially important in granting land rights to build new churches.

Throughout this period the southern Annang region to the west of the Qua Iboe river, the area that would later witness the man-leopard murders, earned a reputation for fierce resistance and lawlessness. Across the region the Government's grip was shaky and seasonal. During the rainy season, when government troops could not travel inland, communities took the opportunity to settle scores. Kirk records a 'little war' between Afa-Ofiong and Etinan in the autumn of 1904. Both were heavily armed with Snider rifles, with the Afa Ofiong having 'sold a number of boys and girls lately and bought war material with the proceeds'.[253] After the expedition to Abak in 1904 the district quietened down, but the country on the other side of the river remained 'unsettled, and men wanted by the Police for their misdeeds found refuge there. Court messengers sent by the District Officer were badly treated and law and order was impossible'.[254]

As a result of a series of inter-denominational delimitation conferences held from 1904 onwards the Annang and Ibibio areas of Calabar Province were apportioned to the Qua Iboe Mission, which therefore became the dominant mission in the region.[255] To the north in Ikot Ekpene Division the Primitive Methodists were given priority, to the east the Calabar and Cross River areas were occupied by the United Free Church of Scotland, and to the west the lower Niger river was covered by the Niger Delta Pastorate of the Church Missionary Society. The Catholic Church refused to participate and their attempts to gain a foothold in Annang and Ibibio territory exercised the Qua Iboe missionaries throughout this period. The first mission station in Abak Division was established at Ikot Idung near Abak in 1904, the same year that Samuel Bill declined an offer of an appointment as the Political Officer of 'Kwa Ibo District'.

The Qua Iboe Mission was able to secure support and enhance its authority in the Annang hinterland stations such as Ikot Idung by vouching for villages and saving them from attack as the expeditionary forces passed through. Evidence from fifteen years of patrols in Annang territory, from Casement's journeys to the founding of Abak station, indicates that the Annang proved a constant irritant to British military forces. While the Ikot Ekpene, Itu and Uyo stations were opened in 1903, it was not until 1909, when the Ikot Ekpene patrol marched south, that the district station was established at Abak. On their route, at Ikwek (north of Abak), the column was attacked by the Obongs, Midims, Ikot Imos and Afaha Obongs with cap guns and matchets.[256] This conflict led to widespread displacement, and many lineages in south-western Annang villages who call themselves *ǹtɔ Abak* (the children of Abak) trace their settlement to this incident. After making tortuous progress with the construction of the new station in Ikot Idung, Smith vouched for the village when troops approached to launch the government expedition against the troublesome Annang district in 1909. He guaranteed that carriers would not be molested after the regular force had passed, and that the village would sell provisions to the troops. Smith himself treated the wounded casualties of the punitive raid from the villages further north.[257] Spared the ravages of the punitive raid, the population of Ikot Idung and neighbouring Annang villages were not slow to recognise the Mission's growing influence.

RESISTANCE AND REVIVAL, 1910–1929

Whether by coincidence or by design the arrival of Europeans at the mouth of the Qua Iboe river was met with the same rites as were used annually to purge Ibibio villages of malevolent spirits and diseases. During the night, women swept the ground in front of their houses, roofs were beaten and torches carried around the village.[1] This chapter examines the ways in which Ibibio and Annang made sense of colonialism and Christianity. It traces their cultural engagements with European rule and religion during the period that led up to the most significant watershed of the colonial period, the Women's War of 1929. It concerns the ways in which uneven relations of power, between men and women, educated and illiterate, titled and non-titled, were negotiated within shifting terrains of social, religious and political contest.[2]

THE LANDSCAPE OF POWER

Territory on the south-western side of the Qua Iboe river joined the newly formed Abak District of Ikot Ekpene Division late in 1910 after being ceded from Aba and Opobo Districts.[3] Repeated disturbances in this part of the District resulted in further troop deployments, and additional police were stationed at Ikot Ekpene until 1912. During this period the process of dismantling the apparatus of the slave trade continued, and in 1910 the compounds of slave-dealing chiefs in south-western Annang were burned, including those of Akpan 'Uko' Udo Ndok, the village head of Ikot Akpa Nkuk, and Inokon Uyo Ubong of Ikot Udo Obobo. A dislike of answering summonses, a tendency to assault court messengers and police, and a habit of 'going for bush' continued, however, as did colonial suspicions of the subversive influence of trading middlemen. In 1911 it was reported of the south-western Annang that:

> The influence of several cunning and avaricious Opobos and Aros is great with the Chiefs. This influence, together with the peculiar semi-passive resistance of the natives renders the task of bringing them into line with the natives on [the north-east] side of the Kwa Iboe River a difficult matter.[4]

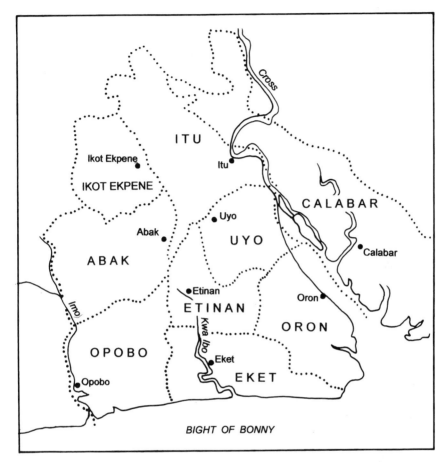

Figure 3.1 Map of Calabar Province

Administrative problems were compounded by the isolation of Abak, the District headquarters located across the river, though successive attempts from 1911 to 1926 to establish a more central site failed. With the outbreak of war in 1914 and the shortage of staff, Abak station was evacuated resulting in a 'serious retrogression. ... The safety of life and property within the area was reduced'.[5] Several cases of highway robbery were reported in the District during 1914, the year of the amalgamation of Northern and Southern Nigeria.[6]

The extension of British rule from the 1910s to the 1940s would later assume the appearance of 'a series of disconnected and reluctant concessions to circumstances which the Government could not ignore but was unable to meet in any other way'.[7] The introduction of courts and the appointment of chiefs as assessors and judges was the sequel to expeditions and the introduction of the Warrant Chief system is a well-known instance of the 're-invention of tradition' since it corresponded less to pre-colonial kinship institutions than to administrative demands for cost-effectiveness and for a buffer to deflect potential political resistance.[8] Before 1914, British political officers sat as judges in the Native Courts with a bench of local Warrant Chiefs who acted as assessors. In the southern Annang region the first courts were established at Utu Etim Ekpo and Azumini. Lord Lugard, reiterating the colonial fallacy of Aro domination over this region, reflected that the Warrant Chief system helped to re-establish the status of traditional authorities among the peoples of the south-east who, he believed, had been rendered 'powerless' by the disintegrating influence of the coastal middlemen and the Aro traders.[9]

Lugard's reforms, the Native Courts Ordinance of 1914 and the Native Authority Ordinance of 1916, were intended to reinforce and recreate an independent paramount chieftaincy by removing British political officers from the court and by introducing the position of the Native Court permanent president. Particular emphasis, therefore, was placed on identifying strong regional and clan chiefs. Indeed, it was not until these reforms that enquiries were held into pre-colonial governance, and attempts were made at founding colonial administration upon 'the less organised forms of government which existed before any European official intervened'.[10] In the Annang context this meant investigating the office of the àkùkù. Very few such chiefs had been appointed as Warrant Chiefs as 'an okuku was taken and hidden in the bush whenever the whiteman came, for it was feared he would catch and carry him off'.[11] Evidence of the àkùkù's power in Abak District was conflicting. 'Some accounts indicate that the least expression of his will, even a gesture, was most punctiliously obeyed: others that he was held as of no importance or could be unceremoniously disposed of by assassination.'[12] Although successors had not been installed in some communities, in many others ŋkùkù were still alive. Nevertheless, the District Officer responsible for implementing Lugard's reforms and for selecting permanent court presidents in Abak District did not pursue this line in his recruitment and concluded that:

> To speak of tribal or clan chiefs in regard to this District is … to employ a quite inapplicable category. No such Chiefs exist, and the problem … is to take the best possible steps towards producing such an institution artificially.[13]

Instead, initially five chiefs were recommended whom he considered superior to all others, including Ebong of Ibesit whom the Resident called 'an able man of no standing', and the charismatic Inokon Uyo Ubong of Ukanafun.[14]

It was on the basis of this reinvention of traditional office that Lugard's legislation, 'set up by a stroke of the pen in parts of the Southern Provinces composed of no more than placemen, persons with no tribal authority whatsoever ...'[15] By 1915 the list of Court Members in Abak and neighbouring Uyo Districts comprised many 'small boys' who were neither recognised chiefs of a town nor possessed any 'qualities which would justify their holding warrants of membership'.[16] The appointment of Native Court permanent presidents petered out, but the imperative of identifying traditional, hereditary chiefs which was initiated by this process, and revisited in Grier's recommendations of 1922, the Commission into the Aba Riots in 1929 and in Cameron's reforms of the 1930s, would dominate colonial discourse on chiefs and courts until the 1940s.[17]

The creation of an autonomous sphere of Annang chieftaincy was premised on the quest for vertical hierarchies of political power. Indirect rule therefore formalised informal and contested local hierarchies. In 1924 the Abak Native Court (including the Ikot Okoro sub-court) had fifty court members who had been appointed from 1915 onwards. Of these, none claimed a hereditary title: ten were classified as government nominees, thirty-nine were placed in a category of 'obscure native title' and one (from Oku) had been appointed on the basis of being chosen by his town. In Utu Etim Ekpo Native Court (including Ikot Odiong), which served the remainder of Abak District, there were forty-seven Warrant Chiefs, who included three hereditary chiefs (all appointed in 1924 including Udo Abassi from Ika), seven government appointees, thirty-six whose title could not be determined, and one who was selected by his town.[18]

The administrative and executive responsibilities of the Warrant Chiefs were quickly overshadowed by their judicial duties in the Native Courts. This was a result of the financial attractions of justice and the administration's conviction that the greatest need was to maintain order and therefore to settle inter-village disputes. Under the Native Courts Proclamation Amendment of 1901 the Warrant Chiefs restricted villagers to taking cases to the newly formed Native Courts. As a result the elders who arbitrated on the various Annang tribunals, notably the village meeting (*èsòp ìkpá ìsòŋ*) and the court of the clan leader (*èsòp àkúkú*), were stripped of their power. The newly appointed chiefs capitalised upon their exclusive rights, as the following observation on the status of chiefs in Calabar Province illustrates:

> They have made no effort to support Government measures, and adopt an attitude of indifference in all matters respecting the public in general, spending most of their time and money in litigation with a view to improve their private fortunes.[19]

In 1910, just a year after the first Native Courts were established in Abak District, several chiefs were found guilty of supplementing their official sitting fees by 'usurping the functions of the Court and trying cases themselves'.[20] These chiefs designated themselves 'Consul Men' and their informal courts represented a semblance of officialdom since they issued their own summons and had uniformed messengers.[21] Such illegal tribunals were popular because they were closer, cheaper, faster and more effective than the few, new and often distant Native Courts, where claimants became frustrated because fees were lost when attendance at court could not be guaranteed, and reviews were delayed when the District Officer could attend court only infrequently. Outside the courts, the new chiefs also capitalised on unexpected opportunities for physical coercion. In 1923, in an incident which confirms observations of the banality of violence associated with indirect rule, a minor 'epidemic' of slight wounds was reported to the District Officer.[22] On investigation he discovered that the chiefs of a number of villages had armed a sanitary patrol with small bows and ordered them to shoot anyone committing a nuisance.[23]

An expanding colonial bureaucracy also meant that where district officers were distant and aloof, clerks, letter-writers and interpreters became part of the local social landscape, and part of personal networks. An analysis of African scribes, clerks and interpreters exposes a sphere of 'working misunderstandings' which opened up between colonialism as practised and colonialism as envisaged by its architects. Court clerks had considerable scope for manoeuvre and their relationship with the chiefs sitting on the court benches created a network of power that linked local political authorities to the bureaucracy of the colonial state. After Lugard's reforms of 1914 the ascendancy of the court clerk was determined by the infrequent presence of political officers and the use of English in the forms and records of the court. The Warrant Chiefs depended on the court clerks' favour. They paid bribes for their seats on the bench, and addressed the clerks as 'master'. Clerks, then, controlled the gateways to colonial courts and bureaucracies and hence exercised great influence over these important sites of struggle for access to resources and the meanings of social relationships and authority. Throughout the 1910s and 1920s clerks in the south-eastern Nigerian provinces gained an odious reputation. Indirect rule provided an 'academy for improvisation' in which these 'auxiliary tricksters', the interpreters, messengers and clerks, could profit from their function as political and cultural intermediaries.[24]

The administration of Abak depended heavily on these intermediaries and hence on district interpreters, clerks and lawyers. The difficulties this generated were apparent in 1915 when relations between the Government and the chiefs ground to a halt. Between them the district interpreter and a local lawyer were thought to have circulated a rumour that the government was about to seize the palm fruit harvest and had played upon these fears to get the chiefs to pay for and sign a petition. The rumour enflamed local opinion to such an extent that European lives were thought to be in danger. Unknown to the signatories the petition was in fact a protest against Lugard's reforms which threatened to exclude the interpreter from court proceedings as British officers withdrew from day-to-day sittings. The chiefs were so angry at having been duped that they insisted that the interpreter was transferred, and the DO reported that the running of the district was 'hung up'.[25]

Popular reaction to the unfamiliar prominence accorded the chiefs during this period found its outlet in 'non-approved' institutions, including the secret societies, as their source of justice and fair play.[26] The imposition of the colonial judicial order was met with overt and covert responses from the elders of the secret societies. The potential revival of 'pre-government days' was a constant fear for the administration and so-called 'revivals' were especially prevalent during the First World War years:

> During the last few months, the secret societies have begun to wake up again. The reason for this is apparently the war at home. Some of the interior people say the day of the white man is over in this country; others, who do not go quite so far as this think that while our hands are full of graver business, we shall not trouble very much about them.[27]

Elsewhere, at Etaha Obong market, two miles from Uyo, *ékpó* meetings were held during which they resolved to restore their 'ancient authority'. Tired of the Native Court, *ékpó* had made arrangements to deal with anyone who sought to frustrate them and demanded 'to rule the whole country again under the old ekpo law'.[28]

Evidence of secret society activities illustrates that they were inspired by particular grievances with the Native Court system. Reports appeared in 1916, for instance, that *ékpê* societies throughout Ikot Ekpene Division, including the Annang villages of Abak District, had revived their former judicial functions. In January, representatives of the *ékpê* society had been called with *àyèì* to meet at Obo market.[29] There they agreed to revive the rule that intruders should be apprehended and killed by the society. The witness statement of Akpan Ekoreko living at Ikot Ama given during the ensuing investigation exposes the clandestine details of its activities:

> The first meeting of the Ekpe Society in connection with the new law was at Ikot Akpan Essiet in the compound of Chief Ebok Idiang (Ikot Ama Court). There an oath was sworn that no one should report what was arranged to the DO. It was then arranged that any[one] caught stealing should be killed and not taken to the DO. Another meeting was held at Ntaw Akpa Oko in the compound of Akpan Nwoko (Ikot Ama Court). Mbiam was again sworn and the same law proclaimed. An order was passed that every town should give their Court Member a goat and 100 manillas because it was their business to get the matter

settled if the DO came to hear of it. After that there was a big general meeting at Edet Akpan Efiong. At this meeting 1200 manillas was subscribed to act as a fund to bribe the police if any one should be killed, and if the family tried to complain to the DO they were to be flogged and turned back. Their townspeople would then deal with them. ... Since then several people have been killed under this law. About 9 days ago a man stole 1 manilla in Etim market and he was seized by the Ekpe people. I can't say if he has been killed, but the matter was not reported to any of the Courts. This law was made because the Native Court could not give them sufficient punishment. This law could never have been made without the Native Court Chiefs who were all present at the meetings.[30]

The Warrant Chiefs were treading a fine line. While the court chiefs in Ikot Ama conspired with the societies, elsewhere they found themselves in conflict with their masked members. In Ukanafun in 1917, *ékpó*, whose laws were in force during September and October, travelled five miles in full regalia to attack the president of the Native Court at Ikot Idiong. Ikot Idiong (Ikot Odiong) was the first Native Court to be established in Ukanafun in 1912 (see Figure 3.2). It was a travelling court whose messenger was based at Utu Etim Ekpo, and was opened because:

> people like their cases heard in their own country by their own chiefs. If they do not get more or less their own way in this matter they do not bring their cases to court. The advantage of having the cases heard in an authorised Court is that the grievance is made public and not heard on the doorstep of some chief's house and the result unknown.[31]

The chief of Ikot Idiong was accused by the *ékpó* society of deliberately requesting the court from the Government. After refusing to contribute to repair costs for the court building, *ékpó* members from the neighbouring village of Ikot Odobia raided the court session on 12 September, released prisoners and attacked the house of Chief Udodung, the court president.[32] Three days later *ékpó* from Ikot Odobia marched again and were joined by members of affiliated societies at Chief Udodung's house where they accused him of having brought 'a Government court into an Egbo country and thus breaking Egbo law'.[33]

The Native Courts were unpopular because of their procedures and their punishments. The courts lacked effective sanctions in calling witnesses, judges were frequently bribed and the review process collapsed under the weight of demand. Re-interpretations of customary law during the early colonial period outlawed 'repugnant' practices, so that recourse to oaths (*ṁbìàm*) and ordeals (*úkáŋ*) was made illegal and investigative procedures, oath-swearing on testimony in the Native Courts, became a parody of traditional practice. Native Court punishments, too, were insufficient to act as deterrents. Punishment for theft became a standing grievance, especially when the penalty was reduced from two years to six months' imprisonment in 1914. Imprisonment was roundly rejected since it carried less social stigma than being publicly shamed in a market. In 1923 chiefs in Abak Division called for the rations given to prisoners to be reduced since their sentences were deemed insufficiently harsh.[34]

Secret society tribunals, in contrast, offered familiar means of investigation, definitive resolution, and harsh punishments, and were popular as a result. In 1924 the *èkpó* society, which was mandated to protect farms from theft, met in Ikot Okoro, Abak District. At the meeting, *m̀bìàm* (of coconut

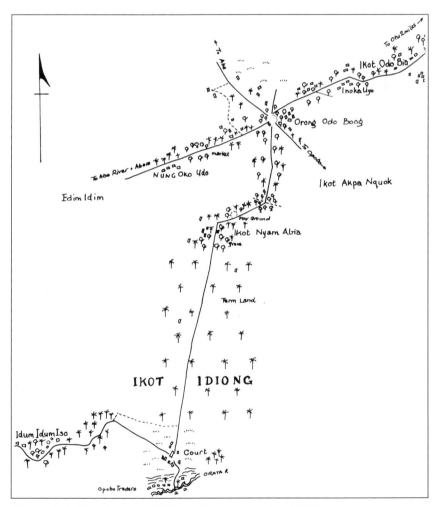

Figure 3.2 Sketch map of 'Okanafon Country', 1917[35]

milk) was distributed to the various villages represented, who were charged with pouring it on village paths and announcing the threat that anyone who sheltered a thief from *ékpó* was to be killed by the *mbìàm*. Thieves caught red-handed were first blinded by having the juice of peppers spat into their eyes, then beaten in the market and finally killed. When the practice was uncovered in October 1924 a village chief and two men holding warrants in the Ikot Okoro Native Court were publicly executed at Nsebe market.[36]

These failings of indirect rule in south-eastern Nigeria were often attributed by the British to the covert activities of the Aro. By 1922 officers recognised the way in which their concerns about the Aro had become all-embracing:

> The Aros are now accused of being responsible for any serious trouble which is anti-government, for a good deal of crime and are further alleged to have re-established the long juju in the Bende district. It is, however, not unnatural that they should use their widespread influence against the Government which has done everything possible to break them.[37]

The ongoing drive to find a political hierarchy across communities in the south-east, however, led the government to re-examine the wisdom of its initial hostility to the influential Aro.[38] Suppression of the Aro, it was now argued, meant the Government had lost the opportunity to harness Aro leadership across the region. The lieutenant-governor of the Nigerian Northern Provinces, Herbert Palmer, for instance, attributed ongoing unrest in south-eastern Nigeria to the failure to recognise the Aro as the ruling family of the Igbo and Ibibio. Palmer's analysis was based on the Hamitic hypothesis of cultural origins.[39] The issue was taken up in 1923 in Grier's major review of indirect rule in south-eastern Nigeria:

> In writing of the Ibos and Ibibios I have so far said nothing about the Aros. Though I agree with Mr Palmer that it is possible that in the early days we might have made use of the domination exercised by this people over a very large area, I am inclined to agree with those who believe that it is impossible to do so now. At the same time the fact must be faced that Aro influence is still a very important factor and will remain so for some time. I am doubtful whether efforts to suppress it have met with much success.[40]

Palmer's thesis was refuted by those who had worked closest with the communities over which the Aro were said to have ruled. M. D. W. Jeffreys, for instance, asserted that the Aro had never sought political control of the Ibibio-speaking areas in which they traded and they 'were never able to rule or dominate the Anangs. ... The Aros were influential traders, not rulers, nor framers of laws, not warriors, nor counsellors, not even members of a fighting race'.[41] Indeed, in commenting on the suggestion that the Aro might have been recruited to suppress the western Ibibio-speakers, Jeffreys observed that 'The influence of the Aro among the Anang depended upon fraud and black magic and it is clear that under such conditions it would not have been possible as suggested ... for us to use the Aros to dominate such people as the Anangs'.[42] Nevertheless, the belief that the suppression of the Aro had left south-eastern Nigeria leaderless persisted.[43] As a result, an anthropological enquiry was appointed to investigate the issue in 1927. It found no corroboration of the idea that the Aro were a regional political power, and concluded that despite their wealth the influence of the Aro did not extend beyond slave-dealing and the *ibini ukpabi* oracle.[44]

The relative absence of powerful rulers, the official relegation of those who may have existed and the growing dissatisfaction with Warrant Chiefs 'reinforced the practical need to tolerate secret societies'.[45] Throughout the inter-war years therefore the Government's policy towards the secret societies was one of 'tolerant forbearance' determined by an overriding priority to maintain cohesion and social integration. Colonial perspectives of the *ekpó* society placed it in an ambiguous space between being essential to the fabric of society and being an 'armed and lawless constabulary'. Discourse on the secret societies shifted as a result of successive acts of political subversion, however, to the point that in 1923 an influential commentator within the province wrote:

> The Ekbo society is not a law-giving or law-making society as has wrongly in the past been considered its functions. Rather it was and is a lawless band of brigands who backed their words with the edge of the matchet. ... as the ghostly Ekbo is malevolent so also is his corporeal representative who destroys property, robs, and plunders and matchets all strangers, non-members and women.[46]

Despite mounting petitions from the missions to outlaw the secret societies, administrators continued to be concerned about launching an assault on the traditional social order and what was conceived as 'communal life'. Only where the balance of power had shifted towards the Christian youth was it considered prudent for the administration to intervene and act against the secret societies. Hence, while the prohibition of *ekpó* was discussed in Uyo District in 1924, it was rejected in the Annang Districts of Abak and Ikot Ekpene for fear of causing a breakdown in the social order.[47] Observations made by the Resident of Calabar Province, for instance, demonstrate a remarkable ambivalence towards a process colonialism itself had initiated:

> The future ... lies with Christianity, and we can afford to let native customs repugnant to our own ideas die a natural death. Those moribund customs, alas, form the only cement which binds together the

communities of this Province at the present day. Christianity means uncontrolled individualism, and chaos in communal life in these parts ...[48]

Confrontations between the secret societies and church congregations involved physical clashes, often when Sunday worship and *ékpó* performances coincided. Attempts to try the cases that arose from these fights were a key indication of the balance of power. During the First World War such litigation proved unrealistic: 'in 1917 it would not have been possible to allow any of these Christian-Ekpo cases to be heard in Native Courts, nearly all the Chiefs are Ekpo Members and the result would have been a foregone conclusion'.[49] In those areas where the court benches were still packed with *ékpó* members, such as Itu, the District Officer continued to hear cases. By 1926, however, courts across the Province were reported to 'hold the scales more evenly between the parties and in many cases have actually punished the Ekpo players when they have proved the aggressors'.[50] Elsewhere, this conflict involved more subtle attempts at undermining the relationship between knowledge and power upon which the cult groups were founded. Chiefs in Arochukwu brought prosecutions against Christians in 1915, for example, for 'revealing the secrets' of *ékpó*, a charge that was sufficiently new in 1915 to require a ruling from senior officers.[51]

By far the most common form of conflict between the churches and *ékpó* concerned disputes over the non-payment of secret society initiation fees by young Christian converts. There was a significant economic dimension to elders' resentment of the youth because they were unable to recoup secret society initiation fees, and because, as Perham put it, 'Christianity has knocked the bottom out of their investments'.[52] In *ékpó* it was customary to cajole and humiliate a non-initiate, but beyond this the political economy of the secret societies depended on an annual cycle of new initiates. While elders consistently opposed any interference with their income from new members' initiation fees, secret society laws, fines and fees were progressively prohibited:

> The Chiefs themselves, petty and mean, have lost a great deal of their power over their towns, owing to the abolition of trial by ordeal and the heavy penalties formerly meted out to offenders by their society laws, of which they were heads. It is customary for the head Chief of a town to hold the headship of the Native Societies Idion, Ekpo, Ekpe, Atat, Ekong and others, their powers were great and fees for consultation, parts of sacrifices, feasts, drinks, and fines constituted, with the Chief's share of the communal palm trees, his entire income. These societies are still in existence but the revenue therefrom ... is practically nil, owing to the inability of the Chiefs to inflict punishment as of old ...[53]

Colonialism and Christianity had created a rift between youth and elders and between their varied bases of political authority. In its Warrant Chief appointments, its efforts to create dependence on its own systems and stipends, and by outlawing 'repugnant' sanctions, colonialism therefore undermined the material base of the very class on which it attempted to base its rule.[54]

Those who converted to Christianity and therefore resisted initiation into the *èkpó* were the subject of considerable and violent coercion: 'The heathen people made palaver, because Christian young men were growing up without joining Egbo, or rather without paying fees to be made members of that powerful society'.[55] The missions sought vigorously to defend their flocks both because they opposed the secret societies as bastions of idol worship, and for more practical, economic reasons. Both the *èkpó* elders and the mission stations needed money. Written contracts between chiefs and young men, between *èkpó* and Christians, and between the church and residents of their compounds, became a common feature of dispute settlement. In April 1915, for instance, Westgarth drew up an agreement between the chiefs and schoolboys of Ediano. The mission boys agreed not to 'spoil' *èkpó*, while chiefs agreed not to attack the school.[56]

The experiences at the Enen out-station of the Qua Iboe Mission, reported by Gamble in 1918, were representative of this ongoing struggle. At Midim the head of *èkpó* and the village chief claimed that *èkpó* would shoot the schoolboys if they refused to join the society. During Gamble's attempts to negotiate, the *èkpó* leaders raised the stakes; they threatened to knock down the school, proposed a law that a boy should pay a fine of a cow and £5 if he refused to join *èkpó*, and intimidated Gamble himself:

> At this stage there was much shouting outside, and about 40 masked men with bows and arrows surrounded the school. I was not at all sure that I wanted to die at that moment, and I inwardly prayed for grace to be kept calm. I first suggested that we should stop talking till the row outside would cease. One of the chiefs went out, and the armed men withdrew to a little awning. Just then one Egbo man inside gave an awful shout, and rushed towards the door. The boys caught him and I cautioned him that he must not move until our palaver was finished. They all charged me with allowing the scholars to break the Egbo regulations, threatening to kill the boys who would not make drums for them. Finally I had to draw a circle, and step inside it, saying that I stood there protected by British law. I have since heard that two boys have been shot.[57]

The main concerns for the Qua Iboe Mission during the 1910s and 1920s involved defending schoolboys from these unwanted attentions of the *èkpó* society; negotiating with chiefs to ward off the Roman Catholic Church as it tried to expand into western Calabar Province; keeping its European missionaries free of the scourge of blackwater fever, and placating the demand for schools and schoolteachers. For the bands of young men who requested schools or teachers church levies were an incentive to organise. Many such bands had established prayer groups in their own rooms or had built their own schools.[58] The standard means by which groups within a village raised money was by securing an area of land either to cultivate crops or to harvest and sell palm fruit, but this fund-raising frequently led to conflict.[59] Particular problems arose when mission boys provocatively chose to cultivate sacred forest land. Mission boys had planted yams on a burial ground in Ududu Ikpe in 1913, for instance, in order to pay money into church collections. During the next seven months eleven people died in the village and *idiɔŋ* claimed the deaths were due to the cultivation of the land. The authorities were amazed that the boys had not been physically assaulted by the village and assumed that the popular feeling there, as elsewhere across the southern provinces, was that the teachers and mission boys were supported by or were agents of the Government.[60]

For young men mission Christianity became more appealing under colonialism. Economic development in general, and trade, urbanisation and schooling in particular, introduced new categories of social status – the literate teacher and clerk – and increased their physical and political mobility. The Qua Iboe church and school in Ikot Akpa Nkuk, a central village in the Ukanafun clan, for instance, was introduced by a group of friends, young men who were just becoming established in the early 1920s. This group included Frank Udosoro, a tailor who had trained in Bonny, Alexander Akpan, a farmer and palm oil trader, Joseph Udo Afa, a storekeeper, Matthew Akpan Umo Obono, another Bonny tailor, and Sampson Ukpono Eyen, who was also a tailor. It is no coincidence that of the five 'pioneer' members of Qua Iboe only one was a farmer and one a storekeeper. The others had trades that were typical of the economic diversification of young men during this period, and those who had trained in Bonny reflected the geographical mobility with which it was associated:

> Hitherto the great desire of all young men in Calabar District has been to become a trader, but that desire is abating now and giving place to a sense of the advantages to be derived from Government service. The great majority of the senior boys at the Hope Waddell Institute and at Duke Town School either sit for the Clerical entrance examination or are employed by the UFC Mission as pupil teachers.[61]

Migration promoted Christianity within south-eastern Nigeria as a whole, but in its rural isolation this process led the Qua Iboe mission to lose many of its brightest recruits. Calabar and Opobo in particular were popular destinations for young men in search of work that they could not get in the villages along the Qua Iboe river. 'This migration is particularly hurtful to the Schools', Bailie noted, 'and generally hinders our whole work because the young people are far more in sympathy than the older people'.[62] Urban migration also gave rise to clear modes of differentiation among young men:

> The one with outstretched hands pleads for the Gospel. The other decked in European clothes returns to his native village, bringing vices of the most degrading sort, learned in some Coast town. He scoffs at those who attend the little mud-and-wattle church. His influence affects the heathen in the town and occasionally its poison kills some of the brightest and most promising boys in our churches. Opposition in this new form is infinitely more subtle and harmful than the antagonism of the old heathen customs.[63]

The administration's increased dependence on supposedly 'traditional' local chiefs meant that despite their literate status and their European leanings, the administration saw the 'new elements' as a threat to the newly established order: 'Mission societies – with exceptions – in the interior have … been a great factor in the decline of the Chief's authority. Most of the Missions have sprung into fierce activity and rivalry against each other, scrambling for power, in most cases creating an entirely new element, those of a "little dangerous knowledge" type, both in education and religion'.[64] The administration's views of the 'indolent' chiefs and ambitious 'new element' meant that by 1924 future administrative options appeared unclear and potentially ill-fated:

> We have undoubtedly taken away the entire revenue from the real Chiefs, revenue which was derived from the sale of slaves and the hearing of cases and we have given them no equivalent in return with the natural result that they would like to see a revival of pre-government days. The young man who has mechanically absorbed a vast amount of book-knowledge does not remember pre-government days and will soon consider he could govern the Country without us. The revival of the former, and the advent of the latter at present, would be equally disastrous for the country.[65]

Despite the complex distinctions and differentiations wrought by colonial rule during the 1910s and 1920s between different forms of chieftaincy, relations between chiefs and secret societies, and distinctions among the young congregations, the political landscape was very quickly polarised and a political opposition emerged along generational lines, the elder backed by colonial policy, the younger by the missions. As colonialism undermined the economic base and coercive power of Annang chieftaincy, young men gained more political room for manoeuvre, which enabled them and their mission supporters to assert themselves.

Writing towards the end of her life from her remote station at Use Ikot Oku in 1913, Mary Slessor observed this trend and petitioned on behalf of her young 'bairns'. Younger people who had experienced social promotion through trade, government service or attendance at mission schools and hospitals 'were at their wits' end', she wrote, as to how they could remain obedient and loyal citizens when they were at the mercy of 'unenlightened' court members and rapacious court clerks. The cleavage between the old and the new, Slessor observed, grew wider and more bitter every week and was most pronounced in contests over particular questions: 'dowry in all its forms, divorce ... the liberty of the citizen to choose, or refuse, to join native Idems ... To be forced to eat corn simply because the feast of new yams has not been held. To let twin mothers stay in the town – to redeem their right to live with other people'.[66]

Very few options were considered by the provincial authorities to bridge the emerging divide between the 'new elements' and the chiefs. One proposal in 1915 was to increase the standard of local administration across the southern provinces by educating chiefs' sons so that in time a ruling caste might be produced. Only by educating heirs to the chiefs to a higher standard of 'integrity and justice' would it be possible to integrate the 'educated' young men into indirect rule.[67] They would become boarders at certain selected schools, it was thought, and would be taught not only 'literary attainments but also and primarily the meaning of discipline, good behaviour and a high moral tone'.[68] In Calabar Province this would have meant sending chiefs' sons to the Hope Waddell Institute in Calabar.[69] Yet chiefs were not only indifferent to this plan but preferred on the whole to avoid education; they were too poor to pay school fees and there was little guarantee that their sons would succeed them given the various and often-changing mechanisms of chieftaincy selection. For instance, the Warrant Chief in Ikot Akpa Nkuk, Iwo Akpan Umana, backed by the village council, ordered that firstborn sons would not be allowed to attend church or school. Fathers who allowed this rule to be infringed were suspended from their positions on the council. This restriction was lifted only when the benefits of having a letter-writing 'son of the soil' become apparent.

The distinction between chiefs and the 'new elements' became translated into a discourse of broad antagonism between elders and progressively better organised youth. The dynamic began in the mission schools with the formation of parties of Christian young men observed across the province in the early 1920s. Here a marked tendency for mission trained youths to form 'societies' was noted, and in some cases they were thought to 'practically rule the community'.[70] A similar process was seen in Abak District in 1925 in the context of the rapidly burgeoning schools, and in the formative influence of school teachers:

The number of mission schools continues to increase steadily and although there is room for doubt as to the excellence of the product of these schools yet a town without the patronage of some mission or other is now hard to meet. The teacher in charge generally has little learning and no education but sooner or later he forms the head of a party in the town who irritate the chiefs and older people with their contempt of ancient customs and institutions.[71]

The 1920s therefore marked a key moment of intersecting dynamics. The progressive criminalisation of the secret societies during these years, under considerable pressure from the mission societies, was mirrored by the dramatic rise of these young men's associations linked to churches, schools and new vocations in villages and towns across the region. Yet, despite the divergent trajectories, this was also a crucial moment of overlap and continuity as these new social forms began to contest and occupy the familiar political space of the secret societies. And conversely, these were moments in which secret societies tried to define themselves within the idiom of the new mutual aid societies.[72] In part the new organisations were an adaptation of the rural lineage structure to colonialism and urbanisation in which lineage members 'translate their experience of it, and their continuing rights and obligations in it, into a new organisation'.[73] More significantly, however, the new 'improvement unions' drew on the idiom of the secret society, not the lineage, in their inception. Like the secret societies, these new unions transcended lineages, and direct parallels can be drawn between unions and societies in common arenas such as burial and performance, in idioms of membership and secrecy, and in the prosecution and punishment of crime.

Throughout the 1920s and 1930s, improvement unions tried to enforce mandatory membership, contributions and jurisdiction. The 'rules' of newly founded unions were frequently submitted to the colonial authorities for approval, and in all cases one of the regulations was the prohibition of litigation without the union's consent. The Annang term given to these earliest unions was *èsòp*, which in general usage means both meeting and, more frequently, court. The increasing political and economic weight of the unions led to fears among the colonial staff that failure to regulate unions would lead them to divert their activities into undesirable channels. The principal dangers were seen to be that unions would be used by village chiefs to enforce their decisions, that sanctions against members might lead to illegal seizure of property, and that the unions might become courts for judging cases beyond civil arbitration. The parallel with the functions of the pre-colonial secret societies was striking. It was the secret societies, and not the lineages, in fact, that acted as the chieftaincy's executive, seized the property of debtors and judged cases among their members. Indeed, this parallel with the secret societies was not lost on the authorities, who also

feared that the unions would assume another of the societies' characteristics and enforce compulsory membership. 'There is a clear danger', the
Resident at Calabar observed, 'that unions will attempt to use compulsion
to swell their numbers in the same manner that indigenous societies such
as Ekpo are not above compulsion'.[74]

Aspects of this process were most visible in the expanding urban centres
where associations emerged among new arrivals to the towns which provided
welfare services and exercised social control over their members. In this
urban context these hometown associations upheld rural moral codes
by screening entrants, repatriating recalcitrant members and in settling
disputes. The Home Branch of the Onitsha Improvement Union in 1935,
for example, screened their members to exclude the 'uneducated, unemployed, and parasitical "natives" or "boys"'.[75] An account of the western
Igbo in Ibadan is also illustrative in this respect. Among the Igbo unions
rules were drawn up ensuring that disputes were heard by a union prior to
judgment in a court of law. These associations would adjudicate in cases of
'fighting, disrespect and insult shown to an elder by a younger, infringement
of marital rights, rivalry in a place of employment, family disputes, suspected
spell-casting, poisoning or witchcraft'.[76]

Comparatively, in assessing the origins of youth associations, the parallel
between the Annang and Banyang of the upper Cross River region is
striking. By the 1930s 'modern' associations, Bands and Clan Unions,
began to emerge in Banyang communities whose form was adapted from
'traditional' patterns typified by *ngbe* (leopard society, known as the *ékpê*
society in Annang). Both the new young men's clubs and the former societies were characterised by elaborate constitutions, a series of offices, fees
for membership and an intricate set of rules punishable by fine.[77] Levels of
secrecy within meetings, the emphasis on internal solidarity and members'
use of the term *eju etok* for the executive committee, meaning 'the secret
community', further highlighted a process of continuity with the societies.
The transformation from secret societies to improvement unions in the
Banyang case, however, was based on continuities which were not merely
of appearance and form. The overriding link was in their common performative roles of village governance. Banyang associations sought the development of their village groups by regulating market prices and awarding
school scholarships, but acquired their 'teeth' and revealed their similarity
to *ngbe* in hearing cases and enforcing community laws.[78]

The formation of Annang and Ibibio 'improvement' unions or 'hometown
associations' took place against this context and within a framework of
increased mobility and migration. Urban interaction and the formation
of 'ethnic associations' also served to crystallise Annang and Ibibio identities. By the mid-1920s, successive Ibibio students had graduated from the
Hope Waddell Institute. The Ibibio elite resident at Calabar included David

Ekot, a court clerk of Calabar Native Court, Paul Bassey Okon, a teacher at Duke Town School, Albert Offiong of the Medical Department, and Nyong Essien. In October 1924, Nyong Essien, an interpreter in the Supreme Court, invited mainland Ibibio to his house in Calabar and formed the Ibibio Association and Community League (commonly known as the Ibibio Union).[79] With branches established across the 'mainland' territory of the province, an overarching body, the Ibibio Welfare Union, was formed at a meeting of thirty-seven school teachers and civil servants on 28 April 1928 at the Qua Iboe Mission House in Uyo, and became the foremost political vehicle of Ibibio and Annang elites during the colonial period.

THE SPIRIT MOVEMENT

Young men flooded to the mission stations during the 1910s and 1920s.[80] While this coincided with the clamour for churches and schools, it is evident that non-instrumental imperatives to conversion were of great significance. As a search for power and protection, the imperatives of health and healing threw the lines of the religious encounter into stark relief. The experiences of Robert Atai, the Qua Iboe evangelist at Ibesit, point to a broad dynamic of religious change during the inter-war period which focused on the tensions over the causes of illness:

> My father died when I was a few months old, when my mother and I came under the care of uncles. These uncles worshipped the gods of their fathers. One was called 'Afang Ukpon'. I was brought up to know and worship this god. My eldest uncle was the priest who ministered to this god. He placed a clay dish at the root of a big tree near our compound. This he filled with water and told us that our souls were in the water, under the shelter of the tree. If a boy or girl became sick then this priest said that the water had dried in the plate. This made the children's souls feel hot. Then he would offer a fowl and put more water in the plate, believing this will cause the fever to leave the children. Once a year we went in a company to this god. The priest damped our bodies with water from the plate and blessed us in the form of a kind of prayer, saying the god would keep our bodies cool. He also put round our necks leaves of the palm tree which had been dipped in the plate. These palm leaves were a sign of our peace and freedom from sickness.
>
> When I was seven years old I began to feel discouraged of going to this god any more. When the feast in its honour was held in my uncle's yard I refused to attend. This made the uncle, who had joined the Church, love me more. He took an interest in me and led me to Christ. He also sent me to live with the native pastor in our town to learn from him more about God. ... Many years passed and some of my uncles had died. Lightning twice struck the tree that sheltered

the plate. This incident made my surviving uncles and my mother to shake and fear that we were all going to die. They trusted the tree to protect us and it failed. They thought the thunder had destroyed our souls, but this made them think, and God opened the hearts of my mother and my uncles to see and know that all souls are in God's care. At Christmas 1918 after the epidemic of influenza, my mother saw that God is above all evil powers and is able to save from death. Thus she came to the Church, and five years afterwards she confessed to the world the reception of her Saviour. ... The old Ju-Ju tree is dead and the land about it is farmed, but we are praising the Saviour. The plate is rotted away and the water dried up, but we are alive and believing that God alone can save both body and soul.[81]

Robert Atai's account reminds us of the very personal motives – of mistrust and discouragement, of being accepted and being loved – that conversion involved. His family's shared trauma in the face of natural calamities contributed to a religious uncertainty in which the power of the Christian churches, like all forms of power in Annang society, was judged on its worldly effects and in terms of its performance against competitors – in this case the power of the *ábáŋ úkpɔ̀ŋ*(soul) shrine. The influenza epidemic of 1918–19 to which Atai refers caused an estimated 4,000 deaths in Opobo District, and a further 12,996 in Uyo and Abak.[82] His mother's conversion was one of a range of religious reactions among survivors of the epidemic. The District Officer at Eket reported that it was popularly believed the influenza deaths were caused by the poison of *ifót* witchcraft and that *esere* bean ordeals had accounted for 110 suspected witches.[83] Across the region the influenza epidemic was also thought to have been caused by poisonous gas released by German troops during the First World War. In Ukanafun, bonfires of scented leaves were lit around family compounds to dispel the fumes. *Ídìɔ̀ŋ* diviners broadcast that the influenza epidemic was the result of the *idìɔ̀ŋ* spirit's anger at the presence of the Qua Iboe Mission. Several church buildings were attacked and razed to the ground during 1918, though the effects on the church's standing did not last. There was a near-total solar eclipse on 29 May 1919. Knowing the importance given to the public testing of religious power the missionaries let it be known that the 'heathen' should be 'dismayed by the signs of the heaven'. The following Sunday the church buildings were crowded.[84]

Economically, the impact of the influenza epidemic on food and labour shortages was devastating and led to the introduction of a new food crop, cassava.[85] Cassava required less labour than the cultivation of yams and was left largely to women to grow.[86] While new roads and government labour increased mobility, the Opobo palm oil traders, the main cultural and economic mediators between the coast and the hinterland, were responsible for the introduction of cassava into the Annang and Ibibio region.

Waterside trading beaches, as we have seen, were also important centres of religious change, and between 1916 and 1918 the traders were instrumental in the spread of the Garrick Braide movement and the Christ Army Church. Prefiguring the expansion of the Niger Delta Pastorate, the movement, which was based on confession and faith healing, spread from Bakana in the Delta through Ikwerre, Etche and across the Ngwa territory of Igboland.[87]

The Garrick Braide movement passed into Ogoni and southern Ibibio-speaking communities in 1919 when its control passed to James G. Campbell, the founder of the West African Episcopal Church. By the early 1920s, therefore, the local religious landscape was shifting, and there was considerable inter-denominational jockeying within Annang and Ibibio villages. The formal agreements signed by the missions in south-eastern Nigeria had enabled churches to claim regional congregational monopolies in only the most superficial sense.[88] In the first major wave of school and church construction during the 1920s the Qua Iboe Mission dominated the southern Annang region when there was usually only one recognised church in a village. Village congregations voted *en masse* between the denominations because churches were built with money raised by the community as a whole through palm fruit sales, and because after 1920 government policy dictated that a mission wishing to open a station had to obtain consent from the local chiefs. When villages switched allegiances they often became mired in protracted legal disputes over the use of church buildings and property. From within and without, however, the meaning of mission conversion was challenged. In part this was a result of friction between Protestant missions and the Roman Catholics who had not signed up to the zonal delimitation conferences. In part also the fluidity of Christian affiliations was driven from within village congregations themselves.

Traders from southern Annang villages who transported oil and kernels by canoe to Opobo encountered the new denominations which had originated in the waterside churches. Having cured an illness of an Igbo or Annang trader the preachers would be invited to open a prayer house in their home village. The arrival of 'spiritual' churches, including the Sabbath and Christ Army Churches, in the southern Annang area was most often linked to healing. The Christ Army Church was invited into Ukanafun, for instance, to treat the 'demonic attacks' suffered by a bicycle repairer, nick-named 'Engineer', who built his workshop by the main Aba-Opobo road on the site of an ancestral remembrance shrine (*ńdùòngò*).[89] The Christ Army, invited from Opobo, settled in the village and opened a prayer house after the healing. A church's practical solution to this form of life crisis was crucial to the founding and growth of Aladura Christianity across southern Nigeria.[90] In this sphere, the spiritual churches articulated familiar modes of healing within a Christian idiom. Very often those drawn to lead the new churches were already religious specialists and borrowed from their own ritual repertoire. In Ikot Afanga, for instance, the African Church was founded by Akpan Etuk Ubong Etotok, an *ábìà ídìɔ̀ŋ* from Nun Ikot Obiodo who burned his *ídìɔ̀ŋ* shrine before assuming his new role. Healing within these churches therefore reflected practices that were common in Annang society, especially forms of healing that were based on the death/rebirth ritual found in *ídìɔ̀ŋ* initiation and in the release of victims whose souls had been 'trapped'. In the Sabbath Church, for example, the ceremony of *òkpùngó úkpɔ̀ŋ* began with the drawing of a grave-shaped outline in talcum powder on the ground of the healing grove. White candles burnt around the outline, with a red candle placed at the head. The victim, praying continuously, lay in the 'grave' and was covered by a white 'burial' cloth. With the intercession of a prophetess in possession the victim jumped out of the grave and was 'reborn'.

Further diversification developed when the Ethiopian Church Movement entered south-eastern Nigeria through Calabar during the First World War.[91] The Ethiopian Church, which had originated in South Africa, was active at Mbiuto (Okat) in 1917. Its political agenda – to exclude European teaching and control – was well known, but it was the church's acceptance of polygamy that made it popular across the province.[92] By 1919 the Ethiopian Movement was regarded as a significant obstacle to the Qua Iboe Mission, which described it as a 'kind of half-way house between heathenism and Christianity' in which many 'evil customs' were countenanced.[93] During 1925 sections within villages began to leave the established mission churches in favour of the 'Ethiopian Movement' usually for the reason that 'They say the Qua Iboe is too strict because we cannot allow polygamists to sit at the Lord's Table'.[94] In Ikot Abia Idem, for instance, the Primitive Methodist Church was asked to leave the village so that younger members might form an 'African' church. Those who seceded to the new church promised the chiefs that they would return to all the old customs and plays.[95] The African Church particularly appealed to chiefs, in fact, since its relaxed rules on polygamy enabled them to retain control over large, extended families. For the church itself, as with all denominations, the conversion of chiefs was especially valuable. The president of the Native Court at Awa who had joined the Ethiopian Church, for instance, used his position to remove Qua Iboe teachers in 1917.[96]

These new churches diversified the religious landscape. Crucially, they also infused Christian beliefs more thoroughly with Annang and Ibibio religious practice than the Qua Iboe Mission. Nevertheless, the Belfast mission was tied, through Samuel Bill's own spiritual awakening, to evangelical revival, and it was from inside, not outside the church, that the most dramatic moments of religious confrontation during the 1920s originated. The routine examinations of the enquirers' classes, the regular reports of 'backsliders' and the discipline demanded by the Mission, most notably in relation to polygamy and most evident in contrast to churches started by Qua Iboe dissidents, meant that while the number of members increased year on year, the mission felt it had not yet captured the popular imagination.

Throughout its history, as a result, the Qua Iboe Mission yearned for spiritual quickening. Returning from furlough in 1901, during which the Ibeno population had been ravaged by smallpox, Samuel Bill found the church in a poor condition. Though reticent to record his thoughts on paper, Bill was worried about the mission's methods:

> I don't feel at all happy about the work out here. Things are not in a good state. There is a general feeling of deadness and a danger of formalism. ... I don't know when there will be another baptismal service – at least not a big one. ... We are commencing to have a Saturday night weekly prayer meeting – just specially to pray for a revival of our own spirits and a blessing on the word on the following Sabbath.[97]

These meetings soon petered out, but the calls for revival persisted. In lamenting the fate of the 'backsliders', David Ekong recognised the need for a popular campaign when he wrote in 1912:

> It is a great thing to get people saved, but I think it is quite as great a thing to hold them when they are saved. And what we need now in Qua Iboe is a revival that will not only bring more people into the Church but will hold them when once they are in.[98]

A decade later news reached the Qua Iboe river of a spiritual movement in Ulster and the mission implored their friends at home to 'pray that this revival may reach Qua Iboe. The Native Churches are in great need of quickening'.[99] By the mid-1920s, faced with resentment over their strict disciplinary codes 'all was not well with the missions'. [100] The Qua Iboe Mission felt it had reached a critical stage 'when a fresh breath of the Holy Spirit is essential to its progress and development ... the Native Church may be cleansed and blessed'.[101] The church advertised its anticipation of a revival in 1924: 'Revival is on the way. If we are faithful it will come, so let us keep praying'.[102]

In July and August 1927 the much anticipated revival appeared to arrive as a wave of religious fervour swept across the Ibibio districts. The Spirit Movement, as it came to be known, began at Westgarth's station in Itu, north of Uyo.[103] At its inception it comprised many elements: the conversion of chiefs and *idiɔŋ*, public confessions, nightly prayers, 'burning of idols' and spirit possession. It was this aspect, spirit possession, that gave the movement's followers their other name, the 'shakers' (*mbɔ̀n síbírìt ǹkék ídém* – 'people who shake with the spirit'). From its inception in Itu, the movement had spread right across Uyo and Ikot Ekpene districts by December 1927 and into Annang villages in Abak and Opobo in January 1928.

Westgarth wrote that the Spirit Movement came 'as a rushing mighty wind and in tongues of flame'.[104] The pressure to enliven the mission was great, as was competition with the Roman Catholics in Itu District. Westgarth would later acknowledge the difficulties he faced in choosing whether to sanction or condemn the Spirit Movement. He was anxious to distance himself from the events of 1927, to stress the spontaneity of the movement, and of course, to claim that its origin was divine. The preface to his account of the movement claims that he 'held no connection whatever with any "Movement" definitely associated with such matters. The whole affair was spontaneous among the natives'.[105] The extent to which he was linked with the Spirit Movement (or at least its origins) bears investigation, however, as most other accounts implicate Westgarth directly and accuse him of indulging visions, dreams and prophecies from among his congregations that prompted the movement. Colonial reports claimed that the revivalist movement was initiated by Mr Westgarth and fostered by pamphlets and occultist literature. They suggested that 'at the beginning of the Spirit Movement a European Missionary [Westgarth] was so far misled by the pious protestations of the Movement as to write a pamphlet in Efik, comparing it to Pentecost. This was followed by the violent outbreak which resulted in many murders and seven hangings'.[106]

Mission Christianity had little tolerance of seers and faith healers, and the place of visions, dreams and prophesy in the Qua Iboe's teaching during its early years is obscured by the fact that Westgarth alone commits these aspects to his journals which he did with ironic humour but without condemning those involved. It is clear from Westgarth's diary entries that prophecies and stories of dreams and visions were circulating in the villages north of Uyo during the First World War, and that he preached on dreams in August 1914. That year he began to record the experiences of the preacher, Etim Akpan Udo.[107] Etim's dreams and premonitions, which began in June 1914, consumed his rambling sermons, and he was despondent when his prophecies did not come to pass. Etim had prophesied the end of the world on 1 January 1915, and responded to his subsequent disappointment by announcing that he had been commanded to lay down, and not wash himself for a month.

It was among the young evangelists and teachers at Itu, and possibly Etim himself, that the Spirit Movement first began. In September 1927 Westgarth took one of the evangelists, Benjamin, aside to discus the origins of the religious fervour. Benjamin said much of it seemed to follow the death of his mother, whom he believed had been poisoned. He wanted revenge, but began to see the error of his thinking:

Whilst still sorrowing for his mother he gave himself to prayer, and reading the Bible. This was followed by a new experience of spiritual things. He said he often spent whole nights in prayer and reading, and writing out parts of the Bible. ...[108]

Benjamin's visitation, which Westgarth recalled had softened the evangelist's heart through the presence of the Holy Spirit, was followed by another, this time to both the evangelist and a teacher. The teacher was an impressionable young man, a 'psychic', and 'had it not been for the gospel he would in all probability have become a heathen practitioner of one of the old native cults'.[109] Afterwards the teacher appeared dishevelled at the weekly scripture lesson, and called everyone to church in order to cite to them the prophecy of Joel, 'In the last days I will pour out my spirit on all flesh. And your sons and daughters shall prophesy'. Some of the teachers insisted that Westgarth suspend the class, but he did not. The teacher returned from the class to his church six miles away, where he 'preached in the unction and power of the Spirit' and the revival began to spread.

At first an *idìɔŋ* man dreamed of seeing a figure through a bright light who placed blood on his right hand and on his chest. His wife was also affected, and burned the *idìɔŋ* house and all of their household shrines. These initial experiences, the seeing of bright, pale-yellow light, and the placing of hands upon a person's chest, became a template for the transmission of the movement. It was common for one of the spirit people to approach those who had not confessed and to pat them on the chest; 'sometimes it was much rougher than patting, and amounted to a rapid pounding as quick as the beats on a side-drum'.[110] Touching the chest in this manner was an echo of the sensations (*ńtúúk*) felt by an *idìɔŋ* in the chest during divination. In fact, a range of elements that became characteristic of the movement shared features with practices of Annang divination, initiation and burial ritual. For many of the spirit people, including the cook at the Itu Station, the spirit possession they experienced was manifest in raising their right arm skywards. This gesture, a connection between soil and sky, and between the god of the soil (*àbàsì ikpá isòŋ*) and the sky god (*àbàsì ényòŋ*), was integral to Ibibio and Annang burial practice. Prophesy also took familiar forms. One village reported that Spirit Movement adherents pointed to passers-by and said, 'You will die tomorrow'.[111] In the village of Ikot Afanga, people said that it was the spirit of *ibɔk* (medicine) that 'worried' the young iconoclasts and led them to see false visions and prophesies. Three 'prophesy people' arrested in Ikot Afanga at the behest of Graddon of the Qua Iboe Mission were children of *idìɔŋ* diviners. In defence of their monopoly on these forms of knowledge, and in a significant precedent of *idìɔŋ*–church conflict, elder *idìɔŋ* men claimed that the 'shakers' were being 'pursued' by the *idìɔŋ* spirit and that since they appeared to be 'playing *idìɔŋ*' they should pay for their initiation.

The Spirit Movement struck a familiar chord and built on a syncretic dynamic already apparent in the region's prophetic churches. The principal belief of Annang followers of the Spirit Movement concerned the Holy Spirit (*Édísáná Ódùdù*), who was dissociated from the Trinity and conceived as a powerful spirit (*ńdêm*) capable of curing all diseases and injuries, ensuring longevity, bringing wealth and combating malicious supernatural forces. In scores of cases the spirit seized a person quite suddenly, caused them great anxiety, fear and trembling, and was followed with a prompting to confession and then by 'unusual elation and ecstatic joy'.[112] The spirit possession of the 'Shakers' manifested itself in bodily convulsions and monotonous dancing. An Opobo chief, David Kapella, recorded the features of a trance-like state of consciousness which spirit possession induced. This included short-sightedness, feeling drunk, and a loss of self-control: 'life and mind are suspending', he wrote, 'I am unable to govern my mind for what I wish ... my left side is burnt inside like fire, and then turned my head by burning like fire inside. Whether I [was] living in the world or not I cannot tell, for I could not govern myself or get my right mind'.[113] Observers pointed to the consumption of raw tree fruits, which are normally soaked for several days, as accounting for the drunken-like behaviour of the spirit people. Others said that their possession and visions were caused by eating very little.

The Spirit Movement attracted young men and women in their teens and early twenties. The dancing associated with the movement was mostly by young women and continued for hours until the dancer fell to the ground exhausted. Where in previous years mothers had prevented their daughters from going to church, they now went along with them, and 'in great anxiety they sat down beside them; hunched themselves into a ball; held themselves together with their arms; dug their chins into their chests and watched until the paroxysm was over'.[114] Falling in this way, like women stripping naked (which some spirit women were reported to have done at Ikpa), was a potent ritual inversion expressing physical and spiritual transformations of the self. The young men who joined the movement included many who had been inquirers at the Qua Iboe Mission stations but had since left the church as they had grown older and had become more intimately involved in the domestic concerns of marriage and reproduction. Those who had received some training in the three 'Rs' expressed themselves in 'unintelligible repetitive writing'.[115]

Bands of young men and women, of between 100 and 300 at a time, entered states of spiritual possession, paraded along the roads and lived in the churches and prayer houses.[116] Here the Holy Spirit was thought to inhabit the church altar, which came to be regarded as a shrine (*idêm*) where prayers and sacrifices could be made to *àbàsì*.[117] Some of the District Officers proposed an especially literal reading of this religious syncretism.

The translation of Christian concepts into Ibibio, and the direct use of Ibibio names for deities and spirits for central tenets of the Christian belief system, was thought to have led to a range of perversions: 'no good is done by using the word Abasi for God, ukpon for soul, when the word ekpo is not used for devil. ... What is being taught the native through the medium of his mother tongue is not Christianity but unwittingly an Ibibio version of it and this is not so much a version as perversion'.[118]

Many women drawn into the Spirit Movement wore *ṁkpàtát* (*Selaginella*) leaves to protect themselves from malicious forces.[119] The confessions of 'sins' that the 'spirits' demanded was directed specifically against suspected witches. Large numbers of cotton trees were felled as witches were thought to dwell in them, and public confessions of witchcraft were coerced as 'they called on persons to confess their sins, and put those who refused to do so to torture'.[120] The movement turned violent very quickly in fact, and its adherents began to compel confession by trussing up suspected witches. The victim was bound with ropes which were tightened with levers. Dousing them in water to shrink the ropes as they dried, the suspected witches were left to die. Trussings to force confessions of witchcraft started on 23 November 1927 and ended on 2 December 1927. In this short period there were thirty-four serious assaults including four murders. Westgarth admitted that the physical manifestations of the movement were difficult to understand and that 'there have been cases undoubtedly where they have not been of God'. What he coyly described to the mission's supporters at home as 'unseemly' acts led the colonial authorities to call in troops. During 1927 eleven 'spirit' people were convicted on murder charges and three were executed.[121]

The colonial authorities associated the wave of religious fervour with similar incidents in the West Indies known as Myalism,[122] and later with the Makka movement in Cameroon.[123] Alarmed that court chiefs were being tied up at Ikot Edong and that court messengers were assaulted, the colonial response to the Spirit Movement was repressive and a police patrol toured areas in Ibiono clan in early December 1927.[124] Jeffreys (whose Ibibio nickname was *Ntokon* – 'hot pepper') was District Officer at Ikot Ekpene in 1927 and sentenced 'spirits' charged with causing the disturbances to short terms of imprisonment. He mustered them in columns of four and made them march in silence around the prison square; anyone breaking the silence was beaten. By evening, after marching all day, the spirit had left them and did not return.[125] The District Officer at Abak recalled that in 1928:

> With promptings from the Political Officers [the chiefs] gave the offenders one month IHL [imprisonment with hard labour] and 12 strokes of the cane in the Native Courts. These strokes were always given in prison in the presence of a Political Officer. I found the best

way was to have 6 strokes given and then ask if the spirit was still present. If the answer was 'no' the other 6 strokes were remitted. If 'yes' they were given. In one incident all the crowd stopped jigging apart from one man who in spite of being cut about with switches refused to be quiet saying that the spirit would not let him do so. A bamboo bed was found on which the man was bound and the other spirit dancers were told to carry him to Uyo some 20 miles. We had not gone far when the man said he would be quiet if he was untied.[126]

A number of questions surrounded the origin of the movement. 'Nothing but a sudden state of alarm', Westgarth claimed, could have accounted for what happened in 1927, especially the dismantling of shrines.[127] Yet, it is far from clear what had caused this alarm. A number of factors contributed to a sense of heightened tension. An underlying aspect was the frustration of the first generation of converts at the continued power of an older class of men who retained control of the courts. It is possible to see the Spirit Movement as part of the ongoing conflict between church congregations and secret society initiates during the 1920s. According to this interpretation, the spirit people, frustrated by inaction on the part of the colonial administration, complained that the Native Courts were dominated by society members, pressed for public action against the societies and ultimately took the law into their own hands.[128] Such a protest would have been galvanised in 1927 when the Evangelical Union of Nigeria covering the eastern part of the country, a powerful coalition made up of the United Free Church of Scotland, the Church Missionary Society, the Niger Delta Pastorate, the Qua Iboe Mission, the Primitive Methodist Mission and the Wesleyan Mission, petitioned the Resident of Calabar to ban ékpó.[129]

There was, however, a peculiar similarity between the 'shakers' and the secret societies which pointed to a persistent cultural ordering; the 'shakers' opposed and attacked ékpó, but their actions, in terms of possession, violence and timing, were very ékpó-like. District officers drew parallels between the Spirit Movement and the annual cycle of the violence associated with the secret societies. Quite apart from the mixing up, as the authorities perceived it, of traditional and Christian beliefs, the Spirit Movement's actions bore the hallmarks of secret society-type operations. 'The atrocities committed by excited adherents of Christian Churches is interesting', the Resident at Calabar noted, 'in view of a recent complaint of the Mission Societies against such pagan institutions as 'Ekpo'.[130] It should be recalled also that the timing of the Movement broadly coincided with the Annang and Ibibio ritual cycle which marked the harvest, the ékpó season and the end of the year during August, September and October. To a limited extent, and in the light of previous points raised concerning the intersection of youth movements and secret societies, it is possible to suggest that the Spirit Movement was shaped by this tradition of renewal in which the secret societies acted as 'social movements in embryo' and who came to the fore as remedial vanguards against hardship and fears of witchcraft.[131]

Another aspect of the Spirit Movement, which resonates with the idea that it was a release of underlying inter-generational tension, was its sexual dimension. It was associated with a high degree of sexual licence, and spirit possession was linked to promiscuity among young people:

> You are well aware that apart from dancing, shaking and making themselves a general nuisance, adherents are for the most part young people of both sexes, who use the movement as a cover for promiscuous sexual intercourse.[132]

As a result, opposition to the Spirit Movement was frequently related in accusations of adultery. Many complaints alleged that by joining the Spirit Movement, and by staying at 'Spirit Settlements' such as the one that developed at Obot Enong Ikot Endem in 1932, wives were deserting their husbands.[133] These complaints were followed by litigation, such as a case of disturbing the peace brought against twenty-three spirit people in November 1932 in Ibiono Native Court, which accused them of committing adultery with wives who had joined the movement.[134] When a 'spirit' woman in possession confessed to adultery at Afaha Utuat and accused her husband of witchcraft, 'the husband then cut her head and that of the adulterer nearly off'.[135] It is difficult to judge whether these accusations were symptoms of the moral panic occasioned by the spirits, devices to discredit them or an opportunity for illicit sexual liaisons. In the light of young men's grievances concerning polygamy, however, it appears that the adultery accusations were further evidence of deep-seated frustrations with the mission's 'discipline'.

Several external factors were also thought to have contributed to the Spirit Movement, including agitation by the Christ Army Church and the distribution of American religious tracts. At Itu the DO secured a pamphlet, 'A Few Important Truths about the Christ Army Church', whose purpose was to perpetuate the movement started by Garrick Braide at Bonny in 1916. 'Emissaries' of the Christ Army Church in Degema Division were reported to have been active in Itu District after the Spirit Movement began and claimed to possess 'supernatural powers'.[136] American religious literature, which had been imported through the post office in Itu, was also thought to have sparked the revival. The authorities found two papers in particular which they considered subversive, both of which emphasised divine healing through prayer and possession. One was the magazine of the Unity School of Christianity,[137] the other was a paper by the Faith Tabernacle.[138]

In fact, it appears that there was a considerable dialogue between those who emerged to lead the Spirit Movement, and the American churches. Although it was initially leaderless, there was a core of young men in Itam, including Michael Ukpong Udo, Richneal Ekit and Akpan Udofia, upon whom the spirit's visitations had a longer and more profound impact than their contemporaries and who began to head the movement. A great deal of correspondence passed between Michael Ukpong Udo and the Faith Tabernacle Congregation in Philadelphia during the height of the Spirit Movement in September 1927, and the Apostolic Faith Mission in Portland, Oregon from 1928 onwards. Michael Ukpong Udo requested and received a significant body of literature from both churches, which he distributed throughout sixty-three villages, which would appear to have had a significant impact on the spiritual revival:

> ... there is no church to control us and direct us accordingly if it were not your pamphlets we would entirely perished off because every church and Missionaries here call us by one name Beelzebub, but being that our Lord Jesus in Gospel Matthew Chapter 10 verse 25 shows plainly we do not grieve much for that. We only mourn for your sake that you should manage through the will of our Lord Jesus to arrange with the Government of Nigeria to permit you to come and establish your Mission here for use ...[139]

As a result of Michael Ukpong Udo's correspondence, the Apostolic Faith began enquiries with the Government to establish the mission in south-eastern Nigeria during 1929. Temporarily bedridden in early 1928, he received detailed advice from the Faith Tabernacle on how to cure himself: 'In order to receive the full benefits of the Atonement, we should put our trust in God alone and not use the slightest remedy of any kind for the healing of our body. ... We should then ask for our healing in Jesus' name'.[140]

Among its varied activities, faith healing was the primary concern for those who directed the teachings and practices of the Spirit Movement. This involved praying, fasting, anointing and laying on hands in curing the sick and infertile. Michael Ukpong Udo, for instance, registered 169 'patients' between November 1927 and May 1928. He noted that in December 1927 'all kinds of diseases [were] brought at Afaha Station from the towns of Osuk, Afaha, Ikot Etim, Utit Obio and many others, and over 60 or 80 people or patients healed in a day without drugs except only touching with hand and all be healed immediately at one or two seconds'.[141] The commonest ailment patients suffered from was a weak body (*mèm ídém*), though other illnesses included swellings (*èfík*), sweats (*úbíák ídíbí,*) chest pain (*úbíák ésît*), ailments brought on by medicine (*ibɔ́k*), witchcraft (*ìfót* and *ùbén*) and suffering from an ancestral curse (*úfèn ǹbìàm yè ékpó*).

Westgarth dismissed the influence of the American pamphlets, but the influence of hypnosis literature and paraphernalia was harder for him to deny. At the height of the religious fervour he found one of the Qua Iboe teachers, David, in a stupor claiming that 'the spirit is coming out of me'.

He had joined the Psychological Society of Bolton, England, several years previously and had followed their teaching on the use of 'mesmeric disks'.[142] By hypnotising himself, David had tried to make contact with, and subject himself to, spirit influences. He had books titled *How to Converse with Spirit Friends* and *How to Know your Future*, and his exercise book was full of automatic 'spirit writing'.[143] David's writings were requests to the spirits to give him power and to influence people in various walks of life to yield up to him all that he required of them. 'To get power the one over the other becomes almost a cult,' Westgarth noted. 'It cuts in two directions, i.e. to prevent the others getting power over him as well as striving to get it over others'.[144]

Although the Mission tried to distinguish between the misguided, like David, and those inspired by the Holy Spirit, the young teachers' experience offers an insight into the cultural meaning of the movement and of Ibibio and Annang Christian conversion more generally. It was a quest for power. A chief who converted during the Spirit Movement said that the thing that kept him away from the church was 'the fear that if he destroyed his "medicine" his enemies would get power over him'.[145] In particular, the Spirit Movement concerned a quest for a special type of power associated with the Europeans of the church and Colonial Office. Westgarth remarked that his congregations had the feeling 'that the European has a knowledge which he does not communicate to his flock, or thinks it wise to withhold … they thought the missionary knew of this power all the time, but had not communicated it to them'.[146] One man who gave testimony during the movement said, 'Lord, we thought this new religion was white man's wisdom, but Thou has visited us thyself and we thank and praise Thee'.[147]

One of the clearest statements that the movement concerned a desire for power and through power, wealth, was contained in an anonymous letter to the DO at Ikot Ekpene which purported to identify the reasons why the Spirit Movement became so popular:

> 1. They said that you and DO know about this spirit it is came from God, that is reason why you white people do not want to put your hands to stop them, because you fear God.
> 2. They said that God has been proved this Spirit to you white people before, and by it you found the mentioned things in the ground. 1. Cement 2. Silver 3. Gold 4. Metal Lead 5. White-wash 6. Iro[n] Materials 7. Kerosene 8. Medicines.[148]

In Ikot Ekpene during 1928 the Spirit 'ringleaders' professed to be able to produce holy water, manillas and salt from holes in the ground, and in later revivals spirit people dug holes 15–20 feet deep in the hope of finding holy water or precious metals.[149] These excavations echo a common means by which powerful substances of unknown origin, such as *mbìàm*, are discovered in Annang and Ibibio society by digging to find a pot buried in the ground.[150] Such pots are doubly empowered, both as the objects of ancestors and because they are of the domain of the earth deity (àbàsì ìkpá ísɔ̀ŋ). It was also reported that spirit men at Ikot Uba station washed their bodies with 'whitewash'. This act might be read literally in terms of seeking access to the knowledge of the 'whites', but may also be regarded as an adaptation of the practice of smearing white ńdôm chalk to 'cool' down the body in healing and to promote fertility in initiations.[151] The letter-writer went on to say that since the Government was resisting the spread of the Spirit Movement it was popularly assumed that they were also deliberately denying the knowledge of these substances to Africans. 'If that be the case', the author concluded, 'they do not want to be under control by anyone again'.[152]

The Spirit Movement cannot, however, be seen as a moment of anti-colonial opposition or indeed a precursor to such a moment. In the main, the movement involved a withdrawal from authority, not a confrontation with it.[153] African religious movements which repudiated both mission Christianity and traditional religion were, of course, striking at the very heart of colonial ideology, and were considered threatening because of this.[154] Yet the thrust of this movement was a search for spiritual power framed within Christianity but which drew on familiar forms in the personal and practical imperatives of healing and security. The Spirit Movement may be regarded, therefore, as a popular struggle of Ibibio and Annang people to adapt their stock of theoretical concepts to the 'explanation, prediction and control' of the social changes wrought by colonialism in the late 1920s.[155] The ambiguous symbolic content of the Spirit Movement, spirit possession, healing and witch-finding, served to bridge the discontinuities of colonial dislocation. As an ill-defined, often leaderless Christian revival, the Spirit Movement captured the youth's groping search for the resources of power from the Holy Spirit, from the soil, and from across the Atlantic; as a witch-finding movement its emergence was linked to the new wealth and status of those who usurped the positions within the political and spiritual hierarchy whose authority was based, in part, on protecting the community against witchcraft. Above all, the Spirit Movement shows that even after two decades of mission presence in the Ibibio and Annang communities affected, and after the weight of material advantage brought by colonialism had swung decisively behind the missions, the religious encounter must be regarded 'as much more of a two-way process of mutual assimilation than a one-way "impact" or imposition'.[156]

After 1927 localised recurrences of Spirit Movement activity continued annually until the late 1930s. 'Cowed into abject submission' by the 'spirits' in 1927, the chiefs took more extensive action against them in the courts when the movement reappeared.[157] One of the longest-running disputes between Spirit People and court chiefs was in Itam which had become the centre of the movement.[158] Key elements of the movement, such as visioning, prophecy, dreaming and speaking in tongues were retained by Michael Ukpong Udo at Itam as he attracted adherents to an independent Christian church called Oberi Okaime, or the Free Healing Church.[159] The church stressed Old rather than New Testament practices, used the Ibibio rather than the European week, and developed its own writing and language, which were taught at its school at Ikpa founded in 1936. [160]

In addition to Oberi Okaime, followers of the Spirit Movement found outlets for their religious expression in various denominations, including the Christ Army Church, the Primitive Methodists, the African Church Mission, the Apostolic Church and the Assemblies of God. This congregational diversity was fuelled by court chiefs who insisted that these 'free spirits' be affiliated to churches:

> The immediate result of the attention of the Clan Councils was to drive the 'shakers' to seek sanctuary under any Mission movement, new or old, who would accept them, and under such protection, to continue their practices.[161]

In 1939 the hand-clapping, singing and playing aloud which were characteristic of services of the Apostolic church, were confused with the Spirit Movement and several cases were brought to court in the Asutan Ekpe Clan in Uyo Division. In its defence the Apostolic Church claimed that it had recruited thousands of former Spirit Movement people and had been able to wean them away from their 'foolish notions'.[162]

During the most widespread revival of the Spirit Movement in 1932 the 'shaking' practice spread across Opobo and southern Annang from Ogoni. Tai Chiefs complained about the religious movement which was being propagated by a Christ Army Church prophetess at Mogho and her followers who professed to cure sickness through prayer and by being anointed with oil and water. During 1932, fifty-nine members of the Christ Army Church in Ogoni were convicted in the Provincial Court for 'shaking'.[163] In Ukan, a village in Opobo Division, for instance, the village elders brought a court case in 1932 calling for the removal of the Christ Army Church. Following the DO's mediation it was agreed that the church could remain providing that:

- The tree beaten to summon Church members should be beaten in the church yard and not the town square;
- No Christians should interfere with Heathen plays and societies;
- Anyone performing spirit shaking in public should be arrested;
- Anyone going round saying that the spirit has entered into them and accusing people of witchcraft should be arrested;
- On the yearly hunting day before the farming season, all the town should hunt and the Christians should take their share of the game to do as they liked with.[164]

With its connections to the 'shaking' movement and the excesses to which it was prone, the District Officer at Ikot Ekpene, claiming support from the clan councils, called for the complete suppression of the Christ Army church in 1934.[165]

Having begun within the Qua Iboe Mission, the effect of the Spirit Movement was to undermine its regional and liturgical monopoly. Even Westgarth, its apologist, would bemoan the superficiality of conviction which he said most 'spirit people' possessed, and claimed that despite the few who had genuinely entered the church, the majority had been subject to 'mass-suggestion'. He concluded that although the movement introduced a 'spirit of prayer' to the mission, and had reinvigorated its preachers and teachers, there was little permanent impact of the 'idol-burning' movement for the mission. Nevertheless, the impact of the Spirit Movement on the rapid expansion of Christianity more generally in the Ibibio and Annang territories was far-reaching. The movement's influence on the construction of discourses of gender and generational conflict, and on contestation over modes of knowledge and explanation, was significant. These issues were also persistent, and the controversies surrounding the congregation, practices and teachings of the Spirit Movement were carried on by the Christ Army Church into the 1930s and 1940s.

THE WOMEN'S WAR

Among the sparks which were thought to have ignited the religious fervour of the Spirit Movement in 1927 was the impending tax collection. In May 1927 it was announced that the first tax was due to be levied in April 1928. At exactly the same time as the tax assessments began in June, investigations were under way to increase Nigerian palm oil production. Locally, the unusual attentions of colonial officers were thought to be connected and rumours circulated that 'the true object of tax assessment officers was to arrange for a confiscation of land and palm trees'.[166] These fears were compounded by the fact that extensive areas of Calabar Province were gazetted as Forest Reserves during the year. The Government was apprehensive about any signs of rebellion linked to the tax collection, and police escorts accompanied the provincial Resident as he toured to quell a number of isolated local protests.[167] The most significant conflict took place in the aftermath of the tax propaganda tours further west, in Warri Province. The resistance in Warri during 1927 established a pattern of anti-colonial protest which took the form of boycotts of the Native Courts, of trade with European factories, of sale of European goods and of palm fruit harvesting. During the protest Native Courts were attacked, and the Warrant Chiefs, who were regarded as being complicit in the introduction of taxation, were stripped of their judicial authority and replaced by self-constituted tribunals.[168]

The tax assessment was calculated on the population of adult men. In

the palm oil-rich divisions of Calabar Province each man paid 7 shillings
tax which was collected by the chiefs of the village. In total £85,000 was
collected in the first tax collection in 1928. While this inspired optimism in
senior official circles and led to a more rigorous assessment in 1929, the
tax was perceived quite differently by its payers, 'the people here imagine
that the tax was a levy, or a kind of collective fine on a large scale. The
real difficulties may begin when the people realise that tax collection is an
annual event'.[169] As the censuses to establish the tax rolls began for the
following year, these 'difficulties' did, indeed, materialise. The reassessment
was postponed in Abak during September 1929 following opposition from
the chiefs. In November when the tax census in Bende Division in neighbouring Owerri Province included counting wives, children, goats and
sheep, rumours spread that women were also to pay tax.[170]

The rumour spread quickly, and had reached Opobo Division in Calabar
via palm oil middlemen and palm wine dealers within a few days. The residents of Ukam in the Ikpa clan of Opobo Division were therefore well
aware of the significance of the arrival, unannounced, of a young cadet,
R. F. Floyer, his interpreter and two messengers on 2 December. Floyer
was conducting the tax reassessment for which he employed a system of
enumerating male adults by means of a 'factor', a ratio, that estimated the
proportion of houses and property to taxable men (of 42 men to every 100
doors).[171] To ensure that they told the truth Floyer took the 'town chiefs'
to an 'Idem' shrine and made them swear that they had not concealed men
or houses. This system was severely criticised in the subsequent enquiries
since it was not only offensive to Ibibio and Annang beliefs, but also did
not have 'the merit of being scientific'.[172] In Ukam the chiefs would claim
that the system resembled the process by which chiefs would order a dead
man's goods to be counted and seized (by which they most likely meant if
the man had been killed by mbìàm).[173] As the counting took place women
became annoyed and shouted at the ADO, 'Why should you leave your town
and come here ... and keep saluting us'. The young men took things further:
'Where you stand is a cemetery where a white man like you was buried',
they told Floyer, 'and if you don't behave yourself you will be buried there
as well'.[174] Floyer's clerk was pushed in the back, a sign, he believed, that
the young men had put 'medicine' on him, and as the two messengers ran
for the police, Floyer and his clerk were beaten up. At a subsequent meeting
in Ukam the villagers explained their fears: that they were going to be made
to pay more tax, that they had heard women were going to be taxed, that
the Government was going to sell their palm trees, and that the dissat-
isfied chiefs were secretly planning to sell land to the Government.[175] On 5
December the Ukam courthouse was destroyed and its telegraph wire cut.

Three similar riots were reported in Owerri Province before a European
doctor drove his car through a protesting crowd in Aba killing two women on

11 December. This was the catalyst that turned a simmering mass protest to violence. Merchants' factories were attacked at Umuahia, Aba, Imo River, Nbawsi, Omoba and Opobo, and Native Courts were attacked across the region.[176] Despite the association of the 1929 riots with the Igbo trading town of Aba, the central theatre of the subsequent violence included Utu Etim Ekpo, Ika, Ikot Ekpene, Abak, Itu, Ikono, Okopedi and Opobo. It was here, in the Ibibio and Annang region in the south-west of Calabar Province, that fifty-five women died and fifty more were wounded in extensive clashes that the women involved called *ékóŋ ibáàn*, the Women's War.[177] Events came to a head in Opobo. Women there demanded written assurances that they would not be taxed and called for the abolition of direct taxation, for the local chief to be replaced, for no personal property to be counted, for the abolition of market tolls and fees for licences to hold plays, and for the authorities to stop arresting prostitutes.[178] On 16 December, when a crowd of women rushed the troops guarding the district office at Egwangwa Beach in Opobo, the troops opened fire and killed thirty-two women.

Coming just months after the formation of the Ibibio Welfare Union in Calabar, the young teachers and clerks among its members were quickly drawn into the turmoil of the Women's War. The Union's role during the conflict offers an initial glimpse into its relationship with the provincial community it sought to represent and with the colonial state, and it addresses an aspect of the Women's War which is often overlooked – the question of why it did not spread. Following the reports of violence in Aba, the Ibibio Welfare Union set up a team to tour 'Ibibio Mainland Territory of Calabar Province to dissuade Ibibio women from participating in such an act of rebellion'.[179] The Union delegation attempted to quell rumours that women were to be taxed, preached 'the Gospel of love, unity and co-operation with the Government'[180] and leafleted affected areas. These written notices were posted from 'Aqua Esop Ufon Ibibio' (the grand meeting for the progress of Ibibio) and informed the public that: 'The members of the Ibibio Welfare Union are your true friends, brothers, and well-wishers. ... for those men, or even chiefs who encourage you to give trouble, have nothing more to do with them. They are not your true friends nor true citizens of Ibibio land'.[181] The Union also reminded the women that 'in the olden days our fathers punished thieves, robbers, and disturbers of the peace'.[182]

In areas of Uyo, Ikot Ekpene, Eket and Itu the Union's campaign claimed success. A crowd of between 3,000 and 4,000 women reached Ikot Osudua, near Ikot Ekpene, for example, and were deflected from their protest only by Reverend Groves of the Methodist Mission and Udo Essien Obot, the President of the Ibibio Union which claimed a membership of fifty 'progressives'.[183] The delegates arrived too late, however, to prevent the events which befell Abak and Opobo Districts. Further measures were taken to prevent the Women's War spreading elsewhere in the province

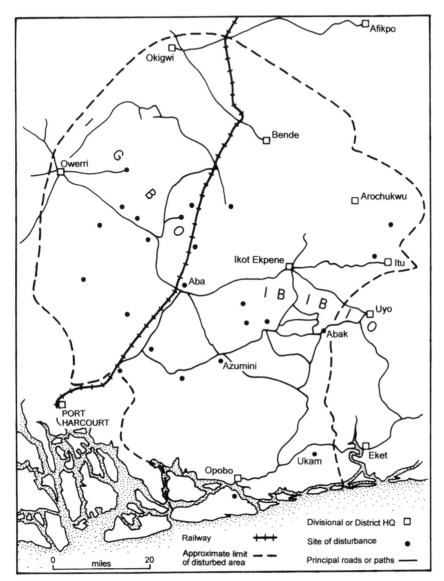

Figure 3.3 The Women's War, 1929[184]

including at Itu where, confronted by marching women on Itu Hill, Dr A.
B. Macdonald the physician in charge of the Itu Leper Colony arranged for
250 lepers to block their way.[185] In Ukanafun a crowd of women carrying
cassava leaves and singing 'white man go' marched from Azumini towards
Ekparakwa, but were persuaded to disband by Chief Ikwo Akpan Umanah
supported by the teacher-preacher and members of the Qua Iboe church.

He was anxious to protect the court from the women's attack, but it was the news he relayed that women had been shot by soldiers at Utu Etim Ekpo that turned them back. In large part, then, it was the extreme violence of the colonial response, especially that troops fired directly at crowds and the indiscriminate burning of compounds, combined with the arrival of larger numbers of troops, that brought the Women's War to an end. It is difficult to overestimate the fear and panic felt by colonial officers during December 1929, which undoubtedly determined their armed response to the revolts. The Resident, Falk, wrote frankly in his journal that 'all this took us by surprise like the Indian mutiny did'. Only thirty police officers were retained in the Provincial headquarters during the conflict. As a result, all of the European women took shelter in the prison and European men insisted on being armed. Falk perceived the women's protests as an Igbo and Ibibio conspiracy bent on an incursion into Calabar Province. As such, holding the left bank of the Qua Iboe river became a strategic imperative. Within official circles it was said that Falk's slogan was burning 'a village a day, keeps the riot away'.[186]

The subsequent commissions of enquiry established to investigate the causes of the Women's War highlighted three main factors: tax collection, dissatisfaction with the courts and falling produce prices. Women themselves identified a number of grievances, among which the following were the most significant:

> Our grievances are that the land is changed – we are all dying. We sang so that you might ask us what our grievances were. We had cause for grievances before the taxation was introduced. It is a long time since the Chiefs and the people who know book ... have been oppressing us. I am related to three Chiefs one of whom is my husband. They don't treat us well at all. ... the new chiefs are also receiving bribes ... Since the white men came, our oil does not fetch money. Our kernels do not fetch money. If we take goats or yams to market to sell, Court messengers who wear a uniform take all these things from us.[187]

Underlying both the issue of tax collection and the provision of justice in the local courts was, as Nwoto's statement above illustrates, the vexed question of the status of the Warrant Chiefs. Attacks on the Warrant Chiefs and the Native Courts they ran indicated that it was not only the imposition of taxes which was resented, but the institutional foundations of indirect rule itself. Direct taxation was introduced into south-eastern Nigeria with the hope that it would 'give a measure of power and responsibility to the chiefs whose position tends to sink lower and lower each year'.[188] The irony was that the association between the discredited Warrant Chiefs and direct taxation increased the unpopularity of both. After the First World War the Native Court system across the south-east had lapsed into a state of crisis.

Courts in Opobo Division were described as 'courts of injustice' where around half of all cases were passed on to the District Officer for review.[189] In Abak District, for example, five Warrant Chiefs were suspended on corruption charges, and Ikot Okoro Native Court was closed because of the behaviour of the chiefs:

> The Chiefs in the Okoro Court had begun to look on it as a means to an end. They considered it was run entirely for their benefit and it was becoming a practice for chiefs never to lose cases. In fact if one's opponent in a Native Court were a chief the odds on winning one's case was 'heads I win, tails you lose'.[190]

In 1922 a major review of the judicial system by S. M. Grier had documented widespread corruption and dissatisfaction with the Warrant Chief system, and described Native Courts as the principal disintegrating force in the eastern provinces.[191] His report recognised that the Warrant Chiefs' authority was derived solely from their relationship with British administration and lacked local legitimacy. Grier's recommendations for reform to the Native Court system aimed to delineate local administrative units by making the Native Court Area coterminous with the clan, and to appoint as Warrant Chiefs elders with customary claims to title.[192] These recommendations were implemented with varying degrees of enthusiasm until the Native Revenue Ordinance of 1927 when the process of reform became systematic and the clan with its council became the basis of local administration.[193] By the outbreak of disturbances in Calabar and Owerri Provinces in 1929, however, the first steps towards the creation of clan courts as Grier had recommended were not sufficiently far-reaching to make people aware that the Warrant Chief system was undergoing substantial change.[194]

The mechanics of how thousands of women were mobilised so quickly shocked and baffled the colonial authorities, whose explanation at the time played on two familiar suppositions. First, that men, especially disgruntled young men, were involved. Second, that the mass rebellion was evidence of covert mobilisation by secret societies. It was reported in the press at the time that men saw the opportunity of engineering the riots as a lever to have all forms of direct taxation removed.[195] The Warrant Chief at Utu Etim Ekpo urged women to riot there on 14 December,[196] and in Abak and at the Imo river station men helped to loot factories. Significantly, the initial anti-tax protest in Calabar Province at Ukam had also included both young men and women who had been 'troublesome since Government had taken away the chief's power [and] would put medicine on anyone who helped Government'.[197] For the Ukam youth the tax assessment was seen as a conspiracy between the new, government-appointed chiefs and the state. Elsewhere during 1929 chiefs waited for clerks to arrive before undertaking the public tax collection for fear of being accused by the youth of personally pocketing the money.[198] Initially, then, the tax protests were seen in much the same light by the provincial authorities as the Spirit Movement which blamed both outbreaks of lawlessness on the frustrations of youth provoked by the Missions, which 'had in the past conducted a campaign to stir up the younger generations against the older one which declined to be converted'.[199] During the subsequent enquiries witnesses were questioned on whether the young men, who were increasingly disrespectful of their elders, were at the back of the movement. Archdeacon Basden, for instance, was questioned at length about the role played in the conflict by 'half-educated youths who ... just hung about the courts'.[200]

Suspicions of male machinations in fomenting what were essentially women's protests, would prove a persistent feature of colonial responses to subsequent tax and trade disputes.[201] Investigations into the Women's War also featured in the ongoing discourse on the subversive role of secret societies in anti-colonial protest. The District Officer at Bende where the tax rumours surfaced, and the Secretary of the Southern Provinces, both believed that there was a secret 'Ogbo society' which exercised control over women and which had been responsible for 'fomenting rebellion'.[202] These views were echoed by provincial officials in Calabar, who thought that 'a big Native Society of the Ibos is working the show',[203] and among the Qua Iboe missionaries who believed that 'secret propaganda must have been very skilfully carried on in the districts where this trouble arose'.[204]

This question of how women from across Owerri and Calabar Provinces gathered so quickly and in such numbers has been taken up by feminist scholars, who point to both social sanctions (like 'sitting on a man')[205] and women's societies (like 'mikiri' in Igbo and ibáàn ìsɔ̀ŋ in Ibibio) by which women were able to express their political and economic grievances.[206] Meaning 'women of the soil', ibáàn ìsɔ̀ŋ was an all-woman meeting led by èkà ibáàn ìsɔ̀ŋ who acted as the chief arbiter and woman's representative. While it had no formal powers over men, ibáàn ìsɔ̀ŋ could enforce its will by besieging a man's house (úfìk ntìè). The group mobilises collectively across a network of villages linked to particular markets and does so for one main reason: when a man insults his wife, especially if he said his wife's genitals smelt (ǹtébé ǹtébé). When 500 women faced the Resident of Calabar Province at Essene they chanted:

> ǹsò ìtébé ǹtùm, ǹkpá ètébé ǹtùm
> What is the smell? Death is the smell.[207]

The rituals of this rebellion point to the way that it expressed contemporary tensions of production and reproduction. On 14 December one of the wives of Chief Akpan Umo at Utu Etim Ekpo beat the women's drum to summon them. As they gathered the women's faces were painted with charcoal and white clay (ǹdôm), and their heads were decorated with *m̀kpàtát* leaves. Elsewhere, thousands of women paraded holding *àyèì* and carrying yam-pounding sticks. In part these aspects, like wearing ragged cloth, painting their faces and dressing like a man, were ritual inversions characteristic of an *ibáàn ísɔ̀ŋ* protest.[208] *Íbáàn ísɔ̀ŋ* dress in men's clothes, sometimes wearing the legs and sleeves of men's clothes only on one side. They will paint their faces blue or with charcoal and parade (*ésàŋá ké údîm*) to besiege the man's compound.[209] These inversions of left and right, male and female, are characteristic of two things: to denote danger and potency in the 'nonsensical' apparel; and to signify the crossing of domains. While male warriors (*ékóŋ*) dress as women to bless fattened *m̀bòbó* women with fertility, so the women's forum (*ísɔ̀ŋ ibáàn*) dress as men when they bring war to a man's compound.

In part, however, the complex symbolism of the protest was also protective. *Àyèì* palm fronds were an injunction of peace and an assurance of safe conduct, and *m̀kpàtát* leaves were employed by the women to protect themselves from malicious spirits (as they had during the Spirit Movement). In the initial commission of enquiry it was also reported that some women 'were nearly naked wearing only wreaths of grass round their heads, waist and knees and some were wearing tails made of grass'.[210] It also claimed that women declared that they were vultures. Women's nudity, a curse of *mbìàm*, was used as 'a bodily insult' against men, an act which highlighted the reproductive significance of women's bodies over which they held unambiguous control.[211] This description of the aesthetic of women's violence is also significant because it introduces an ongoing uncertainty about the meaning of tailed costumes, and a rhetoric of animal transformations. Vultures were important in chieftaincy and *ídìɔ̀ŋ* initiation and were therefore familiar signifiers of transformation and authority. Calling themselves vultures meant that the women were invoking the rites of vultures as messengers of *àbàsì*, and that like vultures in the market, they claimed to be immune from attack.[212] Finally, the symbolism of the Women's War was aimed directly at men and at displaying women's reproductive vitality. The white chalk (*ńdôm*) with which they painted themselves has specific connections to female fertility since it is used to mark a woman's body after fattening and childbirth.[213] Upon the pestles women invoked the power of female ancestors: 'It is I who gave birth to you. It is I who cook for you to eat. This is the pestle I use to pound yams and coco-yams for you to eat. May you soon die'.[214]

★　★　★

Despite the array of factors, both immediate and more remote, that contributed to the outbreak of women's protests in 1929, there are several questions concerning the Women's War that have never been answered satisfactorily. The two most significant and straightforward are: why did women rebel and not men; and why did Ngwa, Annang and Ibibio women rebel and not those elsewhere in the eastern Provinces?[215] If the riots expressed more than anxieties about the rumour of women being taxed and were an expression of resistance against colonial rule and of economic discontent, then why were women more aggrieved? The answers to these questions are twofold. First, that the tax demands coincided with a period of acute domestic tension, and second, that the protests mapped onto a region with a peculiar economic system into which the introduction of taxation was catastrophic.

As the riots showed, and as this symbolism expressed, the shifting balance of power wrought by colonialism from 1909 to 1929 in western Calabar Province had a gendered impact. The Women's War exposed radical changes in the sexual division of labour and the distribution of wealth.[216] It has been suggested, indeed, that by themselves the immediate causes of the conflict would not have generated a mass uprising of women had there not also been a more widespread and fundamental conflict which affected women.[217] The region had indeed witnessed radical agricultural changes. By the late 1920s some women had gained *de facto* control over palm oil production as well as distribution by pledging palm plots.[218] Another factor which was beginning to shift the gender division of labour was the role of cassava. Introduced a decade earlier, cassava was rapidly becoming an important food crop, especially for women for whom cassava cultivation added to their labour burden, but also to their potential economic income.

It was poverty, not profit, however, that led to the events of 1929. The region was hard hit by the collapse of agricultural producer prices during the 1920s and the consequent rising cost of living. A four-gallon tin of palm oil was sold for 15s 6d in Aba during the post-First World War boom which peaked in 1925–26, but had fallen to 5s 10d in 1929.[219] The prices of imported goods also increased and were compounded by a rise in import duties – a head of tobacco rose from 6d to 9d; VH gin from 11 shillings to 15 shillings. Songs from the period lamented the poverty that the changing terms of trade effected:

> *Stand and hear all so that you can laugh at my poverty*
> *Still stand and hear all, hear all and laugh at my honesty*
> *Still stand and hear all*
> *People buy fowls for two manillas – cut cow and enter into inam;*
> *Still stand and hear all*
> *Stand and hear all and laugh at my poverty*
> *Still stand and hear all.*
> *I buy a fowl for ten manillas – my own became ashes*
> *Still stand and hear*
> *Still stand and hear and laugh at my poverty*
> *Still stand and hear.*[220]

The domestic economy functioned on the basis of cash and gift exchanges between husbands and wives. Popular songs from the 1920s captured a set of changing priorities and demands placed upon the economic reciprocity of Annang and Ibibio marriages. These new domestic tensions concerned household budgeting and gifts from husbands to wives. Such gifts were especially important after childbirth. Previously a woman would return to farm work only three weeks after childbirth so long as an elder daughter or relative could care for the newborn. Increasingly during the 1920s, however, Annang women were staying at home for longer and in some villages had formed the habit, and had agreed among themselves, not to go out after the birth of their child until their husbands had bought them new clothes:

> *If my husband does not give me a dress,*
> *I shall return and follow my friend,*
> *A long dress is too costly,*
> *I shall return and follow my friend.*[221]

Postnatal seclusion was even more pronounced for church members, who would wait three months before attending a service and again new demands on husbands were being made. On the appointed Sunday women of the church would escort her and present her with manillas while her husband would buy palm wine for a subsequent feast.[222]

Popular songs of the time illustrate that the church introduced a changing dynamic in the choice of marriage partners arising from the growing proportion of young men who had been to school:

> *There was a woman who married a townsman,*
> *When the church came she married him no longer,*
> *If you want to marry, marry a child in the Ikot Abia Idem school,*
> *The scholars hear the English language ...*
> *If I want to marry a husband I do not marry the husband's idol,*
> *Better to be a harlot than to do that.*[223]

The Qua Iboe Mission recognised some of the trends to which it had contributed. It was desirable, the instructors at the Girls' Institute believed, that a girl should know English 'ways and manners' of doing things; but training a girl to read and write the English language, to dress in 'English style', to cook English food and to keep her house and compound in a purely European fashion was bad. The Institute staff noted that: 'the girl trained to dress like a European may soon find that her husband is unable to keep her in that style and therefore she will have no respect for him. She is often heard saying, "My husband does not love me."'[224] The Mission believed that this tension between the expectations of Christian women and the economic capacities of their husbands was the cause of much 'palaver in the home'.[225]

The strain on marriages was showing. One of the most widespread and well-known critical responses by women to the economic aspect of their marriages was ńdɔ̀k úfɔ̀k èbé ('The Shame of My Husband's House'), a play which illustrates the tension of financial obligations underpinning domestic order at the time. The play, designed to ridicule men's incapacity and unwillingness to buy clothes or provide 'chop' money for their wives, centred on a song which recounted that a woman who had not been shamed had not been married. The women performing the song would parade, with rattles around their ankles, to the marketplace where they exposed their maltreatment.[226] Any husband who did not want the whole village to know that he was poor or was maltreating his wife was compelled to mend his ways. It is not surprising, then, that these new economic tensions corresponded in male responses and in popular slang which referred to extravagant women as isóbó (crab – the destroyer).

The tension over domestic transactions between men and women also suggests why women of the palm oil belt in Calabar and Owerri Provinces were so negatively affected by the slump in the palm oil trade that coincided with the 1929 tax assessment. Once it is harvested from the tree, wives buy the palm fruit from their husbands. This transaction, which takes place before the oil is processed, is known as palm money (òkpòhò áyôp). It was women, therefore, who were not only responsible for the subsequent processing, boiling and squeezing the palm fruit oil (álân áyôp), and drying, cracking and squeezing the remaining kernels (álân isíp – kernel oil), but also for trading both oil and kernels at the market. As Basden testified in his evidence to the commission of enquiry:

> Most of the trade in this country is in the hands of the women, and the complaint which they came and expressed to us was that there was no margin of profit at all, and as they could not make a living, they might as well make a stand ... They do not understand the fluctuations of prices.[227]

The concentration of women's labour on palm oil production and marketing, however, only partly explains why it was women of the palm oil belt who joined the revolt and not men who were similarly affected by the economic downturn.[228] It is with the economic dynamic of underlying currency exchange rates that this issue lies.

The areas within Calabar and Owerri Provinces in which the disturbances took place mapped precisely onto the 'manilla currency zone', the currency originally introduced to the West African coast by the Portuguese as a bracelet. The manilla exchange rate is often ignored as a contributory factor in the various social upheavals of the region during the inter-war period.[229] Yet the effects of the fall in palm oil prices and tax demands on local producers were critically aggravated by the falling manilla exchange rate in 1929.

With the expansion of European trade from the late seventeenth century onwards, currencies became specialised between local uses and trading at the coast.[230] The brass rod, the currency used in Calabar, had been supplanted by English currency by the turn of the twentieth century. Between Oron and Ikot Ubo copper wire currency was displaced by the shilling and the penny by 1920. Yet, elsewhere in Calabar Province, particularly in Ikot Ekpene, Abak and Opobo Divisions, the local manilla currency proved to be a durable medium of exchange until the late 1940s. The persistence of the use of manilla currency was linked to a number of factors. The palm oil trade was a significant source of wealth, and much of it had been retained in manillas. The manilla exchange rate against sterling had also been relatively stable during the late nineteenth century and had therefore become a safe investment.

From the turn of the century, in fact, the manilla began to appreciate. From 1902 to 1912 the local exchange appreciated by almost 1 manilla each year. In August 1914 young men from Atam and Efiat complained to the local mission that 1 shilling was being exchanged for 9 manillas.[231] This shift was attributed to the increase in trade at Opobo and the settled conditions there relative to the 1880s. As Figure 3.4 illustrates, the exchange rate was very sensitive to price fluctuations and rises in producer prices for palm oil and kernels caused the manilla to appreciate. When producer prices were high the supply of British currency increased and the manilla appreciated as more sterling chased the relatively fixed quantity of manillas. Conversely, when there was a depression of palm oil prices, resulting in the contraction of the supply of sterling, the manilla depreciated against sterling.

The introduction of British currency to the manilla zone after the Aro expedition of 1901 had been based on the assumption that the West African token money would displace the manilla, though it was afforded legal status and could be tendered as payment for court fees and fines. An embargo was imposed on the importation of manillas in 1904 which served to fix the overall supply of manillas which was now declining because of attrition, hoarding and its diversion to ritual purposes. By 1907 nickel cash was beginning to percolate into the manilla area. Attempts to stabilise the exchange rate between manillas and sterling in Uyo and Opobo (at 12 manillas to the shilling) were quashed, and although the manilla's status as legal tender was withdrawn in 1911, the colonial state was unwilling to pay the price of manilla redemption. Proposals to demonetise and redeem the manilla in 1913 were dismissed by Lord Lugard, who stated: 'I am not prepared to consent to saddle the general taxpayers of Northern and Southern Nigeria with the cost of solving the difficulties with which the Opobo clique of merchants are confronted, or to defer important and urgently needed public works by applying a large sum of public revenue to an attempt to solve in a hurry by heroic means, a problem which in due course will, in my opinion, solve itself by natural laws'.[232]

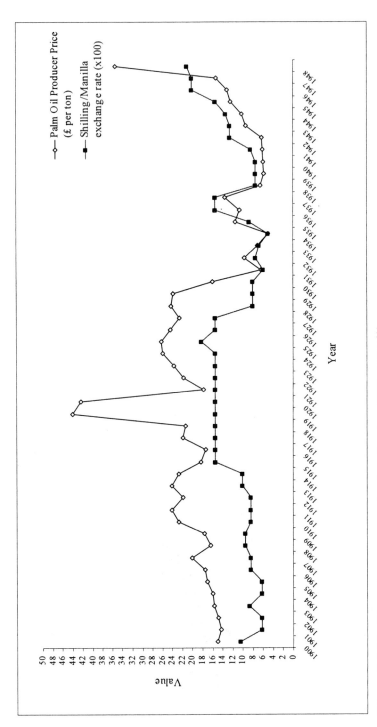

Figure 3.4 Manilla exchange rate and palm oil price, 1900–1948 [233]

The link between manillas and palm oil could not be broken by the natural laws to which Lugard referred. Paper money distributed during the First World War was extremely unpopular and throughout the period the trading firms adopted the manilla in preference because of its stability. An Opobo-based firm at one time carried a stock of over one million manillas. This practice was checked with the introduction of the Manilla Ordinance in 1919 which prohibited Europeans from using the manilla as currency.[234] Thereafter, manillas were confined to trade in local markets and the stocks of manillas previously held by Opobo merchants passed to oil middlemen which further displaced the English currency in the local economy of Abak and Opobo Divisions.

The exchange rate was determined by two factors – the demand and supply of the two currencies and the price of palm oil, the region's main export crop. The way in which the currency market operated is best explained by the main palm oil buyers at Opobo, the United African Company:

> An African middleman, let us suppose, sold a quantity of palm oil to the Company's manager on the wharf, for which he was paid in money of the West African Currency Board. The middleman then went to the Company's store and used some of this money for the purchase of trade goods, which he intended to carry back to his district for sale. With the remainder of his money he then approached one of the manilla dealers and bought manillas from him at the current rate. He then had manillas, and also goods which he could sell in the oil-producing districts. He returned to his village and sold the merchandise for manillas, he then purchased more palm oil, which he brought to the Company's wharf or 'beach' at Opobo; and the series of transactions was then repeated. The main feature of this trade was the use of manillas to purchase produce. The producer, operating direct or through intermediaries, used manillas to purchase imported merchandise or local goods and services in his village market or in Opobo – and it was these returning manillas which fed the manilla market in Opobo.[235]

The manilla–shilling exchange rate affected everyone. Commodity producers and traders, who dealt mainly in manillas, needed to exchange them for sterling with which to conduct official transactions such as paying tax and dealing with European firms. Those who were paid in sterling, the salaried wage-earners, had to buy food or locally produced goods and services which required them to exchange their shillings for manillas. Exchange rate fluctuations, however, affected these two groups alternately. When producer prices were low, the manilla depreciated and commodity producers' purchasing power declined. At the same time the shilling appreciated, and this increased the wage-earner's purchasing power. When the palm oil price was high, however, the manilla appreciated and commodity producers' purchasing power increased, but as the shilling depreciated so the wage-earner's purchasing power decreased. The net effect of the exchange rate fluctuations therefore was to magnify the impact of palm oil export prices.

The intimate link with palm oil prices led to a fluctuating pattern of currency instability. Agitation for the demonetisation and abolition of the manilla came from the salaried classes, who were always at an economic disadvantage in the manilla-using areas. To the manilla-owning peasantry it was not the manilla that fluctuated in ratio to cash, but cash that fluctuated in relation to the manilla, whose value in terms of goods was relatively constant. Throughout the 1920s schemes for the progressive redemption of the manilla were devised, based on allowing litigants to pay fines in manillas which could then be destroyed, and even though the currency issue had figured in 1925 during the market women's riots in Calabar when women had sought to prohibit the use of European coins, the schemes were dismissed one by one.[236]

It was assumed that the introduction of tax in sterling would displace the manilla. It was, ironically, precisely because this could not happen that the tax riots erupted. The tax demand introduced in 1928 was payable only in West African currency. At this time there was only £10 million in Nigeria, a per capita figure of around 10 shillings if it was all in circulation. The per capita figure of West African currency was much lower in the 'manilla zone' than elsewhere, and since the tax rate was 7 shillings it met with an extreme currency scarcity and 'complete economic upset'.[237] Tax collection during the depression years created severe problems and consequent heavy recourse to moneylenders, who exploited the situation and the exchange rate of the manilla:

> Money changers held out for as much as 19 [manillas] to 2/-. The normal rate at that time is about 13 to 2/-. By keeping these manillas until January when they are 6 to the shilling the money changers will make 50% profit in 5 months. The serious part of this is that in order to pay 7/- tax a man has to change the equivalent of 10/- in manillas. This is a great argument for the abolition of manillas. Low produce prices have made tax payment more difficult.[238]

The drain on cash due to tax was such that the shilling almost disappeared from the area and the manilla slumped. Jeffreys calculated that the manilla depreciated to about a third of its former value. This may be true in those districts affected as even using a broad regional average of shilling–manilla exchange the manilla depreciated rapidly from 6.5 manillas per shilling in 1927 to 12.5 manillas per shilling in 1928 and 1929.[239] The impact of the second year of tax was therefore not only felt most acutely

within the manilla zone but also the currency slump it generated disproportionately affected women:

> The native woman is conservative, she is the last to abandon the native
> currency, her fluid wealth is in manillas and on her falls the brunt of
> the manilla fluctuations and the consequent losses.[240]

As we have seen, women were the marketers of palm oil and therefore
felt the impact of manilla depreciation more quickly and more acutely than
men.[241] The falling value of the manilla critically undermined women's
buying power relative to the imported goods they increasingly demanded
of their husbands, and to the shilling, which they would have had to buy
directly had the tax rumours been true. If women were the losers during this
economic shift, then it is also significant that the targets of their protests, the
European firms, Warrant Chiefs and court clerks, who exchanged shillings
for manillas, were the winners as their purchasing power increased.

Seven years after the Women's War, while reviewing ongoing tensions
caused by the manilla exchange rate, District Officer M. D. W. Jeffreys realised
that this aspect of the local political economy had never been considered
in the context of the events of December 1929. Jeffreys argued that the
subsequent enquiries into the Women's War had completely missed its true
origin; the manilla was not once mentioned in the commission of enquiry's
report. He concluded that local currencies such as the manilla should have
been redeemed, and calculated that £75,000 spent on the redemption of
the manilla would have prevented the Women's War.[242]

4

PROGRESSIVES AND POWER, 1930–1938

The Women's War was an important watershed in two respects: first, it captured what had been an emerging trend – resistance to the gendered impact of colonialism within the household; and second, the conclusions drawn from the conflict profoundly shaped the subsequent direction of indirect rule in the south-eastern provinces. The 1930s were years in which colonial rule decisively embedded itself into local Annang society. The proliferation of schools, clinics and courts carried with them British normative principles and procedures in education, medicine and justice. Routines were established as taxes were collected, as weights and measures were checked, and as court fees and fines were recorded. It was a period of administrative bureaucratisation and legal codification as the civil service expanded. Colonial rule between the wars has therefore been characterised as a period of social, political and economic stagnation.[1] The 1930s was indeed the decade of greatest stability in colonial rule, though as this chapter illustrates the calm and routine were superficial. The economic depression of the 1930s not only affected the markets, it also fostered profound changes in class and gender relations.[2]

Despite appearances to the contrary, the years between the Women's War and the outbreak of the Second World War were subject to radical political upheaval within Calabar Province. Reforms in the aftermath of the Women's War designed to resolve an emerging intergenerational rift and to restore 'authentic' rulers instead turned the courts and councils into spheres of intense political contest. The control of local taxation revenue made representation on the council, like seats on the court bench, a prize fought over by new elites and elders alike, and the 'committee class' of young men who made up the 'vociferous, letter-writing minority' formed progressive welfare societies publicly to expose corruption within the Native Administration and privately to usurp its perquisites. This decade witnessed new forms of collaborations – of Africans seeking to establish new forms of access to resources and labour, and Europeans looking for local authorities to fill positions generated by their conceptions of African societies.[3] It was in this context that customary law especially relating to women was redrawn.

AMERICANS AND ANTHROPOLOGY

The Women's War of 1929 is rightly recorded as a significant moment in the history of the colonial period in Nigeria and beyond. Within the legacy of indirect rule it has been seen as one of the great revolts against the imposition of state authority.[4] As important to this story, however, are the processes which the disturbances set in motion. Despite the watershed status of the Women's War the fallout of 1929 has been much neglected, though it was both immediate and long-lasting.[5] In the first place the conflict served to heighten colonial anxieties on a range of issues, especially fluctuations of the palm oil trade, transatlantic trading schemes, and the economic nationalist rhetoric to which they were linked. In the second place it led directly to the long-term restructuring of the political landscape.

Women's capacity for political organisation demonstrated in the Women's War had come as a surprise and a mystery to the government. After 1929 the slightest hint of agitation, of women gathering in unusually large numbers, or of trade boycotts, was met with a swift response, and a police patrol would arrive within hours. The continued economic hardships caused by the economic slump in producer prices during the depression years meant that DOs were prone to misread local events. They were especially vigilant in the months leading up to tax payment, and there was alarm when, in January 1931, a trade boycott was reported in Uyo and Abak Divisions. No palm fruit was being sold to middlemen or to factories such as Ibagwa mill near Abak, which was run by Nigerian Products Ltd. The rumour within government circles was that producers were holding on to their stocks because an American trader was due to visit Ikot Ekpene and would offer them 'fantastic prices'.[6] The price of palm fruit sold at Ibagwa mill had slumped from 2s 9d per gin case to 8d. Indirectly, the price slump was the cause of the boycott, but in fact a number of local chiefs had placed an injunction on palm fruit sales for two months (édìwúk áyôp – palm ban). The subsequent harvest was to be sold so that the proceeds could be used by the chiefs to pay the next round of taxes due in April. What had appeared to be the beginning of another trade or tax protest was in fact a locally adapted mechanism for paying tax. Palm prices were so low that individuals struggled to raise enough to pay their taxes and the chiefs, as tax collectors, were compelled to underwrite the shortfall. Chief Samson of Ekpene Obon near Etinan, where the boycott began, claimed that he had paid out £30 from his own pocket in the 1930 tax collection.[7]

Tax, therefore, had quickly become a factor around which people organised themselves. Poverty and tax featured prominently in songs of the time:

> *Wife I do not marry,*
> *I have no bicycle,*
> *What shall I take to market?*
> *How shall I pay my tax?*[8]

During the depression the ability of those communities most severely hit by the fall in palm produce prices was closely monitored and aspects of the tax collection were changed to accommodate them. After 1932, chiefs, although they still collected the tax, were no longer personally liable for prosecuting tax evaders.[9] It had also become common practice to collect tax during the agricultural season when specific communities were most able to pay, and hence in Opobo Division tax was collected from the Ibibio and Anang clans from May onwards at the height of the palm oil season; from the Ogonis from October to December when they harvested their yams; from the Andonis in November so as to interfere least with their fishing activities; while collection from Opobo itself continued throughout the year.[10]

Rumours circulating during the palm oil 'boycott' during 1931 of American traders and their 'fantastic prices' point to another aspect of the fallout of the Women's War: colonial vigilance regarding subversive American influences. At the time of the disturbances in 1929 the Resident at Calabar had thought that the protests were linked to 'quite a lot of agitation from America, as in the so-called Spirit Movement of 1927'.[11] The American trader at Ikot Ekpene in 1931 was an agent of the Ibibio Trading Corporation, a body formed in 1929 which sought to negotiate direct shipments of palm oil to North America. During the Women's War these agents had held a general meeting of the 'America and Ibibio Co-operation' on 7 December 1929 at Ikot Ubo at which 4,873 people turned out to hear proposals for the radical new trade scheme. In bypassing the European companies and securing higher prices by trading directly with the US, the Ibibio Trading Corporation promised that economic oppression would be lifted and that 'we are sure to have ourselves cut off from this slavery'.[12] Officials in Calabar were sufficiently alarmed that this message was being conveyed just as the women's protests were gaining momentum that the Corporation's agents were warned against inciting the local Ibibio and Annang population by giving them the idea that they were being robbed by the European firms, so that they 'almost claim independency'.[13]

Two men represented the Ibibio Trading Corporation, Henry Walker, an American, and Prince Peter Eket Inyang Udo, an Ibibio. Henry Walker had been touring villages within the province for several months prior to the disturbances. To gain support for the trade scheme it was thought that he had distributed placards which announced that palm oil producers were being cheated, that they need not pay tax and that American 'protection' had arrived.[14] Peter Eket, meanwhile, had received a 'power of attorney' from Ibibio chiefs to sell palm oil to the US and was asking for a levy of £3 per village during these meetings to finance the operation (he claimed that fifty villages had contributed). Walker had returned to the US when the official enquiries were held into the Women's War in early 1930. Peter Eket, however, was called to give evidence. He was questioned robustly on whether he had intended to cause disaffection and discontent in his speech at Ikot Ubo, and whether he had given 'the impression that the United States was more or less taking over the handling of the affairs of trade in Southern Nigeria'.[15] He denied both these claims, of course, though in the Commission's final report the Ibibio Trading Corporation's activities were cited as a 'minor contributory factor' among the various causes of the Women's War.

Eket returned to New York later in 1930 and signed a deal to supply palm oil to the West African American Corporation. By October, however, his New York partners had become impatient and sent an agent, George Macpherson, to Calabar who found that the palm oil supplies had not materialised.[16] Local branches of the Ibibio Trading Corporation had been proposed in Abak and elsewhere to facilitate the purchasing of oil, but those chiefs to whom Eket had presented his plan were reluctant to commit themselves because they would receive only a 50 per cent advance on the price they were paid. Chief Udo Udong in Ukanafun, for instance, 'who sends much oil to Opobo', was approached by the Corporation but was 'shy of dealing with them'.[17]

Throughout the 1930s Eket tried to evade the close scrutiny of the Nigerian authorities, but he was rarely out of their reports. In September 1930 the District Officer in Opobo sent a road labourer to spy, under cover of work, on the activities of a number of men clearing and levelling a site in Opobo town. Though the DO's spy was exposed, it emerged that the building work was for a clerk of Eket's 'American and Ibibio Co-operative Society' who was establishing premises, possibly a factory, from which to buy palm oil for sale in America. A later US State Department investigation into the deal found that only about 600 out of an intended 50,000 tons of palm oil had been exported, that Eket's backers had lost $8,000, and accused him of being 'the African version of a confidence man'.[18]

The Nigerian Government's suspicions of Eket Inyang Udo were linked to both his dubious commercial dealings and, more significantly, his political ideas and connections. He was born in 1897, the youngest son of Inyang Udo Ataku, a wealthy chief in the village of Ikot Ataku seven miles from Eket. He had lived in North America and Great Britain for seventeen years and had served in the British Navy during the Great War.[19] By the late 1920s he had made contacts with several of the most prominent West African 'political entrepreneurs' and nationalists of his generation, including Herbert Macaulay and Wilfred Tete-Ansa. Tete-Ansa (1889–1941) was the most prominent 'nationalist entrepreneur' of colonial British West Africa. Born in the Gold Coast, he studied in the United Kingdom and the US during the 1920s and, on his return to West Africa in 1928, established 'the most coherent and ambitious programme of economic development that had so far been drawn up by a West African'.[20] Eket had worked for Tete-

Ansa's 'West African Cooperative Producers' in 1928, and had founded the 'Ibibio Trading Corporation' under Tete-Ansa's tutelage as part of his wider scheme to link farmers' co-operatives (including cocoa-producing co-operatives in southern Ghana) with the New York-based 'West African American Company', which Tete-Ansa had set up.

The police in Nigeria considered bringing charges of trading under false pretences against Eket, but the interests of aggrieved shareholders were not the Government's main concern. Their concerns were twofold: one was to maintain the status quo among palm oil producers and the European trading companies, and the second was the fear that the nationalist rhetoric which Eket and Tete-Ansa introduced to south-eastern Nigeria would find an audience. In 1931 the Lagos press had carried an article by Tete-Ansa in which he called on readers to 'release yourselves from economic bondage, always bearing in mind that every independent nation must have its own Economic Freedom'.[21] When Eket and Tete-Ansa opened a branch of the Nigerian Mercantile Bank to finance their schemes in 1932 both the police and the United Africa Company (UAC) secretly sent informants to its inaugural public meeting in Aba. The UAC was worried that the outfit would be offering higher prices to producers. The police believed the venture to be 'entirely bogus' since they knew that the men who had pledged large sums to the venture were already heavily in debt to European firms.[22] Of greater concern to the authorities was the network of 'agitators' at the meeting, the means of propaganda they now owned and the political rhetoric they expressed. The committee of the Mercantile Bank included H. Bowari Brown, J. B. George and Obadiah Wilcox, disgruntled commercial and government clerks and former schoolmasters of twenty years' service. They each claimed that they had learned from bitter experience that the Europeans' intention for the African was 'to enslave him'.[23] Their message was carried across the south-east in pamphlets and newspapers printed on Tete-Ansa's new press and distributed by his companies.

From 1929 the colonial authorities had been wary of American trading interests within south-eastern Nigeria, and the network of radical nationalist entrepreneurs engaged in commercial schemes across the Atlantic. The ventures of Tete-Ansa and Eket emphasise that economic independence was an important cornerstone to the development of an agenda for political independence.[24] Intelligence on 'The West African American Corporation of New York' and the various Nigerian bodies affiliated to it (including the Ibibio Trading Corporation) formed the bulk of a file held in Port Harcourt labelled 'Subversive Influences' and which included, among other things, threats of communist sedition, Mahdist propaganda and the literature and lecturers linked to the other main American 'import', religious revivalist literature.

The anti-colonial tone of 'subversive and American' religious tracts during the 1930s was especially associated with the Faith Tabernacle and the Watchtower Bible and Tract Society (Jehovah's Witnesses).[25] The teachings of these churches attacked the essential bases of the colonial ideology. In some instances the effects were felt at a personal level. Shortly after arriving in Okigwe, for instance, a police constable embraced the Faith Tabernacle and was summarily dismissed because he refused to swear on oath in giving evidence before the DO.[26] In other instances these teachings assumed a broader anti-colonial scope. During 1931, for instance, W. R. Brown, a preacher from Jamaica, gave lectures at Native Court houses in the south-east. Senior figures in the administration agreed that 'His utterances, are disguised as religious teaching, but they are intended to subvert all forms of constituted authority' and that in particular they had 'a decided anti-British Government tone'.[27] He displayed tracts of the Bible with the aid of a magic lantern. One passage in particular impressed audiences. Brown explained that God had created seven world powers: Egypt, Assyria, Babylon, Medo-Persia, Greece, Rome and the British Empire. He predicted that British power would fall within months, along with the mission churches which, he said, were suppressing the poor.[28] He sold Jehovah's Witness books written by their president, J. F. Rutherford, in which the British Empire was referred to as part of 'Satan's Organisation', and in which chain stores in America and England sought to control the food supply.[29] These topics – imperialism, agricultural production and economic exploitation – were, of course, particularly sensitive in the aftermath of the Women's War, and the Resident of Owerri Province judged that Mr Brown's lectures would cause unrest amongst the 'semi-educated classes'.[30]

Throughout this period stories circulated in the north of the province of itinerant white American preachers who called meetings and asked for land to build Spirit Movement churches.[31] As a result, during the 1930s the authorities maintained a much greater vigilance over new religious movements, including revivals of the Spirit Movement, and over faith healers and itinerant preachers who were influenced by American churches of 'Christian Scientist leanings'. In December 1933, for instance, over 2,000 people were attracted to the faith healings performed by Sambo of Mbiabong Ikono, and an entirely new village of shelters and palm mats was established on the outskirts of Mbiabong in Uyo Division.[32] Another faith healing settlement sprung up near Ikpe Ikot Abiat, five miles south of Ikot Ekpene.[33] Neither was found to be politically subversive but such settlements were kept under surveillance by plain-clothes police, and were to be discouraged so as to prevent 'hysterical breaches of the peace', 'nocturnal orgies' or anything approaching the 'Spirit shaking'.[34]

By the late 1930s officials and missionaries were alarmed at the potentially subversive effects of the distribution of religious tracts from the likes of the Faith Tabernacle, along with a range of other American religious 'imports'. Post offices across southern Nigeria had set up a blacklist of persons and firms from around the world engaged in 'charlatanistic publications'. One of these mail order suppliers was R. K. Wester of Chicago whose price list indicated that he could supply various ingredients and materials for the production of 'hoodoo' love and luck charms.[35] These American suppliers introduced a range of items and ideas that were appropriated in local ritual practice, especially by *idiɔŋ*, and in due course the language of American 'hoodoo' would be used to legitimate and defend *idiɔŋ* practice against colonial opposition. The most serious threat that these particular American imports posed to imperial rule at the time, however, was the possibility that Wester could satisfy local requests for keys to open all of the government offices in Nigeria.[36]

The association between magic, medicines, drugs and crime that emerged in the 1930s also fell under the expanding scientific orbit of the colonial machinery and its medical and pharmacological departments. Criminal investigations in Calabar in the 1920s had depended on informer's evidence (from a 'Yoruba warrior') for information on 'hashish and other stimulant drugs' which included *'ikiya'* (the giver of courage) and *'agosa'* (the terroriser), both of which were made from compounds of herbs and leaves burnt to powder and which were applied by drinking or rubbing on the body.[37] Interest in specific charms was fuelled by a spate of burglaries across the province in which there was no sign of forcible entry, in which water pots had been mysteriously moved, and in which people complained of waking up with strange scratches on their bodies.[38] The symptoms caused by the stealthy burglar, scratches on the body and shape-shifting abilities point to the invocation of *ùbén* witchcraft in criminal activities, and colonial interest in this type of 'deep sleep'-inducing medicine used in Calabar Province continued.

By the late 1920s inquiries into these substances were being conducted on an academic and scientific basis. An inquiry was held by the Police Intelligence Bureau in 1929, for instance, into 'various charms for invisibility, including heavy sleep etc. used by the criminals of this country'.[39] Particular attention during the inquiry was given to the use of charms and concoctions that had been secretly administered to European officers. Three mixtures were tested by the Government Analyst, which had been given to officers in porridge and puddings. No poisons were detected; rather, the 'medicines' were thought to have been administered to officers as a result of competition for civil service posts and in order to secure favours in the recruitment of domestic servants and houseboys.[40]

Colonial interest in and anxieties about the use of medicines and charms also led to the first moves formally to prohibit Annang secret societies. Initially reported in Abak District in 1931, and then again in Ikot Ekpene the following year *'èkà ékóŋ'* players had paraded with a 'harmful ju-ju' or 'bad medicine'. They forced women to strip off their clothes under penalty of becoming barren, men were made to take off their headgear under penalty of death, and 'The juju used was reported to be so powerful that even Ntinya Chiefs dared not disobey the players when threatened'.[41] As it spread through the Annang and Ika areas the movement became known as 'Obuta-Ibok' or 'New Medicine'. It was supposed to cause sickness and death, and John Nelson, the Qua Iboe Missionary at Ika, reported that many were poisoned.[42] The chiefs in Ikot Ekpene passed a rule banning any play in their respective areas which had 'bad medicine' attached to it.[43] Nelson reported that the Government stepped in, and hundreds of 'medicine men' were imprisoned before the outbreak was suppressed.[44] While there is no surviving evidence of such a concerted campaign, the èkà ékóŋ movement did lead colonial officers to consider the prohibition of 'bad medicine' and the suppression of the ékóŋ society under the criminal code. Ékóŋ had sought to drive the church out of towns across Ibesit in 1932, having partly destroyed the Ibesit church and wounded several converts. Yet the general opinion of the District Officers' conference that year was that the society was unobjectionable in itself.[45] Regarded as a conservative backlash within an ongoing intergenerational conflict, èkà ékóŋ was a reminder that despite Atlantic innovations and new methods of colonial surveillance, the aesthetics of power, and the spiritual apparatus of engagement between emerging classes of men, and between men and women, continued to be expressed in familiar forms.

★ ★ ★

While the Women's War heightened vigilance regarding the potential for anti-colonial protests, especially those linked to or inspired by Americans, the official government response to the disturbances was characterised by the exercise of a colonial rationality in which 'native society', local histories and customs became both an object of colonial knowledge and a field of administrative activity.[46] As a result the fallout of the Women's War witnessed a programme of reforms to Native Administration based on extensive research which itself set the precedent for colonialism's recourse to anthropology and anthropologists in the aftermath of breakdowns of law and order.

In January 1931 Lord Passfield, Secretary of State for the Colonies, decided that no further enquiries would be made into the causes of the Women's War, that those officers administering the districts before the violence would not be blamed for what happened, and that the Government of Nigeria should look to the future. To this end the new Governor, Donald Cameron, held meetings in the Eastern Region headquarters in Enugu as soon as he had arrived from Tanganyika and found that the 1930 taxes, which had been reduced because of the depression, had been paid without incident. While the officers were not held responsible for the disturbances in

1929, however, their policies were. 'It should have been realised', Cameron wrote of the tax revolt, that 'no machinery based on tribal institutions was in existence through which tax might be collected'.[47] The various factors that had contributed to the brief rebellion were therefore reduced to a single concern – the failure to identify appropriate units and institutions through which tax could be collected. What Cameron meant in identifying these institutions was set out in his own memorandum, 'The Principles of Native Administration and their Application', which had been distributed to each of the administrative officers in Calabar Province in September 1931. From that moment appointed 'Native Authorities' were to became the primary arm of local administration, and the guiding principle to its constitution was that 'it consists of the persons who by custom form the ruling authority'.[48] It signalled, in short, an end to the Warrant Chiefs, and the beginning of lineage representation in the courts and clan councils.

The 'Native Administration' reforms were premised on the need for greater and more specific information about those 'who ruled by custom' and the colonial subject more generally. Investigations were to be made into the nature of the social organisation of communities in the south-east to which local government could be adapted, and senior officials looked to the new techniques of anthropology. The scientific authority of the research was, of course, considered all important and 'the anthropologist is presumably a man with a scientific turn of mind', wrote Flood, 'if he has not got the scientific turn of mind he is no use as an investigator'.[49] There was a broad consensus on the importance of anthropological research, and Passfield, for instance, noted that:

> The need for further enquiry into the social organisation of the inhab-
> itants of the South-Eastern Provinces naturally suggests the question
> to what extent the services of investigators trained in anthropological
> science have been, and may still be profitably employed ... I propose
> to take steps to improve and increase the amount of instruction in
> anthropology imparted to newly appointed administrative officers
> who are busily engaged in the work of administration to carry out
> anthropological research of great value.[50]

Coming just two years after the publication of Bronislaw Malinowski's article on the practical uses of anthropology, the post-1929 administration of south-eastern Nigeria was regarded in the highest circles as an exercise in the application of the type of anthropology with which he was associated:[51]

> The great thing is that their enquiries should not be conducted in
> the spirit of antiquarian research, but should be directed to those
> problems i.e. problems presented by native society as a living and
> changing organism, which are of immediate practical importance
> to the Administrative Officer. What is meant is that they should be

followers of the school of which such men as Professor Malinowski are the chief exponents.[52]

While Passfield was keen on training new officers, however, others were reluctant to bring in trained anthropologists from outside. In practice it was administrative officers without any special anthropological training who conducted the work of tracing the antecedents of the 'Native Administrations' Cameron had instituted in Tanganyika. 'The best use to which the Anthropologist can be put', Cameron wrote, 'is to place him at headquarters where he can study reports rendered by officers engaged in the field'.[53] It was the case here as elsewhere, therefore, that the claims of anthropology led to competition, not conspiracy, between anthropologists and officialdom.[54]

Tensions over the nature of the anthropological research, the identity of the researchers and the meaning of the reforms were played out within the 'office politics' of the Eastern Region colonial structure. In Calabar Province, for instance, the proposals for anthropological intelligence work and administrative reform were not well received. Officers in Calabar were guarded about the reforms for a number of reasons. They had been working on administrative reforms along similar lines since 1924, and rigorously defended themselves against the suggestion that these had in any way led to the 1929 Women's War. They were also sceptical about the universal application of the reforms which had been piloted in Warri, suggesting that rather than resuscitating ancient forms of self-government, the 'Warri System was as synthetic as any other – veiled under a cover of vernacular phraseology'.[55] Rather than the time-consuming meetings envisaged by the official guidelines the Provincial Resident, Falk, advised his colleagues to conduct intelligence work from district files, and from the 'great efforts made in the recent past by experienced officers to find natural rulers'.[56] He highlighted several officers in particular – the veteran P. A. Talbot, F. N. Ashley (who compiled texts for new recruits) and M. D. W. Jeffreys (who had become a 'special adviser' to the Province).[57]

Jeffreys was born in Johannesburg and won a Rhodes scholarship to Oxford in 1910. He began his first tour as an administrative officer in Calabar in 1915 and was one of the first District Officers stationed at Abak. From there he circulated small vocabulary cards among his colleagues to collect language information and an array of material artefacts during the 1920s and 1930s.[58] Along with his ethnographic compilations Jeffreys took an interest in emerging political causes attending and addressing a series of meetings of the newly formed Ibibio Union in 1929 and 1930.[59] At the meeting held in Etinan on 3 August 1929 Jeffreys asked to borrow the Union's minute book 'for careful review'. Ostensibly he did so in order to give advice to the fledgling organisation.[60] He advised the Union on administrative matters, minute-keeping, subscription rates and bank accounts as well as discussing issues of the day. Later, however, Jeffreys' use of the minute book was interpreted as the first attempt by the colonial government to spy on the Union.[61]

While in the Civil Service Jeffreys entered the University of London, taking his diploma in social anthropology in 1928 and a PhD in 1934.[62] As a result he was the first trained anthropologist to be employed within the Calabar Provincial service.[63] By 1930 Jeffreys had been placed on special duties in Calabar Province because of his aptitude at 'anthropological matters'. He compiled extensive intelligence reports and wrote on a series of topics – marriage, slavery, currency and land tenure. In each instance, especially in the context of customary law, he argued strongly for codification and showed himself to be frustrated by the pace of reform. In this, Jeffreys, who was a significant and occasionally critical voice within the provincial administration, was something of a 'frustrated radical'.[64]

In 1932 Jeffreys and other administrative officers were instructed to study Cameron's memorandum and prepare intelligence reports that would deal with 'the history and affinities of the people, their administrative and judicial organisation and proposals for reform'.[65] The future of indirect rule hinged on identifying rulers who had traditional authority and were above all legitimate:

> If the people affected are not prepared to accept the orders of the so-called authority, chief or otherwise, unless we compel them to do so then, of course, the administration is not indirect and the Native Authority set up on such a basis is a sham and a snare.[66]

Standard forms were distributed to aid the production of the intelligence reports and officers were given a set of instructions. The first step was to set out briefly the history of the people and the nature of indigenous institutions; the next step was to ascertain what remained of these institutions and in what manner they might be built upon by constituting 'executive authorities' acceptable to the people. The bulk of the report was to distinguish between administrative structures and judicial systems.[67] It needed to identify the smallest unit, the family, through the extended family, quarter, village and clan or confederation until the highest functioning unit, one which had 'executive authority' could be isolated. And in judicial terms the intelligence reports had to distinguish between those employed to judge civil and criminal trials, to show what were regarded as crimes, and how they were punished, and to recommend a Native Court location for each clan.[68] Throughout this process officers were to advise on the degree of social progress in the spheres of Christianity and education and to outline the extent of consultation they had had with local communities especially the 'Christian and educated elements'.

This, then, was the framework within which knowledge of the social organisation of Annang and Ibibio was presented and through which the institutions of colonial rule were reformed. The contradictions apparent in the instructions were barely commented upon: distinctions in indigenous practice between civil and criminal justice, prescriptions to identify geographically integral 'clans', and the exhortations to investigate ancient institutions without producing antiquarian research. The most significant contradictions that appeared from the outset were also overlooked. One of the stated purposes of the 'Native Administration' reforms was to bridge the divide between old and young, between literate and illiterate, yet the proposals to 'revive ancient organisations' were to be drafted with the consent of the 'Christian and educated elements'. Similarly, the nature of the enquiry was retrospective and, despite the pressing need for future reform, little was recorded regarding the conditions of life in Calabar Province during the 1930s themselves.

These contradictions were not lost on the provincial resident. Falk was a 'moderniser' whose political sympathies lay with the 'new elements'. He stressed that twenty-eight years of colonial influence should not be allowed to be undone:

> In making recommendations for any reorganisation you will no doubt be guided by practical administrative considerations and a reflection how impossible it would be in 1930 to return to Government through such powerful pre-conquest influences as the Aro Long-Juju, Egbo, Ekpe or Idiong. Yet these were the 'natural and indigenous rulers' within my own memory in certain parts. [69]

As a result, he advised officers not to take the idea of 'natural rulers' too literally, and argued that to do so 'would be as though a modern Government contemplated administration through spiritual organisations or Free Masons'.[70] It was not long before Falk received a reproach from the Governor for his stance and Mr Hawkesworth, whose presence was deeply resented, was sent from Enugu to prepare a 'model' intelligence report for the anthropological work of reorganisation in Calabar Province.

'WE SHALL NOT BE RULED BY OUR CHILDREN'

The rationalisation and routinisation of the reform process masked the contested fault-lines which emerge from a closer reading of the extensive intelligence reporting upon which it was based. By tracing the political trajectories of youths and elders, new and old elites, in the contest for political legitimacy in Calabar Province, the story of indirect rule is resumed here from where the classic study of the Warrant Chiefs left it in 1929.[71] Narratives that relate the unchecked powers of 'chiefs' under indirect rule, and which demonstrate their unhindered accumulation and misuse of tax and labour rights, do not completely illustrate the ways in which their fortunes waxed and waned or the mechanisms by which their positions were contested and held to account.

Governor Cameron's reforms, in which he hoped 'the educated element of the people would be more adequately represented', were heralded as an important watershed in emphasising the incorporation of the educated elite and recognising the rising tide of political consciousness which they carried with them.[72] Cameron's rhetoric of inclusion and consent was not matched in practice and the net effect of the reforms was to bolster the position of chiefs, in this case the lineage heads represented on village councils, at the youths' expense. At the height of the reform process in 1937 Margery Perham asked, 'Does not reorganisation, the present policy, tend to increase the tendency of a rift between the old and the young, between the ignorant and the educated, between the pagan against the Christian?'[73] The introduction of taxation and of the Native Administration reforms therefore failed to involve the educated elements in local administration in the formal manner intended, but instead generated opportunities in which youths challenged traditional authority and engaged in a contested relationship with the chiefs and the colonial state which was both congruent and conflictual.

There were three significant features of Cameron's reforms: courts and councils should enjoy a clan-based jurisdiction; court and council members should be selected by each lineage; and councils should be responsible for collecting and handling their own revenue. The introduction of the principle of lineage-selected representation transformed public arenas, courts and councils, and sources of accumulation, sitting fees and taxes, into spheres of intense political contestation. The reforms created a system that looked very different when seen from Enugu or Lagos, than from the village itself. From the 'top', as it were, Cameron's instructions were followed to the letter: clan councils were formed by members of village councils, who themselves were members of lineage councils and therefore had a claim to customary office. From below, however, the picture was far more complex. Lineages were not always represented on the village council by the lineage head as the reforms anticipated. Lineages and villages might, instead, send representatives who changed year to year or even month to month. As such, the council membership was highly fluid, the Government knew neither the names of the councillors nor their numbers, and these representatives held no recognised family office and could not be said to possess the customary titles that the Lieutenant-Governor sought. The courts were reconstituted on the same basis: councils selected a number of villages each month to send their representatives to sit on the court bench who may or may not have been the lineage head, and a different person was often chosen each time since the position itself had quickly become a marketable commodity. Across the province it was estimated that there were around 30,000 members of Native Authorities and Native Courts and that at least two-thirds of these were not 'customary elders' in the strictest sense.[74]

Reorganisation in the 1930s was premised on a thoroughly undermined class of shrine priests, and on territorial rather than symbolic principles of inter-village alliance. As a result, the village group or clan level of local administration became the most problematic issue of reorganisation.[75] During the research to compile the intelligence reports it was found that the indigenous political systems had 'swung strongly in the direction of fission and disintegration'.[76] Above the village, clan loyalties were very weak, and clan heads either no longer existed or had lost their political influence.[77] The prospect of future returns from office-holding would not offset the heavy cost of installation ceremonies which meant that no Adiasim clan head (àkúkú), for instance, had been installed since 1917.[78] Revived interest in clan headship led to competition and imitation. In Utu Etim Ekpo during this period it was claimed that 'Okuku regalia may be bought in the market and we have claims to Okukuship in every village'.[79] At the District Officers' conference in 1932 Captain Harvey claimed that 'The "ntinya" [chief's crown] has been greatly in evidence of late because the native knows that District Officers are looking for "ntinya". They are now bought at 2/4 in the markets'.[80]

Proposals to reconstitute clan integrity were hampered both by this reported decline in the position of the àkúkú and because villages sharing a clan affinity (of common ancestry or a common shrine) were often dispersed across a wide territory.[81] Consequently, the principle of territorial cohesion rather than ritual observance shaped the reorganisation process, and Native Administration areas were subdivided into convenient geographical areas in which villages were given a council meeting place, and, in the case of the larger areas, a Native Court of their own.[82] Abak District offers a pertinent example of the ad hoc nature of the reorganisation. Only in the cases of Ika and Ukanafun was a former clan organisation uncovered:

> The remainder of the district is divided into 27 socalled clans which appear to be more like groups of towns with common blood. These towns are not contiguous, but are scattered with towns of other groups between them. Thus it is impossible to get a clan organisation. For years successive District Officers have tried to find a solution and everyone has had to accept the lumping of this heterogeneous mass into council areas …[83]

Those communities, which would be at the centre of the man-leopard murders a decade later, were the subject of comparatively limited investigation for the intelligence reports during the 1930s. Indeed, they were grouped together as 'certain unorganised groups of the Annang tribe' and were made up of twenty-four small clans and fragments of clans within

Abak Division and eighteen on the Opobo side with many who straddled the border between them. Bisected by the Qua Iboe River, this area was also dotted with Opobo and Ogoni trading settlements along the creeks and the river itself. These factors, the shape of the clans and the fact that they straddled the two divisions, made the introduction of reforms to courts and councils extremely problematic in this area; councils were formed on a genealogical basis (as they had been unofficially for some years), and courts on a geographical basis.

The Ibesit clan was one of those that straddled the border, with its population split almost equally between Abak and Opobo Districts. Ibesit was referred to in 1937 as being renowned for inefficient tax collection, a 'chattering' council and the necessity of police work since Ibesit villagers were 'quick with a matchet and few years have passed when for one reason or another some village has not been unwilling host of a body of police'.[84] Covering an area 23 miles long by just 1½ miles wide, Ibesit's geographical shape was a clear example of the Annang dynamic of migration and settlement, and this in itself was thought to militate against the formation of a Native Administration with court and council. The Ibesits, however, refused to attend the neighbouring Abak Native Court. The council was held at Ikot Afanga until the death of Chief Ebong of Uruk Obong who had been a significant influence and a force for clan unity, after which the southern section in Opobo Division had withdrawn twice in 1936 and 1937.

Struggling to reconcile the blueprints for the native administration reforms with the shifting local political landscape, one intelligence report author remarked that 'There is more in local politics than mere geography'.[85] There was also more to local politics during the 1930s than the traditions of descent groups, clans and lineages recorded in the intelligence reports. The reports assumed a static image and overlooked the constant readaptation and reshaping inherent in both the process of lineage fission and instrumental responses to the reforms themselves. Tax collection, along with court and council representation, became a major incentive for such political realignments. The officially recognised unit for taxation and representation (on courts and councils) was the lineage (*ékpûk*). Yet throughout the 1930s, for 'mercenary' reasons, efforts were made annually to split lineages with the aim that these smaller units would gain the status of an *ékpûk* and therefore gain a share in the distribution of tax rebates, along with sitting and council fees. Villages decentralised too. The reforms provided incentives for lineage fission in Ikot Afanga, for instance, as its six lineages declared themselves autonomous villages in the pursuit of their own court independent of Ikot Okoro.

The intelligence reports also failed to grasp the ways in which local political positions were being challenged by educated young men. It was a familiar mode of political practice for elders to enable progressive young men to earn status as mediators. One of the key qualities of defining an Annang youth (m̀kpàráwà) is the ability to speak publicly (átâŋ íkɔ átú – to speak words in public) and to moderate in disputes with equanimity ('to hear from both sides'). The new dynamics of the 1930s, however, upset the balance of these relationships. Taxation created tensions between young and old and shaped the intergenerational landscape upon which the reforms of the 1930s were imposed. 'Youths report chiefs to Government and chiefs punish youths', Akpabio stated, and 'for this they find ways of killing their chiefs'.[86] This relationship between youth and elders was captured in contemporary slang terms such as ńsûŋ (fly), which referred to the impertinent actions, speech and demands of young men and women.[87] These tensions were also played out in the weekly contribution clubs. The contribution club, often referred to as osusu and known in Annang as ùtíbè, operated as a rotating credit and savings society and was especially important for young men in raising money for trading and to pay brideprice. Those subscribers who received the total amount contributed at the beginning were receiving credit while those who received towards the end were building up savings. The process by which turns were selected to receive the money was therefore highly significant. An ùtíbè club in Utu Etim Ekpo Native Court area in 1927 had 132 members. Each member paid 20 manillas on édét day and in rotation each week a total of 2,640 manillas was given to the most senior member still remaining unpaid in the group. Apart from receiving their turns ('hands') at the beginning of the cycle, the ùtíbè heads also received a greater share of the fines paid by defaulters and the small subscription fees paid when a member received their 'hand'. In this way the management of the ùtíbè appeared, 'to be very much in the control of the group heads; the members having but little voice in affairs'.[88]

The colonial period saw several changes in osusu practice as members took precautions against defaulters by documenting transactions.[89] In the Annang context of Ukanafun clan ùtíbè defaulters and corrupt patrons were shamed in songs which presented a cautionary tale to prevent embezzlement. One song, 'Contribution is not given to the young but is given to the big men', is indicative of an underlying economic tension between youths and elders. It refers to the way that young members of an ùtíbè club were not trusted to receive credit by taking their share at the beginning of the group's cycle. Rather, they were forced to save and would receive their turn towards the end, during which time the risk of default or embezzlement increased. The song is sung to a masked performer dressed as the èté ùtíbè:

> Èté ùtíbè, carry your matchet into this field,
> Your belly was big, carry it by yourself,
> Your buttocks are big and point backwards,
> The ùtíbè members swore m̀bìàm which killed you,
> Èté ùtíbè, carry you matchet into this field,

It is the matchet of the one who ate people's money,
We will bury you any place we like,
We will bury you in this pit.

The song ridicules the *ùtibè* club elder who embezzled club subscriptions. In response the members invoked *m̀bìàm* (oath/ordeal) against him from which he died. His corruption was proved by the fact that his stomach, hands and buttocks became swollen, and since he had died from *m̀bìàm* he was not buried but rather thrown into the bush.

The new opportunities afforded by tax collections in the 1930s gave 'progressive' young men the chance to organise themselves outside the *ùtibès* and to link themselves into new relationships of power. Drawing up nominal rolls and collecting taxes imposed administrative demands on lineage elders in which they became increasingly dependent on literate young men:

> Tax collection with its nominal rolls, has revealed the natural rulers, from the village to the family heads, and has placed on them a burden which the older ones are incapable of carrying out without the co-operation of the young and at least semi-literate.[90]

The process by which young, literate non-title holders were able to insinuate themselves into the new niches of indirect rule was reflected across the region and witnessed the emergence of unofficial councils by the 'vociferous, letter-writing minority'. Elsewhere in Nigeria similar 'working misunderstandings' between British administration and decentralised peoples had emerged. With the introduction of taxation between 1912 and 1916, Tiv elders, for example, refused to become tax collectors and instead those forceful often marginal young men who assumed this task were installed as District Heads, given staffs of office and the title of Tor.[91]

An example of Annang responses to the administrative reforms introduced in the aftermath of the Women's War comes from the small southern town of Utu Etim Ekpo, itself one of the sites of the disturbances. Initially, the new clan councils were formed 'close to custom' by lineage heads, but these elders soon found themselves being pushed aside by 'hot-headed and ambitious youths' and were treated with contempt by clerks and secretaries. Giving up the struggle, the elders gave way to youths, who formed themselves into a committee which imitated the procedure of organised and officially recognised councils. The new committee in Utu Etim Ekpo took charge of the court and the council. They charged a shilling from each council candidate and enrolled other young men who shared their outlook without consultation. Members of the court were appointed in similar fashion – their fee being 7 shillings. Income was also obtained from the imposition of 'fines', especially in the course of tax-collecting. These 'unofficial councillors' formed a tax collection committee which processed demand notes extraordinarily quickly because they tortured late payers by tying back their fingers to the wrist. To release himself the victim had to submit to the seizure of his goods and pay a fee of eight manillas (òkpòhò údúk – rope money). By these means the young councillors extorted a fortune in the name of government. The money they raised was loaned out on short-term deals attracting 100 per cent interest. Though this practice was widely reported, few prosecutions resulted as cash and minute books did not implicate the perpetrators, and in Utu Etim Ekpo, as elsewhere in Calabar Province, when asked why they had not done more to resist the usurpation, the elders complained that in relations with Government they were at the mercy of those who could read and write.[92]

As developments in Utu Etim Ekpo illustrate, tax collection had proved a significant stimulus in reconfiguring the relationship between chiefs and new elites and to the youths' collective action. Village tax committees in Calabar Province were seen as the political device of ambitious youths who successfully wrested power from the chiefs. Clubs and societies were formed across the eastern provinces to enable 'the collection of funds for the assistance of members for tax', and in 1936 it was reported that 'Tax Committees composed of the younger element are becoming quite a feature in Annang country'.[93] By 1937 each of the Annang Native Court areas in Opobo Division had a 'tax committee' consisting of progressive men who were responsible for the collection of tax through the lineages. Individual lineages subscribed a sum of money each and the societies then placed the sum on loan to the public, normally to approved men for trading purposes.[94] When the tax-paying period approached, the interest was divided among the lineages to ease the pressure of collecting the values of the demand notes. Commission money, a 10 per cent rebate for taxes paid on time, known as ńkpó m̀fɔn was earned by the young tax collectors.

The young men of Utu Etim Ekpo presented their tax committee as a progressive welfare society, though it was characterised by the DO as 'a pitiful copy of the Ibibio Union'.[95] The economic base of the tax committees, progressive societies and improvement unions during the 1930s was derived from these tax rebates, from clerks' salaries and from the profits of trade. The membership composition of Esop Ufon Anang, a small local union in Ikot Ekpene town, was typical and illustrates this point. The twenty-five members included five teachers, four Native Administration employees, fifteen traders and a court sitting member. The teachers and clerks held the Union's official positions while the traders constituted the bulk of the subscription-paying membership.[96] These progressive Annang traders, who generally dealt in palm oil or piassava, were mission school graduates:

> The product of the Mission school remains a villager and his social life is unaffected ... On the other hand, the product of the larger schools returns to his village discontented and superior to the old village life

... he regards clerical work as his calling in life, and faute de mieux, often takes up trading and exploiting his uneducated brethren.[97]

It is a measure of their engagement with local politics during the 1930s that by 1937 the authorities conceded that 'these societies which abound in the Ibibio and Anang districts and call themselves "Progress Unions" are in fact getting politically powerful'.[98]

A further opportunity for various categories, including young men, to usurp court and council positions emerged because of delays in the reform process most notably within the western districts of Calabar Province. Official clan reorganisation was a haphazard and protracted affair requiring research and public meetings in order to compile the intelligence reports upon which proposals were approved. Courts and councils in Abak and Ibesit, for instance, remained 'unorganised' until 1936. Given the principle of local 'acceptability' upon which Native Administration councils were to be based, unofficial and spontaneous realignments of village affiliations and council membership were often encouraged, especially when the elaborate and time-consuming process of intelligence work had not been carried out. This form of 'unofficial' clan reorganisation therefore offered young men another opportunity to seize the initiative, as they did in 1936 when the young members of a 'society' in Abak town reformed the clan council and disenfranchised the chiefs. Ousted from the council, the chiefs got up a petition whose signatories included Udo Ekong Umana, who had been dismissed as a Warrant Chief sitting on the Abak Native Court several years previously, but had regularly attended the court ever since and because of his influence was thought to have been the 'moving spirit' behind the protest.[99] Udo Ekong Umana complained that:

> Our displeasures ... have arisen from the fact that instead of the 'Re-organisation' being established in accordance with Governmental principles, our Youngmen have both wilfully and unlawfully handled same in quite a very prejudicious and disorderly manner.[100]

The young men of Abak had re-formed the clan council around their own society, which was both a 'talking society' and a 'subscription society' for the purposes of tax-paying, and which had appointed a man to assist villages in revising their nominal rolls. The society had generated sufficient funds to erect a building for its meetings which was later converted into the council hall, and it was the young men of the society who presented themselves as council members. The disenfranchised chiefs complained that as a result of the reforms these young councillors believed themselves to have been empowered by Government to:

> Own, control and become Clan Members of the Abak Native Court, quite independent of all Chiefs,

Possess a Council of their own for the discussion of all Official and Unofficial matters quite independent of all Chiefs, and,

Settle all Village disputes and supply all Government require-ments.[101]

The chiefs, led by Udo Ekong Umana, recognised that the object of reorganisation was 'the Enlightenment or Education of our Youngmen in LEGAL AFFAIRS so that their "Reasoning Faculties" may in graduality [sic] be developed in Official and Unofficial matters'.[102] Yet they saw the new council as a direct challenge to their political status and tax collection authority. They were convinced that members of the council had been 'sworn with a deleterious Juju or Mbiam to never divulge the Agendas of the Meetings to any Chief or Chiefs and that a violation by any Member must be the result of instantaneous death'.[103] The chiefs therefore sought to discredit the young councillors by accusing them of being criminals and ex-convicts, and asserted that 'we shall on no account be ruled by our children'.[104] As such, the events can be read as a power struggle between youth and elders sparked by the Native Administration reforms, and the Resident concluded that 'the petition is due to the annoyance on the part of the signatories [the chiefs] that their power as members of the Native Court or in some other capacity has been interfered with by the new system of village representation and by the fact that they have been left out of the, as yet un-reorganised, Council'.[105]

Young non-title-holders also entered the judiciary during the 1930s and, while nominally recognised by their lineages and villages, established new relationships of power outside the village. Lineage and village heads would complain that links between the District Officers and the new court benches excluded them, and that they had lost all 'countervailing power devoted to them naturally to be exercised over their subjects due no doubt to the whiteman who generally kept correspondence with the court members'.[106] This trend was widely noted in contemporary observations of the compo-sition of the Native Court judiciary: 'The bench is sometimes ... young and inexperienced, whilst old okukus may be seen seated below in the body of the court.'[107] In fact, the work of conducting the court and of cross-ques-tioning the parties and their witnesses rested with the young men: 'They are the men who collect the tax, run the societies etc.'.[108] These observations pointed to the appropriation of chiefly status by a self-made class:

Some of these members are very inexperienced; they marry no wife perhaps but sit to decide marriage cases; they own no land and buy none but sit to decide land cases; this is very unsatisfactory ... there should not be so many self-made chiefs in a village.[109]

The composition of the court benches undermined not only the position of the lineage chiefs but also the authority of the courts as a whole. There was a rapid multiplication of courts after the introduction of the reforms in 1933, and the number of Native Courts in Abak increased from six in 1930 to twenty by 1950. The increased number of courts also caused a new set of problems. New clerks had to be found and trained, but candidates attracted by the relatively low salaries did not have the highest educational qualifications. Hence, the District Officer at Abak reported that while the court clerks of this period learned to keep cash-books and to issue processes, they learned little about court procedure and still less about the law.[110] Yet, while demands for new courts increased, the popularity of the justice they offered, as indicated by litigation rates, declined sharply. Even taking into account the cash crisis during the slump, the decline in litigation, which was most marked after 1936, was attributed to the ease with which 'unscrupulous' men had found their way in to courts:

> The villages have in a number of cases sent unscrupulous young men to represent them on the benches of the court with the result that the people have lost confidence, have probably had to pay too exorbitant douceurs and have therefore preferred to have their disputes settled at home.[111]

The declining palm oil market did not adequately explain the marked decline of formal litigation in Abak Division where the decrease in the number of civil cases was 'remarkable'.[112] The unpopularity of the government-approved courts in civil matters led litigants back to alternative village tribunals and 'The extraordinary low figures point to the setting up of one or more illegal courts, but none of these has been found yet'.[113] Such courts had many merits which were absent in the Native Courts since there was little or no delay, there was no writ of summons, no journey to a distant venue, no fear of adjournment, less fear of bribery, and parties were guaranteed to be heard in full.[114]

During the 1930s the question of illegal courts was extensively revisited.[115] From Grier's 1922 enquiry onwards two questions remained unresolved: whether to embrace illicit courts, and which matters could be settled informally among the village elders rather than being heard in the Native Courts. Officials were aware of the clear distinction which had emerged between parallel systems of adjudication. It was apparent that courts representing various constituencies were being held clandestinely:

> Clan courts not recognised by Government still assemble from time to time in some areas. Their proceedings are kept in the dark, because the fines and fees which they collect are the perquisites of the judges.[116]

Equally, it was recognised that the clandestine courts, along with a broad range of informal tribunals at lineage, village and clan level, were essential to the operation of the colonial legal system. They acted as an effective filter so that most civil matters appearing before the Native Courts were, in effect, appeals arising from decisions given by village elders.[117] Without pre-screening of cases the already overloaded system would collapse:

> Without such multitudinous and sometimes petty societies with their heads and their powers of trying certain cases the village or Native Courts would be full to overflowing with trivial cases; in fact, without them, life would be impossible.[118]

★   ★   ★

It was not only the young men who populated the reformed court benches of the 1930s. The constitution of local courts throughout the decade was hijacked by both these young men and by former Warrant Chiefs. Hence, the authority of the lineage and village heads who were denied access to the court bench, was in fact diminished on two fronts, by the rising class of young men and by powerful chiefs, and was therefore:

> undermined and usurped by Warrant Members and other thrustful energetic and unscrupulous young men who have arrogated to themselves the power and right of trying cases and this alone is today respected.[119]

In every division former Warrant Chiefs levered their way back into power within a year of the reforms.[120] In certain courts former Warrant Chiefs exploited their status to such an extent that they not only sat on the bench but controlled the selection of other court sitting members. In Northern Ukanafun Native Court, for example, leading members, including Chief Jimmy Etuk Udo Ukpanah (Figure 4.1), charged an entry fee of one goat for people to sit on the court bench.[121] Born in Utu Nsekhe in 1894, Ekereuke Etuk Udo Ukpanah was the son of an àkúkú and became a church attendant with the Qua Iboe Mission in Ikot Edong in 1911 where he was christened Jimmy. He entered school in 1914 and the Boys' Institute at Etinan in 1918, from where he became a Qua Iboe teacher in 1920 earning 90 manillas per month. He resigned from the church in 1925 to become a Bench Clerk with the UAC at Ibagwa where he earned £4 per month. It was with this career behind him, and as a relatively young man, that he entered 'Native Administration' in 1928 where he became a warranted chief.[122] Under him, however, the situation in Northern Ukanafun court became so acute that by 1939 several villages petitioned for a new court of their own.[123]

In the context of these complaints, the whole of the Ibesit clan boycotted Abak Native Court because of the 'autocratic rule' of Chief Udo Ekong of Ukpum (Figure 4.1), one of the longest-serving former Warrant Chiefs. Several years later seven chiefs of Abak would lodge a damning petition against Chief Udo Ekong. As 'traditional' chiefs – ŋkúkú ìkpá ìsɔŋ – they claimed the right to raise àyèì during disputes (over land, oil palms or any

Figure 4.1 Chief Jimmy Etuk Udo Ukpanah
(Reproduced with kind permission of Spectrum
Books Ltd)[124]

valuable item) for the sum of eight manillas. While Chief Udo Ekong was
President of the Abak Native Court, however, the petitioners claimed that
he had 'entirely taken the action from us and claimed it to be the business
of the Warrant Chiefs. Then he also uses this matter in taking many bushes
from people and made them his own, or receiving much money for it'.[125]

The example of Akpan Mbori illustrates how and why the Warrant
Chiefs were able to retain their positions. Akpan Mbori was a Warrant Chief
in the Annang Native Court in Opobo Division. Several complaints were
brought against him during the early 1930s which reveal something of the
implicit compromises struck between chiefs, society and the colonial state
during this period. Five complaints (over the previous three years) were
investigated by the Opobo police in 1933 concerning allegations that the
chief had sought bribes from litigants during court adjournments. He was

alleged to have claimed that he could ensure favourable outcomes in cases either in court itself or by settling the cases in his own house. Akpan Mbori was accused by one man of asking for 12 shillings with which to 'settle' his case. The complainant, Udo Usor Udom, paid 6 shillings and was witnessed by three men including a man known as Otoko, the chief's 'go-between', who intimidated other witnesses when the case was investigated by the police.[126] The investigation into the chief was conducted by plain-clothes officers as they believed Akpan Mbori had arranged for the government rest house to be watched so as to identify those who went to inform on him. And the police, who wanted to proceed with a criminal prosecution, believed that the evidence against him, though it was based on witnesses who might be confused by a smart barrister, would be sufficient to secure a conviction. For several reasons, however, the District Officer failed to prosecute the chief:

> For a number of reasons I hesitate to institute proceedings. Annang Native Court serves an area that has not been reorganised. The Court has always had a bad reputation for corruption. Akpan Mbori ... is one of the outstanding personalities of the area. ... I have not met Akpan Mbori, but am told by Mr Usoro, the Ibibio interpreter, who has long experience of the Division, that he is an Ekpuk Head of Ikot Akpan Essien, a village of the Abak clan, and a man of person-ality, though not the Ete Idung (head chief). I have little doubt that Akpan Mbori has received the sums of money alleged, but am not so certain that the money alleged to have been demanded from the complainants, now that they have lost their cases will not prove to have been freely offered before the cases were decided. A conviction will probably lead to a crop of complaints against other chiefs for the same practice, probably just as well-founded, and ending in further convic-tions. This will hinder further reorganisation of the Annang area, as it will become a vast unwieldy body without a head, such authority as exists being impersonal. I feel that the most satisfactory method of combating corruption is by reorganising rather than by individual prosecutions.[127]

Irrespective of the character and performance of those who sat on the council and court benches, and irrespective of whether the District Officer had even met such senior 'personalities', reorganisation was clearly to be pursued at all costs.

As District Officers depended on the chiefs, even former Warrant Chiefs, so these chiefs in turn depended on the power of colonial institutions to maintain their own positions. Their relationship with colonial power, and what that power meant, however, was not interpreted in the literal and obvious ways that might be anticipated. An extraordinary exchange between the Abak chiefs and the Resident of Calabar in 1931 illustrates just how the power of colonial officers was configured and why it was so important to those appointed Warrant Chiefs. In March 1931 the DO at Abak, Captain Cheesman, fell ill and needed to return to Britain for treatment. The depression had left the province chronically under-staffed, so Abak District Office was closed and its functions were transferred to Uyo. The Abak chiefs were furious. They needed access to court files, to staff to enforce decisions, and stated that the administration of the six clans in the Abak District comprising 243 villages necessitated a District Officer. The chiefs' petition, however, was remarkable. The chiefs reminded the 'Governor of the Southern Provinces' that the buildings of Abak station were on Iso Ndem, the site of a former shrine called Ndem Eset (Old Juju):

> The Chiefs were greatly pleased after the fight [the 1909 punitive expedition] when the station was erected on the very spot where the old Ndem Eset was worshipped ... it was the place where all towns under Abak District usually met for the ceremony of the Iso Ndem. Abak is known as the priest, which means Abaka Akan Annang. The reason why good Government exists at Abak is because it had existed since the ancient time.[128]

For the Abak chiefs the power of the colonial order was derived, in part, by its proximity to a central Annang shrine and was configured with what the colonials called 'spirit power'. It is important to remember that Abak was the centre from which Annang communities expanded, and had therefore been a significant ritual nexus. The District Officer's interpretation of this petition illuminates the link between the District Office and the former shrine further. The chiefs addressed the Resident in a meeting by saying 'Without the office, how can the District Officer have power in the bush'. This was what was troubling them, the District Officer decided. 'The office was put on the site of their big shrine and since then peace and prosperity has come. They have invested the office with spirit power and it is this spirit power which makes the DO work so well. If the Office is taken away, that spirit power is withdrawn and the DO will no longer carry on as before. Also the area will go down in prosperity and peace.[129] The power of the ǹdêm animated not only the District Office, but the District Officer too, as the comments on the following exchange illustrates:

> Umana Udom (an Okuku of standing): I am not satisfied. A person given a certain food to eat gets used to it and misses it when it is taken away. Now you have taken our District Officer away.
>
> Resident: He is sick. Look at him.
>
> Umana Udom: Get a doctor to stay with him and make him better.

Resident: He must go to England to get better. I must beg you to be humane. You don't want to bury him here.

Chiefs: He is sick because he has been overtaxed with work. We think if he were given a holiday to rest he would be alright.

(N.B. Probably the question of spirit power is underlying this. The restoration of the office would bring back the spirit power and the District Officer would be alright.). [130]

★   ★   ★

Despite the vernacular interpretations of Governor Cameron's reforms, the public reception focused on the stated aim of resuscitating the 'ancient' institutions of chiefs and clans. At this level, the reforms were very unpopular with two groups – the Christian missions and the educated elites of local improvement unions including the Ibibio Welfare Union. What had been seen as a progressive policy was reversed, the missions believed, because the economic depression and consequent revenue shortfalls had forced the Government to retrench. In Ibesit, Mr Graddon of the Qua Iboe Mission argued that the reforms undermined his work:

> Powers of administration have been put back into the hands of heathen chiefs, resulting in a kind of revival of heathenism. In some places the native Christians are being threatened and intimidated. With the terrible depression on one hand, and the recrudescence of heathenism on the other, many of our little churches are having a hard time ... [131]

The effects of the policy were confirmed in the minds of the church leaders by the 'bad medicine' outbreak in 1932. In addition, by the late 1930s the churches reported that they had lost prominent young men who were leaders within their congregations as a result of the Government's 'Native Administration' policy because they had become attracted to lucrative positions in Native Courts. [132] The world depression of the early 1930s checked the Qua Iboe Mission's plans for expansion. Scores of teachers had their small allowances cut by half in 1932. In 1934, as the value of the manilla fell, so the teachers' allowances were reduced again. It is clear that economic change, currency fluctuation and mission conversion were intimately connected. Throughout this period declines in the palm oil trade and the manilla exchange rate led to unrest from within the Qua Iboe congregations and to demands for less restraint within mission doctrine, especially regarding polygamy. The link here is clear. As times became hard, the demand for additional household and farming labour, that is women's labour to cultivate cassava as a subsistence crop, increased, and calls for male converts to be allowed to marry more wives grew louder. This was the primary reason for the popularity and growth during these years of the 'Missions of native origin' like the African Church which accommodated polygamous unions.

The poverty of the Qua Iboe Mission's enterprise during the mid-1930s in Annang and Ibibio communities translated into a schools programme which was widely criticised. Investment by mission societies in the education sector was limited, and contemporary colonial observers reported of the mission schools operated by the Qua Iboe and Roman Catholic churches in Abak District in 1924 that they were held in 'inadequate bush buildings run by semi-illiterate native teachers. Under these conditions it is doubtful whether more harm than good is being done in the name of Christianity'.[133] In congregations around Abak district Qua Iboe members complained that the church refused to provide higher education since it wished to encourage students to enter the clergy as 'teacher-preachers' rather than allowing them to enter government service which required Standard VI.

The Ibibio Union responded to local educational ambitions with a fund-raising campaign which lasted ten years and culminated in the award of six scholarships in 1938 enabling one student from each of the districts to study overseas: Asuquo Idiong from Abak (medicine at Howard University), Ibanga U. Akpabio from Ikot Ekpene (education at Columbia), Bassey U. A. Attah from Uyo (agriculture at Tuskegee Institute), Obot E. A. Obong from Itu (medicine at Edinburgh), Egbert Udo Udoma from Opobo (law at Dublin and London) and James L. Nsima from Eket (education at Storer College). The impact of university-educated elites, and these six in particular, was to reanimate the Union's social, political and economic agenda on their return and was manifest in demands on the state for support for the Ibibio State College sponsored by the Union, which was inaugurated in 1942.

While it was busily engaged with local educational plans, the Ibibio Welfare Union also expressed its opposition to the council and court reforms of the 1930s, objecting vehemently to the potential disintegrative dynamic they introduced in emphasising discrete clan identities. 'Unity alone', the Union wrote, 'will help us on to progress and advancement. Other tribes, e.g. the Yoruba, advance because of unity. We must develop a pride for things that are Ibibio and unite together to overcome our difficulties'.[134] This rhetoric was further expressed in proposals to strengthen the alliance between the Annang and Ibibio districts by forming a single administrative unit including a scheme for improved conditions of service for clerks (Unified Native Administration Scheme),[135] proposals to relocate the provincial headquarters more centrally, and petitions in support of Nyong Essien, who was nominated as a member of the Legislative Council in 1938 for a new constituency styled 'Ibibio Division' which encompassed the Ibibio Mainland Territory of Calabar Province.[136]

These proposals were undermined, the Union believed, by the Government's 1933 reforms, which reinforced the principle of clan-based jurisdiction in forty-one of the fifty-one Native Courts in Calabar Province in 1932.[137] The union's opposition to these reforms is most clearly expressed in its petition to the Resident of Calabar Province which highlights the critical role of young men in destabilising the process:

> ... Before the advent of the British Government, each tribe [clan] in Ibibio land was secluded from one another by thick forests. ... after the coming of the British Government and the Missions these natural enemity [sic] and misunderstanding were totally eradicated and the old tribal hatred and jealousy gave way to intimate friendship and unity. Some years ago the question of re-organisation of the Native Administration according to the Native Laws and Customs arose. ... the Union, which has the interest of the affairs of Ibibio at heart, take this opportunity to point out most humbly to His Honour that the re-organisation (if to be worked out as is being done now) is not purely native or primitive, that is a wholesale partition of Ibibio into numerous minute clans, which since the advent of the British Government and Missions lived formerly in friendly terms with their neighbours.
>
> ... We believe that the Government embarked on the idea with a good motive but the unscrupulous chiefs and young men desiring to rule and have a sway in everything have caused bitter enemity [sic] and unduly rivalry between one clan and another as a result of this the future of Ibibio seems very uncertain. ... In particular the union observed that the system of administration had led to a situation where a member of one clan could not expect a fair hearing in another clan court and where discrimination on the basis of clan had become widespread in entrance to schools and churches and in the appointment of native administration officers.[138]

The Ibibio Welfare Union's development during the 1930s should be seen in relation to the colonial state and its policies and to the missions and their economic capacities. Its agenda may therefore be viewed as a critical response to the economic and political neglect of the Ibibio-speaking interior of Calabar Province, and in particular to the 'laissez-faire orientation of British policy for administration and development'.[139] It also needs to be set within the emergence of new languages of citizenship developed among the progressive elites of the so-called 'patriotic unions' that stressed unity in the face of division and loyalty in the face of subversion. Tracing this social genealogy of nationalism during the 1930s reveals a complex array of agendas and affiliations, ranging from the young men of local tax committees who covertly usurped their elders' privileges, the provincial elites of the Ibibio Welfare Union who directed their attention to the details and inequities of colonial rule, and nationalist trans-Atlantic political entrepreneurs like Peter Eket. The colonial response to these nascent political movements was more or less blind to localised events, but was rather shaped with one eye on the radicals in Lagos, and the other on improvement union meetings in towns and villages across the east. During this period the agendas of these two groups differed; the former were concerned with the politics of pan-African independence, the latter were occupied with the 'politics of improvement'.[140] There is, therefore, a need to be wary of a teleology which would equate the 'progressives' of the 1930s to the post-war 'political class' since 'There was … a certain disjunction as well as a linkage between "nationalism", *qua* the national anti-colonial movement, and the local political tendencies related to it'.[141]

WOMEN AND THE 'INFAMOUS TRAFFIC'

In late July 1930 M. D. W. Jeffreys witnessed an *èkóŋ* theatrical performance in Nung Ita, Uyo Division.[142] *Èkóŋ* is a good example of the performance of 'humorous masks for serious politics', as the issues tackled in the satirical drama were evidently weighing heavily on local minds.[143] The play was a bawdy romp, a series of sketches, and the afternoon's performance dealt with a range of contemporary issues, including armed robbery, the local politics of tax-collecting and evasion, bribe-taking among court sitting members and the delays of the colonial judicial process. The skits were loosely connected by the recurring presence of a character playing a night guard who was leading a group of young men in search of women. Through his performance the sketches captured various angles on the shifting political terrain of sex, marriage and reproduction, which focused in particular on issues of prostitution, adultery, abortion and desertion.

The play, which was performed by wooden puppets and actors in costume, opened with a story that the annual village sacrifices that were supposed to prevent illness in the village (presumably *ǹdɔk*) had led instead to all the men's testicles becoming swollen. This was interpreted as retribution for their frequenting of prostitutes at Ikot Offiong market. Ikot Offiong was the principal market in the exchange of yams from northern Cross River communities for dried fish from the coast. Swollen testicles, which result from gonorrhoea or elephantiasis, were regarded as punishment for adultery.[144] While men were ridiculed for their adulterous behaviour, the sketches went on to relate tales of new economic tensions between men and women, highlighting the tensions caused by a lover's demands for gifts, and of a wife's desertion, on the Port Harcourt-Enugu train in one sketch, for a wealthier paramour.

Also ridiculed in the play was the transgression and apparent collapse of different forms of moral boundaries. The increasingly permeable gendered boundaries to knowledge associated with the secret societies were satirised, for example, when one of the characters joked, 'If any of you women care to pay me one fowl each I will reveal to you the secrets of ekpe'.[145] Christians too were subject to ridicule as the *èkóŋ* players targeted the apparently lax and ineffective penalties for adultery demanded of church-goers. The final scene, the conclusion of these male–female contests and one which is given little comment by Jeffreys in his notes, might be seen in a rather more ominous light. Of the two central male characters one pays yams for the fattening and circumcision *(èwànà)* of a woman he intends to marry, the other, out of jealousy perhaps, attempts to kill her with poison bought from itinerant Hausa traders.

Evidence from this Ibibio drama illustrates just how contested the fault-lines of gender politics were in Annang and Ibibio villages by the 1930s. There were two conflicting trajectories in this field – a discourse on female emancipation, and a backlash by senior men to control domestic labour and household reproduction. Over time the role of the colonial state in this process had shifted:

> The early impetus to reform African marriage laws in the name of female emancipation was replaced by support from the colonial state for the preservation, and in some cases the extension, of male power.[146]

The watershed marking the shift between these moments, one emancipatory the other less so, was the Women's War. Yet both before and after, the steps taken were faltering and inconsistent.

A series of initiatives in the 1900s relating to the protection of mothers of twins had directly intervened in customary practice within the household so as to ensure that the emerging colonial state, especially the new courts, gave women access to 'avenues of escape'.[147] In 1907, for instance, action for desertion and non-support was taken in Ikot Obong Court against husbands of women who had given birth to twins. Officials had seen them 'adrift' and in a starving condition, and many women were received back into their families.[148] In Oron steps were initiated in 1909 to protect twin children with provisions under the Births and Deaths Ordinance so that parents of twin children had to register their birth and ensure they were presented at court every three months so that they might be seen to be safe from violence.[149]

These limited reforms were not translated into a comprehensive programme, however, despite the efforts of the Commissioner of Calabar Province, Horace Bedwell. Set against suspicions of a revival of the slave trade, and the suggestion that a range of marriage practices, including pawning, child betrothal and divorce settlements, contributed to the 'infamous traffic', Bedwell outlined rigorous plans for the codification of marriage in a draft 'Native Marriage Ordinance' in 1915. During the course of Bedwell's enquiries (he claimed to have met with every Native Court bench in Calabar Province) he found that the chiefs overwhelmingly supported the idea of submitting existing customs to a set of rules enforceable in the Native Courts. The chiefs appeared particularly anxious, Bedwell wrote, that their customary law regarding 'dowries' and marriages should be 'reduced to writing'.[150] Such support for reform was hardly surprising from those older men and chiefs who could therefore establish and extend their own claims in an arena over which they presided.

Commissioner Bedwell's proposals were designed to prevent what was seen as the most prolific and most offensive form of slave-dealing, the trade in young girls under the pretence of child betrothal. His draft ordinance sought to prevent the practice through a process of registration and certification so that failure to provide a marriage certificate would be taken as proof of slave-dealing. Lord Lugard, however, rejected the elaborately drafted plan. He argued that the registration procedures could not address the problem of whether the bride entered the marriage by consent or coercion. Lugard went on to question whether it was advisable to attempt to introduce a legal form of betrothal and marriage at all and doubted the usefulness of rules for the payment of brideprice and for the granting of divorce.[151]

While plans for the codification of customary marriage practices in 1916 were aborted, the issues involved would be revisited regularly. Attempts at reform involved brideprice standardisation, marriage registration and the regularisation of divorce. The Eket chiefs briefly adopted new matrimonial guidelines in 1922 which limited brideprice to £12 and set a minimum age of fifteen before girls could be married, but the chiefs in Opobo opposed these reforms and insisted that brideprice was never less than £30 (2,880 manillas) and that girls could be married at the age of nine. These faltering steps during the 1920s were shaped by the administrative load of matrimonial litigation, mounting uncertainties in the face of variations across the province, and colonial fears of the relationship between marriage practices and slave dealing. Commenting on the way in which men were able to marry a young girl and divorce her with a full refund of brideprice many years later, the Resident at Calabar complained in 1924 that 'the fact that women do not know their state of bondage and degradation does not exonerate us. ... something must be done to prevent injustices in the Native Courts'.[152]

In the first attempt to regulate and limit the refund of brideprice when a couple divorced, Jeffreys, the District Officer at Ikot Ekpene, proposed in 1923 that the amount of recoverable brideprice should be legally restricted to £10 in order to simplify and expedite court work and so reduce the overall number of matrimonial cases.[153] As a result of the changes consequent upon the introduction of British rule, Talbot noted, 'matrimonial "palavers" form a fruitful cause of litigation'.[154] Jeffreys argued that such a step would have the effect of limiting brideprice generally to a fixed sum thereby levelling the 'matrimonial market' and enabling women to have some say in their choice of husband.

Jeffreys' main concern, however, was with what he called 'indirect slavery'. He sought to impress upon the authorities the need to close loopholes in divorce suits, especially the practice of allowing parties other than the woman's parents to be sued for the return of brideprice. He was adamant that only the woman's father, and not any new husband, could be sued for the refund of brideprice and urged the authorities to uphold the local saying that 'the men who ate the dowry must refund it'. In fact, he argued that for the old husband to receive his refund from the new husband, thereby bypassing the woman's lineage and marriage sacrifices, amounted to slavery:

> If it were allowed that a husband secured his dowry from the man to whom the girl has run, a serious train of evils would ensue. The slave trade under the guise of marriage would revive. A wealthy Calabari would come into the Anang hinterland, pay £10–£12 dowry for a girl wife, take her to Calabar and 'marry' her to another man for £15–£18. It is seen at once that the second transaction is not a marriage.[155]

In a 1926 survey of divorce in Calabar Province, called for because of an apparent increase in matrimonial litigation, court benches were asked how they dealt with adultery, divorce and desertion, and who could be sued in each case. The case files from Eket Division showed that divorce action was taken by three sets of people: young girls who had been married when children but refused to live with their husbands once they reached puberty; husbands who had 'tired' of a wife; and women who left because of a dispute with a co-wife or because she went to live with another man. In each scenario Eket courts granted divorce and the refund of part or full brideprice. In Ikot Ekpene, however, brideprice could also be reclaimed through the courts on the death of the wife. The chiefs in Opobo and Uyo stated that the husband was not allowed to sue the person to whom the woman had gone for the return of brideprice and that actions for the return of brideprice should be brought against the woman's parents only. Yet this view was not echoed across the Province. In Abak Division, for instance, the courts allowed the husband to take a civil action against whoever was 'detaining' his wife – either her parents or a new husband.[156] These variations in customary practice concerning divorce and adultery led to renewed calls for codification. The officer in Eket concluded that: 'The whole lack of regularity in procedure is most unsatisfactory, and the introduction of uniformity throughout the Province would be of the greatest benefit'.[157]

The net effect of these albeit uneven and inconsistent innovations was that by the time of the Women's War, popular songs and plays of the time, such as ńdɔ́k úfɔ̀k èbé, captured the greater confidence women had in expressing their choice of marriage partners and the demands they might make of husbands.[158] From Utu Etim Ekpo, scene of the violence in 1929, for example, it was observed that women's status had been improved by the removal of the often inhuman nature and injustices of Native Marriage Laws. It is not uncommon to hear a protest from a Native Court bench that the emancipation of the women, which native custom denies and humanity demands, is causing them to become independent and disobedient to their husbands.[159]

The new freedoms women experienced also found expression in religious conversion. By the early 1930s the Qua Iboe Missionaries noted the increased conversion of young women:

> For long the Anang women appeared indifferent and unimpressionable, but now the light has penetrated their darkness ... About 120 Christian women gather at a special monthly meeting ... It is significant that the number of girls attending the village schools, conducted by our Native Evangelists, reveals an increase of over 140 per cent'.[160]

These young girls, 'surrounded by a cordon of customs', had been largely prevented from engaging their curiosity and attraction to mission teaching. For their mothers conversion meant the shame of a daughter not entering fattening (*mbòbó*), while fathers also feared the loss of brideprice: 'The fact that Christian girls are not fattened for marriage, has made heathen mothers very cautious lest their daughters should come under Gospel influence'.[161] During the early 1920s Christian girls regularly brought cases that they had been forcibly abducted so that *èwàná* specialists could perform body cicatrisation and circumcision. A decade later this coercion had eased, though older women were still concerned that clothing (especially of Christian women) covered *èwàná* markings and concealed the visual means of establishing a woman's character. 'The lament of the elderly Ibibio women', Jeffreys recorded, 'is that today there is no telling whether one is talking to a respectable married woman or to an *uwok* [*àwɔk* – non-initiate], the dress levels all'.[162]

In part these changes were linked to the growth of the Qua Iboe Mission's Girls' Institute. The Institute became a finishing school for young girls to prepare them for a 'useful career as the wives of some of our Christian teachers'.[163] This aspiration was fulfilled in 1920 when two of the 'graduates' married 'Native Evangelists' working at the various out-stations. An evangelist married to one of the 'old girls' was heard to say, 'I thank God for the Girls' Institute, which helped to make my wife what she is, a good house-keeper and a good mother'.[164] In part also, the Girls' Institute had developed as a haven for both the mothers of twins and for the increasing numbers of young girls escaping marriage betrothals in which their fathers had entered them as children:

> Last week a young girl appeared out of the bush .. and asked for shelter. She had run away from Okat, pursued by her people, and

came to us – the old cause so general here – a young girl sold to an old man to be his wife, and in his case given in exchange for another who had died. She objected and after being beaten ran away. The English law now protects such girls if they remain firm and have friends to help them to fight their battles ...[165]

Women often sought sanctuary with the mission churches to extricate themselves from child betrothal pacts. Wives also sought divorce to resist their husbands' religious choices. Cases arose where women left their husbands, for instance, because their husbands sought to determine which church their wives should attend. In one such case the husband insisted in court that his wife leave the Qua Iboe Mission and follow him to the African Church; even though she had invested in the brideprice to marry another woman to the man, 'he still make[s] palaver'.[166] As this instance shows, women could still be sued in Native Courts in spite of the Chief Commissioner's statement to the League of Nations in Geneva that 'in these days of emancipation' a woman converted to Christianity and married to a pagan may leave him if she wishes and does so with no pressure other than moral persuasion on the part of her family or her husband. 'The Native Courts are not invoked to compel her to return,' he claimed, 'nor would they have the power to do so if they were'.[167]

Women's new social mobility was part of a wider generational and gendered dynamic that exercised older men during the early 1930s. The grievances set out by the chiefs of Abak Itenge in Abak District in 1932, for instance, illustrate that specific concerns focused on the sexual politics of the Annang household. Disaffected by witchcraft accusations against them, annoyed that their '*àyèi*' law was regularly ignored by the young, and anxious at the behaviour of women within the lineage, the elders blamed the Qua Iboe Mission and sought to evict the church from their village in which it had been established for over a decade. The chiefs complained:

> 2. That the Qua Iboe Mission forbid our wives neither to obey us, sleep with us at any time nor to do the necessary home businesses for us; and that if any of us died our wives would not mourn for the departed husband nor be present at the funeral. ...
> 4. That the Qua Iboe Mission permit our ladies to roam about, hunting for a man immediately the husband dies without mourning for the husband, contrary to our Native Laws and Custom. ...
> 13. That the Qua Iboe Mission empowered our children to violate our laws and customs, preventing our daughters from marriage, and thus encourage all manner of evils.
> 14. That our daughters are being married in Church without the knowledge and consent of the parents.[168]

Each of these concerns, framed in the colonial discourse on 'native law and custom', related to the anxieties of senior men and their perceived loss of control over dependants.

After the Women's War the colonial authorities became more accommodating of the concerns of senior men. The impact of the Native Administration reforms of the 1930s on the politics of Annang marriage and the social mobility of women has been interpreted in contradictory ways. It has been suggested, for instance, that the introduction of the 'massed benches' in the newly reformed courts of the 1930s further benefited women by eliminating corruption at the hands of the Warrant Chiefs, and that this 'made their persons and property more secure'.[169] This is a common assumption about the effects of the fallout of the Women's War and the reforms of the 1930s in the Eastern Provinces; these may have to be reassessed in the light of evidence of Annang and Ibibio women among whom the rights of person and property after the watershed of 1929 were far from secure. In recognising indigenous judicial institutions, the reforms of the 1930s were represented as a return to 'old ways' and an opportunity for elders and chiefs adjudicating according to 'customary law' to expand their powers over women and junior men. The youth, missions and even the administrative officers therefore complained that support was being given to those who upheld morally unacceptable traditional values:

> Considerable strength has been added to the older ideas by the establishment of tribal courts and the appointment of aged traditional chiefs who support old traditions, though abhorrent to us, in accordance with native law and custom.[170]

Although he was instrumental in bringing many of these issues of marriage and matrimonial litigation to light, Jeffreys recognised that the prospects for reform under this new administration were bleak: 'With these okuku in charge of their tribes old practices are likely to be revised and among them the execution of persons who have won cases against them in the present courts, torture and the flogging of women'.[171] It was against this background, therefore, that the case for codification of 'Native Law and Custom' pertaining to marriage, adultery and divorce was proposed by men like Jeffreys in the 1930s. There was 'no more effective control over rapacious chiefs and avaricious heads of families', Jeffreys argued, 'than public opinion backed by a common knowledge of native law and custom'.[172]

As a direct consequence of the reforms, women's room for manoeuvre was restricted. Yet, for several reasons the chiefs' new-found control over formal judicial mechanisms did not serve as a complete brake on the intra-household dynamics of the 1920s. Under the reformed Native Administration court benches had greater scope to invent legal traditions and bolster the authority of senior men. In this way men could restrain women's attempts to extricate themselves from oppressive marital relationships through the formal courts. But this was not uniformly so. On the one hand, administrative officers retained powers to grant women divorces, thereby undermining the elders' power, so that seeking divorce through the courts became a crucial strategy.[173] On the other, some women would continue to refuse marriage and discover alternative 'escape routes' by supporting themselves through prostitution or beer-brewing in the emerging urban centres or further afield.[174] As the èkóŋ performance illustrated, the 'freedom brought by open highways and trade' could dislocate social and family life in a number of new directions.[175]

These directions are evident if we trace the shifting patterns of colonial discourse on the emancipation of women, and the moral collapse of marriage and the family after the Women's War. In particular this discourse focused on prostitution, migration and slavery. The link between marriage and slavery was part of everyday discourse. In 1931 a case was heard in Utu Etim Ekpo in which a husband had become indebted to a trading firm. In his troubles he 'ran to the church people and profested [sic] becoming a Christian' and 'put away' all of his wives except one. Divorce therefore could be a way of realising one's assets so long as claims to refunded bride-price could be secured. In this instance the husband demanded £8 from his wife to refund her own brideprice. For her part she demanded to be released from the divorce judgment, 'which sold me as a slave'.[176]

Police investigations into slave-dealing in 1935 highlighted the way in which the link between slavery and marriage was fuelled by underlying economic factors including the poverty of parents, the large surplus of girls because young men were unable to pay the increasing proportion of cash brideprices demanded of them, and the pawning of children to raise money and repay debts. Police also cited the procurement of slave children as symbols of wealth among known dealers on the Cross River as contributing to a demand that was serviced by Aro middlemen.[177] The police found little evidence of such practices in the western Annang Division, but in Opobo Division pawning and prostitution were reported causes of child abduction and fraudulent child marriages.[178] The incidence of prostitution in Opobo relative to the rest of the Province was high. In 1937, for example, a police report listed sixty women described as 'living a life of sin' in the township.[179]

Fears of human trafficking and of a revival of the slave trade also developed on a new axis during the 1930s with the dramatic increase in migration of Nigerian workers (mainly Ibibio and Annang) to the island of Fernando Po off the coast of Calabar. With the introduction of cocoa to the island in 1854 its diverse population of indigenous Bubi, colonial Spanish and resettled slaves abandoned trade and launched headlong into cocoa cultivation. By the turn of the century the island was the world's tenth largest cocoa producer. A declining indigenous population combined with the increasing scale of cultivation when big land concessions were authorised to Spanish plantation companies in the 1920s increased the colony's dependence on mainland labour supplies.[180]

Anxieties over the supply of Nigerian labour to Fernando Po were dominated by a need to avoid the kind of international condemnation over indentured labour levelled at Liberia in 1931 when the League of Nations inquiry halted the labour traffic. Nigerian labourers were attracted by the prospect of saving money by working on the island as half of the wages were paid only at the end of a two-year contract. With the outbreak of the Spanish Civil War in 1936, however, conditions on the island deteriorated and recruiters resorted to deception to entice young men to leave their homes. Many travelled to the coast at night and in the darkness were told that they were crossing a river to work at the UAC rubber plantation near Calabar but instead entered ocean-going canoes to cross the treacherous straits to Fernando Po. By 1939 there were 6,100 Nigerian workers on the cocoa plantations on Fernando Po.

The colonial authorities and the 'reading public' were also sensitive to the labour situation in Fernando Po because of familiar fears about slavery and marriage. Rumours surfaced in the late 1930s that young girls from Ibibio and Annang villages were being kidnapped and taken, perhaps to the Enyong Creek and Cross River, where they were sold into slavery or to prostitution in Fernando Po or the Gold Coast. A literate bicycle repairer from Utu Etim Ekpo, John Ibanga, for instance, wrote a 'tip to the Government' in the local newspaper highlighting the continued practice of 'indirect slave-dealing' between Annang villages and Andoni communities on the coast with the connivance of local clerks who wrote out marriage contracts to conceal the trade, especially at taxation time, in young girls between six and ten years old.[181] Such stories focused public attention on the issue of child betrothals. The most heinous of child betrothals was considered to be where the prospective husband was a woman. 'Woman-husbands' on the Cross River, in fact, elderly 'madams' seeking to stock a brothel, gained a dubious reputation for deceiving parents that they represented their brother or other relative who worked as a teacher or a clerk in Lagos, Kano, Jos, Zaria or Accra and had commissioned her to procure a wife for them. Numerous child-stealing and slave-dealing cases were brought to court during the period, and in each of the cases from Arochukwu and Ikot Ekpene it was suggested that the children involved had been taken to the Cross River, chiefly the Afikpo, Obubra and Ikom Divisions.

Many considered that even under the licence of a labour treaty signed with the Spanish in 1943 to regulate recruitment, the transport of labour to Fernando Po still continued illegally and constituted a revival of the slave trade. 'Illiterate, heartless and avaricious' parents in Itu, Ikot Ekpene, Uyo and Abak Divisions were accused of having sold young boys and girls 'like chattels'. One provision in the treaty caused considerable anxiety at the time. Labourers were permitted to take up to two wives and any number of their children under sixteen years with them. The question was, wrote Kay from Ikot Ekpene from where the majority of labourers were recruited in 1943, 'whose wives, and whose children?'[182] He thought the situation was 'fraught with peril' and that the Government would have to address two problems: first, of young women upon whom no brideprice had been paid leaving for Fernando Po without their parents' permission, and second, of 'a number of virgins or near virgins between the ages of 12 and 16 [who] will be sent as "daughters" and it is not difficult to imagine their ultimate occupation in Spanish territory'.[183] In the context of ongoing correspondence with the Gold Coast about the traffic in prostitutes from the upper reaches of the Cross River, Kay argued that marriage registration was necessary to ensure that 'child-wives' were not exported and that no 'alleged' daughters over the age of ten were permitted to go overseas.

In his correspondence with the Governor of the Gold Coast, the Governor of Nigeria claimed that there was hardly a family in the Obubra and Ogoja province without an interest in the trade in prostitutes along the coast.[184] He also claimed that the trade was organised by 'societies' who had representatives in the Gold Coast and who received the women and established them on their arrival. 'It is even claimed', the Governor wrote, 'that the fees extracted from the women have rendered the societies so affluent that they are able to build houses and provide legal assistance for their clients'.[185] There was in fact a growing number of petitions for the repatriation of women which resulted in several initiatives organised by improvement unions to return groups of women found in the coastal cities to their rural villages up-country.[186]

By the 1940s brideprice issues had become a major concern for the authorities. The cost of marriage had become prohibitively high and 'young women either go to husbands who have paid only a small fraction of the dowry demanded with the result that litigation ensues, or else go abroad as harlots'.[187] Administrator-anthropologists like Jeffreys and Kay continued in their attempts to pluck law out of this confusion in order to suppress what they considered the various 'evils' associated with Annang and Ibibio marriages.[188] Despite continued discussion of marriage registration and brideprice standardisation no action was taken and they could only conclude that 'today there is little security or stability in marriage'.[189] The imperative for government intervention in matrimonial practices was justified within a discourse of moral collapse. It was judged that over the previous thirty years of colonial rule, 'with the freedom brought by open highways and trade, the social and family life is breaking up as sons no longer serve their fathers or their gods, and they no longer serve their sons'.[190]

WAR AND PUBLIC, 1939–1945

Throughout the war years the Information Officer, Rex Stevens, conducted briefing tours giving lectures on the progress of the war in public reading rooms and churches across Calabar Province. The war effort gave many causes championed in the progressive discourse of the 'reading public' a new economic and political imperative. A range of economic issues – the manilla exchange rate, tax collection, school funding and palm oil production – would dominate their concerns, along with a growing list of 'social ills' which would fall under their increasingly vigilant and vociferous purview, including court corruption, masquerade violence, child betrothal, human trafficking and juvenile delinquency. Their campaigns were literate, generational, Christian and increasingly nationalist.

The war years witnessed a maturation of 'progressive' political discourse expressed by an expanding 'reading public'. It was not only the educated elites and public letter-writers for whom written English was gaining in importance. An increasing readership of so-called 'semi-literate' traders, school-leaver clerks, bureaucrats and servicemen also fostered a new urban popular culture in the form of the 'Onitsha Market Literature', a pamphlet literature comprised of images from western cowboy movies, love stories and the adventures of legendary merchants.[1] With a broader base of public opinion to which to appeal, the progressives' tone during the war gained in confidence and authority. The spirit of this moment would link the progressive discourse of the educated elites to the radical nationalist discourse of the would-be trader tycoons and their trans-Atlantic trade schemes. Overall the war witnessed a shift in public opinion from petitioning to censure, and an overtly public sphere was cultivated by the improvement unions, the press and the literary societies.[2]

The political ground shifted quickly during the war with the effect that the views of the progressive elite and the radical nationalists began to converge. At the beginning of the war government propaganda efforts sought to deflect local agitation by enlisting the support of the anti-colonial nationalist faction. By the end of the war, however, the nationalist agenda had broadened its constituency and it was not only the radical core that the Colonial Government attempted to outflank but also the improvement unions and the conservative press that had affiliated to and were supporting emergent nationalist political parties.[3]

'JOHN BULL' AND THE READING PUBLIC

During the late 1930s events in Europe had seen the interests of the radical nationalists converge with the views of more mainstream progressive elites. This process was hastened by rumours of the transfer of Nigeria to German sovereignty printed in the *West African Pilot* which reached the Nigeria Youth Movement (NYM) in November 1938. Among the 500 traders, teachers and local chiefs at the NYM meeting in Aba was Prince Peter Eket Inyang Udo. There he heard his friend and new business partner O. A. Alakija condemn the prospect of the transfer of sovereignty:

> The British Nation had never conquered Nigeria but the Nigerians, of their own accord, had invited Britain to be their protector. That in compensation for her protection she had received the mineral and agricultural wealth of the country. Now it was realised that this wealth was diminishing because of the invasion of the country by European firms Britain was prepared to throw off her yoke of responsibility and hand the country to Germany. British policy in Nigeria had broken down the rule of the native chiefs and now that the people were no longer united and in a position to resist interference they were to be handed to a nation who was well known throughout the world to be Negro haters.[4]

Pre-war propaganda by British colonial officers highlighted precisely those aspects of Nazi policy that would affect the anti-colonial elite. Summaries of Nazi policies which curtailed freedoms on citizenship, marriage to Europeans, access to higher or university education, the ability to travel to Europe and the right to strike and form trade unions were circulated to newspaper editors in 1938 and 1939. It was no coincidence, then, that Reverend Potts Johnson, the NYM chairman, reminded his audience that German rule would have significant consequences: no lawyers in court, no police, no trade and no church-going. The fear of such a prospect and the effect of this propaganda were significant. While the resolution passed at the NYM meetings was that if Nigeria was transferred to Germany it would constitute the 'most serious breach of trust ever known in the history of any race', it was passed with 'undivided loyalty to the throne', unanimous support for the launch of the 'Nigeria Defence Fund' and the meetings dispersed to the tune of 'God Save the King'.[5] As the war drew on, however, this loyal chorus faded.

It was a measure of the 'patriotic' ethos of the improvement unions that in 1940 the Ibibio Union asked the Governor not to regard it as a separate body distinct from the Native Authorities because membership of both councils and the Union was so common. The Union outlined to the Governor its desire to be considered part of the administrative structure and represented its role as a mediator: 'To go hand in hand and interpret the policies of the

Government to natives, to see that the laws and orders of the Government were kept, and [to be] a medium through which the government can speak to the Ibibio tribe as a whole'.[6] At the District Officers' conference in 1940, however, delegates deplored the tendency for the Union to consider itself above the authority of the District Officer (and to go over their heads to the Resident or the Chief Commissioner), and they disliked the way in which the clan councils were subjugated to its wishes: 'The councils should be representative of the villages and the people but their opinions were only representative of the Ibibio Union'.[7] The Resident of Calabar Province suggested that it would be unwise to go against the Union, and that it would be 'very bad policy to antagonise them'.[8] He cited the fact that when, through pressure of work, a DO could not attend one of the Ibibio Union's annual meetings, there would be open talk of a boycott.

As the Resident's advice implies, by the outbreak of the Second World War the Ibibio Union had become a significant political force and was increasingly recognised as such both by communities, through the Clan Councils, and by the authorities:

> The Ibibio Union … every year becomes a greater influence in the Ibibio country. It has attracted the best elements of the Native Admin-istrations in addition to Ibibios of the educated and employed classes to its active membership. Its opinions and advice are increasingly followed by the Clan Councils. It is consulted by the Administrative Staff on matters affecting the Ibibios generally as for instance the question of maintaining or reducing the existing tax rates when it was definite in its opinion that they could safely be maintained. It has [also] concerned itself with the conditions of service of the employees of the Native Administrations.[9]

The Union was galvanised by the return of graduates from Britain and America in the mid-1940s, who became instant 'personalities'. Celebrations for the return of Dr Egbert Udo Udoma (see Figure 5.1) on 25 October 1945 included a reception, where, dressed in his barrister's wig and gown, he handed back the packet of 'sand of his fatherland' which had been given to him eight years previously to confirm physically and metaphorically his status as a 'son of the soil'.[10]

Beyond the high-profile groups such as the Ibibio Union it was reported that across the country during the war there was 'a craze for organising improvement unions, leagues, movements and clubs' which, in the rhetoric of the time, were being organised 'with but one common objective which is African re-birth, part of a recent avid thirst for advancement'.[11] The increasing political and economic weight of the unions led to fears among the colonial staff that failure to regulate the unions would lead them to divert their activities into 'undesirable channels'. In the absence of legislation to register the improvement unions, it was recognised by this time that 'Such unions are increasing in number and represent a definite social trend which is a part of the political consciousness of the country'.[12]

In tandem with the Ibibio Union, the arena in which the concerns of the urban elite were debated in Calabar Province was fostered by the bi-weekly journal, the *Nigerian Eastern Mail*. The style and content of Nigeria's newspapers had been influenced by those published in Sierra Leone and the Gold Coast since the 1850s.[13] The wanderings of the coastal intelligentsia and their professional acumen in law and journalism figured directly in the publication of the *Nigerian Eastern Mail*. The *Mail*'s proprietor, C. W. Clinton, had come from Sierra Leone and spent his early career in Accra, where he met and married Muriel McCarthy, daughter of the Chief Justice of the Gold Coast in 1901. He practised law at Sekondi until 1919 when he left for Calabar to become leader of the Eastern Bar. His son, James, was the *Mail*'s editor.

Figure 5.1 Dr Egbert Udo Udoma (Reproduced with kind permission of Spectrum Books Ltd)[14]

When it was launched in 1935 the *Nigerian Eastern Mail* had a circulation of 2,000, rising to 3,160 in 1937.[15] The paper's editorial stance was independent but conservative, and consequently was highly regarded in colonial circles. The Resident of Calabar Province commented, for instance, that it was 'remarkable for its tone of moderation and intelligent criticism'.[16] Indeed, when the government faced increasingly robust populist attacks from the overtly nationalist 'Zik Press' during the war, it had even more reason to welcome Clinton's tempered editorial policy:

> The comparatively healthy tone of public opinion in the Province is due in no small degree to the influence of Mr JV Clinton, Editor of the 'Nigerian Eastern Mail'. In refusing to be coerced into the parrot-like repetition of empty slogans, and in attempting always balanced, reasoned and progressive comment on matters of public interest, Mr Clinton has continued to render most valuable public service.[17]

Just after the war G. I. Jones conducted an unofficial survey among the reading public of the south-east. Five publications figured, including the two government journals (the *Gazette* and the *Nigeria Review*) and three commercial publications (the *Nigerian Eastern Mail*, the *Nigerian Observer* and the *Eastern Nigerian Guardian*). The *Gazette* was popular among civil servants as it was the official organ of the Government; the *Review*'s readership grew during the war because of its coverage of Nigerian troops serving overseas; and almost 30 per cent of Jones' sample read Zik's *Guardian* for whom the charismatic editor's syndicated column 'Inside Stuff' was a particular attraction. In the 1946 survey 15 per cent of the newspaper-reading public took the *Nigerian Eastern Mail*, and did so for the accuracy of its reporting and the balance of its views expressed in Clinton's editorials. These features made it the leading journal in Calabar Province.[18]

The relationship between the *Nigerian Eastern Mail* and the various improvement unions in Calabar Province was close. Several local agents, press representatives upon whom the papers were heavily dependent both to report the news and to sell copies, were leading members of the Ibibio Union. S. E. Hezekiah was the *Mail*'s representative in Uyo and then Port Harcourt before taking up an appointment with the Ibibio Union's National Secretariat as a Field Secretary in 1948. His successor at the secretariat, D. F. E. Essessien, was also a 'freelance journalist' covering stories in Uyo. During 1948–49 the newspaper had a regular 'Ibibio (State) Union' column, and Clinton himself, who was the head of the Calabar Provincial Union, used the paper to present his own political platform.

James Clinton launched a political party through his editorial column in 1944. His manifesto for the People's Party of South-Eastern Nigeria anticipated the future debates that Clinton's editorials would lead. The manifesto proposed a radical agenda of abolishing Native Administration (including all 'traditional dignitaries and chiefdoms'), deciding Native Court benches by ballot, codifying customary law, providing mass education, encouraging stronger consumer co-operative societies, establishing women's representative bodies and defending freedom of speech.[19] While Clinton's political ambitions were far-reaching, his achievements were few. Here it seems likely that his Sierra Leonean heritage almost debarred him from office. In March 1944 the nomination of Gage O'Dwyer as the representative of Ibibio Division to the Legislative Council was met with stinging opposition on the grounds that he was a Sierra Leonean and as such was 'ignorant of the life and thought of the Ibibio people'. Clinton launched his manifesto within a few months. Shortly after its launch, Clinton reported that nobody had signed up for his party. In cosmopolitan Lagos it mattered much less that political careers were launched by newspaper owners who were largely Sierra Leonean descendants. In the provinces it mattered a great deal.

Clinton's *Mail*, however, galvanised another group to this progressive cause during the war – soldiers.[20] Annang solders serving in the Middle East and South-East Asia (Burma) had kept in touch with the public in Calabar Province through the newspapers. The soldiers aligned themselves firmly within the 'progressives'. The 'Annang Boys of Ikot Ekpene' serving in the Middle East, for instance, contributed the sum of £26 7s as a first instalment towards the Ibibio State College Fund in October 1945.[21] Their letters home also called for the development of social infrastructure in Abak. Sergeant Ekpe serving in India, for example, complained that while a fifth of his command came from Abak Division they had heard nothing about the development of the area and called for schools, hospitals, roads and the abolition of the manilla currency.[22] Of all the concerns voiced by eastern Nigerian soldiers on service in India and Burma during the war, reports reaching them from relatives of the escalating costs of brideprice had worried them most. Fears were aired in open letters that servicemen's savings were being spent by relatives on luxuries, in marrying wives and of over-inflating brideprices. The rising cost of brideprice led to calls for councils to set brideprice rates.

In the context of trade, the war years witnessed increasingly vocal opposition to European firms, especially the United Africa Company (UAC), in the local press. The tone of the commentary and criticism during the war was set by the columnists who wrote in the *Mail* under the names Candidus and Impetus and who were stinging in their criticism of the UAC's hypocrisy. They showed how the higher prices for which palm products were bought in Liverpool meant the company had 'fleeced' local producers; how plans for plantations were a ruse to confiscate land; how producers were not trained by the company and could not afford its machinery; and how the comforts for UAC employment applied only to European staff.[23]

This attack on European trading monopolies resonated with earlier campaigns led by the radical tycoon nationalists. By the late 1930s Peter Eket had enjoyed a revival of his fortunes. Returning to New York he established 'American African Overseas Ltd' in April 1937 and secured another deal to export Nigerian palm oil to the United States.[24] Back in Nigeria he had become closely linked with O. A. Alakija, the son of A. A. Alakija, a prominent Lagos lawyer and member of the Legislative Council. Alakija junior was also a lawyer and was based in Aba. He was a member of the Nigerian Youth Movement and a known nationalist agitator. In 1938 during the cocoa hold-up in the Gold Coast he supported palm oil selling boycotts in Warri. Together Eket and Alakija formed the 'New Africa Company' which was to organise the direct export of palm products to the US in conjunction with local suppliers such as the Ibibio Farmers Association, which was formed in 1939. In October that year Alakija addressed 3,000 members of the association in Uyo claiming that the New Africa Company intended to 'represent the entire farmers of the West Coast of Africa on the world market'.[25]

The transatlantic deal fell through because of the war and the difficulties of acquiring export licences when the British brought palm oil purchasing under central control. In the process, however, Alakija had been circulating information in the south-eastern provinces that 'America was willing to assist in the economic development of the Nigerian as a step towards the achievement of native independence'.[26] With the onset of war the threat of the compulsory purchase of palm products, which would prevent local producers from shipping their own commodities, was met with vocal opposition from the Ibibio Farmers Association. The Association claimed that it had the finance in place for a new deal with New York and therefore had contracts to fulfil in America which would be undermined by the Government's proposals.[27] The Commissioner rebuffed their petition saying that their decision 'not to sell your produce to the Home Government at this time of War means that you are for Hitler'.[28] Nevertheless, the threat of a palm oil 'hold-up' was sufficiently serious for the Nigerian Government to petition the Colonial Office to permit the proposed transatlantic trade deal despite the wartime restrictions because of its political implications.[29]

Peter Eket joined the National Council of Nigeria and the Cameroons (NCNC) in 1944 and was quick to support Zik and to make announcements that the future for unity and self-government lay with joining the National Council.[30] Even the relatively moderate members of the literary club in Ikot Ekpene were debating self-government in August 1944.[31] This growing mood of opposition was inflamed by the introduction of a raft of legislation in 1945. The various unions, associations, societies and clubs which made up the NCNC called on the public to oppose the legislation. Of the Bills opposed, the Minerals Ordinance, which vested rights to these resources in the Crown, was especially unpopular and was deemed incompatible with treaty obligations and inconsistent with protectorate status. Opposition from the press and the reading public towards this 'Imperial roguery' galvanised support for self-rule:

> Had we been a democratically self-governing people ruled by a government that effectively reflected the view of the people of the country, that government would be the proper authority to administer our mineral resources in trust for the whole nation.[32]

Collectively, then, the 'educated elements' increased their pressure for progressive, democratic reform. In 1945 Governor Arthur Richards stated that the NAs had to be prepared to adapt themselves to modern conditions: 'The system of indirect rule cannot be static. It must keep pace with the development of the country and at once find a place for the more progressive and educated men'.[33] It is all very well for His Excellency to say this, the *Mail* reported, but '[t]hese old patched bottles can't hold the new wine'.[34] Richards' constitution itself received bitter condemnation and, in an interview with British parliamentary delegates, J. V. Clinton argued that the Richards constitution could never be regarded as democratic.[35] His criticism was directed at the complicity and complacency of the chiefs:

> We are not at all surprised knowing that even our Eastern chiefs who claim no divine descent ... but are just ordinary selfish men grimly clinging to their petty privileges and vested interest, would have swallowed the whole thing with enthusiasm. ... chiefs ruling by right of birth irrespective of merit, education and experience is a dangerous anachronism in modern Nigeria. The attitude of the chiefs all over the country to the Richards Constitution is the best possible propaganda against 'indirect rule' so-called.[36]

As an indication of the conjunction of these factors and the convergence of nationalist interests, Peter Eket had become the president of the Ikot Ekpene branch of the Ibibio Union by 1944, and the Lagos branch of the Ibibio Union joined the NCNC in 1945 on the grounds that it was 'the only body putting up persistent resistance to the Richards Constitution'.[37]

While it increasingly engaged in a political discourse of national and international significance, the reading public in Calabar Province focused their attention on three local issues during the war: corruption, education and the economy. Each of these issues was critiqued for its own failings, and these criticisms in the spheres of local government, economic management and 'development' formed key planks of the nationalist cause.

★   ★   ★

Court corruption controversies were exposed across the Eastern Region during the war years. In most instances familiar abuses came to light

– clandestine courts and court sitting members receiving bribes. In their overt relations with the colonial state the unions conducted anti-corruption campaigns and petitioned for judicial reform. The case of the 'Ukanafun A-Lights' from Abak District illustrates the way in which opposition to court corruption also operated as a political springboard to positions of power. The 'A-Lights' reported cases of court corruption to the District Office in Abak during the 1940s. The 'A-Lights' were the petition writers of colonial Ukanafun and while they had enjoyed very limited formal education, their disposable income, mobility (they each had a bicycle) and resulting access to the hub of the administration made them particularly feared by court sitting members. The 'A-Lights' included cloth traders, money-lenders and farmers who had risen to prominence as founding members of the Qua Iboe Mission churches in their villages. They included Asukwo Ekerikor, a government informer from Nkek; Akpan Anwanyi, a cloth trader and founder of the Qua Iboe Church in the village of Ikot Akpa Nkuk; Udo Akpan Essien, a money-lender, the first man to have a bicycle in the village, and also one of the founders of the Qua Iboe Church in Ikot Akpa Nkuk; Akpan Ebebe, a farmer from Ikot Ukpong; and John Umokan, a cloth trader. In 1945, after the Government called for Native Court sitting members to be named in a move to restrain the excesses of the selection process a petition was lodged at Abak that one of the 'A-Lights' themselves, Udo Akpan Essien, should replace the lineage-backed members representing Ikot Akpa Nkuk on the Southern Ukanafun Clan Court:

> We … beg to state that owing to bribe which is causing much trouble in court … that Ikot Akpa Nkuk village must have only one repre-sentative chief in court instead of four. As such we and the okuku beg to recommend one Udo Akpan Essien of Nto Abak family to your worship, who is a good trader, a well-to-do gentleman, honest and a good justice. That Mr. Udo Akpan Essien dislike[s] bribe and disgraced many representative chiefs reporting them for receiving bribe …[38]

The following year Udo Akpan Essien and Akpan Ekerikor both appeared in an application for the approval of court members made by the Southern Ukanafun Court Chiefs.[39]

Such local contests and controversies were part of a wider dynamic in which the literate elites positioned themselves so that the chiefs and the colonial state might be held to account. Across Nigeria the emerging politics of nationalism were tied to the politics of corruption. In Oyo Province, the Egbe Omo Ibile Ijesa in Ilesha was engaged in an anti-corruption campaign which exploded in a riot in 1941.[40] Drawing directly on colonial administrative practice the Calabar-based *Nigerian Eastern Mail* instituted the 'inspection tour'. The newspaper's editor undertook an annual provincial tour and weekly reports filed by divisional correspondents included regular inspection reports. These divisional agents toured headquarters, schools and clinics, prepared copy on such things as canteen cleanliness and the size of staff accommodation, and presented their report at meetings with the DO or the Resident where they demanded improvements and new amenities.

This process extended to the court room and council hall. During the early 1940s improvement unions sought to broadcast their opposition to court and council corruption more widely. In a manner similar to that adopted by the local newspaper delegations, the Ibibio Union conducted 'enlightenment campaigns' and toured the Ibibio and Annang districts during 1941 and 1942, holding albeit poorly attended public lectures in local council halls. Leading the 'subjects of instruction' of the Ibibio Union's campaign were exhortations to pay tax and oppose bribery. The Union maintained its vocal criticism of bribery within the judiciary and observed a distinct deterioration since the introduction of taxation which had ushered in reforms to the Native Administration system:

> Bribery is practised in courts, councils, villages, everywhere justice or help is sought. No recommendations are made of any person for employment, no case is heard, almost nothing is done ... without first receiving a reward or bargaining for it. ... A host of young persons, indolent and inexperienced; and many self-made poverty-stricken chiefs, who, before the advent of taxation and councils and the system of 6–8 men sitting as court members, were relegated to the background, have today been drafted [into] the courts and councils only to seek dishonestly means of living by practising bribery in its multifarious forms.[41]

In his editorials Clinton bemoaned the 'curse' of bribery which had spread to every government department, court and European firm, and whose net effect, he claimed, was to undermine the war effort: 'We are accustomed to the traditional types of bribery and corruption. The native court clerk, interpreter or messenger on a salary between £1 and £3 a month building a couple of storey houses, owning lorries, keeping harems, and so forth. Or the African head of department fleecing aspirants to appointments ... Then of course there is the court sitting member who sells his judgement to the highest bidder'.[42] The war produced new circumstances in which corruption in the commercial field had reached an 'unprecedented stage'. The papers claimed that the complicity of African big business was just as much to blame and that despite the wartime price controls, 'we will see a crisis if it is all left to the managers of big firms doing deals with traders to sell ... on the black market'. Overall the *Mail* implored public opinion that its hopes of rising to nationhood would be dashed if it continued to be based on venality and corruption in public life. Clinton called upon the improvement unions to take the lead and to exact a pledge from their

members along with civil servants, court members, beachmasters, interpreters, commercial clerks and the like that:

> They might be required, while foreswearing all forms of corruption,
> to abstain from grand entertainments at which much expensive liquor
> flows, from an undue sartorial display, from many wives and they
> might resolve to dress their wife, or wives, if it must be more than one,
> with due moderation befitting their legitimate financial status.[43]

The evangelising message of the Union's tours was explicit: 'Let us refrain
from sowing bribes, so that we may not reap bribes. For if everybody refuses
to demand and to offer these sinful gifts, then bribery shall give place to
just dealings, discipline and prosperity'.[44] Anti-corruption was a key plank
in the progressives' attack on the Native Administration system. The Ibibio
Union's tours were, in fact, a province-wide reflection of similar processes
initiated by progressive young men at village and clan level. The Calabar
Provincial Union, for example, conducted an 'enlightenment' tour of the
province which lectured on the war effort and raised a donation which was
handed over to the Resident in 1942,[45] and Esop Ufon Obong (Obong Clan
Union), formed in 1943, also held 'propaganda' meetings on 'Education,
oil and kernel production, the importance of agriculture to the community,
sanitation and against bribery'.[46]

The progressive discourse broadcast in these tours was also captured in
the editorials of a short-lived publication, the *Ibibio Magazine*. The *Ibibio
Magazine*, edited by H. J. P. Akpankure, was discontinued in 1948 following
the authorities' introduction of publication licences. In its first issues in
1941, however, the *Ibibio Magazine* outlined a range of advice on becoming
an enlightened subject, especially by emulating European civility. Hints on
improving spoken English were published, for example, along with articles
entitled 'How to do what the white men do', which identified the need
to have faith in method, keep good time, be a good judge of character
and commit oneself to service.[47] Nevertheless, while the anti-corruption
tours and such publications upheld colonial ideology in its own terms, this
message ran parallel with a more explicit nationalist tone during the war.
The *Ibibio Magazine*'s inaugural issue, for instance, also described the path
to national independence through individual economic endeavour:

> As long as we do not break these chains, our poverty shall increase
> simultaneously with our book-learning and economic independence
> shall be very far from us. ... he who only waits for the government or
> the benefactors to raise him to riches and independence shall fail; and
> he who will not learn to evade the subtle hands of the oppressors shall
> never be emancipated by sighs and complaints.[48]

★　★　★

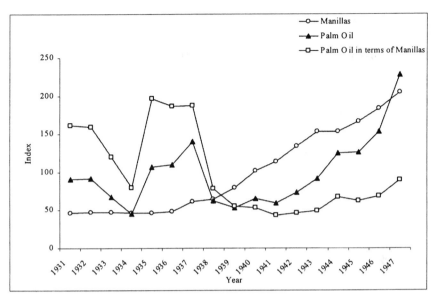

Figure 5.2 An index of manilla exchange rates and palm oil prices, 1931–1947[49]

Throughout the war years one economic issue in Calabar Province above all preoccupied the 'reading public': 'the Manilla menace'. The boom–bust cycle of the 1930s had dramatically exposed the currency instability within the manilla area. In the slump years the manilla depreciated, with 1 shilling exchanged for 20 manillas in 1934. Just two years later, in the boom year of 1936, however, the manilla had appreciated and 1 shilling was exchanged for 5 manillas. A sharp depreciation marked the late 1930s when the exchange rate stood at 13 manillas to the shilling between 1938 and 1940. The manilla subsequently appreciated rapidly in line with the rising price of palm oil because commodity prices were increased as part of the war effort (see Figure 5.2). During 1942 the shilling lost a third of its value against the manilla in less than six months, by 1943 the average exchange rate was 8 manillas per shilling, and by the end of the war one shilling was exchanged for just 5 manillas.

In practical terms domestic budgeting was relatively straightforward when the manilla-shilling exchange rate was 1 shilling to 12 manillas since there was effective parity between a manilla and a penny. Yet the introduction of British currency denominations in the manilla zone was insufficient and ineffective. Daily purchasing of small quantities in the food 'chop' markets required small denominations of currency, which was not matched by the limited supply of halfpennies and tenths. At the same time the conversion rates of such small denominations against the manilla were difficult to calculate; only the shilling was large enough to ascertain its manilla equivalent. The lack of small denominations led to price inflation for those paying in shillings. Food costing 3 manillas was worth 4½ pence when the exchange rate was 8 manillas to the shilling, but the seller would ask for 6 pence as it was the nearest equivalent available coin.

The impact of the wartime economy on the key indices of the palm oil price and the shilling–manilla exchange rate for residents in the manilla districts fell disproportionately on those who received their incomes in West African currency. While wartime economic conditions were hard for commodity producers and wage-earners alike, the fluctuations of the manilla exchange rate in this period exacerbated the situation for the salaried class. Sharp increases in the price of imports during the war (a rise of 226 per cent between 1939 and 1945) were not matched by increases in commodity export prices (which rose by only 180 per cent). The cost of living, therefore, soared and while the national picture was one of high inflation and declining real wages, in the manilla belt the position was exacerbated for those paid in 'coin' by the sharp appreciation of the manilla in 1942. A reduction in the exchange rate from 12–13 manillas for a shilling to 6–8 for a shilling marked almost a 50 per cent reduction in the purchasing power of salaried employees, such as the labourers and clerks employed by the Government and the trading firms who were buyers of local goods and foodstuffs which had to be paid for in manillas. The impact of price rises and the exchange rate was most acutely felt in Abak Division where salary earners in mission and Native Administration employment complained of a shortage of food such that 'at present yams and rice can only be obtained by wealthy people'.[50]

Faced with mounting pressure, the Government responded in 1943 with the Manilla Currency (Amendment) Ordinance, which empowered local councils to fix the exchange rate. A scheme at Opobo to standardise the manilla at the rate of 8 to 1 shilling was introduced under the ordinance but failed because Abiriba traders refused to abide by it when the manilla was steadily appreciating in line with rising palm oil prices. In March 1944 a committee representing the Civil Service Union along with the Yoruba, Igbo, Efik, Hausa and Cameroons community in Ikot Ekpene petitioned the Government on the manilla problem. Their concern was that the new legislation which allowed Native Authorities to standardise the manilla rate was not applied to Ikot Ekpene where the rate had fallen to 6 manillas to the shilling. The economics of the situation was neatly grasped by this committee:

> It is now known that every 1/- rise in the price of palm produce denotes the going down in the number of manilla exchange and eventually devaluation of the King's money. But since the need for oil for war works may necessitate further rise in prices, there is likelihood of

[the] value of manilla currency rising as high as one for one shilling if no steps are taken.[51]

Committees like this, along with meetings of the literary clubs, quickly adopted the editorial lead of the *Nigerian Eastern Mail*. A salary of £5 per month was reduced to £2 10/- in the manilla markets, the paper reported, and the unfortunate average earner was confronted with the universal rise in prices of all commodities with only 50 per cent of their purchasing power. The *Mail* and its 'progressive' readers petitioned continuously during the war for the Government to end the 'manilla menace' and for it either to standardise the exchange rate or remove the currency from circulation:

> This ancient anachronism has been a thorn in the flesh of workers in the Manilla area who receive their pay in his Majesty's coin. The illiterate persons and market women from whom the worker has to buy his daily food have almost a superstitious regard for the Manilla and will receive payment in no other form of currency. It is obvious that the erratic fluctuation of the exchange rate of the Manilla for coin of the realm can hit the worker cruelly hard and at times practically reduce the purchasing power of his salary in the market by as much as fifty per cent.[52]

In this light it has been suggested that during and immediately after the war these economic pressures had reached such a state that the potential was high for 'a major economic crisis with unpredictable political repercussions in the manilla belt'.[53]

★ ★ ★

The politics of education, and the private sponsorship of overseas education for 'sons of the soil', in particular, was a further, highly visible public concern for the literate elites during the war years. The recipient of an overseas scholarship was expected to return as an exceptional 'personality', an overnight big man with his own means. The occupation returning students pursued was their own decision: Udoma became a successful lawyer, Akpabio the headteacher of the Ibibio State College when it opened on 1 March 1946. One avenue, government service, however, was guaranteed to attract the sponsors' chagrin. Another of the returning graduates, U. A. Attah, discovered this when he was accused of deserting the Ibibio Union to enter the Government's agricultural department. Scholarship funds attracted local and national political support and they were not intended to train someone for routine duties or to trade off government training over private initiative. Rather than enter government service, Attah had been expected to launch a largescale commercial farm on behalf of himself and the Ibibio Union.[54]

Schools and scholarships sponsored by local elite unions were funded in various ways including the collective sale of palm fruits, village subscriptions and from the use of rebates that were refunded as an incentive for the timely collection of taxes.[55] Indeed, tax commission funds were highly prized for the contribution they could make to education projects. The imperative for educational facilities in Calabar Province was tangible and was shared by 'A-Lights' and elders alike:

> It was not difficult to convince chiefs that unions were necessary in modern times and that if only they would support 'sons of the soil' who had been abroad … Those sons would import not only bright ideas but also education … Soon these Chiefs were giving up their rebates on taxes so that the unions might have funds.[56]

The path of inter-generational co-operation on investment in education, however, was not always smooth. A notable clash between intellectuals, chiefs and the state concerned the Abak Chief's (Cooperative) Scholarship Fund. The origin of the debate lay in the untimely death in 1942 of Asuquo Idiong, a scholar nominated from Abak District in 1938 and funded by the Ibibio Union to study in Canada. Elites and elders alike sought to secure a replacement from Abak, but by this time the Ibibio Union was financially committed to opening the Ibibio State College at Ikot Ekpene and government scholarships were highly competitive. In April 1945 the chiefs of Abak District who sat on the Divisional Advisory Council (made up of four members from each of the nineteen clans) put forward a plan to appropriate the 10 per cent rebate paid to tax collectors in order to contribute towards a new scholarship fund. The District Officer, F. R. Kay, advised the chiefs that this proposed appropriation was illegal since the tax collectors (1,521 *ekpûk* heads in the District) had not been given any opportunity to consent to this use of their property in this way. Instead, the DO worked for the next three years on the formation of a co-operative society in which the terms of its constitution set out that members would be liable to contribute an equivalent sum of 10 per cent of the tax they had collected. Furthermore, under guidance from the District Officer, the chiefs were persuaded to adopt a rule stating explicitly that the funds should not be used for overseas scholarships, but that a proportion should rather be reserved for local boys' scholarships, and that the co-operative would embark on the construction of a girls' boarding school up to Standard VI.

The controversy caused by this shift from an overseas scholarship to local primary education introduced tensions between the new District Officer at Abak, F. R. Kay, the leaders of the Ibibio Union (notably the returning scholars, Udo Udoma and Ibanga Akpabio), the Abak elite of the Abak District League (including John Ibanga and S. E. Hezekiah) and the Abak chiefs (particularly Chief Udo Ekong). These were the *dramatis personae* who would later come to prominence during the 'man-leopard' murder investigations and the party politics of the 1950s. Frederick Kay had entered service in Nigeria in 1931, and acquired a reputation similar to the former District Officer in Abak, M. D. W. Jeffreys. The two men shared many concerns, and in 1936 they had written a paper together on land tenure in Nigeria and southern Cameroon. Both were pro-codification and pro-interventionist. Before taking up postings in Ikot Ekpene and Uyo, Kay had been instrumental in investigating disturbances at Ayiga in Obubra Division in 1938. He applied to be the Director of Prisons in 1944, and in his tenth tour (February 1945 to May 1946) he was posted as District Officer to Abak. Abak's 'energetic' District Officer had a reputation for being extremely strict; he sacked several Native Administration staff (especially treasurers) within weeks of his arrival.[57] Like his predecessor Jeffreys, who had encouraged the initial collection of contributions for scholarships when he attended Union meetings in the early 1930s, Kay took a keen interest in the Ibibio Union and the development of the intelligentsia.

The Ibibio Union members, particularly those from outside Abak Division, maintained that all funds raised for education should be invested in the Ibibio State College at Ikot Ekpene. The very existence of a co-operative scheme in Abak was seen to undermine the Union. J. U. Eka (Co-operative Inspector and one of the founders of the Ibibio Union) was accused of betrayal in assisting the co-operative scheme, and Kay reported that: 'The Ibibio Union is determined to obtain absolute control over all funds voluntarily raised in the Ibibio-Annang area for education'.[58] Both Akpabio and Udoma were dismissive of the proposed co-operative. They argued that local primary and secondary education should be funded by the Government and implied that Kay himself had appropriated the tax collector's remuneration.[59] In this opposition to the plan the Ibibio Union was joined by the Abak (Division) Improvement League led by J. E. Udom and S. E. Hezekiah, who publicly criticised the scheme in the press. Hezekiah, Secretary of the Abak District League, complained that: 'Abak wants to train her sons overseas so as to take her early stand in the Government Ten-Year Plan'.[60] He went on to urge Abak people to stand together and fight against 'this sort of obscene and dirty business of "divide and rule"', and to resist 'imperialist domination'.[61] The League argued that girls' education was adequately catered for and that unions in Oron and Ikot Ekpene had both used the 10 per cent for overseas scholarships:

> It has been incumbent upon us as the progressive and enlightened natives of this division who are sons, daughters, brothers and relatives of the tax collectors who are the legitimate owners of the 10 per cent tax to view the position critically and to emancipate our respectable chiefs from the grip of ignorance and ill-advice ...[62]

In undermining the Ibibio Union's subscription programme and rejecting the possibility of overseas scholarships, the chiefs had been set on a collision course with local unions. The League's opposition to the scheme 'wears the aspect of a fight for power' between the masses and the upstarts, the *Mail* reported when supporting the scholarship plans:

> The League is torpedoing one of the most sensational educational schemes. It is giving the impression of being a political machine operated from the outside, no doubt by one or two who wish to study law in England at the expense of their country youths.[63]

Such criticisms concerning the use of funds by improvement unions to sponsor overseas university courses had been rumbling on for some time. In 1940 the Ibibio Union apparently learned from a missionary that: 'It was becoming the general opinion of Europeans that the union was a clique of self-interested place seekers and not what it purported to be, an organisation for the betterment of the Ibibio people'.[64]

The dispute over the Abak Overseas Scholarship Scheme became heated and personal. The Ibibio Union's new 'propaganda officer' wrote in the *Mail* that the progressive scheme was being 'frustrated by John Bull's "red tape"', and that this particular 'John Bull', who claimed to be a law student in one of the British universities, wanted the Ibibio Union wiped out.[65] Though most accepted Kay's amendments, it was broadly acknowledged that his intervention had misjudged local expectations. The views and political stances of the reading public themselves, the chiefs and the state were therefore laid bare during the dispute:

> The DO's proposals are reasonable and in our view were made in the best interests of the Abak people as he saw them. However, they did not happen to square with the views and sentiments of the majority of literate natives of Abak Divisions and Ibibio opinion in general ... the members of the Advisory committee were nearly all illiterate and were quite unable to grasp the pros and cons of the matter. Moreover like most of our 'natural rulers' they have been trained to obey the adage 'when in doubt agree with the DO'. So they set aside their original contention. Poor Innocents! Public opinion in West Africa today means the opinion of the educated minority who act as trustees for their illiterate brothers.[66]

During the Second World War the Colonial Office wanted to encourage co-operation between the customary and educated elites – they saw no reason to make any irrevocable choice between them. Yet taken together the disputes over courts, currency and scholarships that occupied the progressive 'reading public' during the war reveal two key developments. First, these incidents signalled the emergence of a self-styled progressive class of young men who were not merely the intelligentsia returning from overseas study but included a broad range of school-leavers, mission converts and traders – the 'A-Lights' who 'straddled' bureaucratic and business classes. And second, these public debates captured an increasingly exasperated tone in the relationship between the 'reading public' and the colonial state's policies and personalities. Increasingly, these frustrations were channelled not only against individual cases, but against the system as a whole.

CASSAVA AND CRIME

Economically, the war tied the colonies closer to the metropole. The direct impact of the war on the Eastern Provinces in Nigeria was threefold. First, 43,000 men from the Eastern Provinces were enlisted in the armed forces. Second, the supply of palm oil, the region's primary cash crop, assumed a strategic significance which increased its demand. And third, the resulting export price gains were outstripped by the cost of living, which rose dramatically as the prices of imported goods almost doubled. The connections between economic conditions during the war and a regional crime wave were imprecise but apparent.

The demand for Nigerian palm exports became especially urgent after 1942 when the Japanese victory over Allied forces in the Far East cut off supplies of fats and oils from Malaya, the Philippines, Singapore and British North Borneo. As a result Nigerian exports were subject to price controls to ensure the supply and affordability of essential goods for the British market, and from 1942 firms were appointed as buying agents for palm oil for the West African Produce Control Board. In order to stimulate the production of palm oil for export the price was steadily increased from £6 3s 4d per ton in 1941–2 to £13 1s 6d per ton in 1945–6. A major campaign to increase the export of Nigerian palm oil was launched in March 1943 which included the threat of compulsory measures to compel farmers to harvest and process palm produce. The corresponding 'kernel drive' was launched with the slogan 'Get cracking with your kernels and knock out Hitler'.[67] Pre-war initiatives to increase production were revived, including the promotion of hand-presses which roughly doubled in number in the Eastern Region to 1,400 between 1938 and 1945.[68] Despite these measures, however, the overall quantity of palm oil exported fell annually. More palm oil was exported in 1938–9 (123,228 tons at £5 18s 9d) than in 1945–6 (110,242 tons at £13 1s 6d per ton), although the price had more than doubled.

The decline in palm oil exports was linked in part to the rise in import prices and the scarcity of 'luxury' goods such as bicycles which palm producers bought with their profits. The price of major imports increased from an index of 100 in 1939, to 166 in 1942, 242 in 1944 and reached 275 in 1947. The conservative estimate of the commission of enquiry into the cost of living was that the price level had doubled between 1939 and 1945. The impact of import prices should not be exaggerated, however. Palm produce revenues were not spent on imported goods alone; in the main they were spent on domestically produced foodstuffs. A later survey showed that Ibibio households were spending 62 per cent of their domestic budget on food; 55 per cent was spent on local foods, including yams, and 7 per cent on imported stockfish.[69]

The Annang economy shifted back to a domestic agricultural rather than an export-led system during the war, and thereby placed renewed pressures on land and labour. Annang farmers looked towards the internal food trade in palm oil and cassava in particular. Within Nigeria during the war more palm oil from the east was sold to the western provinces where cocoa production was expanding, while northern markets also increased the trade of palm oil against cattle which substituted for stockfish in south-eastern diets.[70] Throughout the war cassava, which could tolerate shorter fallow periods than yams, had became an important hungry season food crop and was inter-planted as a joint staple with yams. A decade later, when agricultural surveys were conducted in the late 1950s, cassava had almost completely replaced the cultivation of yams and other starch-based staples on Ibibio and Annang farms. The production and trade of garri (processed cassava) with the north and with the expanding coastal cities increased dramatically during the war.[71] Officials feared that expanding garri production would crowd out palm oil altogether and a temporary ban was imposed on garri freighted by rail in 1944.

The effect of these economic changes was felt differently by men and by women. In the Igbo region of Afikpo cassava cultivation gave rise to 'profound alterations in the economic and social relations between husbands and wives'.[72] The net effect within the Annang household was that off-farm sources of income became more important for men during and immediately after the war. In parallel, the combined pressure to process more palm oil and kernels and to increase production of cassava meant that labour demands fell doubly heavily on women. The war squeezed cash incomes as the prices rose of foodstuffs upon which Annang households were increasingly dependent. This placed greater pressure than ever on land and labour, especially for cassava production. In turn this meant that the rights to land pledges and access to wives and their labour became highly contested. Indeed, coupled with the absence of so many men during the war, the supply of women's labour became a crucial factor in domestic food security.

As the scarcity of luxury imports proved a disincentive to palm oil producers, so the import of essential commodities was also hit during the war (see Figure 5.3). Most essential foodstuffs could be substituted; items like trade gin and dried fish were easily replaced by the illicit gin traffic

and by Andoni smoked fish. Imported salt, however, was particularly problematic as it was an essential rather than a luxury import, and the marketing
of salt was a female not a male activity.[73] As measures to promote local salt
production and to import salt produced elsewhere in West Africa failed,
price controls, restrictions on hoarding and eventually, in 1941, rationing
were introduced. Regular warnings of profiteering were made throughout
the remaining war years especially when, in 1943, salt was selling for 3d per
cigarette tin though the government-controlled rate was 1d. From 1941 the
distribution of rationed salt supplies was managed by local administrative
officers. They oversaw the supply from European companies to chiefs (each
clan council formed a salt committee), who then sold salt to retailers or
directly to the village at the local court house.

The salt-selling system was deeply unpopular and accusations of discrimination and profiteering by the chiefs and court clerks of the salt committees
were quick to emerge. In 1941 Ogoni women in Gokana demanded that salt
distribution return from men's to women's control in the local markets and

Export products	Average pre-war price (1935–38)	Price at outbreak of war (1939)	1941
Palm oil (soft)	£10.14.0	£5.17.6	£6.17.6
Palm kernels	£7.9.0	£5.15.0	£5.2.6

Foodstuffs	Average pre-war price (1935–38)	1941
Yams (Andoni area)	12 for 3/9d	12 for 5/3d
Foofoo (Andoni area)	8d per gin case	1/6d per gin case
Palm oil (Ibibio area)	1/9d per tin	Between 2/- and 2/6d per tin
Smoked fish (Andoni area)	30 frames for 1/8d	25 frames for 1/8d

Imported Goods	Average pre-war price	1941
Rice (2 cwts)	32/-	61/2d (controlled)
Sugar (packet)	3d	7d (controlled)
Corned beef (tin)	7d	1/3d (controlled)
Tobacco (head)	10d	1/- to 1/8d (controlled)
Trade gin (bottle)	7/-	12/6d
Cloth (piece)	8/6d to 10/-	12/6d upwards
Salt (90 lbs)	9/-	10/7d
Dried fish	15/-	None available
Soap (case)	9/9d	14/6d (controlled)

Figure 5.3 Wartime price survey (Opobo Division, December 1941)[74]

that the price (1 manilla per cigarette tin measure) could not be tolerated. They blamed the salt shortage and high prices of cloth in the 'factories' for their refusal to permit their husbands to pay tax.[75] Against this, for example, the Gokana women harassed one of their chiefs, twenty ringleaders were arrested, and a mob blockaded and began to attack the Native Court at which they were held.[76]

Direct intervention, especially through rationing, served to politicise the economy. The Government feared that the salt shortage in particular would create political unrest, especially by anti-colonial labour unions. It was women, however, who were again at the forefront of anti-colonial protests in Calabar Province during these years as they had been in 1929. The wartime economy was the key factor in the most significant breakdown of law and order in Calabar Province during the war, the Women's Riot of 1944. The protests which spread across Ikot Ekpene Division late in 1944, in fact, bore a remarkable resemblance to those fifteen years previously. The riots erupted among the Central Annang, Otoro and Ikono clans in response to misunderstandings over taxation policy, the wartime economic slump and the failure of the Native Courts to deliver justice. As in 1929, reports of conspiratorial communication between Annang and Ngwa Igbo women aroused colonial fears of impending disorder during the tax collection period. The tax collection was due to be completed by 15 November, but several weeks earlier the District Officer reported a rumour that Ngwa women had been telling the women of Nto Edino that they were going to be taxed.[77] In the following days thousands of women gathered in the markets around Ikot Ekpene. They refused to sell garri, paraded with pounding sticks and palm branches, and 'sat on' (úfik ntiê) and swore m̀bìàm against chiefs who continued their tax collection duties.

The impact of the war on the cost of living in Annang villages became apparent in complaints of acute economic hardship voiced during the disturbances. At a meeting on 18 November 1944 representatives of the women listed a range of grievances and demands which included: the low price paid for garri by European agents (from 6s 6d per 90 lb bag to as little as 2 shillings per bag); the high prices paid for imported goods; that tax assessment was made when the price of palm oil was particularly high at 7–10 shillings per tin; that the price of palm oil be fixed at 15 shillings; that women paid tax for their husbands; that they believed that tax would only have to be paid for seven years; that boys under sixteen were forced to pay tax, and that when they failed to pay, the chiefs seized property and their mothers were obliged to pay instead.[78]

Criticisms of the Cameron reforms of the judicial system also appeared in the women's grievances. On this occasion it was not the Warrant Chief system which was targeted, but rather the inability of the reorganised and understaffed courts to respond to popular needs for security, the deterrence of crime and the provision of justice. During an initial investigation on 7 November in Nto Edino women reported to the District Officer that:

> They had not got enough to eat, that thieves came to their farms by night and took all their cassava and pigs destroyed the crops, so they had not enough cassava to make into fufu. ... The women asked for Ufok Usung to be reintroduced.[79]

The District Officer rejected the request for the reintroduction of *úfɔ́k úsúŋ* (night guards) since he assumed that local chiefs had put the women up to telling this story of widespread theft. Yet the women protestors consistently criticised the formal judicial process. The Ikot Ekpene branch of the Ibibio Welfare Union despatched a delegation led by Peter Eket Inyang Udoh to negotiate a peaceful settlement to the dispute and heard the women's grievances on 18 November. At this meeting the women's representatives claimed that Native Court members were taking bribes, thieves were being released by Native Courts to pay their taxes, and their sentences of five months were too short.[80] The women contended that the former custom of rubbing thieves with charcoal and parading them around the market was a more effective deterrent.[81]

Despite assurances from the District Officer concerning the failings of the police and the apparent leniency of custodial sentences, the protests continued. On 21 November small crowds of women were seen along the road to Nto Edino 'daubed in black and white, some wearing sacking on their heads and round them, carrying leaves, throwing dust in the air, presumably invoking mbiam'.[82] On the following day 4,000–5,000 women had gathered to protest in the market at Nto Edino and the District Officer drafted over 150 police from Owerri, Onitsha and Calabar into the area. On 9 December over 1,000 women gathered at Imama where men were seen in the bush armed with bows and arrows, spears, sticks and guns, and were fired upon by the police. The administration's show of force, encamping police in villages where disturbances had occurred, and mediation on the part of the Ibibio Welfare Union, proved effective, however, and the protestors had dispersed by the end of the month.

★ ★ ★

The women's concern with crime in 1944 and their call for the return of familiar judicial practices is one dimension of a significant contest during the war over modes of crime prevention. On the one hand, these contests involved critical responses towards popular forms of informal justice. On the other, they concerned the criminalisation of the secret societies.

One particular issue raised in the women's protests concerned the role of night guards (*úfɔ́k úsúŋ*). The District Officer at Abak, for example, was worried by reports in which communities had resorted to vigilante justice:

I constantly receive complaints from persons who have been assaulted and even made to dance in markets without trial on allegations that they are thieves. They are frequently persons who have been seized by the gangs of men appointed to guard farms. I am of the opinion that these gangs often seize innocent persons with the intention of extorting money by threats. ... A case has just been reported of a woman who hanged herself after being publicly disgraced by being paraded openly in markets as a thief. Lawless elements are taking part in organised blackmail ...[83]

These organised gangs of thief-catchers were night watchmen (úkpèmé ídúŋ, lit. protect village) and were known to the colonial administration as úfɔk úsúŋ (lit. road house) after the awnings they constructed to mount road blocks. Night guard patrols were organised within the familiar structures and routines of the lineage work group (údîm). The various work groups took it in turn to set up road blocks and patrol the main paths within the village, armed with matchets and muskets. They were especially vigilant regarding the theft of farm produce, particularly germinated yams (ìwúòt údiá). Village elders would call out the night guards (úkpèmé ídúŋ) from when the yams were planted to when they were harvested. The guards constructed thatch shelters at the village boundaries and enforced a set of rules which included a ban on carrying yams and goats at night. When apprehended thieves were stripped naked, painted with charcoal, an àyèì was hung around their neck and they were paraded around the village and neighbouring markets. The way in which the thief was represented was evocative of the ékpó ńdêm masquerade figure – a malevolent spirit, a threat to security that held back progress and had to be restrained by human beings. In this symbolically charged context the release of a known thief to wreak havoc and disorder within the village was fraught with danger.

The Government opposed the úfɔk úsúŋ on the grounds that they had 'developed into an organisation for demanding money with menaces'.[84] It was believed that the use of the guards proved a lucrative source of revenue for village chiefs who held illegal trials in which persons arrested by the úfɔk úsúŋ were forced to confess their crime. Sometimes, after the thief had been shamed by being rubbed with charcoal and paraded around the market they were taken to the Native Court, tried and sentenced again.[85] As a result of similar reports, úfɔk úsúŋ had been banned in certain Annang communities such as the Central Annang Council of Ikot Ekpene Division, which prohibited:

  a. the construction and use of Ufok Usung (road houses);
  b. the erection of barriers across roads and paths;
  c. the dancing of alleged thieves in the markets; and
  d. the unlawful prevention of the free use of all public highways.[86]

Opposition to the ban persisted, however, and the President of the Central Annang Council, Sampson Udo, claimed that: 'Ufok Usung had been serving the public very satisfactorily and its destruction will be an encouragement to highway robbers and burglaries which are rampant in this part of the country'.[87]

Conflicting discourses of judicial practice also brought the role of Annang diviners (*idiɔŋ*) into the spotlight during the war years. In 1940 a number of cases came to light in which *idiɔŋ* members were implicated in providing information, leading to revenge killings.[88] In August 1940 the District Officer in Abak, L. T. Chubb, wrote to the local councils to warn *idiɔŋ* members that: 'enquiries into violent or mysterious deaths is a matter for the police and that the *idiɔŋ* society may be made illegal and subject to very heavy penalties if it continues such practice'.[89] The authorities conceived their dilemma as many sided. First, and perhaps surprisingly, they considered it necessary to distinguish those genuinely gifted diviners, 'the man with supernatural powers', from the host of charlatans who 'batten on the fear of the occult'. Second, they raised the question of how to tackle an institution which was concerned with secrets and unexplained events, but which was at the same time integral to the fabric of Annang society.

The District Officer's warning about the naming of suspects came after three cases were reported in 1940 in which *idiɔŋ* members, who were themselves never identified, had named an enemy as being responsible for malicious, usually supernatural, acts against their clients or their families. Udo Nne of Ibiakpan, for example, murdered four people and seriously injured three others in a frenzied attack after an unnamed *idiɔŋ* had indicated that people were trying to kill him. In the second case a man killed the wife and two children of a man an *idiɔŋ* had named as bewitching his family. And in the third a young man lay in wait for and murdered a man at Ikot Ibratim because *idiɔŋ* had indicated that the victim was responsible for killing his father by witchcraft.[90]

The Government's warning prompted leading *idiɔŋ* men in Abak District to call a meeting at Obiakpa in April 1941 and to submit a petition in their defence. They explained that *idiɔŋ* was a scientific profession like 'Necromancy' or 'Crystal Gazing'.[91] It was in this vein that the *idiɔŋ* employed the language of 'hoodoo' introduced to south-eastern Nigeria by American mail order firms during the 1930s to legitimise their profession. They explained the practice whereby a person found guilty by the *idiɔŋ* spirit would be stripped, covered in charcoal and beaten. The *idiɔŋ* were at pains to point out that since the arrival of the Government those found guilty were not killed as they had been before, and they denounced a recent trend by which individuals would report to the District Officer or police that they were about to be killed by *idiɔŋ*. This was a new device, the *idiɔŋ* claimed, 'invented by such persons to try and wipe off the shame of having been declared guilty by *idɔ̀ŋ*.[92]

Passages of the *idɔ̀ŋ*'s petition exacerbated already wide differences of opinion within the colonial administrative hierarchy concerning *idɔ̀ŋ*'s future. The District Officer at Itu complained that *idɔ̀ŋ* (especially those in Abak Division) were responsible for the numerous cases of witchcraft accusation (itself a criminal offence) that came before him. He also highlighted that the petition, in which admissions of murder, assault and adjudication on extrajudicial oath were made, revealed the thoroughly criminal basis of the *idɔ̀ŋ* society.[93] Yet while he argued that continued support or passive acceptance of such a society would be retrograde, the official line was more accommodating. Several officers, including the DO at Abak, felt that to propose a ban on *idɔ̀ŋ* would prove counter-productive because of the serious political effects it would have in undermining senior members of councils who were members of it. While the purpose of *idɔ̀ŋ* was healing and divination, the Resident at Calabar argued that 'like all other Ibibio and Annang societies its general purpose is the formation of a social structure to uphold the authority of the elders and to provide those of them who are its members with an income from the fees of those who join its various grades'.[94] It is important to note that the administration also sought the advice of the Ibibio Union during 1940 over the question of whether to ban *idɔ̀ŋ* because of these apparent criminal connections.[95] The Union was adamantly opposed to its suppression.

The mechanics of indirect rule in 1940 therefore depended on a compromise with the diviners. On this occasion the Government was reluctant to act more firmly against *idɔ̀ŋ* because it believed that that would weaken the authority of the many chiefs in the region who were *idɔ̀ŋ* initiates themselves. Hence, the Resident of Calabar Province was hopeful that the practice of consulting *idɔ̀ŋ* to determine the cause of death would be held in check by 'public opinion coupled with energetic action by District Officers'.[96] The signs, as they could be read from divisional reports, pointed precisely to such a decline. In Ikot Ekpene *idɔ̀ŋ* came to the notice of the authorities only when members forwarded claims in the Native Courts for the initiation fees lost as a result of Christian conversions among the heirs of their fellow members. 'This is a symptom', the DO wrote in 1941, 'that the society is on the decline and is no longer joined by the educated younger generation'.[97]

Throughout the war years initiatory societies across Calabar Province tested the *laissez-faire* colonial stance towards them. The idiom of the secret society had become a powerful explanatory factor in events within the province, with almost all elements of the Annang polity labelled in colonial discourse as a secret society, including divination orders, elders' meetings and any performance. Covert mobilisation in the Women's War, the trafficking of prostitutes and the organisation of village night guards were all aligned in official discourse to the workings of shadowy sodalities of initiates. The secret society also provided an apt idiom with which to conceive of the growing number of criminal gangs. Across the eastern provinces there were more and more reports of robberies and burglaries by gangs and secret societies. Following a theft in Eket, Ben Mbang Nkanta was accused of being a member of *ékóŋ ŋkà ṁbà*, a society of burglars. Nkanta suggested that he should be tried by an ordeal in Annang which he said could reveal secrets. He was found innocent by the ordeal and his three-day celebration in September 1939 was reported in the local newspaper.[98]

The Second World War was in fact a key point in the criminalisation of the secret societies, *ékpó* in particular. The link between the Annang ancestral masquerade, *ékpó* and crime resurfaced during the war amid renewed fears of revivals. Reports of the number of people being assaulted during *ékpó* performances was the key index and was itself a marker of the confidence of converts and 'A-Lights' to report the secret societies to the authorities. In Abak District, for example, there were twelve cases of serious assault attributed to *ékpó* in 1942, and fourteen in 1943.[99] During October 1943, *ékpó* was reported to have 'defiantly taken the law into their own hands', attacking and robbing an Igbo woman, inflicting nine matchet wounds on a man from Ikot Ese, robbing Mr Graddon's houseboy and seriously wounding a Hausa man in Ikot Akpan Esuk.[100]

These reports of *ékpó* activities were not isolated; during 1943 reports flooded in of assaults and extortions from Itu, Uyo, Abak and Ikot Ekpene. Opposition to *ékpó* also came from the progressive letter-writers who framed their objections in economic terms, and pointed to the hindrance *ékpó* had become to the war effort. In making markets insecure, in discouraging 'stranger' traders and particularly in delaying shipments of palm produce to the coast, masked *ékpó* members were accused of being enemies of the Empire and of being 'devilishly spirited Hitlers hitting down our War Effort'.[101] In Itu notices were made in court by the Ibiono Clan Council warning the *ékóŋ* masquerade against interfering with women or people dealing with the palm produce or rubber trades, as both commodities were essential to the war effort.[102]

The apparent revival of *ékpó* met with stiff opposition from the missions and by concerted attempts to discredit, criminalise and suppress it. One of the grounds upon which the Qua Iboe Mission sought the prohibition of *ékpó* in 1943 was that its criminal associations and its various innovations had led it to lose its former legitimacy:

> The present activities are not really a continuation of the old Ekpo, which seemed to be dying or dead, but are moved by propaganda to revive its power. To accomplish this they resort more to the frightfulness of the men who run in the Ekpo dress than to anything else.[103]

By 1944 petitions from Christian groups against the 'criminal activities' of the 'disgraceful societies' were mounting. The United Leaders' Meeting from Ikot Akpan Afaha in Abak Division, for example, petitioned for the suppression of *àtàt*, *ékpó*, *ékóŋ* and *ékpó* on the grounds of the complicity of elders in a campaign of violence towards women and strangers:

> When each starts to play it will roam about and disturbs the public peace. They enter into markets and rob people. They run against women under pregnancy in the markets. They will not allow people the free use of the roads. They hate Hausa, Item people, Abiriba men, and many other traders who used to bring goods to our people. Those from Ikot Afana [Ikot Afanga], Nun Ikot [Nung Ikot], Aya Obiokpa and Ikot Esop along the P. W. D. Aba-Opobo road are especially the terrors of the roads. ... Our old men usually have shares on certain proportion on what they take from strangers [non-members]. These are the reasons why they do not like to check them.[104]

Whether these reports were evidence of a revival or resurgence of *ékpó*, or of a more public and robust opposition from the missions during these years, is difficult to determine. Certainly all observers (mission petition writers, journalists and the District Officers) noted an increase in *ékpó*-related violence and intimidation in 1943 and 1944. Physical violence had always been a central part of the *ékpó* performance: rubbing against non-initiates with one's charcoaled body was a way of humiliating them, and cutting non-initiates with a matchet or hitting them with an arrow was a way of settling a personal score, raising one's status in society and of collecting fines. The violence of the 1940s may have been no more than this common pattern of masquerade violence. There are clues, however, to suggest that several overlapping scenarios contributed to the violence.

Recourse to direct and violent intimidation may have been brought on out of economic frustration. With times being hard, *ékpó* members had progressively fewer initiates when the performance season began. The *ékpó* seasons of 1943 and 1944 also coincided with a spate of public attacks on Igbos in Calabar and Etinan.[105] Throughout the late 1940s the tension of urban identity politics, particularly between Igbo and Ibibio-speaking groups, was high. Efik in Calabar township felt that the Igbo community were gaining control of local enterprises and businesses and held them largely responsible for the prevailing high prices of essential commodities.[106] Various forms of masquerade performance were imported to these urban contexts, especially at Christmas and New Year. Across the continent from the 1920s onwards, most notably during the war years, gangs of youths were reported as a 'menace' to law and order during festive periods.[107] 'Cowboy' gangs emerged in Calabar during the 1946 Christmas festivities, for instance, and 'So far as we can make out they seem to be organised on the lines of the juvenile and adolescent gangs that disturb the peace of the slums of

American cities'.[108] In Calabar Province these forms of 'hooliganism' were also manifest in established masquerade performance. The New Year plays in the growing towns of Uyo, Eket and Calabar were notorious, and secret society members found themselves being charged with the new offence of 'masquerade hooliganism'. In Okopedi in 1940, performances by Obon, Aban, Ekpe and Ekon led to an assault on a police constable.[109] In Eket during Christmas 1945 a woman was shot dead by a relative playing the Abang play.[110]

This apparent deterioration in the conduct of *ékpó* and other societies forced the colonial authorities to reconsider their previously ambivalent stance towards them. In Uyo in 1944 the DO threatened that any *ékpó* men found in their masks would be arrested and charged with conducting themselves in a way likely to cause a breach of the peace.[111] There was, however, no general proscription of secret societies. Again, government restraint was influenced by political sensitivities. In this instance an unlimited ban had become difficult to impose when in 1943 Western-educated Nigerians volunteered to register with the Government their reformed version of a pre-colonial secret cult, the Reformed Ogboni Fraternity.

★   ★   ★

While attempts were made to criminalise *ékpó* during the war years, the idea that the educated elements, and by extension the churches, were gaining at their expense does not tell the whole story. As the economy recovered, the Qua Iboe mission had indeed expanded rapidly during the 1930s. The trade boom of 1936 enabled the mission to supply teachers to those communities, like Azumini, where the church had always intended but could never afford to expand.[112] Classes for women inquirers in Ika and Ibesit were larger and more regularly attended than ever, and the church was buoyed up at seeing so many young women who had yet to reach *mbòbó* seeking admission to the classes.[113] These broad developments, coupled with the annual 'shot' from the Spirit Movement revivals, meant that by 1938 Westgarth could proclaim victory for the Gospel and that 'Plays, which in former days terrorised the district, have completely disappeared almost everywhere'.[114]

The sharp decline in income in late 1938 and early 1939, however, became more pronounced after the outbreak of war, and its effects were felt most profoundly within the church. Beyond the belief that their teachings were discredited by Christian nations being engaged in mortal conflict, it was the familiar link between the economy and conversion that occupied the Mission's concerns.[115] In Ikot Idong Graddon reported that wartime economic conditions of depressed produce prices and the 'abnormal cost of everything' had led to a decline of 35 per cent in the congregations' givings.[116] Mission church attendances fell. Many young men had joined the forces, with many more leaving home to join government service, and the combination of these factors meant that congregations had difficulty in paying their teacher-evangelists.[117] The 'severe ordeal' that the church underwent during the war years, the missionaries argued, was exacerbated by the 'multiplicity of new sects that are swarming all over the place'. The Qua Iboe church lamented that baptisms and attendance at inquirers' classes were declining because new churches, the Christ Army in particular, baptised their adherents without any prior instruction.

The Qua Iboe Mission congregations during the war were therefore marked by a 'spirit of indifference and a tendency to drift'. *Ékpó*'s apparent revival was taken as evidence of this lapse. By January 1945 the Mission was reporting a 'wave of materialism' passing over the country and the missionaries were once again praying for a spiritual revival: 'As everywhere else today, the greatest need here is for spiritual revival. The rising generation does not show the same fervour for the things of God'.[118] In Ika Nelson wrote that: 'Our churches have passed through a time of testing. In many places there seems to be a resurgence of the old heathen customs, and a number of Christians have had to be suspended for taking part in heathen plays. We do pray for a spiritual quickening in the lives of all our Church members'.[119]

Further evidence of the effects of economic suffering in the Annang districts by the end of the war came to light in a protest by the residents of Abak Division who refused to pay their taxes. Tax in 1945 had been assessed according to income rather than a fixed rate. As with previous tax disputes in the region, the cultural interpretation of the assessment criteria was central to this clash. The tax assessment was conducted by a committee of local chiefs appointed by the ever controversial District Officer, F. R. Kay. They estimated income on the basis of palm and yam plots, cassava farms, goats, sheep, dogs and fowls, and were accused of 'casually estimating each man's worth', a process that created a 'hue and cry'.[120]

The Abak Improvement League took up the campaign to petition for a 'stay' of income tax collection in Abak Division:

> People of Abak protest bitterly that they are too wretchedly poor to bear the burden of income tax. Despite trouble and friction in the past this is the first time the argument has been put in a reasonable manner by literates. We do not know whether the people of Abak Division are appreciably poorer than their neighbours of the Uyo, Ikot Ekpene and Opobo Divisions but judging by the few amenities provided out of revenue for the use and comfort of the people of Abak this would certainly seem to be the case. Ibo and Ibibio farmers enjoy the lowest standard of living in the country.[121]

In its protest the League invoked the memory of events in 1929 and expressed their fear of a repetition of 'that shameful women's riot, when our mothers, wives and sisters were unjustly and brutally massacred by this very Nigerian Political Government'.

The dispute also centred on a personal attack on Kay himself, who was criticised for his 'iron-rod administration' and for imprisoning twenty-eight local chiefs on income tax assessment charges. It was wrong, they argued, for Kay to hear a dispute in which he himself was party, and at a 'mammoth mass meeting' organised in March 1946 by the Abak Improvement League, which was promoting the anti-tax campaign, Kay was vigorously cross-examined over the affair. As the meeting disbanded Kay, who was reported to have been 'insulting and autocratic' throughout, was seen whipping the crowd, including the secretary of the Abak District League, Okokon Ita. Okokon Ita subsequently sued Kay for £200 damages for the alleged assault. Kay claimed that as a senior officer he was breaking up an unlawful assembly. He also claimed that Okokon was a letter-writer by profession, and that he had retained Egbert Udo Udoma's professional legal services not from his own money but from the money subscribed to the Abak Improvement League to prosecute the case. Whether the League were a 'pack of rowdy irresponsibles' who had played the part of agitators as Kay claimed, or whether this tax protest reflected the true economic difficulties of Abak Division became obscured by the controversy over the assault. During his visit to Abak in May 1946, the Governor, Sir Arthur Richards, rounded on the Abak District League as 'trouble-makers'.[122] As NCNC supporters who took a critical stance against 'imperialist domination' in the pages of the 'Zik press', the Abak League's position on the 1945 tax assessment captures the conflation of economic and political, livelihood and nationalist concerns that dominated the region at the end of the war.

'AUDACIOUS LEOPARDS' AND 'ATROCIOUS DEEDS'

The political and economic insecurities of the war years were compounded by increased anxiety over the activities of local wildlife, specifically wild leopards. During the dry month of July 1943, leopards were seen prowling closer than normal to villages in Calabar and neighbouring Owerri Province.[123] The introduction of taxation in 1928 had reduced colonial demands for forced labour, especially in road-making.[124] This meant that inter-village roads that had been cleared by compulsory labour reverted to narrow paths along which people could pass in single file only. Requests were made for long bush to be cut back and for hunters to redouble their efforts. Popular opinion was that the dearth of gunpowder needed for Dane guns during the war and the consequent cessation of hunting with dogs was the cause of wild animals boldly stalking into the villages. On 24 July 1943 a leopard suddenly appeared on the Ikot Okoro-Urua Anwa Road in the midst of three pedestrians and attacked one of them before chasing a cyclist for three-quarters of a mile.[125] The successful hunting of a wild leopard during this time was met with considerable relief and jubilation. UAC employee Jackson Akpan was honoured with presents for his bravery when he killed a leopard at Ibagwa in July 1944. The leopard was first deposited with the DO at Abak before being taken round neighbouring villages amid much singing.[126] Though it would not have been reported, it is probable that the DO would have been responsible for the disposal of the leopard's 'poisonous' bile sack and whiskers.[127]

It was not only wild leopards, however, that were on the prowl. These reports from 1943 onwards coincided with local suspicions that a series of attacks on local residents attributed to leopards were not all they appeared. In fact, when one reads the local newspaper from the early 1940s in which several attempts were made to alert the authorities to these rumours, it seems remarkable that an investigation into suspicious leopard-related deaths had not been launched earlier than it was in March 1945. It would be eighteen months before the first official mention was made of human leopards in Abak district in the wake of the first reported man-leopard killing, of Dan Udoffia. Yet the circumstances of a death in Ikot Obong Akan as early as October 1943 cast reports of audacious wild leopard activity in a very different light:

> A young woman called Adiaha Akpan Udo of Ikot Obong Akan was returning from farm in the company of seven other women on 7 October 1943. They were going in a line in a bush path when suddenly an object in the shape of a human being dressed in EKPO mask is alleged to have jumped out of the wood, and attacked the woman like a leopard. He is alleged to have taken her inside the wood and butchered her to death with a matchet. During the incident the rest of the women ran away to their homes and broke the news to the relatives of the woman who upon reaching there, discovered the woman lying dead. A report was made to the police who took up investigations very seriously. Subsequently one Etuk Udo Ekpo Adiaha Akarassi of Ikot Obong Akai was arrested and charged for the murder of Adiaha Akpan Udo. The police also discovered the woman's dresses in his house. The accused has been remanded in custody awaiting trial. The activity of the police in this case has brought to light the series of cases reported here about various people being killed by a leopard and not knowing it was an act done by a wicked human being. The arrest of this man however has reduced the fear and doubts in the neighbouring villages.[128]

These rumours, which cast doubt on the verdict of the Government Medical Officer on a number of local deaths that had been attributed to attacks by wild leopards, also reached Mr Graddon of the Qua Iboe Mission in Ibesit. He and leaders from the Methodist Mission in Opobo believed that these were victims of 'cunningly organised murder'.[129] Repeated and specific calls alerting the authorities to such attacks in Abak and Opobo Districts continued during 1944, yet police investigations were confined to individual cases; they did not address the serial pattern that was emerging, and as a result they failed to quell local suspicions that the murders were in fact widespread. The allegations in a letter to the editor of the *Nigerian Eastern Mail* in January 1944, while refraining from mentioning leopards or man-leopards, provide details that would become very familiar on the suspected scale of the deception, the murder technique and the profile of the victims:

> Sir, Please kindly spare me a short space in your valuable journal to voice out to the relevant authority the state in which the lives of the people in Annang-Opobo Areas has been placed. From October 1942 up to date over 65 souls have died under circumstances that seem mysterious. Some are school children. It is alleged that there are certain sets of people going about with sharp instruments, doing havoc, especially to girls. This information was passed to the police at Abak and Opobo. Investigations have been made with no result. Both police detachments are asked to continue their investigations in the interest of the public whose lives are in jeopardy. Men and women are being butchered, but the culprits could not be tracked down. The relevant authority should please come to the help of the people, for there is no smoke without fire.[130]

Perhaps these rumours were part of a series of popular panics that were later to sweep across Calabar Province during the months immediately after the end of the Second World War. These panics related to crime-waves, kidnapping, slave-dealing, head-hunting and 'market wizardry' which had gripped towns and villages across Calabar Province. 'The end of the war', a columnist wrote of Calabar, 'is generally noted for an unusual wave of crime. But the exceptionally large number of thefts and burglary perpetrated in the heart of the township sometimes in broad daylight and in the most daring manner so soon after cessation of hostilities constitutes a bold challenge to the efficiency of the local Police Force'.[131] Uyo too had become a 'haven for thieves',[132] and a robbery gang was arrested in Abak amidst calls for a stronger police presence.[133] The press reported a spate of 'head-hunting' killings in Umuahia Division where the 'paths, lanes and roads connecting villages are infected with would-be head-hunters'.[134] School attendance, trade and everyday tasks like collecting firewood had been suspended because of these rumours. In November and December 1945 rumours spread that on certain days of the week markets in Ifiayong, Itam and Uyo were attended only by 'witches and wizards', and that on those days people stayed at home.[135] Further anxieties about urban prostitution and violence were captured in newspaper headlines about 'Harlots and Hooligans'.[136] These reports, combined with renewed fears of kidnapping in Ikot Ekpene, slave-dealing on the Cross River and a spate of financial scams perpetrated by con-artists, the so-called 'Wayo' tricksters,[137] suggested that the reports of leopard killings coincided with a post-war moment of considerable disquiet.

Petitioning the district authorities through the press over the rumours of suspicious leopard-related deaths, however, had become a familiar and persistent course of action. That local staff resorted to the *Mail* to alert the District Officer to the peculiarities of Dan Udoffia's death in March 1945 (as outlined in Chapter 1) may not have had the same impact had it not been for DO Kay's posting to Abak that month. The fact that the Udoffia case launched the official man-leopard murder enquiry said as much about the newly arrived District Officer as it did about the case itself, and Kay's own investigations were central to shaping the direction of the police enquiries more generally. Kay was especially concerned at the impact of the murder on the broader community, in particular the chiefs and the 'reading public'. He was most concerned that what he referred to as the invocation of the 'leopard society' had 'sterilised counter-action' and took this as an indication of the very grave hold on public opinion in Abak which the secret societies still had. As a result by March 1945 Kay was considering drastic action to repress what he believed to be the operation of a secret society:

> If I may generalise, I would like to say that I have been in the Uyo
> – Ikot Ekpene – Abak triangle for several years now, and I have shared
> public concern at these leopard-deaths. I incline to think ... that on
> a suitable occasion [a] police escort in support of the Native Author-
> ities ... might profitably search an area for paraphernalia and shrines.
> There are symptoms here of a society which requires suppression, and
> the more enlightened public opinion requires the tonic of vigorous
> administrative action, without which it has no courage.[138]

It would be two years before this large-scale action was approved, but with the Udoffia case 'cracked' DO Kay began to investigate other suspicious deaths from March 1945 onwards with a small contingent of plainclothes police and with the help of the Medical Officer at Ikot Ekpene. Kay's first step was to order that the victims of violent deaths should not be buried without a report being made to the police. In the first seven cases between March and the end of August 1945 the medical evidence suggested death caused by a leopard. The Medical Officer, Dr Le Clezio, at Ikot Ekpene, conducted post-mortem examinations in the presence of police witnesses and was fully briefed of the police's suspicions. Yet in each case he concluded that the victims had been savaged by a wild animal. Despite recognising the peculiar forensic features which were identical in each of the victims, notably that their necks had been removed, the Medical Officer wrote that 'one can easily visualise the same powerful wild beast trailing its victims in the usual fashion attacking them in the same way'.[139]

The mounting circumstantial evidence in these cases, however, pointed to a different verdict. The injuries to John Udo, a public works labourer who died on 24 May 1945, were identical to three cases seen by the Medical Officer in the space of the previous month – decapitation, severe trauma to the upper body and puncture wounds which looked like they had been inflicted by a leopard's claw. At the scene of the crime in Ikot Akpan, however, the police found only human footprints in the sand, the corpse stripped but his clothes untorn, and the man's raffia bag without the manillas it had contained.[140] Peculiar habits, Kay wrote, for a carnivorous animal. Yet in this case and in two further deaths in August in which the DO ordered the bodies of victims to be exhumed, the Medical Officer returned verdicts that leopards were responsible.

Just as the world war was ending in September 1945 clues as to the scope of the war on the man-leopards in Abak began to emerge. Operating undercover in the main market of Urua Anwa, two police constables got wind of a murder. Etok Ebere, a forty-year-old woman, was killed while on her way to visit her daughter at Nung Ikot on 22 September. Her injuries differed from those of previous cases because her masked attacker had been disturbed during the assault. Etok Ebere had died from a deep puncture wound to the neck. It was so deep, in fact, that it could not have been caused by a leopard's claw. As with previous victims the neck area had been removed or severely stripped, which led to the conclusion that the reason for the mutilation was to disguise the fatal wound and hence create confusion about what had inflicted it. In subsequent cases the Medical Officer knew to look for long skewer type wounds by way of a dissection across the top of the body. On the basis of this case the press speculated on the method of murder adopted by the man-leopard:

> Stories of the leopards in Ikot Okoro area of Abak Division stealing people's cattle and taking toll of many lives have been told here time and again. The energetic District Officer, Mr F. R. Kay, recently arranged for special detectives who arrived here early last September. Diligently setting to work and enquiring vigilantly at every village they entered, these men made a careful study of the murder cases said to have been perpetrated by leopards. The recent death, under magic circumstances of one woman named Etok Ebere proved that the atrocious deeds were not perpetrated by the alleged leopards but by savage people known as 'man-leopards'.
>
> A 'man-leopard', as the story goes, would cover himself with a mask and arm himself to the teeth with sharp cutting and tearing implements. On finding a suitable victim he would pounce on him and tear

him to pieces. In this way it is alleged several men and women have been murdered in cold blood. This type of brutal warfare which was started long ago could have continued unabated but for the effort of the District Officer and the keen detective power of the men engaged on the investigations. The District Officer and his detectives deserve public congratulations.[141]

The congratulations, however, were short-lived. Just days before Okon Bassey appeared in court in the last week of November 1945 charged with the murder of Dan Udoffia, two multiple murders rocked Abak Division. On 20 November 1945 four women were found dead in the Ibesit village of Ikot Akam. Three of the women were wives of Willie Akpan Udo Anwa, the other was his sister. A search party had been organised when they failed to return from gathering vegetables the previous night. Two of the women had been pregnant. A matchet was found at the scene, each had been stabbed in the neck and the wounds were thought to have been inflicted by a left-handed person. Willie, a youngish man who had made money from trading dried fish from Opobo and who attended the Qua Iboe Church, was the chief suspect. He was left-handed. The case remains infamous and continues to elicit a range of interpretations. Older women remember Akpan Udo Anwa as having a violent temper: 'he was used to killing', they said, 'it was his custom'. After telling his wives to wash yams they decided to collect *áfâŋ* vegetable leaves to sell in *ékényàŋ* market instead. Akpan Anwa was furious at this and 'had to sharpen his knife'.

Another story suggests that Willie Akpan Udo Anwa had fallen in with the wrong crowd. Local chiefs state that he was variously the 'cousin' or sister's son of the man who would become notorious as the founder of the man-leopard society, Akpan Anyoho. Together, it was claimed, they had formed a gang (*údîm ówó*) to undertake the leopard murders. While this story links the murders to what became a standard narrative of the murders' origin, the interpretation of Willie's half-brother, Atim Akpan Udo Anwa, is more personal and proximate. Atim feared his brother because they were locked in a land dispute and he recalls today that Willie committed his crimes because of insanity. 'The leopard medicine', he said, 'made him mad'. The colonial authorities meanwhile claimed a further motive for the crime – that his affliction was romantic in nature. Since marrying a fourth wife from Ikot Odoro, it was suggested, he had been so 'charmed' by her that he had stopped eating with his first three wives and had attempted to kill one of them, Unwa Udofia, the previous year. The preliminary investigation concluded that Unwa Udofia was again his intended victim and that the other women, one of whom was heard to shout 'don't kill me, I will not tell anybody', were killed to leave no witnesses.[142]

Just two days later, before the furore over the quadruple murder had subsided, three more women were found dead with extensive knife wounds in Abak, this time at Ikot Essiet. The Magistrate at Opobo thought that this case was the high-water mark in unmasking the leopard men. Four men were arrested for the murder and one, Akpan Unwa Etuk Usoro, made a remarkable statement to the police. He confessed that he was one of the killers and a member of an *ékpê* (leopard) society in Ikot Essiet which had undertaken previous murders. There were three key aspects to Usoro's confession. First, he detailed the charms used by the group. Of these the most significant was a black powder held in a calabash. 'It is used', he said, 'for calling a person to the spot where he is to be killed. It is blown into the air calling the name of the person to be killed and it attracts the person to be killed to the spot'. Second, he stated that human body parts were being sold. Up to 80 manillas might be fetched, he claimed, for various body parts, including the left hand, the heart, intestines and skin, which were sold to Ogoni people in Opobo Division. And third, he gave some indication of the scope of the leopard murderer's organisation. He had paid 40 manillas to join while one of his fellow members had paid 60 manillas several years previously to a Hausa man to prepare 'leopard' medicine for the society. He knew of similar groups in other villages, though there were no formal links between them, and he knew that: 'Whenever anyone has someone to be killed he invites us by paying 100 manillas and one goat for sacrifice before we set up for the killing of the victim'.[143] This was also the first case in which lethal weapons, masks and other paraphernalia were seized by the police.

By December 1945, ten months after the Udoffia murder, armed with Okon Bassey's conviction and with this confession, the police could finally claim that there was conclusive evidence that a leopard society had committed the strange murders in the Ekparakwa, Ikot Ibritam and Ibesit Native Court areas. But this certainty was undermined by two remaining doubts: how many murders had already been committed, and had the police, the local government staff and the chiefs known about them all along? In answer to the first, new cases that were opened into old murders seemed to be reported daily and the Resident thought it would take the police two months simply to recover the evidence in cases already under review.

The second issue of complicity led questions to be asked of various groups from the outset. In reviewing the Opobo case files dating back to 1943 DO Allen found it difficult to believe that the Division's police officers, many of them either Ibibios or Annangs, could not have known more about these deaths. When a member of the Opobo Division police detachment claimed he had been aware of the existence of the society since September 1944, the implication was that the police were not only incompetent but in league with the murderers.[144] Allen claimed that the senior police officer in Opobo, Inspector Ntima, had gone out of his way to persuade him that in two cases of murder the cause of death was a leopard. Ntima was immediately posted to Uyo and Allen refused to assign members of the Opobo police detachment to the murders. There was no direct evidence of police complicity beyond this, but the Ibibio Central Native Authority in Opobo Division petitioned against referring any further murder cases to the police 'who regard such cases as a plentiful source of revenue'.[145]

In Abak, Kay made similar accusations about the local staff and claimed that 'whatever the merits or demerits of the police it is abundantly clear that the Native Authority staff – the court clerks, messengers, road overseers, sanitary inspectors and dispensers living in these areas must have been well aware of the position'.[146] In the Udoffia case Kay said that: 'it was knowledge common to the whole of the Native Authority staff, including the Head-master and teachers of the Native Authority school, and the Dispenser, that Okon Bassey was the murderer. As he claimed to be a member of the Leopard Society none dared report'.[147] Kay was dismayed by the fact that the mere invocation of the 'leopard society' had terrorised Native Adminis-tration officials into meek acquiescence. That Native Authority employees had only exposed the first man-leopard murder case anonymously via the *Nigerian Eastern Mail* was significant. In fact, no other member of the local staff, Government or Native Authority provided any information to the investigating authorities up to the end of 1945.[148] It was assumed that one of the principal reasons why information on the murders had not reached the divisional authorities was that the administration was out of touch with the people. The lack of staff and supervision during the war had accentuated the position. 'Many of us in the Eastern Provinces', wrote the Resident, 'have long held the view that except for a few years after the Aba riots of 1929, the numbers of administrative staff have been inadequate. ... events such as these under review show only too plainly the result of under-staffing'.[149] The typical strength of the provincial administration staff for Calabar Province as a whole during the war and immediately after was about a dozen, and the District Officers were on tour in the villages for less than a third of their time.

In the initial investigations Kay lent heavily on the advice and infor-mation of specially selected and trusted chiefs, including Chief Iwok Etuk of Ekparakwa Court and Chief Jackson Ekot of Ibesit. Their assistance led to the formation of a committee aiding the murder enquiries which, by the end of the year, had uncovered nine murders leading to the detention of ten suspects. Many other chiefs, however, became suspects themselves. Unlike the police and the Native Administration staff, the local chiefs were not only blamed for failing to report previous suspicious deaths but were thought to be commissioning and concealing the murders themselves. In Opobo chiefs appeared keen to assist the investigation, but in Abak Kay was convinced that many of the chiefs were themselves 'leopards'. Fear of retaliation by prominent chiefs was thought to be the main reason why people were too frightened to volunteer information on the murders. These suspicions were based on evidence from informers, so-called 'listening posts'. During November 1945 one of the informers said that the headquarters of the leopard society was at Ikot Afanga and that its leader was Chief Joseph Udo of Ikot Akam (part of the Ikot Afanga village group). He was the president of the Branch Native Court, a member of the Divisional Advisory Council and a senior elder of the Qua Iboe church.[150]

Joseph Udo made two statements during December 1945. He confessed that several months earlier he and Chief Udo Akpan Ibanga had revived an 'ancient secret society' known as *àfé ékényòη* whose object was to suppress evil practices, cases of witchcraft and 'other matters' in Ikot Afanga. *Àfé ékényòη* was not in fact a secret society, but an *àfé úkòt*, an elders' meeting which met on the day of the week, *ékényòη*, during which palm wine was presented to the chiefs and its public sale prohibited. The revival of *àfé ékényòη* was most likely linked to the impact of new judicial reforms in 1945. In Sir Arthur Richards' address to the Legislative Council he outlined the post-war policy towards judicial reform and sketched the steps taken to date:

> In the Calabar Ogoja, Onitsha and Owerri Provinces ... Administrative officers with the active cooperation of the people are engaged in a reform of the Native Courts. Their main endeavour is to reduce the large panels and massed benches created as a result of the reorganisation subsequent to the Aba Riots in 1929. Considerable progress has been made in obtaining acceptance of the principle of the selection of the best men for the purpose in many cases literates as Native Court Members. The reduction of the size of the bench has had the effect of increasing the individual earnings, in sitting fees of the members.[151]

Petitions from chiefs who had lost their court seats as a result of this 'best man' policy flooded into the District Office. They included a protest from Southern Ukanafun, which was directed at a familiar target – the ambitious young men who usurped their authority:

> When surveying the Native Administration system of Ukanafun council with respect to the arrogancy [*sic*] of the councillors one can scarcely understand whether the right method of native administration with indirect rule is being correctly applied in this clan. The okukus as the rightful head of the clan and elders of the clan who constitute the Native Authority always murmur about finding themselves as mere rats before the councillors. There [*sic*] rightful rulers of the clan have all driving [*sic*] away from courts and council by these avaricious men who want to enrich themselves.[152]

Àfé ékényòη, as a council of lineage elders and prominent individuals, was therefore thought to have emerged as a clandestine court in direct response to the reforms which had reduced the number sitting on the court benches in favour of younger, more educated men. *Àfé ékényòŋ*'s members had all been court judges, a fact that was reported extensively. But the fact that the majority had lost these lucrative positions when the Native Court panels in Abak Division had been reformed and reduced in 1945, two years before most other divisions in the Province, had apparently been overlooked.

In his evidence Joseph Udo went on to state that an *idìòŋ* man called Udo Nwa Nwa Ekpo from Itung had joined the *àfé ékényòŋ*. He was reputed to have medicine enabling people 'to kill anybody like a leopard' and claimed to have formed a leopard society in Itung and in Ekparakwa. Soon after, most of the *àfé ékényòŋ* members were initiated into his leopard society (*ékpê ówó*, lit. leopard man) and hence into the secrets of clandestine assassination. 'I realise ekpe owo is a dangerous society', Joseph Udo said, 'I regret to have been a member of it. I know it exists solely for the destruction of human life. For a petty grievance a member of ekpe owo will attempt the life of his opponent. For a few manillas a member of ekpe owo will kill any person'.[153] With this confession it was concluded that the leopard men were the henchmen and assassins of the *àfé ékényòŋ* tribunal of elders. Udo Nwa Nwa Ekpo's compound was searched on 9 December 1945. The police found skewers, two masks and a charm identical to those already recovered at Ikot Essiet in the triple murder case along with garments that were believed to have been used by the killers to give them the appearance of a leopard. Udo Nwa Nwa Ekpo's claims that these were actually the instruments and costumes of the *èkóŋ* play were dismissed by DO Kay's hand-picked committee of chiefs.

Allegations that *àfé ékényòŋ*, in league with the leopard men, were guilty of particular crimes, however, proved difficult to substantiate. Accusations were made in two cases. The first concerned the murder in December 1944 of Eka Idem Iduot. During the assault his friend heard him shout out the name of two attackers, including Akpan Ekpenyong the son of Chief Ekpenyong Etuk Adiaha, an *àfé ékényòŋ* member. The victim had married the chief's daughter but still owed him brideprice. The victim's family did not report the murder but instead paid *àfé ékényòŋ* a goat, 100 manillas and four jars of palm wine to hear the case. In settling the matter the two accused men were made to swear their innocence on *mbìàm* and survived its effects. The second case happened in March 1945 when *àfé ékényòŋ* had apparently conspired to murder Benjamin Udofia Udo Ikpat. He was a Christian, a tax collector and a court member and the reason for the attack was claimed to be his various and somewhat zealous attempts to support 'constitutional administration'. He had brought claims against people for refusing to pay tax, for instance, and had prosecuted *ékpó* society members for damage to property and assault.[154]

At best the court and council members of *àfé ékényòŋ*, who were under a duty to report these events, were guilty of taking active steps to prevent news reaching the authorities. Indeed, as events unfolded, it emerged that local chiefs had regularly overstepped their jurisdiction to hear murder cases using familiar methods:

> … An Opobo case is reported where the chiefs are said to have tried a member of the [man-leopard] Society for murder, found him guilty and fined him 1,800 manillas. There is some evidence at Ikot Essiet in Ekparakwa that a man accused of being a member of the Society was told to take 'mbiam' – an oath of denial – before the chiefs.[155]

At worst, it was presumed that *àfé ékényòŋ* and other chiefs had sanctioned 'man-leopard' assassinations. The authorities began to ask themselves why local authorities would exact monetary penalties from known murderers without fear of reprisals unless they themselves had employed them.[156]

The actions of Chief Job Udo Mbodi, the key-holder of Annang Native Administration Treasury, appeared to confirm precisely this suspicion. He and his son were arrested for murder on 26 December 1945 in a case that had initially been attributed to a wild leopard until a witness testified that he had seen the chief's son in the act of stabbing the victim. The victim himself, Udo Udo Idem Udo, had staggered, fatally wounded, to the chief's house to confront him and had repeated his accusations in the village square that it was the chief who had ordered his death. In a surprise raid on the chief's house a bloodstained dagger and two long, pointed skewers were recovered. The chief's own council members in Ibesit further accused him of releasing suspected leopard men held in the court cell on two separate occasions during 1945.

Overall, by the end of 1945 some thirty-one murders had been uncovered, there were ninety-one suspicious deaths under investigation and the police had yet to search more than 200 villages straddling the Abak and Opobo divisional boundary. With the increasing prevalence of the deaths, the roads were deserted after dark. In response to the growing number of cases, the revelations about the secrecy in which they were committed, and the high profile of those involved, the authorities sought to reinforce the small police contingent and to open a new police post closer to the scene of the crimes. The normal police establishment of both Abak and Opobo Divisions, an area of 900 square miles, was less than fifty, half of whom were normally employed at the two government stations. In urgent telegrams to Enugu and Lagos on New Year's Eve 1945, the Provincial Resident in Calabar urged that at least 100 extra rank-and-file police along with four officers should be detailed to the investigation.[157] They arrived within the week.

6

INLAWS AND OUTLAWS, 1946

By February 1946 the murders had resulted in a breakdown in law and order on such a scale that the administrative map was redrawn and eight Court Areas from Abak and Opobo Divisions were amalgamated to create the 'Leopard Area'. This zone was frequently referred to as the 'infected area' and the killings as a whole were discussed in an idiom of contagion and disease. The crisis was called an 'outbreak', and villages in which no suspicious deaths were recorded were said to be 'immune'. The atmosphere and daily routines of people living in the villages around Ibesit and Ikot Afanga were dominated by confusion and fear.

A key index of local security was market day, and the number of people willing to risk the threat of the leopard men in order to trade. Of this period women recall the infrequency with which they ventured from the confines of the compound and that on trips to the market, to distant farm plots or to uncultivated forest areas, they walked in groups and always in single file. People were so frightened of the human-leopard killers that they would urinate in their houses at night for fear of stepping outside in the dark. Parents would lock their children in the house if they were leaving them at home to go to market. These fears, however, were not confined to the anxiety of physical attacks. The fear of being accused of involvement in *èkpê ówó* was also strong and people would not go out for fear of being named as an associate or of being in a particular place at a particular time. The leopard murders constituted what people today call *ìnì àdòt ùyò* (lit. time of slander or false accusation).

'THE TIME OF ACCUSATION'

On 5 January 1946 a police detachment of ninty-five was drafted into the western districts of Calabar Province. There was relief in the villages through which the police marched when it was discovered that they were not there to enforce the tax assessment that was proving so controversial. Even these neighbouring villages were largely unaware at that time of the magnitude of the political crisis unfolding in the area just south of Abak. The death toll was now 'unprecedented in the annals of Nigerian crime', with over 100 deaths under investigation. The huge concentration of rank-and-file police was a powerful show of strength designed to deter further

Figure 6.1 Police camps. Building the police camp at Ediene Atai (top), Police Headquarters, Ediene Atai ('City of Ekpe Owo') (below) (Reproduced with the kind permission of the Bodleian Library, University of Oxford)[1]

murders. Soon after their arrival the mood lifted, the roads were no longer deserted and several hundred people felt sufficiently safe to watch a cinema show at Ikot Akpan Essien on 11 January despite having to return home at eleven o'clock at night.

The respite that the new police force brought with them, however, was fleeting. The large numbers of inexperienced police were little help in stopping the killings or in unravelling the various forensic mysteries which had emerged. This was despite the fact that the police themselves were better educated and trained than ever before. From 1936 onwards the entry qualification was Standard VI. During the 1930s courses held at the Police Training School in Enugu had introduced a range of new investigation techniques including the *modus operandi* system of crime detection, advanced training of CID recruits in photography and fingerprinting, and a greater emphasis on medical forensic evidence.[2] As part of this process the Government Pathologist, Dr P. J. L. Roche, who conducted several examinations during the man-leopard murder enquiries, undertook a course of forensic science in the UK and gave lectures to the CID on his return.[3]

For the authorities investigating the murders there had always been a tension between displaying force and proceeding with stealth. When the investigations began, for instance, Kay had called for a police escort or an armed raid in order to suppress the 'leopard society'. As it was, the large police detachment that was deployed almost a year after Kay's initial request was ill-equipped to investigate the man-leopard murders. A high proportion were Igbo speakers, rendering them both conspicuous and ill-suited to undercover work. Neither they nor the European officers could speak Annang, and the latter therefore frequently laid emphasis on the physical attributes of the suspects, most particularly when they reported that suspects 'looked' guilty. The large number of officers and the scale of the operation, with the construction of camps and rotas of patrols, also militated against detailed, fine-grained investigations. Overall, this police deployment reflected the way in which the authorities conceived and confronted the murders as an act of mass civil disorder and not as a complex and highly localised series of crimes. From the start the enquiry had depended heavily on covert intelligence, on secret, unattributed, overheard hearsay evidence gathered from 'listening posts', from undercover officers, from the committee of chiefs working behind the scenes and from unlikely sources such as the District Officer's cook, who reported on several local rumours about the 'man-leopard' society 'which he overheard while touring'.[4]

The ineffectiveness of the new tactics were quickly exposed. On 10 January Chief Job Udo Mbodi's daughter in-law was murdered just a few hundred yards from one of the large new police camps. Within weeks the police and district authorities recognised that, irrespective of police numbers, the real problem they faced was in gathering hard, corroborative evidence. It was assumed that this was because of the intimidation of witnesses by the ringleaders of the human leopard society and the prominent chiefs who backed them. The fear of reprisals was tangible: 'These people are so terrified of retaliation on the part of the chiefs who are supposed to hire these killers that they will usually endeavour to retract their statements after charging any individual'.[5] It was argued therefore that unless these ringleaders could be detained indefinitely local people would be too frightened to come forward with the evidence that the prosecution needed to secure convictions.

Events following Chief Mbodi's arrest appeared to bear this out as witnesses began to 'flood' in from Ibesit and a further twelve of his victims were identified. The witnesses each claimed that with the chief at liberty they could not come forward for fear that any report against him 'would bring down his vengeance and that of the ekpe society on their heads'.[6] This witness evidence itself, however, proved especially unreliable. Although Chief Mbodi, along with Joseph Udo and his fellow àfé ékényɔ̀ŋ members, were in custody, there was insufficient evidence to charge any of these suspected ringleaders with murder. The prospect of releasing them or of launching flawed prosecutions and allowing them to return 'fortified by their acquittals' to their villages was unthinkable. With many other suspected 'chief executives of the society' at liberty, the imperative to lock up the leopard society leaders was compounded by the need for hard evidence in a growing list of murder cases.

'There are a large number of murders', Kay reported, 'in which there has been direct accusation but the evidence falls just short of the minimum required to make an arrest'.[7] Once the government investigations were launched in earnest towards the end of 1945 bereaved families became the most significant and most problematic source of evidence. While the number of murder charges grew rapidly on the strength of their accusations they could provide little or no corroborative evidence for their claims. The kind of evidence that was available presented its own problems. When questioned as to how they knew a man was a member of the leopard society, people often said things like 'we know he is a leopard man because he says he is one, or he is a bad man so he must be a leopard man, or the suspected leopard man was a known associate of other known or suspected leopard men'.[8] The logic of hindsight meant that accusations were also self-realising. Once it was known that an individual was a suspect, especially if they were already in custody, then apparently corroborative testimony began to materialise.

Common sources of evidence came from reports of threats and accusations. Threats made by alleged killers that 'the leopard society would deal with them' or 'I will see you' were frequent yet insufficient to bring a case to court. Threats based on the interpretation of dreams revealed particular aspects of the underlying epistemological tensions that existed between Annang and colonial ways of knowing. Premonitions and threats apparently played on familiar frameworks of intra-household conflict and on the ways in which husbands intimidated and disciplined their wives. 'We cannot arrest a man', the DO wrote, 'simply because he told his wife that

Figure 6.2 Human-leopard costume (Reproduced with kind permission of the Bodleian Library, University of Oxford)[9]

he dreamed there was a leopard in the bush and that she should not go to farm on a particular morning with the other women of the family because a leopard would kill them – we cannot arrest him even though his dream was deadly accurate'.[10] This description of domestic intimidation involving the prediction of a leopard's appearance at a particular place and time directly echoes the practice of conjuring *èkpê m̀fòró* as a medicinal invocation by husbands to discipline wives suspected of adultery.

The problems caused by sources of evidence such as dreams were compounded by difficulties in identifying material evidence. The authorities could not arrest suspects, for instance, on the basis of finding masks, costumes or weapons similar to those thought to be used by the leopard

Figure 6.3 Human-leopard costume (Reproduced with kind permission of the Bodleian Library, University of Oxford)[11]

men. Masquerade costumes and sharp farming tools could be found in any household – which made distinguishing specific 'man-leopard' evidence almost impossible (see Figures 6.2 and 6.3 for those items that were collected and photographed). There were widespread suspicions, however, that the killers used wooden sticks that were carved at the base in order to fake leopard pad prints when pressed into the mud or sand at the crime scene. During 1946 the police thought they were close to tracking down the 'leopards' when stories reached them of a man who carved wooden leopard pads and that such an implement had been found in a house in Ikot Afanga. Further enquiry, however, revealed that Akpan Umoh Urom, who was a government informer from Ikot Afanga, had commissioned the carving of a

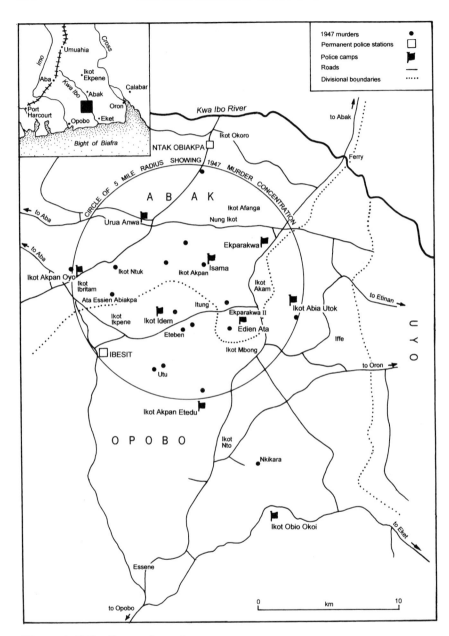

Figure 6.4 The 'leopard area'

leopard pad from the Chukwu family of carvers in Utu Etim Ekpo. He had planted this evidence in the compound of Udo Ukot Enang in order to land him in trouble. The perplexing nature of the material evidence, then, was compounded by the dubious ways in which it was gathered, especially when informants proved so 'ingenious'. Stories about the leopard men were easily invented, though this act betrayed some wider knowledge or suspicion of the use of particular implements and techniques. In fact, no evidence of leopard 'claws' manufactured from locally smelted iron and a common feature of other human leopard incidents was ever recorded, though Ken Barnes, the last British District Officer at Abak, claimed to have seen such a metal claw and a leopard pug mark locked in a drawer of the safe at the Abak District Office in 1959.[12]

Certain practices employed by the police further exacerbated the way in which people could use the strange deaths to accuse and implicate their rivals and enemies. Unwa Offiong, a woman from Ikot Obong Akan, was murdered on 9 February 1946. Her head, left arm and breast had been cut off. The pathologist concluded that: 'These injuries could not have been self-inflicted nor could any agency, other than human, have performed these severances'.[13] After the crime was discovered all the village chiefs were arrested and kept in detention until they named the killer. One of the chiefs implicated a man called Udo Ekpo. When the case came to court the following year the judge considered that the accusation conveniently settled a grudge as Udo Ekpo had built a road over the chief's land without his permission. The chief had previously sold this land and the purchaser now demanded his money back. The judge believed that the chief's accusation was false and he acquitted Udo Ekpo; he noted that the practice by which chiefs were coerced into naming a suspect 'provides excellent opportunities for vindictive men and women to satisfy their vengeance'.[14]

The following story of accusations, judicial politics and encounters with the leopard men illustrates the way in which these accusations worked. In 1945 the marriage between a man from Opobo and an Annang woman was dissolved but the husband sued for the return of debts in Opobo court at the coast. As a result, Nwori Iwo Enang, as she recounts, had to travel by canoe from Edem Idim in Ukanafun to Opobo on what proved an eventful journey:

> I proceeded on journey with the accompaniment of Chief Akpan Anwadem of Ukanafun, Chief Fred Akpanwa of Obete, Chief John Umo Akan of Ukanafun, Mr Inokon-Uyo and four canoe men who were pulling us to Opobo, and when we got to the place I went to the Court and met with the DO Opobo holding reviewed cases in the same court and such presented the [particulars] of my case. On our return, we were attacked by men-leopards whom I believed they were hired by the Plaintiff in the case who is my bitter enemy to kill me

especially. This was the plan that the Plaintiff had, hence he tricklishly transferred the case to Opobo. By the power of the Almighty God we managed to escape and hide ourselves in the compound of Chief Strongface of Opobo, with the exception of Chief Fred Akpanwa who misleadingly took different course. Chief Fred Akpanwa had to return after great suffering from where he was hiding to his home, and consequence to that, he summoned me before his villagers and accused me for betraying him to be killed and I was blamed and ordered to pay him 34 manillas for his expenditure to return home and also for the loss of some of his properties. If, in my first attempt to appear for this case, I met with such a narrow escape from death it means if I venture to continue I will surely lost my life, which I hope your worship does not pray for such.[15]

The letter that Nworie Iwo Enang wrote to the authorities of her unique escape from the leopard men centres on two accusations. First, she accuses her former husband of arranging for the case to be transferred to Opobo in order that he could hire leopard men to ambush her, because only he among her enemies knew where and when she was travelling. Second, the chief who had accompanied her, Fred Akpanwa, accused her of hiring the leopard men and of attempting to kill him because she had arranged the journey and had apparently left him alone to evade the leopard men. Both accusations worked in the same way, as *post hoc* deductions that the leopard men must have been hired by the only person responsible for the potential victim being where they were at a particular time.

A case such as this pointed to two problems when it came to court: the opportunities afforded by the murder for false allegations, and the lack of corroboration for such an allegation despite the presence of witnesses. 'It will be clear to the Judge', wrote Kay, 'that with such a society operating almost any person might be accused of being a member of it and sent to his doom by perjured evidence. ... I view with profound misgiving the inadequacy of the evidence on such of the case files as I have seen'.[16] The Divisional authorities knew that they were prosecuting cases in court with serious flaws and that the lack of corroborative evidence in many cases could be easily demonstrated. It would be clear to the judge in a number of cases, for instance, that if the Crown witnesses' testimony was true, then there should be witnesses to prove it.

Despite the unparalleled intensity of the police enquiry and the limited successes they had made, Kay claimed that under the existing legal restraints government forces were faced with inevitable defeat. Notwithstanding his misgivings about the problematic evidence before him Kay, as leading investigator, did not implement safeguards to deal with witness testimony. Rather, he argued for the opposite – a relaxation of the requirements for arrest, because of the supposed level of risk posed by the 'leopard society'.

As a result Kay made a case for extending the powers of the investigating authorities which he justified by emphasising the scope and scale of the 'man-leopard' society's operations in Abak:

> The Leopard Society effectively dominates an area some 300 square miles in extent (excluding Opobo) containing not less than 100,000 people ... all the prominent members of native society are members, Government and Native authority officials within the area of operations are terrorised, and outside the area of operations are sufficiently frightened to reveal nothing. The police must fight a losing battle alone, or with the aid of a single District Officer who has no time to give the areas, village by village, the intensive attention each requires'.[17]

In making his case Kay also framed the murders as a challenge to colonial authority, and claimed that 'the Leopard Society has been the undisputed authority in these areas for several years, and ... it has had repeated accessions of strength, until it has become sufficiently reckless to challenge Government'.[18]

Under emergency powers the provisions of the existing law could be changed, and in January 1946 Kay urged the Government to impose the Peace Preservation Ordinance on Abak and Opobo Districts. The Ordinance gave the authorities the power arbitrarily to search and arrest suspects, who could then be detained for up to a year. Under this law it was possible to give the Resident more information than he might normally see in a criminal case and it enabled him to order an arrest on suspicion alone. The cost of stationing troops or police in districts proclaimed under the Ordinance was also to be levied punitively upon the inhabitants.[19] It was known to the officers conducting the investigation that the Ordinance was primarily designed to deal with political disturbances of the 'Palestinian type' and that it constituted a significant breach of the constitutional privileges of the subject:

> It constitutes a very grave interference with those liberties, however primitive the subject who enjoys them. But the subjects in this area cannot conscientiously be said to be enjoying them. Hundreds of murders are taking place.[20]

In key respects the enactment of the Ordinance which made Abak and Opobo 'proclaimed districts' in February 1946 was a recognition of failure, as these extraordinary measures were designed for insurgencies, not murder enquiries. Yet this was also an important watershed in the investigation as it introduced the possibility of far greater political repression by the colonial authorities.

The immediate impact of the Peace Preservation Ordinance was to enable the authorities to arrest the twelve members of àfé ékényòŋ in Ikot Afanga, who were immediately transferred to Calabar Prison. Since there was little evidence to link them individually to specific murders, and Joseph Udo had refused to turn King's evidence, it was proposed to charge them with being members of an unlawful society. The àfé ékényòŋ members themselves claimed that before they were transferred the District Officer had given them an oath to swear that their innocence would be proved if they lived for seven days. Four of the members wrote to the Resident to confirm that they had survived the ordeal, were still alive and complained at being detained three months later.[21]

The proclamation also meant that the murders became public. The Peace Preservation Ordinance was one of a number of coercive laws first introduced in Nigeria in 1912 along with the Collective Punishment Ordinance, the Unsettled District Ordinance and the Deposed Chief Removal Ordinance which all became principal targets in the opposition rhetoric of the nationalist elites.[22] Initially, however, all quarters of public opinion in Calabar Province were broadly supportive of the 1946 proclamation. Such was the clamour for definitive judgments and rigorous punishment in the man-leopard murder cases that local chiefs from the Central Annang Council petitioned that those accused of murder should not be allowed access to lawyers, that Government should not use too many witnesses in court and that convicted killers should be hanged.[23]

Press scrutiny of the murder enquiries became intense from this moment onwards. The *Nigerian Eastern Mail* soon devoted its weekly editorial to the murder investigation and what it called the 'outbreak of terrorism' in Calabar Province. The editor himself toured the newly proclaimed districts and interviewed the leading police inspectors. The letter columns were full of speculation about the underlying causes of the murders, with readers invited to write in to provide evidence on particular lines of enquiry. Public calls were made for the improvement unions, the Ibibio Union and the Abak Divisional League, to assist with the enquiry. 'Merely bringing the murderers to book and suppressing the activities of the society is not enough,' the *Mail* argued. 'A thorough investigation of the source and origin of the trouble must be held and in this very necessary work the native administration and the local branches of the Ibibio Union ought to be able to render yeoman service'.[24]

By August members of the Ikot Ekpene literary club were holding a debate on the murders at the public library. There they debated the motion that: 'This house believes the man-leopard society can be eliminated by education'. During the debate the Assistant Superintendent of Police, Mr D. A. Awode, outlined his theories and findings on the man-leopard murders, claiming that within the past four years no fewer than 250 people had been killed by the human-leopards. The aim and object of the society, he said, was to establish in 'unchallenged secret' an opportunity for the members to satisfy their craving for human blood. In his talk he made the first recorded allusion to the link between the murders and cannibalism, and to ethnic cleavages between Ibibio and Annang. Awode said that: 'the man-leopard society exists across Ibibioland but no "real" Ibibio man had been proved to be a member – those so far brought to book belong to the primitive section of Annang'.[25]

Elsewhere, the tone of public discourse in the editorials and correspondence of the 'reading public' placed a consistent emphasis on the links between the killings and the failings of indirect rule. In this framing the murders were thought to have originated as a result of several factors including the lack of administrative supervision in Abak and Opobo caused by the shortage of staff during the war along with the lack of progressive churches, schools, health facilities and roads in the area. Local elites had long been arguing for investment in Abak district because extensive areas of Ikot Ibratim, northern and southern Afaha and Ukanafun were outside easy reach of communication.[26] 'It is disgusting to note', a letter-writer from Afaha commented, 'that the only progressive measures taken here have been to erect court and council buildings at every nook and corner of the division'.[27] The police station was about 35 miles from the more remote communities within the division and their residents travelled even further to Aba, Ikot Ekpene or Uyo for medical services. As a result the progressives petitioned for government investment from the Colonial Development Fund in direct response to the leopard murders:

> Sub-post offices, postal agencies, schools and dispensaries should be established in the heart of the division ... in one word the divisions should be opened up to civilisation.[28]

The progressives' discourse on the murders was to frame them as a revival of the now much reviled secret societies, an insurgency instigated by a rural hierarchy of illiterate chiefs, and a conservative backlash to changes in Annang society, especially innovations in marriage and divorce cases which emerged in the courts. The *Nigerian Eastern Mail*'s view of the cause of the murders, the progress of the investigations and the impact of the Peace Preservation Ordinance, for example, was captured in the paper's first editorial after the ordinance was brought into force:

> The epidemic of men-leopard murders in the Abak and Opobo Divisions has naturally caused Government great worry and concern. Whatever may be the root cause of this outbreak of wanton barbarity and savagery, it has been aggravated by the lack of police supervision caused by the reduction in the Police Force during the war. It is suspected in some quarters that conservative and anti-social elements influential in the tribal life of the areas concerned are using the evil society as a sort of Klu Klux Klan to terrorise womankind and check any tendency to greater social freedom on the part of the women of

their communities, especially in view of the tendency of the native courts to give women greater facilities in divorcing unsatisfactory husbands than had been traditionally allowed them.

Be that as it may, the mass of the people are behind Government in its efforts to put an end to this terror. But public opinion in the areas effected believes that some persons influential in tribal life are behind the malign activities of the society. In the circumstances we consider that Government has acted wisely by declaring the divisions concerned to be proclaimed districts for the purpose of the Peace Preservation (Protectorate) Ordinance. This enables suspected persons to be arrested on a warrant signed by the Resident. The ordinance also provides a penalty for any person who may conceal or in any other way aid a person against whom a warrant has been issued and requires all arms and ammunition in the hands of the public to be delivered up under penalty of three months' imprisonment or a fine of £20.

The situation is sufficiently grave to justify the proclamation of this ordinance and we can only urge the people of the Abak and Opobo Divisions to give the police, the troops (if any are sent there) and the administrative staff their fullest co-operation to stamp out this menace.

The only section in the ordinance we read with some misgiving was that about charging the poor inhabitants of the afflicted district with the cost of any extra police or troops used to restore conditions to normal. The people of Abak and Opobo are among the poorest in Nigeria and may well be let off this extra burden.[29]

The police presence and the Peace Preservation Ordinance had little effect, however, on the murder rate. The press reported that although no official statement of the number killed had been published, it was estimated that well over 100 people had fallen victim to the 'fiends',[30] and that to the outside world the rapid spread of 'leopard mania' was a direct challenge to the local Native authorities and to the Ibibio Union.[31]

'WHAT IS AT THE BOTTOM OF THE LEOPARD MAN EPIDEMIC?'

Since this series of human leopard murders started ... things have gone from bad to worse, until a veritable reign of terror prevails in the division. ... No doubt the police will sooner or later get the horrible situation under control. But knowing that crime waves, even of this nature, have their cause and origin like other social phenomena, we ask ourselves what is at the bottom of the leopard man epidemic? How strong is the society and what causes have revived it and galvanised it into such horrible wholesale activity? Surely the police, the DO Abak and the Resident of the Province must have been asking themselves this question.[32]

Despite the large police operation, and with all the Native Courts in Abak, Midim, Ibesit and Ibiaku now closed, no reliable information regarding the man-leopard society had been gathered. The successes made in prosecuting individual cases were of little use, it was argued, whilst the murders continued and the authorities sought an overarching explanation to tie together the numerous loose ends. With the number of murders growing, the question which dominated the investigation was indeed, what lay at the bottom of the man-leopard epidemic. If the authorities could understand why the killings were taking place, it was assumed they would be one step closer to being able to 'stamp out the menace' completely.

In the course of 1946 a number of theories were proposed to explain the murders. Three related ideas dominated speculation, each of which resonated with familiar colonial and local anxieties – the 'master-juju thesis', the 'secret society revival' and 'witchcraft'. A 'master-juju' theory had formed part of the investigation from its earliest stages. In January 1946 the police began to try to explain why the apparent motives for murder appeared so slight. What else other than some ritual purpose might account for a murder for a 2-manilla debt or 120 manillas in refunded brideprice?[33] Within colonial circles it was widely believed that there was a religious significance to the deaths and that the killers performed appeasement ceremonies before shrines – either in a local village or at a master-shrine reminiscent of the Long Juju of Arochukwu. One of the first lines of enquiry was to examine how 'human beings were being killed at random to satisfy some curious ritualistic need of a juju or society'.[34] Police training, indeed, had emphasised the need for officers to be aware of secret societies and shrines in crime detection. The 1937 issue of *Nigeria Police Magazine*, for instance, had stressed the need for knowledge of 'local superstition' and a study of local fetishes as they were often believed to provide clues to motive.[35] The theory that the murders were linked to the ritual demands of shrines and societies focused the investigation on the role of shrine priests, the *idìɔ̄ŋ* diviners. Kay summed up the range of views held by officers concerning *idìɔ̄ŋ* and the master-juju thesis in early 1946:

> The priests must be in it, though at present there is no evidence to connect the [leopard] society with idiong, the most exclusive of all native societies, whose members are diviners. … Mr Ogbolu (Assistant Superintendent of Police) shares my opinion that there is a master-juju. Mr Allen (DO Opobo) and the other police officers agree that there is a religious significance, but are not sure of the master-juju. They incline to the belief that propitiation ceremonies are carried out before some shrine in the village of the victim or of the murderers, or

possibly in both villages. The evidence is inconclusive, but it is clear that if a master-juju exists we must locate it.[36]

This suggestion resonated with a consistent colonial fear of the Long Juju and of its revival. It also played on a supposed link between the Long Juju and Annang *idiɔŋ* diviners. Reports of the time were replete with cross-references to M. D. W. Jeffreys' earlier research, which suggested two specific associations. The first was his narration of the early history of Aro in which he argued that the Long Juju was formerly an Annang settlement. The second was the ritual and symbolic connection maintained, he claimed, between the shrine and the use of a distinctive white and yellow chalk (*ńdôm*) by *idiɔŋ* priests at their shrines.[37]

More substantive evidence for the 'master-juju's' existence emerged in August 1946 when the police discovered that *ékpê ówó* killers had visited the grave of a former *idiɔŋ* man 'of evil repute' to perform certain sacrifices and to invoke his spirit before undertaking murder. The grave was that of Chief Ukpaka of Ikot Akam who had died thirty years previously. His grandson, who was thought to be one of the originators of *ékpê ówó*, died in Opobo prison on 23 July 1946 awaiting trial on a leopard murder charge. 'There appears almost unanimous belief', the police superintendent reported, 'that if this grave were destroyed there would be no further leopard society murders. Although I am not sufficiently optimistic to imagine we have stumbled across the "master ju-ju", the existence of which has been suggested before, I consider this line of enquiry sufficiently interesting to follow up'.[38] Chief Ukpaka's remains were exhumed, but evidence from other murders suggested to the police that the grave did not have the widespread influence that had been supposed.

While the police were discouraged that the chief's burial site was not a central shrine, it may indeed have had significance for the killers in several other ways. First, it may have been linked to a traditional form of ritual murder in Annang society. This involved the preparation of a charm ring by an *ábíà idiɔŋ*. The ring is left on the grave of a former *idiɔŋ* for seven days after which it can be employed to inflict a spell of madness, sickness or death on its victim by touching them with the ring (*tùàk tùàk ibɔ̀k*, lit. to hit medicine). Second, this chief's grave may have been especially potent because of the violent (*àfái*) way in which he died. Chief Ukpaka's remains were found to show precisely those injuries the Medical Officer had become familiar with from the post-mortem examinations of leopard murder cases. The killers may therefore have been attempting to invoke and prepare a fatal medicine from the grave in order to effect the same form of death that the chief had suffered. If the forensic evidence was reliable, then it was likely that ceremonies were performed at his grave because of the way he died rather than simply because of his status as an *idiɔŋ*. It also suggested the possibility that murders of this type had been committed over the past thirty years. The police concluded, however, that 'the quest for the "master-juju" – though a most attractive idea is a vain dream'.[39]

The suspicion that the murders were linked to a regional network of shrines led investigators back to the problematic evidence of ritual motives. The limited scope of forensic investigations conducted at Ikot Ekpene tended to corroborate a view that, 'where murderers have not been interrupted and the full ritual has been performed, there has been a marked similarity in the condition of the corpses'.[40] A pattern by which male victims had their right arm removed while female victims had their left arm severed began to emerge. The police believed that during warfare in pre-colonial times the head and right arm of an enemy were cut off to be presented to àbàsì ékóŋ, the deity of war. Though it was not fully appreciated at the time, a wild leopard attack on a human being would only very rarely sever the head or any limb.[41] It now appears likely that the killers performed this act, not for the preparation of medicines as the police suspected, but to prevent the spirits (ékpó) of the victims from pursuing the assailants.

In Annang belief the right arm is the source of strength, and by removing it the killer deprived the victim's spirit of the means to furnish a weapon in the spirit world (óbìò ékpó) since it serves to dissipate the úyìb òkpòsòŋ ówó (a person's strong blood). Hence, when a person is killed by mbiàm their body is not buried but thrown into the bush, and the right arm and the head are removed to prevent the mbiàm from returning and attacking other members of the family. The same principle of the right arm applies to women. This means the motive behind the removal of a woman's left arm during ékpê-ówó is more obscure, but it might be explained by the fact that when a libation is poured to a female ancestor, which constitutes direct contact with the spirit world, the pourer uses their left hand. At the time of the killings, however, it was believed that the severed limbs were conferring financial rewards on the killers rather than spiritual protection. Propaganda employed during the man-leopard campaign, based on isolated reports, claimed that the killers were selling flesh and body parts to the ídìòŋ society of diviners and to unidentified buyers in neighbouring Ogoni. In May 1946 reports came to light that the body parts of ékpê-ówó victims were being sold in the Opobo Division, but despite an investigation the connection with Ogoni remained unproven.[42]

The reason for the mutilations to the body of the leopard murder victims, beyond those that disguised the fatal wounds themselves, remained a mystery. The remarkable similarity between individual murders, however, suggested that they were the work of a complex network. The most persistent analogy employed in explaining the killings, in fact, was that they were organised by a secret society – the man-leopard society. The secret society was and remains the dominant local idiom to describe covert mobilisation, and with Annang secret societies thoroughly demonised in Christian rhetoric and on the verge of being criminalised by the colonial state, they became the object of considerable suspicion. Mounting evidence fuelled an underlying colonial fear that the murders were a result of the sort of secret society revival that had been witnessed in the province during the 1910s and 1920s. Kay was partly responsible for shaping the colonial conception of the killers' organisation. During a previous posting in Ogoja Province in 1938 he had investigated head-hunting murders in Obubra District and was struck by the similarity of the mutilation with the leopard killings, as facial tissue was removed from the victims in both cases.[43] In Obubra the killers were members of the Abam society and Kay suspected that the Annang murderers were similarly organised in a secret society.[44] Kay was delighted therefore when the police detachment that arrived in January 1946 included Assistant Superintendent Ogbolu who had served in Abak division during the *ékpê* society revival of 1925.

The theory that the killings marked a revival of an Annang secret society therefore invited confusing comparisons between *ékpê ówó* and the *ékpê* society – between the leopard men and the members of the leopard society. The *ékpê* society's previous role in 'disposing of malefactors' meant that the analogy was quickly applied to the deaths of the 1940s which observers attributed to an *ékpê* society revival. This would suggest that a proportion of the deaths were attributable to executions of criminals carried out clandestinely by *ékpê* turned *ékpê-ówó*. Based on a District Officer's suggestions made in 1946, more recent analysts have therefore subscribed to the view that: 'When ekpe began to use the leopard method as cover, it became ekpe owo'.[45] Further speculation has suggested that the identity of the killers and the methods of their murders were concealed by use of the secret *nsibidi* script used by the *ékpê* society.[46] Such links between the killers and the *ékpê* society, however, are purely conjectural. *Nsibidi*, the script of the Calabar *ékpê* society, was never used by Annang lodges. Also, the *ékpê* society did not kill by imitating a wild leopard, but rather by driving a spike through the head of a victim trussed up at the village's execution grove (*úkâŋ inò*). Furthermore, no evidence emerged from confessions or otherwise that the murders were organised by a revived or reformed *ékpê* society as it had in the 1920s. Eyewitnesses to the murders in the 1940s, in fact, dismiss such suggestions outright and it is apparent that *ékpê ówó* was a quite different development.

Nevertheless, the implications of the connection are wide-ranging. Leopards in this context provided a discursive symbol in which judicial executions were performed and in which executioners were able to evade the attribution of individual guilt. To say that a 'leopard' had 'eaten' a person who was killed by members of the *ékpê* society was an accepted euphemism. The parallels between this and eyewitness testimonies during the murder enquiries that said they had seen a 'leopard' attack their friend or relative is replete with a range of possibilities about the meaning of the word 'leopard' and the way that it could refer to an executioner, animal or assassin. This scenario also raises questions as to whether there was a consensus about the identity of the victims and the reasons why they should be killed. The possibility that killings were sanctioned by collective authorities in the style of an *ékpê* execution had already been suggested during the investigations into *àfé ékényòŋ*. Such a process would suggest that the victims were guilty of some form of moral or criminal transgression. There is no evidence that this was the case, but the idea that the murders represented any form of anti-colonial resistance by village hierarchies was what the authorities feared most.

The local press picked up on the idea that the murders were the result of a leopard society revival, and reported that the society had been known 'from time immemorial'.[47] The press also drew an intriguing historical parallel in reminding their readers that during colonial rule the leopard society had surfaced in an overtly political guise in similar circumstances during the 1914–18 war when there had also been a shortage of administrative staff, an economic crisis and widespread uncertainty:

> At one time … the leopard society held sway all over the country. In 1916, for instance, there used to be an average of three murders a day in Ikot Ekpene. Nowadays if you wanted to remove a relative to inherit his wealth, to kill an enemy or kill your wife's lover in this part of Abak and Opobo Divisions, you pay the Leopard Society 100 manillas. They also make a profit on the corpse by selling part of it to juju men to make medicine. A medicine for hunters to give them a strong heart, was made from the heart of the victim. The skin scraped from his forehead made love medicine. The victim was always clubbed from behind and his forehead scraped to give the appearance of having been scratched by a leopard's claws. The right arm was cut off if the victim was a man and the left if it was a woman. The breast was always torn open and the heart removed.[48]

Various clues suggested that the killers were organised as a formal society. There was evidence of initiation into *ékpê ówó*. Witnesses spoke of members and membership of '*ékpê ówó*'. Police interpreters confirmed that the word '*ádúk*' (initiate or member) was used. Evidence emerged, for instance, that a society of twelve men from Ikot Akan was hired from far and wide and that they met regularly, bringing with them to their meetings goats, cocks and manillas as their contributions to the preparation of charms with which they facilitated the murders.[49] When a suspected leopard man, Jacob Ekanem, was arrested, the police constable noticed four vertical parallel scarification lines on his left wrist. 'We have heard this is the mark of an ekpe owo member', wrote the police superintendent, 'though it seems rather improbable that the society would facilitate our work to the extent of branding its members with such a distinctive device'.[50] Precisely the same puzzle had arisen during the special commission trials during the early 1900s in Sierra Leone.[51] Nevertheless, witnesses came forward claiming to have seen *èkpê ówó* initiations. Unanem Udo was witnessed initiating Etuk Udo Udo, who paid 68 manillas, a cock and a calabash of palm wine for membership and Unanem scratched three or four marks on his wrist and chest.[52]

Why a covert group of murderers would so readily identify themselves with these marks was never answered and indeed undermined the credibility of such evidence in court. It is most likely that these marks were linked, in fact, to a protective cult which was popular in the Abak-Opobo region at the time known as *àním èkìm*. There is no ready translation of this name, though it may be linked to the words to disappear (*ním*) and to become black (*kìm*).[53] *Àním èkìm* entered southern Annang communities through the trading rivers and was founded by Opobo merchants who had settled at waterside markets. The cult provided protection against the predations of malevolent ancestral spirits (*idíók or àfáí èkpó*). Initiation into *àním èkìm* involved the preparation of a protective medicine from the charcoal produced by burning beans, human bone and sand from the burial place of an *idìɔŋ*. This medicine was inserted into seven marks cut into the body, usually three and four cuts to the left and right sides of the chest or hands.

The debate over the constitution of the man-leopard society echoed contemporary discourses about secret societies promoted by missionaries, colonial officials and 'progressives'. Here the argument ran parallel to those that questioned the authenticity of societies during the 1940s and focused on how societies had become 'corrupted' and criminal. At the outset the authorities in Abak and Opobo had been convinced that a type of leopard society, though perhaps not the 'real' leopard society, was in operation. In July 1945 Kay had written that: 'There is a gang of murderers imitating for private gain the methods of the leopard society but the society *qua* society is not operating. It is sheer murder without any ritual significance'.[54] From the evidence of Joseph Udo's confession it was assumed that the original society had been formed at Ikot Afanga and that as its power and fame grew, branches were formed in other villages such as Itung and Ibesit, either because a member of the society had migrated there or because people from the area had been sent to find out the secrets of the society. It was thought unlikely then that there was a central organising body directing the activities of all groups or a 'Chief Leopard Man', but rather that this society was decentralised, and that village 'cells' operated more or less independently of each other.

Armed with this model of the secret society, though lacking any evidence, it was supposed that the society's spread occurred in two phases: first, by authentic 'leopard-men' who employed all of the various devices (costumes, medicines and claws) to disguise their acts, and second, by those who effected crude imitations of the 'leopard-style'. The later phase was thought to have seen the formation of so-called 'imitative societies' in which little was known of the original ritual apart from the method by which a murder could be passed off as a killing by a leopard.[55] The apparent dread and fear in which the society was held enabled these 'imitation' leopard murders to continue undetected:

> It appears that a number of persons have in the past adopted the methods of the leopard society when satisfying their private grudges in the hope of being protected by the fear which it inspires and the cloak of secrecy with which it is surrounded.[56]

Hence, although they had assumed the existence of an 'original' leopard society, the colonial investigative apparatus concluded that the murders they were confronted by in 1946 were only imitations of the 'real' thing. Despite continuing reference to the 'man-leopard society' throughout the enquiries the idea that a formal agency was orchestrating the killings dissolved over time and returned to Kay's original idea of a 'gang of murderers': 'We are up against not an organised society – as the Yoruba Ogboni or Imule Societies – but rather a cult which has grown up gradually mainly through the very prevalent belief in lycanthropy'.[57]

Whether they were linked to shrines or to secret societies remained an unresolved puzzle, but in either guise the man-leopard murders played on existing ideas of Annang shape-shifting and witchcraft. P. P. Grey, who succeeded Kay as District Officer Abak in June 1946,[58] suggested that it was hardly surprising that these ideas were such a prevalent aspect of the enquiries 'when prominent local inhabitants and even some of the police believe that a man can turn himself into a leopard'.[59] At the time ideas of shape-shifting were referred to in colonial discourse as 'lycanthropy', which more accurately refers to the assumption by supernatural means of the form and nature of a wolf (a were-wolf). Contemporary investigators, however, were alive to three aspects of Annang beliefs about human metamorphosis into a leopard – that they were associated with people of powerful status, that the process was internalised, and that the capacity to become a leopard depended on the manufacture of medicines (*ibɔk*):

> The belief in lycanthropy is common. Certain persons in each village or district would gain the reputation of having the power of changing into leopards – a reputation which they would certainly do their best to encourage as it would give them power over other people and add to their prestige and the awe in which they were held. Later they would use their reputed powers to rid themselves of their enemies. ... Possibly he does actually believe that he changed into a leopard at the moment of killing. In any case, he is certain that his medicines will protect him;

that any witness to the crime will see, not him, but a genuine leopard attacking his victim. [60]

In certain respects the deaths attributed to human leopards can be perceived in ways analogous to witchcraft. Most instances of 'leopardism', for instance, played on beliefs in the supernatural powers of bodily transformation. Like witches, the human leopards were also associated with initiations and drew on the polysemic etymology of 'consuming' human flesh. At specific levels the parallels between the leopard men and the forms of witchcraft experienced in Annang society, *ifót* and *ùbén*, are highly suggestive. Like *ùbén* witchcraft the leopard men were thought to be shape-shifters and their attacks were similarly linked to contemporary gender politics and domestic violence. The links with *ifót* are evident in the prior threats of killers, reports of victims identifying the killers on their deathbeds, and stories of the removal of body parts. In this light, the ways in which sudden death is understood through the accusation of Annang witchcraft might be transposed to a 'human leopard murder' context but for two key objections. First, the medical evidence pointed unequivocally, at this stage, to the fact that the victims had been murdered in specific, broadly identical ways. Second, local people in each setting drew clear distinctions between witches and leopard men. Witchcraft cases were reported to the authorities during the period of the leopard murders and there was little apparent reticence in discussing their specifics. Indeed, neither at the time nor since has *ékpê-ówó* been linked to or described as one of the two main forms of witchcraft experienced in Annang society, *ifót* or *ùbén*.

Nevertheless, the argument that the man-leopard killings were ritually motivated and were linked to witchcraft and metamorphosis cults was supported by claims made during the investigations that the killers were using 'medicines' and charms. Medicines (*ibɔk*) were reportedly prepared to give the killers different powers and forms of protection. The combination of medicines and charms were taken by the killers to invoke reactions so as to make people forget (*firé*), to hold someone back (*ńdúɔhɔ*), and to warn of impending danger (*ńdómó*). It remains a commonly narrated story that '*ékpê ówó* used medicine to make people take a particular path or go to market even when they did not want to go'. What is missing from this list, however, is the potion or preparations to effect metamorphosis, the transformation into a leopard or projection of the leopard bush soul *(ékpê úkpɔŋ ikɔt).*

Informants reported in 1946 that a Hausa trader called Abraham, from Bende Division, had sold 'leopard medicine' shortly after the killings began to Akpan Ekpedeme of Itung. Abraham was never traced and officials speculated that he had exploited a niche in the medicines market with remarkably good timing. The medicine described was said to impart the strength of a leopard to its user and was taken to prevent detection by the authorities. Akpan Ekpedeme had died before the investigations into the leopard murders began, which meant that the exact nature of his involvement became the subject of considerable speculation typical of the dilemmas of indeterminacy common to the murder investigations. Akpan Ekpedeme was a prominent *ídìɔ̨* member, a blacksmith who made knives and spears, and the widely acclaimed founder of *ékpê-ówó*.

While the colonial gaze began to shift towards more remote and impersonal causes during 1946, local people were identifying individuals responsible not only for particular murders but for the outbreak as a whole. Leopard murder accusations, like witchcraft discourses, were a way of making sense of a world riven with social tensions and ambiguous relationships and served to 'personalise the universe'.[61] The purported and changing role of Akpan Ekpedeme, for instance, not only gives some indication of the state of confusion to which the various murder theories had contributed, but also to a key ontological disjunction between investigators and their informants. Those stories which name individuals as the architects of *ékpê ówó*, particularly Akpan Ekpedeme and Akpan Anyoho, reveal much of the logic that constitutes Annang modes of explanation. Not only were particular people named, but their associates were said to be related to them. Akpan Anyoho, a middle-aged farmer from Itung, was said variously to be the grandson or sister's son of Akpan Ekpedeme, and was sentenced to death by the Supreme Court at Opobo in November 1946.[62] Willie Akpan Udo Anwa, the person found guilty of the quadruple murder in Ikot Akam in 1945, was said to be the son of Akpan Anyoho's sister. It is in reference to these personal kinship links that speculations are related to another of the enduring mysteries of the leopard murders – why the killings were confined to the villages on the Abak–Opobo border without spreading. The social orbits of the gang members, it is argued, simply did not extend beyond the Ibesit–Ikot Okoro axis (see Figure 6.4).

The story of the leopard men's medicine is an often rehearsed but usually fragmented contemporary story about the charms and preparations they employed. There are many variations of this story. The Ibesit court chiefs, for instance, made a statement on precisely this aspect in January 1946 in which the same individuals are identified but in which the medicine has a far more familiar origin – the grave of a former *ídìɔ̨*:

> Akpan Ekpedeme is the head of 'ekpe owo' society, he is a native of Itung, he is now dead and his son Akpan Anyoho of Itung is now the head of the society together with Akpan Adiaha Otu of Itung. About 4 years ago Akpan Anyoho and Akpan Adiaha Otu went to the grave of Essien Udom and made some 'ekpe' medicine there.[63]

Strands of the narrative therefore focus on the possible identity and location of the specialist responsible for the medicine's preparation. Other aspects of this story include reports of a pot, sometimes described as a palm fruit fermenting pot (*àkò átá*), in which the leopard men washed themselves and first smeared the 'leopard' medicine on their bodies in order to change into a leopard and then its antidote (*àdìtìbé*) to change back to human form.

The following story casts further light on the origin and meaning of the leopard men's medicine. Throughout spells of fieldwork conducted over six years no one had spoken to me of their personal complicity with the leopard men, nor had they betrayed intimate knowledge of the ritual performances attached to the killings. This changed in February 2003, when I visited a man in Nkek called Akpan Idungafa Echiet (whose nickname is 'Seven Tongues') renowned for his possession of supernatural powers to counter witches. Taken by my interest in the leopard men, he recounted the following story. He was the first son of Idungafa Echiet, an *idíɔŋ* who was approached at some point during the Second World War by a man called Akommem from Nung Ikot. Akommem had married Echiet's daughter. Within Nung Ikot village Akommem had been asked for help from a husband in dispute with his intended wife. The husband had sponsored the woman's education, but after finishing school she refused to marry him. The husband wanted to kill her, and Akommem said he knew someone who could disguise the murder. Akommem knew that Idungafa Echiet was a man who could 'make things happen', and that he had knowledge of *ŋkà òkpɔsɔŋ ówó* (the society of powerful men) and *ŋkà ùkpôtìò* (the society of fearless witch-finders). Akommem invited him from Nkek to prepare the means for conducting the first 'man-leopard' murder. Echiet's son who recounted these events to me accompanied him carrying various implements to Nung Ikot, and was therefore an eyewitness to the preparation of *ibɔk ékpê ówó* (the medicine of the leopard men).

Echiet recalled that he and his father prepared the medicine at *Usung Ubom* (a path leading from Nung Ikot Obiodo to Nung Ikot Asanga) which was shielded by tall trees. The means by which the medicine worked was as follows. Somebody with a dispute or an enemy would approach Echiet at *Usung Ubom* and would ask him to prepare the medicine. The medicine's most significant ingredient was the use of palm wine which had fermented for three days but which had not been allowed to touch the ground (*ùfùm ínám úkɔt*, lit. suspended shock drink). Fruits from tall trees that have not touched the ground are commonly used in medicinal concoctions. Partly these ingredients and substances are powerful because Annang exegesis suggests that to touch the ground would be to share the fruit or wine with the ancestral spirits of the soil and hence erode its power. Possibly also the potency of this palm wine is linked to its unnatural method of production since the suspended palm wine subverts the Annang symmetry of up and down, of sky and soil, and fails to resolve the ritual invocation of both *àbàsì ényɔŋ* and *àbàsì ìkpá ísɔŋ*.

The palm wine was kept inside an *àkò átá* pot, used for fermenting palm oil. Into this pot the person undertaking the killing placed a piece of paper with the name of the intended victim written on it along with sand from the grave of a dead medicine specialist (*àbìà ibɔ́k*). Also dipped into the pot was a platted raffia palm leaf known as *áfɔt* (lit. to tie in a loop) whose tip was frayed to create small sharp points. When the killer 'blew drink' (*éfùt ékód*, lit. blow and call) the victim would be lured to their inevitable demise at a predetermined place where the killer could lay an ambush. By flicking the palm leaf (*áfɔt*) at them and spraying them with the medicinal concoction the victim would be stunned (*inám*, a state of possession likened to intoxication and often described as 'not knowing oneself') and could be dragged off to be killed and mutilated. Whether Echiet himself engaged in the killing is moot, but his son reported that as soon as the first police post was established at Ikot Okoro, Echiet carried the medicine home to Nkek, some distance outside the boundary of what would become the 'leopard area', and was never implicated.

Echiet's story is quite remarkable because of the fact that it was told at all. It also links pieces of a story that is not generally known but of which some details had circulated. The link with Akommem, the association with the village of Nung Ikot, and the description of a medicine that used the *àkò átá* pot are all aspects of the story that are corroborated from other sources. Although there is no material evidence to corroborate this story in the form of the costumes, spiked gloves or faked pad prints, it is, nevertheless, supported by the evidence of the pot used to prepare the leopard-men's medicine. Walking far into 'Seven Tongues' recently cleared farm land, at the site of his former compound (*ǹdòn*), we came upon the opening of a pot that had been buried in the ground. This pot is known variously as *ábáŋ útóm ékpê ówó* (pot of the leopard men's work) or simply as *ábáŋ úkpɔ̀ŋ* (pot of the bush soul). Only the lip of the opening and the tops of the three handles are visible. Each of the three handles of the pot is associated with its own medicine – each has its 'own work'. One is for *ékpê ówó*, one is for *ékpê m̀fòró*, and the third is for *ùkpôtiô*.[64] Underneath the pot buried deep in the soil is a wooden mortar upon which the pot rests, and below that is a human skull. Inside the pot there are a number of items, including the claws of a bush leopard, eggs, leaves, water and palm wine. In approaching the pot Echiet appeased the spirit that resides within it and in doing so poured a libation with his left hand.

It is worth pausing to interpret this story in more detail. Compared to colonial accounts, Echiet's story places much greater emphasis on the medicinal powers of the leopard men than the physical means of murder. Echiet mentioned how his father directed the killers to purchase a costume, described as a netting (*m̀bìlé àkpènè*) that could be bought in the market and which covered the entire body including the head. He also directed them to hire or commission the manufacture of the murder weapon, the so-called leopard nails (*m̀bàrá ékpê*) – a glove with three knives bound to the fingers. The meanings attributed to the ritual performance of the leopard medicine preparation were highly functional. The key aspects were stunning the victim and concealing the crime. There was no shape-shifting, no use of body parts and no association with self-empowerment. And far from being the high priest of a subversive anti-colonial movement, Echiet conceived his innovation as a niche market from which he fled as soon as he thought he might be caught. The story is of a highly decentralised operation which was initiated and expanded through personal relations. The individuals who had commissioned the medicine then acted individually and with the utmost secrecy, and it seems likely that Echiet's own identity would have been unknown even to the majority of the killers and especially those who operated in 1946 and 1947. One of the central implications of Echiet's story, therefore, is that his father established a template for murder and later concealed its source by removing himself and the medicine from the area of police surveillance in the early months of 1945.

It is also important to identify the characters in this story, and the role of the key intermediary in the village of Nung Ikot, Akommem. His full name was Akommem Nta (sometimes put as Ako Mmem or Oku Mem). Akommem was a yam farmer and cloth trader who had married four wives. He was a man of means. He had a bicycle and was the first person in the village to build a block bungalow. He joined the Qua Iboe church and took the Christian name Amos. Although Akpan Odu was the court sitting member, Akommem was óbóŋ idúŋ (the village head) and heard cases in his house on édét market day when he would receive gifts of palm wine from members of his lineage. Chief Akommem was linked to two leopard murders. In the first case the victim was living in the chief's compound and was the child of Akommem's sister. In the second case 'Chief Oko Mem Nta of Nung Ikot' was charged in 1946 along with two other men of killing Okoto Nta in September 1943 at the nearby junction and market of Urua Anwa. While the two suspected associates were found guilty and sentenced to death after losing their cases at the West African Court of Appeal, the chief was acquitted.[65] Despite these connections to two murder cases he is remembered as an upstanding and 'progressive' local leader.

In addition, there are important symbolic resonances in Echiet's story to Annang conceptions of ritual murder. The association with tall trees where the medicine was produced suggests witchcraft since ifót witches and their nocturnal cabals are associated with the tall úkpâ tree *(Pentaclethra macrophylla* – oil bean tree). The link between the leopard medicine and pots chimes with the most semiotically significant range of associations. Echiet's pot is similar to that described as being common to powerful Annang men:

Pots of the abang isong type kept in the bush by chiefs or ritual practitioners of such societies as idiong are used in the swearing of oaths or taking of ordeals.[66]

The conjunction of two forms of vessel in the story, between *ábáŋ úkpɔ́ŋ* (pot of the bush soul) and *àkò átá* (the palm oil fermenting pot), points to the association between shape-shifting, palm oil and power. Both pots were associated with transformation. The palm fruit fermentation pot (*àkò átá*) was the principal vessel within this palm oil-producing society for transforming fruit into oil, nature into wealth. Similarly, the pot of animal affinities (*ábáŋ úkpɔ́ŋ*) mediated the boundary between natural and supernatural, human and animal. Both were potent sites of metamorphosis.

The assertion that, from the moment the person was named, they were a 'dead person' and that death was inevitable is also a common feature of conceptions of *ifót* witchcraft in which the date of death is predetermined. In this respect the means of murder also closely resembles the way in which an *idìɔ̀ŋ* would stage a ritual murder – with the writing of names and the predetermining of the time and place of death.[67] The *idìɔ̀ŋ* priest himself would not be present as all *idìɔ̀ŋ* insist that, while they can facilitate a killing though spiritual means, they cannot perpetrate it themselves: 'If you are properly initiated into *idìɔ̀ŋ* your hand cannot kill'. Echiet's story, therefore, also speaks to the ambiguous role of the *idìɔ̀ŋ* diviner.

Today people say that *idìɔ̀ŋ* were the powerful (*òkpɔ̀sɔ̀ŋ*) men of the 1940s. One such figure was Akpan Udo Umana of Ikot Akpa Nkuk village in the Ukanafun clan. His reputation was derived in part from the circumstances of his initiation. Akpan Udo Umana was wearing the *ákpán ékpó* mask during an *ékpó* performance at Udondok market when he ran through the crowd into the bush and was not seen for seven days. When he finally emerged he was holding two wooden rattles (*ékpút*) in his hands, a principal symbol of *idìɔ̀ŋ*. Since he had not bought them in a market and had not paid for his initiation, the source of his power was very secretive and his *idìɔ̀ŋ* was both powerful and popular as a result. When Chief Akommem from Nung Ikot was accused of being a leopard man in the 1943 Okoto Nta case, he asked Akpan Udo Umana to prepare a medicine to protect him (this was known as *áfíá àkpóŋ ùnám átâ ékpó*, refuse to trap a criminal's spirit). It was believed that it was this medicine that assured Akommem's acquittal when he was later investigated.

★   ★   ★

During 1946 various attempts were made to take stock of the killings and to review the authorities' investigation. Most were agreed that a common profile could be established of the leopard murders which identified the common features of the attacks, the victims, and the motives:

The victims:	Children (especially female children between ages of seven and ten).
The time:	Nearly always approximately 7 pm.
The place:	Victims are attacked on a bush path bordered by thick farm fallow and the body dragged 40 yards inside the bush.
The killing:	A heavy stick is used to knock the victim unconscious. And the actual killing is done with a yam spike or stabbing knife.
The mutilations:	Two or three set forms: (i) decapitation with complete or partial stripping of the head of all flesh, removal and stripping of the bones of the neck and removal of one arm and stripping of some of the bones of the severed arm presumably to create the impression that they have been gnawed by a wild animal; (ii) decapitation alone; (iii) as in (i) or (ii), but with removal of the heart and lungs (comparatively uncommon).
The disguise:	Only the most rudimentary forms are ever used. Sometimes a crude form of raffia mask. In several cases witnesses have described the murderers wearing a certain kind of leaf known locally as 'mkpatat' tied round their head. Sometimes a form of spotted cloth. Nine times out of ten no disguise is worn – the leopard man appears to have supreme confidence in his magic.
The eyewitness:	'Strangely enough an eyewitness is nearly always present'. If the murder takes place on a bush path, the eyewitness is invariably walking ahead of the victim. He or she then hears the victim cry out (usually 'iya mie' – the local exclamation of alarm or surprise), turns round, finds he has disappeared and runs for his life. At first they say 'something' attacked the victim; then that a genuine leopard made the attack; and after further interrogation that they recognised so-and-so dragging the victim into the bush. The leopard men are undeterred by the witnesses. The attitude of the leopard men to the presence of eyewitness during the commission of the crime appears to be on a par with the attitude to the question of a disguise i.e. any precautions are unnecessary, since he is fully protected by his medicines and charms and the ritual he carries out before and after.
The pad-marks:	An invariable feature in every case – and indicative of the leopard motif which runs through all cases and links them together as the work of the leopard cult. Self-confessed murderers admit that they use a special implement, but how they are concealed remains a mystery as none has ever been found by the police. Others have said they made the marks with their hands and this is perfectly feasible as I [D.S. Fountain] have tried it successfully myself.

| The motive: | This is always personal. A private quarrel over land, a dowry, a debt or any of the innumerable causes of friction among primitive peoples. Some cases where hired murderers are used but generally speaking it is the aggrieved party who carries out the murder. This is where the idea of an organised society begins to break down. |

Figure 6.5 Murder profile, 1946[68]

By February 1946 the investigators faced a puzzling contradiction regarding the murder motives. The mutilation of many of the corpses corresponded with the ritual of the leopard society, but many of the murders were the outcome of jealousy and revenge. At the same time that the ritual aspects of the mutilations suggested a random pattern to the killings, it became clear in every case under investigation that a motive could be traced linking the victims to their suspected killers. This in turn suggested that the murders were neither a part of religious sacrifices nor were they random.[69] 'It is becoming more and more certain', the *Mail*'s editor wrote in May, 'that the Leopard Society is being used to cloak crimes of theft and vengeance'.[70] The paper reported that there was indeed a perplexing array of motives being investigated:

> One boy had been killed merely because certain parties thought his parents were too proud of him. Another boy, the son of an unpopular schoolmaster, was killed in the hope that this tragedy would make his father ask for a transfer. In another case a woman was killed by someone who was indebted to her. There were some cases in which an angry husband had killed an erring wife and her paramour. Some of the victims were men, some women, some boys, some girls.[71]

In April 1946 all the police and administrators involved in the leopard murder investigations met to attempt to make sense of their enquiries. The chief question they addressed concerned this apparent diversity of murder motives. Specifically the District Officers and police superintendents discussed the following categories of murder:

(a) committed purely for monetary gain with no connexion at all with 'leopard' murders;

(b) as in (a) but the markings of 'leopard' murders were used to disguise the means employed;

(c) purely 'leopard' murders with some unknown ritual significance.

The meeting agreed that the majority of the cases they had encountered up to that point could be placed in classes (a) and (b), that is, assassinations and assassinations with leopard-style disguise. The meeting concluded that there was insufficient evidence to make any definite statement as regards class (c), the ritual motive, though those murders in which the skin of the head had been removed might fall under this category.[72]

In August Grey reviewed the enquiries into the sixty-five murders that had been investigated. Among the victims more women than men had been killed; twenty-seven victims were men, twenty-nine were women, six were boys and fifteen were girls. The means of murder were not entirely consistent, with twenty-five victims murdered by a stab in the neck, twenty-one by matchet, ten by club and nine by other forms of stab wounding. In fifteen of the cases the murderers were reported to have worn masks made from raffia and *m̀kpàtát* leaves, and four cases were reported in which the murderers were said to wear a 'false leopard' mask. No single eyewitness reported the killers wearing special costumes. The police were particularly interested in the increase in multiple murders with six of the seven multiple attacks taking place in 1945 and 1946. This increase was attributed to a perceived need to kill eyewitnesses brought on, it was surmised, either by a loss of faith in the disguising effects of the 'leopard medicine' or by a failure to take the medicine.

As a result of this breakdown of the cases, Grey also reached compelling conclusions about the scope and scale of the 'outbreak'. He argued that most of the murders would quite likely have happened anyway. The motives (disputes over debts) and the profile of the victims (proportionally more women and children) were broadly similar in *ékpê ówó* murders and non-*ékpê ówó* murders. The difference between an *ékpê-ówó* murder and a fatal attack with a matchet or cutlass was simply one of technique in the means of killing and subsequent mutilation.[73] Grey also looked at the scale of the man-leopard murders relative to the overall murder rate across the province. A key question that had been overlooked up to this point was that, if this was a leopard murder 'outbreak', were there appreciably more murders than before? At first sight the reported murder rate for Calabar Province during 1946 of 204 would indicate a remarkable increase on the 1945 figure of 60. Yet, out of these 204 cases, 157 were leopard murders and of these 109 had occurred before 1946. Almost half of the reported murders for 1946, in fact, had actually occurred earlier. Of these, 13 murders had taken place in 1943, 18 in 1944, 17 in 1945 and 17 in 1946. Once the 109 murders were distributed over previous years the increase becomes less significant since the murder rate had risen to 95, not 204. By the end of 1946, 73 out of a total of 157 reported 'leopard' murders had been investigated.[74] Grey's two observations therefore were that the profile of leopard murders and 'normal' murders were actually very similar, and that, set against the regional distribution, the leopard murders were not as unusual as the figures might at first suggest. Both points suggested that the crimes committed in Abak and Opobo were not as exceptional in either their motives or their scale as the attention they received would have implied. In a written reply to a parliamentary question in February 1948 another of the investigators, Schofield, stated that as far as he could tell the incidence of murder in Abak and Opobo was no higher than elsewhere.[75]

The most significant murder motive Grey discovered was revenge. Some 48 murders were reported as revenge killings in which the greatest number were related to marriage (six in which the brideprice was not refunded to the former husband, four of the wife committing adultery, and nine of jealousy). Of the remaining victims nine were innocent witnesses, six owed debts or were involved in land disputes, and six killings were the result of a domestic dispute. In the other cases one man was killed for cutting down an *ńdêm* tree and selling it to Christians (his identity was revealed to the killer by an *idĭɔŋ*); and Udo Udo Usoro confessed that he had beheaded his daughter for medicinal preparation. Only this last case therefore had a ritual motive.[76]

Analysis of each of the *ékpê ówó* cases during 1946 revealed that the accused had a personal motive for killing the victim.[77] The fact that no strangers were killed during *ékpê ówó* appeared to the police to confirm that the killings were 'personal matters'. As a result, official opinion shifted away from the belief that an organised society was directing the murders for ritual purposes, and towards the idea that those accused of committing murder were part of, or had hired, a band of professional assassins, a 'native form of 'Murder Incorporated',[78] compelled by a 'Corsican vendetta'.[79] The District Officer of the 'Leopard Area' asserted that: 'It is a murder society and nothing else'.[80] Apparently mundane motives for murder nevertheless still offered a paradox for the investigators as doubts persisted as to whether these motives could be read as violent domestic disputes or whether they concealed ongoing sacrificial rituals. Although suspicion still hung over the diviners as likely accessories to murder, the police had uncovered no firm evidence to corroborate the ritual murder thesis throughout their investigations in 1946.

The sum of these enquiries, however, is not easy to unravel. Several basic features of the man-leopard murders suggest a similarity with the sociological phenomenon of the 'moral panic'.[81] The murders themselves were quickly identified as a threat to the established social order and witnessed an unfolding of colonial anxieties – secret societies, women's freedoms, prophetic practices and rapacious chiefs. This threat was depicted in what had become an easily recognisable and demonised form: the 'leopard men' as 'folk devils'. The public pressure for a campaign of action to be taken to suppress the threat was another key factor. The model of the moral panic therefore provides an interesting tool in analysing the spiralling of signification and disproportionality associated with the murders. It is also an effective means of addressing why so many varied concerns were drawn into the murder mysteries, and hence it helps us understand how the murder mysteries got out of control.

Playing on public concern about crime and deviance, public interest is diverted away from more fundamental concerns so as to maintain the dominance of the status quo. Public concern about crime, deviance and perceptions of frightening subjects therefore becomes an effective lens that focuses on social organisation itself, and in this context the sense of risk upholds community.[82] Yet it fails to satisfy fully our analytical needs. It is not apparent, for instance, that there was a particular interest group or elite that manufactured the 'scare' and who stood to gain from engineering widespread fear. The moral panic thesis also tends to overlook the specific content of the panics themselves in favour of a more detached interpretation of public discourse. The findings of Grey's report pointed the other way – to the centrality of proximate personal factors in the murder mysteries.

The apparently mundane personal motives, indeed, were crucial not only in unravelling the mystery of individual cases, but in understanding the significance of the ékpê ówó episode as a whole. From this point the investigation shifted from a focus on the 'leopard cult', and what were imagined as its esoteric motives for murder, to a focus on the politics of the everyday life of Annang individuals. As a result the murder investigations began to lay bare the significance of otherwise everyday disputes, and in particular to examine the 'micro-dynamics' of currency and bridewealth.[83]

In July 1946 220 policemen were drafted in from Calabar, Owerri, Onitsha, Warri and Benin Provinces, effectively doubling the special police force operation. The new arrivals were distributed across twenty temporary camps within the 'leopard area'. Villages between the camps were patrolled during the 'danger hours' of the early evening, mobile patrols camped in different villages each night, and a dusk-to-dawn curfew was imposed. However by the first week of September 1946, with two murders in three days, some 20 miles apart, hopes that the large police presence would prevent further killings were dashed.[84] In a further review of the situation some nine months into the investigation, the special police force outlined the key questions it had yet to answer:

> what are the leopard murders?
> what is their underlying cause?
> are they being organised; or are they purely individual?
> does the Leopard Society exist as such or is it a myth?[85]

The lack of progress led to friction between the investigating authorities over the best way to proceed. The police, led by D. S. Fountain, had a repressive plan which included extending the curfew, holding public hangings in the villages in which murders took place, removing and detaining chiefs from those villages, and legislating against 'witchdoctors and sorcerers' to give the police the power to destroy all forms of juju, shrines, groves and oracles and making it an offence to practise any form of 'native medicine'.[86] The

District Officer at Abak, P. P. Grey, however, disagreed with each point of the plan. Grey feared that the measures would send the leopard society further 'underground', and repeated an earlier request that a trained specialist be recruited to the investigation. Grey recognised the widespread stereotype of the Annang that they were quarrelsome and quick to take offence. To combat this he suggested hiring an anthropologist to examine the Annang 'nature' and a sociologist to promote the reform of attitudes.[87] In a clear slight to his colleagues in the police he argued that an anthropologist 'would be in much the best position to expose the underlying organisation of the cult'.[88]

From the start officials were convinced that the deaths were 'deeply rooted in native law and custom, and [were] the highest sanctions that their primitive society ever devised'.[89] At the outbreak of the murders in 1945, however, and despite a decade of previous extensive ethnographic investigation, it became apparent that little was known of the genealogy of violence in Annang society and that a further re-examination was necessary. The names of Siegfried Nadel, Audrey Richards, Phyllis Kaberry and Jack Harris were all mentioned in connection with a proposed anthropological investigation into the means of initiation and modes of operation of the 'man-leopard society'. Sceptical voices in Calabar Province objected that the murder investigation was not 'an anthropologist's playground' and feared that such an outsider would complicate the investigation by introducing concepts that were alien to Annang society.[90] Indeed, the investigation was left, in the main, to that 'Jack-of-all-trades', the police constable.[91]

'THE LEOPARD THAT HIDES ITS SPOTS'

ékpê édídíp ǹkém
The leopard hides its spots

This proverb was popular in Annang courts and tribunals in the late 1940s and early 1950s.[92] Its translation, that the leopard can hide its spots, refers to the way in which the leopard makes itself as small as possible while stalking its victim and is barely distinguishable from a bush cat. When it attacks, however, it extends its limbs, arches its back and reveals its spots. When spoken in a court case the proverb is directed at an opponent and suggests that a dangerous foe has concealed their true intentions and identity under the guise of friendship or kinship.[93] The proverb of the leopard's hidden spots captured local understandings of the nature of competition within the colonial judicial system, a context in which the closest of friends or kinsmen might be suspected of duplicity. It was to these covert contests within the judicial system that the man-leopard murder investigations turned, following the key finding of 1946. Grey's survey had established a link between the murder victims, the suspects and unresolved grievances arising from cases brought before the Native Courts. As a result the police adopted new tactics. As soon as a murder was reported, investigating officers began to ask questions about the victim's prior litigation history for clues of disputes, debts and adversaries.

Since a single, straightforward cause of the killings had proved elusive, the murder investigations became a general enquiry into the ills of indirect rule and legal practice. The focus of the investigation shifted to examine the constitution and capacity of the reformed Native Courts, and the nature of rights that were fought over in a particular set of cases. By 1946 the DOs and police concluded that two decades of reforms to the composition of the Native Courts had failed to address their underlying failings. Widespread popular frustration with the courts had led people to take matters into their own hands, and it was argued that: 'One of the main underlying causes of the outbreak of murders in this area was an existing need by these people for a speedier and more ruthless form of justice than that provided by the British System'.[94]

The theory that the murders were a response to demand for familiar forms of justice was a particularly salient way of explaining the role and rise of àfé ékényɔ̀ŋ as an illegal village court. This idea resonated with over a decade of debate concerning the validity of informal tribunals. It also played on a set of ideas common to officers across Calabar Province that colonial rule should be more 'direct', and that the reforms introduced by Cameron after the Women's War did more harm than good. Kay's concatenation of events in this extract illustrates the basis of this type of reasoning:

> When the country was pacified native courts were established. The Warrant Chiefs backed by the impressive power of the British administration, were jealous of their privileges. Efe Ekenyong they would not tolerate: murder they would report, and the society perforce disbanded. Following the Aba Riots and between 1930 and 1935 reforms in accordance with the Tanganyika memorandum were introduced. The Warrant Chiefs went: the native court criminal jurisdiction was reduced to 3 months imprisonment ... Simultaneously the Protectorate courts were abolished. The Resident lost his jurisdiction; the district officer no longer exercised such jurisdiction as he had. The strange new courts were far away at Opobo and Abak – and strange acquittals were their principal feature. Justice was not merely blindfolded. It was blind and deaf and dumb and the scales had been wantonly tipped. Every Tom, Dick and Harry became a member of the native court, and a state of anarchy alien alike to native custom and British Administration had been introduced. In this compost heap the Efe Ekenyong re-germinated. It may, as the members say, have been born with the best of intentions. Its first few murders may have met with popular approval. Between 1935 and 1945 its motives deteriorated in inverse proportion to the growth of its power.[95]

This review of the post-1929 fallout and of the fluidity and competition that had been introduced into the judicial system also exemplified the way in which official attention had long been focused on the composition and jurisdiction of native courts at the expense of the law they administered.[96] The net result of the disputed interpretations of customary law, as elsewhere on the continent, rendered Annang customary law a negotiable terrain and in many eyes 'neither customary nor legal'.[97] The nature of these contests were not formed out of disputes between Africans and Europeans alone, however, as 'Europeans struggled with other Europeans and Africans with other Africans – women against men, juniors against elders, ruled against rulers – over the form, content and meaning of law in colonial Africa'.[98] In Calabar Province after Cameron's reforms there were two main aspects to this struggle within the courts. First, colonial officers introduced reforms and innovations on the basis of definitions of legal equity. And second, male elders who sat on the court benches reinterpreted customary law to secure their own status. Male and female, Christian and non-Christian litigants sought to exploit the contested terrain in between.

Court hearings throughout Calabar Province were dominated by a particular set of cases – suits for brideprice refunds, contribution club debt payments, and disputed land pledges. The prevalence and contested nature of these legal cases was linked in part to legal innovations, especially by colonial officials:

> Each officer has placed his own interpretation upon the justice or injustice of native court decisions so that contradictions have frequently occurred and the chiefs have been entirely mystified regarding the question of what decisions conform, or do not conform, with other ideas of natural justice.[99]

The reference here to 'natural justice' specifically links colonial innovations and interpretations of customary legal practice with another set of values linked to the legal concept of equity. By definition legal decisions based on equity correct or supplement the provisions of the law in cases in which the law itself fails to provide adequate remedy, or in which its operation would be unfair. Customary law was administered 'where not repugnant to natural justice, good conscience and equity'. Equity, then, was the principal justification for intervention and the imposition of a non-Annang set of values in cases that were heard on review before European district officers.

The importance of this range of court cases – on divorce, debt and land – was also closely linked to the investment priorities of senior men during the inter-war period. Rather than switch to other crops, declining export prices for palm products and rising import prices had led wealthy elders to consolidate their positions through the defence and appropriation of assets (wives, credit and land) in litigation. As a result of these commercial realities village elders across this region between the wars 'showed little inclination to switch their land, capital and labour resources into fresh uses. Instead, they concentrated on issues of ownership and power and began to re-establish their claims to land and palms within the new colonial judicial system'.[100] Senior men, therefore, were using the courts to secure access to rights in productive resources and the courts were employed by elders to underpin new property rights based on cash. It is the nature of these contested rights that the murder investigations illuminate more fully, and here the clue to the relevance of courts and cases to the man-leopard killings is in understanding precisely what was at stake not only for the winners, but especially for the losers in this litigation.

The prevalence and contentious nature of the cases which came to court during the mid-1940s rests on the peculiar vulnerability of rights in land, debt and wives. In each instance arrangements for securing these rights were based on a process of deferred exchange which relied on trust: land pledges might span generations before redemption, loans might pass through several successors before being repaid, and brideprice would constitute many years of labour service, along with intermittent payments of gifts and money, before a marriage was finally agreed. The impact of monetisation was most especially felt on precisely this longer-term range of exchanges. Despite vociferous complaints about immediate, everyday transactions the effects of the introduction of a parallel, shilling-based currency within the manilla zone were most severely felt on those transactions which concerned the reproduction of the long-term social order. Since these longer-term exchanges tend to be correlated to central moral precepts so monetisation, commoditisation and the peculiarities of the dual currency system would expose the social fault lines of Annang society.[101]

Each type of case was a form of debt and its satisfaction was dependent on a number of factors including economic stability, trust between the parties involved and recourse to effective sanctions. Yet each of these necessary conditions was in turmoil during this period. The terms of trade were deteriorating and currency exchange rates were uncertain. Recourse to legal sanctions in the Native Courts was slow, costly and unpredictable. Trust based on a belief in the efficacy of oath-swearing was also undermined by both the expanding Christian congregations, and by a ban on its use as a judicial instrument in the Native Courts.[102] It was precisely because the conditions for conducting and completing contracts were in confusion, therefore, that debt cases proved so contentious in the mid-1940s. The combined influence of arbitrary interference by colonial officers, chiefs capitalising on their positions as court assessors, and the collapse in the morality of exchange, contributed to bring apparently mundane small legal claims to the top of the list of the murder motives.

Of all the cases brought before courts in the Annang districts during this period it was matrimonial cases that were the most numerous. In this light, the leopard murder investigations illuminated the ways in which gender intersected with the economic concerns of the day.[103] It was estimated that 20 per cent of civil litigation in the Native Courts of Calabar Province during the mid-1940s consisted of matrimonial cases.[104] This apparent evidence of tension within the household reflected the potential realisation of two decades of fears about matrimonial litigation, child betrothal and the revival of slavery. It also reflected the broader dynamic of declining economic prospects and a growing mistrust of monetary transactions. In particular, however, it was cases concerning brideprice (òkpòhò ǹdɔ) which became the most popularly attributed causes of the ékpê-ówó killings, 'With a people where the cause of practically all disputes is the failure of some individual to meet his financial obligations, the dowry system provides the most frequent opportunity for this breach of good faith and, as a consequence, is one of the principal factors contributing to this high murder incidence'.[105]

Both the demand for additional rights in women (by men), and the demand for divorce (by women) were high during this period. It is wrong, therefore, to equate social 'stability' (indicated by low divorce rates) with higher degrees of rights husbands and their kin acquired through marriage payments. In the context of colonial judicial practice it was possible to witness both high demand for divorce and an extension of the rights men claimed over women.[106] In principle, Annang marriages were based on an exchange. The wife's parents received brideprice from the husband and were, in the case of divorce, obliged to repay the monetary component. Gifts and labour service were written off. Women might not be remarried until the former husband's brideprice had been repaid, and children born to a subsequent relationship were the custody of the first husband unless the original brideprice had been repaid. One of the most common cases that came to court during this period involved the failure of a wife's family to refund the brideprice to the former husband on divorce. Marriage was the primary reason why men went into debt in Annang society and for this reason, as well as the importance of agricultural labour during and immediately after the war, it was imperative that wives remained in the marriage. Where there was a divorce, however, husbands wanted their brideprice refunded immediately so that they could retire their debts and remarry.[107]

Divorce litigation emerged as the stated motive in a significant proportion of cases. 'Dowry' disputes accounted for sixteen of the ninety-seven murders for which motives were established. Six further murders centred on disputes over children, and four involved the refusal by women to have sex with their husbands. In February 1946, for instance, Adiaha Obudu was ambushed and killed by her husband on the Azumini Road in Ibio. In court the husband, Udo Udo Akpan Esien, claimed that he had married her in church and had paid a heavy brideprice which, when she later divorced him, was not refunded. The grievance he nursed about this forgone investment was the motive, the prosecuting officer, claimed, and Udo Udo was given the death sentence.[108] So why had such disputed claims become murder motives? There were three major parties to marriage: the wife, the husband and the wife's parents. This triumvirate was linked in the oath sworn to confirm the marriage known as *ákán èbé* (lit. to go to husband). In those instances where the details of marriages came to court, it was evident that particular motives drove one of these parties – wives, husbands or wives' families – to destabilise the marriage pledge.

This was a period, as we have seen, when women were rejecting child betrothal arrangements. These betrothals served a variety of purposes, though in the main they were a form of establishing ties with other families, and were ways of offsetting debts. In Manta village, for example, a man claimed that his bride had been given to him some years previously in exchange for a debt of 400 manillas, but she in turn opposed the match through the courts.[109] When a woman rejected a betrothal agreement that had been arranged when she was a child, the effects of the claim for the refund of brideprice were felt especially keenly by the prospective husband. With betrothal from childhood and extended labour for in-laws, the refund of the monetary component of brideprice constituted only a fraction of the true amount already contributed by prospective husbands and which could not be returned: 'When a man thinks about his suffering; the work he did for potential in-laws, who then marry the girl to another man – he would kill'. The Ibibio Union called on the Government to ban child betrothal as they identified the practice as the main cause of the man-leopard murders. When women who had been betrothed as children declined the marriage when they reached maturity:

> The husband who had cared for the girl from youth would not like to see her surviving although in most cases dowries have been refunded. … men who have suffered the same fate narrated their sufferings to their friends either in Osusus club meetings or in social and private gathering – the result was the formation of the evil practice of Man-Leopard society with a view to killing the girls or their parents.[110]

The deferred payment of brideprice meant that the capacity of prospective husbands to complete brideprice settlements depended on the fluctuations in local livelihoods over many years. During the war the failure of prospective husbands to meet rising demands for gifts and to complete the payment of brideprice became a common cause of complaint among women and a significant reason for the failure of marriage agreements. When considering the causes of the *ékpê-ówó* killings, women today talk of a range of economic grievances rather than a breakdown of traditional marriage practices and highlight, for example, men's failure to pay for the final stage of the fattening rites (èwáŋá) without which the woman and her family would be publicly shamed. For èwáŋá a husband would provide oil, cloth, cooking expenses, beads, soap and fees for his bride to dance in the village square, amounting to possibly hundreds of manillas. A man from Ikot Akpan Eyo, for instance, had paid 800 manillas as part-brideprice for his wife when she was in ḿbòbó. Four years later in 1947 he paid 140 manillas, two fowls and 60 manillas to the woman's mother, but was unable to 'tie the cloth' (èwáŋá) and complete the transaction. As a result the woman was married to another man. She then sued for divorce from her first husband, while he sued her and her new husband for adultery.[111] The wartime economy, the costs of ḿbòbó initiation and fear of the shame of becoming a mother without this final stage of initiation (ùwɔ̀k), meant that the girl's parents were more likely to be open to alternative marriage offers for their daughters. Wives' parents were therefore also prone to accepting gifts from two simultaneous suitors in a practice known as 'double dowry'.

Indeed, wife-giving families were generally accused of stalling on brideprice refunds. The murder of a seven-year-old boy, Akpan Dozin, on 19 July 1946 illustrates some of the dynamics at work. Akpan was returning from market at about seven o'clock in the evening. A young girl had been walking just fifteen yards ahead of him. She heard the attack but said that she could not make out what or who had dragged the boy's body away because it was dark. Akpan's body was found half a mile away. The post-mortem found that he had multiple stab wounds at the back of the neck and that his left arm had been severed. The village chief claimed to have found leopard hairs near the scene and villagers pointed to possible leopard pad marks at the spot where the body was found. The police, however, were suspicious of these claims and twenty men were billeted on the village, Ikot Abasi Ufon, where they launched surprise raids during the night and interrogated everyone connected with the case. In the event, the investigation hinged on a complex set of transactions concerning divorce and refund of brideprice and on the dealings of the boy's grandfather.[112]

Akpan's mother, Ekpo Adiaha Udo, had left his father, Lawson Udo, several years previously. Lawson had applied to her father, William Udo, for a refund of his brideprice as a de facto divorce settlement. William himself, as the woman's father, went to demand money from the man with whom his daughter was currently living and received 500 manillas. Instead of handing this over to Lawson as part-refund of the brideprice, however, he kept the money himself. William spent 100 manillas on new clothes, he used 200 manillas to bribe the president of his contribution club to ensure that his 'turn' would be next, and he buried the remaining 200 manillas in his compound as savings. As a disgruntled former husband, Lawson took action against William in court. William, in turn, threatened Lawson that if he did not withdraw the court case 'things would go ill with his children'. He was reported to have repeated this threat on the morning that the case was due to be heard on 19 July, the day of Akpan's murder. As soon as William Udo was detained by the police the village chiefs and several witnesses came forward identifying William Udo as the killer, including the girl who had been accompanying Akpan on his way home. She admitted to concealing the truth at first out of fear, but now claimed that she saw William Udo dragging the boy into the bush.[113]

These details from the Akpan Dozin case precisely fit the general template of murders with which the police were operating during 1946. The injuries he sustained, the disputed debt, the threats, the *volte-face* in the witness's evidence, all these aspects were common. The issue of the stalled brideprice refund was also a typical feature, though the murder of a young boy by his own grandfather, contrary to the laws of complementary filiation (*áyéyìn*), was exceptional. The problem, then, was why such disputed refunds had become so contentious. Why would a father think that he could get away with not returning brideprice on his daughter? Was it that money was in such short supply for senior men just after the war that they resorted to this form of financial crime? Or did he believe that he could see off any legal challenge to this money through the courts?

Reflecting on matrimonial litigation over the previous twenty years, Kay argued that administrative officers in Calabar Province had consistently imported doctrines alien to 'ancient matrimonial customs'.[114] As a result his interpretation of the state of matrimonial law was that the Cameron reforms had legitimised the actions of older men and chiefs to impose greater legal restrictions on women: 'The ingenuity of males in finding fresh causes of action against females must be checked if the courts are not to become instruments for the oppression of womankind'.[115] The moral crises concerning women and marriage went to the heart of colonial policy itself and suggested that it was not only misconceived but bred dangerous contradictory consequences.[116]

In a range of cases that came to court, decisions by court benches and interventions by reviewing officers tipped the balance in favour of wife-takers over wife-givers. Wife-givers suffered increased vulnerability, for instance, in the face of government-enforced bridewealth refunds after many years of marriage.[117] For their part husbands began to claim refunds of their brideprice for a variety of apparently novel reasons. While assessments for the refund of brideprice on divorce were the most numerous cases, the most problematic arose from claims for refund of brideprice on a wife's death. One such instance, for example, was Abak Native Court's decision to uphold a claim for the refund of brideprice in a case where the wife had died seven years previously. The woman's brother who was liable to refund the £30 brideprice claimed this was a 're-enactment of a shabby custom'. He suggested that the practice ran counter to 'British rules and order', and that 'the primitive custom is that, if a man's wife give him no issue and then happen to die prematurely, the husband is entitled to sue for a refund of part or full dowry on the ground of her being barren, our Fatherly Government have long ago abolished this unnatural system'.[118] In another case in Ikot Anta in Northern Ukanafun in 1940 a man sued for refund of dowry three years after his wife had died and the village elders decided that 1,000 out of a total brideprice of 2,800 manillas should be repaid. In front of a District Officer the woman's father, who was liable to refund the money, said of his daughter's husband that 'he is a Christian and knows how to turn things to his taste'.[119]

Cases for refund of brideprice also came to court on numerous other grounds, many of which further contested conceptions of customary practice. A judgment was made in Northern Afaha Native Court in 1939, for example, for the refund of brideprice concerning a mother of twins, despite the claim that 'the court knew it very well that such a thing [was] never available before'.[120] Claims for the custody of children after divorce were also numerous. In childless marriages which ended in divorce, but where brideprice had not been refunded, claims were brought for custody of the children fathered by the wife's second husband. While claiming that this was a matter for 'native law and custom' the DOs who heard such cases agonised over whether 'British justice and equity' should support the refund of brideprice or the natural father's right over his own children.[121]

While plaintiffs and judges were introducing and accommodating innovations in matrimonial litigation, the decisions made on review by the District Officers introduced further complicating factors into the question of settling divorces. Like other deferred exchanges the question of time and of colonial interpretations of the effective duration of marriage contracts figured prominently in these decisions. In a case brought in 1942, for instance, Northern Ukanafun Native Court judged that a man should receive 1,600 manillas as the refund of brideprice after his wife left him, but on review the woman was considered unlikely to be married again given her old age and the ruling was overturned:

> Ignorance of pre-established custom, reinforced by the concept of law entertained by the British, has operated to make for the disregard of certain strongly sanctioned customary behaviour by some District Officers. Thus, when reviewing cases, these officials have permitted divorced women to rejoin their families without refunding the bride wealth; they are of the opinion that once a woman has served her husband for several years and borne him children, the debt is cancelled.[122]

A petition brought to Mbiakot Native Court in April 1946 illustrates the protracted confusions that surrounded the review process. Nine years earlier Chief Akpan Umo Itiat's daughter who had been through *mbóbó* was married to John Umana of Ukanafun Edem Inyang with a brideprice of 1,600 manillas. She died in labour and the husband sued the chief, claiming 3,200 manillas refund. Mbiakot Native Court dismissed the case, as did the Senior District Officer at Abak, Bridges, when the case was heard on review. The decision was overturned, however, when the husband petitioned the very same man, now acting Resident, who ruled that the chief was liable to repay half the assessed brideprice and the chief complained that: 'I did not take this girl from the plaintiff and marry her to another person for money but suffered a loss both in money and the girl'.[123]

Whether these judgments arose from misunderstandings of the law, deliberate or otherwise, or from the payment of bribes is impossible to distinguish. There was a degree to which customary law was re-invented, but these were certainly compounded by financial manipulations of court procedure. It was claimed, for instance, that female children were pawned away in marriage to fund the bribes necessary to defend court cases;[124] and in 1942 it was suggested that: 'In divorcement [*sic*] cases the more bribes a man gives, the greater the amount of dowry to be refunded to him by his parents-in-law. ... his bribed judges will entitle him to twice or two and a half times the correct dowry'.[125]

One instance of legal innovation, above all, figured at the heart of the murder enquiries. This concerned the most recent and controversial innovation in the matrimonial sphere, the so-called 'one manilla divorce':

> Many stories as to what incites these wicked men to wage merciless and relentless war on their innocent country men, mainly womenfolk, have been told ... it is heard on all sides that the alleged vexing decision by the District Officer that a woman might be permitted to divorce her husband with 'one manilla' has had some part to play.[126]

As brideprice during the war years had risen to several thousand manillas the ruling apparently made by Kay, which reduced the amount refunded in a divorce settlement from the wife's family to the husband to just one manilla, was destined to provoke controversy. As the 'one manilla divorce' was reported at precisely the moment the leopard murders went public, it was unsurprising that connections were drawn, as here in the *Mail*'s letter page:

> Now, dear Editor, have you ever asked yourself why it is that mainly women are attacked? Is it because they are weak and helpless? No! The answer is far from it. One of the alleged causes of the revival of the activities of the [leopard] society is that a high official ruled in Abak Division that all divorced women pay their husbands only one manilla to compensate the dowry that they paid on their behalf. The enraged husbands therefore take up this nasty revenge and terminate the lives of such women.[127]

The improvement unions in Abak, already aggrieved by the dispute over the overseas scholarship fund and his actions in the recent tax assessment, seized upon the rumour of DO Kay's intervention in divorce rulings to attack him. The Abak Improvement League, for instance, argued that the District Officer was indeed making Native Courts grant women divorces on payment of just one manilla. The League claimed that the impact of 'This new divorce by one manilla was making husbands to have no control over their wives and introducing prostitution into the country'.[128] They presented their own interpretation of customary practice and argued that women were not entitled to a divorce until they had found a new prospective husband and that this new husband was liable to refund half her brideprice. This was a practice, of course, that had long been opposed by Colonial Officers as it effectively bypassed the wife's parents and was thought to be a common feature of illicit slave-dealing.

Despite the apparent plausibility of this thesis there were three fundamental problems with the link made between the 'one manilla divorce' case and the leopard murders. The first was the question of whether such a court ruling had ever been made. The second was that Annang divorce custom was the same as that elsewhere in the province where there had been no such murders. And the third was that no evidence came to light of the 'one manilla divorce' being relevant to any particular leopard murder prosecution. When the editor of the *Nigerian Eastern Mail*, J. V. Clinton, went on his annual tour of the province in 1946, he interviewed the senior police officers in Abak (Captain Macdonald) and Opobo (S. A. S. P. Hodge) who debunked the theory.[129] Hence, when reports appeared that claimed the man-leopard murders were a protest against the alleged 'one manilla divorce' ruling, they were emphatically denied:

> The most thorough police investigations on the spot and evidence produced before the court in the leopard murder cases show clearly that brideprice (so-called dowry) has absolutely nothing to do with the man-leopard murders either in Abak Division or Opobo Division. … The native law and custom about divorce and refund of dowry is the same in Abak Division as in the rest of Ibibioland administered in the same way. The rumour that the District Officer, Abak has introduced as an innovation a rule that a woman who wishes to leave her husband will be free on the payment of one manilla is not true. It is not true that Abak Division suffers from runaway wives more than any other part of the country or that there is any public disaffection over this issue.[130]

In the face of persistent rumours about 'one manilla divorce' cases being numerous and widespread, however, Clinton invited readers of his paper to send in copies of judgments in which the order had been made. Only one case was ever reported. T.A. Unwah, a schoolteacher from Utu Etim Ekpo,

made several complaints in public meetings, in the press and in a petition
to the Resident that DO Kay had ordered his wife, Matim Frank, to pay
one manilla in her divorce action at Achan Native Court.[131] He claimed that
his wife had been seduced and that he was angry with her. Her reaction
was to divorce him. The brideprice he claimed to have paid was 2,895
manillas plus £15 15s 6½d sterling in 'dressing expenses' (èwáŋá). Yet Kay
ordered Matim Frank to pay just one manilla before leaving him for her
parents' house. It was a punitive decision in response to Unwah's apparent
ill-treatment of his wife after he discovered her having an affair. He was also
ordered to pay 7s 6d. maintenance allowance per month to his wife and his
salary increase of £6 per year was withheld. Unwah himself was quite aware
of the controversy surrounding the judgment and suggested that this would
indeed have motivated a less mature man to murder, and he asked readers
to imagine what the outcome of his treatment would have been, had he been
'an uncultured and illiterate young man'.[132]

The 'one manilla divorce' became a highly contested issue and exercised
local letter-writers. Referring to the allegations that Kay had introduced a
'one manilla divorce', a letter-writer from Abak wrote that: 'Abak area is
very impatient and will be grateful to hear at no distant date whether or not
our kind DO was interviewed or whether or not all the court record books
in Abak Division were scrutinised; for I am sure that should our kind DO
be interviewed re this allegation he would find, as I and all the other sane
people in Abak area have proved our DO to be one of the true District
Officers Abak has ever had'. The correspondent, Akpanik Idighe, continued
to illuminate this point:

> He didn't authorise generally that every woman in Abak Division
> should divorce her husband with one manilla, but that she who has
> been abjectly ill-treated by her husband should do so. Per this order, it
> is alleged that one of the NA teachers who divorced with one manilla
> and as well is compensating the lady with monthly alimony for the
> maintenance of her child. We've heard many other cases of the same
> nature. I myself in two consecutive occasions have witnessed the order
> of the DO Mr Kay, but ... he didn't say any woman can divorce her
> husband with one manilla. The rule previously laid down in our courts
> was ... 1,200 manillas before the divorcement be granted, as many
> unruly women usually cause their husbands to ill-treat them, although
> not in all cases.[133]

It appeared, then, that the incidence of 'one manilla divorce' was relatively isolated. No general order had been given and Kay himself confirmed
this. Rather, he had instituted the reform only for circumstances in which
women had been abused by their husbands. Kay's ruling also undermined
a further device by which men sought to reduce divorce and 'runaway'

wives by insisting that women should pay 1,200 manillas in advance of a divorce agreement. The editor and letter-writers in the *Nigerian Eastern Mail* rallied around Kay, and argued that it was 'obvious that a woman unjustly and harshly treated by her husband should not be compelled to remain in his custody till 1,200 manillas is refunded by her family – it is a gross injustice incompatible with British ideas of justice, equity and fair dealing. Ibibio native law and custom has to move with the times ... and the Abaks cannot succeed in resisting that movement'.[134] Why Kay made no definitive statement on the issue says a great deal about his attitude to explaining himself to the Nigerian public. Recollections of the 'one manilla divorce' confirm that it was the principle rather than the widespread implementation of the punitive settlement which had created the stir. The public outcry highlighted that the rapidly shifting economic circumstances of the period placed a premium on access to labour and credit which served to reaffirm men's control over wives and daughters. The widespread grievance regarding the capacity of the Native Courts to process divorce claims equitably had given rise to a situation in which 'many seekers of divorce therefore take the law into their hands and avoid the courts'.[135]

★   ★   ★

Across the whole range of matrimonial litigation the critical issue was debt.[136] Debts of various kinds, especially linked to contribution clubs and land pledging, figured prominently among the purported murder motives. The main reasons why they had become so controversial was because British ideas of equity and the duration of service gave rise to innovations in the courts, which in turn were singularly ineffective in sanctioning defaulters and recovering debts. The most prolific cause of financial debt (*isùŋ*) during the colonial period was as a result of defaults on contribution club payments. In 1923 the Lieutenant-Governor's ruling that prosecution for *osusu* debts was illegal in the Native Courts took effect at once and without notice, and 'this suddenness entailed considerable hardship'...[137] The decision to stop issuing summonses for the recovery of contribution club debts was met with widespread opposition from the Annang Divisions. The *ùtíbè* was an essential means by which an ordinary man could obtain sufficient money to pay exceptional costs, especially brideprice, or to acquire the use of a plot of land. Furthermore, in Ikot Ekpene Division it was feared by chiefs and officers alike that 'the sudden withdrawal of the constitutional method of recovering contributions from defaulters will lead to a widespread outbreak of illegal seizing and even worse offences'.[138]

A case which appeared before Mbiakot Native Court illustrates the problems arising from colonial reinterpretation of the principle of deferred collective responsibility for debts. A man owing 400 manillas had died and his brother, who assumed the burden, had promised to join an *ùtíbè* club to repay the debt. When he in turn died, however, his son denied liability for the debt. The matter went to the Native Court and on to review where the District Officer judged in favour of the young man and explained that the plaintiff should have formally sued for the debt years earlier since the prosecution now appeared malicious.[139]

Another form of indebtedness was land pledging. The five-year fallowing cycle, plus a dense population, contributed to intense disputes over access to land and 'an incessant grabbing for adequate land illustrated by the countless land disputes and claims which are such a marked feature of clan life today'.[140] One trend was for land tenure to decentralise from lineage (ékpûk) to household (úfɔ̀k) and by the 1930s it was increasingly common to find smaller intra-familial units (idíp) claiming ownership over its piece of farmland. This put greater pressure on temporary land use arrangements. Some DOs completely disregarded land pledging customs (áfáák ikɔ́t ùbî`ɔŋ – land pledge) and awarded pledged land to the person who had worked it for a number of years, holding that occupancy denoted possession without recognising that redemption might take place several generations after the agreement was made.[141] In addition, government land surveying was slow, and customary land inspections during the 1940s were expensive. Court corruption regarding land inspection fees paid to court members was widely criticised by the Ibibio Union and others. In a case in Utu Etim Ekpo in 1943, for instance, the land inspection fee consisted of a goat, five yams, palm wine and cow meat (calculated at a total value of 154 manillas).[142]

Debts in the form of land claims and contribution club defaults figured as known motives in seventeen of out of ninety-seven of the leopard killings for which a motive was clearly established.[143] In the case of Akpogho Icho Ichogho Ekanem, for instance, both forms of debt featured as possible motives as to why Akpan Adiaha Ekpo was accused of her murder. Akpogho's family said that the accused had been in a quarrel with the victim's mother over the use of osusu contribution money. During his trial, however, the suspect confessed that he was in a land dispute with the victim's father, Chief Icho Ichoho of Ibesit.[144]

★ ★ ★

There were three critical reasons why the settlement of debts had become so problematic after the war: the absence of effective debt collection mechanisms, the decline of oath-swearing, and economic pressures exacerbated by the manilla exchange rate. Two forms of customary debt collection were practised in Annang villages. First, if a debt was not repaid the creditor had the right to seize an equivalent amount of property from another person, usually a relative of the debtor. In the Ika clan this principle enabled creditors to apprehend any goat within the village and by selling it thereby realise the debt. The goat's rightful owner was then forced to pursue the original

debtor.[145] The principle of collective kinship responsibility had been undermined in 1918, however, when the Government ruled that debt collection
measures which forced a debtor's family to pay would not be condoned.[146]

The second form of debt recovery was through the *ékpê* and *àbɔ̀n* secret
societies which threatened sanctions and force to bring pressure to bear
upon debtors.[147] It was generally recognised that the secret societies thrived
because of the ineffectiveness of the Native Courts, though it was argued at
the time that they would probably function even if the courts had greater
criminal powers and an efficient debt collection machinery.[148] In the absence
of effective legal instruments for debt recovery and with the imprisonment
of debtors discouraged because the administration believed that debt did
not constitute a crime, there was widespread recourse to more direct means.
The trend was particularly evident in Abak Division where the District
Officer reported that a high proportion of criminal cases were heard in the
courts 'where persons have been prosecuted for taking the law into their
own hands and seizing goods or money to satisfy a debt'.[149]

Given the centrality of the issue of debt recovery to the murder motives,
it might be argued that the murders themselves represented a failure of the
moral economy of Annang exchange relationships. 'We Europeans', Westgarth wrote, 'never quite understand the real value set upon money by our
local people, at least the sense of responsibility felt with regard to money
held in trust by each other'.[150] Each of the exchange relationships at the
heart of the murder cases involved deferred reciprocity (often over extended
periods) in which trust between the parties was contracted on oath. Since
the cost of the assets exchanged were not realised immediately, agreements
were based on the swearing of specific oaths, *m̀bìàm* on land boundaries,
pledges and against *ùtíbè* defaulters, *ékpó m̀kà ówó* against adultery and *ákán
èbé* between parties arranging a marriage. The practice of oath-swearing,
however, was undermined during this period. It was opposed as a general
instrument of social enforcement by Christian congregations, and as a
judicial instrument in the Native Courts.

Oath-swearing constituted a form of ordeal. The terms for oath (*m̀bìàm*)
and medicine (*ibɔ́k*) share a mutable character; their meaning varies
according to context, variously oath, ordeal and poison. In general, *m̀bìàm*
represents both an oath of innocence and a harmful charm, while *ibɔ́k*
means both curative medicine and poison. *M̀bìàm* would be sworn as an
oath of secrecy, as a pact to settle a dispute between rivals and to signify the
spiritual purity of title holders. In a court case *m̀bìàm* was sworn both to
prove the veracity of evidence and as an ordeal to demonstrate innocence.
In all these instances, swearing *m̀bìàm*, often a stone or a phial of salt water
obtained from an oath specialist (*ábìà m̀bìàm*), subjected the oath-taker to a
year-long ordeal during which their premature death signified guilt.

The issue of oath-swearing (Figure 6.6) in the Native Courts drew opposing colonial views. Either *m̀bìàm*-swearing should be discouraged as a dangerous and repugnant practice, or it should be retained because it was a frequent and effective means of bringing litigation to a swift and successful conclusion when faced with conflicting evidence. In two instances in the early 1920s, from Aro and Opobo Districts in Calabar Province, the colonial authorities decreed that swearing of *m̀bìàm* in Native Court cases was permissible only if the *m̀bìàm* substance itself was not consumed by the oath-taker. It was argued that to drink or lick the liquid would be to invite poisoning (the use of carbolic acid was reported) and trickery (with people swapping the substances). The authorities therefore prevented litigants from bringing 'personal' *m̀bìàm* or *m̀bìàm* bought from 'native doctors', and only the 'regular and tested' court *m̀bìàm* was allowed in the court house.[151]

Oath-swearing had been consistently discouraged by the authorities until the late 1930s when the question of prohibiting *m̀bìàm* in the courts of Calabar Province re-emerged. Oaths were never used in criminal cases but were prevalent in certain civil matters. In Ikot Ekpene Division it was reported that oath-swearing arose most commonly in land cases where the original owners and tenants had died and where disputes had been delayed by the fact that land was farmed only once in a cycle of at least five years. Other cases where *m̀bìàm* was sworn included adultery and the refund of dowry.[152] Oath-swearing in these matters was an expected part of the judicial process as 'parties often put cases on review merely because the other has not been told to swear to the truth of his statements', and a refusal to swear in cases of unreliable evidence was 'recognised by the people as quite legitimate, and the parties to the case like it'.[153]

Despite this popularity, however, the provincial authorities sought to prohibit the practice of 'juju-swearing' in the light of shifting religious affiliations:

> The arguments against juju-swearing by Order of a Native Court are obvious. It is a temptation to the Judges to shirk the issue, and it offers opportunities for profitable perjury on the part of the growing class of persons who no longer regard juju with fear and veneration. Moreover it operates unfairly when one of the parties is a Christian and the other a pagan, since a Christian cannot conscientiously swear juju and his 'bible oath' is not accepted in its place. Finally it tends to perpetuate superstitious practices better abandoned.[154]

As a result of views such as this from the Resident in Calabar, a circular was distributed across the Eastern Provinces in 1938 which called for a general ban on the practice of 'juju' oath-swearing.[155]

As the Resident's observations demonstrate, however, significant pressures from Christian congregations were at play in undermining the relations of trust founded on *m̀bìàm*-swearing. As an oath, an ordeal and a poison which could be applied to an individual or *en masse*, *mbìàm* had many uses. And in various contexts oath-swearing became an issue of conflict between Christians and non-Christians in Annang villages. The out-of-court practice of swearing village oaths, for instance, generated an annual conflict between elders and Christian youths:

> It is the usual custom for a village once every year to foregather and proceed to swear everyone on *mbìàm* or juju that they have not been, and are not, thieves. The Christians naturally refused to take this oath and so do all the thieves, who, on the appointed day, declare themselves Christians.[156]

The status of converts, therefore, figured prominently in cases where Christians refused either to contribute to a village levy to pay for specialists (often from Ngwa or Ika) 'to charm the village against thieves',[157] or to testify that they were not thieves, as they did in Afaha Obo in 1937:

> Christians cannot be forced to swear on *mbìàm*, but I have known of many who were glad to rather than be regarded by their fellows as evil-doers. Those who refuse to swear must be able to satisfy that you are baptised Christians and not merely young men who attend church because it has a good osusu club.[158]

The controversy surrounding oath-swearing was common across the Eastern Provinces and by extension began to undermine the very premise of 'customary law and practice'. In Native Courts in Enugu Division, for instance, oath-swearing was banned by the Resident of Onitsha Province in November 1945. 'This begs the question', the *Mail* reported, 'of whether such courts are now regulated by native law and custom as people feel that difficulties will now be encountered in deciding certain civil cases which had previously easily been decided on oath especially matrimonial and debt cases'.[159] Without *mbìàm*, it was suggested there would be no external compulsion for witnesses to tell the truth, thereby placing additional emphasis on circumstantial evidence. Rather than realising that the bans on *mbìàm*-swearing were contributing to the crisis in the courts, the situation was further exacerbated by moves to widen the prohibition on *mbìàm* in direct response to the man-leopard killings. In reviewing the link between murder motives and court cases the Chief Commissioner noted that:

> Native Courts should be prohibited from using the swearing of mbiam as a substitute for evidence. This practice is discouraged now if brought to light through appeal or review but it is considered that this is insufficient and that there should be a definite prohibition.[160]

The Resident of Calabar therefore advised officers to call on all Native Courts to stop swearing oaths and to prohibit the practice in support of a

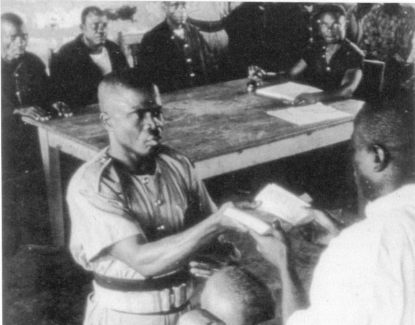

Figure 6.6 Oath-swearing in court, 'Juju' top, Bible below (Reproduced with kind permission of the Bodleian Library, University of Oxford)[161]

claim or in defence outside the court on the grounds that *m̀bìàm* was believed to kill and because it was administered extrajudicially and so usurped the function of the court itself.

While the problems with oath-swearing undermined confidence in colonial justice, economic confidence remained low after the war and this too contributed to amplifying the significance of otherwise petty disputes and minor debts. A number of factors were at play – the return of servicemen from the Second World War, the imbalance between the palm-oil export price and the import prices of scarce and luxury commodities, and the uncertain future of the manilla currency.

It has been suggested that the leopard murderers in Abak and Opobo were recruited from the ranks of unemployed, demobilised soldiers. On returning home to find their possessions distributed among relatives, these veterans were thought to have expressed their disquiet through violence.[162] Servicemen fell under suspicion because of their prior record of local disorder. During the war, for instance, units of military labourers known as 'Pioneers' had rioted in 1943 in Aba and Calabar because of late pay.[163] Servicemen stationed abroad who petitioned against brideprice inflation were also at the centre of a range of economic and political concerns that came to the fore in 1946. One set of fears concerned the politically desta-bilising effects of demobilisation and consequent unemployment. Another was a set of concerns about the post-war economy.

There were, indeed, many unemployed ex-servicemen in the south-east by 1946. There was also a high level of dissatisfaction among ex-servicemen because they had been led to believe during their service that the Government had guaranteed them permanent employment on their return to civilian life. By 1 January 1946 this process of 'resettlement' of ex-servicemen was proceeding slowly: there were 32,764 demobilised soldiers in the country, of whom 16,122 had registered for employment, yet only 4,738 had been placed in formal sector jobs.[164] In Calabar Province only 701 out of 3,611 registered ex-servicemen had been given employment.[165] The governor recognised that there were peculiar difficulties for the 're-absorption' of ex-soldiers in the south-east given the pressure on land that the region experienced, but it was the demand for formal sector jobs that really created the bottleneck since it was widely acknowledged that 'soldiers have lost the inclination to till the soil and rather prefer to join the ranks of their more enlightened colleagues who are pen-pushers'.[166]

There is no evidence at all, however, to corroborate the suspicion that the returning servicemen were connected to the leopard murders. Servicemen did not figure as perpetrators or victims in any of the cases investigated. Most servicemen from eastern Nigeria served in Burma and did not return in any numbers until late in 1946. Indeed, it was reported that demobilised ex-servicemen throughout Calabar Province had conducted themselves with restraint. Ex-servicemen did become associated with a number of financial frauds, and many were arrested for selling their discharge certificates, a document which made it easier for them to find formal sector employment.[167] Yet, there had been no instances of overt 'hooliganism'.[168] Furthermore, in March a suspected leopard man was apprehended and locked in a police cell by an ex-serviceman,[169] and the monthly meeting in November of the Ex-Servicemen's Union in Abak promised to use their influence to exterminate the man-leopard society.[170]

Unemployed ex-servicemen, however, were unquestionably a factor in the general economic disquiet of the post-war period. Official accounts indicated that West African soldiers as a whole held £1.25 million to their credit in army pay accounts with 18,000 servicemen receiving credit balances of over £20. Demobilisation payments were an important factor contributing to the general increase in post-war incomes, wage rates, and the circulation of cash. Overall, prices were rising since the increase in export prices was slower than import prices. The ongoing tax protests in Abak Division were filling the pages of the local newspapers and by June 1946 reports resurfaced across the region of another salt shortage, with prices having returned to wartime levels.[171]

Exchange rate fluctuations served to focus the impact of these economic dynamics during and immediately after the Second World War on particular groups. Accounting for the winners and losers of these fluctuations provides an informative economic background to the man-leopard killings. During this period the manilla appreciated significantly from a low of 13 manillas to the shilling to a high of 4 in 1947. In April 1946 the exchange rate across Ibibio country was 5 manillas to 1 shilling.[172] During the year it was reported from Opobo that 'traders had been making a good thing out of the manilla by buying manillas at 7 or 8 a shilling when people were in need of money to pay their tax and selling at 5 or 6 a shilling later on'. These deals may have only partly offset a more general dynamic. Those who exchanged manillas for shillings – taxpayers, court litigants and women traders – saw their purchasing power increase steadily as a result of the manilla's appreciation. At the same time those most frequently accused of involvement in the leopard murders – chiefs, colonial auxiliaries and their dependants – felt the post-war economic situation more acutely.

More significantly, those with debts calculated in manillas (such as brideprice refunds, contribution club debts and land pledges) saw them appreciate rapidly in shilling terms. For those dependent on salaries paid in shillings the amounts of manilla debts became ever more important. Brideprice, for instance, was calculated in manillas. Yet calculations were made only in relation to the shilling equivalent. This was not an instance in which longer-term forms of exchange had become associated with a particular form of money, but rather concerned currency speculation.[173] Since there was no fixed exchange rate people preferred to make all payments of bride-price in manillas because 'they hope of its fluctuation to make more than the face amount'.[174] Brideprice and its refund was calculated in terms of both currencies: 'It was common … in the Native Court for refund of dowry to be 5 pounds in manillas at six manillas to the shilling, and no litigant would be satisfied if any reviewing officer attempted to render this either as "six hundred manilas" or as "five pounds"'.[175] Security of claim and the speculation on currency rates, then, were part of everyday debt redemption practices. As the terms of exchange shifted so those whose claims could not be secured by legal means saw their losses grow.

The final factor in determining the significance of the exchange rate fluctuations during the murders was uncertainty and fear that the manilla's abolition was imminent. Agitation for and discussion of the redemption of the manilla were widespread throughout the war years and the imminent buying up of the entire stock of manillas was common knowledge. During his annual tour of the province in 1946 the *Mail*'s editor, J. V. Clinton, addressed popular concerns about the 'manilla problem'. The question was, should it be standardised or abolished? Whatever happened, Clinton argued, it should be done with full consultation, especially as 'women had a strong interest in the manilla and might not approve of its abolition'.[176]

> The manilla areas are amongst the least settled of any part of Nigeria, were the focal point of the Aba riots in 1929, have been the scene subsequently of minor outbreaks of disorder and at present include the area of the human leopard murderers. Any misunderstanding of Government's intentions, or any misrepresentation of them, or indeed any rumours of an attempt of Government not to act in good faith – however unjustified – might very well set a spark to the tinder and result in disastrous consequences.[177]

Manilla redemption proposals were more coolly received by women than by men, and the authorities recognised that 'from a political point of view, the unknown factor, and a dangerous one, is represented by the women'.[178]

In April 1946 the decision was finally taken at the regional level to abolish the manilla within a period of two years and was put to the public in October 1946.[179] The precise timing and rate of the redemption, however, were not known and were therefore the subject of considerable speculation. It is reasonable to surmise, however, that high-level political decision-making over the future of the manilla incited a wave of claims and counter-claims over debts. The manilla's uncertain future introduced an economic imper-ative for those creditors holding debts in manillas. Claims to these debts needed to be established quickly and formally, and the debts themselves had to be liquidated while exchange rates were high and before they were set arbitrarily by the colonial authorities.

How exactly these economic pressures affected the man-leopard murders is difficult to determine. The manilla exchange rate affected government employees disproportionately, yet only a handful of all the men convicted for the murders, including Okon Bassey and Chief Mbodi, were salary-earners. On its own the fluctuation in the manilla–shilling exchange rate was probably insufficient to spark the violent protests of the Women's War and the leopard murders. But set against the two most significant economic upheavals of the colonial period – the depression and the Second World War – the exchange rate evidently had a critical effect, and otherwise innocuous debts had become matters of life and death.

DIVINATIONS AND DELEGATIONS, 1947

> Only those who see *ékpê-ówó* know for certain,
> but those who see *ékpê-ówó* will surely die.

By the beginning of 1947 it seemed that the myriad of petty and mundane motives at the heart of the murder mysteries amounted to a damning indictment of the colonial system as a whole. Like the Women's War before it, the man-leopard episode appeared to witness the unravelling of a decade of colonial policy. Both *ékóɲ ibáàn* and *ékpê ówó*, the Women's War and the leopard men apparently exposed the failings of colonial policies relating to chieftaincy, taxation, justice and the palm oil economy. This appeared to apply in equal measure to the judicial apparatus (judges in open court as well as clandestine tribunals), everyday disputes (divorce, adultery, debt and land), political matters (chiefs, pretenders and usurpers) and economic changes (exchange rates and price controls). In several crucial spheres where colonial intervention had disrupted Annang ways of seeing and doing things, those processes had begun to collapse.

Seen against a broader regional perspective the leopard murders might not have seemed so exceptional. There was a regional resonance to the malignant properties of leopard symbolism during this period. Reports were made from the Ogoni town of Kono in Opobo Division, for instance, that chiefs had failed to arrest those men suspected of being in possession of the poisonous whiskers and bile of a leopard shot dead a year previously.[1] And three men were convicted in Calabar when they were found to be in possession of leopard's whiskers. They claimed that they intended to use the whiskers to make preventative and curative medicines but the prosecution maintained that the whiskers were capable of being used for malign purposes.[2] Furthermore, a spate of murders across the region were apparently taking place for precisely the same motives that had been uncovered in the man-leopard cases. These included murders in Abak and Ekparakwa of wives by husbands in March 1947 because they were apparently not 'on terms' or because of charges of adultery.[3]

Nevertheless, the scope of the murders and the scale of the two-year-old investigation in Calabar Province had become a public scandal and were the subject of debate in the highest public circles. Nyong Essien, the House of

Assembly member representing Ibibio Division on the Legislative Council, led a debate on the causes of the murders in March 1947 in which he drew an intriguing parallel with previous acts of resistance in south-eastern Nigeria. 'The Leopard Society', he claimed, 'was caused by a similar situation which gave rise to the Aba riot'.[4] In doing so he laid the blame for the murders squarely on the colonial government thereby bringing the murders within post-war nationalist politics. He claimed that the murders were caused by and exposed the flawed institution of indirect rule. He argued that the reforms of courts and councils recommended in the Aba Riot Commission of Enquiry had not been implemented sufficiently to prevent the very failings in the judicial and political spheres that had apparently led to the murders. In a thinly veiled attack on Kay, he went on to claim that the murders had been provoked by miscarriages of justice caused by the posting of certain administrative officers in Calabar Province.[5]

By the end of 1946 157 'leopard' killings had been investigated. The difficulties in classifying these cases remained. Of the 157 deaths, sixty-four were classified as 'probable' and ninety-three were 'possible' 'man-leopard' murders.[6] During 1947 there were a further thirty-eight murders in Abak and Opobo Divisions. The murder rate alone, however, was only one of a range of factors that would make this one of the most turbulent years in the history of the area. During the events of 1947, authority and the claims upon which it was based shifted quickly and unpredictably. Political authority was competed over by chiefs, diviners, district officers, the police and the new elites, and by surprising alliances of these groups. Judicially, colonial legal codes based on forensic evidence and customary practice based on oaths and ordeals would make unlikely bedfellows. And culturally, colonial rationality would both collide and collude with secrecy and the supernatural.

POLICE AND PROPHECY

By January 1947 evidence of vendetta-style assassinations in which the 'leopard' murder style was imitated for apparently mundane motives was mounting. Then, the murder of one of the investigating police officers, PC Evan Chima, turned the enquiry upside down. When Chima's body was discovered on the morning of 12 January alongside a track outside the village of Ikot Obon Akam, his colleagues considered three possibilities: that he had tackled curfew-breakers the previous night; that he had incurred a personal enmity during the course of his duties; or that his murder was an act of defiance against the police and colonial authorities as a whole. This third fear of anti-colonial resistance certainly raised the stakes, but the death of the policeman was a crucial watershed in the murder investigations because it appeared to expose long-held suspicions of covert, ritual motives.

This was possibly the most significant case in the entire man-leopard murder investigation, yet it was far from straightforward. The scene of

Chima's murder presented the first and most significant clue. It was precisely the spot at which the body of a woman, Adiaha Inyang, had been found murdered by her husband, Chief Udo Ekpo of Ediene Atai, in November 1945. The police were not prone to believe in coincidence, and suspicion quickly fell on the relatives of the chief who had been convicted in March 1946 and executed in September. The assumption was that the chief's relatives had chosen the spot of Adiaha Inyang's death to avenge the chief who had been executed for the murder at Abak Prison just three months previously. It was claimed that before he was executed, Chief Udo Ekpo had specifically instructed his relatives to avenge his death, either on a witness who had given evidence against him, a police constable or a European police officer. When police visited the family's compound they found it deserted. After several days' investigation it was suggested that the chief's second son, Sunday Udo Ekpo, was the most likely suspect, since he was known to have threatened to kill a policeman in retaliation. After a short manhunt, Sunday Udo Ekpo was handed over to the police by Ukpong Eto, who was one of Abak district's most prominent *idiɔŋ* diviners and who had married in excess of thirty wives and had built an 'upstairs' in his village of Ediene Atai.

Sunday Udo Ekpo was detained for questioning along with one of his associates, Etuk Uko, who gave a detailed confession about the death of PC Chima. Etuk Uko would later withdraw his statement but his initial evidence changed the entire investigation. He claimed that Chima had been drinking palm wine with several men in Chief Udo Ekpo's compound on the night he was killed. This party had been arranged in advance:

> One of Chief Udo Ekpo's sons organised a meeting to plan the murder of a policeman as the father had instructed. After the meeting they consulted Chief Ukpong's idiong. Idiong told us that the policeman would not fail to come on that day so we should prepare for him. Chief Ukpong [Eto] instructed us that we should bring back the constable's flesh and tongue to him to be used for medicine for his Idiong so that many people would come to consult him. Chief Ukpong instructed two of his sons to assist us in the murder.[7]

Knowing the route by which Chima would return to his station at Ikot Akpabong, two of the party left early to set an ambush as Chima was accompanied home by the other suspects. Contrary to standing orders, Chima had failed to carry his rifle with which to defend himself. At a prearranged signal the two men lying in wait attacked. Etuk Uko claimed that Chief Ukpong Eto rewarded the assassins with 100 manillas in return for the constable's lips and tongue to propitiate his *idiɔŋ* shrine.[8]

The police were now presented with two explanations of PC Chima's murder. On the one hand, the murder appeared to be linked to revenge against the police for Chief Udo Ekpo's arrest and execution, and on the other, this confession evidence suggested that the murder was linked to a ritual motive and the demands of the *idìoŋ* diviner for human body parts. Both stories implicated the families of Chief Udo Ekpo and Chief Ukpong Eto. From the beginning of the investigation into the constable's murder it was known that the two families were not on good terms. The origin of the dispute was a suit for divorce between Chief Udo Ekpo and his wife, Adiaha Inyang, which was brought to the court on which Chief Ukpong Eto was the court president. During the proceedings Adiaha disgraced her husband by saying that he walked naked in the compound and would not eat her food. Udo Ekpo, having been embarrassed by his wife, threatened her with the words: 'May you still be divorced in the next place, today your head will roll for ground'. Ukpong Eto, as court president, called on Udo Ekpo to withdraw the threat. He would not, and when Adiaha Inyang's body was found later that day Ukpong Eto reported the exchange he had witnessed to the police.

Witnesses reported that Chief Udo Ekpo's family nursed a grievance against Ukpong Eto as the latter had provided the evidence to the police implicating Udo Ekpo in the murder for which he was executed. The police found letters in Sunday Udo Ekpo's house that revealed the level of his animosity.[9] At the time the police admitted that the link between the constable's murder and Chief Ukpong (and hence with the ritual line of enquiry) might have been the result of a malicious accusation:

> There is the possibility that Chief Ukpong and his sons were falsely and maliciously implicated by Etuk Uko's confession. The families of Ukpong and Udo Ekpo were far from being on good terms as Chief Ukpong gave evidence against the late Chief Udo Ekpo and was in some measure responsible for his execution. Everything at present points to the fact that the main motive for the murder was to avenge Chief Udo Ekpo's death but secondary motives such as those attributed to Chief Ukpong may well exist. If Etuk Uko wanted falsely to implicate Chief Ukpong in the murder why should he choose this indirect method of doing it? It would have been easier for him to say that the Chief was present and actually took part in the crime.[10]

Despite their doubts over the truth of the accusation, however, the police began to give these 'secondary', ritual motives greater credence. Subsequent testimony given by the new key witness, Etuk Uko, on the relationship between the leopard men and the diviners apparently confirmed the ritual motive theory. Beyond identifying enemies and opponents wishing to inflict malice through witchcraft, the *idìoŋ* were, according to Etuk Uko, crucial to the planning of murder operations:

> When anyone wishes to kill a person for some personal reason he will go first to an Idiong member and consult his Idiong. The Idiong will

give instructions as to the preparation of certain medicines which will be placed in the bush near a path and which will have the effect of attracting the victim to the spot.[11]

Etuk Uko also claimed that when a killing was conceived, the diviner would instruct that certain body parts, as in PC Chima's case, be returned to the shrine:

> The parts of the body taken to the Idiong member are used to prepare a medicine to give the Idiong juju power and attract people to come for consultations. If these parts were not obtainable the Idiong would lose power and would not be able to answer questions put to it. ... All Idiong men will pay for these human parts. It is mostly the bigger Idiong members who do it. ...[12]

The police found no incriminating evidence when they searched Ukpong Eto's *idiɔŋ* shrine to support this testimony, but nevertheless the leading police investigator remained confident of the significance of this case in exposing a set of ritual motives:

> This is the first case in which any evidence has emerged directly connecting Idiong with the leopard murders, and it suggests a new theory which would fit many of the facts. The question as to the use made by the leopard murderers of the parts of the mutilated bodies of their victims, has always remained a mystery. If these parts are required to propitiate the spirit of the idiong before it will function as an oracle, and the Idiong priests are prepared to pay for any supplied, this would certainly explain such.[13]

Senior police officers thought this evidence was the breakthrough their investigation desperately needed, and that: 'The connexion between Idiong and the murder of the constable as revealed in Etuk Uko's confession certainly suggests that Idiong may be the missing link in the chain connecting all the murders'.[14] The case appeared to establish that these were 'medicine murders' and the direct connection between divination and murder was thought to explain how the apparently trivial motives underlying the murders were, in fact, secondary to sacrifice and the market value of human flesh as the primary motives.[15]

In the light of this revelation the police reviewed three cases from August and September 1946 in which fragments of evidence, the implications of which had not been realised at the time, also appeared to bear out the intimate and criminal association between the diviners and the leopard-men. For instance, the convicted murderer in the Sambo Udofa case of August 1946, his father in fact, was known to be returning from an *idiɔŋ* consultation when the attack took place.[16] Just a few days later, the half-brother of Unwa Udo Osoro of Ikot Obobo Akan had admitted consulting an *idiɔŋ* before killing her.[17] And one of the suspects in the murder of Ekpo Udo Ino confessed the following month that he had taken body parts from the victim to a practising *idìɔŋ* in a neighbouring village.[18] Taken together with the compelling witness evidence in the Chima case a broader conspiracy began to emerge in the police's thinking, which linked the murders squarely to the ritual demands of the Annang divination cult.

Even though it had yet to be prosecuted in court, the Chima case transformed the murder enquiry, and the provisional conclusions drawn from the investigations became the definitive official verdict on the entire man-leopard murder episode. The investigation into the Chima case appeared to confirm suspicions that the murderers were organised in a secret society; it verified suppositions that a 'master-juju' was orchestrating the murders in the form of the *idìɔŋ* society; it tallied with the forensic evidence; it explained the inconsistencies between mundane motives and elaborate mutilations; and it reconciled the contradictions between whether these were ritual or revenge murders:

> Hitherto the most generally accepted theory had been that they were committed with purely personal motives and carried out by individuals by a traditional method i.e. the leopard method. The information obtained concerning the Idiong society, however, made it necessary to revise this theory. It was apparent that the Idiong members required parts of the human body for the preparation of charms and as offerings to their oracle. As far as could be gathered the parts they required roughly corresponded to those missing from the bodies of victims of leopard murders and thus explained the mutilations. The Idiong members employed professional killers to do their work for them and these with the ekpe owo or Leopard Society members. Their victims, however, were not picked haphazard; they preferred to exploit personal enmities as a means of obtaining what they required and spurred on people to kill their enemies offering if necessary to assist them. Thus the personal and the ritual motive would appear to exist side by side in every case.[19]

This conclusion was to be the Government's final word on the murders which was transmitted from the senior police officer Fountain, via the Resident at Calabar to the Colonial Office in London. In his final submission on the subject, the Governor sent the Secretary of State for the Colonies the following conclusions on the leopard murder motives:

> It is believed that the murders are instigated by the members of the Idiong Society in order to obtain human flesh and organs of the body as offerings to the Idiong Juju, and for the preparation of various and complex charms, and that to obtain these the members of the Society and those of the Leopard Society, who are the former's agents,

encourage and counsel the commission of murder as the only means of settling a grievance, real or imaginary and afford the murderers every assistance in the preparation of the crime.[20]

The motives outlined in Figure 7.1 were presented by the Under-Secretary for the Colonies in Parliament on 10 February 1948 when he reiterated the government's suspicion that the 'real motive behind all the murders was ritual and the ... personal motive was secondary'.[21]

Motive	No. of murders
Revenge	19
Jealousy	17
Dispute over dowry	16
Dispute over land	9
Non-payment of debt	6
Dispute over succession to children and property	6
Refusal to allow sexual intercourse	4
Dispute over ownership of property	4
Dispute over 'Esusu' society contributions	2
Dispute over inheritance of widow	1
Concealment of another murder	1
Non-apparent	12
Total	97

Figure 7.1 Motives of 'man-leopard' murders, 1947[22]

These official conclusions, however, were based on a case that itself failed to stand up in court. The Chima case was heard before Mr Justice Ademola, who would later become the Chief Justice of Nigeria, in Opobo on 24 November 1947. By that time, nine months after PC Chima's death, a great deal had changed. The route from investigation to prosecution had been circuitous and surprising, and along the way the question of *idiɔŋ* involvement with the murder had been dropped completely. Not a single detail concerning *idiɔŋ* consultation, Chief Ukpong Eto or sacrificial demands was raised during the trial. Ukpong Eto's two sons, who were among the six initially suspected of the murder, were not prosecuted, and Chief Ukpong Eto himself was not called to give evidence. It is not entirely clear why this line of enquiry was abandoned. Even the junior police constables who gave evidence in the Chima case did not know why Ukpong's sons were not charged since they were implicated by the same source as those who were charged. Perhaps the prosecution counsel thought that the accusations against Ukpong Eto and his family were malicious (as the police had initially suspected). Perhaps the prosecution believed their case was sufficiently strong without muddying the waters with stories of divination, charms and sacrifice. Perhaps the prosecution felt that the two motives presented in the initial investigations – of avenging Chief Udo Ekpo's execution and of ritual for Chief Ukpong's *idiɔŋ* shrine – suggested a contradiction that defence attorneys might exploit. But given the significance of the trial as the 'test case' for the Government's theory on *idiɔŋ*, why did it choose to pursue the revenge rather than the ritual motive in court?

Once in court, the proceedings of the case revealed yet more complications. The prosecution case against Sunday Udo Ekpo and three of his fathers' half-brothers hinged on the evidence of two witnesses. The first was Akpan Ete, who gave four statements to the police. In the first, on 14 January, he pointed out the significance of the location of PC Chima's murder, claiming that he had overheard Sunday Udo Ekpo stating his desire to avenge his father's death on a policeman. In his second statement, given on 22 January, Akpan Ete claimed to have seen Sunday Udo Ekpo and two of the accused men in the company of the policeman on the night of the murder. And in the third and fourth statements, both given on 28 January, Akpan Ete claimed that he had been walking along a road after curfew when he saw two men jump out of the bush and attack the policeman. Not only had Akpan Ete's story become ever more elaborate and inconsistent, but his credibility as a witness was undermined by the fact that he was the father of Chief Udo Ekpo's wife, Adiaha Inyang. This was the same young woman whom the late chief had been hanged for murdering. To complicate matters further Akpan Ete had died (of natural causes it was said) after the preliminary magistrate's investigation, and the men he accused therefore had no opportunity to cross-examine him. In his verdict the judge commented on Akpan Ete's evidence in this way: 'It is useless for me to multiply instances of his ready and ingenious invention of what he did not see. He gave evidence against Chief Udo Ekpo for killing his daughter and the four accused persons are the last stock of Udo Ekpo's household! This is a pregnant fact'.[23]

The other witness was Etuk Uko whose evidence was pivotal to the ritual murder thesis and whose 'confessions' were equally problematic. His initial accounts had implicated himself in the murder, but since his evidence also implicated three others he became a Crown witness, received immunity and was released. At the preliminary investigation held in Abak on 27 July 1947, however, he retracted his statement and would not give evidence against the others because he said he feared that 'the blood of the accused men would trouble him for telling lies'.[24] The police promptly charged him on the strength of his own confession and he was escorted from the witness box and put in the dock. This, the trial judge said, was 'a peculiar situation'.

Etuk Uko's explanation was that his initial 'confession' had been made under torture. After he was detained he claimed that his legs and hands were tied together and that he was suspended by these ropes from the bamboo roof of a house within the Ikot Obong Akpan police camp. There he said that a mixture of red pepper and water was inserted into several of his bodily orifices, that fires were blazing beneath him, that five policemen beat him with their batons, and that they threatened that if he failed to make a statement he would die that day. Etuk Uko claimed that he was told what to say by the police, that what he was reported to have said was false and that three subsequent statements attributed to him were fabricated. The trial judge, however, was unconvinced. It was known that Etuk Uko was seen by a European officer (D.S. Fountain) immediately after making his initial statement and that no comment was made on his appearance or demeanour to corroborate his story. 'Fresh from the fireside where he was hung with pepper applied to all parts of his body', the judge said dryly, 'I should have thought for the next hour, he would not be quite himself'. [25]

Despite his reservations about the claims of police intimidation, the judge (not the defence barristers) found a significant, case-breaking link between the statements given by the two key prosecution witnesses. All the statements made by Akpan Ete and Etuk Uko had been taken by the same police constable. The judge stated that First Class Police Constable Felix Nnaji had shown 'unparalleled zeal' both in this case and others. The evidence of the two witnesses had been expanded upon on successive occasions to the point where they tallied so precisely as to arouse suspicion. Why, the judge asked, would Akpan Ete say that Etuk Uko was not with the policeman on the night of the murder unless it was because he knew that Etuk Uko was a Crown witness?

On the crucial evidence the judge reached what he called an irresistible conclusion: 'Either the evidence of Akpan Ete has been fabricated and his statements were made "ad hoc" to tally with the "confessions" made by Etuk Uko; or the statements of Akpan Ete were made "ad hoc"; they were then put in the form of questions to [Etuk Uko]; and having been assured he would not be prosecuted, [Etuk Uko] accepted them'. Either way PC Nnaji was accused of succumbing to the temptation of 'taking down confessions and statements and supplying at the same time the missing links in the chain'. These critical problems with the eye-witness evidence meant that entirely alternative scenarios – that PC Chima made other calls that night or that he was being stalked by someone else – became possibilities. What was clear, the judge concluded, was that the late Chief Udo Ekpo's family had a number of enemies in the village who might go as far as to invent falsehoods in order to bring the entire household under suspicion. As a result, all four men accused of murdering PC Chima were found not guilty and released.

★　★　★

Figure 7.2 Police investigation (Reproduced with kind permission of The National Archives)[26]

Meanwhile, however, PC Chima's murder had had a significant impact on the scope and direction of the ongoing man-leopard investigations. Following the murder the Resident of Calabar Province held a meeting with the police and the District Officers of Abak and Opobo at which he announced that: 'The strongest possible action must now be taken as the latest murder is considered a direct challenge to constitutional authority'.[27] A rumour was already circulating in Uyo that *èkpè-ówó* would not end its campaign of murder until a European had been killed.[28] In one week eighteen men were hanged at Opobo. A further threat was made that for every ten men hanged one European would die, after which the European police were always armed as a precautionary measure.[29] Indeed, it seems likely that the reason why the Chima case became a turning point, and why the inconsistencies in the case were not fully addressed until the trial, was because it concerned the only death of a serving officer in the colonial administration, and inevitably suggested that the colonial regime itself had become a target of the leopard men.

The authorities responded by intensifying the investigation on three fronts. First, the police stepped up their calls for specialist assistance. Officers had discussed the value of an anthropologist to the enquiries only weeks earlier and on the basis of the evidence against Ukpong Eto, the senior police officer, D. S. Fountain, requested the posting of an anthropologist, Phyllis Kaberry, to the 'leopard area' to investigate *idìɔŋ*. Second, the police reconsidered a number of punitive options, including the closure of markets and courts and the dismissal of court and council members in order to counteract what was perceived as local apathy towards the killings and the investigations. The police recommended that a punitive fine of £7,000 be levied in Abak and Opobo districts at the rate of 6 shillings each in order to cover the costs of the investigation. And third, and most significantly, the Chima case shifted the government's stance towards the *idìɔŋ* diviners.[30]

As a direct result of Etuk Uko's 'confession' evidence in the Chima case, the *idìɔŋ* society was prohibited on 24 February 1947.[31] This order outlawed 'the making, use or possession of any drug, charm, image or other article whatsoever which is associated with the cult of the Juju "Idiong"'.[32] For several weeks prior to this, police efforts had been heavily focused on listing every known shrine and shrine-owner in the area. At five o'clock on the morning of 27 February the police mounted a surprise raid against the *idìɔŋ* in which over 300 shrines were destroyed. The diviners were taken to police camps for questioning, and within two days the regalia of 400 *idìɔŋ* members had been seized (Figure 7.3). In the space of ten days a total of almost 1,000 *idìɔŋ* shrines had been destroyed. Despite the scale of this operation the police did not report finding any suspicious material evidence in the shrines or compounds of the *idìɔŋ* men. Nevertheless the police suggested that, even though no prior warning of the raid had been given, such apparatus 'had undoubtedly been removed and concealed'.[33]

Within days of the initial raid the police were reporting that the suppression of *idìɔŋ* had met with popular support. The implication was that the slenderest of indications of assent from an otherwise fearful and reticent local population amounted to vindication for the police action and of their theory of ritual murder:

Figure 7.3 Confiscated *idìɔŋ* 'regalia', 1947 (Reproduced with kind permission of the Bodleian Library, University of Oxford)[34]

The attitude of the bulk of the people towards Idiong has shown itself clearly in the last few days. They are definitely overjoyed that government has prohibited it and are taking steps to stamp it out. ... When asked whether they wanted Idiong destroyed there were unanimous cries of assent. They know and always have known that Idiong is behind the murders but that they have held – and probably still hold – the cult in such superstitious fear and dread that no one would have dreamt of coming forward on their own initiative and saying so ... There was a distinct feeling amongst the Christians and the younger generations of pagans that such cults as Idiong are holding back progress and that the time has come to get rid of them.[35]

To an extent, therefore, the police justified their stance not merely on the grounds of curtailing the murders, but also in advancing progress, reform and 'development'. The suppression of the *idiɔŋ* was framed in terms of liberating local people, especially young Christians, from the 'despotic' influence of a political and religious hierarchy that had long been, so the police claimed, an 'undisputed power in the land'. In one British officer's words the public's reaction to the seizure of *idiɔŋ* regalia was comparable to what one might expect at home to be 'the attitude of the under-privileged at the dissolution of the House of Lords'[36] In defence of the ban, the authorities also marshalled evidence of the historical judicial roles of *idiɔŋ*. Police informants, therefore, spoke of the way in which *idiɔŋ* had pre-colonial rights to sell slaves or to order executions: 'The present killing by man-leopards is brought into action by these members of Idiong society when they have no more power of killing people or selling people as slaves in those days'.[37] Witnesses claimed that the man-leopard subterfuge had been invented by new younger *idiɔŋ* initiates in the absence of the slave trade, to supply body parts – the skull, tongue, heart, intestines, hair, eyes, lungs, right or left hand – for sacrifice to the *idiɔŋ* shrine deities and for the preparation of charms.[38]

There were alternative, more nuanced, views on the suppression of the diviners, however, which captured something of how local conceptions of knowledge and proof were formed. Accusations in this context became self-fulfilling and arguments were circular. Like the witnesses who came forward to accuse men already in detention, the ban on *idiɔŋ* was one of a number of incidents during the murder enquiries which revealed the 'valuation of history' in Annang society. Here the vantage of hindsight offered an understanding of experience which could only be suspended in the present.[39] After *idiɔŋ* was banned, senior police officers reflected that:

Even assuming ... that the inhabitants of this area have known very much more concerning these murders than they have been willing to divulge, the fact remains that the inner ramifications of Idiong and the Ekpe Owo practice have been kept very secret. It is possible, therefore, that some of the public expressions of approval of the abolition of Idiong may merely have been based upon a deduction that Government, having banned the cult, it must of necessity have been at the root of the evil.[40]

It was far more politically acceptable, however, to accept popular support for police actions at face value. Nobody within the administration wanted to admit that they were going around in circles.

$$\star \quad \star \quad \star$$

This perspective in which diviners and spirit mediums were thought to be leading a movement of crime and anti-colonial resistance has notable parallels in African history.[41] The *idiɔŋ* also share a similar predicament with 'sinister healers' across the continent who are reputed for their association with ritual homicide and their preparation of medicines that endow clients with wealth and power from parts of the human body.[42] Yet, even if the inconsistencies surrounding the evidence in the Chima case are overlooked, it is still difficult to accept the ritual motive theory and the allegation that the *idiɔŋ* diviners were orchestrating the killings. The theory of *idiɔŋ* involvement was certainly convenient for the British authorities. Appearances and evidence, however, were at considerable odds. By highlighting superstition, tradition and custom as the cause of the man-leopard murders, the colonial authorities strengthened the case for their own civilising mission, and deflected attention away from the more immediate issues that dominated each of the murder cases both before and after PC Chima's death. In this way the *idiɔŋ* theory served to distance the authorities from what appeared to be the unravelling of indirect rule and the fatal consequences of successive reforms introduced over the previous decade. To the police, who were as keen as ever to find an all-encompassing hypothesis with which to explain the killings, the theory of *idiɔŋ* complicity began to look perfectly plausible. *Idiɔŋ*, after all, was the most powerful and influential cult organisation in the area; only *idiɔŋ* with its broad and secret client-base could be a link between the killers who were otherwise unrelated; and most of the *idiɔŋ* were men of substance, which fitted with the idea that prominent men, chiefs perhaps, were orchestrating the killings. 'The more the question of Idiong was considered', Fountain wrote, 'the more it appeared to fit into the general pattern of events'.[43]

We should be cautious not to cast the human leopards exclusively as politically repressive and individually self-interested henchmen for rural big men since this view fails to capture the complexity and variation evident in the murder cases.[44] The theory that it was the *idiɔŋ*'s need for human flesh which caused the killings is also highly questionable. The police over-exaggerated the scale of ritual mutilation. There were few instances in which body parts were physically removed from the scene of the crime, and the degree of trauma to the victim's body was such that the precise determination of missing flesh was extremely difficult. As late as June 1947 police remained puzzled that they had failed to discover any flesh removed from victims. In order to find the destination of the flesh and to see who was profiting from the murders, the Commissioner of Police offered a reward of £50 for information leading to the discovery of any person in possession of human flesh from a recent murder victim.[45] Even though the reward had been available for the best part of a year no information regarding the disposal of human flesh from a killing came to light.[46]

It might be argued that *idiɔŋ*'s own prowess held the key. In a manner reminiscent of the *bofima* medicine at the centre of the human leopard murders in Sierra Leone, the capacity of the *idiɔŋ* spirit to divine effectively might have been thought to have waned and to require a sacrifice to be rejuvenated. The post-war period, of course, witnessed intense competition for divination and healing, with the rise of new churches and denominations offering exactly these services. Indeed, a significant proportion of pastors in the new so-called 'spiritual churches' such as the Christ Army Church were converted *idiɔŋ* initiates. Since they operated in mutual competition diviners said, '*idiɔŋ* is market'. Body parts located at a shrine formed important constitutive elements of an *idiɔŋ*'s most powerful medicines, including those which 'magnify' the *idiɔŋ* shrine itself and attracted clients. The skull, for instance, was a requisite feature of an *idiɔŋ* shrine and enabled the diviner to 'see'. These parts were not obtained by commissioning murders, however, but were acquired from two potent categories of the dead: first, from the bodies of prisoners who had been executed and buried in shallow public graves; and second, from the corpses of those who have not been buried at all but had died from *mbiàm* poison and been thrown into the forest (*ájòr*). As transgressors, both categories constituted malevolent spirits (*àfái ékpó*) in marked contrast to the innocents that comprised the leopard murder victims.

Rather than enhancing the power of the *idiɔŋ*, the murders might alternatively have been linked to the killer's own search for power. Perhaps the killings were driven by the desire among young men to acquire a get-rich-quick charm or a concoction for physical immunity from the *idiɔŋ* for which *idiɔŋ* demanded flesh.[47] This would echo common understandings of the way in which *ifót* witchcraft operated. There is, however, no evidence to support this theory either, and the charms that were mentioned included *ńdúóhɔ*, a medicine with the power to conceal, and *èkim*, a protective talisman that can confuse a pursuer and prevent detection. These were familiar parts of the *idiɔŋ* repertoire, however, not new enrichment charms.

Overall, given that no evidence of fresh body parts was ever found at *idiɔŋ* shrines, there was very little proof that could link *idiɔŋ* individually

Figure 7.4 Obong Ntuen Ibok (With kind
permission of Spectrum Books Ltd)[48]

or collectively to the leopard murders. Indeed, despite apparent public
support, opposition to the government's suppression of *idìɔ̀ŋ* was swift to
emerge and came from a rather unlikely source. The ban on the diviners
was met with impassioned and persistent resistance from the leading elites
in Calabar Province, including members of the Ibibio Union. While these
'progressives' might have been expected to embrace the Government's anti-
traditional intervention, the reasons for their stance were varied. Union
leaders were offended that they had been asked to advise the government on
whether a ban should be imposed on *idìɔ̀ŋ* in 1940, but had been snubbed
when the decision was taken hastily and secretly in 1947. The Union also
maintained that the laws of *idìɔ̀ŋ* prevented initiates from shedding blood,
that *idìɔ̀ŋ* would lose the power of divination if they committed murder, and
that the ban had been applied to an order of *idìɔ̀ŋ* known as *ifá*, which was
not even involved in divination.[49] The Union also pointed to the fact that the

Christ Army Church was also offering prophecy and divining motives for revenge, but had not been suppressed. One of the most significant factors in the Union's opposition to the government's action, furthermore, was that one of their most senior, long-standing and influential members, Obong Ntuen Ibok, (Figure 7.4) had fallen foul of the ban.

Ntuen Ibok had impeccable credentials. He had been made a Warrant Chief in Essene near Opobo in 1922. He was among those Ibibio Union members who advised women to keep the peace during the riots of 1929, he contributed personally to the war effort, and in 1943 was awarded the Certificate of Honour for faithful services rendered to the Government. He was also active in the man-leopard murder investigations, and claimed to have traced suspected man-leopards for the police. It was well known that he had accommodated police in his own compound, that he had co-operated in the construction and provisioning of police camps, and that in early 1947 he had appealed to a meeting of the Ibibio Union to take steps to restore law and order in Abak and Opobo. Ntuen Ibok, however, was also an *idìɔ̧ŋ* and as such his house was searched during the police raids of February 1947. Like other initiates in the *idìɔ̧ŋ* order his apparatus was confiscated and burned, but unlike the others Ntuen Ibok was held in Calabar for a further two months.[50] To make this politically sensitive case worse, Ntuen Ibok claimed that after the raid a large sum of money, £1,200, with which he intended to support the education of his son studying in America, was missing, presumed stolen. Outraged, the Ibibio Union protested to the Governor that one of their paramount chiefs had been assaulted, insulted and illegally detained.[51]

Opposition to the suppression of *idìɔ̧ŋ* proceeded on several fronts simultaneously in the public arena, the press and the legislature, and behind the scenes. One of the key aspects of the protest centred on the right of religious freedom. Nyong Essien, the Calabar Province representative in the Regional House of Assembly, said in a speech during the Legislative Council meeting on 20 March 1947 that: 'Idiong should enjoy the protection which other religions in Nigeria enjoy under the law'. He argued that *idìɔ̧ŋ* was an 'age-long religion of the Ibibio people and had no connection with man-leopard society'. He maintained that *idìɔ̧ŋ* was kept absolutely free from bloodshed and in his call for religious toleration demanded the immediate restoration of *idìɔ̧ŋ* regalia and paraphernalia.[52]

During the following month, as evidence that public opinion was shifting, the *Nigerian Eastern Mail* launched a scathing attack on the Government's handling of the murder inquiries. The editor wrote that the 'Government measures seem to worsen rather than abate a situation demanding a great deal of tact'.[53] Two substantive criticisms were levelled in the press. The first concerned the government's failure to consult the Ibibio Union over the *idìɔ̧ŋ* prohibition which was interpreted as evidence of a deteriorating relationship, and that from being the 'darling child' the Ibibio Union had suddenly become an 'eye-sore':

> The Ibibios regard it as a stab in the back of the Union to think that an order-in-council was rushed up on 24 February illegalising [sic] the Idiong society ... On what grounds should this government measure be based: evidence of man-leopards who under stress and storm must play their last cards or is it based on Government's attempt to maintain its own prestige.[54]

The second criticism would keep the controversy over the suppression of the *idiɔŋ* on the political stage for a decade as the editor claimed that the colonial authorities' decision was guided by an ulterior motive, and was an attempt to undermine the future of Annang and Ibibio chieftaincy:

> The proceedings appear to be a covert act by Government to destroy the last semblance of power of our Obongship vested hereditarily [sic] in Idiong as a religious sanctity and we look upon the proceedings as Government collaboration with missionary propagandists to stamp out our religion under cover of leopard murders.[55]

THE IBIBIO UNION TOURING DELEGATION

Just days before the police raid on the *idiɔŋ* shrines during February 1947 the Ibibio Union had held its annual conference at Ikot Akan, Opobo Division. The suppression of the *idiɔŋ* society steeled the Union to its task and during the meeting the man-leopard murders were addressed by the members in detail for the first time. The Union compiled a balance-sheet in which it implicated both government policies and shortcomings and local social practices as being responsible for the outbreak of murders (Figure 7.5). On the government side the Union blamed the lack of 'civilising agencies' (schools and missions), injustice in the Native Courts, oppressive taxation and the repressive tactics of the police investigation. On the local side, the Union attributed the killings to regressive marriage practices (especially child betrothal, 'double dowry' and the refund of brideprice), and to the 'oppression of the common people by the elders, court and council members'.[56] The factors that the Union enumerated were precisely those that had exercised the progressives and the colonial administration for over a decade. From among the array of factors apparently contributing to the unrest, the Union was able to draw out issues precisely focusing its political agenda – for investment and sweeping reforms in the courts, the law and the local administrative hierarchy.

The DO responsible for the 'leopard area', P. P. Grey, addressed each of the points raised by the Ibibio Union. In a written response to the Union he argued that the reform of the court panels during 1945 and 1946 had done something to improve the Native Courts. The proposals to pay salaries

Causes Attributed to Government

a. Lack of civilising agencies in the affected areas, such as schools and real missionary work among the people.

b. Appointment of unsuitable people to be judges and sitting members of the native courts thereby encouraging injustice and where justice is not obtained a means of revenge devised.

c. Inadequate remuneration for native court judges. This gives rise to bribery, corruption and perversion of the course of justice.

d. Introduction of judgement summons in the native courts. This procedure involves very great waste of time and expenses which most natives cannot afford. They therefore choose to adopt a shorter way to end the transaction – man-leopard.

e. One manilla divorce instituted by DO Kay. For example, case of Mr Mbong N.A. dispensary attendant at Abak district versus his wife in the Ikot Ekpene native court. Another case in point is that of Joe Udoma now working at the UAC Uyo versus his wife. These men were ordered to receive one manilla a month for refund of dowry. Many seekers of divorce therefore take the law into their hands and avoid the courts.

f. Improper system of taxation. There were evidences here that taxes were collected on behalf of dead men and invalids. Collectors of their relatives become victimised by the payers.

g. Wrong and malicious over-assessment of income tax. This had helped to aggravate the grievances of the poor native tax payers against the members of tax assessment boards. Appeals to the DOs by the assessment Boards on behalf of the people wrongly assessed had always met with failure.

h. Corrupt action and improper method of investigation by the Police Force in the Leopard areas. That is, they make majority of innocent people to suffer and allow the culprits to go scot-free. The culprits thus set free increased the crime and molest those who gave up their names. Others follow their examples in revenge and claim immunity under the cover of insufficient evidence.

Remedial Measures

a. The establishment of Government, Mission or Native Administration schools and the spreading of real Missionary work in the areas concerned.

b. Suitable, recognised and trustworthy judges should be appointed as permanent employees of the N.A. with monthly minimum wages of £12.10/- for president and £10 for each sitting member. The number of judges should not exceed five in each court. The Presidents or all of the members should be literate persons who will be able to record or read proceedings. Vacancies for Presidents could be filled with any suitable persons from any part of Ibibioland.

c.   The members of appeal courts should comprise all the Presidents of the Native Courts, but no judge from any of the courts should sit when appeals from his court are being heard.

d.   Judgement summons should be abolished and the writ of casa reinstated. This will facilitate collection of debts.

e.   Great care should be exercised in determining divorce cases. Before divorce is granted sound reasons should be given. The grievances of cruelty, adultery and maltreatment should be the basis of granting divorce. Proper compensation should be given to the old husband in addition to refund of dowry. That is if wives are seduced by new husbands.

f.   Matters connected with taxation should be sympathetically dealt with. Only people with sound sense of judgment and spirit of fair play should be appointed to tax assessment and tax appeal boards. Taxes collected on behalf of dead men, invalids and those absent from home for six months and over should be stopped.

Causes Attributed to Natives

a.   Child marriage and the resultant revolt of girls of mature age.

b.   Seduction of married women by men folks.

c.   Oppression of the common people by the elders, court and council members.

d.   Receiving double dowry by parents.

e.   Impoverishment of the people through improper system of income tax assessment.

f.   Claims of refund of dowry for dead wives.

g.   Manufacturers of man leopard murdering apparatus.

Remedial Measures

a.   To prevent frequent cases of divorce girls of not less than 15 years of age should be given for marriage.

b.   Cases of seduction should be severely dealt with.

c.   Heads of families, villages and clan councils should be responsible people who are appointed by the majority of the people. Court and Council members must be popular and experienced people in the customs and traditions of the area.

d.   Where divorce is granted as a result of seduction by new husbands dowry should be refunded to the old husbands in full and immediately. On no account should the father receive from the new husbands dowry higher than the one previously paid except where the full dowry demanded was not completely paid by the first husband. Chiefs should not seduce the wives of others.

e. A man's source of income should be properly gone into before assessing income tax. Properties which yield no income should not be taken into account during the assessment of income tax.

f. Refunds of dowries for dead wives should be stopped.

g. Whenever a member of man leopard society is arrested the complete outfit in his possession should be demanded and taken on charge. The manufacturers of such implements should be traced and punished. If he is a stranger in that area he should be removed immediately.

Figure 7.5 Causes of the 'leopard menace'[57]

to a select and literate set of judges were rejected on the grounds of cost (estimated at £12,680 per annum). The proposal that the court members should be literate would, Grey suggested, disqualify all of the current court members in Abak. On the question of tax, Grey pointed out that no leopard murder case had been the result of unfair or over-assessment of taxation nor of the collectors being victimised. In terms of the matrimonial issues raised by the Union, Grey argued that child marriage had to be dealt with by a Native Administration order, and that the seduction of married women usually incurred £5–£10 damages, though 'there are unfortunately cases where prominent men with several wives are apt to encourage promiscuity in their wives so as to reap a rich harvest by way of court damages'. He said that he was not aware of any 'one manilla divorce' judgment having been given in the 'leopard areas'. Furthermore, Grey reported that considerable time and energy had been devoted to explanations in courts and councils that every divorce action and refund of brideprice should judged on its merits:

> A bad husband who kicks out an old and faithful wife can hardly expect to receive much consideration. Nor can a young and flighty wife who leaves her husband for another man.[58]

Despite these official assurances, inspired by Chief Ntuen Ibok, and urged on in the press, the Union's conference resolved to take the initiative and intervene directly in the murder investigations by sending a delegation to tour the 'leopard area'. Following the model of the inspection tour, the Union demanded from the provincial authorities that it be allowed:

> to take the matter into their own hands in the traditional methods with the view of stamping out the obnoxious society from Ibibiolands. It is also requested that the Government be good enough to provide transport for native Chiefs and important citizens of the six districts of Ibibioland who are to come with their traditional emblems to restore order and peace in the affected areas.[59]

Figure 7.6 Ibibio Union touring delegation (National Archives in Enugu, Nigeria)

The Governor, worried that this initiative would create the impression that the authorities were admitting failure, presented the Union's proposal for a touring delegation in a subversive light: 'The Union's motives are largely political, with the object of diverting from Government to themselves the credit for putting a stop to these crimes'.[60] In part the Ibibio Union's touring proposals were agreed to by the Government to deflect the Union's demand for a commission of enquiry into the ban on the divination order. The Government also feared that the murder rate during the early months of 1947 was increasing, however, and was persuaded by local police officers who thought that the Ibibio Union's peace-keeping ceremonies would prove to be 'the culminating factor in reducing the existing murder rate'.[61] Though these circumstances were extraordinary, the Ibibio Union's actions were not unprecedented. They echoed previous attempts to prevent the spread of women's riots in 1929 and 1944, and built on the idea of the touring delegation which conducted 'enlightenment' and anti-bribery campaigns during the early 1940s. The tour of the man-leopard villages was an opportunity for the Ibibio Union to 'demonstrate its national feeling – to do its civic duty; to help the innocent victims of the murderers; to redeem the good name of Ibibioland, nay the Calabar Province ...'[62]

The Ibibio Union touring delegation (Figure 7.6) comprised thirty-six chiefs, representing the six Ibibio and Annang districts, each possessing 'the ancient judicial rights in capital offences, homicide and manslaughter'. Some of the delegates, such as Chief Udo Ekong, had been involved in the investigations previously as members of DO Kay's Native Authorities Investigating Committee. Usen Udo Usen was appointed as the permanent secretary to the Ibibio Union tour and along with his assistant, W. K.

Ekanem, coordinated the logistics with the police and district officials. An Ibibio from Ikot Offiong in Itu Division, Usen had been interpreter from 1926 for the administrator-anthropologist M. D. W. Jeffreys. Usen Udo Usen had joined the Ibibio Union at its inaugural meeting and was appointed its general secretary in 1933. By 1947 Usen was the district clerk in Uyo, the headquarters of Uyo Division. D. S. Fountain, the senior police officer in charge of the investigations, would later write that in Usen Udo Usen the Union had appointed a remarkably good leader:

> Usen devoted the whole of his energies to his task and showed a most unusual determination to put a stop to the murders at all costs. As an Ibibio himself, he felt that the situation in the area was a stigma on the good name of his tribe and that it was incumbent on him to wipe it away.[63]

The Union's touring deputation was mandated under the Native Authority Ordinance of 1943 to compel villagers to attend public meetings during May, June and July 1947. Court clerks called out the villagers whose attendance was checked against the tax nominal rolls.[64] In this process the Ibibio Union delegation held over eighty meetings at which 213 villages attended, amounting to a total adult population of around 65,000 people. Once assembled the delegation president, an office that was rotated between the chiefs, introduced the aims of the gathering:

> You or your people have taken the law into your own hands by killing the men, women and the innocent children under the guise of leopard. The leopard murder is a society well known to all the elders of the village, the Ekpuk [lineage] and the family heads. You or your elders failed to report to the District Officer or the Police conclusively at the outset of the practice, because it is presumed that you gained by it. You were satisfied that it was the best means you could use to get rid of your offenders. Parts of human body were sold for fat sums of money to your knowledge – you gained by it and were glad that you could make money by selling the relics of your fellow persons.
>
> We are hereby commissioned to be here today not to enquire into the causes of this shameful practice which we well know you will be ashamed to tell, but to order you and or your people to stop killing one another under any cause or guise, but to submit to the laws of this country by preserving peace and order ...[65]

After this speech the delegation investigated previous murders in the village, discussed the extent to which the village had cooperated with the authorities and heard public grievances. Usen Udo Usen recorded this in a tour diary with over 200 typed pages of entries from each of the village meetings. Copies were submitted at intervals to the authorities and appeared in the *Nigerian Eastern Mail* newspaper courtesy of Mr M. T. Uko, reporter for Abak Division, who accompanied the delegates throughout the tour. Every murder case was itemised and local opinions, usually those of the elders, were given as to the cause of the killings. In addition, an official standard questionnaire was compiled for each village attending the meetings. Behind the scenes, diary entries also revealed that several villagers trusted Usen sufficiently to give him clues to the murders. The records that the Union compiled therefore provide a partial census of village life in 1940s Calabar Province. The questions that were asked at each meeting were indicative of the Union's ongoing criticisms of Cameron's version of indirect rule. They identified the number of village heads whose places had been usurped in the courts; the number of villages who had split by lineage in order to acquire a court; and the number of villages in the process of petitioning for Native Courts because they lacked existing representation or because of the distance they had to travel.

The micro-politics of Annang society in the form of jealousies, grudges and litigation histories were drawn out in the Union records of the tour and a number of critical themes emerged, especially the focus on marital strife in Annang households, the contested religious domain, and the focus on categories of strangers. There was near-consensus among villagers as to the causes of the murders. The view of elders in Ikot Akama was typical, and stated that: 'What prompted the people to kill one another was osusu debts, child betrothal, non-payment of dowry, [and] unsatisfactory judgments in the Native courts'.[66] The killers, it was suggested, were 'unsteady' and 'undesirable' types who were motivated by 'hunger and or lack of means of living'. Having personal or family commitments but no means to meet them, a council member from Ekpuk claimed that such men 'jump into this society with hope to be paid readily on completion of the duty of killing'.[67]

Before the tour the Ibibio Union presented a theory that 'native' or 'resident strangers', particularly those of Igbo descent, were possible suspects in the murders. Abiriba settlers, who were often blacksmiths, for instance were suspected of producing the metal 'claw-like' instruments that the murderers were thought to employ.[68] There was never any evidence of this, however, and it seems likely that the accusation came out of the long-running and sometimes violent disputes between the Ibibio, Efik and Igbo communities in Calabar Province throughout the 1940s. Nevertheless, the Union compiled population figures on 'native strangers' in each and every village the delegates descended upon. Most frequently this referred to Opobo, Abiriba and Aro traders who had settled more or less permanently in Annang villages (especially the waterside trading communities such as Warife). The Union asked each village if they wanted the 'strangers' to stay (which they unanimously did), and it emerged that the only complaint against 'resident strangers' was their ability to evade tax.

In other instances, however, it transpired that those people labelled as 'undesirable strangers' were in fact former criminals or accused murderers whose presence in the village was deemed subversive. These included men who had been acquitted of murder charges who, on returning to the village, boasted of their infallibility. They were widely thought to have been injected with medicines or charms that rendered them immune from the law and compelled them to kill again.[69] In the villages of Ikot Obong Akan and Ikot Akpan Eyo, for instance, such men were deemed 'unsteady' and were thought to have friends in the notorious village of Ikot Afanga.[70] A man from Nung Ikot who was accused of being *ékpê-ówó* but who was released on several occasions was referred to locally as *ékpê m̀fòró* (a person who can disappear) on account of his successful evasions. It was a fear of the acquitted person returning home that led to popular calls for a more summary form of justice in murder cases. The Anang Central Council, for instance, requested that if the accused were not hanged but imprisoned, then they should be exiled after serving their sentence.[71]

The threat posed by released suspects was popularly linked to the failures of the judicial process especially to the leopard murder enquiries. Numerous complaints arose during the tour of police failings and abuses. In the village of Ikot Mbong, for instance, the elders were offended by the delegate's opening comment that they had failed to cooperate with the authorities. The chiefs of Ikot Mbong insisted that they had handed suspects over only for the authorities to release them. And in the neighbouring village of Ikot Esenam elders had forced confessions from two suspects after the murder of two young women. Nineteen neighbouring villages produced *m̀bìàm* for the accused to swear, but despite their public confessions the men were released by the police.[72]

In addition to the unanimous complaints about the costs of billeting the police on local communities, and the instances in which police were accused of releasing suspects and collecting large sums of money as ransom for curfew breakers, the tour meetings also exposed serious crimes that had been committed by the police themselves. At Ibesit station a police constable admitted raping a ten-year-old girl.[73] In another instance an ex-serviceman was said to have been beaten to death by two police officers. When the village carried his body to the police, the very same police officers took the statement and passed on the information that the man had died from a drugs overdose. Even when this story was reported to the Union the police accompanying the tour intervened and intercepted witnesses who tried to confirm these allegations to the delegation. Nowhere on the continent, of course, had police been concerned with the notion of policing by consent, 'the police first and foremost served the interests of the state and were little accountable to representative bodies or the community'.[74] The police activities in the 'leopard area' demonstrated this point clearly.

More generally, the village meetings convened by the Ibibio Union delegation highlighted widespread complaints about the judicial practices of Annang elders in the courts. In many villages the murders were directly linked to the failures of the courts to recover debts (court members were accused of embezzling rather than transferring contribution club debts and brideprice refunds), to the bribes and high fees demanded by court sitting members (£15 for a land inspection, for instance), along with the drink and money collected by court clerks without which cases would stand unheard.[75] In several communities these tensions were framed in inter-generational terms. In Ikot Akam, for instance, a young man publicly declared that: 'There would be no peace if the chiefs of the village would not submit to the young elements'.[76] For their part Annang chiefs and elders complained that too many young men were fond of going by bicycle to different villages to return 'with what they happen to see, good or bad' including, possibly, the man-leopard charms.[77]

The Ibibio Union's touring delegation also recorded a wealth of information on the religious changes that underlay these generational tensions in south-western Annang during the 1940s. But it was able to provide few details on *idiɔŋ* because of the ban. The Government's attack on *idiɔŋ*, and the common sight of the roads thronged with men carrying paraphernalia to be destroyed at police camps, was a boon to the Qua Iboe Mission which was reportedly flooded with new converts. The ongoing campaign against the *idiɔŋ* society and the burning of 'idols' by the police gave the Church 'a wonderful opportunity for witness'.[78] In May 1947 Mr Curry of the Qua Iboe Mission at Ibesit wrote:

> Thousands are flocking into our services to evade suspicion. Last Sunday I visited a town where five months ago the church was in ruins and five people formed the congregation. This time there was a neat building, and an attendance of one hundred and fifty. The teacher … said that half the people had not been to church before. At the close of the service the headman asked what should be done about those who wished to destroy their idols. A strange situation has arisen: it is no longer advisable for the Church to take responsibility for this matter, and, therefore, we sent them to the police station, so that they might surrender their idols to the authorities. This scene is being enacted in almost every church in the district … We are alive to the danger of people giving up their idols through fear, and not because they want to serve God. … we are planning to send out bands of voluntary evangelists to conduct a campaign all over the area.[79]

The Qua Iboe Mission capitalised on this turmoil. A ten-day evangelistic campaign was organised with 70 volunteers sent from compound to compound to preach the Gospel. The effects were pronounced:

> So great were the crowds that end walls of the Church buildings had to
> be knocked out for extensions to be made. Many of these people were
> drawn by fear of the police but we know that under the influence of
> the Gospel they could be transformed, and fears give place to praise.
> ... The fruit of the Church's effort was seen when in October 1947,
> four hundred and eighty people bore public confession to Christ in
> baptism.[80]

The Ibibio Union tour records, however, indicate that by 1947 the Qua
Iboe Mission's congregational monopoly had been eroded by the long-
feared incursion of the Roman Catholics along with other foreign missions.
Many villages had two or more church premises and competing congregations. This influx of churches to Abak Division merited press comment:

> Well meaning people wonder if these mushroom churches are not
> stumbling blocks to those groping faithfully after salvation ... It is
> ridiculous and amazing to notice the following churches functioning
> in an area of not more than 200 inhabitants: RCM, Qua Iboe Mission,
> Pentecostal Mission, Christ Army Church, St Peter's Faith Tabernacle,
> Seven Days Adventist, African Church, Holiness Spiritual Church,
> Christa and African Apolstolic, Independent Church, Assembly of God
> Mission, Lutheran Church, Salvation Army, A. M. E. Zion Church
> and a host of others with funny names of obscure extraction.[81]

The press complained about the superfluity of churches in Abak on a number
of grounds: that the schools attached to these churches were a drain on
the government grants they claimed; that new churches emerged because
some factions were unable to adhere to the discipline of a particular church;
that these Christian enterprises were often motivated by the personal gain
of their leaders; and that overall the situation tended to incite religious
antagonism. Nevertheless, religious freedoms had become a more sensitive
issue with the diversification of church denominations operating in Calabar
Province, and particular unease was expressed towards those practising
faith healing. Several civil servants had been dismissed from their jobs for
becoming members of the Jehovah's Witnesses during the war, including
a police constable with sixteen years' experience and a mission school
teacher.

The Union's census of church congregations did not assume any particular salience until mid-way through the tour when complaints were raised
about the churches of African origin: the African Mission, Samuel Spiritual
Church, National Church of Christ, Zion Mission and, most controversially,
the Christ Army Church. As the following comments from Ikot Akama
suggest, 'KRISTAMEM' (Christ Army Church) had quickly assumed an

unusual prominence amid the range of causes popularly linked to the man-leopard murders:

> What may still cause further killing if needs be are certain practices adopted by the Christ Army Church members. Land was given to the members to build their church with the hope that they would adopt the usual Christian teaching. Their movements and adoptions were closely watched. It was revealed that they re-introduced the long-stopped 'Spirit Movement'.[82]

The arrival of the Christ Army Church in the area during the 1940s had brought with it locally familiar spiritual means of prognostication and healing, however, and not 'the usual Christian teaching'. These churches had been the site of the Spirit Movement's first 'outbreaks' in Ogoni and Annang districts during 1927 and 1932, and had become a congregational home to many 'shakers' in later years. The southern Annang areas witnessed a growth of Christ Army churches immediately after the war when their activities came to resemble another 'revival', especially as preachers divined and predicted the dates of people's deaths and named those who had the power to kill by the power of witchcraft.

The controversy surrounding religious practitioners, especially faith healers and seers, had, of course, been inflamed by the ban on the *idiɔŋ*. Opposition to the Christ Army Church was popularly framed by comparison to *idiɔŋ*. The chief of Nung Ikot, for instance, summed up a widespread unease with the practices of this church:

> The members divine like Idiong and cause adultery and recrimina-tions. Idiong members divined against people falsely and murders were committed. Idiong cult was prohibited, but not the practice of divination by members of the Christ Army Church which is the same as Idiong. May I know for information of my people if Christ Army Church is established in the form of Christian church to substitute Idiong? Why should the seers commit adultery with the women in the bush? It is a general taboo throughout Ibibio and Annang to have connection with woman in the bush. Can anything be done to abandon this type of religion?[83]

As a result of the accusations that surfaced during Spirit Movement revivals, and in an attempt to remove the opportunity for adultery in the church compound, the Senior Patriarch of the Christ Army Church had ruled in 1939 that churches 'should not allow women in the compound or prayer hall after 7 pm except accompanied by their husbands or rela-tives and that prayer meetings should begin at 5.30 am and not sooner'.[84] Nevertheless, the church's faith-healing treatments for infertile women continued to be especially controversial. In Ikot Akama village, for instance,

Christ Army members were accused of being adulterers who 'advise women that the Spirit of God had directed that for 7 consecutive days they should go into the bush with one man who would pray for them'.[85] These secretive prayer sessions led to a series of allegations of adultery against the Christ Army pastors and congregations: in Ikot Okpok village the chief complained against the Christ Army's 'worthless preacher and woman hunter'; an accusation of adultery against the elder and seer of the church in Minya was heard before the Union delegation; and in Ibot village the members 'of full standing' were said to be twenty-five young men who were described as 'women hunters' and that women whose husbands were non-members became enemies to their husbands'.[86]

These observations resonated with the delegation's overall findings from this mass public consultation that linked the murders to a complex of issues relating to marriage. Amid the range of social ills identified during the tour, the murders were most closely related to problems with adultery and the refund of brideprice. In Ekparakwa, for instance, Sam Etuk Akpan, whose wife had left him without returning his brideprice, admitted before the delegation that 'last night I was planning to go with my matchet'.[87] In several villages those individuals the elders thought most likely to disturb the peace and commit murder were referred to as 'womanisers'. They were men like Udo Akpakpan in Ikot Esien, who was 'causing trouble in the village by trying to force a woman to remain his wife without payment of dowry'; and Akpan Adia Unwa in Ikot Etim, who 'was in the habit of taking other people's wives and would not pay dowry'.[88]

The touring delegation were specifically charged to refrain from investigating the murders directly since this was an ongoing police matter. Beyond the circulation of rumour, little evidence about the killers was generated as a result. The notable exception was the report of an anonymous informer from Ikot Afanga who spoke with Usen Udo Usen. The informer stated that the man-leopard society had originated when members of the èkóŋ (áwìè òwò) society had injected themselves with charms made from herbs found at the graves of idìɔŋ, murdered persons and important shrines. Human intestines and blood from the human heart, the informer claimed, were put in the charm to protect them when dancing and turning and to make the preparation effective. The charms made them brave, smart and daring. These charms were not taken into the house, but tied to the beams outside for fear that women might touch them. Under the orchestration of àfé èkényòŋ the informer claimed that, when a victim was killed, parts of the body were removed. Some of these were sold, he said, while other parts were 'eaten by the elders who were still cannibals'. The informer went on to claim that prohibition of the idìɔŋ cult had helped to check 'leopard' killing. It was idìɔŋ members, he said, who divined that somebody was being bewitched and provided information which caused the killings to take place.[89]

The local press immediately sought clarification of this allegation of canni-balism on the part of the àfé ékényòŋ elders. The secretary of the Union dele-gation, Usen Udo Usen, told the *Mail* that while body parts were removed there was no evidence that they were consumed by the murderers or anyone else. Rather, he surmised that, whereas in 'ancient dayse [*sic*] these parts of the bodies of victims may have been consumed and ... used for fetish purposes, today they are removed and buried merely to carry out the ancient formalities and to create the same terror that the ancient Leopard Society created. In other words, the modern society is only a money making racket exploiting the practices and superstitions of the Leopard Society of old'.[90]

★   ★   ★

After these public and private discussions on the social ills that contributed to the murders, the communities present at each of the mass meetings were called upon to witness and participate in a ritual oath-swearing. Discussion on the use of oath-swearing in the man-leopard murder investigations had first come to light during the enquiry into the Akpan Dozin murder in 1946. After a police raid on the village of Itung, which had earned a reputation as a 'hotbed' of ékpê ówó activities, the village chief and elders volunteered to collect funds to pay for the preparation of 'a particularly potent form of the "Mbiam Juju" upon which witnesses would be sworn to tell the truth'. Further evidence of the efficacy of such methods had emerged in July 1946 when news was received that Chief Sampson Akpan Ekpo of Ikot Ibak had visited a 'native doctor' (Archibong of Itam, Uyo Division) and had paid £8 for the preparation of a charm which was guaranteed to protect his village against the leopard men and would ensure the arrest of the murderer if a killing did occur. The chief reported that his village had remained 'immune' as a result. The idea that the leopard men were acting under the influence of a set of charms that could make them invisible, leopard-like and uncatchable was clearly widespread. Both the proposed oath-swearing in Itung and the 'counter-charm' used in Ikot Ibak, indeed, suggested the possibilities for the systematic use of indigenous judicial mechanisms in the campaign against the leopard men.

Although he might have been expected to dismiss this proposition given his views on the beliefs and practices he had encountered in Annang villages, the leading police officer D. S. Fountain embraced this idea:

> From all accounts Mbiam is held in very considerable awe by these people and I consider every possible use should be made of it. This may be considered highly unorthodox as no doubt it is, but I am convinced that in dealing with these very primitive people the only satisfactory weapon against 'mumbo-jumbo' is counter 'mumbo-jumbo'.[91]

Desperate for a means of establishing witness evidence that would stand up in court, the investigating authorities therefore began to countenance the use of the very same indigenous methods of judicial enquiry that were thought to have been at the bottom of the man-leopard epidemic. For it was precisely because powerful and potent *m̀bìàm* oaths had been banned in the courts that people had lost faith in the justice they administered. And it was precisely because of the demand for local tribunals and oaths rather than the colonial courts that the leopard men were believed to have surfaced.

Initially, Usen Udo Usen had assured the Resident of Calabar Province that the customary *m̀bìàm* oath 'in the true sense' would not be sworn during the Ibibio Union's tour since it had in effect become a criminalised practice. Reports of the oath-swearing ritual employed by the Union delegation are inconsistent. Nevertheless, notes submitted to the authorities recorded that the ceremony started with the burying of a palm frond (*àyèì*) across the road leading to the village, after which an elephant tusk (*ǹnûk éníìn*) was blown three times. Salt, sand and water from the village were mixed and poured over the buried palm leaf. Villagers then walked across the buried palm leaf in order to undertake the 'solemn agreement' that they would not join or hide *ékpê-ówó*.[92]

This public ritual was also combined with the physical, individual act of swearing that involved the consumption, touching or embracing of an oath substance. No two reports of the substance used in the oath are the same. In May 1947 the Union had sent a telegram requesting permission from the Resident to compel all villagers to drink and rub an antidote. In June the police observed that villagers were asked to 'sign' by touching a pen that they would renounce all evil practices. Later it was decided that the delegates could not swear the entire population of 203 villages in person and a new system was devised in which village heads were to oversee the oath-swearing, sometimes on the following day, and that instead of a pen a 'doll' was used constructed from bamboo and palm leaves that had been smeared with water and sand from the village shrine.[93]

Variations in the oath-swearing practice might be explained by the fact that the delegation did not wish to attract official consternation over the use of *m̀bìàm* and therefore used innocuous objects and practices. It is also possible that the substances were switched between villages in order to prevent the manufacture of an antidote from the same source. *M̀bìàm* can be of any substance, but crucially its origin should be secret (hence a preference for salt water). Today people in Nung Ikot still remember the chiefs who were sent from Abak to swear the villagers against involvement in the leopard murders and describe it as a palm frond (*àyèì*) which was immersed in water and then hung around the neck of the oath-taker.

After the oath was administered Christians and non-Christians separated and prayed to God to stop the 'wicked practice of killing human beings', the former raising their arms above their heads and the latter touching the ground with their fingers.[94] The final element in the oath-swearing then involved a public pledge in which the crowd was told to stand. Each family, lineage and village head had to swear out loud the following:

1. That they bind themselves, their heirs and successors in offices and executors to the Government of Nigeria to keep the peace of this village by seeing that the Traditional emblem is obeyed.
2. That they will report to the authorities any proposal in the village to form any society in connection with the destruction of human life, such as Ekpe Owo, Nka Ibok Mkpa, society of poisonous medicines etc.
3. That they will report without fear any case of murder which they were afraid to report before the police before now.
4. That they or their people will not continue in the leopard murder practice any further.[95]

The contradiction between customary and colonial codes of justice employed during the tour was not lost on observers at the time.[96] Curry of the Qua Iboe Mission wrote that: 'There was much to commend itself in the methods used by the Union, though the swearing of heathen oaths seemed rather inconsistent seeing the authorities had made "Idiong" (the heathen society) illegal'.[97] Assistant Superintendent Williams later wrote: 'With hindsight these counter-measures appear to have been more effective than the normal process of a civilised law and criminal jurisprudence'. The killings continued even as the tour proceeded and eleven more deaths would be reported, but news of the efficacy of the oath and the ill effects of false swearing began to spread. On 25 July 1947, villagers in Ibiana heard of a man from Ikot Akpabong who had begun to suffer from a strange sensation after taking the oath and had offered a cow and 600 manillas to have the oath revoked.[98] The efficacy of the oath was such that villagers asked whether the oath could be sworn against other threats apart from the human leopards, including 'administering poison, Uben, theft of farm produce etc.'.[99] Optimistic about the deterrent effect of such news, the Union was able to proclaim the tour a success and the authorities could justify their approval of it. Police officers like Williams reported that the 'bizarre turn' in the eradication of the killings was therefore brought about by the use of more powerful spiritual means in the oaths overseen by Usen which had effectively neutralised 'the Idiong juju of *ékpê ówó*'.[100]

Both the oral pledges and symbolism of the Union's oath-swearing served to confirm and legitimate these obligations. The ritual performance was especially effective because it combined a remaking of community boundaries, the power of secret substances from the wild and the dead, and the authority of ancestors and elders. The ritual involved reinscribing community boundaries by marking the event on the physical landscape while at the same time confirming its cognitive boundaries. As a way of establishing the boundaries of its own symbols, the presence of strangers in the 'leopard area' was deemed a threat to the 'legitimacy and awe' of the peace-keeping rituals.[101] The 'resident strangers', the Ibibio Union argued, would not believe in the oath-swearing and peace ceremonies that the delegation intended to employ.

The efficacy of the Union's oath-swearing was also determined by the sociology of Annang perception and knowledge.[102] Annang concepts of truth are acquired through the process of testing (*ǹdómó*, to test and see). Oaths (*m̀bìàm*) and ordeals (*úkáŋ*) are the key performative 'rituals of verification' through which hidden truths are determined. They are 'dramas of truth'.[103] In a very patronising manner Fountain reported that Usen had a fairly high standard of education and yet 'firmly believed in the actual supernatural powers of the jujus of his people'. In fact, the 1947 Ibibio Union tour grasped the significance of combating ambiguity and secrecy with the most familiar device of the Annang and Ibibio cultural repertoire, the oath. *M̀bìàm* was both lie detector and deterrent. Failure to swear, and illness attributed to false swearing, were signs of guilt, and mass oath-swearing created a baseline placing the population on notice. In a world in which cause and effect are highly personalised the appeal of oaths and ordeals lies in their very impersonality.[104] Stepping over buried substances was a familiar form of Annang performative ordeal employed to test initiates and suspects alike. It served as an impartial adjudicator, effectively akin to bringing in an outsider to act as judge when existing decision-makers are unable to take responsibility. The oath-swearing was a public drama, then, in which the whole community was present and complicit, and it mobilised the collective ancestors and those linked to localised ancestral shrines.[105]

The symbolic references used in the Union's oath, through the use of the palm frond and elephant tusk, also linked it to traditional authority and the powers vested in *àkúkú* chieftaincy. The use of *àyèì* in the 'peace-keeping ceremonies' invoked a traditional means of imposing order. Burying an *àyèì*, which grows at the highest point of the palm tree, in village soil resolves the familiar Annang high–low opposition which is central to the efficacy of Annang ritual performance. This practice links the ritual to the power of notable ancestors and the earth deity (*àbàsì ìkpá ìsɔ̀ŋ*). Failure to heed the *àyèì*'s injunction would, it was understood, lead to collective ruin in the form of poor harvests, pestilence, difficult childbirth or worse.[106] Elders present at the oath-swearing claimed that they never thought that they would see such ceremonies again in their lifetimes.

Most readings of this ritual process would point to its conservative and re-integrative properties. The delegation's rituals were an attempt to rearticulate fractured cultural frameworks and systems of political domination by those who recognised the significance of the knowledge and practice of routine cultural patterns.[107] As a cognitive process the ritual also acted as a symbolic reference to and legitimation of traditional authority.[108] These associations were particularly salient since appeals to oaths, ordeals or other forms of 'autonomous judges' are most likely to be made at moments of political change when claims to authority are contested and contingent.[109] Indeed, we need to be mindful of the immediate injunctions for oath-swearing too. Re-imagining the past played a powerful role in the ceremonies, but they also concerned the political agency of contemporary actors.

The very process of restoring order during the man-leopard murder investigations was itself a catalyst for change. The oath-swearing campaign that formed a part of the social drama to combat the man-leopard murders witnessed a shift in the authority from elders to a new elite, while retaining at the same time the core symbols and personae of the pre-colonial traditional rituals. Since legitimation was achieved by attaching authority to a process which attempted to transcend the worldly (in its appeals to deities and the dead) this legitimation was ambiguous, unspecific and therefore recoverable by one type of authority from another.[110] Claiming success in bringing the murders to an end, the Union's oath swearing campaign represented the imminence of a fundamental change in relations between the nationalist elites and the colonial state. Having originally set out to do what it called its 'civic duty' – to restore law and order in support of the colonial administration – the political tide was to turn even before the tour had concluded.

★ ★ ★

'It is difficult to assess the effect of the tour in preventing or reducing the murders', the Resident reported, 'but it resulted in the collection of much useful information and calming of public opinion'.[111] Despite its apparent success, however, the Ibibio Union's tour ended in a controversy surrounding the submission of a report on the murders by Usen Udo Usen, who was the district clerk, Ibibio Union secretary and mainstay of the touring delegation. Dr Egbert Udo Udoma, the Union president, claimed that Usen Udo Usen had submitted the report on the tour to the authorities without prior approval from the Union and without it being discussed or signed by other members of the delegation. Whether this was a deliberate ruse or an accidental oversight, the consequences were significant. Usen's report corroborated the police enquiries in key respects, notably that *idiɔŋ* divination and charm preparation had contributed to the murders, and therefore lent backing to the authorities' decision to ban *idiɔŋ* while undermining the Union's opposition to its prohibition.

The diary of the Ibibio Union Tour Delegation demonstrates that Usen consistently defended the government's position in public. When confronted by the village head and former *idiɔŋ* member in Inen Ikot Esien, who asked if

the Government was justified in destroying his *idiɔŋ* shrine while he claimed
to have no knowledge of the man-leopard killing practice, Usen replied:

> When the cases of many killings under the guise of Leopard by your
> people was brought into book, it was proved beyond doubt that
> Idiong diviners were the cause of the many killings. ... I consider that
> the Government was right in the measures taken to prohibit Idiong
> Cult at the time, but in the case of destroying I reserve my opinion.
> ... The answer I give you in connection with Idiong is my personal
> opinion which has nothing to do with the general opinion of the Ibibio
> people.[112]

This speech, along with other passages from the Union's tour diary, was
championed by the Government as evidence justifying the continued ban on
the *idiɔŋ* order while most other African voices in the reports were silenced.
'It must have taken considerable courage', one officer wrote, 'for Mr Usen
to speak out so forthrightly'.[113] Behind the scenes, meanwhile, the more
'politically inspired' among Usen's fellow union members such as Udom, a
clerk at Opobo, were alleged (by Usen) to have collected £122 from *idiɔŋ*
members in Abak Division in July 1947 to finance the fight against the ban
and had asked Dr Udoma, the president of the Ibibio Union, to address a
petition to the Government.[114]

Usen's report was only loosely based on the evidence compiled in the
tour diary, and it seems likely that he had access to police files before he
completed his report. The suspects named by Usen were already well known
to the police, but he created a convincing story about how the murders began
which drew together previous loose ends. Usen claimed that an *idiɔŋ*, Akpan
Ekpedeme, and his sister's son, Akpan Nyoho, had both kept company with
a gang of eleven highway robbers for whom Akpan Ekpedeme prepared
protective charms. 'Most had wives and their wives had lovers', Usen wrote.
One gang member was being harassed by a creditor and another suspected
his wife of adultery; so the robbers, Usen suggested, decided to use their
charms (*ńdómó íbɔ́k*), to eliminate their enemies. They killed the adulterer
first, and then the creditor. The killers wore a costume, Usen claimed, made
of a cloth dotted with chalk and charcoal and a wooden mask.

According to Usen's report the gang's success and apparent immunity
from detection led them to become hired assassins, with agents who would
approach people known to have grudges or disputes asking for 50 manillas as
a consultation fee and 100 manillas for the 'leopard men' to eliminate their
opponent. Usen further suggested that an *idiɔŋ* member, Chief Ukpong Eto
of Ediene Atai, had consulted Akpan Ekpedeme to procure a new human
head for his oracle and as a result not only became familiar with the various
charms used by the leopard men, but also found a market for the sale of
body parts (heads, arms and genitalia) from the victims. Chief Ukpong Eto

had been accused, along with his two sons, of involvement in the murder of PC Chima. A police team investigating the missing body parts of murder victims visited Chief Ukpong Eto in Ediene Atai in June 1946 and reported that: 'He is one of the prominent Idiong men, well known over all Anang. His son Akpan Ukpong Eto was once suspected as ekpe owo man. He has a big house full of different shrines where he divines'.[115] In September 1946 his shrine had been raided and searched by police investigating another local murder: 'On that occasion he was said to have announced that it were better that the police had killed one of his wives or children than that they should have interfered with his juju which was his means of livelihood and that he intended to murder a European Officer or a constable to atone for it'.[116] In his report Usen accused Ukpong Eto of selling body parts to those of his clients he diagnosed as being possessed by the *ibɔk* spirit and who needed to be healed by initiation into *idiɔŋ*.[117]

Usen's theory was that *idiɔŋ* used their knowledge of existing personal rivalries – court disputes over land, brideprice and debts – in order to identify victims for the leopard men. In this way he argued that the ritual and revenge theories which the police had been oscillating between were not mutually exclusive but overlapped. Most of this had long been suspected by the police but coming from Usen, the man who had visited every village affected by the murders, and who had off-the-record evidence and was an Ibibio speaker himself and apparently understood the nature and meanings of charms and rituals, it was adopted as clear confirmation of the police's stance. As a result, Usen was immediately seconded to the police detachment on special duties and became their leopard murder specialist. Indeed, his conclusions became the lynchpin of the police's case. The prohibition of *idiɔŋ* had failed to stop the killings and after six months the government's stance was not only unproved but was also subject to widespread criticism. From their side, the police cited events fifty years previously – the human leopard killings in Sierra Leone – in support of the case that these were ritual murders. Senior officers in the Nigerian investigation had only a limited knowledge of these events, however, as they tried in vain to consult Beatty's 1915 account of the trials in Sierra Leone which was out of print in London. This left Usen's evidence, which was cited directly by the police in their effort to reassure themselves (the CID commissioner in Lagos, and the House of Commons in London) that they had not blundered in their decision to prohibit the *idiɔŋ* diviners.

The Ibibio Union summoned Usen to appear before a public assembly in Ikot Okoro in March 1948 to justify the claims made in his report. Passages of the report in which he had accused prominent personalities of being members of the man-leopard society were read aloud in English, and these individuals questioned Usen directly about the accusations he had made against them. The atmosphere was tense, and Usen had to be protected by a police cordon when the crowd tried to break through and get at him. The most dramatic moments of the meeting arose in a cross-examination of Usen by Ukpong Eto, the man Usen had accused of carrying on Akpan Ekpedeme's role of procuring skulls for new *idi͏ɔŋ* initiates, and who had been arrested along with his two sons for the murder of PC Chima. A record of this conversation appears in Udo Udoma's memoir, albeit this was written with a distinct prejudice against Usen and cannot be corroborated. It is revealing nevertheless and suggests that relationships during the tour were not all they had appeared. It claims that Usen and the chief were actually friends, and that on the three occasions on which Ukpong Eto had been arrested, Usen had stood bail for him:

> *Ukpong Eto:* Usen Udo Usen do you know me well?
>
> *Usen Udo Usen:* Yes I do.
>
> *UE:* You are my personal friend?
>
> *UUU:* Yes, I believe so.
>
> *UE:* You dine in my house with me sharing the same table frequently since you came to Abak?
>
> *UUU:* Yes, that is true.
>
> *UE:* You remember that on three different occasions, I was arrested on suspicion of being a man-leopard and my upstairs building was ransacked and looted?
>
> *UUU:* Yes, I am aware of that.
>
> *UE:* On each occasion I was escorted handcuffed to the Nigeria police station here in Ikot Okoro to be locked up in the guard room, and I had always protested my innocence and denied any knowledge of man-leopard society.
>
> *UUU:* Yes, that is true.
>
> *UE:* On all three occasions it was you as my personal friend who stood bail for me that I was innocent of the accusation and I was released?
>
> *UUU:* Yes, that was so.
>
> *UE:* If you knew that I was a member of the man-leopard society, being one of the original founders with Akpan Ekpedeme then dead, why did you volunteer to take on my bail?
>
> *UUU:* Having associated with you for a long time I had always entertained doubt as to your being concerned with the man-leopard society.
>
> *UE:* Who told you that I am a member of the man-leopard society or that I am associated with it?
>
> *UUU:* Chief, as you know I am not a native of your village and cannot account for all your activities.
>
> *UE:* Are you suggesting that it was a member of my village who told you that I am a man-leopard?

UUU: Yes, that is my answer.

UE: I appeal to you in the name of God to reveal the name of your informer.

UUU: I cannot now remember his name.

UE: I suggest you are lying because no one ever gave you such information.

UUU: [*No answer.*]

UE: Are you prepared to take a solemn oath that I am a member of the man-leopard society?

UUU: I cannot swear.[118]

With this palpable irony, that the very man who had led the touring delegation and who had sworn the inhabitants of eighty villages would not himself be sworn, the plot thickened. At the Ibibio Union meeting on 29 May 1948 a resolution was unanimously passed suspending Usen from the Union and calling for everything possible to be done to bring him to justice for his conduct:

> Feelings ran high when it was discovered that certain portions of the report contain serious but fantastic and groundless allegations against Ibibio chiefs and the Idiong Society. It is believed that Mr Usen, for his own personal advancement and in order to earn honour and promotion from Government, had secretly forwarded the report to Government well knowing that the serious allegations contained in the report are entirely baseless.[119]

According to police reports, the Ibibio Union sought to discredit Usen Udo Usen further by accusing him of acting as a police agent, of taking bribes from chiefs so as not to expose them as *idiɔŋ*, and of embezzling Union funds. A committee of Ibibio Union members formed to investigate Usen's report claimed that it was:

> a carefully planned imaginative fabrication clothed in the garb of realism and half-truths ... Unless Mr Usen Udo Usen was himself a member of the so-called man-leopard society ... he could not have been in a position to disclose all that the report contained.[120]

The Ibibio Union passed resolutions and signed petitions over the next five years for a commission of enquiry into the man-leopard murders and for the authorities to provide proof to justify the ban on *idiɔŋ*. There was considerable speculation as to the reason for this apparently unlikely alliance of the self-styled 'intelligentsia' with the forces of rural conservatism, and why the Ibibio Union supported the *idiɔŋ* so vehemently and for so long. The Union's defence of *idiɔŋ* was assumed to be influenced by senior figures within the Ibibio Union who were themselves *idiɔŋ* members, including Obong Ntuen

Ibok of Essene, who were thought to be using the Union and the devices of colonial law at the disposal of its 'intelligentsia' to fight the ban.

Events at the Ibibio Union's next meeting, its annual conference held in August 1948, were keenly observed despite the precautions taken by the Union, including the use of identity cards to prevent access to unauthorised non-members. Undercover Special Branch police, however, were able to report that at the conference Dr Udoma had come to an agreement with the *idiòŋ* members of the Union that 'in the event of getting the Idiong Cult restored the Union would waive the repayment of a loan advanced to him for his legal training – a sum believed to be in the region of £2,000'.[121] It was reported that Usen 'was the first victim sacrificed in Udoma's campaign' and that he had ordered a former *Nigerian Eastern Mail* journalist, S. E. Hezekiah, to defame Usen in the press. The police claimed that no device to discredit Usen was left untried and that the Union threatened to bring 'conveniently discovered' criminal charges against Usen of embezzling Union funds whilst he was general secretary unless he agreed to make a public withdrawal of his statement incriminating the *idiòŋ* cult.[122] At the conference Usen was dismissed from membership of the Ibibio Union for life, and it was resolved that he be ostracised by Ibibio people everywhere for having 'plotted the destruction of leading personalities by deliberately picking them out, well-knowing that they were innocent, and accusing them falsely of being members of the man-leopard society'.[123] No evidence exists as to whether this was seen as a credible threat or not, but the police also reported that 'Native doctors were employed to prepare charms against him [Usen] in order to bring about his death'.[124]

THE MAN-EATING LEOPARD OF IKOT UDORO

The Union's condemnation of Usen, its own former secretary, coincided with a dramatic twist in the murder investigations. During the Ibibio Union's tour a new District Officer, John McCall, was appointed to administer Opobo Division. Despite the scale of the murder investigations, their final phases would be dominated by the actions of two men alone: Usen and McCall. McCall had been an administrative officer in the Eastern Provinces for eleven years. His assistant, Dennis Gibbs, was a former wing commander with the Royal Air Force and had a distinguished war record. McCall familiarised himself with his new posting by reviewing cases heard in the special sessions of the Supreme Court established to deal with the man-leopard murders. He noted the high number of acquittals and attributed them to the sloppiness with which the police had prepared their prosecutions. Specifically, he claimed that the police had overlooked physical evidence, had ignored discrepancies in eyewitness claims and had coerced confessions from suspects.

McCall reviewed only a small number of the murder cases. Yet those he examined that were brought to court between September and December 1947 exposed significant lapses in the police's ability to prosecute the man-leopard cases. The spate of acquittals which had attracted McCall's attention included a number of cases that had collapsed because of malicious accusations, flawed police procedures, the fabrication of evidence by individual police officers and accusations of police torture. The allegations of police corruption and the illegality of their methods highlighted by McCall were drawn from the judgments by Mr Justice Ademola who heard several cases in late 1947. Having discharged a further three suspects on 1 December Ademola offered his reflections on the prosecutions:

> As I have now tried a number of these 'leopard' murder cases, it will not be out of place for me to state that in one or two of the Police Camps in the area concerned, it would appear that the most cruel punitive methods are being employed for the detection of crimes by some unscrupulous Policemen. ... In one or two cases in this Court not only were they alleged, but they became obvious during the inquiry. The detection of these crimes is undoubtedly difficult but the fruits of these methods do not invariably stand the test in a Court of Law.[125]

Further accusations of police torture which had surfaced in the Chima case were made and were consistent in their details. In his trial for a series of murders in 1942 Akpan Adiaha Ekpo, for instance, gave evidence that he had been badly beaten, and that pepper was put in his nose, eyes, anus and on his penis. Though he swore that he attended the Opobo Hospital for his injuries, no record or witness was found to confirm that he was treated. Although his allegation was rejected, Mr Justice Pollard who heard the case uncovered major inconsistencies in the prosecution's conduct. The statements of both the witnesses and the accused were taken in the same room at the same time. The police constable concerned, David Ekoh, said that this was the usual practice in the 'campaign'.[126] The judge concluded that: 'It is completely beyond my understanding how and why this accused man could have freely and voluntarily made this statement to this Police Constable about a crime that had lain hidden for over 4 years. I intend to say nothing that may embarrass the Crown in the presentation either before me or any other judge ...'[127]

Another common weakness in the cases that McCall highlighted concerned the translation of evidence. Statements would be read out to one of the senior police officers, Brett or Fountain, by the constable who had transcribed and translated the evidence in the presence of the witness, or suspect, who then signed or assented to its veracity. None of the senior police officers spoke Annang, however, and it is unlikely that the witnesses or accused could understand the English translation of their 'statements', so what was presented as confirmation of the truth of a person's statement

Figure 7.7 Unwa Solomon (Reproduced with kind permission of the Bodleian Library, University of Oxford)[128]

concealed the pivotal role of the Annang-speaking police constables, and might very well have concealed their falsification of prosecution evidence. The law on this point was quite specific: 'When the person charged is an illiterate the statement may be read over or interpreted to him apart from some person other than a policeman'. Yet in a number of cases it was apparent that no one other than the police bringing the case had checked that translated written statements accurately recorded the words of prosecution witnesses or accused men.

In the light of these procedural weaknesses McCall attempted to raise the alarm by highlighting what he considered to be blatant miscarriages of justice. The death of Unwa Solomon, an eleven-year-old girl who had died on 9 April 1947, was one such case where McCall argued that the conviction of Isaac Akpan for her murder was a travesty (See Figure 7.7). The case was heard before Mr Justice Ademola in the Supreme Court at Opobo. During the trial two Crown witnesses testified that they had seen Isaac Akpan abduct the young girl on her way home. Another witness claimed that despite severe injuries to her neck Unwa had spoken to him before she died and had said, 'Isaac has stabbed me'. In his defence Isaac Akpan from the neighbouring village of Ikot Abasi Ufon said he had not been in Nkikara village two miles away on the day of Unwa's death and that he and other hunters had gone hunting and had returned when the sun was red. He had witnesses who said they shared a meal with him, listened to gramophone records and saw him home. He admitted that he had run away when the police came to arrest him because he thought he was being pursued for failing to pay his contribution to the police ration. Isaac also stated that he was related as *áyéyìn* to the village of Nkikara and that he could not, therefore, harm those from his mother's natal village. The judge

Figure 7.8 J. A. G. McCall (Reproduced with kind permission of the Bodleian Library, University of Oxford)[129]

was unimpressed by this alibi, particularly as Isaac's own wife disputed the time at which he had returned home, and though it was not necessary to prove motive Mr Justice Ademola noted that Issac Akpan and Unwa Solomon's uncle were at the time engaged in a land dispute as the representatives of their respective villages. Isaac Akpan was found guilty on 29 November 1947 and sentenced to death.[130]

McCall (Figure 7.8) argued that Unwa Solomon was not killed by Isaac Akpan but by a leopard. He stated that the Nkikara villagers knew that they would not be believed if they said a leopard was responsible and that they feared recriminations, in particular a police camp and visitation in their village, if they failed to identify a suspect. McCall's assistant, Dennis Gibbs (Figure 7.9), was told that Nkikara held a meeting in order to pin the murder on someone outside the village, and that several eye-witnesses were nominated to identify Isaac Akpan since he had been a prominent figure in the recent land case. It was the comment of one of these eye-witnesses which cast even graver doubt over the safety of the conviction. McCall himself overlooked this point, but in a handwritten note beneath the verdict

Figure 7.9 Dennis Gibbs hearing a petition (Reproduced with kind permission of the Bodleian Library, University of Oxford)[132]

someone had written 'can a person with a fractured neck speak as the deceased is supposed to have done with very important evidence?'[131]

Shocked at the paucity of hard proof pointing to the existence of the man-leopards, McCall began his own review of the physical evidence. His suspicion was quite simple, that the man-leopard episode had been conjured up not by the *idiɔŋ* society but by mass hysteria, and that the killings were not elaborate simulations but genuine bush leopard attacks. McCall had borrowed a book which had illustrated the bite wounds inflicted on a human victim by a wild dog. The particular similarities with those injuries he saw in Opobo suggested to McCall the real possibility that wild leopards alone had been responsible for the deaths. Gibbs had kept a pet leopard in order to establish its feeding and killing behaviour.[133] He was convinced that too many leopards were hunting too little game. The shortage of gunpowder in Abak meant that leopard hunting had been reduced and during a tour Gibbs found that very little game, especially deer, remained.

Together, McCall and Gibbs became convinced that the answers to the man-leopard murder mysteries could be found at the murder scenes themselves. They tested this theory when they organised a leopard hunt. It was not the first hunt of the investigations but it was more extensive than previous efforts and successfully trapped a number of leopards, including a seven foot 'man-eater' at Ikot Udoro (Figure 7.10). The leopard was shot by a hunter, Akpan Okpokpo, in almost exactly the same spot at which the double murder of a man and a woman had taken place just two weeks previously and for which a fellow villager Sam Udo Ilem had been arrested. The leopard killed on 13 December 1947 was an old male and in poor condition. It had suffered an injury to its paw, two of its canines were broken off and it appeared malnourished. McCall believed that because of these incapacities the leopard trapped at Ikot Udoro had been unable to kill its normal prey, and he would later write that he and Gibbs believed this very leopard to be responsible for the vast majority of the 200 or so killings over the previous five years.[134]

McCall's intervention reminds us of the need to be wary of conflating the various different colonial representations and to delineate the differing motivations of the various colonial agents. There was, therefore, a more problematic correspondence between colonial rhetoric and its agents on the ground.[135] McCall's reports were evidence of a rift that had emerged between the police and the district administration. McCall criticised Fountain's police investigation, and questioned the faith he placed in the speculative findings of Usen's report. Since Kay's initial detective work in 1945, the police, McCall claimed, had approached each case with the preconceived belief that the killing was a human act, that any evidence which might weaken their case had been disregarded (especially initial eye-witness accounts of seeing a wild leopard attack the victim) and that consistent and illegal pressure had been applied on local villages to 'produce' a murderer. McCall not only argued that suspects had been sentenced on hearsay evidence but that the

Figure 7.10 The Man-eating leopard of Ikot Udoro[136]

a. that the killing agent in the majority of 'man-leopard' cases is not a man at all, but a leopard

b. that even if he were mistaken in this belief, the methods of police investigation which have been adopted have resulted in the wrong persons being brought to justice.

In either event Mr McCall's contention is that miscarriages of justice have occurred and may recur. Further points made by McCall:

1. geographical boundaries suggest real leopards.
2. trapping of leopards (including man-eater) has stopped the killings
3. danger of convictions on the evidence of 'eye-witnesses' who keep changing their stories or are contradictory.
4. unreliability of witnesses.
5. in every case the police have investigated with the preconceived belief that the killing was a human act, that they have in every case, 'gone to get their man', and that any evidence which might weaken their case has been disregarded. ... the people are expected to produce a murderer, and if they do not do so, pressure is put upon them.
6. calls for commutation of 18 death sentences
7. protests at his own treatment – being ordered out of his division (with 24 hours' notice) with no reason given.[137]

Figure 7.11 Summary of McCall's argument

entire process of prosecuting the 'man-leopards' had become opportunities for malicious accusations (as outlined in Figure 7.11).

McCall also questioned the forensic evidence. He wondered why many victims had sustained wounds that were no deeper than 2½ inches, and argued that the wounds were inflicted either by a very short-bladed knife, or more likely by a wild leopard. He was further convinced of this when he saw images of the injuries caused on a human by a dog in the book he had borrowed from a police officer.[138] McCall, however, was no forensic specialist. The medical officer, Dr Awoliyi, in one case brought a leopard's head and paws to court as a specimen and proved conclusively that wild leopards could *not* have been responsible. His question was whether it was possible for leopard teeth or claws to have produced the four parallel puncture wounds with cut edges which had been found on the victim's upper body. The doctor said that the wounds inflicted by a leopard's teeth were likely to be lacerated, not clean cut as they appeared, and that if they were clean cut, then they would not be completely uniform and regular.[139]

Nevertheless, McCall raised important questions regarding the evidence of mutilation. Why, he asked, had police attention focused squarely on the use of body parts when in the vast majority of cases they had not been removed from the scene of the crime? Usen's report had suggested that murders were performed to obtain male and female genitalia and skulls for ritual purposes, but there was never any evidence that genitalia or skulls had been removed. McCall directly questioned Usen on this point, who replied that he was 'referring to killing custom which pertained in very olden time, and not during the present series of killings'.[140]

McCall's series of questions turned the entire investigation on its head. He was adamant that even if his theory about the leopards was wrong and that the deaths were the result of murder, the colonial criminal justice system had hanged the wrong men. His theory appeared all the more probable as only one 'leopard' killing was reported after the hunt, and this was outside the 'Leopard Area'. Sixteen convicted men were due to be executed when McCall sent a series of urgent and secret reports detailing his reservations in the days before Christmas 1947:

> I have come to my conclusions in this terribly serious matter unwillingly .... Mr Gibbs, Assistant District Officer, has come to the same conclusions equally unwillingly. We both wish most sincerely that we could agree with the other point of view. We have no desire to stir up a scandal. But we are the men on the spot and I am myself an Administrative Officer of eleven years experience of the Eastern Provinces of Nigeria. Possibly the West African climate has affected my reasoning powers and led me to the wrong conclusions in this matter. The same cannot be said of Mr. Gibbs, whose distinguished war service as one of the youngest Wing Commanders in the Royal Air force and a D.S.O. to boot do not suggest a man of a completely irresponsible type and outlook. Yet of different character, temperament, training and ability, we have formed the same opinions and reached the same conclusions. We are the only Administrative Officers who have travelled extensively in the 'leopard' area. The opinions and conclusions of this report therefore are the opinions and conclusions of the men on the spot, and as such I think that they deserve at least the consideration of the highest authority in Nigeria, and if considered necessary of the highest authority in the Empire.[141]

Not only was McCall's intervention a most serious one, but his insistence that his correspondence be passed to the highest authorities – the Governor and the Secretary of State – threatened to undermine the reputations of all those involved in the investigations. Indeed, in November 1947 when McCall's views surfaced, the Colonial Secretary had already been asked in the House of Commons to justify the punitive measures taken: 'Does the Right Hon. Gentleman really consider that the large number of death sentences passed in these cases has been fully justified, and cannot this very tragic sociological problem be dealt with by other than punitive measures?'[142]

The Government's reaction to McCall's insistent objections in December 1947 was swift: he was given twenty-four hours to leave his post and was ordered to refrain from drawing attention to his transfer to Lagos.[143] By then his reports had become general knowledge, however, and chiefs from Opobo sent telegrams to London petitioning against his hasty transfer.[144] He was given a rousing send-off on 3 January 1948 with a tennis tournament, brass band and dance at the African club organised in his honour. Crucially for the chiefs and the Ibibio Union, however, McCall's allegations gave them firm evidence with which to refute the charge that *idiɔŋ* was involved in the killings. It is no surprise, then, that the principal signatory to the petitions in support of McCall was Obong Ntuen Ibok. Though he had admitted to identifying 'leopard men' for the police prior to his detention in February 1947, he subsequently subscribed to McCall's view that the leopard men had never existed. Taking over as Governor in 1948, Sir John Macpherson reprieved the sixteen men who had been sentenced to death and against whose sentences McCall had lobbied so passionately. Whether this act of clemency was a political device to demonstrate the new Governor's magnanimity, or whether Macpherson saw and believed McCall's claims, is not clear. In February 1948 he also approved a new leopard hunt in Abak and Opobo in which the reward for killing a leopard was increased to ten pounds and funds were made available for gunpowder, shot, cartridges and trap wire.

More generally McCall's stance enabled several groups to redeem themselves, especially the Ibibio Union, which could point to McCall's reservations in its efforts to clear Ibibioland of the 'shameful incident'. Hence the Union both privately and in the press dismissed any suggestions that the killings were conducted by the man-leopard society for ritual purposes:

> It surprises the bulk of the Ibibio people to hear that the Idiong society, a society as old as the hills in Ibibioland, has connection with the recent man-leopard menace, there being no society in Ibibioland known as the 'Man-Leopard Society'. ... we humbly pray to government to repeal the legislation against this purely religious society of the Ibibio people, as freedom of worship constitutes good government.[145]

The Union therefore dismissed the entire investigation claiming that its initial premise had been flawed and that Kay had been unduly influenced by his knowledge of 'the Human Leopard Society among the Sherbros of the former Protectorate of Sierra Leone'.[146]

* * *

In the early months of 1948, Usen Udo Usen was reassigned to the Nigeria Police contingent based in Ikot Okoro. Usen, it was claimed, continued to voice his anti-*idiɔŋ* sentiments, and the Ibibio Union's campaign against him 'did not deter Usen from his self-imposed task ... he gave up his weekends and most of his other spare time to visiting different parts of the area, using his very considerable influence with the local people and continuing to supply most useful information to the police'.[147] There is only one surviving source that details these events during 1948, a secret report prepared for the administration by Senior Assistant Superintendent of Police, Fountain, in 1951. Fountain's report clearly aimed to establish the police's interpretation of the murders and makes no mention of McCall's theories. Rather, it credits Usen Udo Usen with finally bringing the murders to an end.

Backed by Annang court and council members, Usen embarked on a second tour of the man-leopard villages in 1948.[148] He was convinced that murderers had got round the effects of the *mbiàm* oath sworn the previous year by use of an antidote, and despite the inconclusive results of the previous tour he was sure that oath-swearing was the only means by which the killings would finally stop. Hence, Usen set about obtaining various medicines and charms, including an oath he believed was more effective than the 'doll', and an antidote he and the Annang chiefs believed would counteract the leopard society charms. Thus armed, Usen held meetings and repeated the oath-swearing ceremonies in nearly every one of the affected Annang villages. Villagers swore that they had not taken part in any man-leopard activity in the past, and that they would not do so in future.[149] Those who refused to consent to having the antidote applied would automatically become suspects. Fountain reported that from the start Usen was well received and that his second tour was an acclaimed success. The contradictions of Usen's interventions were palpable. Usen backed an anti-*idìɔŋ* campaign with the use of charms acquired from specialists in the same arts.

The final twist came on 21 February 1948 when Akpan Ukpong Eto, the son of Chief Ukpong Eto of Ediene Atai, with whom Usen had clashed over the contents of his report, died suddenly. An exhumation order was obtained by the Medical Officer, who was unable to certify the cause of death. The chief's son was rumoured to have been a leading 'man-leopard' himself, and had been arrested and acquitted for the murder of PC Chima the year before. He had taken Usen's oath when the latter visited the village a fortnight previously during which the *mbiàm* was held against the chest, back and head, parts of the body where Akpan Ukpon Eto complained of pains before he died. Rumours spread that he had died as a result of swearing a false oath and that he had confessed this before his death. Though the pathologist belatedly reported that the chief's son had died of pneumonia, Usen's antidote had had its effect. Usen's reputation, Fountain claimed, was redeemed, and apart from a single death in March 1948 the murders stopped. Among the various factors which had broken the murder cult, Fountain wrote: 'The work of Mr Usen may certainly be given a high place on the list'.[150]

Applauded by the colonial authorities but publicly outcast from his own community, had Usen Udo Usen betrayed his people or was he a scapegoat who fell victim to political intrigue? The Ibibio Union condemned Usen's report on the grounds that he had intended to exploit the gullibility of expatriate administrative officials by a display of his knowledge of the social structure, norms and beliefs of the Ibibio people.[151] He was portrayed as the 'man who knew too much' and his story illustrates the point that 'the colonial politics of knowledge penalised those with too much local knowledge and those with not enough'.[152]

Usen's role in the murder enquiries was crucial because of the structural and personal way in which he acted as broker between institutions, and because of the way he mediated between different ways of knowing. Usen's role as broker depended on convincing chiefs and District Officers of his indispensability based on his claims to knowledge. For the authorities the man-leopard society was an object potentially knowable by colonial rationality which had, so officers mused, evaded detection during the extensive 1930s inquiries conducted for the clan intelligence reports. Usen, in fact, had gained a unique insight into colonial modalities of the ethnographic method as Jeffreys' interpreter and his report was a product of it. Yet Usen also grasped the significance that, in this context of secrecy, knowledge was established by testing and that truth was determined not in a courtroom trial but trial by ordeal. It was because of this that over fifty years later those who remember the events of 1947 and 1948 in the former Abak Division say that it was the oaths Usen and the chiefs administered that brought the killings to an end. Usen's actions therefore demonstrate the improvisation with which colonial clerks subverted colonial modes of authority and how they were translated into locally effective terms. As a link between the domains of district office and village square Usen projected a sense to both sides that he had privileged, esoteric knowledge that was ambiguous, not easily verified, and potentially dangerous.[153] The boundaries to knowledge that Usen attempted to manipulate, however, were impossible to maintain in the full glare of local press coverage and Union scrutiny. As a result his claims to knowledge were exposed.

On the political level, Usen's career shows how the room for manoeuvre of colonial intermediaries could evaporate. The police hailed Usen Udo Usen's role during the tour and alluded to the fast-shifting political loyalties against which his actions were set:

> He has in fact been the Ibibio Union in thought and action and in view of the many politically inspired nationalistic claims to the loyalties of well meaning Africans he has been and is carrying out a task with a fairness and honesty of purpose under most difficult circumstances and without any likelihood of financial or political gain ...'[154]

It is evident that events overtook him quickly, however, both in the micro-politics of the investigation and within the broader sweep of national political change. During the war years clerks had to negotiate the increasingly difficult political contradiction of being from the educated class which criti-cised colonial rule, while at the same time being among those who helped to enforce it. In south-eastern Nigeria, the period of the leopard murders was a key moment for these political trajectories. Specifically, these few months represented the tipping point of a fundamental change in relations between 'improvement unions' like the Ibibio Union and the colonial state. The more explicitly political and anti-colonial trajectory of the unions, and their more confident and strident tone of criticism towards the Government from this moment on, put those among their members who were part of the colonial machinery, like clerks, in a potentially awkward position. Usen had therefore found himself on the wrong side of the line over an issue which may have seemed innocuous enough to him at the time he submitted his report, but which was progressively being recast not in the colonial context of law and order but in a nationalist framework of rights and freedoms.

Despite this shifting ground of political alliances a key puzzle remains. Since Usen knew better than most that the Ibibio Union's line on the *idiɔŋ* prohibition was resolute, why did he persevere in support of the Government and why did he therefore allow himself to be set up to be despised and ostracised by his own people? Usen had been in colonial service for at least twenty-three years. He knew his Bible well, probably from his schooling in the United Presbyterian Church of Scotland in Itu, and in his controversial report he left a record of his views on local people. These fragments combine to suggest the profile of a man whose ethical and political outlook was distinctly shaped by both mission teaching and colonial duty. His view of the local Annang population in the man-leopard villages was of 'savage men who were clever only in practising wickedness'. He noted down passages of sermons from inter-denominational church services which were held on each Sunday during the tour, and attacked what he called the barbarous work of the new 'spiritual churches' which engaged in faith healing. He also drew attention to those he called 'men of character', and distinguished church reverends, village heads and court clerks, who displayed that 'high sense of duty and honesty' of which he himself was so proud. In short, he had become not only an agent of but a champion for the colonial order. He was among those senior, long-serving clerks who not only stood apart from the criticism levelled at ill-educated, bribe-takers within the service, but who were themselves part of an emergent middle class and members of associations that had publicly opposed bribery and corruption in provincial tours in the early 1940s.

While Usen and the tour party were met with grim findings and grave responsibilities at many of their stops, at others they were met with schoolchildren performing dances and, in one instance, Mrs Usen, who had joined him for a few days, was asked by a Catholic church school to hand out the cups on prize day. This was the stuff of a District Officer's or Resident's tour. In his report and his later correspondence he would point out the deplorable state of the roads in certain villages, the illegality of particular local customs, the commendable achievements of mission schools, and how a village group might be better organised to be closer to court. These were precisely the observations and recommendations of senior colonial staff. The Ibibio Union Tour Delegation was part peace-keeping mission and part imperial pageant, and it is difficult to see how this could not have boosted Usen's sense of his own self-importance and sense of where his own prospects were best served.

It was widely reported during 1948 that not only were the Ibibio Union seeking to have the *idìoŋ* restored but that they also wanted Usen 'punished' for submitting what the Union considered to be a fake report. Apparently, however, Usen retained the trust of the Annang section of the Union who had threatened to leave the Union if action was taken against him.[155] Usen worked as interpreter for two new DOs stationed at Ikot Okoro, Brayne-Baker and Alderton, who both toured the parts of Abak and Opobo Divisions in which the murders had occurred. After his secondment to the police, Usen reverted to the provincial administration and was transferred first to Ikot Ekpene, then his home district of Itu, and finally, at his request, to the headquarters of the regional administration in Enugu. There Usen, along with the handful of Annang court members who had supported the investigations in 1948, was awarded the Certificate of Honour on the King's birthday in 1949. The Ibibio Union claimed that Usen's award was a 'face-saving device' on the part of the administration. But Usen, sadly, received his honour only posthumously. Of his death, like much of his life, the archives tell us little, though the little they do tell us is intriguing. In the margin of a report which referred to Usen's death after a short illness in Enugu, Frank Williams, a junior police officer with the investigation, wrote 'Was Poisoned!!' In an article he wrote later for a police journal he expanded:

> This District Clerk died mysteriously shortly afterwards. It is quite probable that he was poisoned for his disclosures, he had obviously incurred the disfavour of some of his fellow tribesmen. The cassava root, grown extensively in the area and the staple diet, is edible only after lengthy processing. In its early stages of preparation for food, it is poisonous and a well-known insidious means in the disposal of unwanted persons.[156]

8

THE POLITICS OF IMPROVEMENT, 1947–1960

The final months of the man-leopard murder investigations in late 1947 represented a key moment in the political trajectory of south-eastern Nigeria. They marked a shift in relations between the 'educated elements' of the improvement unions like the Ibibio Union and the colonial state. During the previous two decades no single issue before the ban on *idiɔŋ* had ruptured relations between the leaders of the Ibibio Union and the Resident of Calabar Province. The provincial authorities, indeed, had consistently sought to nurture the Union as the body around which, one day, an amalgamated Ibibio Division could be organised. Yet coinciding with the Local Government Despatch of 1947 a secret review was under way in the Eastern Provinces of the political fallout of the Second World War. Its focus was to explain why the Native Administration reforms of the 1930s had failed and how the emerging political threat of the improvement unions, which were buoyed by their recent affiliation to the National Council, could be channelled into local administration. This review of the improvement unions in 1947 is a vantage point from which to focus on the historical trajectory of power formations in south-eastern Nigeria to this point.

Despite colonial attempts to divert the elite's energies away from nationalist agitation, the Annang and Ibibio 'reading public' became fully engaged in the party politics of the 1950s, thus realigning regional alliances, remaking collective histories and reinforcing the link between development and the politics of identity. The confident tone of these languages of nationalism shaped a new set of meanings attached to both the murder investigations and a range of issues, contested along the lines of gender and generation, which had become familiar aspects of the social and political landscape. As independence beckoned, the Eastern Region Government commissioned several reviews into pressing concerns of future administration. In view of the analysis of Annang political and social dynamics that came to light in the man-leopard murder investigations, it is no coincidence that the major enquiries launched in the 1950s involved the justice system (investigated by the Brooks Commission, 1953), labour conditions on Fernando Po (1953 and 1957), brideprice (Committee on Brideprice in the Eastern Region, 1955), chieftaincy (the Jones Commission, 1956) and political identities (Willink Commission, 1957–58).

These reviews of the colonial legacy took place in the context of heightened expectations. Politically, the prospect of independence now loomed large; economically, policies shifted from welfarism to development; and socially, the shape of the family was being re-imagined. The cultural indications of these anticipations are all manifest in the imagery in the pages of the *Nigerian Eastern Mail*. After the war, for example, familiar advertisements for British health products, such as Andrews Liver Salts and Beechams Pills, featuring line drawings of white women, were increasingly interspersed with international stories that focused on the achievements of black figures like Joe Louis in the United States, reports on prejudice and discrimination from South Africa, and photographs of fighter jets and modernist architecture.

THE LEOPARDS' LEGACY

'The Death of a Maid'

Adiaha, eldest daughter of a wealthy Annang chief
Was a dark-skinned gentle maiden, but her heart was full of grief.
In her country darkly wooded, where each tribesman fears some ghost
Girls are sold as wives for money to the man who pays the most.
Akpan Udo, hoary chieftain, headman of a Bantu clan
Could afford young Adiaha, tempting bride for any man:
So he bought her for Manillas and she had to be his wife,
Which begins the dismal story, telling how she lost her life.
Akpan Udo was no lover, senile savage past his flame,
But his wives required assistance, so the maiden was fair game.
Days of toil and nights of sorrow Adiaha strove to please,
Till she left him for a stripling, far too poor to pay the fees.
Deep within the virgin forest, hand in hand they used to rove
And they built a palm leaf shelter in a lovely Afang grove.
But by law of Native Custom, Akpan Udo must get back
All he gave for Adiaha, failing which, he might attack.
When the youth refused to pay him, aged Akpan filled with spite
Hid in ambush by a pathway leading to their jungle site
Then he killed the poor wee lassie just to level off the odds,
And he tore her flesh to pieces to appease his pagan gods.[1]

M. T. Williams, Senior Superintendent of Police, wrote two short pieces on the leopard murders in August 1947, one of which he hoped to publish in the *Police Journal*. Included with the manuscript draft were copies of his poem 'Death of a Maid', along with several photographs. They were jaunty pieces extolling the wiles of the police in uncovering the leopard murderers and denigrating those practices – brideprice and divination in particular – which, he believed, had contributed to the crimes. As a serving officer Williams required official permission to publish his views, but this was refused. The uncertainty with which senior colonial officials handled the fallout from *èkpê-ówó*, and the imperative for the authorities to retain a consistent and distanced position, were evident in their refusal to air these unauthorised personal views on the murders. Of Williams' articles the Chief Secretary to the Government wrote: 'It is considered that they contain matters of contention about which no final decision could be or has yet been reached, however accurate time may shew [*sic*] the author's contentions to be. Mr Williams is a Government Officer and if the articles were published it would not be appreciated that the views expressed are not necessarily those of Government'.[2] What troubled the Government most were the doubts that continued to be raised as to whether the attack on the *idìɔŋ* had been wise.[3] On the advice of their lawyers the Government in Lagos decided that nothing should be published until a sense of 'finality' had been reached. There was never any opportunity in what remained of the colonial era, however, for this finality to be achieved.

The police force in Abak and Opobo was progressively reduced and was finally withdrawn on 5 May 1948 when the police headquarters at Ediene Atai closed. There was no formal enquiry or retrospective investigation into the events which had dominated Calabar Province in 1946 and 1947. Only one official report was compiled on the killings subsequently and this was by Derek Fountain, who had spent eighteen months as the officer in charge of the Police Detachment, and who had received the Police Medal for his determination and devotion to duty during that tour. He was subsequently appointed Commissioner of Police for the Western Region based in Ibadan.[4] In 1951 Fountain submitted the report at the request of the Inspector-General of Police in order to help officers in Calabar Province know what to look for when cases of 'killing by leopard' were reported. That the report was commissioned at all was indicative of continuing anxieties that 'leopard murders' might start afresh 'under the guise of killings by leopards'.[5] The report was not intended for public consumption. Indeed, it was not to be removed from the District Office, where the secret file was kept locked in the safe. In it, Fountain's review of the murders naturally privileged the police's view, played down McCall's intervention, praised Usen's role and evaded the problems raised by the messy conclusion to the investigations.

The Government's attempts to distance themselves from the leopard murder saga also included dropping plans for an anthropological enquiry into the southern Annang 'leopard area'. In October 1947, just as the frequency of killings abated, a proposal was drawn up by the Colonial Social Science Research Council for a three-year enquiry into the origin of the 'leopard society murders' looking at the 'wider problems of development in this backward area'. The anthropologists Meyer Fortes and

Raymond Firth were both asked to propose candidates for the project in 1948 which sought to shed light on the murders while posing under the guise of a more general and innocuous study.[6] During the course of the investigations S. F. Nadel, Audrey Richards, Phyllis Kaberry and J. S. Harris were all mentioned in connection with the proposed anthropological study. Apparently unaware of the true nature of the project, Linvill Watson from the University of Pennsylvania, who had applied for a Rhodes-Livingstone Institute appointment, came closest to being hired for the investigation. His application was processed by Max Gluckman, but was questioned on the grounds that, as a Quaker, Watson might unduly sympathise with local opinion against the British.[7]

The issue of religious sympathies had emerged in a meeting between Watson and E. E. Sabben-Clare, the Colonial Attaché at the British Embassy in Washington, on 15 April 1948. Watson had been called to the meeting which concerned research in Africa that the Colonial Office considered needed 'taking in hand urgently'. Afterwards, however, Watson appeared compelled to write at length about his personal convictions: 'I recognise that I would be under obligations of a quasi-political character', he wrote, 'I should probably carry a certain degree of sentimental "pro-Native" bias with me into the field, but honestly feel that I have sufficient flexibility ... to be reliably discreet. I have had a few contacts with African students on this side of the water, who usually expressed more or less a "nationalist" point of view. My sympathies are by no means unequivocally with them, rather the contrary if it came to an immediate practical issue, I suppose; however, I do expect that my activities as a government-sponsored researcher could be arranged so that a role of impartial neutrality could be maintained as plausibly as possible'.[8] Sabben-Clare replied on 8 June 1948 to say that the Colonial Office could not offer Watson the position.

The search for a suitable candidate for the project was officially abandoned for fear that an enquiry would be politically 'unsettling' and that it would lead to 'unpleasant publicity and endless complications'.[9] The failed search for an anthropologist may also be viewed in the context of a shifting relationship between colonialism and anthropology after the Second World War, which saw the colonial administration suspicious of nationalist sympathisers, and anthropology develop as an academic discipline independent of its colonial ties.[10] Yet the administration's private puzzlement about the background to the killings continued into the 1950s. When another American anthropologist, John Messenger, arrived in Ikot Ekpene to conduct fieldwork on religious change in Annang society in 1951, he declined the Colonial Office's request that he make the background to the man-leopard murders the subject of his thesis.[11]

Despite the absence of an official public enquiry or the unofficial sociological research project, the spectre of the man-leopard 'menace' reappeared in a variety of contexts after 1947. The behaviour of wild leopards during the rainy seasons of the late 1940s caused considerable concern. Fourteen leopards were killed in Opobo during 1948 and hunters received the standard rate of £5 per leopard (down from £20 previously).[12] The victims of wild leopard attacks, of which there were four killed and three mauled in Opobo Division in twelve months, were all children. During the investigation into one such case in March 1951, a severed hand, a bloodless crime scene and the absence of paw prints led suspicious CID officers to conduct a detailed enquiry into the matrimonial and litigation history of the victim's family. Since a wild leopard had entered the victim's yard just days before and had carried off a goat from a neighbouring compound two weeks previously, the police concluded that the three-year-old victim had been attacked by a bush leopard. While there were numerous false alarms like this, it seems that the leopard men did reappear in 1955. The death of a schoolboy from the village of Ikot Ukpong Eren in Ibesit was widely thought to be a revival of the 'leopard society', and local church members believed this to be the fourth, not the first, in a new series of murders.[13] Two cases, in fact, were taken to trial in which the 'real' man-leopard method had been adopted.[14]

The leopard murders also reappeared in a range of local discourses on crime, secret societies and civil litigation. Christian petitioners, for instance, invoked the fear of *ékpê ówó* to secure the prohibition of the secret societies; 'if the Government will not take serious steps against the evil movement (*ékpó*) it will soon involve [evolve] into man-leopard …'[15] Apparent miscarriages of justice during the 1950s also reminded people in Abak District of the circumstances which led to *ékpê ówó*. Chiefs in Abak wrote to the District Officer in August 1952, for example, to complain that Udo Ukanga from Ndot had boasted of spending his money to secure his own release from prison after being sentenced to three years and six months for murder, and they claimed that:

> The condition of ekpe owo was carrying on like this and afterwards the part of Abak Division imitate and things became worst. … If Government allow Udo Ukana to free as it is now, [we] believe that a man who gets money will kill his enimies [*sic*] and ready to call lawyer for help to plead and set them free.[16]

Ongoing disputes over the settlement of matrimonial cases also reminded people of the leopard murders. Dick Inyang Udo wrote to remind the DO that adultery cases and disrespect for people's wives had been the 'veritable cause of man leopard murder', and was still causing anger to every husband.[17] Personal threats and violent intimidation also invoked *ékpê ówó*. Moses Samuel suspected his father had poisoned and killed his mother because she was a Qua Iboe Mission convert. While hiding in the bush he wrote notes to the elders of the Ibesit Qua Iboe Church and to the District Officer in Abak to implicate his father if he should carry out his threats, 'my father promises to kill me on my way and be known as ekpe owo'.[18]

Leopards and leopard men were now the archetypal means of intimidation. Even those involved in investigating the murder cases invoked leopards in their own disputes. Chief Sampson Udo Idiong, for instance, who had been praised for his role in the campaign, was sued for an £8 7s 6d contribution club debt in September 1951. Hearing that his creditor had reported this to the District Officer, the chief called the man to his house where he 'rebuked me for having reported him to your worship and swore to heaven that my flesh would feed the leopards (ekpe ikot) in the attempt to claim my money'.[19] The distinction here between *ékpê ìkɔt* (bush leopard) and any other type of leopard had clearly become one that needed to be made.

While the leopard killings had ended, the various political controversies surrounding the investigations continued. In its public addresses during 1948 and 1949, including a welcome address to the new Governor, Sir John Macpherson, the Ibibio Union conveyed its views on the leopard murders in the strongest terms. 'Fictitious and atrocious reports have been submitted to the authorities', it claimed, 'and untold atrocities have been committed by certain investigators'. Usen's report, the Union insisted, was 'absolutely false in its entirety ... and we strongly resent Government's attitude if it believes or takes action on such a report, copied perhaps from files of irresponsible and unscrupulous aliens in Ibibioland. The police investigation was regrettable; atrocious crimes were committed and fabulous stories told, and we will not swallow these lying down'.[20] 'There will be no rest', the Union stated, 'until Government has sent a sincerely independent commission of enquiry to investigate into the root cause and lamentable sequel of the so-called man-leopard murders in the Ibibio territory'.[21]

In 1949 Obong Ntuen Ibok submitted further petitions to the Governor claiming compensation for the money he had said was stolen from his house when he was arrested during the raids on *idìɔŋ*. 'I have been disgraced', he wrote, 'and I am now looked down [upon] by my people'.[22] The Ibibio State Union and the Ibibio representatives in the House of Assembly also launched 'impassioned pleas' for the revocation of the prohibition on *idìɔŋ* into the 1950s. As the union president, Udo Udoma was the chief petitioner:

> I am directed by the Ibibio State Union on behalf of the members of the ancient Idiong society to apply to your good self for the lifting of the ban which has been placed on the Idiong Society by Government. I am to add that the members of the Idiong Society have complained bitterly against the ban so placed on the ground that the ban has brought about untold suffering and hardship, and are extremely anxious that the ban be now lifted by Government and the ancient and religious society be restored.[23]

A murder trial in Eket Division in 1951, however, served to harden the Government's line on the ban. Several witnesses alleged that the identities of the killers had been divined by an *idìɔŋ* and that when these suspects were called upon to clear their names by undertaking the *esere* bean ordeal one of them had died.[24] In the trial that followed, the judge, M. J. Abbott, wrote to the Governor to recommend that the 1947 ban on *idìɔŋ*, which was confined to Abak, Opobo and Uyo Divisions, be extended to the entire Province. Though the judge admitted that *idìɔŋ* played only a preliminary and peripheral role in the murder, officers at the highest echelons of the colonial administration seized upon the case as a vindication of the Government's stance to resist the Ibibio State Union's demands for the ban's revocation.[25]

The colonial rhetoric of the defeat of the *idìɔŋ* society therefore continued in various guises. One of the most bizarre was a presentation made to Arthur Creech Jones, the British Colonial Secretary. Salvaged from the *idìɔŋ* society 'paraphernalia' that had been publicly burned in police compounds and village squares, the Nigerian colonial authorities presented Creech Jones with an *idìɔŋ* head ring (*ókpɔ́nɔ́ŋ*) labelled as an 'Idiong Juju Crown' (Figure 8.1). The exoticisation of this 'trophy' was completed with the description, presumably given to Creech Jones at the time, that the head ring was covered with the skin of an African girl.[26]

Elsewhere in Africa social histories of two contemporary murder inves-

Figure 8.1 Idiong 'juju crown' (Reproduced with kind permission of the Commonwealth Institute)[27]

tigations in Southern Africa[28] and in Ghana[29] shed light on a remarkably similar range of social dynamics, especially on the relationships between rulers and ruled, between individuals and the natural environment, and between health and wealth. Like the man-leopard murders in Nigeria they also occurred immediately after the Second World War and shared a common proximity to the uncertainties wrought by colonial reforms to indirect rule during the 1930s.

The *liretlo* (*muti*) murders in Basutoland, so-called after the body parts removed to make empowering charms and medicines, point to the way in which murders occur in response to situations of social and economic pressure, how the murderers were motivated by the need to increase agricultural output, and to enhance political status and power, or personal 'magnification'.[30] The key problem faced by the authorities in Basutoland was that their suspects were precisely the same chiefs through whom the British sought to rule, and the murders have therefore been interpreted within the framework of a 'crisis of moral authority'.[31] Numerous further parallels can be drawn with the murders in Nigeria. The *liretlo* cases also reveal the problematic nature of witness and accomplice evidence, for instance, along with false allegations and widespread claims of police malpractice. In addition to the engagement of one of south-eastern Nigeria's administrator-anthropologists, G. I. Jones, in the Basutoland enquiries, other intriguing parallels arise in the way in which an 'incipient nationalist organisation', Lekhotla la Bafo led by Joseph Lefela, became engaged in the *liretlo* investigation.[32]

In West Africa attempts to classify types of ritual murder are equally problematic. A distinction can be made between those sacrifices performed to benefit deities or ancestors, and those killings linked to the manufacture of potent medicines which are conducted to benefit an individual.[33] This difference can be seen when comparing concurrent murders in Ghana in 1944 and 1945. The Bridge House killing in the Ghanaian town of Elima in 1945, for example, was a ritual murder. Body parts and flesh from a young girl were used to prepare medicines to enable the murderers, a faction in a chieftaincy dispute, to win a court case.[34] The Kibi (Kyebi) murder, the death of Akyea Mensah in 1944, however, was a mortuary ritual.[35]

The Kibi murder investigation leads us to examine an intimate portrait of the way in which the royal dynasty of Akyem Abuakwa came to terms with the loss of the chief architect of its political accommodation with Mission Christianity and colonialism.[36] Two points from the analysis of the enquiry run parallel to events in Nigeria. First, the thesis that the murder was the result of social, political and economic tensions built up during the inter-war period. And second, that the protracted case (February 1944 to March 1947) bore witness to the poisoning of relations between the intelligentsia and the colonial authorities, and the emergence of a specifically anti-colonial agenda.[37] Within a month of the conclusion of the Kyebi case in July 1947 the defence lawyer, Dr Joseph Boakye Danquah, launched the United Gold Coast Convention, the first nationalist party in Ghanaian history.[38]

Like these comparative instances, the man-leopard murders coincided with a moment at which the various narratives of governance, chieftaincy, nationalism, marriage, economics and justice all became the subject of heightened public and political contestation.

NATIONALIST TRAJECTORIES

In its editorial at the end of the Ibibio Union's tour of the man-leopard area the *Nigerian Eastern Mail* hailed the delegates for having 'saved Nigeria from further embarrassment'.[39] The tour had enhanced the Union's reputation as a 'patriotic' body, it claimed, and added that 'this is the sort of thing we call a practical and constructive effort towards the attainment of self-government'.[40] The national interest, nationalism and the prospect of self-government now constituted the key themes of the politics of 'improvement' and the end of empire. Perceptions of the appropriate pace of this change and the legitimate horizons of expectations, however, differed markedly between London and Calabar, and between radical and progressive.

High-profile incidents immediately after the Second World War fostered the appearance, if not the reality, of widespread militant nationalism and this accelerated moves to independence.[41] The agenda of the key nationalist players was rapidly unfolding. Azikiwe held press conferences in 1947 to unveil a fifteen-year plan at talks in London in which he would demand either dominion status or complete independence for Nigeria.[42] Locally, his supporters, such as E. Essessien, held meetings across the region in which they reiterated their opposition to 'the spirit of imperialism'.[43] Within the colonial bureaucracy, however, progress towards self-government was perceived in gradualist terms, and fears of nationalist subversion were shaped by the perceived imperative of embracing and outflanking the progressive majority:

> It is the whole-hearted co-operation of the progressive elements of the population that must be obtained if the pace of reform is to be accelerated. It is the wishes and aspirations of this class especially that should be treated with respect.[44]

The Second World War came to be perceived by the colonial authorities as a political watershed in Nigeria, marking the parallel decline of the chiefs and the dramatic rise of young men's progressive unions. In March 1947 Sir Bernard Carr, the Chief Commissioner of the Eastern Region, urged the provincial Residents to consider what active measures could be taken to secure a greater degree of cooperation between these two sections of society in order to be able to proceed towards a more progressive and stable local administration in the Eastern Provinces:

Some twenty or so years ago we started the introduction of Native Administration into the Eastern Provinces. We had detailed enquiries into indigenous systems of organisation and gradually councils of sorts evolved composed largely of aged family heads. ... Now alongside these Councils there grew up various Unions comprising the more progressive elements and these were apt to operate outside the orbit of the Councils ... They did, at times, make advances towards the Native Authorities but such advances were viewed with considerable suspicion as evidencing a desire to usurp the functions of the Councils ...

At about this stage came the war. Supervision of Native Author- ities was perforce relaxed as also was contact with the Unions. ... The Unions ... continued and, I should say, became stronger and more influential but probably with less interest in Native Authorities (except perhaps to criticise and prod from outside) ... Many influ- ences were at work during these years of which we know only too little but I should say that a large section of the communities have jumped say some fifty years in outlook. ... I think we must recognise that it is vital to the policy behind our New Constitution that the Native Authorities should absorb and move forward with the best of the progressive element: unless we can achieve this in time the New Constitution will fail in its object.[45]

Carr's observations set in motion a series of reviews in 1947 in which District Officers from across the Eastern Provinces reflected on the political ramifications of the reform process in the 1930s and 1940s. Their responses were compiled in a secret dossier of reflections on the post-war status of improvement unions, and reports on the potential role that the unions might play as outlets for emerging nationalist ambitions in the context of the new constitution.[46]

The increasing political and economic weight of the unions led to fears among the colonial staff that failure to regulate unions would lead them to divert their activities into 'undesirable channels'. In the absence of legis- lation to register the improvement unions, it was recognised by this time that: 'Such unions are increasing in number and represent a definite social trend which is a part of the political consciousness of the country'.[47] In his review of post-war Nigeria, Lord Hailey observed that there was a danger of underrating the force which the improvement unions could exert on the authorities, as 'developments in the Eastern Provinces have shown their co- operation can be of great value ... and when they are in opposition they can prove a source of standing embarrassment to the course of good adminis- tration'.[48] After 1945 it was the improvement unions, as vehicles of the elite's political interests, which had become the foremost critics of local admin- istration. The success or failure of the 1946 Constitution, therefore, was considered to rest on precisely the task of bringing the improvement unions within the orbit of local administration and on absorbing the progressives within the Native Authorities:

> Unless the two halves of society – the elders and the progressives – can be brought together to work as one for the common good, the Native Authorities on whom the Richards Constitution is based will become more and more of a sham ...[49]

In 1947 the shortcomings of successive administrations in the Eastern Provinces were attributed to the neglect of village organisation and local-level social dynamics. Native Administration in the Eastern Provinces had been shaped by models of Government in the North and West, but substituting 'amorphous councils for well organised chiefs and councils long recognised by Native Custom'.[50] Despite the 'anthropological' intelligence reviews upon which the Native Administration reforms were based, Carr and his colleagues conceded that the intelligence reports told them very little about the social dynamics at play when they were written in the 1930s. In turn, it was judged that the reforms of the 1930s were unsuccessful because contemporary investigations failed to appreciate the shifting balance of power that was apparent after the introduction of taxation:

> It is true, I think, to say that in many cases, councils are not genuinely representative of the people, since their formation was established with too much of an eye on indigenous custom and too little on the constantly changing conditions of village, clan and tribal life and the emergence of a strongly vocal, active, even iconoclastic body of men who have outstripped placid village life and look for better things.[51]

Indeed, it was realised by 1947 that the tone in which the 'grasping' and 'unscrupulous' young men were described in the intelligence reports had ignored an important political reality. The 1930s were witness to contests for political, financial and judicial power between a complex of opposing forces broadly configured as youth and elders. Contrary to its intention, the Native Administration reform process, however, had compounded the disenfranchisement of the educated youth who had become increasingly resentful of the conservatism of the elders in whose hands power had been placed:

> At the time when the majority of the Intelligence Reports were written and all that could be found of indigenous organisations were councils of elders I do not think the influence that the young men must have had on the elders in pre-Government days was sufficiently realised and, though in some reports, the young men's societies were mentioned there appeared at that time no way in which any of their representatives could be brought into the organisation, even when their influence was realised.[52]

Recent events had made promoting better dialogue between unions, elders and the state a political imperative as it was argued that unions should be informed of issues being debated by the councils and of contentious legislation: 'Had the recent "Mines Bill", "Deposition of Chief's Ordinance", and "Public Lands Acquisition Amendment Ordinance" been discussed freely with Unions and explained to them, a good deal of the demonstration against these Ordinances would not have arisen'.[53] 'How then can we use the Unions?' was the question which dominated submissions from across the Eastern Provinces. Despite negative reports and apparent obstacles to engaging certain unions in the local administrative structure, the overall goal was identified as seeking an accommodation between new elites and elders. A number of solutions was proposed which included their assuming consultative, affiliate or more fully representative status:

> The alternatives seemed to be: a. For the Unions to remain outside the Native Authority and for District Officers to make a point of consulting them b. For the Unions to remain outside the Council but to form a sort of 'Lower House' thereto; c. For the Unions to be represented as such on the Council.[54]

The Senior District Officer of Opobo Division, for example, recognised that the Ibibio Union had long been engaged in attempts to unite clans fragmented under the Native Administration reforms, and suggested that since its members included most of the councillors 'there is no reason why it should not in the future form the skeleton of a unified Ibibio State'.[55]

By 1947, therefore, there was a congruence of views between progressives and the colonial authorities on the need for political reform born out of both a hard-fought local power struggle and the 'high politics' of the Colonial Office. Before all the replies in the secret review had been sent back to Enugu, the Commissioner received a copy of the Secretary of State's Local Government Despatch.[56] The Despatch issued by the Colonial Office in 1947 ushered in the end of Lugard's indirect rule and of Cameron's Native Administration and acknowledged that these policies and democratic self-government were mutually incompatible.[57]

The review of improvement unions in the Eastern Region during 1947, therefore, anticipated a significant part of the ongoing process of administrative reform. As a result of the imperatives identified the previous year, an all-African select committee of the Eastern House of Assembly toured the entire Eastern Region in 1948 to discuss future local administrative reforms with Native Authority councils and improvement unions.[58] It concluded that the system was in need of 'drastic reform'.[59] The different perceptions of the pace of reform, however, remained critical. The committee's recommendations were incorporated in a memorandum adopted by the Eastern Region House of Assembly in 1949 which introduced a three-tier system of local government councils formed along the lines of English local government and enabled open access on an elective basis.[60] The reforms of the 1940s did not intend decolonisation in the sense of self-government, however, but rather the achievement of reformed or modernised forms of African local administration.[61] As an illustration of the range of views on the speed of change, the issue of the *Nigerian Eastern Mail*, which published the details of the Local Government Bill, also carried a story of Azikiwe's visit to Washington. In the call he made for independence during his trip, he claimed that Nigeria was 'near breaking point and it might be difficult to control extremists and prevent a revolt'.[62]

Indeed, it was the unions' potential involvement in subversive activities and their affiliation to nascent nationalist political parties that stimulated the urgency of these enquiries. The fear of the unions' direct association with nationalist causes, which were spearheaded by the National Council of Nigeria and the Cameroons (NCNC) in 1944 and had eighty-seven 'ethnic union' affiliates by January 1945,[63] was high on the agenda:

> We must do all that is possible to prevent them becoming centres of agitation. ... with an eye on the new Constitution and all its implications and with a view to combating the unhealthy machinations of the so-called National Council I cannot escape feeling that positive and early action is necessary.[64]

During this period, in fact, improvement unions were kept under surveillance as fear of social upheaval began to take a grip after the general strike of 1945, and as Cold War suspicions started to filter through the colonial administration.[65] In late 1947 in Calabar, for instance, police records show that the activities of workers' and progressive unions came under close scrutiny and that their potential affiliation to the Zikist Movement was of particular concern. Following the introduction of the Richards Constitution in 1947 it was not the fledgling political parties, but rather the pan-ethnic associations which assumed the political initiative and which acted as the principal centres of 'political ferment in Nigeria during the growth of nationalism'.[66] The majority of nationalist politicians of the 1950s were prominent in the associations; a survey of the House of Representatives showed that 55 per cent of members from the Eastern Provinces were officials or active in 'ethnic associations'.[67]

★ ★ ★

Two distinct versions of vernacular nationalist discourse had coexisted in the immediate post-war period.[68] On the one hand was Zik's threat of impending violence; on the other was the long-standing discourse on patriotism and good citizenship. The civic outlook of the so-called 'patriotic' unions had been based on exhortations to keep the peace and for people to pay their taxes and refrain from accepting bribes. Another dimension to this conception of citizenship articulated inter-ethnic dialogue, integration and harmony. The language was of a 'common citizenship' in the context of urban communities which might think of themselves not as an Igbo, Ibibio, Ijaw or Efik but as citizens of Calabar, Aba or Port Harcourt.[69] Loyalty and cooperation were the watchwords necessary for the 'inter-tribal cohesion' of a future nation. Clinton and his *Nigerian Eastern Mail* had consistently preached that loyalties should be transferred from the 'tribe to the nation'. This discourse was framed against the background of simmering distrust and suspicion that existed between the Efik, Ibibio and Igbo communities in Calabar Province. The simple paradox, however, was that the progressive elites who preached this idea of common citizenship had long been organised in parochial, ethnic-based unions which were radicalised during the war and now anticipated self-rule. By 1948, with the formation of Egbe Omo Oduduwa the pan-Yoruba union, Clinton, for instance, recognised that his vision had failed and that the time had come when 'we who started this tribal nationalism must teach the country that we meant no harm'.[70]

The constitutions of 1947 and 1951 raised the political stakes and by mid-1953 national political parties became clearly demarcated as ethnic blocs. Constitutional reform led to a decisive rift in the NCNC's cross-ethnic support with the 'Calabar bloc' resigning from the party in 1953 amid personal animosities and accusations that the NCNC had become an exclusively Igbo political instrument.[71] Professor Eyo Ita, Dr E. U. Udoma and Jaja Wachuku formed the National Independence Party (NIP) in March 1953, which has been seen as 'the embryo movement of the ethnic minorities in the Eastern Region'.[72] Following the 1953 Constitutional Conference NIP opposed the NCNC's agreement to set up three 'strong' regions with a 'weak' centre, because in the Eastern Region the Igbo would inevitably take the lead. Inspired by the separation of the Cameroons from Nigeria as a strategy to satisfy the demands of minority ethnic groups, NIP, backed by the Ibibio State Union, inaugurated the movement for Calabar-Ogoja-Rivers State (COR State) in December 1953.[73] Envisaged as a broad coalition of non-Igbo groups from Divisions across the three provinces, the COR State Movement, led by Udo Udoma, Okoi Arikpo, O. O. Ita, and Harold Dappa Biriye, represented an attempt to galvanise the Ibibio State Union's existing claims to sub-regional autonomy.[74]

The COR State proposal was based on an allegation of orchestrated political marginalisation. Injustice and 'immorality', it argued, had arisen as a result of the Government's creation of the Eastern Region under the 1947 constitution. Of the 84 seats in the House of Assembly for which the 1957 elections were fought, 55 (65 per cent) represented predominantly Igbo constituencies. The COR State minorities maintained that this political domination translated into an Igbo hegemony in the legislative and judicial spheres, and in the control of investment projects, contracts and schol-arships. Debates between COR and the NCNC over the minority issue during the 1950s were bitter. By the 1959 Federal elections the pro-COR campaign claimed that the vote represented a choice between freedom or 'perpetual orphanage to the Igbos'.[75] And on the other side, the NCNC 'never disguised its abhorrence of the COR state idea, because of our deep-seated belief that this specious movement not only violates the principle of self-determination but ... is based on inspired hatred for the most populous linguistic group in Eastern Nigeria for no just cause'.[76]

The fear of cultural hegemony was pervasive and the submission to the 1958 Minorities Commission from Abak Division highlighted the process which COR State supporters sought to reverse:

> Our market rules are no longer respected, our customs about leasing of lands and even selling have been set at nothing to suit the strangers within our gates. Our Chiefs are not respected and our rules and regulations have no meaning among our strangers. Even our children are misled to flout our authority. Our women are now being openly insulted and beaten up in open markets without any justifiable causes. The Police force is out of our control, the court is out of our control, and the so-called Native Court has no power to match the growing disorders in our mixed communities.[77]

In various ways, therefore, it was argued that the 'Ibos have succeeded in adding economic and financial power to their political power'.[78] Local griev-ances from Abak focused on the role of Igbo palm oil traders, whom the Annang petitioners believed were receiving loans from the Eastern Region Government to invest in the trade to oust local competition.[79]

The COR State supporters also based their petition for liberation from the Igbo majority on the grounds of the cultural and historical unity of the minorities, on constitutional arguments, and on popular legitimacy. Histor-ically, it was argued that the southern minorities shared a common heritage and social institutions which distinguished them from the Igbo. Hence, the COR State petition invoked a remaking of their collective histories based on a diffusionist representation of disparate migrations and languages focused on a common origin:

> The Efik-Ibibio and Ekoi of Calabar Province, the Yakur-Ekoi tribal complex which inhabits the non-Ibo areas of Ogoja Province and Ijaw of the Niger Delta originally formed part of the negro populations that once inhabited the open terrain of the Western Sudan. ... [and] were pushed south-wards in the forest regions of Nigeria by waves of Hamitic and Semitic invaders and by population pressures from north-west and eastern Africa.[80]

Despite their linguistic differences, the petitioners also suggested that these various groups were united by characteristically non-Igbo social institutions, and as we shall see, this debate over chieftaincy would become a key marker in the party politics of the decade.

The COR State proposal also argued that trade links dating back to the sixteenth century bound the minority groups in commercial dependencies, and invoked the nineteenth-century treaties of protection to establish their objections. The submission of the COR State movement to the Minorities Commission in 1958, for instance, asserted that:

> The minority people's of Calabar-Ogoja-Rivers area … are bound to the British crown by Treaties of Friendship and Protection. To this extent they consider themselves different from the rest of the population of the Eastern Region, some of whom had been brought under the British crown by conquest and cession.[81]

The signatories, therefore, sought to claim their separation from the Igbo on the basis of boundaries created by the declaration of the 'semi-sovereign entity' embraced by the Oil Rivers Protectorate in 1885. On this basis they argued that: 'It is therefore to be regretted that Her Majesty's Government in direct contravention of these various Treaties should have 'handed us over' as it were to major tribal groups without consultation and without our consent'.[82]

The COR State movement also based their claims to popular legitimacy from returns at the polls. The minorities issue had become a national one when, in 1955, Awolowo's Action Group party adopted the cause of COR State along with the Middle Belt State in the North and the Mid-West State. In the House of Assembly elections of 1957, Action Group and UNIP[83] favoured grouping all the minority groups of the south-east in one territory, while the NCNC proposed the creation of three separate states (Ogoja, Rivers and Cross River). The Commission would later report, however, that Azikiwe admitted that the motive behind its submission was 'to break that atmosphere in the unanimity of the COR demand on the one hand and to save our faces with our people on the other hand'.[84]

The 1957 election results indicated that the political loyalties of the southern minorities, however, were far from solidly behind the proposals for COR State.[85] The heartland of COR support was confined to the key Ibibio District of Uyo, but elsewhere loyalties were fractured. The vote in the Annang centres of Abak and Ikot Ekpene were deeply split. Annang and Ibibio support for COR had been undermined by the NCNC thanks to several tactics, including the appointment of the leading Annang politician Ibanga Udo Akpabio to the post of Regional Minister of Education, and the proposed creation of Annang and Uyo Provinces. The reforms undermined the cohesion between Ibibio and Annang communities that the Ibibio State

Union had sought to preserve, as they created 'new centres of loyalty and solidarity among the Anang and Ibibio and detracted from the cohesion which the Union aspired to maintain'.[86]

The COR State leaders were confident that the creation of the new COR State would be recommended in the presentation of the Minorities Report in 1958, though the authorities undertook elaborate precautions to curb potential protests in those areas that were to be disappointed.[87] All four state creation proposals from the former Eastern Region were rejected by the Willink Commission. The Government rejected the COR State proposal on the grounds that it was 'inspired only by a negative dislike for the Ibo tribe'.[88] The Ibibio and Annang of Calabar Province, who had led the COR State movement, would have become a new majority, it argued, and it had become apparent that 'neither Ogoja nor Rivers showed themselves very anxious to be subject to Calabar'.[89] The divergent loyalties of the Annang and Ibibio constituencies, in fact, were cited by the Willink Commission, which noted that 'the Annangs and Ibibios recently have fallen out, and in evidence before us many Annang leaders expressed themselves as hostile to the idea of the State'.[90] The subsequent 1958 Constitutional Conference deferred the decision on state creation on the grounds of impending independence.

EXPECTATIONS REVISITED

The 1947 Local Government Despatch marked a significant shift in colonial thinking about the timing of the transfer of power and was introduced both to promote the post-war British concept of local government and to maximise the efficiency of grants made under the Colonial Development and Welfare Act of 1945.[91] British officials believed that their development initiatives would make colonies simultaneously more productive and more ideologically stable in the tumult of the post-war years: 'Welfare – social services in the short run and a higher standard of living in the long – was the antidote to disorder'.[92] The 1950s therefore witnessed a wave of 'last-minute' development and redoubled efforts to increase production in order to promote stability. 'Once a stable African Government is established it is essential that Government should be able to show results in the sphere of economic and social development', Cohen at the Colonial Office wrote, 'otherwise it is bound to disappoint the people and likely to lead ... to the transfer of power to irresponsible extremists'.[93] In Nigeria Governor Macpherson outlined his intentions in 1949:

> The people of Nigeria want agricultural development, they want industrial development, they want educational development, they want political development; and the prime concern of my administration is to meet this general demand for progress as quickly, as soundly and as comprehensively as possible.[94]

In the fields of adult literacy, co-operative credit and loan societies, and a variety of cottage industries, the District Officers in Calabar Province 'embarked on an all-out drive of self-help'. In 1950 the Ibibio State Union sought representation on the Eastern Region Development Board to stimulate investment in Ibibioland.[95] Yet, by that year it had become apparent that the regional development plan, supported by the Colonial Development and Welfare Fund, would fall woefully short of expectations. The Eastern Region as whole was allocated around £5 million, and the Chief Commissioner advised Provincial Residents and members of 'Tribal Unions' to convince people that 'if they wanted social services they would have to pay for them'.[96]

At the local level, petitions for funding continued to be met with familiar responses. In relation to the most popular demand the government ruled that 'Community Development Funds should not be used to assist in meeting the cost of construction of schools'.[97] Rather, officers argued that external assistance would undermine collective contributions and 'the semi-compulsory levy for the village school fund [which] is now almost part of Native Law and Custom'.[98] Such levies were commonplace in Annang communities where they were organised on the basis of palm fruit harvesting in which after a month's embargo on all village palm stands, a general collection was undertaken and the sale of the fruit went towards paying levies.

These initiatives also gave rise to a number of rating schemes, levies added to taxes for particular programmes. Such rates, like the education rate in Enyong and the cottage hospital rates in Abak, caused their own difficulties. Between February and May 1953 in Eket Division the supposed imposition of an education rate of 5 shillings on women was met with violent protest. At one point census-takers were mistaken for tax collectors and were attacked by a large number of women at the Eket District Council headquarters. A police detachment was stoned by a crowd which included, it was said, several men in female dress, and fifty leading women were convicted.[99]

The most significant investment in post-war development in south-eastern Nigeria was in the major potential growth sector, palm oil, and was also met by opposition along familiar gender lines. Post-war development discourse increasingly linked development to growth, though in Calabar Province it would confront familiar obstacles.[100] Despite the effects on supply caused by the Korean War, Nigeria's share of the world's palm oil export market had been declining. And despite various initiatives, including locally owned plantations and hand presses, the failure of these measures was obvious and the 'menace from the East' had not been confronted.[101] In 1946, the Nigerian Local Development Board allocated £60,000 to the Department of Commerce and Industries for the construction of Pioneer Oil Mills. The Pioneer was a 'self-contained power-driven mill' first developed by the United Africa Company in the 1930s. It could not increase the quality of oil produced, but it could increase the quantity by recovering 85 per cent of the oil (compared to 60 per cent by a hand-screw press), and the automated steaming of the fruit reduced labour time by half. The first was installed at Akpabuyo in 1949. In 1950 the Eastern Regional Production Development Board sponsored a scheme for the installation of Pioneer Oil Mills throughout the oil palm belt with Costains, the engineering contractors, undertaking a plan which was intended to include twenty-two mills. By the end of 1950 eighteen mills were in operation, ten of which were run by private individuals and eight by the regional Production Development Board.

Opposition to the Pioneer Oil Mills surfaced quickly and was most acute in Abak Division. In October 1950 objections were raised in Abak over the leases for new sites for the oil mills. A mob of women gathered in protest against a site being leased to the Board in Utu Etim Ekpo and invaded the Native Court. The disturbance spread and by 24 November 3,000 women appeared in Uyo to rescue previously arrested ring-leaders. Various views were proposed to explain the women's protests. The most obvious source of resistance was thought to be those whose income depended on the hiring of hand presses, of which there were over 600 in the province. The colonial authorities also pointed to a lack of information and consultation with women and that mill locations tended to provoke land disputes. The press and 'progressives' blamed disaffected middlemen and produce buyers who feared the loss of their trading monopoly.[102]

These diagnoses, however, failed to grasp the key explanation for why women protested. Although the mills offered to sell back the nuts for hand-cracking, they effectively took control of palm kernels out of women's hands. Women's rights over the processing of kernels was an established correlative of their considerable economic obligation in doing most of the work in preparing palm oil. In a polygamous society where women control separate economic interests from their husbands, palm kernels, along with the unrefined portion of the oil, the fibres of the husks and usually a cash share of her husband's trading profits offered women a source of income from the palm oil trade. Despite the fact that women's dependence on the kernel market was offset by cassava cultivation, the protests in the 1950s also came against a steady rise in the palm kernel price, making control of the trade even more economically significant. With the advent of the new mills men who cut the fruit could take it straight to the oil mill where they received a higher price than the women could pay.[103]

Evidence from the protests themselves illustrate that the women were predominantly motivated by the threat of the loss of this resource as a result of the entrance of men into the palm kernel trade. In the Ekparakwa area of Abak Division, gangs of women attacked men in 1951, for instance, as they returned from the market with palm fruit they had bought. The men were roughly handled and their palm fruits were seized. The disturbance was stopped when Chief Iwok Etuk placed *àyèi* on the surrounding roads.[104] The following year women of the Nung Ikot Women's Society announced that they were writing to Dr Hon. Udoma (by then their representative in the House of Assembly) asking him to have a law passed that would stop men from buying palm fruit.[105]

The politics of 'improvement' and the more confident tone of the nationalist elites cast a new light on familiar social issues in Calabar Province after the war. The public discourse of these years was marked by both a reflection on the colonial legacy and a keen anticipation that modernist imaginings would be realised. Nowhere was this dynamic more evident than in the ongoing debate over the future of marriage practices and judicial procedures. In a newspaper column entitled 'These Old Customs' published in the *Nigerian Eastern Mail* in 1947, the attention of the reading public was directed to apparently anachronistic ritual practices. Among these the columnist focused on issues concerning marriage, oath-swearing and court corruption. He argued that the 'fattening ceremony' should cease, that 'woman-husbands' brought women into servile labour, 'child betrothal' made the prospective wife a domestic servant, that the dishonesty of juju priests made *mbìàm* a sham, and that the swearing of *mbìàm* in court led to miscarriages of justices.[106]

The fact that these fields of marriage and justice remained intimately connected to the politics of indirect rule is illustrated by a case in Abak in 1952. In his submission to the Brooks Commission on Native courts E. E. Umanah, the Abak reporter for the *Nigerian Eastern Mail*, stated that if the government genuinely wanted the 'educated elements' to learn the art of self-government, then the old chiefs should step down. A prominent former Warrant Chief in Abak, Chief Udo Ekong, was offended by this, and consequently proposed to prosecute Umanah for adultery with his wife.[107] Umanah responded by suggesting that this prosecution rather proved his point and claimed that Udo Ekong was typical of precisely 'this type of court chief, who, having gained the position, uses it to revenge their enemies, or ancient wrongs done them'.[108]

'Ever since there had been a Nigerian Press', a 1950 commentator announced, 'it had been discussing the problem of brideprice'.[109] By 1949 brideprice had reached £30–£40 or more with a further £8–£10 for marriage drinks. In Abak Division brideprice was assessed for girls with elementary education at £45–£50.[110] If the prospective bride had reached Standard VI, her parents were liable to demand the refund of the school fees. This would make the cost of marriage £50–£60, or the equivalent of two years' income for an average farmer, fisherman or labourer. At such high rates it was unsurprising that fathers turned a deaf ear to reports of mistreatment because they were unable to refund the dowry should their daughter want to divorce.[111]

The debate on brideprice was framed not only in terms of the costs for young men, but also in terms of the moral rhetoric of the progressives, who argued that 'the transaction now becomes akin to selling into slavery'.[112] Progressive voices also decried the 'evil social consequences' and the 'slough of sexual immorality' to which the situation had given rise: perpetual debt, promiscuity and urban prostitution. 'Nothing prevents an adequate reform of the system of native marriage', the *Mail*'s editor argued, 'except the greed of the older generation who regard their daughters as a form of property and are not ashamed to barter them to the highest bidder'.[113] Calls for reform and for easier brideprice terms grew and were matched in places by efforts led by improvement unions to limit brideprice costs. Overall the colonial discourse on the collapse of marriage was appropriated by the 'progressives', who complained that wives were leaving for the cities to lead independent lives of prostitution.[114] It was as a result of this that improvement unions like the Banyang Clan Unions passed rules against prostitutes during the 1950s and even hired vehicles to 'repatriate' women who were perceived to have abandoned their rights and monetary obligations to work as prostitutes in plantations and cities.[115]

The Eastern Region House of Assembly passed a motion in February 1954 to establish a government committee to probe the brideprice question. Speakers in the debate complained that ad hoc formulae devised by families and clans across the region reduced women to commodities. Others, including Mrs Margaret Ekpo, explained that women were bought and sold like slaves and called for brideprice to be abolished.[116] The subsequent inquiry received oral evidence and 413 letters, mainly from young men, and identified precisely those problems with brideprice which had arisen during the 1930s and which were the root of those personal rivalries which had motivated the *ékpê-ówó* murders in the mid-1940s. In general it found that Nigerian soldiers were largely responsible for the increase in brideprice during the war years. Servicemen had asked their parents to arrange marriages for them in order to claim marriage allowances. The net effect of their requests and of more cash in the economy, the commission noted, was that extended betrothal with instalments of brideprice in cash and in kind spread over many years had given way to an expensive one-off cash transaction.[117] The legislation which emerged from the committee's investigation included limiting brideprice, registering marriages, pronouncing divorces in court and abolishing child betrothals.[118]

The regional debate over the future of brideprice in 1954 was also linked to long-running criticisms of the credit associations, *osusu* and *ùtìbè*, which were popularly used by young men to save brideprice money. Letters to the newspapers during this period called for the 'isusu evil' to be destroyed. In December 1954, amid claims that 'members requesting isusu in times of need must be prepared to pay £5 in way of expenses and greetings of palm wine',[119] the Eastern Region Government approved bye-laws for District Councils like Uyo to protect *ùtíbè* members from unscrupulous leaders. The new laws made it illegal for a collector or headman to demand entrance fees of more than a shilling or to refuse a member their share when it was their turn.[120]

★   ★   ★

In 1953 the former Governor, Sir Walter Buchanan-Smith, gave evidence to the Commission of Inquiry into the Native Courts of the Eastern Provinces. He commented that since the introduction of the Native Court system the Colonial Government had unwittingly destroyed the basis of native law and custom. He argued that the indigenous legal and administrative system continued to function, even after the Second World War, in a covert fashion, and that the single accomplishment of the colonial reforms had been to drive it underground. Indeed, Buchanan-Smith contended that in cases of theft the colonial system had been responsible for many murders, and:

> If we were to treat certain other crimes in the same way we shall in my opinion most certainly encourage trial by ordeal, invocation of the fetish and again murders. In other words we shall once again drive the native legal system underground.[121]

The Native Courts were increasingly ridiculed. The corruption with which they were associated gave rise to groups specifically organised around this issue, such as the League of Bribe Scorners.[122] The following provides a satirical local perspective on the state of the courts after the war:

> COMPOSITION: the present generation – are nothing more than a pack of incivil [*sic*], illiterate, nasty and obstructive set of self-made chiefs, popularly known as 'snuff chiefs' or 'pipe chiefs'. Along with them is a semi-educated clerk commonly called 'writer' who attributes to himself a toga of arrogance and superiority even though he knows that he knows not, in a class of intelligentsia with experience of English Court procedure. PROCEDURE: the procedure in a native court is simply ridiculous and full of laughter. President first asks the defendant if he has anything to say: if he is a grammarian he will be laughed at. Big grammar, as the chiefs would put it, is an offence and a contempt in a native court ... JUDGMENT is a travesty of justice – the chiefs are more concerned by their pinch of snuff or pipe, and miss most of the proceedings outside [going to the toilet].[123]

The Brooke Commission on Native Courts was established in 1955 to investigate the law administered in the courts, along with the courts' own constitutions and practices. It identified 'an urgent desire for more certainty in the law to be administered'.[124] The Commission proposed that handbooks on customary law be prepared by a Native Courts Advisor. The Commission further recommended that the renamed 'customary courts' should have more specific lines of review and appeal which excluded British officers, and that reforms instigated to reduce the size of court benches should be consolidated.[125]

The contested terrain of law and order exposed familiar contours right into the 1950s. After the Second World War, Annang secret societies came under increasing official purview. While the leopard murder investigations were ongoing, attempts to suppress *ékpó* had been framed in a narrative of the criminalisation of secret societies: 'There is a grave danger that it [*ékpó*] will develop into an organised robbery society, on all fours with the murder society of Abak and Opobo'.[126] The Uyo Divisional Advisory Committee had recommended that the *ékpó* society be declared illegal in 1947, though the first bye-laws restraining *ékpó*'s activities were enacted only later, in 1952. In Ikot Ekpene the plays were not banned, but their activities were restricted. Otoro Rural District Council instituted regulations, for example, which applied to *ékpó*, *èkón* and *ékpê*, and which demanded that the societies were registered with District Councils (including the names of the members), registration fees paid, permits arranged before any procession, and that no society carried a weapon.[127] The District Officer in Uyo reported of *ékpó* that:

> Its continuance is certainly not in any way essential to the people, except to those individuals who use it as a protection racket for extorting money. In these days its proper place is in museums and history books.[128]

Criminals after the Second World War were consistently framed within the idiom of the secret society.[129] Armed robbery was first reported as the 'menace of a secret society of criminals' known as *amauke* ('your money or your life') in Uyo in 1959.[130]

In the light of new crime threats, calls for official recognition of night guards (*úfɔk úsúŋ*) re-emerged in 1951 when the Ikot Ekpene County Council argued that the continued activities of the *úfɔk úsúŋ* patrols demonstrated a genuine need for more protection than was being provided by the Nigerian police.[131] Despite the long-running government opposition to the night watchmen, the state sanctioning of vigilante patrols saw their fortunes reversed in 1952:

> An interesting development in the Ikot Ekpene Division has been the establishment of a system of Rural Police Patrols. Small, uniformed bicycle patrols now visit outlying villages at regular intervals in order to collect information and to maintain contact with the people. Side by side with these patrols there exists the traditional system of village guards which again became active during the crime wave which was

reported in 1951. With a view to regulating these institutions, and to co-ordinate their activities with those of the Nigerian Police, an embryo 'Watch Committee' has been set up consisting of representatives of the County Council and the Local Police Authority. It is an informal body.[132]

The symbolic repertoire of the Annang night guard was also translated into political spheres, especially in the association between lanterns and good character.[133] While the NCNC were represented by the cockerel and the Action Group by the palm tree,[134] independent Annang political candidates, including Frank Akpan Umoren, used the hurricane lantern in their campaigns during the 1950s as a sign of their good character.

Legal authority continued to be side-stepped in other ways too. In 1955 it was reported that village councils in Abak Division were progressively usurping powers that properly belonged to the Native Courts.[135] In Ikot Ekpene a number of convictions were secured when illegal courts were uncovered which had not only usurped judicial rights, but had also assumed its entire paraphernalia, including printed process forms and uniformed messengers.[136] Events to the north-east, in Abakaliki Division during the 1950s, indicated just how far these usurpations and illegal courts could extend. In the early 1950s Ezzikwo County in Abakaliki Province experienced an apparent series of murders. Secret investigations which began in December 1957 led to the arrest of Chief Nwiboko Obodo and members of the 'Ndi Obozi Obodo society'. It appeared that his group had instituted its own tribunal and had killed suspected thieves and adulterers. The society itself was therefore thought to be 'a perversion of an Ibo customary guard system' and it transpired that a considerable number of the victims were thieves or had been accused of crime.[137] During the Odozi Obodo affair 114 deaths were investigated in three clans (Isioko, Igboji and Ikwo) and 148 people were charged with murder, including the most prominent chief in each clan.[138] By March 1959 fifty-five members of the society, including its leader Chief Nwiboko Obodo, had been condemned to death.

There were many similarities between events in Abakaliki and those in Abak and Opobo a decade earlier. As with *ekpê ówó*, the authorities agonised over whether Ndi Odozi Obodo could be considered a 'secret society', and speculated on various pre-colonial precedents. Reflecting on the underlying causes of the murders, the Odozi Obodo killers, like the leopard men before them, were thought to have exploited chronic under-policing.[139] The Abakaliki murders were therefore associated with demands for more intensive policing (and rural police posts), and with calls, like that of the Ibibio Union's in 1947, for infrastructural development (particularly primary schools, roads and bridges) to prevent further breakdowns of law and order.[140]

The Abakaliki murders exposed the widespread and violent nature of illegal courts and vigilante justice in Eastern Nigeria during the 1950s. The broader picture, however, was a power struggle over the new wealth that was accumulating in the hands of the 'native authorities', the chiefs, as the result of post-war financial reforms which devolved increased taxation and spending powers to local councils. Objections to overcharging and the accumulation of funds in the hands of certain well-placed men such as Chief Obodo were met with punishment beatings and murder.[141] The 'unauthorised oppressions by chiefs and councillors', as the police called it, meant that Odozi Obodo represented a violent culmination of a tension in the Eastern Provinces between chiefs and society.

★   ★   ★

Chieftaincy became a major political fault-line between the NCNC and the UNIP/AG alliance, and the politics of 1956-58 represented a crucial watershed and realignment of attitudes towards the chieftaincy. In the late 1940s and early 1950s the popularity of the chieftaincy had ebbed significantly. Opposition to individual chiefs was voiced in petitions against their monopoly of the numerous offices which were now recognised as politically significant. A village head might be àkúkú (èté ídúŋ), 'president' of the village council, a court sitting member and a Native Administration councillor. During the war the material benefits of office-holding had been galvanised in the responsibilities they held for controlling prices and distributing rationed goods like salt.[142] Villagers in Abak also accused chiefs of embezzling village development funds collected through collective palm fruit harvesting.[143] Opposition to the chiefs' expanding material base was also expressed less visibly in witchcraft accusations. After catching a man preparing a cocktail of 'bad medicines' and chanting his name, Chief Thomas Chukwu of Ibio Nung Achat claimed that he 'did not know that when one build as an upstairs [two-storey house] the other party who cannot build this [is] jealous [of] the builder'.[144] The man, Akpan Okori, was apparently preparing three different charms to effect the chief's murder – ówóhó ékpó ('the one which bites the chest and kills'), útóró ékpó (which causes fatal diarrhoea) and útúák (which is put in a charm ring and causes madness or sickness when it is touched against its victim).

It has been suggested that the NCNC's programme towards the chiefs was influenced less by demands from the more chieftaincy conscious minorities than by the need to counter Action Group propaganda that the 'republican Igbo' were anti-chieftaincy.[145] In February 1957 Azikiwe addressed over 5,000 people at an NCNC rally in Ikom. He had brought with him ex-Olobi of Ikobi from the Western Region to demonstrate the attitude of his party towards the chiefs. 'The NCNC, he said, believed in the institution of chieftaincy and his government had therefore appointed a Professor of Social Anthropology to advise it scientifically about chieftaincy'.[146] His Government, he stated, had not deposed any chiefs, unlike the Action Group which had deposed six, including the ex-Olobi.[147] Zik introduced him as an example of what the Eastern Region would have in store if the Action Group won the election.

Following a House of Assembly debate, the Eastern Region Government approached the Colonial Office for assistance in appointing a commissioner to ensure that the proposed inquiry was divorced from politics and commissioned G. I. Jones to undertake a review of the status and position of chiefs.[148] He concluded that the balance of power between elites and elders, which had favoured the elites immediately after the war, needed to be tipped back in favour of the chiefs:

> In 1956 the pendulum has swung the other way and in the direction of fusion. Obong Isong are now very much in evidence, they feel and other people feel with them that they have a right to ex officio representation on local and other government councils.[149]

Indeed, Jones reported widespread criticism of the post-war reforms which had sought to engage the educated elite into local administration. They had gone too far, he claimed, especially in the Ibibio-speaking divisions:

> People appear to feel that the recent local Government reforms represent too great a swing in the direction of elected representation which they associate with the young, illiterate and 'progressive elements' and away from the 'traditional elements' as equated with chiefs, elders, titled men and other persons holding their offices for life. Certainly conditions in some of the Ibibio divisions where the traditional element has been almost completely excluded from Local Government Councils seems to bear this out.[150]

Jones also found that this realignment of the balance of power between elites and elders was strongly supported by the 'professional and progressive elements', who were determined to revive clan chieftaincy and secure its political place within the regional House of Chiefs.[151] The Ibibio Union had petitioned for a Conference of Chiefs in 1941.[152] In 1956, therefore, the Ibibio State Union submitted its position to the Commission in which it repudiated the suggestion that:

> The inherent traditional authority did not go far beyond the confines of family and that such authorities were incapable of development. This might well have been so in other parts of the Region, but in the Ibibio Country there have been inherent traditional authorities with influence over large clans and are from the remotest periods.[153]

The Ibibio Union argued that àkúkù or óbɔ́ŋ ìkpá ísɔ̀ŋ were the political, judicial, and ritual heads of the 'clans' identified in the government intelligence reports. The Union demanded that all such chiefs be represented on local government councils, and that:

In order to make for orderly progress and stable political community, the Nkuku natural rulers should take active part in the business of government and therefore respectfully recommends a House of Chiefs in the Eastern Region.[154]

With the publication of the Jones Report,[155] and with debates on the classification of chiefs continuing at an all-party conference on chiefs in Enugu, chieftaincy had become a high political priority.[156] Chieftaincy also emerged as a key distinction drawn between the Igbo majority and the southern minorities in the 1958 submissions to the Willink Commission as outlined by the COR State Movement:

> The resentful disrespect for elders and traditional authority and the complete disregard for the customs and traditions of other tribal groups displayed by some tribal leaders have deprived the Eastern Region of moderating and stabilising influence and the rich experience of the chiefs of the Region; and has made cooperation between the young and the old in the administration of the Region almost impossible. For this reason we make bold to insist that the creation of a House of Chiefs in the proposed Calabar, Ogoja and Rivers State is indispensable.[157]

The degree to which party politics among the minorities led to the political resuscitation of the Eastern chiefs is unclear. Nevertheless, the Regional House of Chiefs, which was established in 1959, was evidently a political device. Most of the members of the inaugural House, from Igbo and non-Igbo communities alike, were NCNC supporters.[158] In April 1959 the 56-year-old Chief Ibanga Idiok of Nung Ita Obio Nkan in Abak Division was installed as the clan head of Southern Annang in succession to his father (Chief Ibanga). During his installation he declared his confidence in the Eastern Region Government and urged his people to help check what he called 'the menace of the Action Group'.[159]

By the 1950s *ékpê ówó* was framed in a popular political discourse of radical social change and marked discontinuity between traditional and modern beliefs, cultures and leaders. *Ékpê ówó* was represented as a conservative reaction to the collapse of Annang moral and political frameworks and as a backlash by traditionalists against Christianity and colonial law.[160] The victims, it was suggested, were those who had manipulated colonial remakings of customary law which contradicted established notions of Annang justice. Being too *mbàkárà* (ruler/white man), it was suggested, was to court death at the hands of the 'leopard men', and as such the killers' motives found sympathy with Annang elders elsewhere.[161] These re-evaluations did not emerge at the time of the killings and cannot be neatly reconstructed, but the argument that in retrospect the human-leopards should be considered within a framework of 'heroic criminals' is based in part on the fact that they killed without opposition from their own communities.[162] Witnesses failed to come forward, informants kept silent and local leaders failed to rally resistance. This interpretation of the murders as a conservative, chieftaincy-led response to colonialism and its innovations drew upon the dominant political discourse of the post-war years – the tensions between elites and elders.

The apparent paradox of these events was that between 1947 and 1959 the argument for self-government had been won by the political elites, but by independence the status of the chiefs had been rehabilitated. The interesting thing about history, however, is that the favourites at the start do not always go on to win.[163] The events of the 'leopard-murder' investigations demonstrated the chiefs' symbolic and ritual significance as interlocutors between elites, state and the population at large, and their party-political support was equally essential in subsequent years. The conflict between 'A-Lights' and elders had been a political contest throughout this period and did not reflect the absolute social contradiction which it was represented to be in colonial discourse.

9

ECHOS OF EKPE OWO

In many senses the Annang past is a 'scarce resource'.[1] Annang history is hedged in by the practice of past and present religious injunctions, by concepts of knowledge and by the interplay of 'hierarchies of credibility'. The past's scarcity is derived very simply from the fact that very few people living in the villages of the 'leopard area' today talk freely and directly about *ékpê ówó*. There is good reason for many older people to be uncomfortable with the past of the leopard murders. They swore oaths that they would have nothing to do with leopard men, oaths ingested and consumed into their bodies for a lifetime in unknown substances of fearful power.

My main contemporary interlocutors, those willing to talk, have been those who were in some way associated with the colonial authorities at the time of the murders as court clerks, interpreters or house-boys for the police. Indeed, official acknowledgement from the regional administration of assistance during the leopard-murder investigations, in the form of a letter of recognition, has become a seal of honesty, trustworthiness and good character in present day claims to chieftaincy titles and in obituaries. Being part of or close to the investigations provides an authority with a degree of immunity from suspicion and a space for social commentary. It also contributes to a circularity in the historical narrative. Since the historical record of the leopard-murders was never published, those Annang closest to the investigating authorities and who acted as intermediaries and auxiliaries for the colonial power have become instrumental in recycling the colonial narrative.

Memories of the leopard men are also 'scarce' because there is an imperative to retain authority and consistency between narratives. These stories are not infinitely susceptible to contemporary invention. There are limits to this process determined by the needs for versions and charters of the past to demonstrate access to authoritative sources along with the need to illustrate the interdependence and continuity of one version with others.[2] The tension between invention and interdependence in memories of the murders has to be explored in what elderly men and women still remember and how these memories relate to the official reports which sit on the shelves of archives and libraries. It not only concerns the degree of 'fit' between what happened and received narratives about the past, but also points us to examine the management of meaning. The relationship between memory and history in this context is a productive one and is fraught with echoes, tensions and contradictions. It is important therefore to emphasise the mutuality of memory and history rather than their opposition.[3]

It is in this light that we should address the most common and widely accepted formula of the past that has circulated since the investigations. This story identifies just one village, Ikot Afanga, the scene of the quadruple murder in 1945, as the site, sometimes the sole site, of the murders. The accusation is captured in the song: 'Ikot Afanga, *idúŋ ékpê ówó*' (Ikot Afanga, the village of the leopard men). This core narrative also identifies a small group of men led by the mysterious figure of Akpan Ekpedeme, and his sister's son, the convicted killer Akpan Anyoho, as the principal leopard men, even though they were both dead during the height of the enquiries. Of the various murder motives to have been voiced at the time of the enquiries, it is the refund of brideprice and in particular the 'one manilla divorce' that are recalled today. Narratives told by Africans to Africans during the Ibibio Union tour have fixed the representation of the leopard men, and in turn contemporary narrators are able to distance themselves from the murders spatially, temporally and in terms of kinship. Stories told today of other known protagonists in other places are relocated and reconnected with this particular village and these men.

Epistemologically the past is also a scarce and expensive resource in Annang concepts of knowledge. To know, as in 'to see something', is *dìɔŋ*; historical knowledge (or wisdom) in Annang, however, is *fìɔk*. In turn these concepts of knowing correspond to two different forms of access to knowledge: *adijiara* (self-apparent) and *ndungo* (to go and pay for findings). For Annang elders and their juniors there is an imperative to protect and conceal that which may prove politically useful or, alternatively, embarrassing. In practical terms this especially applies to lineage genealogies, settlement histories, land cases, childless marriages and succession issues. As a result, and within a conception that access to knowledge will benefit the recipient without compensating the holder, Annang say: *afo ajem ifiok, ana mkpo ukpa ke ubok* (however you want knowledge you have to spend something). In some instances the prohibitive costs of access to knowledge lead ambitious young men to covert means by which to access sensitive historical data. One former schoolteacher, for example, concealed tape-recording equipment while investigating his family's heritage and claims to title. Many years later he used this information to stake an unlikely but successful claim to the village headship.

Informants' testimony on the murders, therefore, is shaped by the scarcity of knowledge it has produced. Other circulating memories of *ékpê ówó* are constructed differently according to gender, generation and authority, and have shifted over time. Those who were not involved in the prosecutions but are old enough to remember the leopard murder investigations recall little or no detail of the stories about the murders themselves. Rather, they remember the things that affected their everyday lives most directly: the compulsory collection of water, fuelwood and the supply of food for the police, along with the clearing and keeping open of paths. Through these labours the police occupation was carved on the Annang landscape. In the village of Nung Ikot, for instance, the path leading to Ikot Okoro is still known as the 'man-leopard road'. Of the investigations people remember the public face and the humiliations of mass village meetings. Some also recall the methods used by the police, especially their techniques of torture. These included stories of suspects holding heavy logs above their heads for as long as their strength held out, or of having their thumbs tied back to the wrist to make them talk. These recollections serve to illustrate that the memories of the murder investigations continue to be steeped in violence and fear. The enquiries were an opportunity for colonial excess, opportunities that were sanctioned under an official policy that the police should make a 'nuisance' of themselves.

For younger generations the leopard men are strikingly absent from contemporary discourse. The stories of the killings have not passed down through the generations, and this silence is related to the effects of shame and the collapse of trust. While shame in itself has a powerful silencing effect, its material consequences suggest a presentday imperative for these evasions. The shame of being associated with disorder carries with it the fear of being labelled 'unprogressive' and hence undeserving of the dividends of the politics of improvement. The nature of the murders themselves may also explain the silence of past generations. *Ékpê ówó* was an internal, domestic conflict in which the killings were the result of a collapse of trust. Trust was an essential factor in an array of social transactions that apparently led to the murders. As these transactions began to fail during the 1940s so did trust in the means of redress in the new courts of the colonial administration. With the outbreak of the killings trust collapsed between fellow villagers and neighbours, commonplace agreements were fraught with danger and idle accusations had serious implications. In this context of internecine conflict trust not only evaporated at the time, but has not been reconstituted subsequently in order to provide the necessary confidence for people to recount events.[4]

Pentecostal Christianity in the southern Annang villages has also had a profound effect on remembering the past. The appeal to 'time' as an epistemological category enables Pentecostals to draw a line between 'now' and 'then', a modern God-loving 'us' and a traditional Devilish 'them'.[5] The stress on rupture with the past as a result of the 'pentecostalisation' of most denominations ministering in south-eastern Nigeria in recent times has meant discussion of the past itself becomes difficult, and of murder and 'medicines' especially problematic. Women, especially younger women active in the congregations of churches infused with Pentecostalism, are called on to renounce any discursive engagement with the past. In their confessional experience of becoming 'born again', they strive to make a 'complete break' with a past populated by juju and demons. As a result, many women not only deny knowledge of the leopard murders but sometimes actively prevent their brothers, uncles or fathers from passing on their own recollections.

Young men, in contrast, are more likely to reconstruct than to reject stories of the leopard men. Their conception of *ékpê ówó* conforms closely with present-oriented notions which conceive memory as a means of reconfiguration rather than a tool of reclamation. The leopard murders are perceived by young men today as a conflict, a 'communal clash', of the type they frequently hear about in the Niger Delta. This conception resonates with contemporary discourses on disorder, marginalisation, minority politics, youth protest and the rhetoric and means of violence by which disputes are pursued in contemporary Nigeria.[6]

Indeed, the only contemporary reference to leopard men that I encountered during this research arose in the context of a dispute over the property, rights and resources of the Exxon Mobil oil company.[7] Members of a militant youth group abstained from sex before invoking '*ekpe ikpa ukot*' ('the leopard who walks in shoes'). Though quite different from the narratives of Annang man-leopard societies of the 1940s, the significance of the story is how localised genealogies, rhetorics and aesthetics of violence are articulated to a regional political discourse which focuses on justice and accountability. The rhetorical invocation of the human leopards in the oil dispute would appear to confirm recent observations that lineage-based societies are peculiarly adaptive to new bureaucratic, economic and criminal environments.[8] Comparative evidence draws links between shape-shifting secret societies and contemporary conflict in Sierra Leone and Liberia in which secret societies are rich repositories of idioms of youth initiation, modes of collective covert action and of the aesthetics of violence. This historical narrative of human leopards, however, tends to be more implied than documented and more dependent on embodied rather than discursive memories.[9] In pressing political and economic claims during the oil dispute today, the leopard men briefly re-emerged with the intention of conveying the threat of violence and disorder. In south-eastern Nigeria, therefore, there is both a dynamic, contingent history of secret societies to trace and an active, discursive use of the past in the present.

NOTES

ABBREVIATIONS

NAE National Archive of Nigeria (Enugu)
PRONI Public Records Office of Northern Ireland (Belfast)
RH   Rhodes House Library (Oxford)
TNA The National Archives (Kew)
WUL   Witwatersrand University Library

CHAPTER 1

1. *Daily Mail*, 30 June 1947.
2. SASP, Ediene Atai to Commissioner, CID, Lagos, 10 May 1947, NAE: ABAKDIST 1/2/88.
3. DO Abak to Resident, Calabar, 31 March 1945, NAE: CALPROF 17/1/1594.
4. Dan Udoffia had been buried naked on a bamboo stretcher. To implicate Okon Bassey further, the prosecution argued that this itself was an offence against custom (*Nigerian Eastern Mail*, 22 December 1945).
5. DO Abak to Supt. Police, Calabar, 22 April 1946, NAE: ABAKDIST 1/3/2.
6. Resident, Calabar to Secretary, Enugu, 14 January 1946, NAE: CALPROF 7/1/1421.
7. Hutton, 1920; Maling, 1939; Kennerley, 1951; Lindskog, 1954; Joset, 1955; Foran, 1956; Rich, 2001.
8. Mudimbe, 1988; Dirks, 1992 p. 20.
9. Sierra Leone Govt. Archives, Native Affairs Minute Papers 118, 1882 in Kalous, 1974 p. 50.
10. Abraham, 1975. The animals with which these *boni hinda* murders were associated (leopards, crocodiles and chimpanzees) are peculiar, Richards has argued, in that they are the only animals of the forest that attack humans in a premeditated fashion for food or sport, unlike other forest creatures, like snakes, which attack only when provoked (Richards, 1993).
11. Jackson, 1990 p. 73.
12. Jones, 1983; Ferme, 2001 p. 193.
13. Richards, 1996 p. 147.
14. Jackson, 1990 p. 72.
15. *Bofima* was a term of 'Mandingo' origin meaning 'black bag' or 'medicine bag' (Beatty, 1915 pp. 22–3). On the properties of 'medicine' (*hale*) on the Guinea Coast more generally see Jedrej, 1976.
16. MacCormack, 1983 p. 55.
17. Whitehead, 2000 p. 750.
18. Richards argues that 'It is an open question whether or not boni hinda murders actually take place, or are largely or mainly conjured up in the minds of those who fear the possibility' (Richards, 1996 p. 143). While the West African

'cannibal' may be considered the ontological equivalent to the witch, Richards notes that this does not preclude the possibility that a politically useful belief may be bolstered by well-timed assassinations or mutilations (Richards, 2001 p. 168). More generally see Arens, 1979; Brown and Tuzin, 1983; Barker, Hulme and Iversen, 1998; Goldman, 1999; Beaver, 2002.

19. 'it is a grave scholarly error', MacCormack says, 'for literal-minded historians to use this material without any anthropological interpretation' (MacCormack, 1983 p. 52). MacCormack cites the work of Milan Kalous as an example of this. Kalous compiled a collection of over-edited and poorly referenced sources from the Sierra Leone government archives (Kalous, 1974). By extension one might extend this note of caution to those who depend uncritically on Kalous' book as an historical source, especially Shaw, 2002 chapter 8. For further criticism of Kalous' collection see Abraham, 1975 pp. 120–30.

20. The supposed connection between the human-leopards and the Poro society was dismissed at the time of the investigations in 1912 (Beatty, 1915). Subsequent historical links between acts of leopard-style ritual murder and the Poro society (Ellis, 1995; 1999; 2001) have been criticised for 'imputing to the shadowy 'cannibal' associations the same ontological organisation and legal status as to Poro and Sande, the real secret societies' (Richards, 2001 p. 168).

21. Burrows, 1914 p. 143.

22. Alternative views, though no less speculative, linked the human leopards directly to the Atlantic slave trade itself. Torday claimed that leopard societies were formed to defend the population against chiefs who attempted to sell their own subjects to the slavers. Their members were 'cloaked in the skins of leopards and provided with iron imitation claws', he claimed, in order to execute these chiefly culprits (Torday, 1931 p. 121).

23. Shaw, 2002 Chapter 8.

24. Ibid. p. 246. This approach to the material and the conclusions to which it leads are limited in two respects. First, it inevitably elides the intervening narrative between the eras of slave and legitimate trade by relying on an ill-defined conceptual device, the 'historical imagination'. Second, it depends on the most unreliable transcription of the colonial records available (compiled by Milan Kalous), and then from a highly selective set of references to slavery. There are, it should be noted, as many references in Kalous which do not link leopardism to slavery, and those that there are might equally, and more likely, be references to contemporary forms of wealth which included domestic slavery.

25. Stanley would later claim that the 'mark' distinguishing members of the leopard society was hopelessly discredited by the Special Commission Court, and that common sense alone would undermine the idea of secret society members identifying themselves in this way (Stanley, 1919 p. 9).

26. Beatty, 1915 p. 42.

27. Ibid. p. 83.

28. Stanley, 1919 p. 4.

29. Walker, 1877; De Cardi, 1899; Fitzgerald Marriott, 1899; Watt, 1903.

30. The Royal Museum at Terverun acquired an *anioto* costume and iron paw as used by the Mobali from M. Delhaize, who had collected them from the area around Stanley Falls (Maes, 1911). Various images are also reproduced in Lindskog, 1954.

31. Lindskog, 1954.

32. Roberts, 1996 p. 69.

33. The eastern Congolese districts in which the lion and leopard men were reported were iron smelting areas. The association with metalwork also featured

in other reports. In south-eastern Angola in 1943, for instance the lion-men practice was thought to have originated among blacksmiths (Joset, 1955).

34. Roberts, 1996 p. 68.

35. Cited in Lindskog, 1954 p. 38. This analysis can be compared with the ambiguities arising from a series of man-leopard cases in Libreville, the capital of the French colony of Gabon in the late nineteenth century described in Rich, 2001. These murders began in 1877 and ended two years later without a formal investigation. What was clear, however, was that the murders exposed the contradictions of colonial rule on the city's shifting social landscape. Free townspeople suspected that former slaves, who introduced new charms and beliefs to the city, were responsible for the killings and accused Catholic missionaries of harbouring them. The missionaries, meanwhile, sought to convince officials that clan chiefs and elders were responsible for the murders and that they employed the leopard men to intimidate their dependents (slaves and women) in order to retain their political autonomy.

36. On the debate regarding social bandits, resistance, criminals and deviants in Africa, see Austen, 1986a; 1986b.

37. Cyrier, 1999.

38. Joset, 1955 pp. 24–5.

39. Schneider claimed that before the 1920s the word *mbojo* meant something like 'bogeyman' and was used by Turu mothers to discipline their children (Schneider, 1982 p. 96).

40. Many of the 103 reported cases were deaths caused by real lions (Wyatt, 1950 p. 7).

41. Ibid. p. 5.

42. Schneider, 1962 p. 127.

43. A. W. Wyatt, 'The Lion Men of Singida', 13 April 1949, NAE: OPODIST 1/10/3.

44. Wyatt, 1950 p. 8. Unlike other big cat killings no direct link was made in Tanganyika between the human lions and a secret society. A striking parallel existed, however, with the women's *inmala* performance during which neophytes were sent into the bush to retrieve a lion and initiates prepared a drum to imititate a lion's roar.

45. Schneider, 1982 p. 99.

46. D. C. Neillands, 'Notes on the Leopard Society', 13 May 1946, NAE: CALPROF 17/1/1595.

47. One of the first fictional references to leopard men is in H. G. Wells' 1896 *The Island of Dr Moreau*.

48. Grant, 1900.

49. Gaunt, 1923. On the theme of the 'educated African' in the literature of this genre and period, see Killam, 1966.

50. Crosbie, 1938. See also White, 1916.

51. 'Toi, y en a connaître les Aniotas? ... Non? ... Ça y en a société secrète pour lutter contre Blancs. ... I am telling you there is a secret society, called "Aniota." They organised to stop civilisation by white men!' (Hergé, 1982). For an excellent discussion of the visual imagery employed in *Tintin au Congo* see Hunt, 2002.

52. Shaw, 1953.

53. Ginzburg, 1991 p. 90, emphasis in the original.

54. Trotti, 2001.

55. Peel, 1995 pp. 582–3.

56. De Certeau, 1988 p. 89.

57. Ibid. p. 97.

58. Comaroff and Comaroff, 1992 p. 38.
59. Sahlins, 1985 p. ix.
60. Stoler and Cooper, 1989 pp. 17–18.
61. Stoler, 2002 p. 100, emphasis in the original.
62. Guyer, 2004.
63. Bayart, 1993 p. 133.
64. Cameron, 1933; 1937; 1939; Graham, 1976; Noah, 1987.
65. Tamuno and Horton, 1969 p. 50.
66. Peel, 1990; 2000; 2002.
67. Bayart, 1993 p. 114.
68. See in particular Cooper and Stoler, 1989; Dirks, 1992.
69. Dirks, 1992 p. 3.
70. Asad, 1991 p. 322.
71. Pels, 1996.
72. Cooper and Stoler, 1989 p. 18.
73. Bayart, 1993 p. 113.
74. Riesman, 1986 p. 98.
75. Hodgson and McCurdy, 2001 pp. 5–6.
76. McCaskie, 1981 p. 492.
77. Nwaka, 1983 p. 87.
78. Mamdani, 1996.
79. Smock, 1971 p. 9.

CHAPTER 2

1. Beattie, 1980; Riesman, 1986; Fardon, 1996.
2. At birth the nature of these relationships is gendered. To bring good fortune in this patrilineal society a male child should be born face up so the top of its head (*ètíŋ ìwúòt* – source of life) sees the soil first. The umbilical cord was buried at the base of the plantain or palm wine tree (Talbot, 1923 p. 204).
3. See Sangree, 1974; McCall, 1995.
4. Ukpong, 1982 p. 167.
5. McCall, 1995.
6. This analysis of local narratives of settlement implies the rejection of the once common idea that the Annang and Ibibio were forcibly displaced from Ibom, a village near Arochukwu, as an attempt to explain and validate regional Aro influence.
7. Messenger, 1957 p. 21.
8. Jones, 1988 p. 412.
9. For the classic exposition on lineage as an instrument of expansion, see Sahlins, 1961.
10. Horton, 1967 p. 103.
11. In addition to population and land pressures, marriages which deliberately contravened rules of lineage exogamy in order to keep daughters close, to reduce brideprice costs, to promote reciprocity, and to circulate wealth also contributed to segmentation within Ibibio society (Charles, 1996 p. 89).
12. The *àkúkú*'s first fruits 'harvest' is generally distinguished from the new yam festival. See Forde, 1949.
13. The relationship between communities centred on a parent village is sometimes also referred to as *údúk* (rope), a term referring to any descent group, or *ìmân* (Messenger, 1957 p. 19).
14. In the late nineteenth century trans-Qua Iboe river Ukanafun villages recognised Ukpanta of Ikot Odiong as *àkúkú* until he failed to share a leopard

carcass. Allegiances subsequently shifted to 'Inokon' Udo Uyo of Ikot Udo Obobo. In this way distinctions were produced that were represented during the colonial period as the difference between the 'weak chiefs' (eldest males of the lineage) and 'strong men' (who were able to maintain law and order) (Jones, 1970 p. 315).

15. McCaskie, 1992 p. 241.
16. Ruel, 1969 p. xiv.
17. Anderson, 1999 p. xi. This practice has a broad regional currency. On its contemporary use in Cameroon, see Geschiere, 1997 p. 178fn.
18. A wife maintained her own shrine with figures representing her father's lineage along with that of her husband's, but it was not maintained after her death. A woman who had been initiated into *inám* might be represented within the household ancestral shrine (*isó ékpó*).
19. Wives in mourning (*ákpé*) were not allowed to leave the compound or to cut their hair for a period of seven weeks. At the ceremonial 'second' burial a chicken was touched on the woman's head to signify separation from the person destined for the world of spirits (*óbió ékpó*). A wife's parents attended on that day in order to accept their daughter and release her from bonds to her dead husband.
20. For the ceremony a large tapestry was made of a rich and highly coloured pattern on which the events of the dead person's life were depicted in appliqué (see cover). This was hung on a wooden frame, like a tall hut, known as *ńwómó* in which the spirits of the dead were housed to prevent them from wandering about in desolation. The size and aesthetics of the *ńwómó* were determined by the gender, wealth and status of the deceased (Ekefre, 1992; Salmons, 1980).
21. Akpaide, 1982 p. 29. This is in contrast to Mbiti's suggestion that categories of the dead are determined by time depth and the capacity of the living to remember them (Mbiti, 1969 pp. 83–4).
22. Goldie defines *àfái* as 'violently and outrageously', and also as an executioner, a cruel, bloody man and a murderer (Goldie, 1862).
23. Messenger refers to this category of spirits as 'souls of above' (*ékpó ényòŋ*). They included the souls of poisoners (*ifót ékpó*), murderers (*ṁfùmfùm*), thieves (*inò*), those killed in combat (*àfái*), and those which were homeless and without relatives.
24. Talbot, 1923, p. 143.
25. Talbot wrote that the Annang were 'credited with going to the graves of those newly dead, and there making a sacrifice to ensure the aid of evil spirits. After this they beat upon the ground with a plantain stem – the African tree of life – calling, at each stroke, on the name of the corpse, till, at length, the dead man is said to arise from his grave …' (Talbot, 1923 p. 63).
26. As Tonkin reminds us, power also resides in the mask itself, and in the case of *ékpó* most masks are kept at and enhance the power of a family, lineage or diviner's shrine (Tonkin, 1979 p. 243).
27. Simmons, 1957. See also Messenger, 1973 pp. 121–3.
28. Umoren, 1995 p. 81.
29. The consumption of these roots differs from the contemporary smoking of cannabis (known as *ikɔŋ ékpó*) by the general parade of masked *ékpó* performers.
30. The *ékpó ńdêm* mask cannot bend forward to look at the ground for fear of invoking the god of the soil (*àbàsì ìkpá ìsóŋ*), and because its potency is derived from an inability to resolve the high–low opposition. During its performance onlookers are safe in a confrontation with *ékpó ńdêm* only if they kneel or

bow before it. The performance of *ékpó ńdêm* is mimicked in a child's play known as *kpɔ̀kɔ̀ íwúòt* (hit on the head). One boy ties a palm wine tapper's rope around himself and a sack over his head while his friend pulls him around towards bystanders to collect coins. The performance is also represented in the punishment of thieves (see section on *úfɔ̀k úsúŋ* in Chapter 5).

31. Murphy, 1980.
32. van Gennep, 1977.
33. One such protective practice was made in worship to the child's spirit mother (*èkà àbàssì*) and involved making cuts close to the eyes known as *ékìm* which were filled with a medicine, and are prescribed to save the child from sickness and to provide protection against evil powers.
34. It remains unclear as to whether age grades have ever existed among Annang communities, though a system of 'companies' (*ŋkà*) was reported in the Obong and Ika clans (Jeffreys, 1950).
35. There has been considerable confusion over the definition of the *ékóŋ* and *èkóŋ* societies in Annang. This confusion has arisen in part because of the subtle tonal distinction in their pronunciations, and because they both involve young men. *Ékóŋ* is the Ibibio name of a warrior cult known in Annang as *áwìè òwò* while *èkóŋ* is a masquerade comprising a number of dramatic performances, including puppetry, costumed acting and acrobatics.
36. The right hand of a non-initiate was tied to the backside instead of being raised to *àbàssì ényòŋ*, and only the death of initiates were memorialised in the construction of *ŋ́wómó* (Salmons, 1985; Udoka, 1984).
37. By the early twentieth century *áwìè òwò* had become a prestige association and membership was confined to those who could afford to pay its high fees. It is probably the distinction in status at burial that gave rise to the conception of *áwìè òwò* as a society of wealthy elders who were recognised in death by the construction of *ŋwòmò*.
38. Author, 1997 and 2001.
39. Fitzgerald Marriot's presented the following to the Royal Anthropological Society in 1899, 'Human sacrifices are … also done at the performance of a religious play called Aikon. The victim, who is a slave, may be of either sex, but a boy or girl is preferred to an adult. The victim is held down while the executioner beheads him with a sharp matchet, not with one but with several blows. Each person present is supposed to tap the head with a small knife. The skull is finally put in the King's Juju house. This play is performed yearly at the yam digging season. The people wear red cotton caps which they dip in the blood of the victim' (Fitzgerald Marriott, 1899 p. 24). See also *QIM Occasional Paper*, January 1898, (18), PRONI, D/3301/EA/1.
40. Salmons, 1985 p. 60.
41. Talbot, 1923 p. 180.
42. WUL: Jeffreys Papers File 259.
43. Messenger, 1984 p. 71.
44. WUL: Jeffreys Papers File 259.
45. Recorded at Ikot Edem Ewa village, Adat Ifang clan. October 2001.
46. Talbot recorded that the initial cost of *ékpê* (egbo) initiation was 900 manillas, 15 pots of palm wine, 20 fowls, 20 sticks of dried fish, 23 seed yams and 23 cooking yams (Talbot, 1923 p. 173).
47. Messenger, 1957 p. 70; Ruel, 1969 p. 248.
48. Talbot, 1914 p. 245.
49. Brink, 1989; Ema, 1940; Jeffreys, 1956; Malcom, 1925. Brink's work has also illustrated how *m̀bòbó* was a survival strategy for young women providing them

with nutrient reserves for themselves, their foetus and their breast-feeding infant during periods of restricted food supply (Brink, 1989 p. 136).

50. The term *àwɔk* is also a pejorative reference to non-initiates.

51. In the southern Annang region the terms *èbrè* and *ibáàn isɔŋ* (women of the soil) were used interchangeably.

52. In the late nineteenth century, for example, Unwa Iyang from the village of Nkek was a regionally renowned *èbrè* leader and initiated the wives of prominent chiefs including the wife of Chief Nyoyoko from Adiasim near Ikot Ekpene.

53. Diviners (*idɔ̀ŋ*) are said to be buried at night, in secret, because of the potency of the powers acquired as a result of spending a night in the forest during initiation.

54. Talbot, 1923 p. 175. Seven is the most significant ritual number in Annang (Messenger, 1957).

55. Author, 2001 (left), Talbot, 1923 p. 180 (right).

56. The skull was therefore a highly valued body part. Talbot relates that chiefs were buried in secret to prevent the desecration of their graves for their skulls. He also reported the suppression of a gang of thirty 'body-snatchers' discovered near Eket in 1913 digging up graves for skulls (Talbot, 1914 p. 246).

57. Jeffreys noted that *m̀fá* was a type of palm oil fruit used by *idɔ̀ŋ* in divining practices (Jeffreys, 1931) and that the term was not linked to the four grades of initiation he delineated: the novice (*idɔ̀ŋ*), the full member (*ábià idɔ̀ŋ*), one who had initiated another (*àkúkú idɔ̀ŋ*), and one who had presented the society with a cow, 2,800 manillas and goats and pigs (*óbɔŋ idɔ̀ŋ*) (Jeffreys, 1931).

58. Talbot, 1923 p. 171. Talbot recorded the following cost of initial *idɔ̀ŋ* initiation: 900 manillas, one pot of palm wine, twenty fowls, twenty sticks of fish, twenty-three seed yams, and twenty-three cooking yams, followed a week later by the presentation of 100 manillas to the chief *idɔ̀ŋ* and ten each to others, and a further 400 to the chief *idɔ̀ŋ* and sixty each to the others the following day (Talbot, 1923 p. 173).

59. Comparatively of Lele conceptions of agency Douglas says that it is the very person whose position is most critically ambivalent, the diviner, who is potentially a sorcerer. They are ascribed the power of metamorphosis and are believed to be able to transform themselves into a leopard to meet other sorcerers at night (Douglas, 1963 p. 130).

60. See, for example, Little, 1949.

61. Horton, 1967 p. 122; Tamuno and Horton, 1969 p. 37.

62. Murphy, 1980, and more broadly, Meillassoux, 1978.

63. Stories from the southern Annang village of Ikot Edem Ewa, for instance, relate the killing of an *àkúkú* for removing a player's mask thereby breaking *ékpó* laws.

64. Horton, 1967 p. 112.

65. Messenger, 1962 p. 67.

66. Northrup, 1978 p. 109.

67. Tonkin, for instance, rejects a dichotomised view of 'open' chieftaincy government and 'closed' secret societies, and argues for a 'totalising' analysis to the study of masks, secret societies and power which recognises the effects of complexity within a single system (Tonkin, 1979 p. 245).

68. McIntosh, 1999.

69. Guyer, 2004 p. 82.

70. Parkinson, 1906 pp. 121–2. Parkinson's source was Richard Henshaw, Agent for Native Affairs, an authority much cited by Talbot.

71. Jeffreys, 1931.

72. Messenger refers to the soul as *ékpó* and distinguishes between the bodily soul (*ékpó*) and the bush soul (*ékpó íkɔ́t*) (Messenger, 1984 p. 67; 1957 p. 150).
73. Goldie, 1862 pp. 315–316.
74. Cf. Jedrej, 1986 p. 502.
75. Parkinson, 1906 p. 122.
76. A woman without such a pot was generally derided and considered poor. A man wishing to divorce his wife might remove the pot to signal his intention (WUL: Jeffreys Papers File: 258).
77. Ruel, 1970 p. 335.
78. Talbot, 1915 p. 88.
79. Ruel, 1970 p. 334.
80. Ibid. p. 338. Talbot observed similar distinctions across the region (Talbot, 1932 p. 142).
81. Talbot, 1923 p. 121. Annang conceptions of shape-shifting and soul attacks, however, should be set within a complex of ideas and practices known to be circulating among the peoples of the eastern Delta region. Kalabari, Okrika, southern Igbo, Ibibio, Aro, and the societies on the Cross River each shared elements of beliefs in the trapping of bush souls, the use of pots for divination and medicinal preparation, and of shape-shifting (Talbot, 1932 pp. 139–42).
82. Malcolm, 1922 p. 220.
83. Talbot, 1914 p. 244. Accounts from the early twentieth century illustrate how 'soul-trapping' rituals included the equipment of the slave trade era: 'should a medicine-man wish to injure anyone, he drops a key within [a black pottery pot], letting it lie for seven days beneath the magic water. On the eighth he takes it out again and holding it in his hand makes movement as of locking up. From that moment the man, whom it is sought to injure, falls sick and must die' (Talbot, 1932 p. 141). These accounts also resonate with stories of the most prominent chiefs in the region having pots so large that turned upside down they could cover and suffocate a person.
84. Jeffreys, 1931.
85. In libations (*ádùɔk úkɔ́t* – pour drink) drink is presented to the sky and poured to the soil. At the loss of milk teeth a child throws a tooth over the house to ensure that a new set grows (Ekandem, 1957 p. 170). Before an *ékpó* masquerade performer fires his bow and arrow he must point it first to the sky and then to the earth. Warriors (*áwiè òwò/ékóŋ*) must jump over a net or small fence to signify that they are authentic initiates, an ordeal which renders them immune to attack if completed successfully (Salmons, 1985 p. 58). They also jumped over a fellow *áwiè òwò* member's corpse during burial (M'Keown, 1912 p. 42). Stepping over ritually charged substances, including dead bodies, to pledge or prove innocence forms part of various ordeals (*úkáŋ*). And during marriage ceremonies bridegrooms must successfully jump down from a high clay platform (*m̀bót*) to prove their strength and courage (Messenger, 1957 p. 73).
86. Jeffreys, 1955 p. 135; Lieber, 1971.
87. Messenger, 1984 p. 66.
88. These lines are taken from a 1920s *m̀bòbó* song recorded by Jeffreys (WUL: Jeffreys Papers File: 256).
89. For a detailed description see Udo, 1973 pp. 31–33.
90. Messenger, 1957 p. 109.
91. Broadly this cycle divides between an active season of clearing and planting from January to June/July and a slack season from August to December.
92. Messenger, 1957 p. 87.
93. Positioned in the rear of the compound, the yam barn contains several latticed

bamboo racks thirty feet long and eight feet high to which tubers are tied with piassava rope. The racks are covered with palm branches to protect the yams from the sun.

94. On 'yam-barning' titles in the Igbo community of Ohaffia see Arua, 1981. The significance of yam accumulation was also manifested, according to some accounts, by annual human sacrifices (Groves, 1936 p. 52).

95. Talbot, 1923 p. 181.

96. Charles, 1996.

97. *Ékpó ǹkà ówó* is not found in every Annang community (Nwahaghi, 1997). The main factor explaining its relative intensity is the presence of a female ancestor within a lineage who has been 'killed' by the ordeal of *ékpó ǹkà ówó*.

98. A procedure that acknowledges male impotence, albeit secretly, is known as *údɔ*, where, under *idìɔ̀ŋ* supervision, a wife will be allowed to sleep with a friend of the husband (Jeffreys, 1956 pp. 18–19).

99. Messenger, 1957 p. 118.

100. Ibid. p. 119. Offiong has correctly refuted Tuden and Plotnicov's generalisation that slaves in Annang society were dedicated to cult shrines in the same way as Igbo *osu* (Offiong, 1985).

101. Goldie, 1862; Northrup, 1979a p. 16; Jones, 1967 p. 78.

102. Lovejoy and Richardson, 1999 p. 335.

103. For an extensive overview see Klein, 2001.

104. Ibid. pp. 58–61.

105. Ibid. p. 65.

106. Edwards, 1967 p. 20.

107. Northrup, 1978 p. 141.

108. Dike, 1956 p. 45.

109. Northrup, 1979b p. 50.

110. Account of a journey ... from Esene on the Opobo River to Ikorasan ... on the Qua Ibo river, 1894a, TNA: FO 2/64 30B.

111. Aro Origin, Anthropological papers on the basis of the wide spread of Aro influence, (H. F. Matthews), 1927, NAE: ARODIV 20/1/15; Talbot, 1926 p. 182; Dike and Ekejiuba, 1990 p. 135fn.

112. Notes on Report on the Eastern Provinces by the Secretary for Native Affairs, by M. D. W. Jeffreys, 1924, NAE: IKOTDIST 15/8/2.

113. Watt, 1903 p. 105.

114. Harris, 1942; Northrup, 1978 pp. 78–9.

115. In the case of the Cameroonian Grassfields, Warnier argues that kidnapping exposed an inter-generational cleavage. Young men could bypass the economic control of their elders by kidnapping and selling their juniors in order to finance marriage (Warnier, 1989).

116. Udo Akpabio from the Ukana clan became a Warrant Chief in Ikot Ekpene. See Groves, 1936.

117. The birth of twins, was believed to have been the result of an association with a malevolent ancestor (*idiók ékpó*). For a discussion on twin infanticide in Africa, see Renne and Bastian, 2001 and articles in the same volume.

118. Groves, 1936 p. 47.

119. It was this mode of debt bondage that British traders and Efik merchants adapted at the coast to secure credit (Lovejoy and Richardson, 1999; 2001).

120. Groves, 1936 p. 49.

121. On the role of *okonko* in the slave trade of southern Ngwa see Oriji, 1982.

122. Ottenberg and Knudsen, 1985.

123. William Snelgrave had documented *ékpẽ*'s existence in 1713 and it is likely to

have been introduced several decades earlier (Snelgrave, 1734 pp. 7–12 cited in Lovejoy and Richardson, 1999 p. 347fn).

124. Jones, 1984.
125. The *èkpè* society took control of the *esere* bean ordeal in 1850 (Latham, 1972 p. 250).
126. 'Comey' (or 'breaking trade') constituted a payment made by European merchants to Delta rulers which guaranteed the right to trade unmolested (See Jones, 1963 p. 96). Before it was abolished in 1888 in favour of a flat annual rate paid to the Government, 'comey' had been levied on each ship entering the Qua Iboe river to the value of a puncheon of palm oil for each mast, £70 for each trader, plus an export tax of one iron bar for each puncheon of oil shipped (Ashley, 1937. 'Ibibio Subtribes: Short Historical Sketches', NAE: CALPROF 3/1/1637).
127. Latham, 1973 pp. 38–9.
128. Signed on board HMS Minx, 19 September 1855. Cited in Ashley, 1924. 'Ikot Ekpene Division', NAE: IKOTDIST 15/8/2.
129. Latham, 1973 p. 80.
130. Walker, 1877 p. 121.
131. F. Braudel, *L'Identité de la France. Espace et histoire*, p. 156, cited in Bayart, 1993 p. 112.
132. For further interpretations of the origin of 'Moko' based on language use see Jeffreys, 1935 p. 12 and Ejituwu, 1991 p. 67 and 75 (Obolo/Andoni), Northrup, 1973 p. 5 (Ibibio), Noah, 1980 p. 3 (Caribbean), and Hair, 1967 p. 263 (Igbo).
133. Alonso de Sandoval, *Natureleza de Todo Etiopies* cited in Hair, 1967.
134. For a comparison of these vocabularies see Northrup, 1973 p. 4.
135. Koelle, 1963 p. 18 See also Northrup, 1978 p. 63.
136. Koelle, 1963 p. 18.
137. Northrup, 1973 p. 2 See also Winston, 1965 p. 123.
138. On the impact of slavery on rice production in Guinea-Bissau see Hawthorne, 2001.
139. Pereira, 1937 p. 132.
140. Barbot, 1699 p. 465. Agbisherea (or Egbo Sairra) was a pre-colonial name for the Ibibio, and Goldie's 1862 Efik Dictionary records Annang as 'a district of Egbo Sherry distant from Calabar'.
141. Jones, 1989a p. 25.
142. The literature on the 'middle passage' refers to two limited daily rations of palm oil, pepper, rice and 'slabber' sauce, but makes little mention of the significance of yams to the diet of slaves (Sheridan, 1981 pp. 605 and 618; Kiple and Kiple, 1980 p. 199).
143. Barbot, Hair, Jones and Law, 1992 pp. 699–700.
144. Northrup, 1976 p. 355.
145. Adams, 1823 p. 132. See also Northrup, 1976 p. 356.
146. Taking only half of Barbot's recommended yam quota Jones argues that the annual demand was in excess of 1 million yams (Jones, 1989a p. 41). Northrup estimated that at least 400,000 yams annually entered this trade at the beginning of the eighteenth century and 1.2 million yams per year by the end of the century (Northrup, 1976 p. 363; 1978 p. 251).
147. Northrup, 1972 p. 225. This point is also illustrated for neighbouring Ogoniland in Kpone-Tonwe, 1997.
148. On Eastern Delta currencies of this period see Jones, 1958; Latham, 1971; Northrup, 1978 pp. 157–64.

149. Jones, 1989a p. 41.
150. Northrup, 1979a p. 5.
151. Northrup, 1976.
152. Lynn, 1981 p. 332.
153. James Badgley 'Report on the Old Calabar River' enclosure in Baron to Hay, 20 June 1828, PRO, CO 82/1 cited Northrup, 1979a p. 9.
154. Hugh Goldie, 'Journal' for 23 October 1848 and 20 November 1850, in Missionary Record, IV (September 1849, 130 and VI (September 1851), 131 cited in ibid.
155. Amadiume, 1987 p. 27.
156. Martin, 1984 p. 413.
157. Lynn, 1997 p. 79.
158. Martin, 1956 p. 15.
159. Lynn, 1997 p. 126.
160. Comparatively on Sierra Leone see Leach, 1994 pp. 132–4, 144–5 and Ferme, 2001 p. 194.
161. Messenger, 1957 p. 226.
162. In Mende society a similar 'spiral of ferns' was used to regulate farming, to ban fishing and the collection of palm fruit and was supposed to bring death or sickness to anyone who disregarded it (Little, 1949 p. 206). Domestically, palm products were the gifts which secured a man's rights during the betrothal of a child. To stake his marriage claim to an unborn child, a man presented a gift of a palm kernel on a plate to the expectant mother, and if the child was a girl then the prospective husband tied *àyèì* to her wrist.
163. Information called for under para 3 of His Excellency's minute to the Report on the Eastern Provinces by the Secretary for Native Affairs, (M. D.W. Jeffreys), 1922, NAE: CALPROF 5/12/510.
164. On several occasions the Messengers, anthropologists who worked in Ikot Ekpene in the early 1950s, dressed the wounds of men on the morning following such visitations (Messenger and Messenger, 1981). The Messengers refer to this witchcraft as *ifòt*, but in the southern Annang region it is known as *ùbén* and the two forms of witchcraft are sharply delineated.
165. Talbot, 1923 p. 108.
166. On cats, witches, sex and shape-shifting, see Evans-Pritchard, 1976 p. 237.
167. Messenger and Messenger, 1981.
168. There is a regional currency to this form of medicine. In Ikwerre this charm is known as *ebube agwu* (surprise leopard).
169. Goldie, 1890.
170. Talbot, 1926 p. 207.
171. Dike, 1956 p. 197.
172. Ashley, 1924. 'Ikot Ekpene Division', NAE: IKOTDIST 15/8/2.
173. 'Memorandum submitted by the Chiefs and People of Ikot Inyang Udo Village, Abak Division, South-Eastern State to the Irikefe Panel', September 1975.
174. On the networks of brokers and interior suppliers see Lynn, 1997 p. 71.
175. King Jaja to Granville, 28 July 1881, TNA: FO 403/18.
176. Hailey, 1951 p. 157.
177. Ashley, 1924. 'Ikot Ekpene Division', NAE: IKOTDIST 15/8/2.
178. R. D. Casement, 'Report on an Attempted Journey from Itu ... to the Opobo River', TNA: FO 2/63/328.
179. Northrup, 1979b p. 49.
180. Peel, 2000 p. 7.
181. David Ekong: First Pastor of the Qua Iboe Church, (G. Bill), 1964, PRONI:

D/3301/GB/5. Talbot referred to the deity as the great Juju Ainyena (Talbot, 1923 p. 103).

182. Egbo Egbo: Ibuno Chief and Christian, (R. L. M'Keown), n.d., PRONI: D/3301/GC/4/1.

183. The late Ukat Ibuno, (D. Ekong), n.d., PRONI: D/3301/GA/6.

184. David Ekong to Mr Niblock, 10 June 1897, PRONI: D/3301/AB/1.

185. S.A. Bill to Edward, 12 October 1901, PRONI: D/3301/AG/1.

186. David Ekong: First Pastor of the Qua Iboe Church, (G. Bill), 1964, PRONI: D/3301/GB/5.

187. Peel, 2000 p. 227; 1990.

188. The term *ukpötia* or *ùkpòtiô* continues to be associated with the Eket region. 'Nka Ukpotio' was the name taken by bands of young men during a witch-hunt in the 1970s (Offiong, 1982), and which re-emerged in Eket in 2002.

189. Jeffreys noted another category of witch-finders in Eket, young children. In 1928 a young boy had accused eight people of witchcraft, who all succumbed to the *esere* bean ordeal. The boy told Jeffreys that he could leave his body at night and join the dances of the witches who themselves had the power of looking like trees (Jeffreys, 1966 p. 97).

190. Peel, 1990 pp. 350–9.

191. Three thousand coffee seedlings were given by the Government for the scheme but the low price of coffee made the scheme uneconomic and it was abandoned after only one season.

192. Watt, 1951 p. 88 (facing) and M'Keown, 1912 (frontispiece).

193. *QIM Occasional Paper*, August 1901, (32), PRONI, D/3301/EA/2. 'We give them a little secular education to develop the intellect and make them better able to understand the Great Truths we wish them to grasp. We give them domestic training, that they may develop wifely instincts and we insist on their continuing their manual or out-door work as necessary to the training of an African girl ...' (*QIM Occasional Paper*, November 1908, (61), PRONI, D/3301/EA/2). See Bastian, 2000 for an analysis of the reconfiguring of gender roles through such schools in an Igbo context.

194. Cf. Meyer, 1999; Peel, 2000 pp. 255–65.

195. Peel, 2000 p. 219.

196. Cf. ibid. p. 137 on the Yoruba case.

197. S.A. Bill to Mr Hamilton, 20 March 1899, PRONI: D/3301/AG/1.

198. M'Keown, 1912 p. 74.

199. *From Darkness to Light: The Story of Etia*, (G. Bill), n.d., PRONI: D/3301/GC/9/24.

200. Peel, 2000 p. 238.

201. David Ekong to Mr Keown, 16 July 1923, PRONI: D/3301/AB/1.

202. David Ekong to Mr Keown, 28 October 1925, PRONI: D/3301/AB/1.

203. *QIM Occasional Paper*, August 1901, (32), PRONI, D/3301/EA/2.

204. *QIM Occasional Paper*, February 1903, (38), PRONI, D/3301/EA/3.

205. The Qua Iboe Mission Makes History (J. W. Westgarth), 1946, PRONI: D/3301/GA/2.

206. M'Keown, 1912 p. 127.

207. Ibid. p. 114.

208. Akpan Udo-Ema, (J. Kirk), n.d., PRONI: D/3301/GA/3.

209. Peel, 2000 p. 155.

210. *QIM Occasional Paper*, February 1904, (42), PRONI, D/3301/EA/3 *QIM Occasional Paper*, February 1904, (42), PRONI, D/3301/EA/3. He subsequently burned down his own compound and shot himself.

211. *QIM Occasional Paper*, February 1902, (34), PRONI, D/3301/EA/3.
212. Piot reports that pre-colonial Kabre witches did not kill but rather ate small holes in their victims' arms, a practice which sounds similar to *ùbén*. Like the Annang case, Kabre beliefs in more lethal forms of witchcraft coincided with the advent of wage labour in the mines and plantations of southern Togo and Ghana in the 1910s and 1920s (Piot, 1999 p. 68).
213. Latham, 1972.
214. The physical effects of the *esere* bean ordeal are detailed in Simmons, 1956 pp. 225–6.
215. Dayrell, 1913 p. 34.
216. For some, like Samuel Akpan Ekang who became a mission evangelist, Harford's presence on the river had prompted his intellectual path to conversion: 'When I was about eight or nine years of age, my father gave me to one of Mr John Harford's clerks to live with him and learn English' (*QIM Occasional Paper*, February 1905, (46), PRONI, D/3301/EA/3).
217. M'Keown, 1912.
218. S. A. Bill to Mr Niblock, 16 December 1898, PRONI: D/3301/AG/1.
219. S. A. Bill to Mr Niblock, 20 August 1899, PRONI: D/3301/AG/1.
220. *QIM Occasional Paper*, January 1898, (18), PRONI, D/3301/EA/1.
221. See Fardon, 2002.
222. *Daily Journal*, S. A. Bill, 2 December 1902, PRONI: D/3301/DA/1.
223. *Qua Iboe Mission Quarterly*, August 1906, (52), PRONI, D/3301/EA/4.
224. Noah, 1984 p. 42.
225. *QIM Occasional Paper*, May 1899, (23), PRONI, D/3301/EA/2.
226. S. A. Bill to Mr Hamilton, 20 March 1899, PRONI: D/3301/AG/1.
227. *QIM Occasional Paper*, November 1899, (25), PRONI, D/3301/EA/2.
228. Anene, 1956 pp. 21, 23.
229. *QIM Occasional Paper*, August 1901, (32), PRONI, D/3301/EA/2.
230. Afigbo, 1971 p. 3.
231. Ekechi, 1985.
232. Groves, 1936 p. 53.
233. Afigbo, 1971 p. 6.
234. S. A. Bill to His Excellency the High Commissioner, Southern Nigeria, 20 October 1904, PRONI: D/3301/AG/1.
235. *QIM Occasional Paper*, August 1901, (32), PRONI, D/3301/EA/2.
236. In 1888 a small society called the 'Qua Iboe Missionary Association' was formed in Belfast and raised just £70 in its first year. These original sponsors cut their funding in 1891 and advised Bill to move to the Congo. Instead, he returned home to Belfast that year and following a series of talks in Mission Halls formed an interdenominational council which became the auxiliary of the mission.
237. M'Keown, 1912 p. 96.
238. Ibid. p. 169.
239. Ibid. p. 162.
240. Ibid. pp. 96–7.
241. Ibid. p. 90.
242. *QIM Occasional Paper*, May 1900, (27), PRONI, D/3301/EA/2.
243. *QIM Quarterly*, August 1908, (60), PRONI, D/3301/EA/4.
244. *QIM Occasional Paper*, August 1900, (28), PRONI, D/3301/EA/2.
245. Peel, 2000 p. 229.
246. *QIM Occasional Paper*, August 1905, (48), PRONI, D/3301/EA/3.
247. M'Keown, 1912 p. 73.
248. *QIM Occasional Paper*, February 1905, (46), PRONI, D/3301/EA/3.

249. *QIM Quarterly*, May 1906, (51), PRONI, D/3301/EA/4.
250. *QIM Quarterly*, February 1908, (58), PRONI, D/3301/EA/4.
251. *QIM Quarterly*, May 1908, (59), PRONI, D/3301/EA/4.
252. A. Bailie to McKeown, 6 February 1905, PRONI: D/3301/AD/5.
253. *QIM Occasional Paper*, August 1904, (44), PRONI, D/3301/EA/3.
254. The Qua Iboe Mission Makes History, (J. W. Westgarth), 1946, PRONI: D/3301/GA/2.
255. Udo, 1972.
256. Johnson, 1932. 'Afaha Obong, Annang Sub-Tribe, Abak District', NAE: CSE 1/85/4782A.
257. M'Keown, 1912 pp. 144–6.

CHAPTER 3

1. David Ekong: First Pastor of the Qua Iboe Church, (G. Bill), 1964, PRONI: D/3301/GB/5. The missionaries were describing *ńdɔk* which refers to the end of year and the annual purification of evil spirits. Leonard's account of *ńdɔk* in Duke Town is one of the fullest: 'Early in the morning of the day appointed, usually about 3 a.m. the closing ceremony begins with a deafening outburst of noise, that can only be likened to the descent of an approaching and ever-increasing tornado rushing into a valley of deep and deathlike silence. Immediately in every house the mimic thunder of cannon is heard, mingling with the rattle of musketry, the beating of drums, and the clatter of pots, pans, doors or of everything in fact which is capable of making a noise. ... those spirits who are evil and inimical to the interests of the community at large ... must go ... and [they] make all the noise that is possible in order to effect this removal. ... the observer would see sincere and genuine outbursts of grief on the part of various individuals, invariably slaves, on behalf of and in remembrance of departed relatives, whose spirits and therefore personalities, had in this rude way been expelled, as far as they were concerned for all eternity. ... on the appearance of the sun upon the scene ... the houses by now are all thoroughly set in order and garnished, having been swept from the roof to the floor, and the dirt which has been so collected, along with the remains of old fires ... are carried by the members of each household down to the river's bank and thrown into the water. Thus is the town purged of all its evil spirits' (Leonard, 1966 p. 449). See also MacGaffey's comments on Portuguese arrivals in Kongo (MacGaffey, 1986 p. 199).
2. Roberts, 1999 pp. 390–2.
3. With a population estimated at 190,000 Abak was administered as a sub-Division of Ikot Ekpene Division until proposals to gazette Abak and Uyo as Divisions were made in 1929.
4. 'Annual Report, Abak Division', 1911, NAE: CALPROF 14/6/1304.
5. Senior Resident, Calabar Province to Honourable Secretary, Southern Provinces, 11 September 1929, NAE: MINLOC 6/1/48. In 1916 E. Dayrell was the only political officer at Ikot Ekpene, and from there he administered the districts of Abak, Uyo, Itu and Arochukwu. As a result many parts of the Division were not visited for over a year (Afigbo, 1972 p. 152).
6. 'Annual Report, Calabar Province', 1914, NAE: CALPROF 5/4/645.
7. W. M. Hailey, Native Administration in the British African Territories, Part III: West Africa, Nigeria, Gold Coast, Sierra Leone, Gambia (HMSO, London, 1951), p. 2.
8. Afigbo, 1972 p. 50.
9. Lugard, 1920, Report on the amalgamation of Northern and Southern Nigeria,

and administration, 1912–1919, London: HMSO. See also Nwabughuogu, 1981.

10. 'Annual Report, Abak Division', 1914, NAE: CALPROF 5/4/359.

11. 'Information called for under Para. 3 of His Excellency's Minute to the Report on the Eastern Provinces to the Secretary for Native Affairs' by M.D.W. Jeffreys, 1934, NAE: ABAKDIST 1/2/44.

12. 'Annual Report, Abak Division', 1914, NAE: CALPROF 5/4/359.

13. DO Abak to Commissioner, Calabar, 23 March 1914, NAE: CALPROF 5/4/90.

14. Resident's Views on Native Court Structure (Notes on Mr Palmer's Report on the History of Native Administration of the Old Southern Nigeria), 1915, RH: Mss Afr.s.1873. In 1922 Chief Ebong, President of Abak Native Court, admitted that the true position of clan chief of his own clan of Ibesit had not been recognised by the government since the previous chief, his grandfather, Akpan Etuk Udo Nwa, died three years prior to government rule (Report on the Eastern Provinces by the Secretary for Native Affairs, (S. M. Grier), 1922, RH: 723.12.v.43 (12)). Inokon Uyo Ubong's influence increased across the southern Annang region as a result of his appointment and because he had been instrumental in persuading the Afahas to take their cases to the Azumini Native Court (Spence, 1936. 'Afaha Clan of the Annang Sub-Tribe', NAE: CSE 1/85/6495).

15. Cameron, 'Principles of Native Administration and their Application', cited in Kirk-Greene, 1965 p. 202.

16. ADO Uyo and Abak to Commissioner, Calabar, 17 March 1915, NAE: CSE 3/7/3.

17. In 1922 Brooks, the Resident in Calabar, ruled that no paramount chiefs should be replaced (Afigbo, 1972 p. 171).

18. DO Abak to DO Ikot Ekpene, 22 April 1924, NAE: CALPROF 5/12/510.

19. Report by the Commissioner on Calabar Province, 31 December 1913, NAE: CALPROF 5/4/544.

20. 'Annual Report, Abak Division', 1910, NAE: CALPROF 14/6/96.

21. Noah, 1984 p. 31. The private court of Chief Udo Eyop of Afaha Udo Uyop in Ibesikpo was reputed to be the most notorious (Anene, 1966 p. 267).

22. Mamdani, 1996 p. 59.

23. Sumner, 'Tours of Southern Nigeria', 1923–28, Mss.Afr.s.538.

24. Bayart, 1999 p. 46. See also Derrick, 1983. While we can distinguish between official roles – letter-writers, clerks, interpreters – we should also be mindful of the fact that these categories often overlapped and that people's roles were improvised. Robert Cudjoe, a Ghanaian, worked in south-eastern Nigeria during from the 1910s as an interpreter though his official role was district carpenter (Cudjoe, 1953).

25. DO Uyo and Abak to DO Ikot Ekpene, 16 March 1915, NAE: CSE 3/7/3.

26. Tamuno and Horton, 1969 p. 53.

27. Revival of Secret Societies in Igbo country, (J. N. Cheetham), 1915, NAE: RIVPROF 8/3/261.

28. J. W. Westgarth, Qua Iboe Mission to Provincial Commissioner, Calabar, 15 January 1918, NAE: CALPROF 5/8/71.

29. DO Ikot Ekpene to Resident, Calabar Province, 25 August 1916, NAE: CALPROF 4/5/42.

30. Statement of Akpan Ekereke of Ikot Esukpon, 25 June 1916, NAE: CALPROF 4/5/42.

31. DO Uyo to DO Ikot Ekpene, 6 October 1917, NAE: CALPROF 5/7/674.

32. Udodung Nko from Idung Urom Iso was one of the wealthiest men in southern Ukanafun during the 1930s. He became the president of the Native Court and a Warrant Chief. He built a two-storey ('upstairs') house in 1938.
33. DO Uyo to DO Ikot Ekpene, 6 October 1917, NAE: CALPROF 5/7/674.
34. 'Annual Report, Abak Division', 1923, NAE: CALPROF 5/14/50.
35. Okonafon Patrol, 1917, NAE: CALPROF 5/7/674.
36. 'Annual Report, Calabar Province', 1924, NAE: CALPROF 5/14/550.
37. DO Ikot Ekpene to Resident, Calabar, 21 November 1922, NAE: CALPROF 5/12/510.
38. Afigbo, 1971 p. 22.
39. On the historiography of the Nigerian Hamitic hypothesis see Zachernuk, 1994.
40. Report on the Eastern Provinces by the Secretary for Native Affairs, (S. M. Grier), 1922, RH: 723.12.v.43 (12).
41. Notes on Report on the Eastern Provinces by the Secretary for Native Affairs, by M. D. W. Jeffreys, 1924, NAE: IKOTDIST 15/8/2.
42. Ibid.
43. WAG Ormsby-Gore Cmd 2744 Report on a visit to West Africa, 1926. p. 19, cited in Afigbo, 1971 p. 24.
44. Aro Origin, Anthropological papers on the basis of the wide spread of Aro influence, (H. F. Matthews), 1927, NAE: ARODIV 20/1/15.
45. Nwaka, 1983 p. 191.
46. 'Annual Report, Abak Division', 1923, NAE: CALPROF 5/14/50.
47. DO Ikot Ekpene to Resident, Calabar, 15 February 1924, NAE: CALPROF 5/1/156.
48. Resident, Calabar Province to The Secretary, Southern Provinces, 14 June 1927, NAE: CALPROF 5/1/156.
49. DO Opobo to Resident, Calabar, 13 May 1927, NAE: CALPROF 5/1/156.
50. Extract from the Annual Report of the Calabar Province, 1926, NAE: CSE 1/12/2.
51. ADO Arochukwu to DO Ikot Ekpene, 29 April 1915, NAE: CALPROF 5/5/242.
52. Perham, 1937 p. 239.
53. DO Ikot Ekpene to Resident, Calabar Province, 1 June 1918, NAE: CALPROF 4/7/14.
54. Unlawful societies were defined under the Criminal Code (Ordinance 15) of 1916 which also provided sanctions against trials by ordeal, worship or invocation of 'obnoxious' spirits, witchcraft accusations and the possession or sale of drugs and charms.
55. M'Keown, 1912 p. 73.
56. Diary, J. W. Westgarth, 14 April 1915, PRONI: D/3301/CB/1.
57. *QIM Quarterly*, February 1918, (97), PRONI, D/3301/EA/8.
58. This was a common process and in Yorubaland was organised in terms of bonds of fellowship common to age groups or clubs known as *egbe*: 'The solidarity of male age-peers was strikingly manifest in the common practice by which groups of young men, once as large as forty, came to see the missionaries, out of curiosity to see what they were about … ' (Peel, 2000 p. 56).
59. The formation of one of the most notable unions of the Eastern Provinces, the Abiriba Communal Improvement Union traced its origins to subscriptions collected to pay teachers' salaries and for the maintenance of the Church of Scotland Mission School which were enforced in the Native Court. See Abiriba Improvement Union to Chief Commissioner, Eastern Provinces, 20

October 1947, NAE: UMDIV 3/1/612.

60. District Commissioner, Ikot Ekpene to Provincial Commissioner, Eastern Province, 22 December 1913, NAE: CALPROF 13/6/108.

61. DO Calabar to Commissioner, Calabar, 29 December 1915, NAE: CALPROF 5/5/528.

62. *QIM Occasional Paper*, May 1905, (47), PRONI, D/3301/EA/3.

63. *QIM Quarterly*, May 1917, (95), PRONI, D/3301/EA/8.

64. DO Ikot Ekpene to Resident, Calabar Province, 1 June 1918, NAE: CALPROF 4/7/14.

65. 'Annual Report, Calabar Province', 1924, NAE: CALPROF 5/14/550.

66. Mary Slessor to Mr MacGregor, 1 October 1913, NAE: CALPROF 13/6/108. See also Proctor, 2000 p. 57.

67. District Commissioner, Ikot Ekpene to Provincial Commissioner, Eastern Province, 22 December 1913, NAE: CALPROF 13/6/108.

68. Secretary, Southern Provinces to Commissioner, Calabar, 26 August 1915, NAE: CALPROF 5/5/528.

69. On the development and content of education in Calabar see Taylor, 1984. Schools themselves became sites of conflict. The government school in Bonny witnessed what was described as a 'rebellion' over food and conditions in 1913. Within the Qua Iboe sphere during this period there were numerous complaints about teachers' conduct (especially that they were guilty of adultery) and a corresponding number of disputes between teachers and pupils (particularly over excessive punishment). During 1914, for instance, Westgarth reported 'a lot of trouble everywhere with schoolboys and teachers' and two cases came to light in which teachers were beaten by schoolboys (Diary, J. W. Westgarth, 7 November 1914, PRONI: D/3301/CB/1). The trajectory of violence in Nigeria's schools and universities may be traced to these tensions.

70. Report on the Eastern Provinces by the Secretary for Native Affairs, (S. M. Grier), 1922, RH: 723.12.v.43 (12).

71. 'Annual Report, Abak Division', 1925, NAE: CALPROF 5/16/45.

72. Kalu cites an instance in June 1920 when the Okonko society in Amuozu Ihie (Ngwa) begged the DO to permit the formation of a club called Amuzo Ihie Okonko Society with a motto ('Bear ye one another's burden') with the aim to foster unity, relieve one another in times of trouble, distress and death and encourage interest in their country (Kalu, 1977a p. 83).

73. Southall, 1975 p. 223.

74. Resident, Calabar to Secretary, Eastern Provinces, 25 January 1944, 1943–44, NAE: CALPROF 3/1/2906.

75. Henderson, 1971 p. 237.

76. Okonjo, 1967 p. 111.

77. Ruel, 1969 p. 259.

78. Ruel, 1964 p. 10.

79. Active in covering burial and repatriation costs, the union came to prominence when, in 1927, it hired barrister V. W. Clinton and brought libel proceedings against E. N. Amaku. Amaku was a teacher in the Duke Town school and the author of a book which was to have sensational consequences, though it was written innocuously as an aid for learning Efik in the United Presbyterian Church of Scotland Mission. Amaku claimed in his book, *Edikot Nwed Mbuk* ('A History of the Efik People'), that the Ibibio were, ' ... knaves who were heavily endowed with dynamism, wisdom, industry and cunning but were unworthy of trust' (Udoma, 1987 p. 28). In 1927 the Ibibio Association and Community League dropped its legal case and a settlement was organised by

the church with Amaku in which the Mission authorities agreed to destroy the booklet and Amaku tendered an apology.

80. Details of church numbers from this period are scant. The DO at Ikot Ekpene estimated that within his Division of 600,000 people (including Itu, Uyo, Ikot Ekpene and Aro Districts) there were 30,000 mission converts, some 5 per cent of the population (DO Ikot Ekpene to Resident, Calabar, 21 November 1922, NAE: CALPROF 5/12/510).

81. *QIM Quarterly*, August 1930, (146), PRONI, D/3301/EA/14.

82. Flu Epidemic: Calabar Province, 1919, NAE: CALPROF 5/9/69.

83. Jeffreys, 1966 p. 96.

84. *QIM Quarterly*, November 1919, (103), PRONI, D/3301/EA/9.

85. Ohadike, 1981.

86. Ibid. p. 386.

87. Kalu, 1977b; Tasie, 1975.

88. There was no law to enforce the regulation that missions seek approval from the political officer before opening a new church, and it was frequently ignored. This gave rise to rivalry and antagonism between the missions, 'The Roman Catholics will do their utmost to convert the heretics of other denominations, the African Mission ambitious to establish itself as the one religion of Africa will lose no opportunity of increasing their membership at the expense of other denominations. The Wesleyans and Methodists have their returns of membership and communicants to send in and a decrease in their members would be regarded as unsatisfactory' (Resident, Calabar to Secretary, Southern Provinces, 27 June 1921, NAE: CALPROF 5/11/341).

89. With the mission arrivals the practice of the second burial declined and in place of ŋwòmò cement monuments were constructed from 1917 onwards (Butler, 1963 pp. 118, 122. See also Beier, 1956). Many families relocated in the early colonial period in order to gain access to the new roads, especially the Aba-Opobo road which traversed Abak District. Former, abandoned compounds (ǹdòn) subsequently became sites for the construction of ŋ́kúkú ékpó shrines and spiritually charged spaces commonly used in ritual performance.

90. Horton and Peel, 1976 p. 497.

91. On Ethiopianism and nationalism in South Africa see Laouel, 1986; Chirenje, 1987. The first Ethiopian Church in Lagos was founded in 1918 by S.A. Oke who preached that Africa should have her own religion. In these sentiments there was an affinity between Ethiopianism and the ideas of Aladura churches such as the Cherubim and Seraphim (Peel, 1968 p. 134). The Zion Movement, another South African independent church, was active in Calabar Province in 1928.

92. The doctrine of the United Native African Church on polygamy read as follows: 'This organisation did not preach polygamy but tolerates it wherever that is the custom of the people ... It abhors the forcing of monogamy of foreign systems of marriage on its members firmly believing that their monogamy not polygamy is essential to their salvation and since it cannot be proved from the Holy Scriptures that polygamy is a sin, the United African Church did not regard polygamy as a sin' (Notes on the Constitution of the United Native African Church, nd, Jeffreys Papers File: 263).

93. *QIM Quarterly*, May 1919, (109), PRONI, D/3301/EA/9.

94. *QIM Quarterly*, February 1925, (124), PRONI, D/3301/EA/11.

95. Reverend W.T. Groves to Lieutenant-Governor Southern Provinces, 12 January 1927, NAE: CALPROF 5/1/156.

96. *QIM Quarterly*, May 1917, (95), PRONI, D/3301/EA/8.

97. S. A. Bill to Edward, 14 September 1901, PRONI: D/3301/AG/1.
98. David Ekong to Mr Keown, 6 January 1912, PRONI: D/3301/AB/1.
99. *QIM Quarterly*, November 1922, (115), PRONI, D/3301/EA/10.
100. Abasiattai, 1989 p. 499.
101. *QIM Quarterly*, May 1923, (117), PRONI, D/3301/EA/10.
102. *Qua Iboe Field Notes*, 1924, PRONI, D/3301/EA/11.
103. The spheres of the various missions (the Qua Iboe, Presbyterian and Methodists) intersected in the area around Itu (Uyo, Itam, Ibiono and Ikono) which was therefore at the periphery of mission activities (Abasiattai, 1989 p. 500).
104. Westgarth, 1946 p. xiii.
105. Ibid.
106. ADO Enyong Division to Senior Resident, Calabar Province, 22 February 1933, CALPROF 3/1/210. The pamphlet referred to was Utom Spirit, (J. W. Westgarth), 1928, WUL: Jeffreys Papers File: 263.
107. Diary, J. W. Westgarth, 2 January 1915, PRONI: D/3301/CB/1.
108. *QIM Quarterly*, November 1927, (135), D/3301/EA/12.
109. Westgarth, 1946 p. 16.
110. Ibid. p. 53.
111. DO Uyo to Clan Councils of Uyo Division, 9 February 1939, NAE: ABAKDIST 1/2/81.
112. Westgarth, 1946 p. 50.
113. Paper entitled 'The Trouble Began' by David Kapella, n.d., PRONI: D/3301/OA/12.
114. Westgarth, 1946 pp. 54–5.
115. Jeffreys, 1952–53 p. 101.
116. In a register of 'Spirited Souls' (probably from 1927) the numbers involved in nineteen villages across Ikot Ekpene Division totalled 1,912, an average of 100 'spirits' per village. (Extract from ledger 'Registering Tribe of Ibibio Spirited Souls', nd, WUL: Jeffreys Papers File: 263).
117. Messenger, 1962 p. 287.
118. 'Annual Report, Abak Division', 1923, NAE: CALPROF 5/14/50.
119. Report of the Commission of Inquiry appointed to inquire into the disturbances in the Calabar and Owerri Provinces, December 1929, 1930b, RH: 723.13.s.4/1930.
120. Sumner, 'Tours of Southern Nigeria', 1923–28, Mss.Afr.s.538; Extract from Annual Report, Calabar Province, 1927, NAE: CALPROF 3/1/210.
121. Jeffreys, 1952–53 p. 102.
122. Jeffreys, 1935 p. 22. Waddell described Myalism in Jamaica as manifesting itself in 'fearful paroxysms, bordering on insanity, accompanied with acts of violence on those who attempt to restrain it (Waddell, 1863 p. 188).
123. Acting Secretary, Southern Provinces to Chief Secretary to the Government, 10 February 1939, NAE: CALPROF 3/1/1954. The Makka movement originated in the Mambilla area of Gashaka District of Bamenda Division in 1938. The Annual report of that year described it as 'a frenzied dance in which most of the population, men and women, joined. The dancers would gyrate in a frenzy to the drum, waving their arms like a windmill. They would then begin to shake as in an epileptic fit to the ground, apparently senseless: '... Anyone who fell down in such a trance was admitted a member of the society. On recovery such a one appeared to be endowed with supernatural powers and went about the villages denouncing people as witches. ... it appears that those who originally introduced it said that Makka would purge the country of witches, cure all illnesses, increase the yield of the farms and even raise the

dead from the grave' (Acting Secretary, Southern Provinces to Chief Secretary to the Government, 10 February 1939, NAE: CALPROF 3/1/1954).

124. Report on Outbreak of lawlessness by Spirit-possessed, Itu District, (D. Itu-Enyong), 1927, NAE: CALPROF 3/1/209.
125. Jones, 1989b p. 517.
126. Sumner, 'Tours of Southern Nigeria', 1923–28, Mss.Afr.s.538.
127. *QIM Quarterly*, August 1928, (138), PRONI, D/3301/EA/13.
128. Offiong, 1989 p. 65; Nwaka, 1978 p. 193.
129. Secretary to the Evangelical Union of Nigeria (East of the Niger) to Resident, Calabar Province, 28 April 1927, NAE: CALPROF 5/1/156.
130. Resident, Calabar Province to Secretary, Southern Provinces, 20 December 1927, NAE: CALPROF 3/1/209.
131. Cross, S. 1972. The Watchtower, Witch-cleansing and Secret Societies in Africa. Paper presented to the Conference on the Religious History of Central Africa, Lusaka, 1972. cited in Ranger, 1986 p. 50.
132. DO Uyo to Clan Councils of Uyo Division, 9 February 1939, NAE: ABAKDIST 1/2/81.
133. Extract from Quarterly Intelligence Report, Calabar Province, March 1932, NAE: CALPROF 3/1/210.
134. DO Opobo Division to Resident, Calabar Province, n.d., NAE: CALPROF 3/1/210.
135. Report on Outbreak of lawlessness by Spirit-possessed, Itu District, (D. Itu-Enyong), 1927, NAE: CALPROF 3/1/209.
136. Resident, Calabar Province to Secretary, Southern Provinces, 20 December 1927, NAE: CALPROF 3/1/209.
137. Founded by Myrtle and Charles Fillmore in Kansas City in 1889, the Unity School of Christianity followed Christian Science teachings with an emphasis on divine healing. Myrtle believed she could heal by repetition of the phrase 'I am a child of God and therefore I do not inherit sickness'. Their official publication, *Unity Daily Word* began in 1924 (see Melton, 1996 pp. 637–8).
138. Peel, 1968 p. 63fn.
139. Shepherd Michael Ukpong Udo to The Apostolic Faith Mission, December 1928, WUL: Jeffreys Papers File: 263.
140. Edwin Winterborne to Michael Ukpong Udo, 16 February 1928, WUL: Jeffreys Papers File: 263.
141. Register for patients and the names of sickness (vol. 1), (M. U. Udo), 1927–1928, Jeffreys Papers File: 263.
142. Westgarth, 1946 p. 33.
143. The rough and gruesome drawings of snakes and fetters Westgarth saw in the teacher's exercise book led him to think they were Satanic. He burned them.
144. Westgarth, 1946 p. 34.
145. *QIM Quarterly*, November 1927, (135), D/3301/EA/12.
146. Westgarth, 1946 pp. 16–17.
147. Ibid. p. 45.
148. Abasiattai, 1989 p. 506; Anon. to DO Ikot Ekpene, c. January 1928, NAE: IKOTDIST 13/1/174.
149. DO Ikot Ekpene to Resident, Calabar, 20 January 1928, NAE: IKOTDIST 13/1/174.
150. WUL: Jeffreys Papers File 259.
151. The link between sources of healing powers and materials related to Europeans was evident in other contexts too. Pregnant women commonly rubbed mud from bicycle tracks on to their waists, and the rubber from burned bicycle tyre

tubes on to their infants to prevent and heal diseases in their children (Jeffreys, 1940 p. 379). A woman arrived at the Enen station in 1912, for instance, with her child in pain. It appeared that some months before Smith from the Qua Iboe Mission had been cycling through her village. Her child was ill and she had taken some of the sand from the track made by the tyres of his bicycle and put it on the child's body. The child got better and she attributed its recovery to the 'magical' power from the bicycle (*QIM Quarterly*, February 1912, (74), PRONI, D/3301/EA/6).

152. Anon to DO Ikot Ekpene, c. January 1928, NAE: IKOTDIST 13/1/174.

153. On this debate more generally see Ranger, 1986.

154. Fields, 1985 pp. 274–7.

155. Horton, 1971 p. 95.

156. Peel, 2002 p. 137.

157. Extract from Quarterly Intelligence Report, Calabar Province, March 1932, NAE: CALPROF 3/1/210.

158. Michael Ukpong Udo was sentenced to two years' imprisonment in 1932 nominally for trespass but in fact because the court members feared the Spirit Movement's charismatic leader. Two hundred women demanded his release and on review the DO quashed his sentence (ibid.).

159. See Abasiattai, 1989; Adams, 1947; Hau, 1961.

160. In 1927, aged fifteen, Akpan Akpan Udofia had a series of dreams while at Ididep Central School which led him to believe that he was intended to be a teacher for Seminant, the Spirit of God. Udofia joined the Spirit Movement and lived in isolation while he was instructed by Seminant (the Secret Teacher). For twenty years from the time he left school until 1948, Udofia was forbidden by his Secret Teacher to study the Efik Bible, any history book or to read, write or speak English. During his seclusion knowledge of the Oberi Okaime symbols, language and Holy Books appeared only to Udofia and the leader, Michael Ukpong Udo (Hau, 1961).

161. DO Uyo to Resident, Calabar Province, 15 December 1939, NAE: CALPROF 3/1/210.

162. Rev. J. T. Vaughan, The Apostolic Church, Ikot Abia Idem, Ikot Ekpene, to ADO Uyo, 26 April 1939, NAE: CALPROF 3/1/210.

163. DO Opobo to Resident Calabar, 2 April 1935, NAE: CSE 1/85/5348.

164. DO Opobo to The Rev. J. G. Campbell, Patriarch of Christ's Army Church, 4 February 1932, NAE: CALPROF 3/1/210.

165. DO Ikot Ekpene to Resident, Calabar, 12 January 1934, NAE: IKOTDIST 13/1/174.

166. Resident, Calabar to Secretary, Southern Provinces, 3 December 1927, NAE: CALPROF 5/17/611.

167. Ibid.

168. Report of the Commission of Inquiry appointed to inquire into the disturbances in the Calabar and Owerri Provinces, December 1929, 1930b, RH: 723.13.s.4/1930 See also Okonjo, 1974 pp. 184–90, and Ikime, 1966.

169. Notes by Resident, Ogoja in Notes on the History of Taxation affecting Eastern Province and more especially Calabar Province, (E. M. Falk), February 1933, RH: Mss Afr. S. 1000(1).

170. Noah, 1985 p. 28. Chief Okugo was convicted and imprisoned for two years on charges of spreading news likely to cause harm and assault.

171. Report of the Commission of Inquiry appointed to inquire into the disturbances in the Calabar and Owerri Provinces, December 1929, 1930b, RH: 723.13.s.4/1930.

172. Ibid.
173. Notes of Evidence taken in the Calabar and Owerri Provinces on the Disturbance, 1930, RH: 723.17.s.1.1929.
174. Ibid.
175. Ibid.
176. For a more detailed account of the Women's War see Afigbo, 1966; 1972; Gailey, 1970; Ifeka-Moller, 1975; Akpan and Ekpo, 1988; Dike, 1995.
177. Van Allen, 1976.
178. 'Report of the Commission of Inquiry appointed to inquire into certain incidents at Opobo, Abak, Utu Etim-Ekpo in December 1929', RH: Mss 723.13. s.4/1930. During the 'Dancing Movement' (*nwa obolia*) in Owerri, Onitsha and Ogoja provinces in 1925 women also demanded an end to prostitution, better medical services, improved fertility, safeguards for women traders and that wives should not be given to Christians (Report of the Commission of Inquiry appointed to inquire into the disturbances in the Calabar and Owerri Provinces, December 1929, 1930b, RH: 723.13.s.4/1930). See also Afigbo, 1966 pp. 549–50.
179. Udoma, 1987 p. 59.
180. Noah, 1988b.
181. The Message from the Ibibio Welfare Union, 18 December 1929 in ibid. pp. 227–9.
182. Ibid.
183. Noah, 1995 p. 110. Reverend Groves attended several meetings of the Ibibio Welfare Union from 3 August 1929 onwards.
184. Adapted from Report of the Commission of Inquiry appointed to inquire into the disturbances in the Calabar and Owerri Provinces, December 1929, 1930b, RH: 723.13.s.4/1930; Ifeka-Moller, 1975 p. 130.
185. McMahon, 1936 p. 24, cited in Noah, 1985 p. 29.
186. Journal of H. Falk, 11 December 1929, RH: Mss.Afr.S. 1000(1).
187. Notes of Evidence taken in the Calabar and Owerri Provinces on the Disturbance, 1930, RH: 723.17.s.1.1929.
188. ADO Abak to DO Ikot Ekpene, 22 August 1924, NAE: CALPROF c.582/22.
189. Afigbo, 1972 p. 190.
190. 'Annual Report, Abak Division', 1923, NAE: CALPROF 5/14/50.
191. Report on the Eastern Provinces by the Secretary for Native Affairs, (S. M. Grier), 1922, RH: 723.12.v.43 (12).
192. Though a subsequent review conducted in 1923 by G. J. F. Tomlinson was highly critical, Grier's reforms were supported by Governor Clifford.
193. Reform in Calabar Province was more rapid and extensive than elsewhere. In Ikot Ekpene Division Jeffreys and Ashley had facilitated the opening of clan courts for Ibiono, Ikpe, Ikono, Ika and Itam as early as 1924. And in Otoro clan, for example, consistent attempts were made between 1920 and 1927, 'to appoint as "warrant-chiefs" only village heads' (Dewhurst, 1935. 'The Otoro Group of the Otoro Clan, Abak District', NAE: CSE 1/85/6323).
194. Afigbo, 1972 p. 244.
195. *Daily Times*, 24 March 1930.
196. 'Report of the Commission of Inquiry appointed to inquire into certain incidents at Opobo, Abak, Utu Etim-Ekpo in December 1929', RH: Mss 723.13. s.4/1930.
197. Report of the Commission of Inquiry appointed to inquire into the disturbances in the Calabar and Owerri Provinces, December 1929, 1930b, RH:

723.13.s.4/1930. Falk and Ford, respectively the Resident and the Commissioner of Police marched to Ukam on 11 December where in meetings with the chiefs Falk noted that, 'it was clear that they had no control over the young men' (Journal of H. Falk, 11 December 1929, RH: Mss.Afr.S. 1000(1)).

198. Afigbo, 1972 p. 232.
199. Notes on the History of Taxation affecting Eastern Province and more especially Calabar Province, (E. M. Falk), February 1933, RH: Mss Afr. 1000(1).
200. Notes of Evidence taken in the Calabar and Owerri Provinces on the Disturbance, 1930, RH: 723.17.s.1.1929.
201. Women held up the local markets around Oron in May 1933 in a protest that was blamed on male middlemen (Resident, Calabar to Secretary, Southern Provinces, 12 June 1933, NAE: CALPROF 3/1/444).
202. Gailey, 1970 p. 130fn.
203. Journal of H. Falk, 20 December 1929, RH: Mss.Afr.S. 1000(1).
204. *QIM Quarterly*, February 1930, (144), PRONI, D/3301/EA/14.
205. Van Allen, 1972.
206. Van Allen argues that the women's injunction of 'sitting on a man' was the cultural blueprint for the entire process of the women's mobilisation. Ifeka-Moller, in contrast, suggests that while 'sitting on a man' was a common village-based method for women to protest, it did not explain the inter-village (and indeed inter-ethnic) character of the rebellion as a whole. *Ibáàn isòŋ*, however, is organised on such an inter-village basis (cf. Offiong, 1997 p. 430). On the cultural precursors to protest among Igbo women see Bastian, 2001 in which the consequences of senior women's control of young women is also illustrated.
207. Cited in Ekpo, 1995 p. 66.
208. This is contrary to those who have suggested that the women dressed in order to represent *ékpó* (Umoren, 1995 p. 69).
209. *Ibáàn isòŋ* also supervised the rites of widowhood (Talbot, 1914 p. 249). See also Ekpo, 1995 pp. 52–4.
210. 'Report of the Commission of Inquiry appointed to inquire into certain incidents at Opobo, Abak, Utu Etim-Ekpo in December 1929', RH: Mss 723.13.s.4/1930.
211. Ifeka-Moller, 1975 p. 135.
212. Akpan and Ekpo, 1988 pp. 56–7.
213. See also Umoren, 1995.
214. Harris, 1940 pp. 143–5 cited in Van Allen, 1972 p. 175.
215. The report of the Commission of Enquiry stated that no evidence was presented to show why some areas rose in the riots and others did not: 'We have not before us evidence to show why other parts had not disturbances. To enquire into that would have extended unduly the labours of this commission' (Report of the Commission of Inquiry appointed to inquire into the disturbances in the Calabar and Owerri Provinces, December 1929, 1930b, RH: 723.13.s.4/1930).
216. Ifeka-Moller, 1975 p. 137.
217. Ibid. p. 142.
218. Ardener, p. 900.
219. Jones, 1989a p. 96. At Umuahia the palm oil price (per 4 gallon tin) fell from 13s before the depression to 7s 4d in 1928, and 5s 11d in 1929 (Akpan and Ekpo, 1988 p. 13). See also Onwuteaka, 1965 p. 277.
220. Feast songs (*ikúɔ úsɔ́rɔ́*) in WUL: Jeffreys Papers File: 256.
221. Ibid.
222. WUL: Jeffreys Papers File 259.

223. WUL: Jeffreys Papers File: 256.

224. *QIM Quarterly*, August 1932, (158), PRONI, D/3301/EA/15.

225. Byfield's analysis of the effects of the extension of British rule in Egba at the turn of the century shows how young women began to challenge the authority of senior lineage members to regulate their marriages, and how mutual attraction, concern over physical well-being and economic interests all became factored into their marriage deliberations as a result (Byfield, 2001 p. 38).

226. Akpabot, 1975 p. 58; Abaraonye, 1997 p. 219.

227. Notes of Evidence taken in the Calabar and Owerri Provinces on the Disturbance, 1930, RH: 723.17.s.1.1929.

228. Martin, 1988 p. 117.

229. Naanen, 1993. Naanen's excellent analysis highlights the way in which the manilla exchange rate was a crucial factor behind the violent disturbances in Umuahia in 1925, across the region in 1929 and in Okigwi District in 1938. It is also possible to map this factor onto the analysis of the Spirit Movement. During 1927 the exchange rate dropped dramatically from 6 or 7 manillas for one shilling in 1927, to 12 and 13 manillas in 1928. Those exchanging shillings for manillas (chiefs and clerks) gained, while those exchanging manillas for shillings (women traders and court litigants) lost out. In part, this reflects those categories who became 'Spirits' (young men and women), and those who were targeted by the 'cleansing' movement (chiefs and society elders). For an overview of currency instability in south-eastern Nigeria over the past century see Ekejiuba, 1994.

230. Jones, 1958; Latham, 1971; Northrup, 1978 pp. 157–64.

231. Diary, J. W. Westgarth, 29 August 1914, PRONI: D/3301/CB/1.

232. Cited in Draft Report on Manilla Currency, 1946, NAE: OPODIST 1/1/2.

233. Adapted from Naanen, 1993 p. 431 (Table 1). Naanen cites the following sources in the compilation of the manilla exchange rate figures: Helleiner, 1966; Manillas, 1948–49, NAE: IKOTDIST 13/1/499.

234. Manilla Ordinance Cap 125 Vol. II L/N p. 1151 Lagos, 1923. This explains the static exchange rate recorded in Figure 3.4 when the palm oil price rocketed during the early 1920s.

235. United Africa Company, 1949 p. 46.

236. A 1922 proposal calculated that 350,000 manillas could be disposed of annually in this manner at a cost of £3,000 per annum in forgone court income ('Annual Report, Abak Division', 1922, NAE: CALPROF 5/13/110). On the Calabar market women's riot of 1925 see Akpan and Ekpo, 1988 pp. 18–20.

237. Land Tenure in Nigeria by M.D.W. Jeffreys, 1 October 1936, NAE: CSE 1/85/6334.

238. 'Annual Report, Abak Division', 1930, NAE: CALPROF 2/11/10.

239. Naanen, 1993 p. 431.

240. DO Special Duties to Assistant Treasurer, Calabar, 15 May 1933, NAE: IKOTDIST 13/1/482.

241. Byfield's account of the decline of women's *adire* cloth production in the Yoruba town of Abeokuta illustrates similar dynamics in the gendered impact of the depression in colonial Nigeria (Byfield, 1997; 2002).

242. Land Tenure in Nigeria by M. D. W. Jeffreys, 1 October 1936, NAE: CSE 1/85/6334. The extent to which Jeffreys' view was shared by his contemporaries is not clear. In the margin of the report next to the calculation someone had written 'what nonsense'.

CHAPTER 4

1. Crowder, 1985 p. 596.
2. Byfield, 1997 p. 99.
3. Roberts and Mann, 1991 p. 23.
4. Mamdani, 1996 p. 41.
5. Despite brief discussions in work by Perham, Nicolson and more recently Martin, the only assessment of the immediate post-1929 era, albeit on administrative reorganisation, is Noah, 1987; 1988a.
6. Manager, Nigerian Products to DO Abak, 23 February 1931, NAE: UYODIST 1/2/27.
7. PC Onwumere to DO Uyo, 18 January 1931, NAE: UYODIST 1/2/27.
8. WUL: Jeffreys Papers File: 258.
9. DO Opobo to Resident, Calabar, 27 July 1934, NAE: OPODIST 1/1/19.
10. DO Opobo to Resident, Calabar, 31 January 1934, NAE: OPODIST 1/1/19.
11. Journal of H. Falk, 20 December 1929, RH: Mss.Afr.S. 1000(1).
12. Minutes of a general meeting held at Ikot Ubo, Eket District, 7 December 1929,' Herbert Macaulay Papers, University of Ibadan: 30.7.5, cited in Harneit-Sievers, 2001.
13. Prince Eket Inyang Udo, interview with Resident, Calabar Province, 21 December 1929, Herbert Macaulay Papers, University of Ibadan: 30.7.5 cited in Ibid.
14. Report of the Commission of Inquiry appointed to inquire into the disturbances in the Calabar and Owerri Provinces, December 1929, 1930b, RH: 723.13.s.4/1930.
15. Ibid.
16. These schemes were also hampered by the difficulties of transferring money from the United States to Nigeria (Noah, 1987 p. 45).
17. 'Annual Report, Abak Division', 1930, NAE: CALPROF 2/11/10. This is the same Chief Udo Udong of Ikot Idiong who had been attacked by *èkpó* in 1917.
18. Investigation of the activities of Prince Peter Eket, 17 June 1940 (R. L. Bennerman, Special Agent), U.S. National Archives: RG 59 848/L0011/4, cited in Harneit-Sievers, 2001.
19. Notes of Evidence taken in the Calabar and Owerri Provinces on the Disturbance, 1930, RH: 723.17.s.1.1929.
20. Hopkins, 1966 p. 140; Crowder, 1968 pp. 469–70; Webster, 1985 pp. 585–7.
21. *Lagos Daily News*, 27 May 1931, cited in Hopkins, 1966 p. 145.
22. Assistant Commissioner of Police, Aba to Commissioner of Police, Owerri Province, 3 August 1932, NAE: RIVPROF 2/1/19.
23. Report of the Meeting in connection with the formal opening of the Nigerian Mercantile Bank, (E. Egejuru), 29 July 1932, NAE: RIVPROF 2/1/19.
24. Crowder, 1968 p. 470.
25. See Fields, 1982a; 1985 on the missionary radicalism of Watchtower movements in east-central Africa during the 1910s and 1920s.
26. File Note on Faith Tabernacle pamphlets, 6 January 1931, NAE: RIVPROF 2/1/19.
27. Resident, Owerri to Secretary, Southern Provinces, 11 June 1931, NAE: RIVPROF 2/1/19.
28. Inspector of Police, Aba to Assistant Commissioner of Police, Aba, 30 April 1931a, NAE: RIVPROF 2/1/19; Report of Mr SI Simon, Qualified Interpreter, Aba, 30 April 1931b, NAE: RIVPROF 2/1/19; Resident, Owerri to Secretary, Southern Provinces, 11 June 1931, NAE: RIVPROF 2/1/19.

29. Rutherford's texts included *Prosperity Sure* and *Light* published in 1928 and 1930 respectively by the International Bible Students Association in New York.

30. Resident, Owerri to Secretary, Southern Provinces, 11 June 1931, NAE: RIVPROF 2/1/19.

31. DO Itu to Resident, Calabar, 22 February 1933, NAE: ITUDIST 7/1/261.

32. DO Uyo to Resident, Calabar, 5 December 1933, NAE: IKOTDIST 13/1/174.

33. An Assistant District Officer returned to the site several weeks later after it had been abandoned. In a room at the back of the faith healer's house the A.D.O. found 'all the paraphernalia of the average native doctor, skulls, bundles of feathers, small wooden figures, eggs etc'. (DO Ikot Ekpene to Resident, Calabar, 14 June 1934, NAE: IKOTDIST 13/1/174).

34. DO Ikot Ekpene to Resident, Calabar, 1 February 1934, NAE: IKOTDIST 13/1/174, and DO Enyong to Commissioner of Police, Calabar, 5 April 1934, NAE: ITUDIST 7/1/497.

35. Enclosure, 27 May 1941a, NAE: ABADIST 14/1/798.

36. Secretary of the Synod, Diocese on the Niger to Captain Shepherd, 27 May 1941b, NAE: ABADIST 14/1/798.

37. WUL: Jeffreys Papers File 259

38. Sumner, 'Tours of Southern Nigeria', 1923–28, Mss.Afr.s.538.

39. Nigeria Medical Dept., 1929, Annual Medical and Sanitary Report, Govt. Printer: Lagos.

40. Ibid.

41. Report on Ikot Ekpene Provincial Court Case No.86/1932, 1932, NAE: CALPROF 2/13/142.

42. Bailie reported on the effects of a box of bad medicine (*idiók ibɔk*) in 1905: 'a fire flashes from it to consume his enemies, if a man is touched by it he instantly falls down dead, shake it at a crowd and immediately they are covered with loathsome sores, scatter it in a town and the women are rendered barren' (A. Bailie to McKeown, 17 April 1905, PRONI: D/3301/AD/5).

43. Report on Ikot Ekpene Provincial Court Criminal Case No.101/32 (Rex versus Akpan Udo Usoro and 21 others), 1932, NAE: CALPROF 2/13/155.

44. *QIM Quarterly*, May 1932, (153), PRONI, D/3301/EA/15.

45. Conference of District Officers, Calabar Province, 24–25 March 1932, NAE: CALPROF 5/9/341.

46. Wilder, 2000 p. 45.

47. Governor to Secretary of State for the Colonies, 17 August 1931, NAE: OPODIST 1/1/18.

48. Secretary, Southern Provinces to Resident, Calabar, 18 September 1931, NAE: CALPROF 3/1/224.

49. Minute by Flood, 19 December 1930, TNA: CO 583/176/9.

50. Secretary of State for the Colonies to Officer Administering the Government of Nigeria, 27 January 1931, TNA: CO 583/176/9.

51. Malinowski, 1929. Lucy Mair was appointed as a lecturer in Colonial Administration in Malinowski's department at the London School of Economics in 1933.

52. Minute by Tomlinson, 3 January 1931, TNA: CO 583/176/9.

53. Governor to Secretary of State for the Colonies, 17 August 1931, NAE: OPODIST 1/1/18.

54. James, 1973 p. 46.

55. Notes on the History of Taxation affecting Eastern Province and more especially Calabar Province, (E. M. Falk), February 1933, RH: Mss Afr S. 1000(1).

56. Resident, Calabar to DO Opobo, 12 February 1930, NAE: OPODIST 1/1/18.
57. Talbot, 1914; 1914; 1923; 1926.
58. Jeffreys, 1944; 1955.
59. C. S. Bennington, Supervisor of Qua Iboe Mission schools, Rev. R. W. Grove of the Primitive Methodists in Ikot Ekpene, and R. J. Taylor who was Principal of the Etinan Institute also attended Union meetings during this time.
60. Noah, 1988b p. 104.
61. Udoma, 1987.
62. Jeffreys, 1931; 1935.
63. Jones, 1974; Lackner, 1973; Tonkin, 1990.
64. James, 1973 p. 49. Mervyn Jeffreys retired from colonial service in 1945 and joined the University of Witwatersrand as Senior Lecturer in Social Anthropology. He died in 1975 (*The Star*, 15 May 1970 and 24 March 1975; Dictionary of South African Biography Vol. V., Human Sciences Research Council, Pretoria, 1987 cited at http://sunsite.witsac.za/jeffreys/).
65. Secretary, Southern Provinces to Resident, Calabar, 23 February 1932, NAE: CALPROF 5/1/185.
66. Secretary, Southern Provinces to Resident, Calabar, 2 October 1935, NAE: CALPROF 5/1/185.
67. Secretary, Southern Provinces to Resident, Calabar, 23 February 1932, NAE: CALPROF 5/1/185.
68. Ibid.
69. Resident, Calabar to DO Opobo, 12 February 1930, NAE: OPODIST 1/1/18.
70. Ibid.
71. Afigbo, 1972.
72. Cameron, 1933.
73. Perham, 1937 p. 251.
74. Resident, Calabar to Secretary, Southern Provinces, 20 June 1935, NAE: CALPROF 5/1/185.
75. Jones, 1956, Report on the Position, Status and Influence of Chiefs and Natural Rulers in the Eastern Region of Nigeria, Government Printer: Enugu p. 40.
76. Ibid.
77. Ibid. p. 41.
78. Resident's covering report on The Adiasim Tribe of Ikot Ekpene District, 1936, NAE: CALPROF 3/1/1750.
79. Harding, 1937. 'Certain Unorganised Groups of the Annang Tribe in the Abak District and the Opobo District', NAE: MILGOV 13/1/20.
80. Conference of District Officers, Calabar Province, 24–25 March 1932, NAE: CALPROF 5/9/341.
81. 'Annual Report, Calabar Province', 1932, NAE: CALPROF 5/18/213.
82. Jones, 1956, Report on the Position, Status and Influence of Chiefs and Natural Rulers in the Eastern Region of Nigeria, Government Printer: Enugu p. 40.
83. 'Annual Report, Abak Division', 1930, NAE: CALPROF 2/11/10.
84. Harding, 1937. 'Certain Unorganised Groups of the Annang Tribe in the Abak District and the Opobo District', NAE: MILGOV 13/1/20.
85. Chapman, 1932. 'Certain Unorganised Groups in the Utu-Etim Ekpo Native Court Area, Abak Division', NAE: MILGOV 13/1/21.
86. Groves, 1936 pp. 57–8.
87. WUL: Jeffreys Papers File: 258.
88. DO Ikot Ekpene, 'Notes on Osusu (Ibibio – Utibe)', 16 February 1928, NAE: IKOTDIST 1/4/131.

89. Falola, 1994 p. 170.
90. Harding, 1937. 'Certain Unorganised Groups of the Annang Tribe in the Abak District and the Opobo District', NAE: MILGOV 13/1/20.
91. Dorward, 1974 p. 465.
92. Chapman, 1932. 'Certain Unorganised Groups in the Utu-Etim Ekpo Native Court Area, Abak Division', NAE: MILGOV 13/1/21.
93. The Resident, Calabar to the Secretary, Southern Provinces, 10 June 1936, NAE: MINLOC 16/1/1329.
94. On age grades and tax collection, see Jeffreys, 1950 p. 163.
95. Chapman, 1932. 'Certain Unorganised Groups in the Utu-Etim Ekpo Native Court Area, Abak Division', NAE: MILGOV 13/1/21.
96. ADO, Ikot Ekpene to Resident, Calabar, 24 July 1933, NAE: CALPROF 3/1/707.
97. Johnson, 1933. 'Ukanafun Clan, Abak District', NAE: CSE 1/85/5214.
98. Extract from SP 12502, GHF Findlay, 1937, NAE: CSE 1/85/7523.
99. Resident, Calabar to Secretary, Southern Provinces, 10 June 1936, NAE: CALPROF 3/1/1301.
100. Abak Chiefs to Chief Commissioner, Enugu, 6 April 1936, NAE: MINLOC 16/1/1329.
101. Ibid.
102. Ibid.
103. Ibid.
104. Ibid.
105. The Resident, Calabar to the Secretary, Southern Provinces, 10 June 1936, NAE: MINLOC 16/1/1329.
106. Afaha Ikot Essien to DO Abak, 1 October 1953, NAE: ABAKDIST 1/2/22.
107. Harding, 1937. 'Certain Unorganised Groups of the Annang Tribe in the Abak District and the Opobo District', NAE: MILGOV 13/1/20.
108. Marshall, 1931. 'Ika Clan, Abak District', NAE: CSE 1/85/4718.
109. Report of the Touring Deputation of the Ibibio Union, July and August 1941, NAE: ABAKDIST 1/2/80.
110. Resident, Calabar to Secretary, Southern Provinces, 3 December 1927, NAE: CALPROF 5/17/611.
111. 'Annual Report, Calabar Province', 1939, NAE: MINLOC 17/1/43.
112. Ibid. The recorded number of civil cases in Abak fell from 11,839 in 1937 to 5,906 in 1939.
113. 'Annual Report, Abak Division', 1930, NAE: CALPROF 2/11/10.
114. Nigeria, 1953, Report of the Native Courts (Eastern Region) Commission of Inquiry, Lagos: Government Printer p. 12.
115. Report on the Eastern Provinces by the Secretary for Native Affairs, (S. M. Grier), 1922, RH: 723.12.v.43 (12). In 1934 Governor Cameron recommended that since the villages were the unit of future administration they should at least settle petty civil disputes along the lines of the 'village republics' discussed in his 'Tanganyika Memorandum' (Secretary, Southern Provinces to Resident, Calabar Province, 12 March 1934, NAE: CALPROF 3/1/505). Hence, the arbitral powers of village courts were acknowledged in Calabar Province, though they were not formally gazetted as they were in Owerri, Warri, Ogoja and Onitsha Provinces (Perham, 1937 p. 243).
116. 'Annual Report, Calabar Province', 1930, NAE: CSE 1/86/188. All of the Native Courts in Abak by 1946 belonged to category D which meant they held the most minimal level of powers and jurisdiction.
117. Ibid.

118. Marshall, 1932. 'Obong Village Group, Abak District', NAE: CSE 1/85/4905A.
119. Ibid.
120. Jones, 1970 pp. 320–1.
121. DO Abak to Resident, Calabar, 27 April 1939, NAE: ABAKDIST 1/2/21.
122. Ukpanah, 1965. Ukpanah went on to become the President of Western Annang Local Council until 1950.
123. Omo Odok and others to DO Abak, 19 March 1939, NAE: ABAKDIST 1/2/44.
124. Udoma, 1987, p. 352 (facing).
125. The meeting of Nkuku Ikpa Ison of seven tribes to DO Abak, 16 October 1948, NAE: ABAKDIST 1/2/9.
126. Assistant Commissioner of Police, Opobo to Senior Resident, Calabar, 22 July 1933, NAE: OPODIST 1/1/14.
127. DO, Opobo to Senior Resident, Calabar, 24 July 1933, NAE: OPODIST 1/1/14.
128. Abak Chiefs to Governor of Southern Provinces, 20 March 1931, NAE: UYODIST 1/1/32.
129. DO Abak to Resident, Calabar, 21 March 1931, NAE: UYODIST 1/1/32.
130. Ibid.
131. QIM Quarterly, November 1932, (155), PRONI, D/3301/EA/15.
132. QIM Quarterly, May 1939, (2), PRONI, D/3301/EA/18.
133. 'Annual Report, Abak Division', 1923, NAE: CALPROF 5/14/50.
134. Report of the Touring Deputation of the Ibibio Union, July and August 1941, NAE: ABAKDIST 1/2/80.
135. Minutes of meeting of the Ibibio Union held at Uyo, 5 December 1936, NAE: CALPROF 5/1/307.
136. Udoma, 1987 p. 72.
137. 'Annual Report, Calabar Province', 1932, NAE: CALPROF 5/18/213.
138. Ibibio Union to Senior Resident, Calabar Province, 9 January 1932, NAE: CALPROF 5/1/307.
139. Nwaka, 1983 p. 86.
140. Peel, 1983 p. 179.
141. Ibid.
142. Jeffreys, 1951. For further descriptions of èkóŋ theatre, see Scheinberg, 1977; Ebong Inih, 1990.
143. Ottenberg, 1972.
144. Messenger and Messenger, 1981.
145. Jeffreys, 1951 p. 46.
146. Channock, 1989 p. 77.
147. Channock, 1982 p. 57.
148. Extract from Annual Report on the Ikot Ekpene District, 31 December 1907, NAE: CALPROF 14/4/19.
149. Oron Native Council Law, 8 March 1909, NAE: CALPROF 14/4/19.
150. Provincial Commissioner to Colonial Secretary, 23 October 1915, NAE: CALPROF 13/6/103.
151. Minute by Governor, 26 April 1916, NAE: CALPROF 13/6/103.
152. Resident, Calabar to Secretary, Southern Provinces, 2 December 1924, NAE: CALPROF 5/11/777.
153. M.D.W. Jeffreys to F. N. Ashley, 27 December 1923, NAE: CALPROF 5/11/777.
154. Talbot, 1923 p. 204.

155. DO Ikot Ekpene to Resident, Calabar, 28 September 1926, NAE: CALPROF 5/16/191.
156. ADO Abak to Resident, Calabar, 20 July 1926, NAE: CALPROF 5/16/191.
157. DO Eket to Resident, Calabar, 4 August 1926, NAE: CALPROF 5/16/191.
158. For an excellent case study of these dynamics in south-western Nigerian, see Cornwall, 2003; 2005.
159. Chapman, 1932. 'Certain Unorganised Groups in the Utu-Etim Ekpo Native Court Area, Abak Division', NAE: MILGOV 13/1/21.
160. QIM Quarterly, May 1933, (157), PRONI, D/3301/EA/15.
161. QIM Quarterly, November 1915, (89), PRONI, D/3301/EA/7.
162. Jeffreys to Senior Resident, Calabar, 25 October 1933 cited in Jeffreys, 1956 p. 27.
163. QIM Quarterly, November 1919, (103), PRONI, D/3301/EA/9.
164. QIM Quarterly, May 1933, (157), PRONI, D/3301/EA/15.
165. QIM Quarterly, February 1908, (58), PRONI, D/3301/EA/4.
166. Resident Calabar to DO Abak, 16 May 1938, NAE: ABAKDIST 1/2/20.
167. W.E. Hunt Minute of 26th Session. League of Nations. p. 12 Geneva. 1934 cited in Land Tenure in Nigeria by M. D. W. Jeffreys, 1 October 1936, NAE: CSE 1/85/6334.
168. Chief Udo Obong Akpan et al., Abak Etenge to DO Abak Division, 19 August 1932, NAE: CALPROF 2/13/176.
169. Van Allen, 1972 p. 177.
170. DO Itu to Resident, Calabar, 23 May 1927, NAE: CALPROF 5/1/156.
171. 'Information called for under Para. 3 of His Excellency's Minute to the Report on the Eastern Provinces to the Secretary for Native Affairs' by M.D.W. Jeffreys, 1934, NAE: ABAKDIST 1/2/44.
172. Land Tenure in Nigeria by M.D.W. Jeffreys, 1 October 1936, NAE: CSE 1/85/6334.
173. Compare this to the Nuer case in which government chiefs and courts from the 1930s introduced the possibility of divorce that did not depend on the wife's kinsmen to cooperate in the return of bridewealth (Hutchinson, 1990 p. 401). Also see Roberts, 1999 on the ways in which matrimonial litigation was linked to domestic tension in French Soudan at the turn of the century.
174. Shadle, 2003.
175. Minute on the treatment of adultery in Native Courts, Acting DO Ahoada, 1937, NAE: AHODIST 14/1/396.
176. Frank Uko vs Aka Udofia, 31 March 1931, NAE: ABAKDIST 1/2/13.
177. Assistant Commissioner of Police to Inspector General of Police, 4 February 1935, NAE: OPODIST 1/1/39.
178. DO Opobo to Resident, Calabar, 20 June 1935, NAE: OPODIST 1/1/39.
179. Prostitutes and Undesirables, Opobo Township, 1937, NAE: OPODIST 1/1/53.
180. Few sources deal with post-1931 labour to Fernando Po but on the earlier period, see Sundiata, 1974; 1996; Lynn, 1984; Clarence-Smith, 1994.
181. Nigerian Eastern Mail, 30 March 1940.
182. DO Ikot Ekpene to Resident, Calabar, 28 April 1943, NAE: CALPROF 5/1/193.
183. Ibid.
184. Governor Nigeria to Governor Gold Coast, July 1941, NAE: IKOTDIST 13/1/461.
185. Ibid.
186. Ruel, 1969 p. 266.

187. Degema to The Resident, Owerri Province, 20 September 1945, NAE: PHDIST 7/1/74.
188. Channock, 1982 p. 62.
189. Minute on the treatment of adultery in Native Courts, Acting DO Ahoada, 1937, NAE: AHODIST 14/1/396.
190. Ibid.

CHAPTER 5

1. Obiechina, 1971; 1972.
2. On the influence of these 'paracolonial' networks, see Newell, 2001.
3. Lynn, 2000.
4. DO Aba to Resident, Owerri, 17 November 1938a, NAE: RIVPROF 2/1/48.
5. Report of a Public Meeting arranged by the Nigerian Youth Movement, Port Harcourt, (I. A. C. Willoughby), 17 November 1938b, NAE: RIVPROF 2/1/48.
6. Minutes of a meeting of a deputation of the Ibibio Union with the officer administering the Government of Nigeria (C. C. Wooly), 3 May 1940, NAE: ABAKDIST 1/2/80.
7. District Officer's Conference, Uyo, 10 August 1940, NAE: ABAKDIST 1/2/80.
8. Ibid.
9. 'Annual Report, Calabar Province', 1939, NAE: MINLOC 17/1/43.
10. *Nigerian Eastern Mail*, 15 December 1945.
11. *Nigerian Eastern Mail*, 30 December 1939.
12. Report on the Afaha People's Union by Mr H. R. Ross (ADO, Eket), 4 January 1944, NAE: CALPROF 3/1/2906.
13. Omu, 1978 p. 22.
14. Udoma, 1987 p. 352 (facing).
15. Omu, 1978, p. 264.
16. Annual Report, Calabar Province, (C. J. Mayne), 1946, RH: MSS Afr. S.1505.1.
17. Annual Report, Calabar Province, (C. J. Mayne), 1947, RH: MSS Afr. S.1505.2. Clinton was later awarded the OBE.
18. Jones, 1946. Unpublished MS. He took his sample from 101 prospective local government staff in Owerri Province. The Government prevented G. I. Jones from publishing his survey.
19. *Nigerian Eastern Mail*, 9 December 1944; 16 December 1944; 23 December 1944.
20. Olusanya, 1973; 1968; Crowder, 1985.
21. *Nigerian Eastern Mail*, 13 October 1945.
22. *Nigerian Eastern Mail*, 30 March 1946.
23. *Nigerian Eastern Mail*, 26 August 1939.
24. Returning to Nigeria by boat to set up his deal Peter Eket was again secretly watched by the Nigerian police. On this occasion suspicions were aroused because of his conversations on deck with Mary Shaw, a West Indian lawyer and known Communist agitator.
25. *The African Advertiser*, 16 October 16 (enclosed in RG 84 Lagos Consulate, Despatch No. 1, 31 October 1939) cited in Harneit-Sievers, 2001.
26. Minute, 20 February 1940, NAI CSO 26/36183/S.2.
27. *Nigerian Eastern Mail*, 12 January 1940.
28. Public Declaration by The Ibibio Farmers in support of the Farmers Committee of British West Africa, 11 May 1945, NAI, CSO 26/36148/S.167.

29. The Colonial Office refused the request in May 1941. In 1949 the Ibibio Farmer's Association became a licensed buying agent for the Palm Produce Marketing Board.
30. *Nigerian Eastern Mail*, 18 November 1944.
31. *Nigerian Eastern Mail*, 12 August 1944.
32. *Nigerian Eastern Mail*, 3 March 1945.
33. 'Political and Constitutional Future of Nigeria', Governor of Nigeria' Despatch to the Secretary of State for the Colonies, 6 December 1944.
34. *Nigerian Eastern Mail*, 24 March 1945.
35. *Nigerian Eastern Mail*, 18 January 1947.
36. *Nigerian Eastern Mail*, 8 September 1945.
37. *Nigerian Eastern Mail*, 30 March 1946.
38. Udo Unwa Edo, Udo Udo Udo Inyang Etuk and Akpan Imo to DO Abak, 23 April 1945, NAE: ABAKDIST 1/2/16.
39. Court Chief's Meeting, S. Ukanafun to DO Abak, 14 October 1946, NAE: ABAKDIST 1/2/16.
40. Peel, 1983 pp. 191–6.
41. Subjects of Instruction by a Deputation of the Ibibio Union to the clans of the six Ibibio Districts, March to April 1942, NAE: CALPROF 5/1/308.
42. *Nigerian Eastern Mail*, 20 October 1945.
43. *Nigerian Eastern Mail*, 9 October 1943.
44. Report of the Touring Deputation of the Ibibio Union, 1942, NAE: ABAKDIST 1/2/80.
45. Secretary, Calabar Provincial Union to Resident, Calabar, 14 October 1943, NAE: CALPROF 7/1/1246.
46. Secretary, Esop Ufon Obong to Chief Commissioner, Eastern Provinces, 9 September 1944, NAE: CALPROF 7/1/1320.
47. Ibibio Magazine Vol. 1 No. 2, June 1941, NAE: ABAKDIST 1/2/80.
48. Ibibio Magazine Vol. 1 No. 1, May 1941, NAE: ABAKDIST 1/2/80.
49. United Africa Company, 1949.
50. *Nigerian Eastern Mail*, 11 August 1945.
51. Community Committee, Ikot Ekpene to Resident, Calabar, 20 March 1944, NAE: IKOTDIST 13/1/482.
52. *Nigerian Eastern Mail*, 18 March 1944.
53. Naanen, 1993 p. 439.
54. *Nigerian Eastern Mail*, 30 March 1946.
55. Since 1942 a flat rate of 7 shillings had been levied instead of 5 shillings (the official rate). The extra 2 shillings was collected for educational development. As a result £7,000 had been raised for a secondary school at Ikot Aba Ibekwe in Egwanga District.
56. Aloba, 1954 p. 637.
57. *Nigerian Eastern Mail*, 2 February 1946.
58. DO Abak to Resident, Calabar Province, 6 March 1946, NAE: CALPROF 7/1/638.
59. I.U. Akpabio to F.R. Kay, 7 March 1946, NAE: CALPROF 7/1/638.
60. *Daily Comet*, 29 July 1946.
61. Ibid.
62. *Nigerian Eastern Mail*, 5 January 1946.
63. *Nigerian Eastern Mail*, 9 February 1946.
64. Resident's Inspection Notes, Uyo Division, August 1940, NAE: CALPROF 5/1/307.
65. *Nigerian Eastern Mail*, 8 September 1945.

66. *Nigerian Eastern Mail*, 12 January 1946.
67. *Nigerian Eastern Mail*, 24 July 1943.
68. Colonial attempts to stimulate palm production during the 1930s centred on the introduction of new seed technology and the formation of co-operative societies since plantations and mechanised processing were largely resisted. In 1933 C. F. Strickland's attempts to supplant the cocoa producers' co-operatives from the Western Provinces into the palm belt, however, failed roundly. With the government's inspections and insistence on record-keeping, farmers were reluctant to provide records of their incomes for fear that it would be used in tax assessments (Strickland, 1934, Report on the Introduction of Co-operative Societies in Nigeria, p. 17).
69. Martin, 1956 p. 19.
70. Cattle transported south to Umuahia doubled in number to 30,000 between 1939 and 1940, and rail transportation of palm oil to the north rose from 4,857 to 8,575 tons per annum between 1942 and 1944 (Martin, 1988 p. 123).
71. Agricultural Officer, Umuahia to Resident, Owerri, 14 May 1943, NAE: ABADIST 1/26/907. Cassava was originally eaten as *akpu* (a hungry season food) and only later as garri.
72. Ottenberg, 1959 p. 215.
73. Falola, 1992.
74. Secretary, Southern Provinces to Chief Secretary to the Government, 16 February 1938, NAE: OPODIST 1/1/56.
75. DO Opobo to Resident, Calabar, 13 October 1941, NAE: OPODIST 1/10/45.
76. DO Opobo to Resident, Calabar, 19 October 1941, NAE: OPODIST 1/10/45.
77. R. A. Stevens, 'Activities of Women in Ikot Ekpene Division', November and December 1944, NAE: CALPROF 7/1/1329. Only fragments of Stevens' report have survived in the National Archives in Enugu.
78. Ibid.
79. Ibid.
80. Sentences in all cases had been reduced by one third during the war.
81. R. A. Stevens, 'Activities of Women in Ikot Ekpene Division', November and December 1944, NAE: CALPROF 7/1/1329.
82. Ibid.
83. DO Abak to Resident, Calabar, 10 October 1941, NAE: CALPROF 3/1/1956.
84. Acting Resident, Calabar to Secretary, Eastern Provinces, 19 May 1942, NAE: CALPROF 3/1/1957.
85. Ibid.
86. Native Authority Ordinance (No. 43), 1933, NAE: CALPROF 3/1/1957.
87. President, Central Annang Council to Chief Commissioner, Eastern Provinces, 26 February 1942, NAE: CALPROF 3/1/1957.
88. Secretary, Eastern Provinces to Resident, Calabar Province, 5 November 1940, NAE: CSE 1/85/9284.
89. DO Abak to The Councils, Abak Division, 21 August 1940, NAE: CALPROF 3/1/1955.
90. Resident, Calabar to Secretary, Eastern Provinces, 23 October 1940, NAE: CALPROF 3/1/1955.
91. Mass Meeting of Idiong Society to Resident, Calabar, 15 April 1941, NAE: CALPROF 3/1/1955. Three of the twenty-five signatories to this petition are of particular note: Ukpong Eto from Ediene (because of the later allegations concerning the Chima case), Akpan Udo Umana (who was the leading *idiɔŋ*

in the Ukanafun village of Ikot Akpa Nkuk and who was said to have prepared medicine to release man-leopard suspects), and Udo Ekpo Udom (from Ikot Edem Ewa village in Adat Ifang clan who was the uncle of my present day *idi̇̀ŋ* informant).

92. Ibid.

93. DO Itu to Resident, Calabar, 27 June 1941, NAE: CALPROF 3/1/1955.

94. Resident, Calabar to Secretary, Eastern Provinces, 23 October 1940, NAE: CALPROF 3/1/1955.

95. Secretary, Eastern Provinces to Resident, Calabar Province, 5 November 1940, NAE: CSE 1/85/9284.

96. DO Abak to Resident, Calabar Province, 5 May 1941, NAE: CALPROF 3/1/1955.

97. DO Ikot Ekpene to Resident, Calabar, 8 July 1941, NAE: CALPROF 3/1/1955.

98. *Nigerian Eastern Mail*, 28 October 1939. On burglary gangs in Lagos and Abeokuta during the late 1930s see Tamuno, 1970 pp. 190–1.

99. Resident, Calabar, to Secretary, Eastern Provinces, 14 March 1944, NAE: CALPROF 5/1/156.

100. *Nigerian Eastern Mail*, 6 November 1943.

101. *Nigerian Eastern Mail*, 4 September 1943.

102. *Nigerian Eastern Mail*, 15 July 1944.

103. J.W. Westgarth, Qua Iboe Mission to Senior Resident, Calabar Province, 13 January 1943, NAE: CALPROF 5/1/156.

104. The United Leaders' Meeting, Ikot Akpan Afaha to The Resident, Calabar Province, 16 December 1944, NAE: CALPROF 5/1/156.

105. Annual Report, Calabar Province, (C. J. Mayne), 1947, RH: MSS Afr. S.1505.2.

106. *Nigerian Eastern Mail*, 18 November 1944.

107. On 'cowboy' gangs in Dar Es Salaam see Burton, 2001 and La Hausse, 1990 on Durban.

108. *Nigerian Eastern Mail*, 18 January 1947.

109. *Nigerian Eastern Mail*, 12 January 1940.

110. *Nigerian Eastern Mail*, 12 January 1946.

111. *Nigerian Eastern Mail*, 19 August 1944.

112. *QIM Quarterly*, May 1936, (168), PRONI, D/3301/EA/17.

113. *QIM Quarterly*, May 1937, (173), PRONI, D/3301/EA/17.

114. *QIM Quarterly*, May 1938, (177), PRONI, D/3301/EA/18.

115. *QIM Quarterly*, May 1942, (14), PRONI, D/3301/EA/21.

116. *QIM Quarterly*, May 1939, (2), PRONI, D/3301/EA/18.

117. *QIM Quarterly*, May 1945, (26), PRONI, D/3301/EA/21.

118. *QIM Quarterly*, May 1944, (22), PRONI, D/3301/EA/21.

119. *QIM Quarterly*, May 1942, (14), PRONI, D/3301/EA/21.

120. *Nigerian Eastern Mail*, 5 January 1946.

121. *Nigerian Eastern Mail*, 10 January 1946.

122. F. R. Kay, Personal Papers, 3 June 1946, NAE: CALPROF 5/1/25.

123. *Nigerian Eastern Mail*, 24 July 1943; 4 August 1943.

124. Compulsory labour continued during this period with unskilled labourers having to work a maximum of sixty days during 1934 (DO Opobo to Resident, Calabar, 13 July 1933, NAE: OPODIST 1/1/38).

125. *Nigerian Eastern Mail*, 24 July 1943.

126. *Nigerian Eastern Mail*, 22 July 1944.

127. Anderson, 1999 p. xi.

128. *Nigerian Eastern Mail*, 18 December 1943. In June 1946 an informant from Ikot Akpa Obong Efim waterside alleged that the leopard murders had started in 1940 by Etuk Udo Ekpo Akarassi and his friend Akpan Nyoho, and that the rampancy of the subsequent murders was a result of Akarassi's acquittal in this case (Report of Enquiry re. missing part of Murdered Persons by Ekpe Owo Men, 6 June 1946, NAE: ABAKDIST 1/2/90).

129. The Leopard Men, n.d., PRONI: D/3301/GC/9/3.

130. *Nigerian Eastern Mail*, 29 January 1944.

131. *Nigerian Eastern Mail*, 22 September 1945.

132. *Nigerian Eastern Mail*, 15 September 1945.

133. *Nigerian Eastern Mail*, 16 February 1946.

134. *Nigerian Eastern Mail*, 17 November 1945.

135. *Nigerian Eastern Mail*, 1 December 1945.

136. *Nigerian Eastern Mail*, 16 March 1946.

137. In February 1946 these 'Wayo' tricksters were reported for a scam in which they posed as agents of a 'New York Currency Note Firm' and sold a small box containing black blank paper. When a liquid was applied it turned into a currency note. The box was sold for £195 on the promise that it would produce an unlimited amount of money (*Nigerian Eastern Mail*, 9 February 1946).

138. DO Abak to Resident, Calabar, 31 March 1945, NAE: CALPROF 17/1/1594.

139. DO Abak to Resident, Calabar, 19 July 1945, NAE: CALPROF 17/1/1594.

140. Ibid.

141. *Nigerian Eastern Mail*, 3 November 1945. Akpan Udo Adiaha of Ikot Odoro in Opobo Division was arrested for the murder of Etok Ebere on eye-witness evidence but was acquitted in May 1946.

142. Willie was a member of the Qua Iboe Mission. His father had entered *inám* and was said to have ordered *èkóŋ* to kill his son because of his conversion. On 30 November 1945 Akpan Iwok made a statement about the quadruple murder in Ikot Afanga. Within four hours Akpan Iwok himself was murdered. Sunday Iwok and Peter Okure were later convicted for his murder.

143. Rex Versus Akpan Etuk Usoro, Udo Udo Ebok, Eka Ibok Akpan Obot and John Ukwa, 22 November 1945, NAE: CALPROF 7/1/1420. Though his alleged accomplices were discharged and he retracted his confession in court Akpan Unwa Etuk Usoro was found guilty of murder in April 1946 and was sentenced to death. The motive for the murder remained unclear.

144. DO Opobo to Supt. Police, Calabar, 24 December 1945, NAE: ABAKDIST 1/3/2.

145. Ibid.

146. DO Abak to Resident, Calabar Province, 17 January 1946, NAE: CALPROF 17/1/1596.

147. Ibid.

148. Ibid.

149. Extract from His Honour the Chief Commissioner's Inspection Notes, Calabar Province, 5 February 1946, NAE: ABAKDIST 1/3/2.

150. The informant, Francis Egbeuonu, volunteered to join the *àfé ékényòŋ* to obtain evidence of the next murder but DO Kay refused and removed him to Calabar for fear that his life was in danger (DO Abak to Resident, Calabar, 11 July 1946, NAE: CALPROF 17/1/1598).

151. *Nigerian Eastern Mail*, 11 May 1946.

152. Ufere Akpaidem, Ikot Akpankuk, to DO Abak,, 15 July 1945, NAE: ABAKDIST 1/2/16.

153. DO Abak to Resident, Calabar Province, 13 March 1946, NAE: CALPROF 17/1/1596.
154. Ibid.
155. DO Abak to Resident, Calabar Province, 17 January 1946, NAE: CALPROF 17/1/1596.
156. Comments on Notes of Mr D.C. Neillands on the Leopard men by F. R. Kay, 21 May 1946, NAE: CALPROF 17/1/1595.
157. Telegram: Resident Calabar to Secretary Enugu, 31 December 1945, NAE: CALPROF 17/1/1594.

CHAPTER 6

1. RH: Ms Afr. S. 1063.
2. Where Cohn traces the development of forensic techniques, fingerprinting, photography and anthropometric criteria in India to 1835, it is interesting to note that there is no record of such investigative modalities being employed in the Nigerian leopard murder enquiries which depended primarily on informants and confessions (Cohn, 1996 pp. 10–11).
3. On the history of the Nigeria Police Force see Tamuno, 1970; Clayton, 1985 and Shirley, 1950.
4. DO Opobo to Supt. Police, Calabar, 24 December 1945, NAE: ABAKDIST 1/3/2.
5. Ibid.
6. DO Opobo to Resident, Calabar Province, 24 December 1945, NAE: CALPROF 17/1/1594.
7. DO Abak to Resident, Calabar Province, 17 January 1946, NAE: CALPROF 17/1/1596.
8. General Report on the activities of the Police on Special Duty in the Abak and Opobo divisions – December 1945 to May 1946 (SASP Police Abak/Opobo), 27 May 1946, NAE: CALPROF 13/1/8.
9. RH: Ms Afr. S. 1063.
10. DO Abak to Resident, Calabar Province, 17 January 1946, NAE: CALPROF 17/1/1596.
11. RH: Ms Afr. S. 1063.
12. Ken Barnes, personal communication.
13. *Rex* versus *Udo Ekpo* in the Supreme Court of the Calabar Judicial Division holden at Opobo before His Honour Noel Pollard, 4 September 1947, NAE: OPODIST 1/1/8.
14. Ibid.
15. Nworie Iwo Enang to DO Abak, 8 March 1946, NAE: ABAKDIST 1/2/16.
16. DO Abak to Resident, Calabar Province, 17 January 1946, NAE: CALPROF 17/1/1596.
17. Ibid.
18. Ibid.
19. Ibhawoh, 2002 p. 66.
20. DO Abak to Resident, Calabar Province, 17 January 1946, NAE: CALPROF 17/1/1596.
21. Idem Isawere, Udo Akpan Ibanga, Udo Udo Onose and Akpan Akpan Aboho to Resident Calabar, 13 July 1946, NAE: CALPROF 17/1/1596.
22. Ibhawoh, 2002.
23. Extract from His Honour the Chief Commissioner's Inspection Notes, Calabar Province, 5 February 1946, NAE: ABAKDIST 1/3/2.
24. *Nigerian Eastern Mail*, 16 February 1946.

25. *Nigerian Eastern Mail*, 10 August 1946.
26. *Nigerian Eastern Mail*, 8 December 1945.
27. *Nigerian Eastern Mail*, 9 February 1946.
28. Ibid.
29. *Nigerian Eastern Mail*, 23 February 1946.
30. *Nigerian Eastern Mail*, 9 February 1946.
31. *Nigerian Eastern Mail*, 19 February 1946.
32. *Nigerian Eastern Mail*, 16 February 1946.
33. Asst. Supt. Police, Abak to Supt. Police, Calabar, January 1946, NAE: ABAKDIST 1/3/2.
34. Two Articles, with photographs, on Leopard Society murders, E. Nigeria, (M. T. Williams), 1947, RH: MSS. Afr. 1063.
35. Clayton, 1985.
36. DO Abak to Resident, Calabar Province, 17 January 1946, NAE: CALPROF 17/1/1596.
37. Jeffreys, 1931.
38. D. S. Fountain to Superintendent of Police, Calabar, 19 August 1946, NAE: CALPROF 17/1/1598.
39. D. S. Fountain to Superintendent of Police, Calabar, 12 September 1946, NAE: CALPROF 17/1/1598.
40. DO Abak to Resident, Calabar Province, 17 January 1946, NAE: ABAKDIST 1/3/1.
41. Tim Coulson (Department of Zoology, University of Cambridge), personal communication.
42. Report of Enquiry re. missing part of Murdered Persons by Ekpe Owo Men, 6 June 1946, NAE: ABAKDIST 1/2/90.
43. R. S. Mallinson, 'Annual Report, Obubra Division', 1939, NAE: OBUDIST 11/1/58. Kay's successor in Obubra Division, however, noted his tendency to exaggerate the extent of the head-hunting murders (DO Abakaliki to DO Obubra, 1 March 1941, NAE: CALPROF 2/1/1995).
44. DO Abak to Resident, Calabar Province, 17 January 1946, NAE: CALPROF 17/1/1596.
45. Nwaka, 1986 p. 428.
46. Okon, 1982 p. 68.
47. *Nigerian Eastern Mail*, 4 May 1946.
48. *Nigerian Eastern Mail*, 18 May 1946.
49. D.S. Fountain to Superintendent of Police, Calabar, 12 August 1946, NAE: CALPROF 17/1/1598.
50. D.S. Fountain to Superintendent of Police, Calabar, 27 July 1946, NAE: CALPROF 17/1/1598.
51. Beatty, 1915.
52. D.S. Fountain to Superintendent of Police, Calabar, 28 August 1946, NAE: CALPROF 17/1/1598.
53. Kaufman, 1972 p. 230.
54. DO Abak to Resident, Calabar, 19 July 1945, NAE: CALPROF 17/1/1594.
55. General Report on the activities of the Police on Special Duty in the Abak and Opobo divisions – December 1945 to May 1946 (SASP Police Abak/Opobo), 27 May 1946, NAE: CALPROF 13/1/8.
56. DO Opobo to Resident, Calabar Province, 16 January 1946, NAE: CALPROF 17/1/1594.
57. D.S. Fountain to Superintendent of Police, Calabar, 12 September 1946, NAE: CALPROF 17/1/1598.

58. Kay was invalided in June 1946. In January 1947 he was transferred to Mamfe in Cameroons Province and on 22 May 1951 he died as Resident of Bamenda Province. Governor Macpherson said his passing was a 'grievous loss to the Eastern Region and to Nigeria'.

59. The Leopard Society of Southern Annang, (P. P. Grey), 26 May 1946, NAE: ABAKDIST 1/2/90.

60. D. S. Fountain to Superintendent of Police, Calabar, 21 September 1946, NAE: CALPROF 17/1/1598

61. Geschiere, 1997 p. 22.

62. D. S. Fountain believed Akpan Anyoho was responsible for four murders in addition to the one for which he was convicted (Annual Report, Calabar Province, (C. J. Mayne), 1946, RH: MSS Afr.S.1505.1).

63. Statement of Ibesit Native Court Members, 23 January 1946, NAE: CALPROF 17/1/1596.

64. In this context Echiet described the *èkpê mfòró* medicine as enabling its user to disappear and to change form without any reference to leopards.

65. *Nigerian Eastern Mail*, 23 March 1946.

66. Nicklin, 1973 pp. 185–6.

67. The same system is echoed in contemporary formulae employed in the ritual sacrifice required for the production of 'quick money' which the *idìɔŋ* also directs. A skull is buried beneath a table at the shrine *isó èkpó*. Here the name of the person to be 'sacrificed' and the date upon which the attack is to happen is written down and placed inside a box. On the appointed day the sacrificial victim begins to vomit blood before dying and a vast sum of money appears on the shrine's table (see also Smith, 2001 p. 818).

68. D.S. Fountain to Superintendent of Police, Calabar, 21 September 1946, NAE: CALPROF 17/1/1598.

69. General Report on the activities of the Police on Special Duty in the Abak and Opobo divisions – December 1945 to May 1946 (SASP Police Abak/Opobo), 27 May 1946, NAE: CALPROF 13/1/8.

70. *Nigerian Eastern Mail*, 4 May 1946.

71. Ibid.

72. Extract from the Chief Commissioner's Inspection Notes, Calabar Province, 9–15 April 1946, NAE: CSE 1/85/9284.

73. The Leopard Society of Southern Annang, (P. P. Grey), 26 May 1946, NAE: ABAKDIST 1/2/90.

74. Ibid.

75. Written reply for PQ1/2 Dr Segal, Labour, Preston, 2 February 1948, TNA: CO 583/294/4.

76. The Leopard Society of Southern Annang, (P. P. Grey), 26 May 1946, NAE: ABAKDIST 1/2/90.

77. D. S. Fountain to Resident, Calabar Province, 4 January 1947, NAE: CALPROF 13/1/8.

78. The Man Leopard Murders of Calabar, n.d., RH: Mss.Afr.s.1784 (18).

79. D. C. Neillands, 'Notes on the Leopard Society', 13 May 1946, NAE: CALPROF 17/1/1595.

80. The Leopard Society of Southern Annang, (P. P. Grey), 26 May 1946, NAE: ABAKDIST 1/2/90.

81. Cohen, 1972; Goode and Ben-Yehuda, 1994; Thompson, 1998.

82. Douglas, 1992.

83. Guyer, 1986.

84. D. S. Fountain to Superintendent of Police, Calabar, 6 September 1946, NAE:

CALPROF 17/1/1598.

85. D.S. Fountain to Superintendent of Police, Calabar, 21 September 1946, NAE: CALPROF 17/1/1598.
86. Ibid.
87. The Leopard Society of Southern Annang, (P. P. Grey), 26 May 1946, NAE: ABAKDIST 1/2/90.
88. DO Abak to Resident Calabar, 7 October 1946, NAE: CALPROF 17/1/1598.
89. DO Abak to Resident, Calabar Province, 17 January 1946, NAE: ABAKDIST 1/3/1.
90. Comments on Notes of Mr D. C. Neillands on the Leopard men by F. R. Kay, 21 May 1946, NAE: CALPROF 17/1/1595.
91. Williams, August 1947. Unpublished MS. RH: Mss Afr. 1063.
92. Messenger, 1959 p. 72.
93. Ibid. p. 69.
94. SASP, Ediene Atai to Commissioner, CID, Lagos, 19 May 1947, NAE: ABAKDIST 1/2/88.
95. DO Abak to Resident, Calabar Province, 13 March 1946, NAE: CALPROF 17/1/1596.
96. Nigeria, 1953, Report of the Native Courts (Eastern Region) Commission of Inquiry, Lagos: Government Printer p. 31.
97. Channock, 1989.
98. Roberts and Mann, 1991 p. 9.
99. Nigeria, 1953, Report of the Native Courts (Eastern Region) Commission of Inquiry, Lagos: Government Printer p. 35.
100. Martin, 1988 p. 78.
101. Parry and Bloch, 1989.
102. Nigeria, 1953, Report of the Native Courts (Eastern Region) Commission of Inquiry, Lagos: Government Printer p. 51.
103. Byfield, 1997 p. 87.
104. Kay, 1947. Thesis on some aspects of the impact of English law on custom relating to matrimonial cases in Calabar Province, cited in Nigeria, 1953, Report of the Native Courts (Eastern Region) Commission of Enquiry, Lagos: Government Printer, p. 41.
105. SASP, Leopard Campaign to Commissioner, CID, Lagos, 21 July 1947, NAE: CALPROF 17/1/1599.
106. Hutchinson, 1990.
107. Byfield, 1997 p. 87.
108. *Nigerian Eastern Mail*, 23 March 1946.
109. Uko Obot to DO Abak, 17 August 1947, NAE: ABAKDIST 1/2/9.
110. Ibibio Union to Resident, Calabar, 26 November 1946, NAE: CALPROF 3/1/1928.
111. Adiaha Etim to Resident, Calabar Province, 19 September 1947, NAE: ABAKDIST 1/2/25.
112. D. S. Fountain to Superintendent of Police, Calabar, 23 July 1946, NAE: CALPROF 17/1/1598.
113. D. S. Fountain to Superintendent of Police, Calabar, 27 July 1946, NAE: CALPROF 17/1/1598.
114. Kay, 1947. Thesis on some aspects of the impact of English law on custom relating to matrimonial cases in Calabar Province, cited in Nigeria, 1953, Report of the Native Courts (Eastern Region) Commission of Enquiry, Lagos: Government Printer, p. 43.
115. Ibid., p. 41.

116. Hunt, 1991 p. 471.
117. Cf. Hutchinson, 1990 p. 407.
118. Akpan Akpan Ekong to DO Abak, 27 June 1949, NAE: ABAKDIST 1/2/9.
119. Akpan Essiet to DO Abak, 24 July 1940, NAE: ABAKDIST 1/2/20.
120. Udo Akpan Udo Oso and Nwa Inyan Ada to Chief Commissioner, E. Provinces, 18 July 1939, NAE: ABAKDIST 1/2/20.
121. Adiaha Etim to Resident, Calabar Province, 19 September 1947, NAE: ABAKDIST 1/2/25.
122. Messenger, 1962 p. 298.
123. Chief Akpan Umo Itiat to DO Abak, 20 April 1946, NAE: ABAKDIST 1/2/19.
124. Report of the Touring Deputation of the Ibibio Union, July and August 1941, NAE: ABAKDIST 1/2/80.
125. Ibid.
126. *Nigerian Eastern Mail*, 26 January 1946.
127. *Nigerian Eastern Mail*, 2 March 1946.
128. *Nigerian Eastern Mail*, 18 May 1946.
129. *Nigerian Eastern Mail*, 4 May 1946.
130. *Nigerian Eastern Mail*, 6 April 1946.
131. Achan Ika Civil Case 279/45 as reported in *Nigerian Eastern Mail*, 17 August 1946.
132. Ibid. Unwah resigned from his post in September 1946 to take up a position with the Assemblies of God Mission in Ikot Ekpene.
133. *Nigerian Eastern Mail*, 20 July 1946.
134. *Nigerian Eastern Mail*, 31 August 1946.
135. Ibibio Union to District Officers, Abak and Opobo, 18 February 1947, NAE: CALPROF 17/1/1595.
136. Byfield, 1997 p. 88.
137. 'Annual Report, Abak Division', 1923, NAE: CALPROF 5/14/50.
138. ADO to DO Ikot Ekpene, 3 March 1923, NAE: IKOTDIST 1/4/131.
139. Unwafia Akpan to DO Abak, 6 December 1941, NAE: ABAKDIST 1/2/19.
140. Population density of the Ukanafun Clan was estimated at 536 per m² in the 1932/33 census (Johnson, 1933. 'Ukanafun Clan, Abak District', NAE: CSE 1/85/5214).
141. Messenger, 1957 p. 212.
142. *Akpan Archibong* v. *Udokrok Udo Ukpong*, April 1943, NAE: ABAKDIST 1/2/13.
143. D. S. Fountain to Superintendent of Police, Calabar, 8 August 1946, NAE: CALPROF 17/1/1598; D. S. Fountain to Superintendent of Police, Calabar, 12 August 1946, NAE: CALPROF 17/1/1598; D. S. Fountain to Superintendent of Police, Calabar, 19 August 1946, NAE: CALPROF 17/1/1598.
144. *Rex* v. *Akpan Adiaha Ekpo*, 4 September 1947, NAE: OPODIST 1/10/8.
145. Marshall, 1931. 'Ika Clan, Abak District', NAE: CSE 1/85/4718.
146. Afigbo, 1972 p. 266.
147. Dewhurst, 1935. 'The Otoro Group of the Otoro Clan, Abak District', NAE: CSE 1/85/6323.
148. Resident, Calabar Province to Secretary, Eastern Provinces, 28 October 1942, NAE: CALPROF 3/1/1958.
149. 'Annual Report, Calabar Province', 1939, NAE: MINLOC 17/1/43.
150. *Nigerian Eastern Mail*, 21 July 1945.
151. Resident, Calabar to Divisional Officers, 24 November 1920, NAE: CALPROF 3/1/1879.

152. DO Ikot Ekpene to Senior Resident, Calabar, 27 July 1937, NAE: CALPROF 3/1/1879.

153. Ibid.

154. Senior Resident, Calabar, to Secretary, Southern Provinces, 6 August 1937, NAE: CALPROF 3/1/1879.

155. Nigeria, 1953, Report of the Native Courts (Eastern Region) Commission of Inquiry, Lagos: Government Printer p. 51.

156. Marshall, 1932. 'Obong Village Group, Abak District', NAE: CSE 1/85/4905A.

157. Etuk Udo Inana, Qua Iboe Mission, Ikot Ese to DO Abak, 8 October 1949, NAE: ABAKDIST 1/2/11.

158. DO Abak to Afaha Obo Ata Esien (Court members), 2 December 1937, NAE: ABAKDIST 1/2/20.

159. Giving evidence on juju oath before the Native Court, 1947, RH: MSS Afr. S. 1900.

160. Nigerian Eastern Mail, 10 November 1945.

161. Chief Commissioner's Inspection Notes – Calabar Province, 21 April 1946, NAE: CALPROF 3/1/1879.

162. Okon, 1982 p. 186.

163. Clayton, 1985.

164. Nigerian Eastern Mail, 9 March 1946.

165. Annual Report, Calabar Province, (C. J. Mayne), 1946, RH: MSS Afr. S.1505.1.

166. Nigerian Eastern Mail, 16 March 1946.

167. The Ex-Servicemen Ordinance 1945 (No.48) required Government departments and private firms to register.

168. Annual Report, Calabar Province, (C. J. Mayne), 1947, RH: MSS Afr. S.1505.2.

169. Nigerian Eastern Mail, 30 March 1946.

170. Nigerian Eastern Mail, 23 November 1946.

171. Nigerian Eastern Mail, 8 June 1946; Nigerian Eastern Mail, 22 June 1946.

172. Nigerian Eastern Mail, 27 April 1946.

173. Parry and Bloch, 1989 p. 26.

174. E. Offiong, 'Manilla as used in the eastern provinces', RH: Mss.Afr.s.1556/7(b). These observations refute the claim that brideprice repayments were being paid in sterling during the 1940s (Offiong, 1989 p. 68).

175. Grey, 1951 p. 63.

176. Nigerian Eastern Mail, 11 May 1946.

177. Draft Report on Manilla Currency, 1946, NAE: OPODIST 1/1/2.

178. Ibid.

179. By early 1948 the increase in the production of palm produce and the award of cost of living allowances to civil servants meant that the exchange rate in Opobo had shifted sharply with the manilla appreciating from 12 to 4 to the shilling (Nigerian Eastern Mail, 31 January 1947; 24 May 1947). Speculation that the manilla was to be redeemed only served to sustain its appreciation against the shilling. When the redemption started on 1 October 1948 the most common òkpòhò manilla was exchanged at four to the shilling (Nigerian Eastern Mail, 11 September 1948). By 1949 the manilla redemption exercise had removed 23,175,890 manillas valued at £289,562:13 (Annual Report, Calabar Province, (C. J. Mayne), 1949, RH: MSS Afr.S.1505.4).

CHAPTER 7

1. *Nigerian Eastern Mail*, 26 April 1946.
2. *Nigerian Eastern Mail*, 25 January 1947; 19 April 1947.
3. *Nigerian Eastern Mail*, 8 March 1947; 22 March 1947; *Eastern Nigerian Guardian*, 2 April 1947.
4. *Eastern Nigerian Guardian*, 2 April 1947.
5. New Leg Co Hon Nyong Essien's (representative for Ibibio Division) address to the Legislative Council 20 March 1947.
6. D. S. Fountain, 'A Report on the Leopard Society Murders', July 1951, RH: Mss.Afr.s.1784 (18).
7. Ibid.
8. D. S. Fountain to Commissioner C.I.D., Lagos, 20 January 1947, NAE: CALPROF 17/1/1598.
9. Sunday Udo Ekpo, who was the prime suspect, had written that 'Chief Ukpong had killed him [his father] ... he paid £30 to the police Sergeant at Abak to bear false witness to my father and also paid £10 to police constable Joseph to change all the statements made by our father. The statements made in the court the day of the trials baffled everyone of us ... ' (ibid.).
10. Ibid.
11. D. S. Fountain, 'A Report on the Leopard Society Murders', July 1951, RH: Mss.Afr.s.1784 (18).
12. Ibid.
13. D. S. Fountain to Commissioner C.I.D., Lagos, 20 January 1947, NAE: CALPROF 17/1/1598.
14. M. T. Williams to Commissioner C.I.D., Lagos, 29 January 1947, NAE: CALPROF 17/1/1598.
15. D. S. Fountain to Commissioner C.I.D., Lagos, 20 January 1947, NAE: CALPROF 17/1/1598.
16. D. S. Fountain to Superintendent of Police, Calabar, 8 August 1946, NAE: CALPROF 17/1/1598; D.S. Fountain to Superintendent of Police, Calabar, 12 August 1946, NAE: CALPROF 17/1/1598; D.S. Fountain to Superintendent of Police, Calabar, 19 August 1946, NAE: CALPROF 17/1/1598.
17. DO Opobo to Resident, Calabar, 17 July 1947, NAE: OPODIST 1/1/47.
18. No material evidence was found to support this claim (M. T. Williams to Commissioner C.I.D., Lagos, 29 January 1947, NAE: CALPROF 17/1/1598).
19. Annual Report, Calabar Province, (C. J. Mayne), 1947, RH: MSS Afr. S.1505.2.
20. Officer Administering the Government, Nigeria to the Secretary of State for the Colonies, 30 December 1947, TNA: CO 583/294/3.
21. *Nigerian Eastern Mail*, 28 February 1948.
22. Officer Administering the Government, Nigeria to the Secretary of State for the Colonies, 30 December 1947, TNA: CO 583/294/3.
23. *Rex* v. *Sunday Udo Ekpo, Etim Ekpo, Otu Nkpo and Etuk Uko*, 24 November 1947, NAE: OPODIST 1/10/8.
24. Ibid.
25. Ibid.
26. TNA: CO 583/294.
27. Resident, Calabar Province to the Secretary, Eastern Provinces, 22 January 1947, NAE: ABAKDIST 1/2/90.
28. Ibid., The Leopard Men, n.d., PRONI: D/3301/GC/9/3.
29. The Leopard Men, n.d., PRONI: D/3301/GC/9/3.
30. Resident, Calabar Province to the Secretary, Eastern Provinces, 22 January

1947, NAE: ABAKDIST 1/2/90.

31. Order in Council No.9, 1947, NAE: CSE 1/85/9284.
32. Ibid.
33. M. T. Williams to Commissioner C.I.D., Lagos, 3 March 1947b, NAE: CALPROF 17/1/1598.
34. RH: Mss. Afr. S. 1063 p. 21.
35. Idiong – Report by Mr Fountain SASP, 3 March 1947a, NAE: CALPROF 17/1/1598.
36. DO Opobo to Resident, Calabar, 17 July 1947, NAE: OPODIST 1/1/47.
37. The Leopard Murders and the Idiong Society (D. S. Fountain), 24 February 1947, TNA: CO 583/294/3.
38. Ibid.
39. Ferme, 2001 p. 20.
40. M. T. Williams to Commissioner C.I.D., Lagos, 3 March 1947b, NAE: CALPROF 17/1/1598.
41. On the role of shrine priests in the *maji maji* rebellion in Tanganyika, see Iliffe, 1967; Becker, 2004; on the role of *orkoiik* diviners in political upheavals in Kenya's western highlands, see Anderson, 1993; and, on the *mhondoro* spirit-medium's part in the Zimbabwean war of independence, see Lan, 1985.
42. On the role of *inyanga* in the preparation of *muti* medicines, see Ngubane, 1986.
43. D. S. Fountain, 'A Report on the Leopard Society Murders', July 1951, RH: Mss.Afr.s.1784 (18).
44. Blok, 1972.
45. Governor to Secretary of State for the Colonies, 20 June 1947, TNA: CO 583/294/3.
46. DO Opobo to Resident, Calabar Province, 22 December 1947, NAE: OPODIST 1/10/8. Of course, this did not prevent such stories from circulating. In a report to supporters at home the Qua Iboe missionaries reported that bottles were found containing human fat in the house of a chief in a surprise raid and that they were being sold for large sums as very potent medicine (The Leopard Men, n.d., PRONI: D/3301/GC/9/3).
47. Rosemary Harris, personal communication.
48. Udoma, 1987 p. 352 (facing).
49. It became a given of the investigations, repeated in numerous reports, including those written by Ibibios themselves, that *idiɔŋ* had two branches or grades – *ibɔk* and *ifá* (Udoma, 1987 pp. 148, 152). *Ibɔk* related to the manufacture of charms, medicines and prognostication, while *ifá* was thought to represent a higher echelon, a titled class of the wealthy and powerful. The Ibibio Union claimed that since *ifá* did not engage in divination they could not have aided the leopard men. What was read as hierarchy was specialisation. Only the most senior and successful *idiɔŋ* could initiate into more than three or four separate spirits.
50. Fountain argued that three of the most prominent *idiɔŋ* men in Abak and Opobo were restraining potential witnesses from presenting evidence to the Police. As a result Chief Ntuen Ibok of Essene, Chief Wilson Akpan Nya of Ibekwe, and Chief Ukpong Eto of Ediene were detained in Calabar. Ntuen Ibok was 'deported and exiled' to Calabar purportedly because he failed to produce the killers responsible for the murder of two victims in his village (*Nigerian Eastern Mail*, 17 May 1947). Though he was never charged in the Chima case, police argued that Ukpong Eto remained a threat.
51. *Nigerian Eastern Mail*, 29 March 1947.

52. New Leg Co Hon Nyong Essien's (representative for Ibibio Division) address to the Legislative Council, 20 March 1947 cited in *Nigerian Eastern Mail*, 26 April 1947.
53. *Nigerian Eastern Mail*, 12 April 1947.
54. Ibid.
55. Ibid.
56. Ibibio Union to DO Abak and DO Opobo, 18 February 1947, NAE: OPODIST 1/10/5.
57. Ibid.
58. DO Abak to Resident, Calabar, 22 February 1947, NAE: OPODIST 1/10/5.
59. Ibibio Union to DO Abak and DO Opobo, 18 February 1947, NAE: OPODIST 1/10/5.
60. Governor to Secretary of State for the Colonies, 20 June 1947, TNA: CO 583/294/3.
61. Ibibio Touring Delegates Diary, 25 July 1947, NAE: CALPROF 7/1/1418.
62. *Nigerian Eastern Mail*, 11 October 1947.
63. D. S. Fountain, 'A Report on the Leopard Society Murders', July 1951, RH: Mss.Afr.s.1784 (18).
64. The congregation of the Faith Tabernacle refused to attend the meetings and were each given six strokes of the cane and a collective fine of £13 (Ibibio Touring Delegates Diary, 16 July 1947, NAE: CALPROF 7/1/1418).
65. 'Propaganda against the Leopard-Men' *African Affairs* 46, 185 pp 218–219.
66. Ibibio Touring Delegates Diary, 27 June 1947, NAE: CALPROF 7/1/1418.
67. Ibibio Touring Delegates Diary, 25 July 1947, NAE: CALPROF 7/1/1418.
68. DO Opobo to Resident, Calabar Province, (I. F. W. Schofield), 20 February 1947, NAE: OPODIST 1/10/5.
69. SASP Leopard Campaign to Commissioner, CID, Lagos, (M. Williams), 28 May 1947b, NAE: CALPROF 7/1/1418.
70. Ibibio Touring Delegates Diary, 10 June 1947, NAE: CALPROF 7/1/1418; Ibibio Touring Delegates Diary, 16 June 1947, NAE: CALPROF 7/1/1418.
71. Extract from His Honour the Chief Commissioner's Inspection Notes, Calabar Province, 5 February 1946, NAE: ABAKDIST 1/3/2.
72. Ibibio Touring Delegates Diary, 21 June 1947, NAE: CALPROF 7/1/1418; Ibibio Touring Delegates Diary, 23 June 1947, NAE: CALPROF 7/1/1418
73. Ibibio Touring Delegates Diary, 28 June 1947, NAE: CALPROF 7/1/1418.
74. Anderson and Killingray, 1991 p. 8.
75. Ibibio Touring Delegates Diary, 2 July 1947, NAE: CALPROF 7/1/1418.
76. Ibibio Touring Delegates Diary, 28 May 1947, NAE: CALPROF 7/1/1418.
77. Ibibio Touring Delegates Diary, 16 June 1947, NAE: CALPROF 7/1/1418.
78. The Leopard Men, n.d., PRONI: D/3301/GC/9/3.
79. *QIM Quarterly*, May 1947, (34), PRONI, D/3301/EA/22.
80. The Leopard Men, n.d., PRONI: D/3301/GC/9/3.
81. *Nigerian Eastern Mail*, 13 September 1947.
82. Ibibio Touring Delegates Diary, 27 June 1947, NAE: CALPROF 7/1/1418.
83. General Secretary, Ibibio Union to DO, Opobo, 27 June 1947, NAE: OPODIST 1/10/5.
84. The Rev. J. G. Campbell, Patriarch of Christ's Army Church to DO Uyo Division, 25 October 1939, NAE: CALPROF 3/1/210.
85. Ibibio Touring Delegates Diary, 27 June 1947, NAE: CALPROF 7/1/1418
86. Ibibio Touring Delegates Diary, 11 June 1947, NAE: CALPROF 7/1/1418; Ibibio Touring Delegates Diary, 9 June 1947, NAE: CALPROF 7/1/1418; Ibibio Touring Delegates Diary, 7 June 1947, NAE: CALPROF 7/1/1418.

As a result of the Union's findings the police conducted intelligence on the 'spiritual churches' from the camp at Ediene Atai during August 1947. Of the Christ Army Church at Ikot Ndien PC Patrick Omenukor wrote 'information from reliable sources has it that women who go to the Church never agree with their husbands and do not marry their husbands any more immediately they step to church' (Police Report: Spiritual Churches, 17 August 1947, NAE: OPODIST 1/10/1).

87. Ibibio Touring Delegates Diary, 2 June 1947, NAE: CALPROF 7/1/1418.
88. Ibibio Touring Delegates Diary, 4 June 1947, NAE: CALPROF 7/1/1418.
89. Ibid.
90. *Nigerian Eastern Mail*, 30 August 1947.
91. D. S. Fountain to Superintendent of Police, Calabar, 27 July 1946, NAE: CALPROF 17/1/1598.
92. An alternative ritual format was also reported which involved the sacrifice of a goat and a chicken. Palm leaves were dipped in the goat's blood and put on the two roads leading to the village and each villager stepped over the blood-stained leaves (SASP Leopard Campaign to Commissioner, CID, Lagos, (M. Williams), 28 May 1947b, NAE: CALPROF 7/1/1418).
93. Ibibio Touring Delegates Diary, 18 July 1947, CALPROF 7/1/1418.
94. SASP Leopard Campaign to Commissioner, CID, Lagos, (M. Williams), 11 June 1947b, NAE: CALPROF 7/1/1418.
95. 'Propaganda against the Leopard-Men' *African Affairs* 46, 185 pp 218–19.
96. The blind eye the authorities turned to the use of oath-taking in the Nigerian murder campaign resonated with the response of administrators in Malawi, Tanganyika and Zambia who were confronted by the use of *mucapi* witch-cleansing medicine when they launched a large witch-cleansing campaign in the early 1930s in direct contravention of the Witchcraft Ordinance (Fields, 1982b). See also Kershaw, 1997 p. 237 on the counter-oathing led by L. S. B. Leakey in Kenya during the Mau Mau rebellion in Kenya in 1952.
97. *QIM Quarterly*, January 1948, (36), PRONI, D/3301/EA/22.
98. Ibibio Touring Delegates Diary, 25 July 1947, NAE: CALPROF 7/1/1418.
99. Ibibio Touring Delegates Diary, 2 July 1947, NAE: CALPROF 7/1/1418.
100. The Man Leopard Murders of Calabar, n.d., RH: Mss.Afr.s.1784 (18).
101. Ibibio Union to Resident, Calabar, 15 May 1947, NAE: CALPROF 7/1/1418.
102. Douglas, 1970 p. xiii.
103. Tonkin, 2000.
104. Ibid. p. 381.
105. Cf. Green, 1990.
106. Ekandem, 1955 p. 55.
107. Fields, 1982b p. 593.
108. Bloch, 1986; 1989; Green, 1990.
109. Tonkin, 2000 p. 374. In other reports the delegates presented themselves as alternative healers. In his address to Ikote Esiet village T. S. B. Inyang, one of the delegates, reported that the leopard society members drank a charm mixed with human blood from which the delegates had the power to cure. If the leopard men came privately for confession and showed that they were truly sorry for having entered the society, Inyang said, they would be given an antidote (*Nigerian Eastern Mail*, 21 June 1947).
110. Bloch, 1986 p. 191.
111. Annual Report, Calabar Province, (C. J. Mayne), 1947, RH: MSS Afr. S.1505.2.
112. Ibibio Touring Delegates Diary, 21 June 1947, NAE: CALPROF 7/1/1418.

113. DO Opobo to Resident, Calabar, 17 July 1947, NAE: OPODIST 1/1/47.

114. Udoma was thought to have refused saying that he wanted to wait until the murders had ended, but another barrister, Ibeziaku, wrote the petition for a fee of 30 guineas (DO Opobo to Resident, Calabar, 21 July 1947, NAE: OPODIST 1/1/47).

115. Report of Enquiry re. missing part of Murdered Persons by Ekpe Owo Men, 6 June 1946, NAE: ABAKDIST 1/2/90.

116. M. T. Williams to Commissioner C.I.D., Lagos, 10 March 1947, NAE: CALPROF 17/1/1598.

117. U. U. Usen, 'Report of the tour by the Ibibio Delegates in the Man-Leopard Areas of the Abak, Opobo and Uyo Divisions of Calabar Province, 26 May to 31 July 1947', NAE: OPODIST 1/10/6.

118. Udoma, 1987 p. 166.

119. *Nigerian Eastern Mail*, 3 July 1948.

120. Udoma, 1987 p. 142.

121. Extract from Special Branch Secret Report (SBE/22/124) to Chief Commissioner of Police, 16 August 1948, NAE: OPODIST 1/10/3.

122. Ibid.

123. Udoma, 1987 p. 178.

124. Extract from Special Branch Secret Report (SBE/22/124) to Chief Commissioner of Police, 16 August 1948, NAE: OPODIST 1/10/3.

125. *Rex v. Benjamin Udo Mbat, Udo Ibana and Akpan Usen Ekong*, 1 December 1947, NAE: OPODIST 1/10/8.

126. Akpan Adiaha Ekpo was charged with the murder of a girl called Akpogho Icho Ichogho Ekanem at Ibesit in 1942. This was the second 'man-leopard' case heard by Justice Pollard which had collapsed because of the dubious provenance of the evidence gathered by PC David Ekoh (*Rex v. Akpan Adiaha Ekpo*, 4 September 1947, NAE: OPODIST 1/10/8).

127. Ibid.

128. Unwa Solomon, 1947, RH: MSS. Afr. 1063.

129. Close-Up of 'Sanders', 1947, RH: MSS Afr. S. 1900.

130. *Rex v. Isaac Akpan*, 29 November 1947, NAE: OPODIST 1/10/8.

131. DO Opobo to Resident, Calabar Province, 22 December 1947, NAE: OPODIST 1/10/8.

132. The District Officer (Dennis Gibbs) Listening to Complaints, 1947, RH: MSS Afr. S. 1900.

133. Gibbs was not the only colonial officer raising big cats during this period. In Umuahia, for instance, J. H. Ball had reared two leopards and an antelope before taking on a two-spotted palm civet in 1952 (Ball, 1955 p. 64).

134. McCall, 1986 p. 442.

135. Stoler, 1992.

136. McCall, 1986 p. 443.

137. DO Opobo to Resident, Calabar Province, 22 December 1947, NAE: OPODIST 1/10/8.

138. Ibid.

139. *Rex v. Isaac Oton, Akpan Edem Idiong and Akpan Afana*, 6 December 1947, NAE: OPODIST 1/10/8.

140. DO Opobo to Resident, Calabar Province, 22 December 1947, NAE: OPODIST 1/10/8.

141 DO Opobo to Resident, Calabar Province, 22 December 1947, NAE: OPODIST 1/10/8.

142. Dr Segal to Mr Creech Jones (Colonial Secretary), reported in *Evening*

Standard, 19 November 1947. Compare this relatively mild enquiry, however, with the furore of protests and petitions played out around Whitehall in the wake of the Kyebi case in Ghana (Rathbone, 1989 pp. 450–6).

143. McCall stood by his claims throughout his life and put his case in reply to articles concerning 'man-eating' big cats in the British press and academic journals (McCall, 1986).

144. *Nigerian Eastern Mail*, 17 January 1948.

145. *Nigerian Eastern Mail*, 10 July 1948a.

146. Udoma, 1987 p. 147.

147. D. S. Fountain, 'A Report on the Leopard Society Murders', July 1951, RH: Mss.Afr.s.1784 (18).

148. The influential Annang chiefs were Udo Ekong (Permanent President Abak Native Court); Iwok Etuk (Permanent President Ekparakwa Native Court); Udofia Etuk Udo (Council member Mbiakot Clan Abak Division); Samson Udo Idiong (Court and Council member Abak); Effiong Umo (Court and Council member Abak); Thomas Ukot (Court and Council member Nung Ikot); Silas Unanam (Council member Ikot Ikoror and Abak); Abraham Akpan (Council member Utu Etim Ekpo); and Jeremiah Akpan (Council member Ikot Okoro) (*Nigerian Eastern Mail*, 28 May 1949).

149. D. S. Fountain, 'A Report on the Leopard Society Murders', July 1951, RH: Mss.Afr.s.1784 (18).

150. Ibid.

151. Udoma, 1987 p. 163.

152. Stoler, 2002 p. 101.

153. Murphy, 1981 p. 680.

154. D. S. Fountain, 'A Report on the Leopard Society Murders', July 1951, RH: Mss.Afr.s.1784 (18).

155. Annual Report, Calabar Province (C. J. Mayne), 1948, RH: MSS Afr. S.1505.3.

156. Two Articles, with photographs, on Leopard Society murders, E. Nigeria, (M. T. Williams), 1947, RH: MSS. Afr. 1063 In its unprocessed form cassava contains toxic prussic acid.

CHAPTER 8

1 Ibid.

2. Chief Secretary to the Government to Commissioner of Police, Lagos, 30 September 1947, RH: MSS. Afr. 1063.

3. Acting Chief Secretary to the Government to the Commissioner of Police, Lagos, (M. T. Williams), 3 December 1947, RH: MSS. Afr. 1063.

4. Martin Lynn, personal communication.

5. I. Stourton (Inspector-General of Police), 'Foreword – A Report on the Leopard Society Murders', July 1951, RH: Mss.Afr.s.1784 (18).

6. P. Canham (Secretary, Colonial Social Science Research Council) to Professor R. Firth, 8 December 1948, CO 583/294/4; p. Canham (Secretary, Colonial Social Science Research Council) to Meyer Fortes, 17 January 1949, TNA: CO 583/294/4.

7. Colonial Social Science Research Council to Dr. M. Gluckman, 23 February 1948, TNA: CO 583/294/4. Dr Linvill F. Watson attended the University of Pennsylvania earning a B.A. in 1938 and a Ph.D. in 1953 based on research in northern Igboland. He subsequently taught at the University of Saskatchewan 1966–86.

8. Linvill Watson to E. E. Sabben-Clare, Colonial Attache, British Embassy,

Washington D.C., 17 April 1948, University of Saskatchewan Archives 1999–064 File 1–11.

9. Chief Secretary to the Government to The Secretary, Eastern Provinces, 9 December 1948, NAE: CALPROF 7/1/1419.

10. James, 1973 p. 43.

11. John Messenger, personal communication.

12. The Resident at Calabar observed that, 'The rewards unquestionably encourage hunting, and they ensure that the hunters produce the animal's bodies: there is no chance, therefore, of the parts with magical significance falling into mischievous hands, because the police destroy them before the hunter draws his money, (Resident, Calabar. Memo., 6 October 1950, NAE: CALPROF 7/1/1419).

13. *QIM Quarterly*, January 1956, (68), PRONI, D/3301/EA/16.

14. Sgt. John Okekere to Regional CID, Enugu, 9 November 1955, NAE: CALPROF 7/1/1419.

15. Okon Esien Akpan and Sam Akpan Nka to Chief Commissioner, Eastern Provinces, 18 February 1952, NAE: MINLOC 16/1/1883.

16. Anon. to DO Abak, 18 August 1952, NAE: ABAKDIST 1/2/12.

17. Dick Inyang Udo to Resident, Calabar, 26 November 1953, NAE: ABAKDIST 1/2/27.

18. Moses Samuel to DO Abak, nd, NAE: ABAKDIST 1/2/12.

19. Udofia Anwa to DO Abak, 27 September 1951, NAE: ABAKDIST 1/2/12.

20. *Nigerian Eastern Mail*, 12 June 1948; 10 July 1948b.

21. *Nigerian Eastern Mail*, 18 December 1948.

22. Obong Ntuen Ibok to Governor, Nigeria, 14 January 1949, NAE: CALPROF 3/1/1955.

23. Udo Udoma to Resident, Calabar, 24 May 1949, NAE: CALPROF 3/1/1955.

24. Resident, Calabar to Secretary, Eastern Provinces, 28 June 1951, NAE: CSE 1/85/9284.

25. Secretary, Eastern Provinces to Chief Secretary to the Government, 13 August 1951, NAE: CSE 1/85/9284.

26. Commonwealth Institute Collection: T/NIGE/160.

27. Ibid. Donated by Mr Creech Jones, 15 May 1964.

28. Evans, 1993; Marwick, 1940; Ngubane, 1986; Murray and Sanders, 2000; Jones, 1951, Basutoland Medicine Murder: A Report on the Recent Outbreak of 'Diretlo' Murders in Basultoland, 8209, HMSO: London.

29. Rathbone, 1989; 1993; Gocking, 2000.

30. Marwick, 1940 p. 211.

31. Murray and Sanders, 2000 p. 51.

32. Weisfelder, 1974.

33. Law, 1985.

34. Gocking, 2000. The medicine in question was thought to be of Ewe origin and to have had properties that would cause its user to succeed in law suits (Gocking, 2000 pp. 198–9). As such, its properties were comparable to Annang *ńdúɔ́hɔ* medicine which figured critically in the man-leopard murder investigations.

35. Cf. Wilks, 1993; McCaskie, 1989; Goody, 1962.

36. Rathbone, 1993.

37. Comparatively on the relationship between chiefs, colonialism and murder in Ibadan, Nigeria see Watson, 2000.

38. Rathbone, 1989 p. 458.

39. *Nigerian Eastern Mail*, 18 October 1947.

40. *Nigerian Eastern Mail*, 26 July 1947.
41. Pearce, 1982.
42. *Nigerian Eastern Mail*, 12 July 1947
43. Ibid.
44. Annual Report, Calabar Province, (C. J. Mayne), 1947, RH: MSS Afr. S.1505.2.
45. Chief Commissioner, Eastern Provinces to Resident, Rivers Province, 8 March 1947, NAE: RIVPROF 2/1/87.
46. It is important to signal the contradiction here between the open and conciliatory thrust of Carr's proposals and the fetishised mode of concealment (the 'secret' review) in which it was undertaken. As Stoler suggests this code of concealment was not usually intended to hide the subject matter but rather the 'conflict among officials about how to act on the problem, [and] their desperate assessments of what was the cause (Stoler, 2002 p. 108).
47. Report on the Afaha People's Union by Mr H. R. Ross (ADO, Eket), 4 January 1944, NAE: CALPROF 3/1/2906.
48. Hailey, 1951 p. 20.
49. Resident, Rivers Province to Chief Commissioner, Eastern Provinces, 31 March 1947, NAE: RIVPROF 2/1/87.
50. Resident, Cameroons Province to Secretary, Eastern Provinces, 26 May 1947, NAE: RIVPROF 2/1/87.
51. Senior DO, Umuahia Division to Chief Commissioner, Eastern Provinces, 8 April 1947, NAE: RIVPROF 2/1/87.
52. DO, Degema to Resident, Rivers Province, 22 March 1947, NAE: RIVPROF 2/1/87.
53. Resident, Ogoja Province to Chief Commissioner, Eastern Provinces, 5 April 1947, NAE: RIVPROF 2/1/87.
54. Resident, Cameroons Province to Secretary, Eastern Provinces, 26 May 1947, NAE: RIVPROF 2/1/87.
55. Senior D.O., Opobo Division to Resident, Calabar Province, 27 March 1947, RIVPROF 2/1/87.
56. No. 64 of February 1947 (*Nigerian Eastern Mail*, 16 August 1947).
57. Kirk-Greene, 1965 p. 28.
58. Coleman, 1971 p. 315.
59. Report of the Select Committee of the Eastern Region House of Assembly set up to review the existing system of Local Government in the Eastern Provinces and to formulate general principles for the reform of that system, 1948, RH: 723.13.s.10/1948 (1).
60. Memorandum on Local Government Policy in the Eastern Provinces of Nigeria, 1949, RH: 723.17.r.14/1949(2).
61. Crook, 1986 pp. 79–80.
62. *Nigerian Eastern Mail*, 14 January 1950.
63. Sklar, 1963 p. 58.
64. Chief Commissioner, Eastern Provinces to Resident, Rivers Province, 8 March 1947, NAE: RIVPROF 2/1/87.
65. See, for example, Nwokweji's comments on the formation of the Informal Committee on the Political Significance of Colonial Students in Great Britain in 1947 which sought to prevent students from running 'intellectually wild' during their formative years at English universities (Nwokeji, 1994).
66. Sklar, 1963 p. 64.
67. Coleman, 1971 p. 384.
68. Pels, 2002.

69. *Nigerian Eastern Mail*, 19 April 1947.
70. *Nigerian Eastern Mail*, 17 January 1948; 14 January 1950.
71. Sklar, 1963 p. 205fn.
72. Nnoli, 1978 p. 169.
73. Report of the Commission Appointed to Enquire into The Fears of Minorities and the Means of Allaying Them, 1958, TNA: CO 957/41.
74. Other prominent COR State Movement supporters included Sampson Udo Idiong (Abak), Ekpenyong Udo Ekong (Uyo), U. A. Oton (Opobo), Chief Robert Umo Inyang (Ikot Ekpene), Professor Eyo Ita, Andrew Bassey (President of the Efik State Union), Etubom Enaing Essien, Hannah B. Otudor, Elizabeth Henshaw, Chief U. E. Ede Iduok of Oniong Nung Ndem, Michael Ogon and Macdonald Ogon (Ogoja).
75. *Eastern States Express*, 7 November 1959.
76. *Eastern Outlook*, 31 October 1957.
77. Memorandum by the Chiefs, Elders, Women and Representatives of all sections of Abak Division to the Minorities Commission, 1958a, TNA: CO 957/21.
78. Memorandum to the Minorities Commission submitted by the Chiefs and People of Ibekwe County, Opobo Division, 1958b, TNA: CO 957/21.
79. Memorandum by the Chiefs, Elders, Women and Representatives of all sections of Abak Division to the Minorities Commission, 1958a, TNA: CO 957/21.
80. COR State Movement, 1958, Memorandum Submitted to the Minorities Commission by the Central Executive Committee of the Calabar-Ogoja-Rivers State Movement, St. Therese's Press: Calabar p. 21.
81. Memorandum submitted by the Calabar, Ogoja and Rivers State Movement, Calabar Branch, to The Governor-General, 18 July 1955, NAE: CALPROF 7/1/1446.
82. Ibid.
83. The NIP and the United National Party (formed in 1952 by NCNC dissidents) merged as the United National Independence Party (UNIP) in August 1954, and was later absorbed as the Eastern Wing of the Action Group. The formal merger was not announced until July 1957
84. Committee of South Easterners, 1974, The Case Against the Creation of A Cross River State, Goodwill Press: Port Harcourt p. 5.
85. The AG/UNIP alliance won eighteen out of thirty non-Igbo seats in the Eastern Region in 1957 on the strength of the COR State issue.
86. Nwaka, 1983 p. 92.
87. Akinyele, 1996 p. 81.
88. Committee of South Easterners, 1974, The Case Against the Creation of A Cross River State, Goodwill Press: Port Harcourt.
89. *West Africa*, 22 November 1958. Of the other parties to the COR State proposal, the commission found that the Ijaws had switched their support to the Niger Delta Congress and the peoples of Iko, Obubra and Ogoja Divisions had returned to the NCNC (Post, 1963 pp. 364–5).
90. Report of the Commission Appointed to Enquire into The Fears of Minorities and the Means of Allaying Them, 1958, TNA: CO 957/41.
91. Pearce, 1982 pp. 171–2.
92. Cooper, 1997 p. 67.
93. Cited in ibid. p. 80
94. *Nigerian Eastern Mail*, 15 January 1949.
95. Resolution passed by the Ibibio State Conference-in-Session against the failure on the part of the authorities to develop Ibibioland, 19 August 1950, NAE: CALPROF 5/1/308.

96. Record of an interview granted to delegates of the Ibibio Union by His Honour, the Chief Commissioner, Eastern Provinces, 2 March 1950, NAE: CALPROF 5/1/308.

97. Minutes of District Officers Conference, Port Harcourt, 10 December 1952, NAE: PHDIST 10/1/544.

98. DO Brass to Resident, 17 April 1950, NAE: PHDIST 7/1/253.

99. Annual Report, Calabar Province, (C. J. Mayne), 1953, RH: MSS Afr. S.1505.7.

100. Cooper, 1997 p. 71; Van Beusekom and Hodgson, 2000 p. 31.

101. Meredith, 1984 p. 325.

102. Nwabughuogu, 1985.

103. *Nigerian Weekly Record*, 4 August 1950.

104. DO Opobo to Resident, Calabar, 27 February 1952, NAE: CALPROF 7/1/2339.

105. ADO to DO Opobo, 10 February 1952, NAE: CALPROF 7/1/2339. By 1954 forty-one mills were in operation, but doubts remained as to whether they could be run as commercial propositions without the plantations to supply them. Writing in 1956 Martin reported that women had begun to accept men buying kernels from the mills for resale. At the same time, she noted, men were taking more responsibility for children's education and 'the inter-sexual division of labour, perquisites and obligations is today extremely fluid' (Martin, 1956 p. 4).

106. *Nigerian Eastern Mail*, 18 January 1947; 25 January 1947; 1 February 1947; 8 February 1947; 22 March 1947.

107. E.E. Umanah to ADO, Abak, 8 November 1952, NAE: ABAKDIST 1/2/10.

108. Ibid.

109. *Nigerian Weekly Record*, 4 August 1950.

110. Nigeria, 1955, Report of the Committee on Brideprice in the Eastern Region of Nigeria, Lagos: Government Printer p. 43.

111. The Committee also heard that Ibibio condemned the use of the term 'brideprice'. Brideprice translated in Ibibio is translated as 'Ekom Uru Ando' – a person bought as a slave – and demanded that 'Nkpo Ndo' should used instead, which means 'those things which a man gives when he marries a woman' (ibid. p. 42).

112. *Nigerian Eastern Mail*, 12 July 1947.

113. *Nigerian Eastern Mail*, 14 May 1949.

114. Hunt, 1991 p. 480.

115. Ruel, 1969 p. 266.

116. *Eastern Outlook and Cameroons Star*, 25 February 1954.

117. Nigeria, 1955, Report of the Committee on Brideprice in the Eastern Region of Nigeria, Lagos: Government Printer p. 5.

118. The Limitation of Dowry Law was enforced on 20 November 1956 and stipulated that dowry and incidental expenses should not exceed £30 (£25 as dowry and £5 as incidental expenses). Anyone found to be exceeding this amount was liable to a fine of £100. On the question of divorce the committee advised that it should only be permitted on the grounds of desertion, cruelty, adultery, impotency or lunacy, and that the refund of brideprice should be the wife's liability if found guilty of causing the divorce, and that a culpable husband should not be entitled to a refund at all. Child betrothal below the age of sixteen was abolished (ibid. pp. 46–7).

119. *Eastern Outlook and Cameroons Star*, 8 July 1954.

120. *Eastern Outlook*, 30 December 1954.

121. Sir Walter Buchanan-Smith's evidence to the Brooks' Commission in Nigeria, 1953, Report of the Native Courts (Eastern Region) Commission of Inquiry, Lagos: Government Printer p. 38.

122. League of Bribe Scorners, 1950–54, NAE: PHDIST 10/1/1196.

123. *Nigerian Eastern Mail*, 4 March 1950.

124. Nigeria, 1953, Report of the Native Courts (Eastern Region) Commission of Inquiry, Lagos: Government Printer.

125. By December 1960 the 24 Native Courts with 200 judges in Abak had been replaced by 16 newly established customary courts with 109 judges. Five customary court judges made up the Abak County Court of Appeal.

126. Resident in charge, Uyo Division to The Resident, Calabar Province, 12 March 1946, NAE: CALPROF 7/1/380.

127. District Council (Control of Traditional Societies) Bye Laws, 1952, NAE: CALPROF 7/1/380.

128. DO Uyo to Senior Resident, Calabar Province, 1 March 1952, NAE: CALPROF 7/1/380.

129. Tamuno's historical survey includes accounts of the police's encounters with several criminal gangs during the late 1940s and 1950s (Tamuno, 1970).

130. *Eastern States Express*, 22 April 1959; Udoma, 1987 p. 495. In November 1958 the Amaukes in Uyo were broken up by the police with twenty-one arrested and eighteen convicted of robbery (*Eastern Outlook*, 4 June 1959).

131. Secretary, Eastern Provinces to Chairman, Ikot Ekpene County Council, 14 August 1951, NAE: CALPROF 3/1/1957.

132. Annual Report, Calabar Province, (C. J. Mayne), 1952, RH: MSS Afr. S.1505.6.

133. *QIM Quarterly*, January 1958, (76), PRONI, D/3301/EA/27.

134. AG loyalties are still recalled in *ékpó* society songs from the period: *Isin nwed ino ajop, Isin nwed ino ajop Nigeria* (Vote for the palm tree, Vote for the palm tree, Nigeria). Recorded at Ikot Edem Ewa village, Adat Ifang clan. October 2001.

135. ADO Abak to Acting Resident, Calabar, 8 May 1955, NAE: CALPROF 17/1/2702.

136. Annual Report, Calabar Province, (C. J. Mayne), 1950, RH: MSS Afr. S.1505.5.

137. A.O. Abakaliki to Chief Secretary to the Premier, 26 November 1958, NAE: AIDIST 2/1/462.

138. Asst. Supt. Police to Commissioner of Police, Enugu, 9 June 1958, NAE: AIDIST 2/1/462.

139. Tamuno and Horton, 1969. Cf. House of Representatives Debates, 16 Feb 1959 (columns 600–1); 26 February 1959 (column 1285). Annual Reports (Nigeria Police Force, 1958), p. 9.

140. In 1959 it was suspected that Odozi Obodo's activities were being revived under the guise of new 'Murder Incorporated Societies' known as Imiko Adinma (devils who know no mercy) (*Eastern Outlook*, 7 May 1959; *Daily Times*, 26 May 1959).

141. Rosemary Harris, personal communication.

142. See Nwokeji, 1994 p. 75.

143. Village Council, Utu Idung Akpan Udom, to DO Abak, 26 June 1952, NAE: ABAKDIST 1/2/27.

144. Chief Thomas Chukwu to DO Abak, 9 November 1949, NAE: ABAKDIST 1/2/11.

145. Afigbo, 1972 p. 35fn.

146. *Eastern Outlook*, 21 February 1957.
147. The ex-Olobi said he was dethroned for refusing to obey an Action Group instruction to ring a bell in his town to announce that voting for the NCNC be forbidden.
148. *Eastern Outlook*, 13 October 1955.
149. Jones, 1956, Report on the Position, Status and Influence of Chiefs and Natural Rulers in the Eastern Region of Nigeria, Government Printer: Enugu p. 40.
150. Ibid. p. 55.
151. Ibid. p. 40.
152. Notes on a Meeting with a Deputation from the Ibibio Union at the Residency Calabar, 20 May 1941, NAE: CALPROF 5/1/308.
153. A Memorandum submitted by Ibibio State Union to Professor GI Jones Commission of Enquiry into the Position, Status and Influence of Chiefs and Natural Rulers in the Eastern Region of Nigeria, 1956 (G. I. Jones Papers).
154. Ibid.
155. Jones' report received a sensitive reading and his interpretation of Igbo chieftaincy in particular was unpopular: 'The insinuation in the Jones Report that most Ibo chiefs did not exercise influence outside their villages should not be perpetuated' (*Eastern Outlook*, 30 April 1959).
156. *Eastern Outlook*, 29 May 1958.
157. Memorandum submitted by the Calabar, Ogoja and Rivers State Movement, Calabar Branch, to The Governor-General, 18 July 1955, NAE: CALPROF 7/1/1446.
158. Sklar, 1963 p. 445.
159. *Eastern Outlook*, 23 April 1959.
160. Compare this 'reading' of the 'man-leopard murders' with the way in which the Kyebi case in the Gold Coast in 1944 was used in the press by some of the 'educated elite' against 'traditional rulers' who wished to use evidence from the case of apparent vestigal feudalism to accelerate the diminution of chiefly authority and the enhancement of the intellectual aristocracy (Rathbone, 1989 p. 458).
161. I am grateful to John Messenger for his recollections from Ikot Ekpene in 1951–52.
162. Hobsbawm, 1969; 1972.
163. Bayart, 1993 p. 115.

CHAPTER 9

1. Appadurai, 1981.
2. Ibid. p. 203.
3. Zemon Davis and Starn, 1989 p. 5.
4. Jonathan Spencer, personal communication.
5. Meyer, 1998 p. 183.
6. Gore and Pratten, 2003.
7. Ibid. pp. 238–240.
8. Bayart, 1999 p. 40.
9. Ellis, 1999; Shaw, 2002.

REFERENCES

NIGERIAN NATIONAL ARCHIVES, ENUGU

The following series were consulted:

ABADIST   (Aba District Office, 1903–1957)
ABAKDIST   (Abak District Office, 1915–1956)
CALPROF   (Calabar Province Office, 1906–1963)
CSE   (Civil Secretary, Enugu, 1896–1951)
DEGDIS   (Degema District Office, 1902–1956)
EKETDIST   (Eket District Office, 1909–1960)
IKOTDIST   (Ikot Ekpene District Office, 1911–1960)
ITUDIST   (Itu District Office, 1922–1958)
MILGOV   (Military Governor's Office, formerly the Premier and Civilian Governor's Offices)
MINLOC   (Local Government Ministry, 1907–1963)
OPODIST   (Opobo District Office, 1900–1956)
PHDIST   (Port Harcourt District Office)
RIVPROF   (Rivers Province Office, 1900–1960)

INTELLIGENCE REPORTS

Adiasim Tribe of Ikot Ekpene District, MILGOV 13/1/12, file EP 15480, by C. P. Thompson (1936).

Afaha Clan of the Annang Sub-Tribe, CSE 1/85/6495, file EP 13117A, by W. D. Spence (1936).

Afaha Obong, Annang Sub-Tribe, Abak District, CSE 1/85/4782A file CP 1932, by S. E. Johnson (1932).

Certain Un-reorganized Groups of the Annang Tribe in the Abak District and the Opobo District, MILGOV 13/1/20, by H. J. M. Harding (1937).

Certain Unorganized Groups in the Utu Etim Ekpo Native Court Area, MILGOV 13/1/21, by G. B. G. Chapman (1939).

Ediene and Itak Clans of the Ikot Ekpene Division, MILGOV 5/1/6, file EP 7989A, by R. J. M. Curwen (1931).

Ika Clan, Abak District, CSE 1/85/4718, file EP 9012A, by H. H. Marshall (1931).

Ikpe Clan, Ikot Ekpene Division, CALPROF 3/1/53, file CP 63, by K. V. Hanitsch (1932).

Northern Annang Group, Ikot Ekpene Division, MILGOV 13/1/7, by E. G. Hawkesworth (1932).

Obong Village Group, Abak District, CSE 1/85/4905A, file EP 9652A, by H. H.

Marshall (1932).

Okun and Afaha Clans Intelligence Report, Ikot Ekpene Division, CSE 1/85/4228, file EP 7731B, by S. E. Johnson and E. G. Hawkesworth (1931).

Otoro Group of the Otoro Clan, Abak District, CSE 1/85/6323, file EP 12721A, by J. V. Dewhurst (1935).

Ukanafun Clan, Abak District, CSE 1/85/5214, file 10546A, by S. E. Johnson (1933).

THE NATIONAL ARCHIVES, KEW

The following series were consulted:

CO537   Colonial concerns at the rise of political activism in the 1950s.

CO583   Calabar Province: outbreak of leopard society murders, 1947.

CO957   Commission on Minority Groups in Nigeria, 1958.

PUBLIC RECORDS OFFICE OF NORTHERN IRELAND, BELFAST

The following series were consulted:

D/3301/AA Letters from the Superintendent in the Field, Mr S. A. Bill, to the General Secretary of the Mission Council in Belfast. Mr R. L. Mckeown, 1900–1942.

D/3301/AB/1 Letters from David Ekong, 1897–1929.

D/3301/AB/3 Letters from Various Natives in Qua Iboe to Mr R. L. Mckeown, 1912–33.

D/3301/AB/4 Letters from Mr A. V. Willcox to Mr R. L. Mckeown, 1912–33.

D/3301/AD Letters, A. Bailie, 1889–1905.

D/3301/AG/1 Letter Book, S. A. Bill, 1898–1907.

D/3301/AH Letters from All Parties Involved Concerning a Derogatory Article in the Qua Iboe Local Press About Wages Paid by the Missions to Their Native Teacher. May–June 1939.

D/3301/AJ/1 Letters to and from Representatives of the British Government in Nigeria, 1895–1900.

D/3301/AM Letters from Various Natives to People Connected with the Mission, 1897–1924.

D/3301/CA Diary of the Qua Iboe Mission, 1887–1941.

D/3301/CB Diary, J. W. Westgarth, May 1914–September 1919.

D/3301/DA Daily Journal, S. A. Bill, April 1902–August 1922.

D/3301/EA Qua Iboe Mission Occasional Papers, 1892–1962.

D/3301/GC/4/1 Egbo Egbo: Ibuno Chief and Christian. In Qua Iboe Mission Booklet, edited by R. L. M'Keown, n. d.

D/3301/GC/5/1 Jimmy Udo Ema: Evangelist and Pastor. In Qua Iboe Mission Booklet, edited by J. W. Westgarth, n. d.

D/3301/GC/6/1 Samuel Ibekwe Ekaluo: A Qua Iboe Christian Leader. In Qua Iboe Mission Booklet, n. d.

D/3301/GC/9/3 The Leopard Men. n. d.

D/3301/GC/9/24 From Darkness to Light: The Story of Etia, in Qua Iboe Mission Booklet, edited by Gracie Bill, n. d.

D/3301/LB/1 Report to the Home Council by Mr E. Heaney from Ikotobo Missionary Station. 31 December 1904.

D/3301/OA/7 Note Telling How Death is Dealt with in the Customs of the Qua Iboe Natives. n. d.

D/3301/OA/12 Paper Entitled 'the Trouble Began' by David Kapella, an Opobo Chief Apparently Relating His Physical Condition During State of Consciousness Resembling Trance, as Found in Some Primitive Religions. n. d.

Westgarth, J. W. The Holy Spirit and the Primitive Mind: A remarkable account of a spiritual awakening in darkest Africa, London: Victory Press, 1946.

JEFFREYS PAPERS, UNIVERSITY OF WITWATERSRAND LIBRARY

The following files were consulted:

221	Afaha Abong
222	Customs of Annang
224	Uyo District
225	Tribal Organisation: Ikpe, Okoro, Northern and Central
227	Okun and Afagha Clans
228	Tribes and Clans Eket District
229	Ehum
230	Egbo Society
231	Uwet Burial Customs
232	Customs of the Nka or Udim Ekpo in Ika
256	Ibibio Notes
258	Ibibio Language
259	Ibibio Notes
260	Ibibio Notes
261	Ibibio GramMarch
262	Ibibio Thesis
263	Ibibio Spirit Movements
270	Opobo District
278D/XX	Democratic Institutions in Primitive Societies
278D/XIX	Some Notes on Palm Wine among the Ibibio
278/V	Some Folklore Stories among the Ibibio

RHODES HOUSE, OXFORD

S. M. Grier, Report on the Eastern Provinces by the Secretary for Native Affairs, 723. 12. v. 43 (12), (Government Printer, Lagos, 1922).

E. S. James, 'Minorities in Biafra', Mss Afr. s. 1927 (Unpublished MS, 1969).

John Armstrong G. McCall, The 'Man-Leopard' Problem, Calabar Province, Nigeria, MSS. Afr. S. 1704 (1947).

Notes of Evidence taken in the Calabar and Owerri Provinces on the Disturbance, 8 volumes, 723. 17. s. 1. 1929 (1930).

Report of the Commission of Inquiry appointed to inquire into the disturbances in the Calabar and Owerri Provinces, December 1929, Sessional Paper No. 28, 723. 13. s. 4/1930 (Waterlow and Sons, London Wall, London, 1930c).

Report of the Native Courts (E. Region) Commission of Inquiry, 723. 5. v. 20/1953 (1) (1953).

C. F. Strickland, Report on the Introduction of Co-operative Societies in Nigeria, 723. 14. s. 1934 (1) (1934).

Montgomery Trevor Williams, Two Articles, with photographs, on Leopard Society murders, E. Nigeria., Written as Senior Asst. Supt. of Police, Ediene Atai, MSS. Afr. 1063 (1940–57).

G. J. F. Tomlinson Report on a tour in the Eastern Provinces by the Assistant Secretary for Native Affairs, 723. 17. v. 14/1923 (1), (Government Printer, Lagos, 1923).

Report of the Committee on Brideprice in the Eastern Region of Nigeria, 723. 12. 145/1955 (2) (Lagos, Government Printer, 1955).

OFFICIAL REPORTS (SOAS)

'Report on the Position, Status and Influence of Chiefs and Natural Rulers in the Eastern Region of Nigeria', by G. I. Jones, (Government Printer, Enugu, 1956).

'Report of the Committee on Brideprice in the Eastern Region of Nigeria' (Lagos, Government Printer, 1955).

G. I. JONES' PAPERS

Ibibio State Union, A Memorandum submitted by Ibibio State Union to Professor GI Jones Commission of Enquiry into the Position, Status and Influence of Chiefs and Natural Rulers in the Eastern Region of Nigeria (Ikemesit Co. Ltd., Aba, 1956).

Western Annang County Council, The Local History of Ukanafun Clan, Submission to Local History Project (1965).

UMOREN PAPERS

Dealing with the period after 1970, these are the papers of the former Clan Head of Southern Ukanafun Clan. The papers include judgement books for the various courts over which the Clan Head presides and wide-ranging correspondence.

NEWSPAPERS

Nigerian Eastern Mail (from the collections held by Northwestern University Library and the Library of Congress).

Eastern States Express (British Library Newspaper Collection).

Eastern Outlook and Cameroons Star (British Library Newspaper Collection).

THESES

Anikpo, M. O. 1980. Patterns of Integration: A Study of the Ibo Ethnic Identification in Jos, Nigeria. PhD thesis. University of Cambridge.

Eboreime, O. J. 1992. Group Identities and the Changing Patterns of Alliances Among the Epie-Atissa People of Nigeria 1890–1991. PhD thesis. University of Cambridge.

Jeffreys, M. D. W. 1931. Notes on the Ibibio. Diploma in Anthropology. University of London.

Kpone-Tonwe, S. 1987. The Historical Tradition of Ogoni, Nigeria. MPhil thesis. SOAS University of London.

Messenger, J. C. 1957. Anang Acculturation: A Study of Shifting Cultural Focus. PhD thesis. University of Michigan Microfilms Ann Arbor.

Okon, S. E. 1982. The Man-Leopard Society in Annang/Ibibioland of Old Calabar

Province, 1939–1948: An Anti-Colonial Movement. PhD thesis. University of Calabar.

SECONDARY SOURCES

Abaraonye, F. I. 'Gender Relations in Ibibio Traditional Organizations', *Dialectical Anthropology* 22(2), 1997, pp. 205–22.

Abasiattai, M. B. 'The Oberi Okaime Christian Mission: Towards a History of an Ibibio Independent Church', *Africa* 59(4), 1989, pp. 496–516.

Abraham, A. *Topics in Sierra Leone History: A counter-colonial interpretation*, Freetown: Leone Publishers, 1975.

Adams, J. *Remarks on the Country Extending from Cape Palmas to the River Congo*, London: G. and W. B. Wittaker, 1823.

Adams, R. F. G. 'Oberi Okaime – a New African Language', *Africa* XVII(1), 1947, pp. 24–34.

Afigbo, A. E. 'Revolution and Reaction in Eastern Nigeria, 1900–1929: the Background to the Women's Riot of 1929', *Journal of the Historical Society of Nigeria* 3(3), 1966, pp. 539–57.

—— 'The Eclipse of the Aro Slaving Oligarchy of South-Eastern Nigeria, 1901–27', *Journal of the Historical Society of Nigeria* 6(1), 1971, pp. 3–24.

—— *The Warrant Chiefs: Indirect Rule in South-Eastern Nigeria, 1891–1929*, London: Longman, 1972.

Akinyele, R. T. 'States Creation in Nigeria: the Willink Report in Retrospect', *African Studies Review* 39(2), 1996, pp. 71–94.

Akpabot, S. E. *Ibibio Music in Nigerian Culture*, Michigan, 1975.

Akpaide, U. U. 'Ibibio Concept of the Mask: the Otoro Community Example', *Nigeria Magazine* 141, 1982, pp. 24–39.

Akpan, E. O. and V. I. Ekpo *The Women's War of 1929*, Calabar: Government Printer, 1988.

Aloba, A. 'Tribal Unions in Party Politics', *West Africa* July 10, 1954, p. 637.

Amadiume, I. *Male Daughters, Female Husbands: Gender and Sex in an African Society*, London: Zed, 1987.

Anderson, D. and D. Killingray 'Consent, Coercion and Colonial Control: Policing the Empire, 1830–1940', in *Policing the Empire*, Anderson, D. and D. Killingray (eds), Manchester: Manchester University Press, 1991, pp. 1–15.

Anderson, D. M. 'Black Mischief: Crime, Protest and Resistance in Colonial Kenya', *The Historical Journal* 36(4), 1993, pp. 851–77.

Anderson, R. G. (ed.) *Palm Wine and Leopard's Whiskers: Reminiscences of Eastern Nigeria*, Central Otago, 1999.

Anene, J. C. 'The Protectorate Government of Southern Nigeria and the Aros 1900–1902', *Journal of the Historical Society of Nigeria* 1, 1956, pp. 20–6.

—— *Southern Nigeria in Transition, 1885–1906: Theory and Practice in a Colonial Protectorate*, Cambridge: Cambridge University Press, 1966.

Appadurai, A. 'The Past as a Scarce Resource', *Man* 16(2), 1981, pp. 201–19.

Ardener, E. W. 'A Rural Oil-Palm Industry', *West Africa* 1909, 26 September 1953, pp. 921–23.

Arens, W. *The Man-Eating Myth: Anthropology and Anthrophagy*, New York: Oxford University Press, 1979.

Arua, E. O. 'Yam Ceremonies and the Values of Ohafia Culture', *Africa 51(2)*, 1981, pp. 694–706.

Asad, T. 'From the History of Colonial Anthropology to the Anthropology of Western Hegemony', in *Colonial Situations: Essays on the Contextualization of Ethnographic Situations*, Stocking, G. W. (ed.), Madison, WI: University of Wisconsin Press, 1991, pp. 314–24.

Austen, R. A. 'Criminals and the African Cultural Imagination: Normative and Deviant Heroism in Pre-colonial and Modern Narratives', *Africa* 56(4), 1986a, pp. 385–98.

—— 'Social Bandits and Other Heroic Criminals: a European Concept and its Relevance to Africa', in *Social Banditry and Rebellion in Africa*, Crummey, D. (ed.), London: James Currey, 1986b, pp. 89–108.

Ball, J. H. 'Rearing the Two-spotted Palm Civet', *Nigerian Field* 20(2), 1955, pp. 64–6.

Barbot, J. *A Description of the Coasts of South Guinea*, London, 1699.

Barbot, J., P. E. H. Hair, A. Jones and R. Law *Barbot on Guinea: the Writings of Jean Barbot on West Africa, 1678–1712*, London: Hakluyt Society, 1992.

Barker, F., P. Hulme and M. Iversen (eds) *Cannibalism and the Colonial World*, Cambridge: Cambridge University Press, 1998.

Bastian, M. L. 'Dancing Women and Colonial Men: The Nwaobiala of 1925', in *'Wicked' Women and the Reconfiguration of Gender in Africa*, Hodgson, D. L. and S. McCurdy (eds), Portsmouth, NH: Heinemann; Oxford: James Currey, 2001, pp. 109–29.

Bayart, J. -F. *The State in Africa: The Politics of the Belly*, London: Longman, 1993.

—— 'The 'Social Capital' of the Felonious State or the Ruses of Political Intelligence', in *The Criminalization of the State in Africa*, Bayart, J. -F., S. Ellis and B. Hibou (eds), Oxford: James Currey, 1999, pp. 32–48.

Beattie, J. 'The Self in Traditional Africa', *Africa 50(3)*, 1980, pp. 313–20.

Beatty, K. J. *Human Leopards: An Account of the Trials of Human Leopards before the Special Commission Court; with a Note on Sierra Leone, Past and Present*, London: Hugh Rees Ltd., 1915.

Beaver, D. 'Flesh or Fantasy: Cannibalism and the Meanings of Violence', *Ethnohistory* 49(3), 2002, pp. 671–85.

Becker, F. 'Traders, "Big Men" and Prophets: Political Continuity and Crisis in the Maji Maji Rebellion in Southeast Tanzania', *The Journal of African History* 45(1), 2004, pp. 1–22.

Beier, H. U. 'Ibibio Monuments', *Nigeria* 51, 1956, pp. 318–36.

Bindloss, H. *The League of the Leopard*, London: John Long, 1904.

Bloch, M. *From Blessing to Violence: History and Ideology in the Circumcision Ritual of the Merina of Madagascar*, Cambridge: Cambridge University Press, 1986.

—— *Ritual History and Power: Selected Papers in Anthropology*, London: Athlone Press, 1989.

Blok, A. 'The Peasant and the Brigand: Social Banditry Reconsidered', *Comparative Studies in Society and History* 14(4), 1972, pp. 494–503.

Brink, P. J. 'Fattening Room among the Annang of Nigeria', *Medical Anthropology* (NY) 12(1), 1989, pp. 131–43.

Brown, P. and D. Tuzin (eds) *The Ethnography of Cannibalism*, Washington, DC:

Society for Psychological Anthropology, 1983.

Burrows, D. 'The Human Leopard Society of Sierra Leone', *Journal of the Royal African Society* 13(50), 1914, pp. 143–51.

Burton, A. 'Urchins, Loafers and the Cult of the Cowboy: Urbanization and Delinquency in Dar Es Salaam, 1919–61', *Journal of African History* 42, 2001, pp. 199–216.

Butler, V. F. 'Cement Funeral Sculpture in Eastern Nigeria', *Nigeria Magazine* 77, 1963, pp. 117–24.

Byfield, J. 'Innovation and Conflict: Cloth Dyers and the Interwar Depression in Abeokuta, Nigeria', *Journal of African History* 38, 1997, pp. 77–99.

—— 'Women, Marriage, Divorce and the Emerging Colonial State in Abeokuta (Nigeria) 1891–1904', in *'Wicked' Women and the Reconfiguration of Gender in Africa*, Hodgson, D. L. and S. McCurdy (eds), Portsmouth, NH: Heinemann; Oxford: James Currey, 2001, pp. 27–46.

—— *The Bluest Hands: a Social and Economic History of Women Dyers in Abeokuta (Nigeria), 1890–1940*, Portsmouth, NH: Heinemann, 2002.

Cameron, D. *Principles of Native Administration and Their Application*, Lagos: Government Printer, 1933.

—— 'Native Administration in Tanganyika and Nigeria', *Journal of the Royal African Society* 36(145), 1937, pp. 3–29.

Cameron, D. C. *My Tanganyika Service and Some Nigeria*, London, 1939.

Channock, M. 'Making Customary Law: Men, Women and Courts in Colonial Northern Rhodesia', in *African Women and the Law: Historical Perspectives*, Hay, M. J. and M. Wright (eds), Boston: Boston University, 1982, pp. 53–67.

—— 'Neither Customary nor Legal: African CustoMarchy Law in an Era of Family Law Reform', *International Journal of Law and the Family* 3, 1989, pp. 72–88.

Charles, J. O. 'Marriage and lineage segmentation in Ibibioland', *Anthropologica (New Series)* 38(1), 1996, pp. 81–92.

Chirenje, J. M. *Ethiopianism and Afro-Americans in Southern Africa, 1883–1916*, Baton Rouge: Louisiana State University Press, 1987.

Clarence-Smith, W. G. 'African and European Cocoa Producers on Fernando Po, 1880s to 1910s', *The Journal of African History* 35(2), 1994, pp. 179–99.

Clayton, A. *The Thin Blue Line: Studies in Law Enforcement in Late Colonial Africa*, Oxford: Rhodes House Library, 1985.

Cohen, S. *Folk Devils and Moral Panics: The Creation of the Mods and Rockers*, London: MacBibbon and Kee, 1972.

Cohn, B. S. *Colonialism and its Forms of Knowledge: the British in India*, Princeton, NJ: Princeton University Press, 1996.

Coleman, J. S. *Nigeria: Background to Nationalism*, Berkeley: University of California, 1971.

Comaroff, J. L. and J. Comaroff *Ethnography and the Historical Imagination*, Boulder, CO: Westview Press, 1992.

Cooper, F. 'Modernizing Bureaucrats, Backward Africans, and the Development Concept', in *International development and the Social Sciences: Essays on the History and Politics of Knowledge*, Cooper, F. and R. Packard (eds), Berkeley: University of California Press, 1997, pp. 64–92.

Cooper, F. and A. L. Stoler 'Introduction Tensions of Empire: Colonial Control and

Visions of Rule', *American Ethnologist 16(4)*, 1989, pp. 609–21.

Cornwall, A. 'To be a Man is More than a Day's Work: Shifting Ideals of Masculinity in Ado-Odo, Southwestern Nigeria', in *Men and Masculinities in Modern Africa*, Lindsay, L. A. and S. Miescher (eds), Westport, CT: Heinemann, 2003, pp. 230–48.

—— '"In the Olden Day": Histories of Misbehaving Women in Ado-Odo, Southwestern Nigeria', in *Christianity and Social Change in Africa: Essays in Honor of J. D. Y. Peel*, Falola, T. (ed.), Durham, NC: Carolina Academic Press, 2005, pp. 117–38.

Crook, R. C. 'Decolonization, the Colonial State, and Chieftaincy in the Gold Coast', *African Affairs* 85(338), 1986, pp. 75–105.

Crosbie, J. *The Lion Men*, London: Sampson Low, Marchston and Co., 1938.

Crowder, M. *West Africa under Colonial Rule*, Evanston, IL: Northwestern University Press, 1968.

—— 'The 1939–45 War and West Africa', in *History of West Africa*, Ajayi, J. F. A. and M. Crowder (eds), London: Longman, 1985, pp. 596–621.

Cudjoe, R. 'Some Reminiscences of a Senior Interpreter', *The Nigerian Field* XVIII, 1953, pp. 148–64.

Cyrier, J. 1999. Anioto: 'Putting a Paw on Power'. Leopard Men of the Belgian Congo, 1911–36. Paper presented at the 4th Annual Midwestern Graduate Student Conference for African Studies, East Lansing, Michigan, 1999.

Dayrell, E. *Ikom Folk Stories from Southern Nigeria*, London: Royal Anthropological Institute, 1913.

De Cardi, C. N. 'Ju-Ju Laws and Customs in the Niger Delta', *Journal of the Anthropological Institute* 29(1/2), 1899, pp. 51–64.

De Certeau, M. *The Writing of History*, New York: Columbia University Press, 1988.

Derrick, J. 'The "Native Clerk" in Colonial West Africa', *African Affairs* 82, 1983, pp. 61–74.

Dike, C. (ed.) *The Women's Revolt of 1929*, Lagos: Nga, 1995.

Dike, K. O. *Trade and Politics in the Niger Delta, 1830–1885: an Introduction to the Economic and Political History of Nigeria*, Oxford: Clarendon Press, 1956.

Dike, K. O. and F. Ekejiuba *The Aro of South-eastern Nigeria, 1650–1980. A Study of Socio-economic Formation and Transformation in Nigeria*, Ibadan: Ibadan University Press, 1990.

Dirks, N. B. 'Introduction', in *Colonialism and Culture*, Dirks, N. B. (ed.), Ann Arbor, MI: University of Michigan Press 1992, pp. 1–25.

Dorward, D. C. 'Ethnography and Administration: A Study of Anglo-Tiv "Working Misunderstanding"', *The Journal of African History* 15(3), 1974, pp. 457–77.

Douglas, M. 'Techniques of Sorcery Control in Central Africa', in *Witchcraft and Sorcery in East Africa*, Middleton, J. and E. H. Winter (eds), London: Routledge and Kegan Paul, 1963, pp. 123–43.

—— 'Introduction', in *Witchcraft Confessions and Accusations*, Douglas, M. (ed.), London: Tavistock, 1970, pp. xiii–xxxviii.

—— *Risk and Blame: Essays in Cultural Theory*, London: Routledge, 1992.

Edwards, P. (ed.) *Equiano's Travels*, London, 1967.

Ejituwu, N. C. *A History of Obolo (Andoni) in the Niger Delta*, Oron: Manson

Publishing Company, 1991.

Ekandem, M. J. 'The Use of Plants as Symbols in Ibibio and Ibo Country', *Nigerian Field* 20(2), 1955, pp. 53–64.

—— 'Ibibio Farmers and Some of their Customs', *Nigerian Field* 12(4), 1957, pp. 169–75.

Ekechi, F. K. '"The War to End all Wars": Perspectives on the British Assault on a Nigerian Oracle', *Nigeria Magazine* 53, 1985, pp. 59–68.

Ekefre, J. D. 'Nwomo Monument: the Funerary Art of the Anang and Ibibio', *Nigerian Heritage* 1, 1992, pp. 27–37.

Ekejiuba, F. 'Currency Instability and Social Payments among the Igbo of Eastern Nigeria, 1890–1990', in *Money Matters: Instability, Values and Social Payments in the Modern History of West African Communities*, Januarye, I. G. (ed.), Portsmouth, NH: Heinemann and London: James Currey, 1994, pp. 133–61.

Ekpo, V. I. 'Traditional Symbolism of the Women's War of 1929', in *The Women's Revolt of 1929*, Chike, D. (ed.), Lagos: NGA, 1995, pp. 49–74.

Ellis, S. 'Liberia: 1989–1994. A Study of Ethnic and Spiritual Violence', *African Affairs 94*, 1995, pp. 165–97.

—— *The Mask of Anarchy: The Destruction of Liberia and the Religious Dimension of an African Civil War*, London: Hurst and Company, 1999.

—— 'Mystical Weapons: Some Evidence from the Liberian War', *Journal of Religion in Africa* 31(2), 2001, pp. 222–36.

Ema, A. J. U. 'Fattening Girls in Oron, Calabar Province', *Nigeria Magazine* 21, 1940, pp. 386–9.

Evans, J. 'Where Can We Get a Beast without Hair? Medicine Murder in Swaziland from 1970 to 1988', *African Studies* 52, 1993, pp. 27–42.

Evans-Pritchard, E. E. *Witchcraft, Oracles, and Magic among the Azande*, Oxford: Clarendon Press, 1976.

Falola, T. '"Salt is gold": The Management of Salt Scarcity in Nigeria during World War II', *Canadian Journal of African Studies* 26(3), 1992, pp. 412–36.

—— 'Money and Informal Credit Institutions in Colonial Western Nigeria', in *Money Matters: Instability, Values and Social Payments in the Modern History of West African Communities*, Januarye, I. G. (ed.), Portsmouth, NH: Heinemann; London: James Currey, 1994, pp. 162–87.

Fardon, R. 'The Person, Ethnicity and the Problem of "identity" in West Africa', in *African Crossroads. Intersections between History and Anthropology in Cameroon*, Fowler, I. and D. Zietlyn (eds), Providence, RI: Berghahn, 1996, pp. 17–44.

Ferme, M. C. *The Underneath of Things: Violence, History, and the Everyday in Sierra Leone*, Berkeley: University of California Press, 2001.

Fields, K. E. 'Christian Missionaries as Anticolonial Militants', *Theory and Society* 11(1), 1982a, pp. 95–108.

—— 'Political Contingencies of Witchcraft in Colonial Central Africa: Culture and the State in Marxist Theory', *Canadian Journal of African Studies* 16(3), 1982b, pp. 567–93.

—— *Revival and Rebellion in Colonial Central Africa*, Princeton, NJ: Princeton University Press, 1985.

Fitzgerald Marriott, H. P. 'The Secret Societies of West Africa', *Journal of the Royal Anthropological Institute* 29(1/2), 1899, pp. 21–7.

Foran, W. R. 'Lycanthropy in Africa', *African Affairs* 55(219), 1956, pp. 124–34.

Forde, D. 'Integrative Aspects of the Yako First Fruits Rituals', *Journal of the Royal Anthropological Institute of Great Britain and Ireland* 79(1/2), 1949, pp. 1–10.

Forde, D. and G. I. Jones *The Ibo and Ibibio speaking people of South-Eastern Nigeria*, London: International African Institute, 1950.

Gailey, H. A. T. *The Road to Aba: a Study of British Administrative Policy in Eastern Nigeria*, New York: New York University Press, 1970.

Gaunt, M. *The Arms of the Leopard*, London, 1923.

Geschiere, P. *The Modernity of Witchcraft: Politics and the Occult in Postcolonial Africa*, Charlottesville, VA: University of Virginia, 1997.

Ginzburg, C. 'Checking the Evidence: The Judge and the Historian', *Critical Inquiry* 8(1), 1991, pp. 83–4.

Gocking, R. 'A Chieftaincy Dispute and Ritual Murder in Elimina, Ghana, 1945–6', *Journal of African History* 41(2), 2000, pp. 197–219.

Goldie, R. H. *Dictionary of the Efik Language*, Edinburgh: United Presbyterian College Buildings, 1862.

—— *Calabar and its Missions*, Edinburgh: Oliphant Anderson and Ferrier, 1890.

Goldman, L. (ed.) *The Anthropology of Cannibalism*, Westport, CT: Bergin and Garvey, 1999.

Goode, E. and N. Ben-Yehuda *Moral Panics: the Social Construction of Deviance*, Oxford: Blackwell, 1994.

Goody, J. *Death, Property and The Ancestors: a Study of the Mortuary Customs of the LoDagaa of West Africa*, London: Tavistock Publications, 1962.

Gore, C. and D. Pratten 'The Politics of Plunder: The Rhetorics of Order and Disorder in Southern Nigeria', *African Affairs* 102(407), 2003, pp. 211–40.

Graham, J. D. 'Indirect Rule: The Establishment of "Chiefs" and "Tribes" in Cameron's Tanganyika', *Tanzania Notes and Records* 77(78), 1976, pp. 1–9.

Grant, J. C. *The Ethiopian: A Narrative of the Society of Human Leopards*, Paris: Libraires, 1900.

Green, M. 'Mau Mau Oathing Rituals and Political Ideology in Kenya: A re-analysis', *Africa* 60(1), 1990, pp. 69–87.

Grey, R. 'Manillas', *Nigerian Field* 16(2), 1951, pp. 52–66.

Groves, R. W. 'The Story of Udo Akpabio of the Annang Tribe, Southern Nigeria', in *Ten Africans*, Perham, M. (ed.), London: Faber and Faber, 1936, pp. 41–61.

Guillot, R. *Michel Fodai and the Leopard-Men*, London: Harrap, 1969.

Guyer, J. *Marginal Gains: Monetary Transactions in Atlantic Africa*, Chicago: Chicago University Press, 2004.

Guyer, J. I. 'Indigenous currencies and the History of Marriage Payments: a Case Study from Cameroon', *Cahiers d'Etudes Africaines* 26(4), 1986, pp. 577–610.

Hailey, W. M. *Native Administration in the British African Territories, Part III: West Africa, Nigeria, Gold Coast, Sierra Leone, Gambia*, London: HMSO, 1951.

Hair, P. E. H. 'Ethnolinguistic Continuity on the Guinea Coast', *Journal of African History* VIII(2), 1967, pp. 247–68.

Harneit-Sievers, A. 'Dreams of Free Trade in Colonial Nigeria: Peter Eket Inyang Udoh and his Ibibio Ventures, 1929–1941', in *Afrikanische Beziehungen, Netzwerke und Räume (Festschrift for Leonhard Harding)*, Marchfaing, L. and B. Reinwald (eds), Münster/Hamburg: LIT, 2001, pp. 187–97.

Harris, J. S. 'The Position of Women in a Nigerian Society', *Transactions of the New York Academy of Sciences* 2(5), 1940, pp. 141–8.

—— 'Some Aspects of Slavery in Southeastern Nigeria', *Journal of Negro History* 27(1), 1942, pp. 37–54.

Hau, K. 'Oberi Okaime: Script, Texts and Counting System', *Bulletin de l'IFAN* XXIII Ser. B(1–2), 1961, pp. 291–308.

Hawthorne, W. 'Nourishing a Stateless Society During the Slave Trade: the Rise of Balanta Paddy-Rice Production in Guinea-Bissau', *Journal of African History* 42, 2001, pp. 1–24.

Helleiner, G. K. *Peasant Agriculture, Government and Economic Growth in Nigeria*, Homewood: II: R. D. Irwin, 1966.

Henderson, R. N. 'Generalised Cultures and Evolutionary Adaptibility: a Comparison of Urban Efik and Ibo in Nigeria', in *Nigeria: Modernization and the Politics of Communalism*, Melson, R. and H. Wolpe (eds), East Lansing, MI: Michigan State University, 1971, pp. 215–52.

Hergé *Les aventures de Tintin: Reporter du Petit 'Vingtième' au Congo*, Tournai: Casterman, 1982.

Hobsbawm, E. *Bandits*, London: Weidenfeld and Nicolson, 1969.

—— 'Social Bandits: Reply', *Comparative Studies in Society and History* 14(4), 1972, pp. 503–5.

Hodgson, D. L. and S. McCurdy 'Introduction: "Wicked" Women and the Reconfiguration of Gender in Africa', in *Social History of Africa*, Hodgson, D. L. and S. McCurdy (eds), Portsmouth, NH: Heinemann; Oxford: James Currey, 2001, pp. 1–24.

Hopkins, A. G. 'Economic Aspects of Political Movements in Nigeria and the Gold Coast, 1918–1939', *Journal of African History* 7(1), 1966, pp. 133–52.

Horton, R. 'Stateless Societies in the History of West Africa', in *History of West Africa*, Ajayi, A. and M. Crowder (eds), London: Longman, 1967, pp. 72–113.

—— 'African Conversion', *Africa* 41(2), 1971, pp. 85–108.

Horton, R. and J. D. Y. Peel 'Conversion and Confusion: A rejoinder on Christianity in Eastern Nigeria', *Canadian Journal of African Studies* 10(3), 1976, pp. 481–98.

Hunt, N. R. 'Noise over Camouflaged Polygamy, Colonial Morality Taxation, and a Woman-Naming Crisis in Belgian Africa', *The Journal of African History* 32(3), 1991, pp. 471–94.

—— 'Tintin and the Interruptions of Congolese Comics', in *Images and Empires: Visuality in Colonial and Postcolonial Africa*, Landau, P. S. and D. D. Kaspin (eds), Berkeley: University of California, 2002, pp. 90–123.

Hutchinson, S. 'Rising Divorce Among the Nuer, 1936–1983', *Man, New Series* 25(3), 1990, pp. 393–411.

Hutton, J. H. 'Leopard-Men in the Naga Hills', *Journal of the Royal Anthropological Institute of Great Britain and Ireland* 50, 1920, pp. 41–51.

Ibhawoh, B. 'Stronger than the Maxim Gun: Law, Human Rights and British Colonial Hegemony in Nigeria', *Africa* 72(1), 2002, pp. 55–83.

Ifeka-Moller, C. 'Female Militancy and Colonial Revolt: The Women's War of 1929, Eastern Nigeria', in *Perceiving Women*, Ardener, S. (ed.), London: Malaby Press, 1975, pp. 127–57.

Ikime, O. 'The Anti-Tax Riots in Warri Province, 1927–1928', *Journal of the Historical Society of Nigeria* 3(3), 1966, pp. 559–73.

Iliffe, J. 'The Organization of the Maji Maji Rebellion', *The Journal of African History* 8(3), 1967, pp. 495–512.

Jackson, M. 'The Man Who Could Turn into an Elephant: Shape-shifting among the Kuranko of Sierra Leone', in *Person and Agency: the Experience of Self and Others in African Cultures*, Jackson, M. and I. Karp (eds), Uppsala: Acta Universitatis Upsaliensis, 1990, pp. 59–78.

James, W. 'The Anthropologist as Reluctant Imperialist', in *Anthropology and the Colonial Encounter*, Asad, T. (ed.), London: Ithaca Press, 1973, pp. 41–69.

Jedrej, M. C. 'Medicine, Fetish and Secret Society in a West African Culture', *Africa* 46, 1976, pp. 247–57.

—— 'Cosmology and Symbolism on the Central Guinea Coast', *Anthropos 81*, 1986, pp. 497–515.

Jeffreys, M. D. W., *Old Calabar and Some Notes on the Ibibio Language*, Calabar: Hope Waddell Press, 1935.

—— 'The Bicycle Traffic in Calabar Province', *Nigeria Magazine* 21, 1940, pp. 378–9.

—— 'A Contraceptive Girdle from Calabar Province, Nigeria', *Man* 44, 1944, p. 80.

—— 'Age Grade Among the Ika and Kindred People', *African Studies* 9(4), 1950, pp. 157–66.

—— 'The Ekon Players', *Eastern Anthropologist* 5(1), 1951, pp. 41–7.

—— 'African Tarantula or Dancing Mania', *Eastern Anthropologist* 6(2), 1952–53, pp. 98–105.

—— 'The Burial Bird for an Okuku', *African Studies* 14(3), 1955, pp. 134–7.

—— 'The Nyama Society of the Ibibio Women', *African Studies* 15(1), 1956, pp. 15–28.

—— 'Witchcraft in Calabar Province', *African Studies* 25(2), 1966, pp. 95–100.

Jones, A. *From Slaves to Palm Kernels: a History of the Galinhas Country (West Africa)*, 1730–1890, Wiesbaden: F. Steiner, 1983.

Jones, G. I. 'Native and Trade Currencies in Southern Nigeria during the Eighteenth and Nineteenth Centuries', *Africa* 28, 1958, pp. 43–54.

—— *The Trading States of the Oil Rivers: a Study of Political Development in Eastern Nigeria*, London: Oxford University Press, 1963.

—— 'Olaudah Equiano of the Niger Ibo', in *Africa Remembered: Naratives by West Africans from the Era of the Slave Trade*, Curtin, P. (ed.), Madison, WI: Waveland Press, 1967, pp. 60–98.

—— 'Chieftaincy in the former Eastern Region of Nigeria', in *West African Chiefs: Their Changing Status under Colonial Rule and Independence*, M. Crowder and O. Ikime (eds), Ile-Ife: University of Ife Press, 1970, pp. 312–24.

—— 'Social Anthropology in Nigeria During the Colonial Period', *Africa* 44(2), 1974, pp. 280–9.

—— *The Art of Eastern Nigeria*, Cambridge: Cambridge University Press, 1984.

—— *The Background of Eastern Nigerian History*, New Haven CT: Human Relations Area Files, 1988.

—— *From Slaves to Palm Oil: Slave Trade and Palm Oil Trade in the Bight of Biafra*, Cambridge: African Studies Centre, 1989a.

—— 'Recollections of the Spirit Movement in the Ibibio Area of Calabar Province', *Africa* 59(4), 1989b, pp. 517.

Joset, P. -E. *Les Sociétés Secrètes: Des Hommes-Léopards en Afrique Noire*, Paris: Payot, 1955.

Kalous, M. *Cannibals and Tongo Players of Sierra Leone*, Trentham, NZ: Wright and Carman, 1974.

Kalu, O. U. 'Missionaries, Colonial Government and Secret Societies in South-Eastern Igboland, 1920–1950', *Journal of the Historical Society of Nigeria* 9(1), 1977a, pp. 75–90.

—— 'Waves from the Rivers: the Spread of the Garrick Braide Movement in Igboland, 1914–1934', *Journal of the Historical Society of Nigeria* 8(4), 1977b, pp. 95–110.

Kaufman, E. M. *Ibibio Dictionary*, Leiden: Cross River State University Ibibio Language Board and African Studies Centre, 1972.

Kennerley, J. *The Terror of the Leopard Men*, New York: Avon Publishing Co., 1951.

Kershaw, G. *Mau Mau from Below*, Oxford: James Currey, 1997.

Killam, G. D. 'The "Educated African" Theme in English Fiction about Africa, 1884–1939', *Phylon* 27(2), 1966, pp. 155–64.

Kiple, K. F. and V. H. Kiple 'Deficiency Diseases in the Caribbean', *Journal of Interdisciplinary History* 11(2), 1980, pp. 197–15.

Kirk-Greene, A. H. M. (ed.) *The Principles of Native Administration in Nigeria: Selected Documents, 1900–1947*, London: Oxford University Press, 1965.

Klein, M. A. 'The Slave Trade and Decemberentralized Societies', *Journal of African History* 42, 2001, pp. 49–65.

Koelle, S. W. *Polyglotta Africana, Graz*, Austria: Akademische Druck u. Verlagsanalt, 1963.

Kpone-Tonwe, S. 'Property Reckoning and Methods of Accumulating Wealth among the Ogoni of the Eastern Niger Delta', *Africa* 67(1), 1997, pp. 131–58.

La Hausse, P. '"The Cows of Nongoloza": Youth, Crime and Amalaita Gangs in Durban, 1900–1936', *Journal of Southern African Studies* 16(1), 1990, pp. 79–111.

Lackner, H. 'Social Anthropology and Indirect Rule: the Colonial Administration and Anthropology in Eastern Nigeria 1920–1940', in *Anthropology and the Colonial Encounter*, Asad, T. (ed.), London: Ithaca Press, 1973, pp. 123–53.

Lan, D. *Guns and Rain: Guerrillas and Spirit Mediums in Zimbabwe*, London: James Currey, 1985.

Laouel, B. 'Ethiopianism and African Nationalism in South Africa before 1937', *Cahiers d'Études Africaines* 26(4), 1986, pp. 681–8.

Latham, A. J. H. 'Currency, Credit and Capitalism on the Cross River in the Pre-Colonial Era', *Journal of African History*, 1971, pp. 599–605.

—— 'Witchcraft Accusations and Economic Tension in Pre-Colonial Calabar', *Journal of African History* 13(2), 1972, pp. 249–60.

—— *Old Calabar, 1600–1891: the Impact of the International Economy upon a Traditional Society*, Oxford: Clarendon Press, 1973.

Law, R. 'Human Sacrifice in Pre-colonial West Africa', *African Affairs* 84(334), 1985, pp. 55–6.

Leach, M. *Rainforest Relations: Gender and Resource Use among the Mende of Gola, Sierra Leone*, Edinburgh: Edinburgh University Press, 1994.

Leonard, A. G. *The Lower Niger and its Tribes*, London: Frank Cass, 1966.

Lieber, J. W. *Efik and Ibibio Villages*, Ibadan: Institute of Education Ibadan University, 1971.

Lindskog, B. *African Leopard Men*, Uppsala: Almqvist and Wiksells Boktryckeri AB, 1954.

Little, K. 'The Role of the Secret Society in Cultural Specialization', *American Anthropologist* 51, 1949, pp. 199–212.

Lovejoy, P. and D. Richardson 'The Business of Slaving: Pawnship in Western Africa, c. 1600–1810', *Journal of African History* 42, 2001, pp. 67–89.

Lovejoy, P. E. and D. Richardson 'Trust, Pawnship, and Atlantic History: The Institutional Foundations of the Old Calabar Slave Trade', *The American Historical Review* 104(2), 1999, pp. 333–55.

Lynn, M. 'Change and Continuity in the British Palm Oil Trade with West Africa 1830–1855', *The Journal of African History* 22(3), 1981, pp. 331–48.

—— 'Commerce, Christianity and the Origins of the 'Creoles' of Fernando Po', *The Journal of African History* 25(3), 1984, pp. 257–78.

—— *Commerce and Economic Change in West Africa: the Palm-oil Trade in the Nineteenth Century*, Cambridge: Cambridge University Press, 1997.

—— (ed.) *Nigeria. Part I. Managing Political Reform 1943–60*, London: Stationery Office, 2000.

MacCormack, C. P. 'Human Leopards and Crocodiles: Political Meanings of Categorical Ambiguities', in *The Ethnography of Cannabalism*, Brown, P. and D. Tuzin (eds), Washington: Society for Psychological Anthropology, 1983, pp. 51–60.

MacGaffey, W. *Religion and Society in Central Africa*, Chicago: University of Chicago Press, 1986.

Maes, J. 'Les Anioto des Mobali', *La Revue Congolaise* 2, 1911, pp. 314–15.

Malcolm, L. W. G. 'Short Notes on Soul-Trapping in Southern Nigeria', *The Journal of American Folklore* 35(137), 1922, pp. 219–22.

Malcom, L. W. G. 'Note on the Seclusion of Girls among the Efik of Old Calabar', *Man* 25, 1925, pp. 113–14.

Maling, R. W. 'The Were Leopard', *Uganda Journal* VII, 1939, pp. 93–5.

Malinowski, B. 'Practical Anthropology', *Africa* 2, 1929, pp. 22–8.

Mamdani, M. *Citizen and Subject: Contemporary Africa and the Legacy of Late Colonialism*, Princeton, NJ: Princeton University Press, 1996.

Martin, A. *The Oil Palm Economy of the Ibibio Farmer*, Ibadan: Ibadan University Press, 1956.

Marchtin, S. M. 'Gender and Innovation – Farming, Cooking and Palm Processing in the Ngwa Region, Southeastern Nigeria, 1900–1930', *Journal of African History* 25(4), 1984, pp. 411–27.

—— *Palm Oil and Protest: An economic history of the Ngwa region, south-eastern Nigeria, 1800–1980*, Cambridge: Cambridge University Press, 1988.

Marwick, B. *The Swazi*, Cambridge: Cambridge University Press, 1940.

Mbiti, J. S. *African Religions and Philosophy*, London: Heinemann, 1969.

McCall, J. A. G. 'Comment on the "Leopard" Killings', *Africa* 56(4), 1986, pp. 441–5.

McCall, J. C. 'Rethinking ancestors in Africa', *Africa* 65(2), 1995, pp. 256–70.

McCaskie, T. C. 'State and Society, Marriage and Adultery: Some Considerations towards a Social History of Precolonial History', *Journal of African History* 22(4), 1981, pp. 477–94.

—— 'Death and the Asantehene: A Historical Meditation', *Journal of African History* 30, 1989, pp. 417–44.

—— 'People and animals: Constru(ct)ing the Asante experience', *Africa* 62(2), 1992, pp. 221–47.

McIntosh, S. K. (ed.) *Beyond Chiefdoms: Pathways to Complexity in Africa*, Cambridge: Cambridge University Press, 1999.

McMahon, A. B. *The Hill of Healing: the Marchy Slessor Hospital in Itu*, Calabar, 1936.

Meillassoux, C. '"The Economy" in Agricultural Self-sustaining Societies: a Preliminary Analysis', in *Relations of Production: Marxist Approaches to Social Anthropology*, Seddon, D. (ed.), London: Frank Cass, 1978, pp. 127–58.

Melton, G. J. 'Unity School of Christianity', in *Encyclopedia of American Religions*, Detroit: Gale Research Inc., 1996, pp. 637–8.

Meredith, D. 'Government and the Development of the Nigerian Oil-Palm Export Industry, 1919–1939', *The Journal of African History* 25(3), 1984, pp. 311–29.

Messenger, J. C. 'The Role of Proverbs in a Nigerian Judicial System', *Southwestern Journal of Anthropology 15(1)*, 1959, pp. 64–73.

—— 'Religious Acculturation among the Anang Ibibio', in *Continuity and Change in African Cultures*, Bascom, W. R. and M. J. Herskovits (eds), Chicago: University of Chicago Press, 1962, pp. 279–99.

—— 'The Carver in Anang Society', in *The Traditional Artist in African Society*, Azeredo, W. L. d. (ed.), Bloomington: Indiana University Press, 1973, pp. 101–27.

—— 'Ancestor Worship among the Anang: Belief system and Cult Institution', in *African Religious Groups and Beliefs*, Ottenberg, S. (ed.), Chanakya, Puri, Meerut, India: Archana Publications, 1984, pp. 63–75.

Messenger, J. C. and B. T. Messenger 'Sexuality in Folklore in a Nigerian Society', *Central Issues in Anthropology* 3(1), 1981, pp. 29–50.

Meyer, B. '"Make a Complete Break with the Past": Memory and Postcolonial Modernity in Ghanaian Pentecostal Discourse', in *Memory and the Postcolony: African Anthropology and the Critique of Power*, Werbner, R. (ed.), London: Zed Books, 1998, pp. 182–8.

—— *Translating the Devil: Religion and Modernity among the Ewe in Ghana*, Edinburgh: Edinburgh University Press, 1999.

M'Keown, R. L. *Twenty-five Years in Qua Iboe: the Story of Missionary Effort in Nigeria*, London: Morgan and Scott, 1912.

Mudimbe, V. Y. *The Invention of Africa: Gnosis, Philosophy, and the Order of Knowledge*, London: James Currey; Bloomington: Indiana University Press, 1988.

Murphy, W. P. 'Secret Knowledge as Property and Power in Kpelle society: Elders versus Youth', *Africa* 50(2), 1980, pp. 193–207.

—— 'The Rhetorical Management of Dangerous Knowledge in Kpelle Brokerage', *American Ethnologist* 8(4), 1981, pp. 667–85.

Murray, C. and P. Sanders 'Medicine Murder in Basutoland: Colonial Rule and Moral Crisis', *Africa* 70(1), 2000, pp. 49–78.

Naanen, B. B. B. 'Economy within an Economy: the Manilla Currency, Exchange

Rate Instability and Social Conditions in South-eastern Nigeria, 1900–48', *Journal of African History* 34(3), 1993, pp. 425–6.

Newell, S. '"Paracolonial" Networks: Some Speculations on Local Readerships in Colonial West Africa', *Interventions: International Journal of Post-colonial Studies* 3(3), 2001, pp. 336–54.

Ngubane, H. 'The Predicament of the Sinister Healer', in *The Professionalisation of African Medicine*, Last, M. and G. L. Chavanduka (eds), Manchester: Manchester University Press, 1986, pp. 189–204.

Nicklin, K. 'Abang Isong: the Ibibio Ceremonial Palm-wine Pot', *Nigerian Field* XXXVIII(4), 1973, pp. 180–9.

Nnoli, O. *Ethnic Politics in Nigeria*, Enugu: Fourth Dimension Publishers, 1978.

Noah, M. E. *Ibibio Pioneers in Modern Nigerian History*, Uyo: Scholars Press, 1980.

—— 'The Establishment of British Rule among the Ibibio, 1835–1910. Part One: The Military Approach', *Nigeria Magazine* (148), 1984, pp. 38–51.

—— 'The Establishment of British Rule among the Ibibio, 1835–1910. Part Two: The Judiciary', *Nigeria Magazine* (149), 1984, pp. 24–34.

—— 'The Role, Status and Influence of Women in Traditional Times: the Example of the Ibibio of Southeastern Nigeria', *Nigeria Magazine* 53, 1985, pp. 24–31.

—— 'After the Warrant Chiefs – Native Authority Rule in Ibibioland 1931–1951', *Phylon* 48(1), 1987, pp. 77–90.

—— 'The Ibibio Union 1928–1966', *Canadian Journal of African Studies-Revue Canadienne Des Etudes Africaines* 21(1), 1987, pp. 38–53.

—— 'Native Authority Rule in Ibibioland 1931–51', in *Proceedings of the Ibibio Union 1928–1937*, Noah, M. E. (ed.), Uyo: Modern Business Press, 1988a, pp. 21–45.

—— 'Aba Women's Riot: Need for a Re-definition', in *The Women's War of 1929*, Chike, D. (ed.), Lagos: Nga, 1995, pp. 105–16.

—— (ed.) *Proceedings of the Ibibio Union 1928–1937*, Uyo: Modern Business Press, 1988b.

Northrup, D. 'The Growth of Trade among the Igbo before 1800', *Journal of African History* 13(2), 1972, pp. 217–236.

—— 'New Light from Old Sources: Pre-Colonial References to the Anang Ibibio', *Ikenga* 2(1), 1973, pp. 1–5.

—— 'The Compatibility of the Slave and Palm Oil Trades in the Bight of Biafra', *Journal of African History* 17(3), 1976, pp. 353–64.

—— *Trade Without Rulers: Pre-Colonial Economic Development in South-Eastern Nigeria*, Oxford: Clarendon Press, 1978.

—— 'Nineteenth Century Patterns of Slavery and Economic Growth in South-Eastern Nigeria', *International Journal of African Historical Studies* 12(1), 1979a, pp. 1–16.

—— 'Roger Casement and the Aro', *Ikenga* 4(1), 1979b, pp. 46–50.

Nwabughuogu, A. I. 'The Role of Propaganda in the Development of Indirect Rule in Nigeria, 1890–1929', *The International Journal of African Historical Studies* 14(1), 1981, pp. 65–92.

—— 'Oil Mill Riots in Eastern Nigeria, 1948–51: A study of Indigenous Reaction to Technological Change', *Journal of African Studies* 12(4), 1985, pp. 194–202.

Nwahaghi, F. N. 'Fidelity in Ibibio Marriage: the Role of Ekpo Nka Owo, the ancestral Spirit of Adultery', *Africa Marchburgensia* (Special Issue 16), 1997, pp. 48–59.

Nwaka, G. 'Secret Societies and Colonial Change: A Nigerian Example', *Cahiers d'Études africaines* 18(1/2), 1978, pp. 187–200.

—— 'The Ibibio Union and Colonial Change', *Nigeria Magazine* 146, 1983, pp. 85–94.

—— 'The "Leopard" Killings of Southern Anang, Nigeria, 1943–48', *Africa* 56(4), 1986, pp. 417–45.

Nwokeji, G. U. 'Britain's Response to post-Second World War Colonial Crisis, 1947–50: Findings and Reflections from the Nigeria Research', *Frankfurter Afrikanistische Blätter* 6, 1994, pp. 75–86.

Obiechina, E. N. *Literature for the Masses. An Analytical Study of Popular Pamphleteering*, Enugu: Nwankwo-Ifejika and Co., 1971.

—— (ed.) *Onitsha Market Literature*, London: Heinemann Educational, 1972.

Offiong, D. A. 'The 1978–79 Akpan Ekwong Anti-Witchcraft Crusade in Nigeria', *Anthropologica* XXIV, 1982, pp. 27–42.

—— 'The Status of Slaves in Igbo and Ibibio of Nigeria', *Phylon* 46(1), 1985, pp. 49–57.

—— *Continuity and Change among the Traditional Associations of Nigeria*, Zaria: Ahmadu Bello University Press, 1989.

—— 'Conflict resolution among the Ibibio of Nigeria', *Journal of Anthropological Research* 53(4), 1997, pp. 423–441.

Ohadike, D. C. 'The Influenza Pandemic of 1918–1919 and the Spread of Cassava Cultivation on the Lower Niger: A Study in Historical Linkages', *Journal of African History* 22(3), 1981, pp. 15–56.

Okonjo, C. 'Sranger Communities: The Western Ibo', in *The City of Ibadan*, Lloyd, P. C., A. L. Mabogunje and B. Awe (eds), Cambridge: Cambridge University Press, 1967, pp. 97–116.

Okonjo, I. M. *British Administration in Nigeria 1900–1950: A Nigerian View*, New York: Nok, 1974.

Olusanya, G. O. 'The Role of Ex-Servicemen in Nigerian Politics', *The Journal of Modern African Studies* 6(2), 1968, pp. 221–32.

—— *The Second World War and Politics in Nigeria, 1939–1953*, London: University of Lagos, 1973.

Omu, F. I. A. *Press and Politics in Nigeria, 1880–1937*, London: Longman, 1978.

Onwuteaka, V. C. 'The Aba Riot of 1929 and its Relation to the System of "Indirect Rule"', *Nigerian Journal of Economic and Social Studies* 7(3), 1965, pp. 273–82.

Oriji, J. N. 'A Re-Assessment of the Organisation and Benefits of the Slave and Palm Produce Trade Among the Ngwa-Igbo', *Canadian Journal of African Studies* 16(3), 1982, pp. 523–48.

Ottenberg, P. V. 'The Changing Economic Position of Women among the Afikpo Ibo', in *Continuity and Change in African Cultures*, Bascom, W. R. and M. J. Herskovits (eds), Chicago, 1959, pp. 205–23.

Ottenberg, S. 'Humorous Masks and Serious Politics among Afikpo Ibo', in *African Art and Leadership*, Fraser, D. and H. M. Cole (eds), Madison, WI: University of Wisconsin Press, 1972, pp. 99–121.

Ottenberg, S. and L. Knudsen 'Leopard Society Masquerades - Symbolism and Diffusion', *African Arts* 18(2), 1985, pp. 37–44 and 93.

Parkinson, J. 'Notes on the Efik belief in "Bush Soul"', *Man* 6, 1906, pp. 121–2.

Parry, J. P. and M. Bloch 'Introduction: Money and the Morality of Exchange', in *Money and the Morality of Exchange*, Parry, J. P. and M. Bloch (eds), Cambridge: Cambridge University Press, 1989, pp. 1–32.

Pearce, R. *The Turning Point in Africa: British Colonial Policy, 1938–48*, London: Frank Cass, 1982.

Peel, J. D. Y. Aladura: *A Religious Movement among the Yoruba*, London: Oxford University Press, 1968.

—— 'Syncretism and Religious Change', *Comparative Studies in Society and History* 10(2), 1968, pp. 121–41.

—— *Ijeshas and Nigerians: The Incorporation of a Yoruba Kingdom, 1880s–1970s*, Cambridge: Cambridge University Press, 1983.

—— 'The Pastor and the Babalawo – the Interaction of Religions in 19th-Century Yorubaland', *Africa* 60(3), 1990, pp. 338–69.

—— 'For Who Hath Despised the Day of Small Things? Missionary Narratives and Historical Anthropology', *Comparative Studies in Society and History* 37(3), 1995, pp. 581–607.

—— *Religious Encounter and the Making of the Yoruba*, Bloomington, IN: Indiana University Press, 2000.

—— 'Gender in Yoruba Religious Change', *Journal of Religion in Africa*, 2002, pp. 136–66.

Pels, P. 'The Pidginization of Luguru Politics: Administrative Ethnography and the Paradoxes of Indirect Rule', *American Ethnologist* 23(4), 1996, pp. 738–61.

—— 'Creolisation in Secret. The Birth of Nationalism in Late Colonial Uluguru, Tanzania', *Africa* 72(1), 2002, pp. 1–28.

Pereira, D. P. *Esmerelda de Situ Orbis*, London: Hakluyt Society, 1937.

Perham, M. *Native Administration in Nigeria*, London: Oxford University Press, 1937.

Piot, C. *Remotely Global: Village Modernity in West Africa*, Chicago: University of Chicago Press, 1999.

Post, K. *The Nigerian Federal Election of 1959: Politics and Administration in a Developing Political System*, London: Oxford University Press, 1963.

Proctor, J. H. 'Serving God and the Empire: Mary Slessor in South-eastern Nigeria, 1876–1915', *Journal of Religion in Africa* 30(1), 2000, pp. 45–61.

Ranger, T. O. 'Religious Movements and Politics in Sub-Saharan Africa', *African Studies Review* 29(2), 1986, pp. 1–69.

Rathbone, R. 'A Murder in the Colonial Gold Coast: Law and Politics in the 1940s', *Journal of African History* 30(3), 1989, pp. 445–61.

—— *Murder and Politics in Colonial Ghana*, New Haven, CT and London: Yale University Press, 1993.

Renne, E. P. and M. L. Bastian 'Reviewing Twinship in Africa', *Ethnology* 40(1), 2001, pp. 1–11.

Rice Burroughs, E. *Tarzan and the Leopard Men*, Tarzana: ERB, Inc., 1935.

Rich, J. 'Leopard Men, Slaves and Social Conflict in Libreville (Gabon) c. 1860–1879', *International Journal of African Historical Studies* 34(3), 2001, pp. 619–38.

Richards, P. 'Natural Symbols and Natural History: Chimpanzees, Elephants and Experiments in Mende Thought', in *Environmentalism: the View from Anthropology*, Milton, K. (ed.), London: Routledge, 1993, pp. 144–59.

—— 'Chimpanzees, Diamonds and War: The Discourses of Global Environmental Change and Local Violence on the Liberia–Sierra Leone Border', in *The Future of Anthropological Knowledge*, Moore, H. (ed.), London and New York: Routledge, 1996, pp. 139–55.

—— '"Witches", "Cannibals" and War in Liberia (Book Review)', *Journal of African History* 42(1), 2001, pp. 167–70.

Riesman, P. 'The Person and the Life Cycle in African Social life and Thought', *African Studies Review* 29(2), 1986, pp. 71–198.

Roberts, A. F. '"Like a Roaring Lion": Tabera Terrorism in the Late Nineteenth Century', in *Banditry, Rebellion and Social Protest in Africa*, Crummey, D. (ed.) London: James Currey and Heinemann, 1996, pp. 65–86.

Roberts, R. 'Representation, Structure and Agency: Divorce in the French Sudan during the Early Twentieth Century', *Journal of African History* 40(3), 1999, pp. 389–410.

Roberts, R. and K. Mann 'Introduction', in *Law in Colonial Africa*, Richard, R. and M. Kristin (eds), London: James Currey, 1991, pp. 3–58.

Ruel, M. 'The Modern Adaptation of Associations among the Banyang of the West Cameroon', *Southwestern Journal of Anthropology* 20(1), 1964, pp. 1–14.

—— *Leopards and Leaders: Constitutional Politics among a Cross River People*, London and New York: Tavistock Publications, 1969.

—— 'Were-animals and the Introverted Witch', in *Witchcraft Confessions and Accusations*, Douglas, M. (ed.), London: Tavistock Publications, 1970, pp. 333–50.

Sahlins, M. D. 'The Segmentary Lineage: an Organisation of Predatory Expansion', *American Anthropologist* 63, 1961, pp. 322–45.

—— *Islands of History*, Chicago: University of Chicago Press, 1985.

Salmons, J. 'Funerary Shrine Cloths of the Annang Ibibio, Southeast Nigeria', *Textile History* 11, 1980, pp. 119–41.

—— 'Martial arts of the Annang', *African Arts* 19(1), 1985, pp. 57–63, 87–88.

Sangree, W. H. 'Youths as Elders and Infants as Ancestors: the Complementarity of Alternative Generations, both Living and Dead in Tiriki, Kenya and Irigwe, Nigeria', *Africa* 44(1), 1974, pp. 65–70.

Scheinberg, A. L. *Ekon Society Puppets: Sculptures for Social Criticism*, New York: Albert Gordon and Leonard Kalm, 1977.

Schneider, H. K. 'The Lion Men of Singida: A Reappraisal', *Tanganyika Notes and Records* 58/59, 1962, pp. 124–8.

—— 'Male–Female Conflict and Lion Men of Singida', in *African Religious Groups and Beliefs*, Ottenberg, S. (ed.), Cupertino, CA: Folklore Institute, 1982, pp. 95–109.

Shadle, B. L. 'Bridewealth and Female Consent: Marriage Disputes in African Courts, Gusiland, Kenya', *The Journal of African History* 44(2), 2003, pp. 241–62.

Shaw, J. J. *The Leopard Men*, London: Frederick Warne, 1953.

Shaw, R. *Memories of the Slave Trade: Ritual and the Historical Imagination in Sierra Leone*, Chicago: University of Chicago Press, 2002.

Sheridan, R. B. 'The Guinea Surgeons on the Middle Passage: The Provision of Medical Services in the British Slave Trade', *The International Journal of African Historical Studies* 14(4), 1981, pp. 601–25.

Shirley, W. R. *A History of the Nigerian Police*, Lagos, 1950.

Simmons, D. C. 'Efik Divination, Ordeals and Omens', *Southwestern Journal of Anthropology* 12(2), 1956, pp. 223–8.

—— 'The Depiction of Gangosa on Efik-Ibibio Masks', *Man* 57, 1957, pp. 17–20.

Sklar, R. L. *Nigerian Political Parties: Power in an Emergent African Nation*, Princeton, NJ: Princeton University Press, 1963.

Smith, D. J. 'Ritual Killing, 419, and Fast Wealth: Inequality and the Popular Imagination in Southeastern Nigeria', *American Ethnologist* 28(4), 2001, pp. 803–26.

Smock, A. C. *Ibo Politics: The Role of Ethnic Unions in Eastern Nigeria*, Cambridge, MA: Harvard University Press, 1971.

Snelgrave, W. *A New Account of Some Parts of Guinea and the Slave Trade*, London, 1734.

Southall, A. W. 'From Segmentary Lineage to Ethnic Association – Luo, Luhya, Ibo and Others', in *Colonialism and Change: Essays presented to Lucy Mair*, Maxwell, O. (ed.), The Hague and Paris: Mouton, 1975, pp. 203–29.

Stanley, W. B. 'Carnivorous Apes in Sierra Leone', *Sierra Leone Studies* 11, 1919, pp. 3–19.

Stoler, A. L. '"In Cold Blood": Hierarchies of Credibility and the Politics of Colonial Narratives', *Representations* 37, 1992, pp. 151–89.

—— 'Colonial Archives and the Arts of Governance', *Archival Science* 2(1–2), 2002, pp. 87–109.

Stoler, A. L. and F. Cooper 'Between Metropole and Colony. Rethinking a Research Agenda', in *Tensions of Empire: Colonial Cultures in a Bourgeois World*, Cooper, F. and A. L. Stoler (eds), Berkeley: University of California Press, 1989, pp. 1–56.

Sundiata, I. K. 'Prelude to Scandal: Liberia and Fernando Po, 1880–1930', *The Journal of African History* 15(1), 1974, pp. 97–112.

—— *From Slavery to Neoslaver: The Bight of Biafra and Fernando Po in the Era of Abolition, 1827–1930*, Madison, WI: University of Wisconsin, 1996.

Talbot, D. A. *Woman's Mysteries of a Primitive People: the Ibibios of Southern Nigeria*, London: Cassell, 1915.

Talbot, P. A. 'The Land of the Ibibios, Southern Nigeria', *The Geographical Journal* July–December, 1914, pp. 287–306.

—— 'Some Ibibio Customs and Beliefs', *Journal of the Royal African Society* 13(51), 1914, pp. 241–58.

—— *Life in Southern Nigeria. The Magic, Beliefs and Customs of the Ibibio Tribe*, London: Frank Cass, 1923.

—— *The Peoples of Southern Nigeria: A Sketch of their History, Ethnology and Languages, with an Abstract of the 1921 Census*, London: Oxford University Press, 1926.

—— *Tribes of the Niger Delta: Their Religions and Customs*, London: The Sheldon Press, 1932.

Tamuno, T. N. *The Police in Modern Nigeria 1861–1965: Origins, Development and Role*, Ibadan: Ibadan University Press, 1970.

Tamuno, T. N. and R. Horton 'The Changing Position of Secret Societies and Cults in Modern Nigeria', *African Notes* 5, 1969, pp. 36–62.

Tasie, G. O. M. 'Christian Awakening in West Africa, 1914–1918: a Study in the Significance of Native Agency', *West African Religion* 16(2), 1975, pp. 31–42.

Taylor, W. H. 'Missionary Education in Africa Reconsidered: The Presbyterian Educational Impact in Eastern Nigeria 1846–1974', *African Affairs* 83(331), 1984, pp. 189–205.

Thompson, K. *Moral Panics*, London and New York: Routledge, 1998.

Tonkin, E. 'Masks and Power', *Man* 14(2), 1979, pp. 237–248.

—— 'West African Ethnographic Traditions', in *Localizing Strategies: Regional Traditions of Ethnographic Writing*, Fardon, R. (ed.), Edinburgh: Scottish Academic Press, 1990, pp. 137–52.

—— 'Autonomous Judges: African Ordeals as Dramas of Power', *Ethnos: Journal of Anthropology* 65(3), 2000, pp. 366–86.

Torday, E. 'Things that Matter to the West African', *Man* 13(116), 1931, pp. 110–13.

Trotti, M. A. 'Review Essay: The Lure of the Sensational Murder', *Journal of Social History* 35(2), 2001, pp. 429–43.

Udo, E. A. 'The Missionary Scramble for Spheres of Influence in Eastern Nigeria, 1900–1952', *Ikenga* 1(2), 1972, pp. 22–36.

—— 'The Ibibio Pre-Colonial System of Land Tenure', *Ikenga* 2(1), 1973, pp. 29–40.

Udoka, A. 'Ekong Songs of the Annang', *African Arts* 18(1), 1984, pp. 70, 94.

Udoma, U. *The Story of the Ibibio State Union*, Ibadan: Spectrum Books, 1987.

Ukpanah, M. *Nsekhe Family*, Port Harcourt: Goodwill Press, 1965.

Ukpong, J. S. 'Sacrificial Worship in Ibibio Traditional Religion', *Journal of Religion in Africa* 13(3), 1982, pp. 161–88.

Umoren, U. E. 'The Symbolism of the Nigerian Women's War of 1929: an Anthropological Study of an Anti-colonial Struggle', *African Study Monographs* 16(2), 1995, pp. 61–72.

—— 'Symbols of Religion as Sanctions of Morality in Annangland (Nigeria)', *Cahiers des religions africaines* 29(57), 1995, pp. 75–86.

United Africa Company 'The Manilla Problem', *Statistical and Economic Review* 3, 1949, pp. 44–56.

Van Allen, J. 'Sitting on a Man: Colonialism and the Lost Political Institutions of Igbo Women', *Canadian Journal of African Studies* 6(2), 1972, pp. 165–81.

—— 'Aba Riots or Igbo Women's War? Ideology, Stratification and Invisibility of Women', in *Women in Africa*, Halfkin, N. J. and E. G. Bay (eds), Stanford: Stanford University Press, 1976, pp. 59–85

Van Beusekom, M. M. and D. L. Hodgson 'Lessons learned? Development Experiences in the Late Colonial Period', *Journal of African History* 41(1), 2000, pp. 29–33.

van Gennep, A. *The rites of Passage*, (trans.) Caffee Gabrielle, L. and M. Vizedom. London: Routledge and Kegan Paul, 1977.

Waddell, H. M. *Twenty-nine Years in the West Indies and Central Africa*, London, 1863.

Walker, J. B. 'Notes on the Politics, Religion, and Commerce of Old Calabar',

Journal of the Anthropological Institute 6, 1877, pp. 119–24.

Warnier, J. -P. 'Traite sans raids au Cameroun', *Cahiers d'études africaines* 29, 1989, pp. 5–32.

Watson, R. 'Murder and the Political Body in Early Colonial Ibadan', *Africa* 70(1), 2000, pp. 25–48.

Watt, J. 'Notes on the Old Calabar District of Southern Nigeria', *Man* 3, 1903, pp. 103–5.

Webster, J. B. 'Political Activity in British West Africa, 1900–1940', in *History of West Africa*, Ajayi, J. F. A. and M. Crowder (eds), London: Longman, 1985, pp. 568–95.

Weisfelder, R. F. 'Early Voices of Protest in Basutoland: The Progressive Association and Lekhotla La Bafo', *African Studies Review* 17(2), 1974, pp. 397–409.

Westgarth, J. W. *The Holy Spirit and the Primitive Mind: A Remarkable Account of a Spiritual Awakening in Darkest Africa*, London: Victory Press, 1946.

White, S. E. *The Leopard Woman*, London: Hodder and Stoughton, 1916.

Whitehead, N. 'Hans Staden and the Cultural Politics of Cannibalism', *Hispanic American Historical Review* 80(4), 2000, pp. 721–51.

Wilder, G. 'Practicing Citizenship in Imperial Paris', in *Civil Society and the Political Imagination in Africa: Critical Perspectives*, Comaroff, J. L. and J. Comaroff (eds), Chicago: The University of Chicago Press, 2000, pp. 44–71.

Wilks, I. 'Space, Time and Human Sacrifice', in *Forests of Gold: Essays on the Akan Kingdom of Asante*, Wilks, I. (ed.), Athens, OH: Ohio University Press, 1993, pp. 215–40.

Winston, F. D. D. 'Nigerian Cross River Languages in Polyglotta Africana: Part II', *Sierra Leone Language Review* 4, 1965, pp. 122–8.

Wyatt, A. W. 'The Lion-men of Singida', *Tanganyika Notes and Records* 28, 1950, pp. 3–9.

Zachernuk, P. S. 'Of Origins and Colonial Order: Southern Nigerian Historians and the 'Hamitic Hypothesis' c. 1870–1970', *The Journal of African History* 35(3), 1994, pp. 427–55.

Zemon Davis, N. and R. Starn 'Introduction: Memory and Counter-Memory', *Representations* 26, Special Issue: Memory and Counter-Memory, 1989, pp. 1–6.

INDEX